STUDIES IN AESCHYLUS

TO MY WIFE

CONTENTS

PREFACE

In this book I have assembled most of my previously published work on Aeschylus – and have added to it. All the extant tragedies are covered, and I trust that what emerges, from the old and the new taken together, is a fairly comprehensive interpretation of Aeschylean tragedy as it touches the god-given destinies of individual, family and city, and of the whole human race. The core of the book consists of five chapters on *Oresteia*, where alone we encounter at its height the majesty of the poet's art and the profundity of his thought. But there was a problem here. Chapters 5–8 all deal with distinct and, to some extent, separable themes; and it seemed desirable that in each case the full evidence and argument, without need of constant cross-reference, should be before the reader; the texture of the trilogy being, however, so close, some repetition was unavoidable; I have endeavoured to reduce it to the minimum.

The bibliography of Aeschylus is vast, but fairly accessible; and I have sometimes referred to works which are strong in this line. (*The Cambridge History of Classical Literature*, Vol. I, will include an extensive bibliography.) I have myself made no attempt at a comprehensive or well balanced list: my Bibliography of Short Titles has a strictly practical aim, being limited to works which are referred to on a number of occasions. I have made one exception: there has been such a proliferation of books and articles dealing with *Septem* (and the role of Eteocles) that it seemed more convenient to the reader, in chapter 2, to retain and update the existing bibliographical note from *Yale Classical Studies* rather than scatter the references in a general list. In the text, the reader will observe that, in a controversial field, space is only given to the exposition and discussion of variant interpretations where this is directly relevant to my argument: otherwise the book would have been much longer and not, I fancy, more

useful. As in my recent book on Sophocles, Greek – untranslated or
unparaphrased – has been kept out of the text so far as possible, in the hope
that the book may be of interest to some Greek-less readers.

My debts are manifold but not always easy to define. My love of
Aeschylus goes back to the early 1920s, when in the Sixth Form at Clifton I
read *Agamemnon* with that gifted teacher C.F. Taylor and by him was
introduced to a great tradition of Aeschylean interpretation, that of Walter
Headlam; and I share the debt we all owe to my old friend and
contemporary George Thomson for the publication and continuation of
Headlam's work. The 1930s were for me, where Aeschylus is concerned, a
period of continuous excitement which led to prototypes of chapters 1, 6
and 7. After the Second World War came important works by Reinhardt,
Solmsen and Kitto, and Fraenkel's great edition of *Agamemnon*, which
resumed with massive scholarship a long tradition of work on Aeschylus
and added his own insights, sometimes fallible but often acute. Fraenkel in
Oxford and Page in Cambridge were potent influences. From the quiet
seclusion of the metropolis it was possible to view the work of these two
outstanding scholars with some detachment, absorbing here and rejecting
there. It is partly no doubt to their influence that we owe the welcome
efflorescence of Aeschylus studies in this country in the work of Garvie,
Dawe, Taplin, Griffith and other younger Aeschyleans, among whom I
mention with sadness the late Colin Macleod. The flow of valuable work
continues, and there are recent publications of which I have been unable to
take account in this book.

For permission to reprint published articles I am grateful to the Council
of the Society for the Promotion of Hellenic Studies, to the Director of the
University of London Institute of Classical Studies, to the Classical Journals
Board and the Oxford University Press. I wish to thank a number of
friends for their encouragement and for help of various kinds: Mrs P.E.
Easterling, Dr Oliver Taplin, Mr Ewen Bowie, and especially Mr Edward
Whittle, who performed the ultimate service of reading my proofs. In the
Press, I am greatly indebted to the skill and consideration of Ms Pauline
Hire and Ms Susan Moore.

When friendly reviewers of my *Sophocles* used the term 'old-fashioned'
of my critical approach, it was not, I fancy, in disparagement. Of course all
authors like to think that their work is, if anything, in advance of its time,
but there is one respect in which I am bound to admit the soft
impeachment. Towards more fashionable lines of interpretation I have no
hostility in principle, but merely a certain reserve (due partly to ignorance)

and a strong conviction that the possibilities of a more conventional approach are by no means exhausted; that it is still possible to say helpful things about society without being a Marxist, about sex without being a Freudian, and about structure without being a 'structuralist'. Indeed the more one is concerned with structure in the sense of form, the further 'structures' seem to retreat into their subliminal fastnesses. For structure is something imposed by the artist, deliberately, upon his material; and the greater the rational control, the more sense it makes to ask what the artist 'meant'; and, with a poet and dramatist, patiently to study his text in the hope of discovering what he 'meant'. 'Polysemic' interpretation may be all very well in certain fields of criticism, but in the case of the Greek tragedians, who combined an unrivalled power in the depiction and evocation of emotion with a strong rationality, it may be little better than evasion of choice. Literary criticism need not end, but should begin, with the attempt – desperate though it may be – to enter into the mind of the author. Such an attempt is made in this book.

London, February 1983   R.P.WINNINGTON-INGRAM

BIBLIOGRAPHY OF
SHORT TITLES

Broadhead: H. D. Broadhead (ed.) *The Persae of Aeschylus* (Cambridge 1960)

Daube: B. Daube, *Zu den Rechtsproblemen in Aischylos' Agamemnon* (Zürich & Leipzig 1938)

Di Benedetto: V. Di Benedetto, *L'ideologia del potere e la tragedia greca: ricerche su Eschilo* (Turin 1978)

Dodds (1): E. R. Dodds, *The Greeks and the irrational* (Berkeley & Los Angeles 1951)

Dodds (2): E. R. Dodds, *The ancient concept of progress* (Oxford 1973)

Dodds (3): E. R. Dodds, 'Morals and politics in the Oresteia', *PCPS* n.s. 6 (1960) 19–31 (= *The ancient concept of progress* 45–63)

Dover: K. J. Dover, 'The political aspect of Aeschylus's *Eumenides*', *JHS* 77 (1957) 230–7

Edwards: M. W. Edwards, 'Agamemnon's decision: freedom and folly in Aeschylus', *CSCA* 10 (1977) 17–38

Fraenkel: E. Fraenkel (ed.), *Aeschylus Agamemnon* (Oxford 1950) 3 vols.

von Fritz (1): K. von Fritz, 'Die Gestalt des Eteokles in Aeschylus' *Sieben gegen Theben*', in *Antike und moderne Tragödie* (Berlin 1962) 193–226

von Fritz (2): K. von Fritz, 'Die Danaidentrilogie des Aeschylus', *Philologus* 91 (1936) 121–35, 249–69 (= *Antike und moderne Tragödie* 160–92)

Gagarin: M. Gagarin, *Aeschylean drama* (Berkeley & Los Angeles 1976)

Garvie (1): A. J. Garvie, *Aeschylus' Supplices: play and trilogy* (Cambridge 1969)

Garvie (2): A. J. Garvie, 'The opening of the *Choephori*', *BICS* 17 (1970) 79–91

Griffith (1): M. Griffith, *The authenticity of Prometheus Bound* (Cambridge 1977)

Griffith (2): M. Griffith, 'Aeschylus, Sicily and Prometheus', in *Dionysiaca*, ed. R. D. Dawe *et al.* (Cambridge 1978)

Groeneboom: P. Groeneboom (ed.), *Sept., Prom., Ag., Cho., Eum.* (Groningen 1930–53), *Pers.* (German transl., Göttingen 1960)

Haldane: J. A. Haldane, 'Musical themes and imagery in Aeschylus', *JHS* 85 (1965) 33–41

Kaufmann-Bühler: D. Kaufmann-Bühler, *Begriff and Funktion der Dike in den Tragödien des Aischylos* (Bonn 1955)

Kitto (1): H. D. F. Kitto, *Greek tragedy* (London 1939, 3rd ed. 1961)

Kitto (2): H. D. F. Kitto, *Form and meaning in drama* (London 1956)

Kitto (3): H. D. F. Kitto, *Poiesis: structure and thought* (Berkeley & Los Angeles 1966)

xii

Knox: B. M. W. Knox, *The heroic temper* (Berkeley & Los Angeles 1964)

Lebeck: A. Lebeck, *The Oresteia: a study in language and structure* (Washington 1971)

Lesky (1): A. Lesky, 'Eteokles in den *Sieben gegen Theben*', *WS* 74 (1961) 5–17

Lesky (2): A. Lesky, *Die tragische Dichtung der Hellenen* (3rd ed., Göttingen 1972)

Lloyd-Jones: H. Lloyd-Jones, *The justice of Zeus* (Berkeley & Los Angeles 1971)

Lucas: D. W. Lucas, *The Greek tragic poets* (London 1950, 2nd ed. 1959)

Macleod (1): C. W. Macleod, 'Politics and the Oresteia', *JHS* 102 (1982) 124–44 (a revised and expanded version of 'L'unità dell' Orestea', *Maia* n.s. 25 (1973) 267–92)

Macleod (2): C. W. Macleod, 'Clothing in the *Oresteia*', *Maia* n.s. 27 (1975) 201–3

Mazon: P. Mazon (ed.), *Eschyle* (Budé, 6th ed., Paris 1953) 2 vols.

Méautis: G. Méautis, *Eschyle et la trilogie* (Paris 1936)

Murray: R. D. Murray, Jr, *The motif of Io in Aeschylus' Suppliants* (Princeton 1958)

Page: (where the reference is to a commentary) J. D. Denniston and D. L. Page (eds.), *Aeschylus Agamemnon* (Oxford 1957); (where the reference is to a text) D. L. Page (ed.) *Aeschyli septem quae supersunt tragoediae* (Oxford 1972)

Peradotto: J. J. Peradotto, 'The omen of the eagles and the $H\Theta O\Sigma$ of Agamemnon', *Phoenix* 23 (1969) 237–63

Petrounias: E. Petrounias, *Funktion und Thematik der Bilder bei Aischylos* (Göttingen 1976)

Pohlenz: M. Pohlenz, *Die griechische Tragödie* (2nd ed., Göttingen 1954) (2 vols.)

Reinhardt: K. Reinhardt, *Aischylos als Regisseur und Theologe* (Bern 1949)

Rose: H. J. Rose, *A commentary on the surviving plays of Aeschylus* (Amsterdam 1958) 2 vols.

Stanford: W. B. Stanford, '*Γυναικὸς ἀνδρόβουλον ἐλπίζον κέαρ* (*Agamemnon* line 11)', *CQ* 31 (1937) 92f.

Stinton: T. C. W. Stinton, 'The first stasimon of Aeschylus' *Choephori*', *CQ* 29 (1979) 252–62

Taplin: O. Taplin, *The stagecraft of Aeschylus* (Oxford 1977)

Thomson (1): G. Thomson, *Aeschylus and Athens* (2nd ed., London 1946)

Thomson (2): G. Thomson (ed.), *Aeschylus, the Prometheus Bound* (Cambridge 1932)

Thomson (3): G. Thomson (ed.), *The Oresteia of Aeschylus* (Cambridge 1938) 2 vols. [Rev. ed. (Prague 1966) 2 vols.]

Tucker (1): T. G. Tucker (ed.), *Aeschylus, Seven against Thebes* (Cambridge 1908)

Tucker (2): T. G. Tucker (ed.), *The Choephori of Aeschylus* (Cambridge 1901)

Vernant: J.-P. Vernant and Vidal-Naquet, P., *Mythe et tragédie en Grèce ancienne* (Paris 1973)

Vickers: B. Vickers, *Towards Greek tragedy* (London 1973)

West: M. L. West, 'The Prometheus trilogy', *JHS* 99 (1979) 130–48

Wilamowitz (1): U. von Wilamowitz-Moellendorf, *Aischylos Interpretationen* (Berlin 1914)

Wilamowitz (2): U. von Wilamowitz-Moellendorf (ed.), *Aischylos Orestie* II (Das Opfer am Grabe) (Berlin 1896)

Winnington-Ingram: R. P. Winnington-Ingram, *Sophocles: an interpretation* (Cambridge 1980)

CHAPTER ONE

Zeus in *Persae*[1]

Aeschylus was a dramatist of ideas – of religious ideas. His ideas may have
been old or new, clear or confused, crude or profound, but it was in terms
of religious ideas that he interpreted the story of the house of Argos; and it
was in terms of religious ideas that he interpreted a great event in the
history of his own time. It is, therefore, of considerable interest and
importance to discover, if we can, a relationship between the way he
thought in 472 and the way he thought in 458. In 458 he made a Chorus
reject[2] an old doctrine: that prosperity and good fortune in themselves give
rise to disaster – the doctrine, that is to say (though the word is not used),
of the jealousy of the gods (φθόνος τῶν θεῶν). No, sings this Chorus, it is
the impious deed that begets after its kind, the old *hubris* that gives birth to
new and to a train of evil consequences. In 472, in *Persae*, we seem to find
both doctrines. We find the Chorus singing of the crafty deceit of a god
from which no mortal can escape, and we find the Messenger speaking of
the jealousy of the gods. But we also find Darius speaking of the stern
punishments of Zeus and attributing the disasters of the Persians to their
own acts of *hubris*. As though such seeming contradictions were sent to test
our ingenuity, eminent scholars – I mention no names[3] – have tied
themselves in knots to demonstrate that the contradiction does not exist. I
would suggest that the contradiction not only exists but is essential to the

---

[1] This chapter is reprinted with minor alterations from *JHS* 93 (1973) 210–19, which was a volume in
honour of Professor E. R. Dodds.

[2] *Agam.* 750ff.

[3] Except to say that Dodds is not among them. 'What to the partial vision of the living appears as the
act of a fiend, is perceived by the wider insight of the dead to be an aspect of cosmic justice' (Dodds
(1) 39). If there is any originality in this chapter, it is in regard to the art rather than to the thought of
Aeschylus.

thought of the play, and that it has, to some extent, dictated the play's form.[4]

This form is very simple, just as the dramatic action is simple. The Persian elders express their anxiety at the long-delayed return of Xerxes and his mighty army; Atossa tells them about her sinister dream; a messenger brings news of the disaster at Salamis. By the closing words of Atossa, before she leaves the stage at 531, the poet seems deliberately to have left open in the mind of his audience the possibility of a speedy arrival of Xerxes;[5] and, if the news of Salamis had been followed, after a short choral ode, by the return of Xerxes in rags and a scene of lamentation closing the play, it would have been a sequence very gratifying to Athenian pride. But it does not happen that way. Between the news of disaster and the return of Xerxes comes the evocation of Darius from his tomb. Not only so, but this episode occupies roughly a quarter of the play, of which, in point of action, it is manifestly the most striking – and surprising – feature. We are of course free to say that Aeschylus, observing that his play lacked action, decided to expand it with a characteristic exhibition of what ancient critics called τὸ τερατῶδες – 'the portentous', 'the sensational'. We can even regard Darius as a rather uneconomical device for introducing the battle of Plataea. Such explanations are, however, best kept in reserve to be brought forward if no reason more creditable to the dramatic skill of the poet can be found.

We are faced, then, with a formal problem. Why does Aeschylus hold up the return of Xerxes, while the ghost of Darius is evoked from the tomb? And why does he devote so large a part of the play to this scene? It is perhaps by asking ourselves such questions and attempting to answer them that we stand the best chance of reaching plausible interpretations of Aeschylus. There is another question – not this time of form – which should be asked and can be answered.[6] Why, in a play produced in Athens about the Athenians' finest hour,[7] is the goddess Athena mentioned only once (no more often than Poseidon or Hermes, Phoebus or Pan) and not even then as herself the saviour? The answer is that Athena would be too

---

[4] I am not concerned to deny that the play has patriotic and political aspects. It is indeed obvious that, in some degree, it was bound to evoke a patriotic response, at which certain features may have been aimed, but Kitto (3) gets the emphasis right. On the political aspect, cf. A. J. Podlecki, *The political background of Aeschylean tragedy* (Ann Arbor 1966) 8–26, and my review in *Gnomon* 39 (1967) 641ff.; Dodds (3) 22 n. 1.

[5] Cf. R. D. Dawe, *PCPS*, n.s. 9 (1963) 27; Taplin 92–8 (who, however, doubts the text and argues for a radical solution).

[6] The point is made by Pohlenz I 61.

[7] Cf. Aristoph., *Frogs* 1027.

patriotic, too local. Aeschylus is going to interpret the campaign, not in terms of Athena saving her city, but of Zeus maintaining a moral order in the world. The answer to this question will perhaps enable us to answer the other question – the question of form.

It is unnecessary to expatiate upon the importance of Zeus in the thought of Aeschylus. But that great name is not bandied about in his plays. In *Persae* it occurs five times: five times as often as the name of any other Olympian god, but five times only. Three of these occurrences are in the Darius-scene, out of the mouth of Darius himself (740, 762, 827). One opens the choral ode (ὦ Ζεῦ βασιλεῦ, 532) which ends the first half of the play and precedes the evocation. The remaining instance lies on the far side of the Darius-scene, in the first outburst of Xerxes on his entrance (915). After that outburst Zeus is not mentioned in the closing scene; he is not mentioned in the first half of the play at all (until 532). Perhaps, then, it would not be unfair to say that Zeus belongs particularly to the Darius-scene and its immediate environment. This said, let us now return to the beginning and consider the religious standpoint which is expressed in the play's first half.

The Chorus of Persian elders, faithful counsellors of the King, are anxious because no news has come from the great host. They recall the vast manpower and the vast wealth of the Persian realm; they recite the names of princes from all parts of the empire who had departed. If this gives the measure of their anxiety, it is also their ground of confidence. For who could resist this great army advancing like a wave of the sea? 'The host of Persia is not to be withstood, its people valiant' (91f.). At this point we come up, as so often alas in Aeschylus, against a textual problem. Is the order of stanzas, as we find it in the MSS, correct? Many editors have followed O. Müller in placing the pair of stanzas θεόθεν γὰρ . . . λαοπόροις τε μηχαναῖς (101–14) before δολόμητιν δ' ἀπάταν . . . ἀλύξαντα φυγεῖν (or whatever we read there, and whether we accept 93–100 as a mesode or make a pair of stanzas out of it); and for a variety of reasons I am sure they are right.[8] With this transposition, the Chorus now explain the irresistible character of Persian might by singing of a *moira* or allotted portion of divine origin (*theothen*) which has imposed

[8] The case for the transposition is well argued by Broadhead on 93–106. D. Korzeniewski's suggestion (*Helikon* 6 (1966) 573ff.) that the mesode should be placed between Str. γ' and Ant. γ' seems an awkward and unrewarding compromise. The MS order is defended by W. C. Scott, *GRBS* 9 (1968) 25–66, who argues that, in the mind of the Chorus, it is the Greeks who, in resisting the Persians, are victimized by the divine deceit; and by two recent writers: di Benedetto 8f., G. Paduano, *Sui Persiani di Eschilo: problemi di focalizzazione drammatica* (Rome 1978) 45.

upon the Persians a career of wars and sieges and sacks. (No specific god is mentioned, and this, as we shall see, is characteristic. The idea of *moira*, of a divinely appointed portion or lot, is a common feature of Greek thought in the archaic period.) When the Chorus add that the Persians learnt to look upon the rough waters of the sea, the audience may perhaps wonder whether this was something that was not (in the Homeric phrase) *kata moiran*, but that idea cannot be in the minds of the Chorus. When they sing that their countrymen have put their trust in 'slender cables and devices for transport of a host', *they* will be thinking of ships, but (after 71f.) the audience may well remember the bridging of the Hellespont.[9] And thus on two levels this stanza leads into the sinister themes which follow. For, if the audience thinks of the rash act of Xerxes, the Chorus is pursuing a different train of thought. May not the power and success of Persia be in itself a cause for alarm? They have sung of a dispensation divinely given: but can men trust the gods? δολόμητιν δ' ἀπάταν θεοῦ τίς ἀνὴρ θνατὸς ἀλύξει; (107f.). 'What mortal man can escape the crafty-minded deceit of god (or of a god)?'

Again we run into textual difficulties, but fortunately they do not obscure the nature of the ideas employed, which are familiar common-places of archaic thought.[10] With a false show of fawning friendliness the god (a god) leads a mortal man on into a net from which he cannot escape. The subject of the sentence (97–100 *or* 111–14) may be ἀπάτα, but more likely it is ἄτα: in any case the notion of *ate* is introduced and means here 'infatuation'. For the smiling favour of heaven induces the mortal victim to commit some fatal error which brings him down at the height of his prosperity. So far as the language of the Chorus goes, the notion is quite unmoralized, though of course the audience may already be disposed to supply a moral. There is a strong emphasis upon *deceit* (δολόμητις ἀπάτα), which implies that the divine purpose is concealed, until it is too late. If the gods are deceitful, they are also fickle: friendly at one moment, hostile at the next. Notice, then, the words with which the Elders greet their queen, when she enters at the end of the *parodos*: 'To a god of the Persians were you bedfellow, and of such a god the mother – unless its former *daimon* has now deserted the host': (θεοῦ μὲν εὐνάτειρα Περσῶν, θεοῦ δὲ καὶ μήτηρ

---

[9] Broadhead (on 100–3) and A. H. Coxon (*CQ* n.s. 8 (1958) 46) argue conclusively that the first part of the stanza refers not to the Hellespont but to the sea in general. It is therefore very awkward if, as Broadhead (on 104–6) holds, the subsequent lines refer to the bridge of boats, the Chorus having 'passed from the general to the particular'. Coxon and Groeneboom (and others) seem to be right that the Chorus is thinking of the sea, generally, throughout.

[10] The textual problems are discussed at length by Broadhead *ad loc.*

ἔφυς, εἴ τι μὴ δαίμων παλαιὸς νῦν μεθέστηκε στρατῷ, 157f.). *Daimon* here is perhaps something less than 'god', certainly something more than 'destiny' (in the faded sense which we find in Euripides and later writers). It is related to the *theothen moira* of the *parodos*. It was characteristic of the archaic period[11] to use this half-personification of the *moira* which stressed its divine origin – most commonly of course of the individual destiny, but here of the *moira* and *daimon* of the Persian host, though these are closely linked to the personal fate of the despotic ruler. But the *daimon* is changeable (μεθέστηκε): the man or nation that was once *eudaimon* may become *dusdaimon*.

If the elders are anxious, so, because of her dream, is Atossa. Like them, she fears a great reversal of fortune. She fears that the prosperity which Darius raised 'not without some god's aid' will be overturned. Again the text – or its interpretation – is perplexed (163f.),[12] but the general sense must certainly be that, as the gods gave, so they may take away; and again we have a vague expression: 'not without some god's aid' (οὐκ ἄνευ θεῶν τινός). Atossa has nothing more to add to our understanding of the situation, as she goes on to tell her dream to the elders and receive their well-meant if futile advice.

The first speech of the Messenger reveals that the fears of Atossa were justified: 'At one stroke great wealth has been destroyed, the flower of the Persians is fallen and gone away' (ὡς ἐν μιᾷ πληγῇ κατέφθαρται πολὺς | ὄλβος, τὸ Περσῶν δ' ἄνθος οἴχεται πεσόν, 251f.). Her fear for the wealth, her fear for the men.[13] Note that to the Chorus, despite their earlier forebodings, this is a monstrous and unlooked-for blow which they describe as κακὰ νεόκοτα (256) and πῆμ' ἄελπτον (265). The Messenger, when he has assured Atossa of the personal survival of Xerxes, gives a catalogue of fallen princes which echoes ironically the catalogue in the *parodos*.[14] With the details of his narrative we are not now concerned, but only with the light in which he sees the events recounted. He sees, naturally, the operations of a god or gods. It was a god that gave the glory of the naval battle to the Greeks (454f.); a god that raised the storm in Thrace and froze the Strymon, so that men prayed who had previously been indifferent to religion (495ff.). His last words speak of the evils that a god had brought down upon the Persians (514).

This closing comment echoes more briefly the judgement which he had

[11] Cf. Dodds (1) 23 n. 65, 42, 58 n. 79.
[12] See n. 22 below.
[13] On the difficulties of 159–69 see my review of Broadhead in *CR* n.s. 12 (1962) 124.
[14] On the third catalogue see n. 37 below.

already expressed in answer to a question from Atossa. She had asked
whether the numbers of the Greek ships had been so great. No, he replies, it
was the Persians who had the advantage: ἀλλ' ὧδε δαίμων τις κατέφθειρε
στρατόν, | τάλαντα βρίσας οὐκ ἰσορρόπῳ τύχῃ. | θεοὶ πόλιν σώζουσι
Παλλάδος θεᾶς (345ff.). It was a *daimon* that destroyed the Persian navy,
weighting the scales of fortune against them; it was the gods that saved the
city of the goddess Pallas. But the most interesting piece of interpretation is
that with which the Messenger begins his narrative, again in answer to a
question from Atossa. Who began the battle? 'The whole trouble began,
lady, when from somewhere there appeared an *alastor* or an evil *daimon*'
(353f.). And the destructive spirit, the *daimon*, we learn was incarnate, as
divine agencies in Aeschylus so often are, in a human person[15] – in the
emissary that Themistocles (not here named) sent to Xerxes. Xerxes, when
he had heard him, gave the fatal instructions, 'for he did not know the
future that the gods ordained' (οὐ γὰρ τὸ μέλλον ἐκ θεῶν ἠπίστατο, 373).
More significant still is this expression: 'not understanding the trick of a
Greek man or the *phthonos* of the gods' (οὐ ξυνεὶς δόλον | Ἕλληνος ἀνδρὸς
οὐδὲ τὸν θεῶν φθόνον, 361f.). The word *dolos* recalls the *dolometis apata* of
107 (93); the *phthonos* makes explicit what was only implied in the *parodos*
and attributes a motive to the gods.

Atossa has her comment, and so does the Coryphaeus have his. At 471
there is a pause in the narrative. ὦ στυγνὲ δαῖμον, exclaims the queen, ὡς
ἄρ' ἔψευσας φρενῶν | Πέρσας (472f.). 'Hateful *daimon*, how you have
cheated the Persians of their wits.'[16] The comment from the Chorus at the
close of the Messenger's speech is similar in tone: 'Burdensome *daimon*,
with what excessive weight have you trampled on the whole Persian race!'
(ὦ δυσπόνητε δαῖμον, ὡς ἄγαν βαρὺς | ποδοῖν ἐνήλου παντὶ Περσικῷ
γένει, 515f.). The disaster is seen, then, as a cruel and excessive blow dealt
by a deceptive divinity.

Neither here nor elsewhere, in this part of the play, is there mention of
any specific god. Chorus, queen and messenger, are alike in speaking
always of *theos* or *theoi*, *daimon* or *daimon tis*.[17] There are two reasons for
this which amount to much the same thing. (i) The name of the great god

---

[15] On double causation or 'over-determination' in Homer and Aeschylus see Dodds (1) 30f. (with
specific reference to this passage) and Dodds (3) 27 n. 5.

[16] See Broadhead on 472 (and App.): the scholiast is wrong. This is the *apate/ate* of the *parodos*. Cf. 552,
724f.

[17] Here I reluctantly part company with Professor Kitto who has so much of value to say about the
play, when he asserts (Kitto (3) 56) that 'it is a matter of indifference to Aeschylus' how the divine
power is named. Not, surely, where the attitudes of his characters and the form of the play are
concerned.

who is ultimately responsible for all will come with the greater effect for the preceding anonymity; and it does in fact come at the beginning of the following stasimon: ὦ Ζεῦ βασιλεῦ (532). (ii) The set of ideas in terms of which the events are interpreted by Chorus, Queen and Messenger, were in fact associated in Greek popular thought, not so much with clearly envisaged personal gods as with vaguely conceived divine powers − with a *daimon*, with *theōn tis*, with *to theion*. We have the evidence in Homer and Herodotus. It has been observed that, in Homer, while the poet attributes events to the intervention of a named Olympian god, his characters often use the vaguer terms;[18] and in Herodotus we are familiar with this unspecific use of *to theion* and *ho theos*.[19] Indeed Herodotus is the best commentator on the first half of the *Persae*, giving us the range of ideas within which the Aeschylean characters are moving. The ideas are these: that the gods are jealous, that they grudge men excessive prosperity; that they deceive men, luring them on; that their favour cannot be depended upon; that their ways are unpredictable; that they are cruel, deceptive, and fickle. The view of the supernatural taken in this part of the play is, I suggest, hardly at all moralized. True, since Xerxes has met with disaster, Xerxes has evidently made a big mistake. This is part of the process by which the gods curtail the prosperity that has earned their jealousy; they lure the prosperous man into making such a mistake, and he makes it in over-confidence, believing, in the words of Atossa, that, when his *daimon* is in fair course, the same wind of fortune will blow for ever (601f.).[20] So Atossa asked if it was Xerxes that began the battle: 'proudly confident in the multitude of his ships' (πλήθει καταυχήσας νεῶν, 352), but I do not think she means to criticize her son in moral terms. No more do the Chorus imply criticism, when they speak of the Persians as 'greatly proud' (τῶν μεγαλαύχων, 533). But here the word, coming as it does immediately after the address to Zeus the king, may, like that address, be the poet's way of pointing forward to the scene which is to follow.[21]

[18] Cf., e.g., M. P. Nilsson, *Greek piety* (Oxford 1948) 59f.; Dodds (1) 10ff. (with special reference to the *Odyssey*); P. Chantraine, *Fondation Hardt Entretiens* I 50ff. (with special reference to *daimon*). The name of Zeus is sometimes used to stand for the divine world in general, which perhaps facilitates the transitions in *Persae*, the Aeschylean Zeus fading in at 532, fading out at 915.

[19] The possible influence of *Persae* on Herodotus is too big a question to be handled here: the modes of expression which we find, e.g. in Herodotus 1 and 7, are in any case appropriate to the proverbial wisdom which he is expounding.

[20] αἰεὶ (*uel* ἀεὶ) δαίμον' codd. αἰὲν ἄνεμον Weil. The emendation is compelling. One cannot accept the attempts of Groeneboom and Broadhead to defend δαίμονα . . . τύχης by reference to such expressions as θεοῦ μοῖρα, τύχη δαίμονος, which clearly are not reversible.

[21] Contrast 827, 831. This seems to be an example of the way in which the implications of a word or theme are unfolded during the course of an Aeschylean play, on which see App. A, with particular reference to the use of οἴχομαι in this play.

The divine world is jealous of human success, of human prosperity; the tangible evidence of prosperity is wealth, and the pre-eminent symbol of wealth is gold. So, in the opening anapaests of the Chorus, the word πολύχρυσος occurs four times. So Atossa leaves the gold-bedecked palace (χρυσεοστόλμους δόμους, 159) to express her fear not only for the men but for the wealth of Persia. Textual and interpretative difficulties again, but she seems to be saying that great wealth may be a danger and may overthrow the prosperity it represents.[22] And the Messenger, in his first words, apostrophizes Asia as 'a great haven of wealth' (πολὺς πλούτου λιμήν, 250): not only the flower of the Persians is gone, but great prosperity (ὄλβος) has been overthrown at a blow. We are not surprised that the theme recurs in the Darius-scene, in association with the motives and the punishment of Xerxes. For there is a problem in the relationship between wealth and disaster. In *Agamemnon*, the Chorus reject the notion that it is prosperity and good fortune that are the cause of misery; if the goddess of Justice leaves 'gold-bespangled mansions' (χρυσόπαστα ἔσθλα), it is when hands are defiled (σὺν πίνῳ χερῶν).[23]

We thus return to our original issue. The beliefs which are, if I am right, reflected in the utterances of Chorus and characters up to this point of the play were common beliefs of the average Greek. If I say (what is obvious) that they were not the beliefs of Aeschylus when he wrote *Agamemnon*, I am not of course suggesting that his rejection of the old *phthonos*-doctrine was a revolutionary innovation, though nowhere else is this rejection so strongly and sharply put. In that amalgam of ideas and feelings which Gilbert Murray called 'the Inherited Conglomerate' there was more than one explanation of the disasters which befall mankind. If the Greeks often felt the gods to be malevolent, they longed for them to be just,[24] and generations before Aeschylus writers such as Hesiod and Solon had seen disasters in the light of punishments. Yet Aeschylus, when he wrote that chorus in *Agamemnon*, thought it was worth while explicitly to reject the doctrine that wealth and prosperity were in themselves sufficient to generate woe, in favour of the Solonian doctrine which found in *hubris* a middle term between *koros* and *ate*. He found it worth while, I am

---

22 πλοῦτος should by all means be retained, but the force of the image has not been determined beyond doubt. See recently Korzeniewski, op. cit. 577ff.; Taplin 78 (with n. 2).

23 *Agam.* 773ff.

24 Dodds (1) 32: 'Man projects into the cosmos his own nascent demand for social justice; and when from the outer spaces the magnified echo of his own voice returns to him, promising punishment for the guilty, he draws from it courage and reassurance.'

suggesting, to interpret a historical event of his own time upon exactly the same lines. To give this interpretation is the function of Darius.

He serves this function mainly by what he says but also, partly, by what he is and was. The choral ode which follows the news of Salamis (532ff.) closes the first half of the play with a lamentation. In the first stanza, the Chorus put the full responsibility upon Xerxes, whose name is thrice repeated. They go on: τίπτε Δαρεῖος μὲν οὕτω τότ' ἀβλαβὴς ἐπῆν τόξαρχος πολιήταις, Σουσίδαις φίλος ἄκτωρ; (554–7). Some editors have wished to change the text, and some perverse interpretations have been given. But, as Broadhead has seen, there is only one natural interpretation: 'Why was *Darius* (μέν) in his time so undisastrous a lord of the bow over his citizens?' And there is only one difficulty, which is why the Chorus should (as Broadhead puts it) 'have chosen to express their judgement in the form of a question'. Perhaps they are made to do so, because this is a question they cannot answer and Darius can. And he will do so in terms of the Zeus whom the Chorus had, we might say, ignorantly hailed (532). Note, then, the words with which the ghost of Darius is first addressed by the queen: ὦ βροτῶν πάντων ὑπερσχὼν ὄλβον εὐτυχεῖ πότμῳ, | ὡς ἕως τ' ἔλευσσες αὐγὰς ἡλίου ζηλωτὸς ὢν | βίοτον εὐαίωνα Πέρσαις ὡς θεὸς διήγαγες, | νῦν τέ σε ζηλῶ θανόντα πρὶν κακῶν ἰδεῖν βάθος (709ff.).[25] He had exceeded all men in prosperity and good fortune; he had been the object of envy (ζηλωτός); taking Πέρσαις ὡς θεός together, as they should probably be taken, he had been regarded by his subjects in the light of a god. All of which things, according to the traditional view of the jealousy of heaven, were a prescription for ultimate disaster. And yet he lived out (διήγαγες) a life of blessedness through to the end and, by dying before ill befell, was truly *eudaimon* in the Herodotean sense. What, then, was Darius? He was the good king who brought no great disaster upon his people; and his career of lasting success was evidence that wealth and prosperity and enviability are harmless, if men know how to bear them.[26]

Let us now turn to what Darius says. As soon as he hears that an

[25] I should take ὡς (with Groeneboom) as explanatory rather than exclamatory. The only real problem in the lines concerns Πέρσαις, and the best solution seems to be in taking it with ὡς θεός (cf. 157f., 654f., 856). This carries matters a step beyond the normal Greek description of continuous prosperity (cf. Plato, *Gorg.* 473c).

[26] The point is made again at 852ff., on the placing of which see Taplin 126. A portrait of doubtful historicity, no doubt. But Aeschylus treats history as myth – and could do so, as long as he did not flagrantly disregard facts well known to his audience. Marathon could not be omitted but demanded – and received – cautious handling. Darius' bridging of the Bosphorus is quietly disregarded. (Cf. J. H. Quincey, *CQ* n.s. 12 (1962) 184). Kitto (3) 74ff., has a good discussion of the relationship between the historical events and the dramatic treatment. See also n. 31 below.

expedition has been made against Athens, he recognizes it as an act of folly
(719). Then Atossa tells him of the bridging of the Hellespont (722). 'Did
he actually do that (καὶ τόδ' ἐξέπραξεν)', exclaims Darius, 'close the great
Bosporus?' 'Yes,' replies the queen, 'some *daimon* surely lent its aid to his
decision' (or however we should translate γνώμης . . . ξυνήψατο).[27]
'Alas, it was some great *daimon* that came upon him so that his judgement
was at fault.' Darius gives no name, though he soon will; and I think it was
of deliberation that Aeschylus here, at first, makes him use language which
recalls the theology of the early part of the play. Inded what he has said so
far hardly carries us beyond the range of ideas we have already met. Atossa
knew that the Persians had been cheated of their wits (472f.); the elders
knew that the trickery of the gods led the prosperous man into a state of
infatuation (111ff.). But why was Darius so struck by the bridging of the
Hellespont? This he tells us in a speech which begins with Zeus and ends
with Poseidon. For he has recognized that Xerxes, by his own impetuous
folly, had brought an early fulfilment of destined and prophesied disasters
(739–41). In his ignorance and youthful rashness he had precipitated the
fatal train of events, putting shackles upon the Hellespont, thinking that he,
a mortal, could master the gods (744–50).

The modern reader may at first feel some disappointment here. Was it
all, then, a formal insult to the gods in general and to Poseidon in
particular? But of course the act of Xerxes was symbolical, as the act of
Agamemnon in treading the scarlet draperies was symbolical; and the
significance of a symbolical act must be seen not only in what it is but in
what it symbolizes. Agamemnon's act symbolized (as I believe) a state of
mind,[28] and so did that of Xerxes. But the act of Xerxes does more: it
symbolizes the wider implications of the whole expedition. *Persae*, in one
aspect, interprets world-history.

By bridging the Hellespont, Xerxes was in effect seeking to abolish a
natural boundary between East and West. The contrast between the two
races – the Greeks and the oriental barbarians – diverse in their ways of
thought and life must have impressed itself strongly upon this generation
(and was later to dominate the history of Herodotus). In *Persae* Aeschylus
seeks to give an intelligible account of this world-fact. The two races were
different, and they were intended by Zeus to remain different. It is no
accident that the comments of Darius upon the bridging of the Hellespont
are immediately followed by another of the infrequent mentions of the

[27] See n. 30.
[28] See ch. 5, p. 90.

name of Zeus – but in a new connection. Never, says Darius, had such a disaster befallen the Persians, 'since lord Zeus assigned this honourable state (τιμὴν), that one man should hold the sceptre of direction and rule all Asia nurse of flocks' (762ff.). It was Zeus, then, that had ordained monarchy as the proper mode of government for Asiatics. No less, however, was it the will of Zeus that Greeks should be free. This is not stated – it could hardly be stated by Persians – but it is implied. And this is also the significance of Atossa's dream, in which she saw the futile attempt of Xerxes to yoke to one chariot the two women, Greek and barbarian: ἅρμασιν δ᾽ ὕπο | ζεύγνυσιν αὐτῶ καὶ λέπαδν᾽ ὑπ᾽ αὐχένων | τίθησι (190ff.). There can be little doubt that the yoking of the two women and the yoking of the Hellespont have the same symbolical reference.[29]

Why, then, should Xerxes have attempted this fatal enterprise? Why should he have inaugurated it with an act so ominous as the bridging of the Hellespont? There was the initial folly of the expedition (719), but it is in the context of the symbolical act that Darius speaks of the faulty judgement of his son (725, 749), of a 'disease of the mind' (νόσος φρενῶν, 750). For such a disease a divine cause is likely, and indeed it is clear that Darius accepts Atossa's view that the ill-judged act of Xerxes was done under divine influence. He accepts her very word (ξυνήψατο, συνάπτεται), but prefaces it with the phrase: ὅταν σπεύδῃ τις αὐτός (742). Disaster for Persia was among the inscrutable purposes of the gods, but it was Xerxes – and not the gods – who was in a hurry. To Atossa, when she first raised the theme (472), the failure of judgement was due to a cheating *daimon*. But Darius, who equally believes in divine distraction, sees farther into the causes which evoke it: it is when a man is himself bent upon an evil course that the ironical divine helper lends his aid.[30] It is when Xerxes has come to feel that at all costs he must add by conquest to his wealth that he is immediately inspired with the maddest and most fateful of all ways of doing so. It is no accident that in the closing words of Darius' speech we return to an earlier theme, when he fears that the wealth he laboured to acquire is now at the mercy of the first-comer (751f.).[31] And this leads

---

[29] Observe the phrases which come so close to one another in the *parodos*: ζυγὸν ἀμφιβαλεῖν δούλιον Ἑλλάδι (50), ζυγὸν ἀμφιβαλὼν αὐχένι πόντου (72). On the yoking – and indeed the whole chariot-theme in the play – see Taplin 78.

[30] Groeneboom has helpful notes on 724 and 742. His parallels suggest strongly that συνάπτομαι has a sense akin to συλλαμβάνω, and we can therefore compare the use of συλλήπτωρ at *Agam.* 1508. These are the passages in which Aeschylus comes closest to formulating the relationship between divine and human responsibility: on which see the admirable discussion in Dodds (3) 25ff.

[31] For his purposes Aeschylus deliberately and grossly exaggerates both the military and the economic effects of the Persian defeat (cf. Lloyd-Jones 89). When we read 751f., we should not however forget that the aims of the Delian Confederacy included reprisals as well as liberation.

Atossa to reveal how her son had been taunted for not adding to that wealth (753ff.).[32]

Responsibility lay on Xerxes, but not, humanly, on Xerxes alone, for he had been led astray by evil associates. Human responsibility radiates in widening circles. First Xerxes, then his counsellors, but soon we find the whole Persian host to blame; and the moral climax comes in the context, not of Xerxes and Salamis, but of Plataea.

For the knowledge which Darius had of the oracles enabled him to foretell yet more disasters. Aeschylus may have had more than one reason for wishing to introduce Plataea (dramatically forced though his means of doing so may appear). In any case we need not be surprised that he reserves his strongest condemnation – and his clearest statement of the principles of crime and punishment – for this context. He was writing for an audience which had seen the sanctuaries of the Acropolis plundered and burnt. And so he makes Darius state that the blood shed in the plain of the Asopus was the 'penalty of *hubris* and godless thoughts' (ὕβρεως ἄποινα κἀθέων φρονημάτων, 808) on the part of those who had not reverenced the images, altars and temples of the gods. 'Therefore, having done ill, they suffer – and will suffer – no less ills' (τοίγαρ κακῶς δράσαντες οὐκ ἐλάσσονα | πάσχουσι, τὰ δὲ μέλλουσι, 813f.). The heaps of dead will bear silent witness even to the third generation 'that a mortal man should not have overweening thoughts, for *hubris*, flowering, bears a crop of *ate*, from which the harvest reaped is one of tears' (ὡς οὐχ ὑπέρφευ θνητὸν ὄντα χρὴ φρονεῖν. | ὕβρις γὰρ ἐξανθοῦσ᾽ ἐκάρπωσεν στάχυν | ἄτης, ὅθεν πάγκλαυτον ἐξαμᾷ θέρος, 820ff.). But these are terms no less applicable to Xerxes; and it is to Xerxes that the minds of the audience will turn back, when Darius says: 'Nor let a man, scorning his present fortune (*daimon*), lust after other things and so spill great prosperity' (μηδέ τις | ὑπερφρονήσας τὸν παρόντα δαίμονα | ἄλλων ἐρασθεὶς ὄλβον ἐκχέῃ μέγαν, 824ff.), and when he sums up the moral lesson in the tremendous couplet: 'Zeus is set over to chastise thoughts which are over-proud and heavy is his correcting hand' (Ζεύς τοι κολαστὴς τῶν ὑπερκόμπων ἄγαν | φρονημάτων ἔπεστιν εὔθυνος βαρύς, 827f.). These then are the causes of disaster: not wealth, but the lust to add to it; more than mortal thoughts, and the acts of *hubris* and impiety to which they lead. It is Zeus who judges these matters and inflicts the heavy punishment. At 515f., the

---

32 Of the two motives attributed to the Persians in Herodotus (cf. H. R. Immerwahr, *TAPA* 87, 1956, 241–80) – retaliation and expansionism – Aeschylus, for fairly obvious reasons, places the emphasis on the latter. Atossa speaks of retaliation at 473ff., but after that the theme is silent, except for divine *talio*.

Coryphaeus had apostrophized the 'troublesome *daimon*' that had trampled heavily on the Persian race. Now we can give him a name;[33] now we know on what principles he acts.

Nothing, to my mind, is more interesting in the artistic technique of *Persae* than Aeschylus' handling of the closing scene. Darius has come and gone, having interpreted events upon the highest moral and religious level. His closing instructions to the Chorus are that they should bring Xerxes to a proper understanding by the admonitions of reason (εὐλόγοισι νουθετήμασιν, 830), so that he may cease in his overweening rashness (ὑπερκόμπῳ θράσει) to offend the gods. Atossa leaves the stage on an errand concerned rather with his body than his mind.[34] The Chorus remain to greet their king. Is there any sign whatever that they have taken the words of Darius to heart? When Xerxes enters full of remorse, he is received with lamentations and recriminations. But of the 'admonitions of reason' there is no trace. For the Chorus, loyal subjects and faithful counsellors though they may be, are but ordinary Persians. Xerxes and his subjects are upon the same moral level, and it is not the level of Darius. The last scene returns to the moral level and to the religious ideas of the first half of the play; and it is as though Darius had never spoken.

Most significant of all are the opening words of Xerxes. 'Miserable am I to have met this hateful *moira* most unforeseen. How cruelly has a *daimon* trampled upon the race of Persians.' (ἰώ, δύστηνος ἐγὼ στυγερᾶς μοίρας τῆσδε κυρήσας ἀτεκμαρτοτάτης, ὡς ὠμοφρόνως δαίμων ἐνέβη Περσῶν γενεᾷ, 909ff.) The words arouse echoes: of Atossa's 'hateful daimon' (472), of the final comment of the Coryphaeus on the news from Salamis (515f., just cited). When Xerxes complains of the *daimon* that has now turned against him (δαίμων γὰρ ὅδ' αὖ μετάτροπος ἐπ' ἐμοί (942f.)), we can compare the words of the Chorus at 158: 'unless the former *daimon* has now deserted the host' (εἴ τι μὴ δαίμων παλαιὸς νῦν μεθέστηκε στρατῷ) and Atossa's reference to a shifting wind (601f.). Xerxes attributes his disaster to the cruelty of a fickle *daimon* who has turned against him – has turned against him inexplicably. His hateful *moira* he describes as *atekmartotatē*: 'most unforeseen', 'most unforeseeable'. But he can only call

---

[33] Some might prefer to see the βαρὺς δαίμων as a minister of Zeus: perhaps it does not matter greatly.

[34] On the instructions of Darius (832ff.). A device no doubt for removing her from a scene in which she is not needed. But also preparation for the man who has by his folly squandered his great wealth. Darius' closing words (839–42) have caused difficulty, but they too have a point in reintroducing the *ploutos*-theme, with a reminder of the ultimate futility of amassing wealth. Cf. B. Alexandersen, 'Darius in the *Persians*', *Eranos* 65 (1967) 7.

it so, because he fails to understand the principles upon which it is based. He
uses the vague anonymous *daimon* and *moira*, but couples them with a call
upon Zeus (915) – without, however, understanding the role of Zeus. This
final naming of the name of Zeus is of course intended to remind the
audience of the words of Darius; and it might also seem to be the cue for the
Chorus, if they had learnt their lesson, to repeat it. But nothing comes from
them except the familiar mention of a *daimon* of destruction (921).[35] At
1005ff. the text is unfortunately corrupt, but there is a reference to *ate*, a
reference to a *daimon* or *daimones*, and to an 'unlooked-for' evil (ἄελπτον
κακόν) that has been wrought. When Xerxes picks up the theme, he uses
the very words (πῆμ' ἄελπτον, 1028) which the Chorus had applied to the
news from Salamis (265).

That Aeschylus should return at the end of the play to words and themes
from the beginning is not surprising. This is a traditional device of style
which in Aeschylus is so common as to be almost regular – in speeches, in
odes, in scenes and in entire plays – a device to which the term
ring-composition has been given.[36] Nor do the echoes I have already
mentioned stand alone.[37] It is a traditional device of style, but it is not
merely a piece of formal symmetry. By these repetitions – and particularly
by those which have religious implications – Aeschylus is deliberately
recalling the mood, the ideas, the standards and the religion of the *parodos*
and indeed of the whole first half of the play. Everything is made to seem
the same. And yet everything is different, because Darius has spoken. By
designing the play, as it were, in three panels, of which the third repeats the
first, the dramatist has given to the central section the greatest possible
emphasis. Through this design, the religious thought of Darius, which is
also the poet's, is made to stand out like a peak above the lowlands of
traditional commonplace belief which surround it on either side.

Everything has been transformed by the Darius scene. But not, it would
appear, for the Chorus. Aeschylus must have hoped that his audience

---

[35] Note that Atossa addresses the *daimon* at 845.

[36] Many instances will be found in Korzeniewski, op. cit., and in E. B. Holtsmark, 'Ring composition
and the *Persae* of Aeschylus', *SO* 45 (1970) 5–23, who however seems to attach an exaggerated
importance to this stylistic feature. One can agree that ring-composition has an 'ideational' as well
as a structural purpose, since it can be used as a mode of emphasis and is perhaps most effective when
what intervenes between the two occurrences casts a new light upon word or theme. It is interesting
to find Mr Antony Hopkins (*Talking about sonatas* (London 1971) 18) saying much the same about
the effect of Recapitulation in sonata-form – and reminding us (ibid. 52) that it is not the
'ground-plan in itself' which has significance but the use to which it is put.

[37] There are echoes of the *parodos* in 916 (cf. 1 and n. 21 above); 925 (cf. 59); 926 (cf. 26); 1013 (cf. 87ff.,
esp. 91). The catalogue of fallen princes (955–1001) – cf. Holtsmark, op. cit. 19f. – echoes not only
the *parodos* (21–58) but the Messenger's report (302–28).

would be more perceptive. Yet the subsequent course of fifth-century history may well make us doubt whether the lesson of Ζεὺς κολαστής was really grasped by the Athenians. Aeschylus might indeed have felt it a deplorable thing, if the patriotic emotions which the play aroused did more to determine Athenian policy and actions than the warning against acts of *hubris* which he had employed the resources of his art to make effective.

In conclusion, *Persae* is not the greatest of the surviving plays of Aeschylus: it may well be the least great. The interpretation of East–West relations which it embodies is interesting, but does not seem to go much farther than might be expected from an intelligent Greek of the time. Morally, it is a study in black and white, and so lacks subtlety. The theological doctrine is fundamentally the same as that of Aeschylus at his greatest, but it is not put to the severer tests – that is to say, it is not developed in a context which, like those of *Oresteia* or the Danaid trilogy, raises wellnigh insoluble problems about the nature of Zeus and his justice. The victims are all guilty! Perhaps *Persae* demonstrates the superiority of myth over history as a theme for tragedy; perhaps it shows how wise Aeschylus was, normally, to write trilogies; perhaps, in 472, there were depths of thought and insight to which he had not yet attained. But all this, if true, is no reason why the play should not be given its due. I suggest that, in point of construction and dramatic craftsmanship, it is a finer piece of work than it is sometimes credited with being.[38]

[38] The artistic unity of the play is strongly defended by G. Paduano (op. cit. in n. 8).

CHAPTER TWO

Septem contra Thebas[1]

Septem carries the stamp of greatness: in the entrance-song of the chorus (for instance) and in the sombre rhetoric of the so-called *Redepaare*. Indeed, throughout we catch what Longinus called 'the resonance of a great mind'. It has, moreover, a feature which was not to be found in *Persae* and will not be found in *Supplices*: the dramatic issues are focused upon an arresting individual figure. Eteocles has been called 'the first Man of the European stage', and the play 'our earliest tragedy of character'.[2] Yet what *is* the character of Eteocles? The question has fascinated recent writers, but no agreement has been reached upon the answer.[3] This great play and this great dramatic figure continue to baffle us.

[1] The text of this chapter remains virtually as printed in *YCS* 25 (1977) 1–45; the annotation has been revised to take account of some subsequent work. I have had the benefit of comments on various drafts from a number of friends since it was first drafted at the Institute for Advanced Study at Princeton in 1964.

[2] Kitto (1) 54. 'The first clearly studied individual character in dramatic literature' (Gilbert Murray, in the preface to his translation). 'Der erste "tragische" Mensch der Weltdichtung': O. Regenbogen, *Hermes* 68 (1933) 69, who deliberately avoids the word 'Charakter'.

[3] A number of more specialized articles are cited with full details in subsequent footnotes. The following publications have appeared since 1958 and are cited, if at all, by name of author only or (in some cases) by name and date: H. H. Bacon, 'The shield of Eteocles', *Arion* 3.3 (1964) 27–38; A. L. Brown, 'Eteocles and the Chorus in the *Seven against Thebes*', *Phoenix* 31 (1977) 300–18; Anne Burnett, 'Curse and dream in Aeschylus' *Septem*', *GRBS* 14 (1973) 343–68; R. S. Caldwell, 'The misogyny of Eteocles', *Arethusa* 6 (1973) 197–231; H. D. Cameron, 'The debt to Earth in the *Seven against Thebes*', *TAPA* 95 (1964) 1–8; ' "Epigoni" and the law of inheritance in Aeschylus' *Septem*', *GRBS* 9 (1968) 247–57; 'The power of words in the *Seven against Thebes*', *TAPA* 101 (1970) 95–118; *Studies on the Seven against Thebes of Aeschylus* (The Hague 1971); R. D. Dawe, 'Inconsistency of plot and character in Aeschylus', *PCPS* 189 (1963) 21–62, esp. 31–42; C. M. Dawson, *The Seven against Thebes by Aeschylus*, transl. with comm. (Englewood Cliffs, N.J. 1970); F. Ferrari, 'La decisione di Eteocle e il tragico dei *Sette contra Tebe*', *Annali della Scuola N.S. di Pisa* ser. 3.2[1] (1972) 141–71; K. von Fritz, 'Die Gestalt des Eteokles in Aeschylus' *Sieben gegen Theben*', *Antike und moderne Tragödie* (Berlin 1962) 193–226; L. Golden, 'The character of Eteocles and the meaning of the *Septem*', *CPh* 59 (1964) 78–89; *In praise of Prometheus* (Chapel Hill, N.C. 1966) 42–61; A. Hecht and H. H. Bacon, *Seven against Thebes*, transl. (London and New York 1973); G. M. Kirkwood, 'Eteocles *oiakostrophos*', *Phoenix* 23 (1969) 9–25; A. Lesky, 'Eteokles in den *Sieben*

There are difficulties. *Persae* is complete as a single play; *Oresteia* is a complete trilogy. The remaining extant plays of Aeschylus are truncated works of art which cannot be fully understood in isolation from their lost companions. *Septem* was the last play of a trilogy; it was preceded by *Laius* and *Oedipus*, and of these plays we know little. As though this were not obstacle enough, there is grave suspicion – amounting in the view of many to virtual certainty – that the ending of the play, as we find it in the manuscripts, is not genuine. It seems that, for some later revival, an interpolator has modified the archaic simplicity of the action by adding a theme from the *Antigone* of Sophocles. But, even if we decide to excise the suspect passages, we cannot be quite sure how much of the original ending survived the interpolator's activities. Our approach to the interpretation of this play must therefore be modest, and discussion is bound to be interrogative and discursive. We can afford to neglect no evidence, no suggestion, but must beware of imposing patterns of interpretation. Without the earlier plays, the problem may well be insoluble.

Laius had been warned by the oracle of Apollo that he should die without offspring, if he was to keep his city safe. He disobeyed, and Oedipus was born, to kill his father and wed his mother. Having discovered the truth, Oedipus blinded himself; and then he cursed his sons. They quarrelled. Polynices, in exile, brought a foreign army against his native city. Thebes is besieged and about to be assaulted. Eteocles leads the defenders. It is with the last phase only of this well-known legend that *Septem* deals, and its action is of extreme simplicity. The play opens, unlike *Persae* and *Supplices*, with a spoken prologue. Eteocles addresses the citizens: it is a general's speech before battle.[4] He is joined by a spy, who tells him that the attack is imminent and that seven Argive champions will lead their forces against the seven gates of Thebes. Eteocles prays, and the prologue is over. The Chorus enters, not sedately marching, but dancing and singing to the excited dochmiac metre. They are the virgins of Thebes, panic-stricken by

gegen Theben', *WS* 74 (1961) 5–17; G. R. Manton, 'The second stasimon of the *Seven against Thebes*', *BICS* 8 (1961) 77–84; Brooks Otis, 'The unity of the *Seven against Thebes*', *GRBS* 3 (1960) 153–74; H. Patzer, 'Die dramatische Handlung des *Sieben gegen Theben*', *HSCP* 63 (1958) 97–119; A. J. Podlecki, 'The character of Eteocles in Aeschylus' *Septem*', *TAPA* 95 (1964) 283–99; T. G. Rosenmeyer, '*Seven against Thebes*: the tragedy of war', *Arion* 1.1 (1962) 48–78; O. L. Smith, 'The father's curse', *ClMed* 30 (1969) 27–43; W. G. Thalmann, *Dramatic art in Aeschylus's Seven against Thebes* (New Haven, Conn. and London 1978); K. Wilkens, *Die Interdependenz zwischen Tragödiensstruktur und Theologie bei Aischylos* (Munich 1974) 24–118; E. Wolff, 'Die Entscheidung des Eteokles in den *Sieben gegen Theben*', *HSCP* 63 (1958) 89–95.

4 Either he addresses the audience, as commonly held, or, as Taplin 129ff. argues, a token force 'on stage' which exits at 35.

the sounds of the enemy; and they have come to throw themselves upon
the altars of the city's gods in passionate prayer. Eteocles rebukes them for
indiscipline (in a scene which we shall have to consider with some care). At
the end, saying that he will himself fight at one of the seven gates, he leaves
the stage. After a choral ode, the Spy and Eteocles return in haste. The Spy
has discovered the order of battle of the invaders: that is, he now knows
which Argive champion will assault which gate. Each warrior is
described – his bearing, his words, the blazon upon his shield; and against
each Eteocles announces the dispatch of an appropriate defender. Six
attackers and six defending champions. But at the seventh gate is Polynices.
This is the dramatic climax of the play. Eteocles recognizes the working of
his father's curse and prepares to fight his brother in single combat. The
Chorus pleads with him, unavailingly, and he leaves the stage in full
armour. They then sing of the Erinys which is accomplishing the curse of
Oedipus; they sing of the disobedience of Laius and so place the present
crisis in relation to the disastrous history of the house. During their song the
battle is decided. A messenger brings the news that the city is saved, but the
two brothers have slain one another. Their bodies are brought on, and the
play (the genuine play) ends with a lyric lamentation, or *threnos*.

The summary is flat – deliberately flat, to avoid taking issue on matters
of controversy, with one exception, which is that the spuriousness of the
closing scene has been assumed. And on this something must be said,
though it can be said briefly here. The manuscripts contain, first (861–74),
an entry of Antigone and Ismene to lead the lamentations over their
brothers and then, later (1005–78), the entry of a herald, who, speaking on
behalf of the community, forbids the burial of Polynices. Antigone plays
her familiar Sophoclean role and defies the edict, supported by half the
Chorus, and two separate funeral processions move off. (What fate awaits
Antigone we can only surmise.) Here are two separate questions. The first
is whether Aeschylus introduced the sisters at all, and it is of minor
importance: some critics who reject the Herald accept Antigone and
Ismene. Since this has little effect upon the general interpretation of the
play, no words need be wasted on it. It is different with the Herald-scene.
The real argument against the genuineness of this scene is not linguistic or
stylistic (though such objections have been raised), but dramatic. It has
seemed to many in the last degree improbable that at the very end of a
trilogy Aeschylus would raise a new issue – and fail to carry it to a proper
conclusion. And, since there was motive and opportunity for interpolation,
it has seemed preferable to believe that the trilogy was not murdered by its

own creator. As it stands in the manuscripts, the close of the trilogy is ragged: *Oresteia* leaves no loose ends.[5] It is of course an assumption, founded on a subjective judgement, that Aeschylus in 467 was writing trilogies upon the same principles of art and thought as in 458, but it is the assumption one prefers to make.[6]

This view also assumes that, if the interpolated passages are removed, we are left with a conclusion which is artistically satisfactory, consistent with what we know or can reasonably conjecture about the trilogy as a whole. For the content of the lost plays our most important evidence is in the second *stasimon* (720–91) – the choral ode which intervenes between the departure of Eteocles for the battle and the news of its outcome.[7] In its explicit reference to past generations it is unlike any other feature of the surviving play; and its purpose is, obviously, to place the immediate action in a long perspective, to pull the threads together in preparation for the final act, which closes not this play only, but the trilogy as a whole. The ode is constructed with great care and with characteristic Aeschylean symmetry.

It opens with a word of fear; and fear was the keynote of the Chorus' earlier songs – fear for the city and for their fate as citizens. What they now fear is the Erinys, the grim goddess that is like to accomplish the curse of Oedipus upon his sons (720–6). 'I shudder at the destroyer of a *house* (τὰν

---

[5] See ch. 3 for the Danaid trilogy, and ch. 9 for *Prometheia* which, whether by Aeschylus or not, should come into consideration.

[6] H. Lloyd-Jones, 'The end of the *Seven against Thebes*', CQ 9 (1959) 80–115, sought to demonstrate, not that the suspected passages are undoubtedly genuine, but that the objective evidence adduced against them falls short of establishing that they are spurious. The weight of recent opinion is against their authenticity: cf., e.g., E. Fraenkel, 'Zum Schluss der "Sieben gegen Theben"', *MH* 21 (1964) 58–64; R. D. Dawe, 'The end of Seven against Thebes', CQ 17 (1967) 16–28: id. *Dionysiaca* (ed. R. D. Dawe *et al.*, Cambridge 1978) 87–103; P. Nicolaus, *Die Frage nach der Echtheit der Schlusszene von Aischylos' Sieben gegen Theben* (diss. Tübingen 1967); A. L. Brown, 'The end of the *Seven against Thebes*', CQ 26 (1976) 206–19 (who defends 1005–25 and 1054–78); Taplin 169ff.
'Recent writers agree that the essential question is whether a new theme is likely to have been introduced at the end of a trilogy' (Cameron, 1968, p. 249). For me the answer is clearly no, certainly not in this way. 'Was folgt aus dem so unerbitterlich Verbot? Nichts folgt, ganz und gar nichts; nichts geschieht, nichts wird oder kann geschehen' (Fraenkel, op. cit.). As to the sisters, whom W. Pötscher, *Eranos* 46 (1958) 140–54, tried to rescue, I would only say that, if Aeschylus introduced them, he did not do so with the anapaests which stand in the text. It is simply incredible that the lines 854–60 – one of the finest and most moving sustained metaphors in Aeschylus – were separated by this poor stuff from the *threnos* they were written to lead into. (For a different view of these lines, which are admittedly corrupt, see Dawe, *Dionysiaca* 89f. A. L. Brown, *Eranos* 74 (1976) 6–21, argues that 848–60 are misplaced and should precede 832–47.) If no sisters, 996f. should be deleted with Wilamowitz and Fraenkel.

[7] For a careful examination of the ode see Manton, who conducted a series of seminar discussions on the play at the University of London Institute of Classical Studies in May 1960: after this lapse of time it is hard to be sure what I owe to him and to other participants.

ὠλεσίοικον)'. At the end (790f.), after the terms of the curse (or something close to them) have been given, the ode concludes with the words: 'I tremble lest the swift Erinys bring it to accomplishment.' This is the familiar ring-composition. But, in addition, rather more than half-way through the ode (764f.) there is a third word of fear (followed immediately by a third reference to curses, a third word of accomplishment).[8] And the fear is different. 'I fear lest along with the princes the city be subdued.' What has intervened to cause this change in the object of fear is the story of Laius and his disobedience. His disobedience to Apollo, who thrice spoke in his Pythian shrine to say that it was by dying without progeny that Laius would keep his city safe (θνᾴσκοντα γέννας ἄτερ σῴζειν πόλιν). We can be sure that in these or similar terms the audience had heard the oracle before (perhaps in the prologue of *Laius*). The terms were chosen with care, so that neither Apollo nor Aeschylus was committed to the final destruction of the city. Oracles are traditionally ambiguous. This oracle might mean that the city would certainly be destroyed, if Laius had offspring: it was not excluded, however, that, if the family that should never have come into being were to perish, the city would be saved.[9] One thing is certain: since the birth of Oedipus, the city has been in jeopardy.[10] Thus, when the Messenger announces that the city has been saved (πόλις σέσωται), the words of the oracle (σῴζειν πόλιν) are clearly recalled.[11] But, if the city has been saved, the princes are dead and their ill-fated family has come to an end.[12] The fates of both city and family have been in the balance; and of this double issue there is a double outcome. There is, as the Messenger says, cause for rejoicing and for tears, and his words are picked up by the Chorus (814ff., 825ff.).

The *polis*-theme which runs through *Septem* – and must have run through the trilogy – is underlined by the metaphor of the ship of state, of the ship in storm (there is no better example of a recurrent metaphor in

---

8　Curses, 725, 766, 787; fear: 720, 763, 790; accomplishment: 724, 766, 791. The theme of wealth also appears at the beginning, middle and end of the ode: see pp. 43f. below.

9　Cf. Manton 80. The oracle in this form was no doubt the invention of Aeschylus. What was the question, and in what circumstances was it put? Better than the commonplace enquiry of childless couples, it would suit a consultation on the safety of the city (cf. Herodotus 6.19). In any case the answer, as Manton points out, is paradoxical, 'since normally a king would regard it as his duty to provide for the carrying on of his own guardianship of the state by begetting a son'.

10　And was certainly jeopardized on a previous occasion by the Sphinx: see p. 41. below.

11　The passage 803–21 has suffered dislocation, and scholars are not agreed upon a remedy: see most recently H. Erbse, 'Interpretationsprobleme in den Septem des Aischylos', *Hermes* 92 (1964) 19–22; C. W. Willink, 'A problem in Aeschylus' *Septem*', *CQ* 18 (1968) 4–10; Taplin 168 n. 1. Both 804 and 820 open with πόλις σέσωται, followed by a reference to the fate of the royal brothers. If not both, then at least one or the other is genuine.

12　Line 828 (ἀτέκνους); cf. 690f.

Aeschylus). It is used with economy, and thus the more effectively, at salient points: in the first words of Eteocles (1ff.); towards the end of the Spy's first speech (62ff.); in the choral ode which follows the departure of Eteocles (758ff.); in the first words of the Messenger (795f.).[13] It is specially associated with Eteocles. Eteocles is steersman of the ship of state; he is lord of the Cadmeians ($Καδμείων\ ἄναξ$) and so first addressed (39). But he is also 'son of Oedipus' and so addressed by the Chorus (203). Thus the two issues are both focused upon him; his words and actions and decisions affect them both. In the earlier part of the play we see him primarily in his 'political' role. As king of Thebes, he speaks as the situation requires ($λέγειν\ τὰ\ καίρια$, 1), and his generalship is wise. When he speaks and acts as son of Oedipus, will his words and deeds be as timely? It seems as though Aeschylus may have intended to invite this question. It is perhaps worth noticing a contrast brought out in the earlier part of the play. Note the words of the Spy at the end of his first speech (67f.): 'through my clear reports you will have knowledge of the state of the external foe ($τὰ\ τῶν\ θύραθεν$) and will come to no harm'. As defender of his city against this external enemy, we see Eteocles as vigilant (3), undeceived (38) and well-informed (40, 67), saying as well as doing what is seasonable. May it not be that in his role as the accursed son of Oedipus, caught off his guard, caught in a trap, summoned to deal with a foe internal to his house, internal to himself, he will display a different quality?[14] Perhaps it is no accident that the Spy, as he leaves the stage after announcing that Polynices is at the seventh gate, is made to recall the prologue by reverting to 'the ship of state' (651f.).[15]

His speech (631–52) is the great hinge upon which the structure of the play

[13] The same comparison is used by Eteocles at 208–10. Dawson, 18f., reviews the passages, together with related metaphors of wind and wave. Cf. also Kirkwood 19–22; Thalmann 32ff.; Petrounias 34–51.

[14] Cf. Bacon 29f.: 'there is a danger "outside" which must not be let in, and a danger "inside" which must not be let out'; Caldwell 205; Thalmann 38ff. Bacon points out that images of storm and animality are used of both the internal and the external enemy.

The expression $τὰ\ τῶν\ θύραθεν$ recurs in 193, contrasted in the following line with $ἔνδοθεν$; since 194 is so true of Eteocles and his house, Aeschylus may have intended a double meaning. (If, with Headlam, reading $ὀφέλλεται$, we could translate 193 as 'things outside are going as much as possible in our favour', the point would emerge more clearly, but this is a doubtful sense for the verb.) The contrast recurs at 201f.: the women should leave 'external' affairs to the man, their place is within the house. But the house will be the source of danger, in relation to which Eteocles will need – and will reject – their counsels.

[15] It is commonly, and perhaps rightly, held that 619 is spurious. It may seem uncalled-for as a comment on the Delphic oracle. If it was 'dragged in', it was in order to remind the audience of line 1, before the seasonableness of Eteocles' speech is put to the final test. Dawson, *ad loc.*, defends the line, also with reference to 1, but on rather different grounds.

turns; and his final words round off the whole first portion of the play. The
sharp, the shattering, contrast between what has gone before and what
comes after is enhanced by the extraordinary way in which Aeschylus has
handled the exposition of this play – with a boldness only an 'archaic' poet
would have dared to employ. Though the occasion of the war is the quarrel
between Eteocles and Polynices, and though the climax of the action is to
be their single combat, no word is spoken of the quarrel, nor is Polynices
named or his presence in the invading army mentioned, until the play has
run more than half its course (576ff.). Though the quarrel and the duel are
the working-out of the curse of Oedipus, that curse is only mentioned once
in the earlier portion of the play, when Eteocles (69ff.), praying the gods to
save the city, joins to Zeus and Earth and the city's gods the name of the
Erinys that is his father's Curse. Then the theme drops out until (655)
Eteocles recognizes in the conjunction of himself and his brother at the
seventh gate the fulfilment of that curse. From then on, it is never out of
mind.[16] This arrangement makes for a sheer dramatic effect of great
power, for a moment of 'astonishment' (ἔκπληξις) such as Aeschylus
loved; and this might be explanation enough. But it has made critics ask in
what the unity of the play resides, if it has unity; and what is the
relationship between the Eteocles of the first part and the Eteocles of the
second part, if they are related. It may be worth while to list some of the
views which have been held upon these questions.

Aeschylus has taken from different versions of the myth two themes
which are not really consistent and has combined them mechanically to fill
out the action of his play (Wilamowitz). He has made Eteocles play
different roles as each scene demanded, being interested in the dramatic
effect of individual scenes rather than in the consistency of the whole
(Howald). There is no inconsistency, no change in the bearing of Eteocles,
who is from first to last the unselfish patriot, and who accepts the pollution
of a brother's blood as the last and greatest gift he can make his country
(Pohlenz). The complete change in Eteocles from the calm patriot of the
first half to a man lusting after his brother's blood is the best possible
evidence of the power of the Erinys now suddenly working upon him
(Solmsen). There are these views and variations upon them.[17] Closely

---

[16] Lines 655, 695, 700, 709, 720ff., 766, 785ff., 819, 833, 841, 887, 977; cf. 987.

[17] U. von Wilamowitz: e.g. *Aischylos Interpretationen* (Berlin 1914) 66f.; *Griechische Verskunst* (Berlin
1921) 199. E. Howald, *Die griechische Tragödie* (Munich 1930) 73. Pohlenz 193ff. F. Solmsen, 'The
Erinys in Aischylos' *Septem*', *TAPA* 68 (1937) 197–211 – an article which initiated a generation of
debate. Add the view of Golden, for whom Eteocles is from first to last a self-seeking politician with
no real belief in the Erinys.

related to this controversy is another. To what extent should we regard Eteocles as a free agent? Is the decision that he shall fight his brother at the seventh gate his own or imposed upon him by the gods? Or do his own desires go along with the decrees of destiny? Are we right to speak of a *decision*? What did he decide and when did he decide it? Perhaps it will be best to take this last question first. It involves, for one thing, the effect and significance of the most striking single feature of the play.

Aeschylus liked to build an imposing feature in the middle of his plays (or rather later): the Darius-scene in *Persae*, the Cassandra-scene in *Agamemnon*, the great *kommos* in *Choephori*. So here, in the centre of the play, 300 lines – nearly a third of the whole – are taken up with seven pairs of speeches (with brief lyrics between each pair): the Spy describes one by one the seven Argive champions at the seven gates and Eteocles names a Theban to oppose each one of them. (It is convenient to refer to this scene by the German term *Redepaare*.) The scene is unrealistic (and provoked a jibe from Euripides),[18] but the day is doubtless past when it had to be defended from the charge of being undramatic. The drama resides primarily in the fact that Eteocles does not know, though the audience and the reader foresee, that he will meet his brother at the seventh gate; and, as each Theban champion is posted to meet an adversary who is not Polynices, the more certain it becomes that the brothers will meet, so that we see Eteocles, as it were, being forced down a narrowing tunnel towards his doom. If, as Kitto suggested,[19] there are always good reasons why Eteocles should not post himself at one of the first six gates (and particularly if the sixth chance, because of the virtues of Amphiaraus, proves to be no chance at all), there is a strong effect of dramatic irony. The idea is attractive, but has met a powerful challenge.[20] When did Eteocles make his choices? He states (at 282ff.) that he will post seven champions, himself included, to the seven gates 'before the swift and hasty-rumoured words of a messenger arrive and set all ablaze under pressure of need'. This is explicitly said, and (so the argument goes) it should be assumed, in default

[18] *Phoen.* 751f.: cf. *Arethusa* 2 (1969) 139, n. 18.

[19] Kitto (1) 50f. Kitto is excellent on the general effect of this scene, but goes too far when he speaks of Eteocles as 'a man of acute moral perceptions', who appoints against each attacker 'the man best fitted by his moral character to meet that particular assailant'. Neither the attackers nor the defenders are quite so clearly differentiated as that. A special importance seems to attach to Tydeus (and Kitto may be right that the first person singular in 397 suggests, for a moment, that Eteocles will go against him), and to the virtuous Amphiaraus against whom he cannot go; and it may not be accidental that these, together with the seventh gate, are the three cases in which a future tense is used (see n. 21). (Delete 472, with Fraenkel and Page.)

[20] By Wolff and Patzer in *HSCP* (1958).

of evidence to the contrary, that it is carried out and that, therefore, when
he meets the Spy, his postings have already been made; and, since the
Argive order of battle has been determined by lot (55f., 376), it is the gods,
not Eteocles, who have paired the two brothers at the seventh gate; and it is
this divine appointment that he recognizes by his outburst at 653ff. This
view also has its attraction, but encounters a difficulty. Having described
the first of the Argive warriors, the Spy asks: 'Whom will you post against
him?'; and in due course Eteocles replies: 'I will post against Tydeus the
good son of Astacus.' τίν' ἀντιτάξεις τῷδε;, τόνδ' ἀντιτάξω (395, 408).
That the Spy, who cannot know what has been happening, should use the
future tense is natural enough. But surely, if Aeschylus wished it to be clear
that the postings had already been made, the one thing he should not have
done was to make Eteocles use the future tense of the very first posting. In
fact different tenses are used in different instances: three futures, two
perfects, an aorist and a present; and this has perplexed the commentators.
More perhaps than it need have done. Taking the tenses at their face value,
a spectator will suppose that Eteocles has been interrupted at his work, that
some champions have been posted and some not. It could even be that, as
Lesky suggests, he aimed deliberately to combine two impressions both
vital to the effect of the scene – the sense of an inexorable destiny, the sense
that something is developing before our eyes. And the second impression *is*
vital. Indeed it is hard to see that there is any real advantage, dramatic or
religious, in making the conjunction of Eteocles with Polynices arise
automatically from decisions taken prior to this scene. The duel is in any
case contrived by the Erinys. How much better that the spectator should
feel that the Erinys has been working under his very eyes, through words
and decisions of a character upon the stage![21]

And perhaps it does not make all that difference whether Eteocles takes
his decisions now or then, for when we come to the seventh gate, his

---

[21] My criticism of the Wolff–Patzer view follows much the same lines as Lesky (1) and (2) 95; see also
von Fritz (1) 200–5, and Kirkwood 12f., who criticizes Erbse's laboured attempt (op. cit. in n. 11) to
justify the use of future tenses referring to a posting which has already been made, on the grounds
that the time referred to is the (future) time of Eteocles' *answer*. 'Ich will deine Mahnung mit
folgender Disposition beantworten.' Surely it would have needed a very sharp-witted member of
the audience to take the point. As to 285f., the lines are certainly preparation for the simultaneous
entries of Eteocles and Spy at 369ff., being clearly recalled by the language of 371 and 373f. Surely,
this cuts both ways. It could indicate that Eteocles has forestalled the situation envisaged, but it
could equally mean that that situation has in fact arisen, interrupting Eteocles at his work. This was
the view of Wilamowitz, Groeneboom and Italie (*Aeschylus' Zeven gegen Theben*, Leiden 1950); and
(*pace* Kirkwood and others) I prefer to accept it, not believing Aeschylus used his tenses without
precise intention. See n. 19 (futures used for the most significant choices) and n. 45 (a special point
about Hippomedon and Hyperbius). For a recent defence of the Patzer-view, see Burnett 346f.
(with notes 12 and 13); and on the whole problem Wilkens 61ff., Taplin 142ff., 152ff.

position is the same and equally fatal.[22] He is committed to fight, and now this is the only gate at which he can fight, and it is his brother's gate. On both hypotheses, he has the same alternative – to fight or go back on his word. And that is how the issue of freedom presents itself: is he free – and does he wish – to change his mind, to go back on his decision? He does not change his mind. And, if we ask why, we are not importing a modern speculation, for he gives his reason. He seems to give more than one reason. The whole scene, which begins with the speech of Eteocles at 653ff. and continues up to his final exit, needs – and will receive – close examination, but one dominant factor, one strand in a complex fabric, is his recognition that the curse of Oedipus is being fulfilled, that it is thus futile to struggle, because he and his house are dedicated to destruction by the gods. The Erinys, to which he prayed in the prologue, and of which the Chorus will sing, is at her fatal work.

It is often said or implied that, except for the prayer of Eteocles, the curse and the Erinys which embodies it are absent altogether from the first portion of the play and, with that same exception, from the mind of Eteocles. And it is true that Aeschylus has excluded any other direct reference to the curse or the quarrel or even to the presence of Polynices with the invading army. But the explicit is not everything, least of all in Aeschylus. Here, as so often, we suffer from the loss of the preceding plays. It is, however, tolerably certain that *Oedipus* contained the curse; and that the audience listened to *Septem*, from the start, with the curse in their minds.[23] We then must read it so and remember, when the first speaker introduces himself as Eteocles, that this is a man who has been cursed by his father. Whatever the terms of the curse, and in whatever sense they were understood, for a man to lie beneath a father's curse was to the Greek a most terrible thing: it had the force of an Erinys and is recognized by Eteocles as 'great in power' (70; cf. 977). The mental state of such a man might well be abnormal and show itself in his words. Of course, Aeschylus often frustrates modern expectations, but, supposing that he wished to convey such a hint, he would be likely to do it early. It is thus worth

---

[22] The point is made by A. L. Brown (1977) 307.

[23] Having the curse in mind, an audience might be alert to the double aspect in which Earth is presented in the prologue as in the whole play (see Cameron, 1964, and Dawson 19–22). A kindly mother to be defended (16ff., cf. 415f.), she is also associated with death, drinking shed blood, and receiving the bodies of the dead. Hence the ironical fulfilment of the curse: the brothers, who have quarrelled over their share in earth as the giver of wealth, receive equal shares of earth in burial. Perhaps the idea of the world of the dead as 'all-hospitable' (860, cf. *Suppl.* 156f.) was so familiar that πανδοκοῦσα at 18 conveyed a double meaning (cf. Dawson 21, n. 45).

considering the words of Eteocles, when first he gives his name. 'If we should fare well, god's is the credit; but, if . . . disaster should befall, the name of Eteocles – and of Eteocles alone – would be loudly sung throughout the city by the citizens, with muttering preludes and with groans' (4ff.).[24] Do the words express an attitude of mistrust, a sense of isolation, not only from other men but also from the gods, such as a man under a curse, the member of a doomed family, might feel? It is a hint, no more, but it prepares us for the equally strange tone of other references by Eteocles to the gods. But Eteocles, in his civic capacity, must pray to them. About the terms of his prayer there has been much debate.

And the debate turns on a particle. 'O Zeus and Earth and the city-gods, and the Erinys-Curse of my father that has great power, do not utterly uproot the city in total destruction by enemy-sack . . .' The word for city is followed by the particle γε, which can have limiting or restrictive force: 'the city at least'. And, if it has limiting force, it can hardly fail to suggest a distinction between the city which is to be saved and the house which is to be destroyed, and to the destruction of which the terms (πρυμνόθεν πανώλεθρον ἐκθαμνίσητε) are so appropriate.[25] It would be blindness to deny that this distinction is deliberately suggested by Aeschylus. The doubt is whether the distinction is in the mind of Eteocles or whether his words, by the familiar device of dramatic irony, convey more than he means. Much has been built on this particle. For, if Eteocles is in effect saying: 'Destroy me and my house, if you must, but spare the city', this prepares the way for an act of un-selfregarding sacrifice on his part at the climax of the play. Decision on this issue is precarious and bound to be subjective. In Aeschylus, the word is apt to be more important than the man (the word with a life of its own), which should make us lean towards an interpretation

---

24 The sentiment can be paralleled, with progressive secularity, from Thuc. 2.64.1–2 (cited by Dawson 4, n. 10) and Dem. *de Corona* 212, discussed by E. Fraenkel in *MH* 18 (1961) 37, who suggests that Aeschylus may be using a familiar form of contemporary oratory. The phraseology of our passage is, however, remarkably suggestive. (i) There is the relationship of Eteocles to the *polis* (6, 9) – and his potential isolation from it. (ii) There is his relationship to the gods, brought out by the hymn-and-prelude metaphor. (There will be a hymn indeed, but directed *against* Eteocles – and Eteocles alone. It will have a prelude in groans and mutterings, prior to something worse.) The preceding plays might have thrown light on this theme. (iii) There may be a play on the name of Eteocles. On this – and on the drama as a whole – see J. T. Sheppard, *CQ* 7 (1913) 73–82, which is still valuable.

25 As the text stands, Eteocles goes on to couple with πόλιν the expression δόμους ἐφεστίους, which, if it means anything, must mean houses where dwells a group united by common worship at the hearth. This is a prayer that, as regards houses, cannot be answered in respect to the house of Oedipus. R. D. Dawe, *The collation and investigation of manuscripts of Aeschylus* (Cambridge 1964) 180f., has launched so powerful an attack on the genuineness of 73 that it may be unsafe to base interpretation upon it. Page, in his Oxford Text, deletes with Dawe, but the line is defended by Lloyd-Jones in *CR* 16 (1966) 20f. See now G. Zuntz, *PCPS* 27 (1981) 90f.

in terms of the theme (and the action) rather than in terms of psychology. But the principle must not be pressed too far. If there is other evidence for the mental state of Eteocles in this earlier phase of the play, we should perhaps say that, with these words, he vaguely forebodes the destruction of his house and of himself: to say that he offers himself as a willing sacrifice to save the city seems more than should be read into the words.[26]

We must now turn to the scene between Eteocles and the women of the Chorus. Nowhere in the play have critical judgements been more sharply opposed. It seems to be a matter of temperament whether or not one finds an excess of violence in the abusive words with which Eteocles rebukes the frightened women. Clearly a commander is entitled to restrain those who, he fears, will spread panic among his troops; a religious – or superstitious – man might well fear words of ill-omen, even when they are addressed to the gods;[27] a Greek, in either case, is likely to base himself upon a general principle. Yet, this sweeping condemnation of women! 'Neither in trouble nor in prosperity may I share my house with the female sex. When a woman is dominant, her confidence [her criminality?] is intolerable; when she has become afraid, she is an even worse evil to house and city.' The double reference to the *house* (188, 190) in this *political* context should perhaps be noted; and it is not surprising that a French critic leans towards a psychological interpretation and regards the violence of Eteocles as a reaction to his accursed state. 'C'est la maternité qu'Étéocle haït, car il ne l'a connue, dans sa famille, que souillée par l'inceste.'[28] The point is well taken – may indeed have been obvious to those who had seen *Laius* and *Oedipus*. One may agree that Eteocles was affected by the horror of the relationship between the sexes in his family, linked as it was to his accursed state. But did Aeschylus ever write a speech of twenty lines mainly for the purpose of characterizing a personage? Here too the words may be more important than the man. And perhaps we shall never seize the significance of the words without the help of the lost plays, in which, probably, a woman played a role. But to this we will return.[29]

In the scene which follows (203–44), the Chorus plead against the threats of Eteocles their fears and the piety which leads them to place all their hopes in the gods. Their piety as such he cannot rebuke (236), but urges them to

[26] Cf. Lesky (1) 10f. 'Una eventuale dissociazione fra le sorti di Eteocle e della città non implicherebbe di per sè un rapporto di causalità, e *almeno* [sc. γϵ] non significa in ogni caso che Eteocle pensi a se stesso come ad un olocausto per la salvezza della città' (Ferrari 145).

[27] Cf. Cameron (1970) 99, but see n. 33 below.

[28] Méautis 108f. Cf. Patzer 103, Podlecki 284, and others.

[29] See pp. 45f. below.

discipline: they should stay at home and keep quiet and leave the required religious observances to the men. On the realistic plane this is reasonable enough, but the tone of much that he says arouses question. Words such as 'pragmatism', 'cynicism' and 'insincerity' have been used by critics.[30] Or is it rather that disillusionment of a man who has himself no hope in the gods which we found (rightly or wrongly) in the early lines of the play? The ephirrhematic scene is followed by *stichomythia*, which resumes and concentrates the earlier themes: the fears of the Chorus; the abuse of women; the appeal for discipline. The Chorus yield compliance (263). Their compliance comes suddenly rather than by a gradual process of persuasion;[31] and the terms they use may be more significant than the fact that they comply. 'I keep silence;' says the Coryphaeus (263), 'along with others I will suffer what is fated.' But what is fated for the city? What is fated for Eteocles? It is of sinister import, when he says: 'I choose that word of yours instead of those' (264) and (by ring-composition) closes the main section of his speech by a return to their word: 'None the more shall you escape what is fated' (281). Immediately he announces his intention of fighting, the seventh with six others at the gates.[32]

When Aeschylus emphasizes a theme by the repetition of words, we should take note. The theme is silence. Four times with the same word, Eteocles urges silence on the Chorus (232, 250, 252, 262); and the *stichomythia* comes to its climax with: 'Be silent', 'I am silent'.[33] But can silence alter facts? The Chorus *are* afraid, and with good reason (and they *do* hear the horses neighing, 245f.); and in fact, despite their promise, they do go on singing about fear,[34] though, on the realistic plane, it was the part of a prudent general to make them desist. It may, however, be suggested that there is another kind of silence about another kind of fear. It has already

---

[30] Dawe (*Collation* 142) speaks of 'Eteocles's half-cynical, half-pessimistic religious attitude (cf. *vv* 4ff., 217–18, 719)'. Cf. Golden, *passim*; Podlecki 287ff. (who speaks of 'insincerity'); Dawson 5 ('sardonic irony'), 7 ('a very pragmatic view of the gods'). At 236, his δαιμόνων . . . γένος has been seen as derogatory: this is doubtful, but his 256, after 255, approaches blasphemy.

[31] Cf. *Eum.* 892ff.

[32] The expression used does not necessarily imply that he will be seventh in order, i.e. at the seventh gate, though it was doubtless chosen to suggest it.

[33] At 258 παλινστομεῖς is explained by a scholiast with δυσφημεῖς: see the notes of Tucker and Rose, who puts the point as follows – 'If you cannot speak properly, say nothing at all.' One is reminded of the familiar double sense of εὐφημεῖν, εὐφημία: well-omened speech or (to be on the safe side) silence. For the employment of this theme in the *Agamemnon*, see App. E, esp. 214. Either kind of evasion is futile; and I suspect that this is the real significance of the passages examined by Cameron (1970).

[34] In metre – and no doubt in music and dance – the first *stasimon* is calmer than the *parodos*. The *parodos*, while envisaging the sack of the city, was concentrated upon the immediate sounds and sights which threatened battle. The *stasimon* is devoted to a vivid evocation of the sack itself – the fate from which the champions of the *Redepaare* are to save the city and its inhabitants.

been pointed out how remarkable it is that, in the earlier part of the play, except for one line, silence is preserved about the curse of Oedipus – unbroken silence about the presence of Polynices in the invading army. Yet these are facts which will determine the outcome of the action, and silence cannot alter them. The fact of the Erinys is a ground for fear; and Mme de Romilly has shown, in a brilliant book,[35] how intimate is the association in Aeschylus between the idea of an Erinys and the idea of fear – an association which is developed, with formal art, in the choral ode (720ff.) we have already studied. This association has not yet been made explicit in the play, but the audience of Aeschylus may have been ready to assume that a man who is the object of an Erinys is a man in fear. It may be suggested, then, that throughout the first part of the play Eteocles is in fear, which is not fear of battle or of death (for in human affairs he is courageous), but fear of the Erinys. This fear, except for one outburst, he conceals in silence, but the excessive character of his reaction to the fears of the Chorus derives from his own – and different – fear. This fear is vague and intermittent; it does not prevent him from using words which imply his survival and victory in the struggle (271ff.) or enable him to see the sinister implications of the references to fate. But the words of Aeschylus cannot be silenced.

If it is indeed true that the Eteocles of the prologue and the first episode is shown, behind the façade of a resolute king and general, to be filled with a vague sense of doom, with fear of the Erinys, with despair in his relation to the divine world, we shall not see this aspect of him in the earlier part of the *Redepaare*. The outburst at 653ff. will be the more effective, the more completely Eteocles is calm and *sophron* in the preceding phase. It is now his function to do and to say what is timely (τὰ καίρια), to interpret the accounts of the Spy, to turn the arrogant words and symbols against the boasters and, with the right words, to send against each the right man.[36]

On the broad dramatic effect of this scene something has already been said. A tension is generated which justifies the suspension of all obvious dramatic action during nearly one-third of the play. But Aeschylus had set himself a technical problem in giving ordered variety to an episode which, prior to the seventh gate, consisted merely of six pairs of speeches. The over-riding pattern is that of boasters on the one side, men of modest courage on the other. This pattern he was enabled to break by presenting the prophet Amphiaraus as a good man fatally involved with evil

[35] *La crainte et l'angoisse dans le théâtre d'Eschyle* (Paris 1958).
[36] On this process of 'verbal magic' see Bacon 32; Rosenmeyer 68; Cameron (1970) 97, 100ff.

companions. He was still left with five boasters; and all the resources of his rhetoric, all his command of visual and auditory images, might – without his constructional skill – have left a monotonous impression. It is worth studying how he dealt with this problem, and more may emerge than mere technical skill.[37]

First is Tydeus, and against him Melanippus. Tydeus lusts for battle, and abuses the prophet who will not let him fight. So is first introduced the sixth champion Amphiaraus; and in the Spy's sixth speech Amphiaraus answers Tydeus in kind – and then passes judgement on Polynices (his first mention in the play); looking backward and forward, the speech rounds off the first phase and introduces the second. Tydeus is bloodthirsty, a cruel and barbaric figure, arrogant (or unfortunate?) in his choice of blazon for his shield,[38] but he does not blaspheme against the gods. He is in a sense more human than those that follow, as he is closer to the story. (And, as will be seen, his description bears on Eteocles.) Between him and Amphiaraus stand the figures of Capaneus, Eteoclus, Hippomedon and Parthenopaeus. Capaneus is the very paradigm of blasphemers, notorious for his Zeus-inflicted punishment, which Eteocles foretells. Eteoclus is a minor figure under the shadow of Capaneus; he blasphemes, not against Zeus, but merely (on his shield) against Ares; and Eteocles can deal with him briefly. With Hippomedon Zeus returns, but in a skilful variation. As Capaneus was the human being who challenged the thunder of Zeus, so Typhon was his great superhuman adversary. Hippomedon has Typhon upon his shield; and this is shown to be ill-omened for him, since, by a lucky chance, his opponent has Zeus upon his. Parthenopaeus – an enigmatic figure, by whose legend the imagination of Aeschylus had perhaps been caught[39] – has the Sphinx for blazon, and with it we move back a step towards the present story and are ready for Amphiaraus and his comments upon Tydeus and Polynices. It seems, then, that these four figures move upon a different, a remoter, plane than Tydeus, Amphiaraus, Polynices

---

[37] For a different view of the relationship of structure and theme, cf. Wilkens 61ff., who places great emphasis upon the fourth gate (Typhon/Zeus), as also does Thalmann 106, 114.

[38] Cf. Bacon 32.

[39] On the Parthenopaeus-speeches see the interesting discussion of Cameron (1970) 104–6; also Thalmann 114f. At 532 Διός and δορός are ancient variants (for the evidence see Dawe, *Collation* 152–4, and Page's apparatus). βίᾳ with a dependent genitive elsewhere in Aeschylus has the sense of 'despite', and most modern editors favour Διός. It seems strange, however, in view of the care with which Aeschylus has patterned his blasphemers, that this supreme blasphemy should be thrown out so casually and then dropped, picked up by neither Eteocles nor the Chorus. Looking at *Sept.* 47, one may suspect that the sense was complete at the end of 531, and the first word of 532 was mainly illegible, both Διός and δορός being reasonably intelligent attempts to supply the missing word. Perhaps δεινόν or (with Blaydes' τάδ') δεινῶς?

– and Eteocles. Their defeat is certain, if the gods are just and moral (though their opponents may not escape death),[40] but it is Tydeus and Amphiaraus – the first and the last – who stand closest to the story.

The significance of Tydeus is clear: that, as he lusts after the blood of his enemies, so Eteocles will lust after the blood of his brother. This is so, if verbal reminiscences mean anything.[41] Against Tydeus was sent Melanippus, a man who worshipped the 'throne of Shame' and shrank from shameful deeds and from such deeds alone. So was Eteocles preoccupied with his honour.[42] Blood-lust and honour are two of the themes which complicate the judgement of the scene to which we must now turn.

When Eteocles hears that his brother is at the seventh gate, threatening to kill him or drive him into exile, as he claims to have been driven, claiming, with no boastful words[43] but through the modest figure of Justice on his shield, that he has right on his side, what will Eteocles say and what will he do? The Spy, whose function was in relation to the external enemy and has been performed, now leaves the stage. And we are at the heart of the difficulty of interpreting the piece. What will Eteocles say? In a long speech (653–76) he will reject the claims of Polynices, identify himself as the proper adversary of his brother, and will send for his armour. When the Coryphaeus pleads with him, he will answer in terms of his honour (677–85). When the full Chorus takes up the plea with the power of song, he remains obdurate, speaking bitterly of his father's curse and the hostility of the gods (686–711). All this time, it seems, his panoply is being brought out by slaves and his arming for battle takes place before the eyes of the audience.[44] A fine visual effect of the kind that Aeschylus loved. As each

---

[40] Some members of the audience would remember that Melanippus and Megareus – both *spartoi* (412, 474) and so a special class of Thebans with a special relationship to their native soil – died in their defence of Thebes (cf. C. Robert, *Oidipus* (Berlin 1915) 131ff., 247).

[41] 380: μαργῶν καὶ μάχης λελιμμένος; 392: μάχης ἐρῶν. Compare the phraseology of 686–8, 692.

[42] See pp. 35ff. below. At 415f. we cannot be sure whether ὁμαίμων is a nominative adjective agreeing with Δίκη or a genitive plural (as maintained by K. Wilkens, *Hermes* 97 (1969) 117–21). In any case, the combination is bound to make us think not only of Polynices, who is attacking his native land on a claim of right, but of him and Eteocles, blood-kinsmen between whom an issue of right has arisen.

[43] Cf. Otis 164; Dawson 10.

[44] Cf. Rose I, 217f.; W. Schadewaldt, 'Die Waffnung des Eteokles', *Eranion* (Festschrift H. Hommel) 105–16 = *Hellas und Hesperien*² I. 357ff.; Bacon 27ff. Other references in Taplin 158 n. 1. Taplin 158ff. does indeed raise serious objections to this otherwise attractive hypothesis, notably that 'the action would not in any proper sense be accompanied by the words', and that 'the putting on of armour or of any costume is a difficult thing to manage on stage'. He is inclined to believe that Eteocles is armed throughout the play and to delete 675f. as an interpolation. His objections carry weight, though I am reluctant to abandon the effect described in my text (not to mention the first half of 675). Opinions differ as to the points at which the various pieces of armour are brought out

piece of armour is put on, the more impossible that he should withdraw. In a final *stichomythia*, when he speaks as a hoplite (717), he is fully armed – armed as a soldier against the possibility of withdrawal. The Coryphaeus shoots her last bolt. 'Will you reap the harvest of a brother's blood?' And Eteocles replies: 'When the gods give, evil cannot be escaped.' He leaves the stage; and the Chorus goes on to sing of the Erinys. Every aspect and every theme in this densely-written sequence must be examined.

In his long speech (653–76), when he has spoken of his father's curse, the fulfilment of which he recognizes in this conjunction of his brother and himself, he turns to Polynices and his claims. What has Polynices to do, what has he ever in his life had to do, with Justice? If Justice associates with this criminal, she will be falsely so called (670f.). It is in this confidence (672) he announces that he will fight his brother. As in every other case an appropriate champion has been matched with an invader, so now he finds himself the proper adversary. 'I will stand with him, ruler with ruler, brother with brother, enemy with enemy.'[45]

The tone of his speech has been differently judged – particularly the tone in which he rejects the claims of Polynices. His words have a tense vehemence: but does he pronounce as a judge the verdict of impartial truth or speak as a personal enemy, in whom bitterness is welling up out of a long history of antagonism? If the answer depended merely upon subjective impression, critics would have to agree to differ. We must look for any relatively objective grounds that we can find. We need help; and the help that *Oedipus* might have given us is not at our disposal. So some writers have turned to the reported words of Amphiaraus (580ff.), and not without reason. An impartial judge roundly condemns Polynices for bringing a foreign army against his native land; and it is as certain as such things can be that this condemnation is endorsed by Aeschylus. But it does not settle the question of the rights of Polynices or the mood of Eteocles when he rejects

---

(if brought out they were), and this is something which can hardly be determined. If the shield of Eteocles is brought out, did it have a blazon which was visible to, and recognizable by, the audience? Bacon suggests that it bore an Erinys. Another possibility might be the figure of Dike, the iconography of which can be carried farther back than that of Erinys. But would either – or any – blazon have been clearly recognizable in the theatre? Of course, if Taplin is right, this is a non-question, since we can hardly suppose Eteocles to have been carrying a shield throughout, including the *Redepaare*.

45 The word is ἐχθρός, expressive of personal enmity and feud; the notion has already been introduced at 509. The aptness of the conjunction of Hippomedon and Hyperbius, ascribed to Hermes, consists not only in their respective blazons, but in a pre-existent personal enmity. Note that in this case at least it is clearly implied that Hyperbius had already been assigned his gate, not only by the tense of ἡρέθη, but because it would be futile to ascribe to Hermes what was Eteocles' own doing.

them. 'What right shall quench the mother's fount?' says the prophet in his oracular style (584).[46] That is to say, whatever rights Polynices might claim (and however well they might be founded), this did not justify him in ravaging his native land. But Eteocles' condemnation of his brother goes back, hyperbolically, to the very moment when he left his mother's womb: neither then nor as a child nor as a youth nor as a young man did Justice deign to look on him.[47]

If Amphiaraus cannot help us, can the Chorus? We must of course beware of assuming that, because they are a chorus, they are necessarily right – that they necessarily express a view which the poet intends us to accept. In this scene it may well be that their view of the gods is too simple, but it is surely likely that their view of the mind of Eteocles is correct. (Why should Aeschylus make them mislead the audience on such a point? Why should we presume to know better than they?) We must therefore pay close attention to what they say – and also to the form in which they say it.

The form of the scene between Eteocles and the Chorus is epirrhematic, that is to say, it combines song and speech in alternation; the Chorus sings short lyric stanzas, after each of which Eteocles speaks three lines. It has often been observed that, though slightly shorter (by a pair of stanzas), this scene has the same form as that which follows the first rebuke of Eteocles to the Chorus. The similarity of form might have suggested that Aeschylus wished the two scenes to be considered together, even without the similarity – and contrast – of subject-matter. Each is a scene of persuasion, an appeal for the restraint of ungoverned emotion. In the first Eteocles rebukes the women of the Chorus for their hysterical fears and tries to reduce them to calm; in the second the roles are reversed – it is Eteocles

---

[46] Lines 580–6 are of course an answer in advance to 639–48, where Polynices calls to witness the kinship gods of his father's land (cf. 582, 585f.) and claims that Dike will give him back his father's city. Lines 584–6 are taken by Hermann, Rose and Fraenkel as a paratactic comparison, but, whether this is correct or not, the first element has independent validity. The earth is itself a mother and fount of nourishment, which will be quenched when the invading army ravages the land. The behaviour of Polynices is thus the exact opposite of that of Melanippus, who, prompted by Dike, defends the earth his mother. One might perhaps say that 584 and 585f. look at the same situation, the first in terms of a mystical bond, the second in more realistic terms ($\sigma\acute{\upsilon}\mu\mu\alpha\chi\sigma\varsigma$). But there is nothing to deny that Polynices may have a claim of right. In fact the phrasing of 584 rather implies that he has or may have.

[47] This hardly sounds to me an 'analytical and deliberate rejection' (Kirkwood) of his brother's claim, nor do I detect (with one critic) 'the undertone of regret and disappointment at a life of promise steered in the wrong path'! One would like to believe that Eteocles and Polynices were twins, that Polynices the younger twin had behaved like Jacob to Esau, but such a story would probably have left a trace!

who is now seen by the Chorus as filled with a mad lust for blood – and for
the blood of his brother, from which they seek to restrain him.[48]

Their judgement is first given in the first words of the Coryphaeus.
'Dearest of men, son of Oedipus, do not show yourself like in wrath' (or 'in
temper') 'to him who has the worst of names.' This is probably the best
way in which to take the Greek expression ($\tau\hat{\wp}$ $\kappa\acute{a}\kappa\iota\sigma\tau$' $a\mathring{v}\delta\omega\mu\acute{e}\nu\wp$),[49]
with a reference – one of several in the play – to the etymology of the
name of Polynices: 'the man of much contention'. In any case, the
Coryphaeus is saying: 'do not show yourself like Polynices'. If this stood
alone, it might justify us in interpreting the mood of the speech of Eteocles
as one of hatred and contention. But it does not stand alone. The first two
lyric stanzas of the Chorus speak of a 'spear-mad infatuation filling the
heart', of 'an evil lust', of 'a longing' (like the longing to eat raw flesh)
which is driving him 'to accomplish a man-slaying which will bear a bitter
fruit in unlawful blood'. The expressions are not only unequivocal in
themselves, but reminiscent of the description of Tydeus, who was seen by
the Spy 'raging madly and longing for battle'. The same blood-lust that
showed itself in the cruel and barbaric Tydeus now shows itself in Eteocles,
but the blood is that of a brother.

What then does Eteocles say to this? Does he deny his fierce lust for a
brother's blood, his $\grave{\omega}\mu o\delta a\kappa\mathring{\eta}s$ $\mathring{\iota}\mu\epsilon\rho os$? No, he explains it (695–7):[50] he
explains it in terms of the curse. Now we can look back to the first word
which he spoke when the Spy withdrew: 'maddened by the gods'
($\theta\epsilon o\mu a\nu\acute{e}s$), spoken of the family of Oedipus, that is to say, of himself and
of his brother. Much later in the play, after they are dead, the Chorus will
sing of their 'mad strife' ($\mathring{\epsilon}\rho\iota\delta\iota$ $\mu a\iota\nu o\mu\acute{e}\nu a$, 935); and that will be a word
they have already used of the heart of Oedipus when he blinded himself
and cursed his sons ($\mu a\iota\nu o\mu\acute{e}\nu a$ $\kappa\rho a\delta\acute{\iota}a$, 781).

[48] The inconsistency in the role of the Chorus, who turn from panic-stricken virgins into counsellors
of moderation (even addressing the king as 'child', 686), is mitigated – if Aeschylus would have felt
that mitigation was necessary – by the fact that in both situations they take the line of piety: in the
earlier scene placing all their hopes in the gods, in the present scene seeking to dissuade Eteocles from
an act of impiety (cf. 831). A. L. Brown (1977) 316 speaks of 'the same contrast that we saw earlier
between a sombre realistic fatalism and a trusting intuitive feminine piety'.

[49] Elsewhere in Aeschylus $a\mathring{v}\delta\hat{a}\sigma\theta a\iota$ is middle: Eum. 380, P.V. 766 and ($\mathring{\epsilon}\xi a\upsilon\delta\hat{a}\sigma\theta a\iota$) Cho. 151, 272;
but we find the passive sense 'to be called' in Sophocles: Trach. 1106, Phil. 240, 430. Corrupt and
difficult as 576–8 are (cf. Cameron, 1970, 106, n. 35), Amphiaraus is clearly playing on the name of
Polynices, as does Eteocles at 658. It is not unlikely that the etymology of 'Eteocles' is in mind at
683–5 (see p. 36 below) and possibly at 5ff. (see n. 24); and that, at 830, $\kappa a\grave{\iota}$ $\pi o\lambda\upsilon\nu\epsilon\iota\kappa\epsilon\hat{\iota}s$ was
preceded by a similar reference. Hecht and Bacon, 14f., suggest a double etymology, from kleos but
also from klaio.

[50] Lesky (1) 14 rightly called attention to the vital significance of that $\gamma\acute{a}\rho$ (695); and before him
Regenbogen in Hermes (1933) (see n. 2 above).

The family is 'maddened by the gods' and 'greatly hated by the gods'; and in the following scene Eteocles comes back again and again to his conviction that the gods have decreed the destruction of his race.[51] He regards the position as hopeless, delay as futile (704). He speaks of the gods in general (702), of Phoebus that hates the whole race of Laius (691), and of his father's curse, which he knows to be an Erinys (70, cf. 700). (It is such a convergence of upper and nether powers driving a man to an impious act as we shall meet again in *Choephori*.) It is fair to say – and was said with great emphasis by Solmsen in his influential article – that the mind of Eteocles is now, in some sense, dominated by the Erinys. This does not, however, exclude the attribution to him of other mental states – or one had better say, the description of his mental state in other terms. It does not exclude, but entails, hatred of his brother. It is in terms of the curse that he explains this hatred; it is through this hatred that the curse fulfils itself. If curse and hatred are two strands in the fabric, they are much of a colour. But there is a third strand – and perhaps a fourth.

The third strand is that of shame and honour, glory and disgrace. When the Coryphaeus begs him (677–82) not to be contentious like his brother and refers to the pollution of fratricide,[52] Eteocles replies, not – or so it

---

[51] Eteocles knows from the beginning that he is under a curse which is likely to be fulfilled and could mean the destruction of the family. When he learns that his brother is at the seventh gate, it is a moment of revelation in which vagueness is turned into clarity (cf. Lesky (1) 10f.). Though at 672, as at 271–8, he speaks as if he might survive, he really knows that he and his brother will die. Cf. Dawe 41, n. 1. Burnett, pp. 356ff., has recently put forward an interesting suggestion. There were two sources of information about the future, the Curse and the dream (see n. 64 below). The Curse was bitter, speaking of an iron-bearing hand; the dream, of a foreign mediator, was less discouraging. Eteocles has now come to realize (710f.) that the dream was no less sinister than the curse. In the following *stasimon*, as in the concluding *threnos*, the terms of the Curse and the imagery of the dream are fully integrated. This hypothesis, developed in great detail by Burnett, would clarify a number of obscurities, though it can hardly be established with certainty in the absence of the preceding play.

The attitude of the Chorus, until they sing their *stasimon*, is not so clear – or so important. Line 681 need not imply both deaths (see Cameron, 1970, p. 111 on αὐτοκτόνος), though it is so worded as to suggest them; 718 implies the death of Polynices only.

[52] There is a difficulty about the reference to *miasma* (and about the precise meaning of καθάρσιον at 680 and καθαρμούς at 738, which has been much, and inconclusively, debated). The earlier plays may or may not have thrown light on this. The killing of Laius by his son must have caused such a pollution, and in Sophocles it leads to the plague and so to the revelation of Oedipus' identity. Whether this theme was used by Aeschylus is quite uncertain. Perhaps we should assume that *miasma*, so far as it affected the city, was extinguished by the death of Oedipus; and that the *miasma* of fratricide was extinguished by the deaths of both brothers (cf. Cameron, 1970, pp. 109ff.). There is no hint of a persisting pollution in the closing scene: even if 843 is taken to imply that the city is still in danger, this is not linked with the notion of *miasma* (and in the 'spurious' portion ἄγος attaches only to Polynices, 1017f., and for a different reason). Aeschylus, while accepting notions of pollution and purification as part of traditional religious belief, may not himself have been happy within this range of ideas. L. Moulinier, *Le pur et l'impur dans la pensée des Grecs* (Paris 1952) 193–5, finds different standpoints in the *Oresteia*; and Dodds (3) 23 argues convincingly that, in *Eumenides*,

would appear – in terms of hatred, not in terms of the curse, but on the grounds of honour (683–5). 'If a man is to suffer evil (κακόν), let it be without shame (αἰσχύνης ἄτερ).[53] For that is all that profits among the dead. But no good repute (εὐκλείαν) is won from things which are both evil and shameful (κακῶν τε κἀσχρῶν).' The text of 685 is in doubt, but not the general sense of the passage or the word *eukleia*. And in the use of this word Eteocles (or Aeschylus) may well be playing on his name 'the man of true glory' as the coryphaeus had played upon the name of his brother 'the man of much contention'. When he speaks of evil – objective evil (κακόν) – he may mean pollution or death, but, when he speaks of good repute as 'gain among the dead', he clearly envisages that he may die. When he speaks of shame and glory, it is generally supposed that he is thinking of his honour as a soldier and a ruler; and we may recall – may be meant to recall – the words with which he dispatched Melanippus against Tydeus (407ff.).

A third strand has been identified – and perhaps a fourth: but what is the pattern? What is the relationship between curse and blood-lust on the one hand, honour and patriotism on the other? Or has Aeschylus just laid the two double strands side by side in an attempt – a crude early attempt – to suggest a mixture of motives within the same personality? This could be so, and much of the controversy which the decision – and the character – of Eteocles have evoked could be attributed to the crudity of Aeschylus and the unwillingness of modern scholars to believe him crude. But it may be worth looking at the scene again – and at three lines in particular, three difficult lines which have not yet been taken into consideration.

The Chorus has sung that an excessive cruel desire is driving Eteocles towards fratricide. Instead of denying it, he identifies the driving force with his father's curse which haunts him, and whose words he quotes. In answer the Chorus sings: 'Yet do not you be driven.' The general connection of thought is thus clear, but in the three lines spoken by Eteocles (695–7) there is uncertainty of text and interpretation.[54] It matters little that we do not

---

the importance of the formal purification of Orestes is 'deliberately *minimized*'. Cf. ch. 7, p. 146.

[53] Or: 'If a man should suffer evil without shame, then let it be.' It is not easy to choose between the two punctuations.

[54] In Page's text the lines read as follows:

φίλου γὰρ ἐχθρά μοι πατρὸς †τελεῖ† ἀρὰ
ξηροῖς ἀκλαύτοις ὄμμασιν προσιζάνει
λέγουσα κέρδος πρότερον ὑστέρου μόρου.

In 695 Weil's μέλαιν' is excellent in itself, contributing visually to the personification, but, despite 832, there is no compelling reason to believe that Aeschylus wrote it here. One is as reluctant to

know what was the penultimate word of 695, what contribution it made to this astonishing personification. Nor does it matter greatly how we take the following line. Whose eyes are dry? Does the Curse haunt the dry eyes of Eteocles or haunt him with dry eyes? It does not matter, because at this point the line of distinction between the Curse and the mind of Eteocles is hard to draw, because the Curse is working on him and in him. At least it is certain that what the Curse says to Eteocles is also what Eteocles is saying to himself. What then does the Curse say? (Even this is disputed, but argument can be left to a footnote.)[55] The Curse speaks of 'gain (profit, advantage) first; death (fated death) afterward'. Either there is a gain which will be followed by death; or there is a gain which ranks superior to death; the meanings are not mutually exclusive, and both could be intended. The word for 'gain' is *kerdos*; and it occurred thirteen lines previously, also in a context of death. We might expect it to have the same meaning here. Since there it meant freedom from disgrace, a good reputation after death, and since here the Chorus replies that Eteocles will *not* be called base (κακὸς οὐ κεκλήσῃ), if he complies,[56] it might indeed seem that the meanings are the same. But there is an objection, which is not so much that in this latter passage the gain is spoken of as prior to death (since the act which gains posthumous glory is, in time, prior to death). The objection is that the words are put into the mouth of the Curse and it is, at first sight, no proper function of the Curse to speak to Eteocles of his honour – of his honour as a soldier. The interest of the Curse is in the mutual fratricide, and its means of bringing it about is the mutual enmity of the brothers. The gain, therefore, that it would be proper for the Curse to hold before the eyes of Eteocles is the death of Polynices; and it is his fierce desire for that death he is seeking to explain. But, if we take *kerdos* of the death of Polynices, we seem to be

jettison the τελει (with varying accentuation) of the manuscripts as one is incapable of accommodating it. In 696, the eyes are perhaps more probably those of the Curse, in which case Butler's ἄκλαυτος is attractive, if not requisite.

[55] So good a commentator as Groeneboom took the words as meaning that an earlier death is preferable to a later one, i.e. better die quickly and get it over. But how can πρότερον be other than an epithet of κέρδος as ὑστέρου is of μόρου? It is equally intolerable, with Verrall and Rose, to take πρότερον of value and ὑστέρου of time. Pauw and others emend the text to read: κέρδος πρότερον, ὕστερον μόρον – an easy correction, but, in view of the Greek tendency towards correlative expressions, an unnecessary one. (Dawe is far too scornful of the received text.)

[56] One cannot feel happy about βίον εὖ κυρήσας, least of all with an interpretation which refers the phrase merely to the preservation of life. The scholia have: καλῶς πράξας, εὐτυχήσας, εὖ πράξας. Tucker (1) could be on the right lines: 'The word [βίον] includes material prosperity, which will enable him to offer the (liberal) sacrifices next mentioned.' This suits the reply of Eteocles at 703, the meaning of which is established by 772ff. Oedipus was respected by the gods for his lavish sacrifices: the only gift (χάρις) that the gods will welcome from his sons is their death. Still, one cannot feel quite happy about the phrase.

opening up a breach between its meaning here and its meaning thirteen
lines above. The conclusion seems as inevitable as it is unwelcome. On
reflection, however, how large is the breach? And indeed does it exist? It all
depends on what honour means to Eteocles – or rather on what meaning
is, in this context, intended to be conveyed by such words as αἰσχύνη,
αἰσχρός, εὔκλεια (which we translate by 'shame', 'shameful', 'good
repute'). The answer to this question could have some importance for the
interpretation of the play and of the trilogy.

Aeschylus was writing in the fifth century, in a city-state, for an audience of
men who had fought the Persians. It has therefore been natural to assume
that, when he speaks of shame and glory, using terms of praise and blame so
characteristic of Greek morals, the terms were intended to bear the
connotations which they had acquired within the city-state. But he was
writing about the heroic world. In that world the hero prized his honour
above everything – his honour and his prestige. And his prestige depended
upon his ability to maintain his status and privileges; to resent, retort and
retaliate a slight; to humiliate and destroy his enemies. This was his virtue,
his excellence, his *arete*. If he failed, his prestige was gone; he was despised
and felt the shame it was the main object of his existence to avert. The only
'failure' countenanced by the code was an honourable death in battle. In
due course this heroic ideal of *arete* was modified, by addition rather than
by subtraction. Courage in battle had always been cardinal to it, but, as the
city-states developed, the important context of courage became the
defence of the community, not, as in the relatively anarchic world of
heroes, defence of one's prestige, property, family and friends. But the old
emotional attitudes died hard, if they died at all.[57] If justice became a virtue
in the city-state, it could still be formulated in the late fifth century as
'doing good to your friends and harm to your enemies', though the
application of this principle was limited by various factors and particularly
by the existence of legal process under the aegis of the state.

There was an issue of justice between Polynices and Eteocles – an issue
which could not be settled in any court. The 'rights and wrongs' of it we do
not know, but each thought that he was in the right. Polynices claimed that
he had been dishonoured – deprived of his τιμή – by the brother who had
driven him into exile;[58] and he was determined to avenge this injury by
death or by repaying him in kind. The image of Justice on his shield says

---

[57] Cf. A. W. H. Adkins, *Merit and responsibility* (Oxford 1960) *passim*.

[58] The text of 637 is quite uncertain, but must contain the idea that Eteocles had deprived Polynices of
his τιμή by driving him out.

(647f.): 'I will bring back this man, and he shall have the city of his fathers and the range of his house.' The city, like the house, is a patrimony; Polynices (like Orestes in *Choephori*) is deprived both as son and as ruler (or so he claims). What he has lost (with what justice, we do not know) Eteocles enjoys; and the return of Polynices is a menace to his enjoyment. Hence their enmity – the personal enmity conveyed by the word ἐχθρός; hence the appropriateness that (673ff.) ruler should fight against ruler, brother against brother, enemy against enemy.[59]

When, therefore, Eteocles speaks at 683–5 of shame and honour, what has he in mind? What is it that would destroy his fair fame in the eyes of men and, should he die, deprive him of the only *kerdos* among the dead? Cowardice, of course. So he must go out against the foe, full of rage for battle like a Homeric hero; and it is no accident that, in the stanzas which the Chorus sings at 686ff. and 692ff., some of the vocabulary – and much of the spirit – are Homeric.[60] But, by heroic standards, he would lose his honour, not only by cowardice, but also by not resenting a wrong, by not standing up for his rights, by not taking vengeance, by not inflicting upon his enemy the ultimate harm. Since his gaze is now fixed upon his personal quarrel, it is surely not unreasonable to suppose that this is what he has in mind by shame and good repute. (And that is the view of a scholiast, who, being a Greek if late in time, understood these things, and who wrote: ἐν κέρδος τὸ αὐτὸν ἐκδικῆσαι ἀδικούμενον.) If that is so, there is no essential difference between the two 'gains', between honour after death (684) and the destruction of Polynices (697), since it is by the pursuit of effective vengeance that Eteocles will establish his good fame – and, one might add, will justify his name. Seen in the light of the present argument, the two names which seemed so far apart – the man of much contention, the man of true glory – come close together.

This line of interpretation simplifies the pattern of the scene we have been considering. It is not merely that hatred and honour converge towards the same result: they are motives so closely related as to be almost identical, both serving the Erinys that now dominates the mind of Eteocles. The pattern is simplified. Has it become too simple? It is perhaps time to insist again on the disadvantages from which we suffer in interpreting this

---

[59] ἄρχοντί τ᾽ ἄρχων (674). The fact that Adrastus and not Polynices was in command of the invading army is disregarded here, as it is at 816 and 828. It was the easier to do so, in that both brothers claimed the rule in Thebes.

[60] Cf. μέμονας (686), ἀνδροκτασίαν (693) and – later (698) – ἐποτρύνου. On ὠμοδακής (692) Tucker (1) cites *Il.* 4.35; 24.212; he also refers to Soph fr. 799.5 P for the cannibalism of Tydeus. Did Aeschylus expect his audience to recollect this feature of the legend? See also p. 48 for a possible, but uncertain, act of 'cannibalism' on the part of Oedipus. Such points are not to be pressed.

play. We do not know the rights and wrongs of the quarrel: we do not even know how important it would have been to know them. In the Danaid trilogy the rights and wrongs of the quarrel between Danaus and Aegyptus seem to have been left, deliberately, vague. It could have been so in the Theban trilogy, but this is not so probable, since it contained a play which will have demanded a handling of the relationship between the brothers. It may be useful at this point to consider what we know or can without extravagance conjecture about the earlier plays.

Our fragments of *Laius* and *Oedipus* are inconsiderable. Our most valuable piece of evidence for the content of these plays is the choral ode in *Septem* which relates the impending fratricide to the past history of the house (720ff.), but it has to be used with caution. It is easy to list the series of events.[61] The oracle; the disobedience; the birth of Oedipus and his exposure; the killing of Laius; the marriage of Oedipus to his mother (presumably following his victory over the Sphinx). Then a long interval of time. Oedipus discovers the truth, blinds himself, curses his sons. His sons quarrel; Polynices makes friends abroad and plots his return from exile. Oedipus and Jocasta (if she was called Jocasta) are dead before *Septem*. There is altogether too much, and some of these events must have lain outside the economy of the two lost plays. One of our difficulties is that, while we know *Oresteia* and can form a fair idea of the Danaid trilogy, we do not know quite how Aeschylus may have constructed a trilogy in 467. *Agamemnon* is much longer than either *Choephori* or *Eumenides*, but it would be rash to assume that either *Laius* or *Oedipus* had a length or an action out of scale with the brevity and simplicity of *Septem*.

In any case, some unity of time is likely to have been preserved in both plays. If Laius was a character in *Laius*, the action will have included his death, in which case the oracle and the birth of Oedipus lie well to the past. A scrap of papyrus has now made it highly probable that Laius spoke the prologue to this play. Prologue and *parodos* between them (the Chorus being Theban elders) will have put the audience in possession of the facts, including the oracle and the disóbedience. Perhaps Laius announced his intention of leaving – but why and whither? – and left, never to return.

---

[61] It is possible that the trilogy took the story back to the rape of Chrysippus: see Lloyd-Jones 120f., Thalmann 9ff. The advantage of this hypothesis is that it motivates the oracle: Laius is to be punished for a crime, if he obeys the oracle or for that matter if he disobeys, by the extinction of his race. The trouble is that, unless one accepts Thalmann's interpretation of παρβασίαν at 743 as a reference to the rape, there is no hint of this in the extant play, where all the emphasis is upon the disobedience.

Later, a narrative of his death and the advent of Oedipus. (But in which order?) Oedipus can hardly have arrived without vanquishing the Sphinx[62] and winning the hand of Jocasta. Did Jocasta play a part? Laius, Messenger, Jocasta and Oedipus would hardly be too large a cast; and the action would not be out of scale. In reading the second *stasimon* of *Septem*, we are tempted to assume that 742–57 cover the action of *Laius*, while 772–90 cover that of *Oedipus*. But this is too facile. The second of these passages refers to the honours paid to Oedipus 'when he had removed the man-seizing *Ker* from the land'. A long interval of time must have elapsed between the first and the second play, long enough for sons to grow to manhood. Lines 772–7 could well give us the close of *Laius*: a triumphant Oedipus celebrating his victory, his marriage and his kingship, with lavish sacrifices to the gods and feasts for the people. A saviour whose sons will bring a deadly threat.

It could have been so. The real difficulty is with *Oedipus*. The *stasimon* (fifth strophe and antistrophe 778–90) gives us the revelation, the self-blinding and the curse. *Stasimon* or no, one feels that, without the curse in the preceding play, the development of *Septem* would have been barely intelligible to an audience, however familiar with the myth. One may doubt too whether Aeschylus would have dared to withhold all reference to Polynices until 576, unless there had been something about the quarrel, some hint of his activities abroad. (Is the death of Oedipus tacitly assumed? And that of Jocasta?) Revelation, blinding, curse, death, quarrel. Almost too much for a short play; and certainly little room is left for the means of revelation, whatever those may have been. Teiresias – and Apollo? Or a recognition by tokens? A plague?[63] We shall not know, but the revelation may even have taken place before the play began. The characters? Oedipus for certain. Did Jocasta (again?) have a role? Both sons? And did Polynices have a role which balanced that of Eteocles in *Septem*? Eteocles on Polynices (662ff.) sounds allusive: were the audience in a position to judge for themselves? Was the curse delivered on stage: a big central feature?

These – and many more – questions can be asked and not answered. It might seem hopeless to proceed farther. If we cannot settle the broad action of these plays, what can we know of their character and their themes? Except that in the Aeschylean trilogy (to judge by what evidence we have) themes tend to persist from play to play. The second *stasimon* seems

---

[62] The fact that Aeschylus used the Sphinx story for his satyr-play might suggest that it was not given detailed treatment in the trilogy, but it must have come in (as it comes into the second *stasimon*, 776f.), doubtless in the form of a narration.

[63] Fr. 691 M may or may not come from *Oedipus*.

intended to be a drawing together of threads. It gives us the oracle (the thrice-given oracle) and the involvement of the city with the progeny of Laius: the threat. The threat comes to fulfilment in *Septem*. Not for the first time. The Sphinx had been a threat to the city and its population (775f.). Oedipus saved the city from this danger; perhaps it was the danger from the Sphinx that prompted the mission of Laius, so that the trilogy began with the city in danger and the first play ended with the city saved. Ironically, because Oedipus who saved Thebes from the Sphinx endangered it when he cursed his sons.

The city was endangered by the disobedience of Laius and by the curse of Oedipus; and, though both come into the *stasimon*, in neither case (because of difficulties of text and interpretation) can we be sure why the act was committed. But we know (roughly) what the curse was: that they should divide their inheritance sword in hand. With iron ($\sigma\ell\delta\eta\rho\sigma$). We can be fairly certain that this word was used, together with a reference to lots or shares. The Chorus sing first of the iron sword under a riddling image (characteristic of archaic poetry); since iron came from the Black Sea region, it is a Chalybian foreigner that casts lots and distributes the shares equally between the sons, to each so much of the ancestral land as burial required. It is possible that this image was an echo from *Oedipus*, and was first the image of a dream.[64] But this we cannot know for certain.

Nor do we know what version of the quarrel between the brothers was followed – or devised – by Aeschylus. It is certain that it was a quarrel over inheritance and over shares.[65] What should they have done? Perhaps

---

[64] Only 787ff. purport to give the terms of the curse (cf. Manton 78f.). What then was the source of the riddling image at 727ff. (picked up at 941ff.)? Cameron (1970) 116, following Tucker, holds that the language of the curse itself 'must have said that the sons would have to submit the question of the division of their inheritance to a foreign arbiter from over the sea, born of fire, and who would give them exactly equal shares'. But this, which does not sound quite like a bitterly-worded curse, is difficult to reconcile with the fairly specific 787ff. Manton suggests that the source of the image was a dream; and Eteocles had just referred to dreams (710f.). Hermann saw that the dream or dreams *must* have been in the preceding play. If Eteocles had merely said 'the dreams were all too true', it might have stood on its own, but, when he describes their content as $\pi\alpha\tau\rho\dot{\omega}\omega\nu$ $\chi\rho\eta\mu\acute{\alpha}\tau\omega\nu$ $\delta\alpha\tau\acute{\eta}\rho\iota o\iota$, it becomes intolerably obscure, unless the dreams had been reported in *Oedipus*. Who dreamt the dream or dreams? Eteocles, according to the scholiast, but this could be a guess, if a good one. Conceivably Jocasta. See Manton and, most recently, the full discussion by Burnett (cf. n. 51 above). There seems little doubt that the dream-figure was seen casting lots; and Burnett relates this to frequent occurrences of the lot-theme earlier in the play. H. Engelmann, 'Der Schiedsrichter aus der Fremde', *RhM* 110 (1967) 97–102, provides an interesting review of the evidence for foreign arbitrators. See now Thalmann 62–78.

[65] Cameron (1968) argues that the issue was between two contrasted systems of inheritance, by primogeniture and by division of the property – and that this issue had a topical relevance. This seems a great deal to extract from 902f. (where Cameron finds a clue to the sense of $\grave{\epsilon}\pi\iota\gamma\acute{o}\nu o\iota s$ in Plato's *Laws*, i.e. younger sons who do not inherit). If this was a prime issue, it is rather extraordinary that there is no hint of it in the *Redepaare*, 631–76.

they should have been joint rulers and held the wealth in common, in which case the 'monarchy' of Eteocles (883) should have been no monarchy at all.[66] Failing that, perhaps they should have shared out the wealth equally; and in the end, ironically, they get equal shares. Unless it was a question of dividing inheritance, why say that they shall divide it *with iron*? It should have been done by the casting of lots (as Zeus, Poseidon and Hades cast lots for theirs), and in the image lots are cast by the Chalybian foreigner. Or by an arbitrator, himself casting lots, if the parties could not agree; and it is in this capacity that the sword (or Ares) is seen to act. Who, then, was to blame? Eteocles or Polynices or both? By no word does the Chorus support one claim against the other; and in the closing *threnos* the two brothers are treated upon an equality.[67] This might be easier to understand, if Eteocles had been at fault in driving his brother into exile, just as Polynices was at fault in seeking redress the way he did.[68]

However this may be, one thing is clear. Power and wealth were too tempting; and the emphasis is upon wealth. Wealth and the rich land from which it was derived. 'They have their share allotted of the god-given apportionments.[69] Under their bodies there shall be earth's unplumbed wealth' (947ff.). They will lie in their graves 'without share in the great plains' (733). The treatment of this theme in the second *stasimon* may be particularly instructive. The reference to the great wealth-giving lands is led up to by the double stress of $\kappa\tau\epsilon\acute{a}\nu\omega\nu$ $\chi\rho\eta\mu\alpha\tau o\delta\alpha\acute{\iota}\tau\alpha\varsigma$ (and the quantitative $\acute{o}\pi\acute{o}\sigma\alpha\nu$: so much and no more). In the last stanza, returning to the curse and rounding off this theme, the word $\kappa\tau\acute{\eta}\mu\alpha\tau\alpha$ stands alone. But in the middle of the ode comes another emphatic reference to wealth. The Chorus has been singing of the successive waves of trouble – and the towering wave that now threatens the city also, so that they fear it may perish with the princes. From this they pass to a general reflection on the dangers of wealth. 'Destruction passes by the poor,[70] but, when the prosperity (wealth) of gain-getting man has waxed too great, it brings a

---

[66] Joint rule, as envisaged at Eur. *Phoen.* 69f. (cf. the joint rule of the Atridae at Argos, much stressed in the *parodos* of *Agam.*, e.g. 43f., 109f.). In which case, at the outset of our play (6), the emphasis on Eteocles as sole ruler might be calling attention to a situation which ought not to have existed. Cf. also 674, 816, 828, and esp. 882f. (rival claims to 'monarchy'). Cf. Golden (1964) 83.

[67] Cf. Gagarin 122f.

[68] On 923ff. ($\grave{\epsilon}\rho\xi\acute{a}\tau\eta\nu$ $\pi o\lambda\lambda\grave{a}$ $\mu\grave{\epsilon}\nu$ $\pi o\lambda\acute{\iota}\tau\alpha\iota\varsigma$, $\xi\acute{\epsilon}\nu\omega\nu$ $\tau\epsilon$ $\pi\acute{a}\nu\tau\omega\nu$ $\sigma\tau\acute{\iota}\chi\alpha\varsigma$ $\pi o\lambda\upsilon\phi\theta\acute{o}\rho o\upsilon\varsigma$ $\grave{\epsilon}\nu$ $\delta\alpha\acute{\iota}$) Page justly observes 'phrasis perobscura'. However, the dual verb and the notion of much harm done to citizens and foreigners seem authentic. 'What follows is collectively, not individually true' (Rose). The dual suggests, however, that both limbs of the statement were true of both, which would be the case, if they were jointly responsible for the war. Cf. Podlecki 299.

[69] Reading $\lambda\acute{a}\xi\epsilon\omega\nu$ (Fraenkel).

[70] There is great uncertainty about the text, and $\pi\epsilon\nu o\mu\acute{\epsilon}\nu o\upsilon\varsigma$ is merely a plausible suggestion.

jettisoning from the stern' (769ff.). Then comes the particular application. 'For (γάρ) what man was so admired by the gods who share the city's hearth and by the great throng of mortals[71] as then they honoured Oedipus when he had banished the man-seizing Monster from the land?' By banishing the Sphinx Oedipus had gained the wealth of Thebes. Sacrifice and feast. For what should the gods admire a man except for the lavish scale of his offerings?[72] But wealth is dangerous, when it grows too great.

Wealth at the beginning, middle and end of this ode. Dangerous wealth. We might guess that the wealth which went with the royal power of Thebes had been a leading theme of the trilogy; and it might be a good guess. There caution would stop, with the observation that it was the lure of wealth that ruined the sons of Oedipus. But the generalization about wealth stands between the lyric handling of two crucial episodes. The disobedience of Laius; the cursing of his sons by Oedipus. Why did the one disobey, the other curse? Thanks to obscurities and corruptions in the text (and to our ignorance of the earlier plays), we do not know.

Or rather, as to the disobedience, we are told that Laius 'overmastered by ill counsels begat his own death, Oedipus the father-slayer, who endured to sow the pure field of his mother where he grew and raise a bloody stem; it was madness that brought together man and wife, their wits destroyed' (750–7). Which man and wife? The point is controversial. If the language (παράνοια . . . φρενωλής) seems too strong for those who, like Jocasta and Oedipus, came together in ignorance, it is fair to say that, on the other hypothesis, 'the plural form of νυμφίους applied to Laius and Jocasta would suggest that both were responsible' (Manton).[73] But it was Laius who consulted and disobeyed the oracle. Add that Jocasta's role in the preceding sentence is to be impregnated by Oedipus, and the argument seems little short of decisive. It is virtually decisive, unless there is reason to attribute responsibility to Jocasta.

[71] Weil's ἀγών (αἰών codd.) is virtually certain and πολύβατος highly probable (see Page's apparatus). The text of 773 is doubtful.

[72] It could be of course that the gods admired him for his cleverness (as the gods at Plato, *Symp.* 180a, admired Achilles for his devotion to Patroclus – the word is ὑπεραγασθέντες). Taking 772 and 703 together, it seems more likely that in both cases there is a context of sacrifice, hinted at perhaps by ξυνέστιοι.

[73] Manton 81 lists a number of considerations which he holds to favour a reference to Oedipus and Jocasta. This is the most weighty. Cf. *BICS* 13 (1966) 92, n. 12. In that article I have examined in greater detail *Septem* 187–90 and 750–7 and the bearing the two passages may have upon one another and I refer the reader to it. The same evidence is discussed by Caldwell, whose Freudian interpretation of 'the misogyny of Eteocles' I do not feel competent to criticize.

In the translation given above, one Greek word has been omitted: the first line runs κρατηθείς ἐκ φίλων ἀβουλιᾶν. All attempts to take φίλων as an epithet (perhaps in the form φιλᾶν) founder in one way or another.[74] If it is a dependent genitive, then Laius was over-persuaded by the bad advice of 'friends', which at first sight gives a poor meaning. But a scholiast suggests that the reference is to his wife (ἢ ἀντὶ τῆς γυναικός).[75] The stanza immediately gains coherence. If Jocasta shared the guilt, then, as Laius was punished by death at the hands of his son, so she suffered the incestuous marriage. The interior of the stanza deals with the double punishment, the role of Oedipus within it being subordinate to that of his parents; the madness at the end balances (on the principle of ring-composition) the ill counsels at the beginning. Certainly the case for taking the closing sentence of Laius and Jocasta is much strengthened.

But, apart from these phrases of doubtful interpretation, what reason have we to suppose that Jocasta played such a role? Let us return to Eteocles rebuking the Chorus (181ff.). We have already noted with surprise the sweeping abuse of the female sex and – most surprising of all – a generalization (a *gnome*), half of which seems quite inappropriate to the context.[76] Which is one of fear. Why, then, is Eteocles made to say to the frightened virgins of Thebes that woman, when she holds the upper hand (κρατοῦσα), is an intolerable *thrasos*, a word which connotes arrogance or criminal boldness? One answer might be that, early in the story, a woman had over-persuaded her husband to a criminal act. Had given him bad counsel. 'Let not a woman give counsel (βουλευέτω): that is the man's affair' (200). 'Laius, overmastered (κρατηθείς) by the ill counsels (ἀβουλιᾶν) of his near ones . . .' (750). We know from other evidence that Aeschylus was much interested in the relationship between the sexes; we know that he chose to depict Clytemnestra as a women of 'manly-counsel'

---

[74] Cf. *BICS* 13 (1966) 90f. The popular view that φίλων/φιλᾶν here is used in the supposedly Homeric sense of 'own' is quite unacceptable, in the light of A. W. H. Adkins, *CQ* 13 (1963) 30ff., esp. 32f. (With ἀβουλίᾳ or ἀβουλίαις, which are possible readings, φίλων is clearly a noun.) For a different view, see A. L. Brown (1977) 306, n. 21.

[75] The suggestion is by no means obvious, and one would like to believe it was made by someone who knew the lost plays. There is, however, no clear evidence of such knowledge elsewhere in the scholia. On 710 it is implied that Eteocles was the dreamer, but this could be a guess.

[76] It is closely examined by H. Friis Johansen, *General reflection in tragic rhesis* (Copenhagen 1959) 106ff. It belongs to a type which he classifies as foil-antithesis, in which the generalization consists of two contrasted elements, one of which (generally the former) has no relevance – or no immediate relevance – to the situation illustrated. He compares other Aeschylean examples, but if anything emerges from the comparison it is the exceptional lack of relevance in this case and the choice of κρατοῦσα for emphasis (cf. *BICS* 13 (1966) 88f.). Tucker (1) writes: 'κρατοῦσα is at first sight a peculiar antithesis to δείσασα, but the real opposition of the latter is with θράσος.' Yes, but why put it that way?

and to display the appalling consequences of her desire for mastery.[77] Did he, then, depict Jocasta as a proud and masterful woman playing a harmful role? No wonder in that case that Eteocles was determined to keep women in their place! Clearly, no certainty could be claimed for this suggestion, though it does help to explain a troublesome feature. Suppose it were true, one is led to ask: if Jocasta over-persuaded Laius to beget a son in defiance of the oracle, what was her motive? It could have been the natural desire of a woman for children, playing on the natural desire of a man (and a king) for heirs. Or she too may have had dynastic thoughts.[78] If the theme of wealth was, as one would like to think, carried back to the beginnings of the story, perhaps it was tolerable to neither king nor queen that the royal wealth of Thebes should go out of the family for want of an heir.

The two fatal moments – fatal decisions – crystallized in the second *stasimon* are the disobedience and (after the blinding) the curse. There is a distinct possibility that the first was linked to the theme of wealth. What was the motive of the curse? In the study of Aeschylus we have to steel ourselves against the obstructions of a corrupt text, but it is really too bad that the text should have been corrupted at just this point (783–7).[79]

[77] Cf. ch. 6 below, where I seek to bring out the importance in this connection of words for mastery (κρατεῖν, κράτος) and counsel (e.g. ἀνδρόβουλος). Johansen, op. cit. 106, n. 17, shows how elaborately the notion of 'counsel' is developed in *Sept.* 182–202, with echoes of political terminology. I would add two further points of a speculative character. (i) What is at issue between Eteocles and the Chorus is a question of discipline and obedience. When he speaks in praise of πειθαρχία (224), an audience might well remember Laius' failure to obey – and might be encouraged to do so by the way in which he is made to express himself, in terms of a family of abstractions. It is possible that, in this riddle, the combination μήτηρ γυνή was intended to suggest Jocasta who was mother and wife to the same man. Both her husbands should have been saviours but endangered the city. The mother-wife encouraged the disobedience of a husband and brought to birth the opposite of εὐπραξία. It is conceivable that when Sophocles (*O.T.* 928) used the same combination to ironical effect he recollected this passage in *Septem.* (ii) At 196–9 Eteocles threatens any that disobeys: ἀνὴρ γυνή τε χὤ τι τῶν μεταίχμιον (197). The critics are puzzled: what an odd way of putting it! 'The phrase has no specific connotations; he is just too angry to speak with complete coherence' (Dawson, whose explanation is that commonly offered). Eteocles may have been out of control: but was Aeschylus? What does lie between a man and a woman? An effeminate man, but one can hardly suppose a reference to the Laius–Chrysippus story. Or a masculine woman, cf. γυναικὸς ἀνδρόβουλον κέαρ. This is immediately followed by 200 on the male prerogative of counsel. Jocasta as a pilot-model for Clytemnestra!

[78] When, at Soph. *O.T.* 1078f., Oedipus accuses Jocasta of family pride, it is conceivable that he was attributing to her, wrongly, a motive which she truly had in Aeschylus.

[79] I print Page's text of 781–86. He adopts two emendations: ἀρχαίας Wilamowitz ἀραίας codd., ἐπίκοτος Heath -κότους codd.

μαινομένᾳ κραδίᾳ
δίδυμα κάκ' ἐτέλεσεν
πατροφόνῳ χερὶ †τῶν κρεισσοτέκνων δ' ὀμμάτων† ἐπλάγχθη.
τέκνοις δ' ἀρχαίας
ἐφῆκεν ἐπίκοτος τροφᾶς,
αἰαῖ, πικρογλώσσους ἀράς

Not only is the reference to the blinding (783f.) manifestly corrupt, with a tantalizing possibility

Oedipus launched bitter-worded curses upon his children, because he was angry (reading ἐπίκοτος). Angry at what? There is, apparently, a dependent genitive, which in the manuscripts is τροφᾶς, meaning 'rearing' or 'nurture', together with an epithet (though this is less certain) ἀραίας, meaning 'accursed' or (in some way) concerned with a curse. If τροφᾶς is right – and in this play we should be most reluctant to alter it – does it refer to the nurture, the tendance, of Oedipus or to the rearing of his sons? According to some critics,[80] Oedipus cursed Eteocles and Polynices for their mere existence; and a case can be made for this interpretation. In the maddening pain of his discovery, he blinded himself so that he might not see them (another corrupt text) and cursed them so that they might perish. They were reared under a curse, and he cursed them. But the objections too are weighty. 'Wrathful' does not seem the right word (yet ἐπίκοτος echoes περιθύμους in the first stanza) for a curse uttered in sheer disgust. And why, specifically, this curse? If he cursed his sons for their mere existence, one could understand his imprecating upon them an early death: but why that they should divide the property with the sword? It sounds like a punishment to fit a crime. Suffering in Aeschylus is not always deserved, but there is perhaps a difference between suffering because you belong to an accursed family and being cursed by your father for belonging to it. Erinyes are agents of punishment and associated with wrath; and one of the special fields in which they operate is where a parent has been offended. Is there any known case in which the Erinyes of a parent are not called to pursue an offence? There is offence in the epic tradition.

There are two offences, both attributed to the lost cyclic epic *Thebais*.[81] According to one account, Oedipus cursed his sons because, at the feast which followed a sacrifice, they served him with the haunch and not the shoulder (which was the more honourable portion); according to the other, he cursed them because Polynices set before him the silver table and the golden cup of Cadmus which he had forbidden to be used. Aeschylus will have known both versions, but need have used neither. The cup story has at least this advantage that it is linked to the theme of the fatal wealth of the family: if it was pride of wealth that caused the sons to bring out luxurious articles from the family treasure (τιμήεντα γέρα), this might have revealed

---

that it also referred to children, but emendation of some kind is needed either in 778 or in 785, since they fail to correspond metrically. The whole problem is hideously complicated, and I confine myself to the main features only.

[80] Schütz, Hermann, Weil and, most recently, H. C. Baldry, 'The dramatization of the Theban legend', *G&R* 25 (1956) 31, n. 1.

[81] Athen. 465e; Schol. Laur. in Soph. *O.C.* 1375 (frs. II and III Allen).

that state of mind which brought about their quarrel. But to make the text
fit, we must emend it, hazardously.[82] The scholiast to whom we owe the
haunch-and-shoulder story refers specifically to *Septem* (not to *Oedipus*).
He thought the reaction of Oedipus mean and petty, and so may we
(though of course we do not know how he was presented in the trilogy).
Aeschylus could well have had his own variation on the theme of sacrifice
and feast, but in this realm of uncertainties one must be content to review
the evidence, with one final comment. Which is that, if the sons were
culpable – or thought culpable by their father – Eteocles was presumably
no less so than his brother. (To a school of critics for whom Eteocles can do
no wrong this is intolerable.)[83]

Once again we come back to the point that in interpreting *Septem* we are
hampered, disastrously, by our ignorance of the earlier plays. Not only of
their action, but of the tone and of the roles. We have our idea of Oedipus
from Sophocles: the Aeschylean Oedipus, if we knew him, might surprise
us. But in what way? Fragments out of context should not be relied upon
too much, but there is a testimony which could imply that he tasted and
spat out the blood of his victim;[84] we do not have the story of the killing of
Laius or its motivation. It is not unlikely that Jocasta had a role, and there is
at least one good reason for supposing it was deleterious, but we do not
know. Nor do we know whether Polynices and Eteocles – either or
both – were presented and prominent in *Oedipus*, though it seems likely.
We suffer from blank ignorance on some points tempered by greater or
lesser probabilities on others. Yet too many critics courageously assume
that we can understand *Septem* – and Eteocles – without that knowledge
of the background at which the play hints again and again, but which is
withheld from us by the malignity of fate.

   We get at least an impression that the story of this noble family, with its
fame of wealth, was a grim one – grim perhaps by reason of the deliberate,
as well as the unwitting, acts of its members. Aeschylus is, traditionally,
regarded as a writer of tragedies in which impiety and *hubris* are punished,
in which, whatever superhuman forces may operate, divine and human
motivations run in parallel and the individual agent does not escape

---

[82] We need not only Wilamowitz's ἀρχαίας (printed by Page), which admits more than one
   interpretation, but also Robert's (op. cit. in n. 40) τρυφᾶς, to which the objection is not so much
   that the root τρυφ- is not known to be Aeschylean as that, in this play, a word of 'nurture' should
   not be eliminated without the most compelling reasons. Cf. Cameron (1964) 2ff.
[83] Cf. G. Müller, *Hermes* 94 (1966) 264ff.
[84] Fr. 173 Mette.

responsibility for his own decisions. With such a picture would consist a guilty Oedipus. And a guilty Eteocles? For Eteocles also is a member of the family.

We can form more than one picture of Eteocles, as we select – and interpret – the evidence. Sharing with his brother responsibility for the wrong, whatever it may have been, that was done to their father; equally responsible for their disastrous quarrel – conceivably more responsible, if he drove his brother into exile; at the moment of crisis consumed with a passionate hatred indistinguishable from his brother's; preoccupied, like him, with status and power and possessions and the values they dictated to the heroic world; sharing with him an impious disregard of the bond of kinship, so that in the end, justly, they share the narrow territory of their graves. Compatible with the words of Eteocles in the hour of decision (as they have been interpreted above), compatible with the final undifferentiating verdict of the Chorus, this picture has a seductive self-sufficiency and a recognizable affinity to Aeschylean tragic thought. One would like to be content with it. But has something been left out? Is there a strand whose place in the pattern has not been identified?

There is another Eteocles, familiar to modern scholarship, about whom little has yet been said. The iron hero, the unselfish patriot, the man of the *Opfertod*. The notion of a sacrificial death, though it has left a legacy in the invincible reluctance of some recent critics to admit any disparagement of Eteocles, has now (in its pure form) been largely abandoned, on the grounds that Aeschylus has given no indication in the text that the fratricidal duel was, as such (and immediately), necessary to the preservation of Thebes. But does not every soldier who dies for his country sacrifice his life? And did not Eteocles, when he went out to fight his brother, go out as a patriot in defence of his city?[85]

At this point we must return, briefly, to the seventh gate and to the Spy, who opens his report (631–8) with the sinister prayers of Polynices. They are complex and revealing.[86] First comes the city (632). No more than Eteocles, it seems, does Polynices envisage a duel as part of the assault. He prays (with a word of cursing) that he may mount the city's defences and

---

[85] Cf., e.g., B. Snell, *Aischylos und das Handeln im Drama, Philologus*, Supplb. 20 (Leipzig 1928) 83, who, drawing a sharp distinction between the Homeric and Aeschylean views of honour, says that for Eteocles it is not his own fate that stands in the foreground, but that of the city.

[86] Von Fritz saw the importance of these lines, and his discussion (206ff.), including an interesting comparison with Eur. *Phoen.*, is most valuable. I cannot, however, stay with him when he goes on to advance a modified version of the *Opfertod*, which seems to rest on assumptions which Aeschylus could have made clear if he had wished, e.g. that, if Eteocles had survived the duel, he could hardly have lived on, still less continued to rule.

raise the paean of capture, and then that he may deal with his brother. Infinitives after participles, this comes as a climax. Either his brother will fight him in single combat to the death (and, extravagantly, he says he is willing to die if only he can first kill) or, if Eteocles prefers to live, he shall be driven into a dishonourable exile.[87] These are the threats – the threat to the city, the threat to Eteocles. To which will the latter respond? We wait to see. And when he perceives his father's curse at work, cries ὤμοι and is close to tears, and then checks his tears 'lest there be begotten a more intolerable lamentation' (657), we wonder if he is thinking of the deaths which will attend the fall of the city.[88] And when, in answer to the Coryphaeus, he speaks of disgrace and honour (683–5), we wonder if he is thinking of his honour as a soldier, his duty as a citizen. We wait for a word of the *polis*, and it does not come.[89] Why, if the poet intended us to see the decision of Eteocles in terms of patriotism, has he made things so difficult for us? It would have been so easy – and so clear – if Eteocles had taken up the theme of his earlier prayer (71f.) and said that, come what may to him and his house, he will strive to preserve the city at least from destruction.[90] He says nothing of the kind. (Wilamowitz saw this, but drew the wrong conclusion.)[91] Instead, as to tears, we learn that his eyes – or those of the Curse which now inspires him – are dry with a hot longing for his brother's blood; as to honour, that the *kerdos* that it offers and demands is the death of Polynices. This is his answer to the challenge.

Still one ransacks the scene for anything that may bear upon the city.[92]

[87] I omit reference to the second half of 634, where text and meaning remain extremely dubious. At 636, when Polynices says κτανὼν θανεῖν πέλας, it is an extravagant way of expressing, not a wish, but a readiness to die (parallels in Tucker (1)'s note): it is chosen for obvious reasons.

[88] The sense of the line must be intentionally elusive, for Aeschylus is clear when he wants to be. γόος *can* be used of sufferings other than death (cf. *P.V.* 33), and so Eteocles might be thinking of the pain of disgrace, but, since it is most commonly used of lamenting the dead, he might be thinking of his fellow-countrymen. Which is it? In any case, the γόος which actually ensues (and τεκνωθῇ is a carefully chosen word) is that lamentation for the πανδάκρυτον Οἰδίπου γένος which we find in the *exodos* (cf. 853, 917, 967).

[89] Without attaching undue significance to such statistics, I note that, in a play in which πόλις, πολίτης, and other words of the same root, occur on the average once in every 15 or 16 lines, this (648–748) is the longest stretch without such a word. To play fair, one should observe that Eteocles does refer at 668 to his father's land (πατρῷα χθών), mishandled by Polynices.

[90] If he had said of the future what the Sophoclean Oedipus said of the past: 'So long as I have saved this city, I care not' (ἀλλ' εἰ πόλιν τήνδ' ἐξέσωσ', οὔ μοι μέλει, *OT* 443).

[91] Wilamowitz (1) 67.

[92] Dawe, on the same evidence, still argues for an *Opfertod*. 'We continue to get the impression that the death of Eteokles saved Thebes from destruction.' But one must distinguish effect and motive. It is one thing to say (rightly) that the death of the accursed brothers saved the city, another to say that Eteocles died to save the city. The formulation of the prayer at 71f. need not foreshadow an *Opfertod*, but rather (as Dawe himself writes) 'by inserting the particle [γε in 71] Aeschylus implants in the minds of the audience the idea that [the fate of Eteocles and that of the city] are *not* the same, but one is conditional upon the other'. See p. 26 above and Podlecki 296ff.

At 717 Eteocles, now in full armour, uses the word *hoplites*. How one would like to know whether the audience, when they watched the arming of Eteocles, remembered their Homer or their hoplites, the Trojan or the Persian War! Did they think of the armed citizens of the contemporary world who marched out to defend their city-states? Without the *Redepaare*, such a suggestion might be dismissed as a fantasy. Yet six such defenders were dispatched, with suitable eulogies; and Eteocles is the seventh. His own references to shame and honour can, as we have seen, be related to his personal quarrel and to the curse. But an ambiguity remains, since similar terms were used of Melanippus, when Eteocles sent him out to defend his native soil. Does it make *no* difference that, while Polynices attacks their native land, Eteocles defends it? And is this too a strand in the fabric? And is there not perhaps one question we have not yet asked?

Eteocles has two roles, two functions, a twofold address: he is 'lord of the Kadmeians' and 'son of Oedipus', in virtue of which he is the common focus of a twofold issue, the destinies of the city and the family, dangerously intertwined. In everything he says or does, he is one or the other. There is a view of the play that sees him as two men, the one suddenly transformed into the other by the arbitrary intervention of a sinister divine force. This is altogether too simple and below the level of Aeschylus. It is too simple because the circumstances in which he found himself lord of the Kadmeians are bound up with his sonship to Oedipus, his emotions and motives as lord are bound up with his brotherhood to Polynices; it is un-Aeschylean because the gods of Aeschylus work through human motive and emotion. Nevertheless, we may yet find a further dimension in the tragedy of Eteocles, if, asking ourselves a question which should be asked of any Aeschylean personage: 'In what situation did he find himself?', we answer that he found himself between two worlds.[93]

In so far as we can discern a basic pattern in the play – and in the trilogy – it is the entanglement and disentanglement of house and city. At the end, the city which has been in danger since the disobedience of Laius is

[93] Cf. V. L. Ehrenberg, *From Solon to Socrates* (2nd ed. London 1973) 207 (with n. 39): 'The individual suffers the tragedy of standing between the demands of family ties and those of the polis, between past and future.' Vernant, in his chapter entitled 'Tensions et ambiguïtés dans la tragédie grecque', 28, writes: 'Le vrai personnage des *Sept.*, c'est la cité, c'est-à-dire les valeurs, les modes de pensée, les attitudes qu'elle commande et qu'Etéocle représente à la tête de Thèbes aussi longtemps que le nom de son frère n'est pas prononcé devant lui. Car il lui suffit d'entendre parler de Polynice pour que, sur le champ rejeté du monde de la *polis*, il soit rendu à un autre univers: il se retrouve le Labdacide de la légende, l'homme des *génē* nobles, des grandes familles royales du passé, sur lesquelles pèsent les souillures et les malédictions ancestrales.' (First published in an English version in *Interpretation: theory and practice*, ed. C. S. Singleton (Baltimore 1969) 111.)

saved, but the house perishes. Some critics, oddly enough, have found this outcome disconcerting and not what they would have expected in an Aeschylean trilogy; and it has even been greeted as an advance in the thought and theology of Aeschylus that, in *Oresteia*, means were found – by him, by the gods, by the myth? – to save a doomed family from utter destruction! Suppose, however, that it was an essential point of the Theban trilogy that the family should be destroyed?[94]

Neither Aeschylus, when he wrote his plays, nor his audience, when it came to the theatre, laid aside all awareness of their contemporary world. *Persae* was contemporary history, but treated like myth; *Oresteia* was myth, but had without doubt a relevance to contemporary history, and not least to the troubled political drama which had seen the assassination of Ephialtes.[95] If Aeschylus dramatized the salvation of a city which had been endangered by a *genos*, he could have had in mind a political process which had been carried towards completion in his own lifetime. It had been a result, if not a purpose, of the constitutional reforms of Cleisthenes to disembarrass the political life of the city-state from the dangerous influence of the *gene*, the clans, with their loyalties and rivalries and feuds. The clans were an archaic element in the body politic, deeply rooted in an earlier world and in its standards of value, inimical to the order of the *polis* and menacing its security.[96] The Theban legend may have offered to Aeschylus the opportunity of dramatizing this process of disentanglement. On the one hand, the *genos*, an archaic relic – a family of dynasts preoccupied with their wealth and privileges – endangering the state. On the other hand, the *polis* that must be saved by the selfless devotion of its citizens, who find their highest excellence in its defence and their greatest shame if they fail to defend it. These are the two worlds between which Eteocles finds himself – the old world and the new. He dies as member of a doomed and disastrous family, despairing of his race, filled with mad hatred, seeing his honour in the ruthless prosecution of a feud. But he also goes out, the seventh, to fight for that city which in the extremity of his hatred he has forgotten, and saves it by a crime.

For, if Eteocles is allowed some footing in a new and more civilized world, mainly he lives and dies in the old one. Lives and offends and dies. Offends against the religious basis of the family, in a family quarrel. The

[94] Cf. Thomson (1) 315f.
[95] The precise relevance is of course debated. Cf. Dover 230ff.; Dodds (3) 19–31; Podlecki, *The political background of Aeschylean tragedy* (Ann Arbor 1966) 63–100 (on which see *Gnomon* 39 (1967) 641–6); Macleod (1) 129ff.
[96] Cf. Knox 77f.

rights and wrongs of it are never settled; and the theme of justice drops right out of the play as soon as the princes are dead.[97] One might indeed ask whether there is any case in Aeschylus in which an issue of human justice is settled on human terms. It is not claims that matter but conduct, and particularly conduct in relation to the gods.[98] What shocks the Chorus, in their piety, is that Eteocles no less than Polynices should disregard the sanctity of kindred blood. When they hear the news, they condemn both brothers impartially with a single phrase. 'They perished with impious mind' (ὤλοντ' ἀσεβεῖ διανοίᾳ, 831). But there was another paramount field of religious obligation – to the wider kinship group, which is how the Greeks conceived the city-state. Whatever his claims of right, Polynices condemns himself, when he attacks his native land. Melanippus and Megareus paid with their lives the debt they owed to the land which nourished them. Perhaps there is one field at least in which Eteocles cannot be deprived of all moral advantage.

This seems at least a possible pattern of interpretation, reconciling some seeming contradictions in the evidence and in the emotional responses which one can, tentatively, assume in an audience of Greeks. There were the city and the family, both in danger. Zeus and the city-gods have saved the city (822ff.); the prayer of Eteocles (69), the prayers of the Chorus in the *Redepaare*, have been answered. Thanks must be given, but not yet. The expressions of joy at the salvation of the city are almost perfunctory, before the Chorus turns to lamentations for the two brothers upon whom their father's curse has been fulfilled. They address the black accomplishing Curse that Oedipus laid upon his sons (832ff.). The father's prayer has done its work without fail (840f.); no less have the disobedient counsels of Laius had their effect (842). It was an Erinys that ratified the words of Oedipus (885f.); it was Apollo, the Messenger had said (800ff.), who took to himself the seventh gate and 'ratified' upon the family of Oedipus the ill-counsels of Laius of old. There is a multiplicity of gods in *Septem*. There is Zeus, and the *polissouchoi theoi* particularized in the frantic prayers of the *parodos*. There is Apollo, with his special concern to punish the disobedience of Laius. There is the Erinys, 'a goddess unlike the gods', a dark power of the underworld to whom the sons of Oedipus are given over. It is the gods who give (719), and the gods by whom Eteocles sees his race as maddened, hated and abandoned (653, 702). It was the simple faith of the Chorus that, if the gods received their sacrifices, the black-aegised Erinys would leave

---

[97] And one can hardly believe that it was reintroduced, and so oddly, at 1070ff.
[98] Cf. Kaufmann-Bühler, *passim*.

the house (699ff.), but the doomed Eteocles had the deeper insight, when he saw that one great sacrifice alone would win the respect of the gods, which was the destruction of his race (703). There are Olympians and Chthonians; divine powers of different and contrasted orders, they are seen in the last analysis – and this is Aeschylean[99] – to converge towards the same end. Eteocles prayed to the Curse–Erinys, along with Zeus and the city-gods, to save the city; and his prayer was answered, paradoxically, by his own impious act, which destroyed the family and liberated the city from its contagion.

This could be true. If we possessed the entire trilogy, we might or might not see it clearly to be true. As things are, a critic can only hope that he has clarified rather than confused the issues.

[99] Cf. ch. 8 below, *passim*.

CHAPTER THREE

The Danaid trilogy[1]

A scrap of papyrus has told us two things: that an Aeschylean trilogy ended with *Danaides*, *Amymone* being the satyr-play,[2] and that this trilogy was in competition with Sophocles. It is virtually certain that the first play was our *Supplices* ('Ικέτιδες); and since Sophocles first competed in 468, this means that a play once regarded as early Aeschylus must be dated to the 60s, possibly to 463. It is less certain, though highly probable, that the second play of the trilogy was *Aegyptii* (as conjectured long ago by Schlegel). That *Supplices* demands a sequel should always have been clear. Now single plays that formed part of trilogies are at once tantalizing and challenging, and it is natural — and indeed proper — that scholars should use their ingenuity in the attempt to recover at least the general trend of the lost plays. It is proper because it affects the interpretation of the extant play. It is natural and proper, but whether it is prudent one begins to doubt when one observes how widely the speculations of scholars on tenuous evidence diverge from one another. Yet, in the case of the Danaid trilogy, one is haunted by a feeling that the necessary evidence is at our disposal, if only we could use it rightly. In what does the evidence consist?

There are the fragments attributable to the missing plays. With one important exception, these do not amount to much. But fr. 125 M from *Danaides* gives us seven famous lines on the universal power of love in

[1] This chapter goes back to a lecture delivered to the Society for the Promotion of Hellenic Studies in 1958, which was published in *JHS* 81 (1961) 141–52. The text remains substantially as printed, but I have revised the annotation to take account of subsequent work. I would mention in particular Garvie (1), which is indispensable. The trilogy is dealt with in his ch. 5, pp. 163–233 (with full bibliographical references). I regret that I have been unable to take into account H. Friis Johansen and E. W. Whittle (edd.), *Aeschylus: the Suppliants* (Copenhagen 1980), which discusses the trilogy in I 40–55.

[2] P. Oxy. 20 (1952) 2256 fr. 3 (fr. 122 M) is printed by Garvie (1) viii and its not inconsiderable problems are fully discussed in his ch. 1. As to *Aegyptii* for the second play, having due regard to Taplin's cautionary remarks (194ff.), I still think (with Garvie) that it is the best working hypothesis.

nature, and we know that they were spoken by Aphrodite herself.[3] There is the mythographical tradition – Apollodorus and Hyginus; Pausanias; certain scholia. The constant feature – that the Danaids killed their bridegrooms – is known to us from *Prometheus Vinctus*. Apart from this, it is clear that both before and after Aeschylus there were different versions of the story in circulation. We must have independent reasons for saying that any particular late account depends upon him; and it is only Aeschylus himself who can give us these reasons. It is Aeschylus who provides the primary evidence. I am not thinking of the story of Io and her descendants as told in *Prometheus* (846ff.): though this passage corresponds so closely to *Supplices* where it covers the same ground – even including the figure of the hawks and doves – that it is not unreasonable to suppose that it summarizes those aspects of the Danaid trilogy at least which were relevant to the later play (as I believe it to have been).[4] The primary evidence is provided by *Supplices* itself. In *Oresteia* we can see how themes introduced in *Agamemnon* are carried over into *Choephori* and, in many cases, find their culmination in the closing scene of *Eumenides*. It is a reasonable assumption that Aeschylus used similar methods in the Danaid trilogy and that themes which are developed in *Supplices* were taken up and developed further in the succeeding plays. It is also worth bearing in mind that, if any feature in the extant play seems to lack relevance or to receive emphasis disproportionate to its dramatic value there, it may look forward to the missing sequel.[5] These are assumptions; and the biggest assumption that one makes – optimistic and perhaps ill-founded – is that we can begin to understand the artistic methods and modes of thought of Aeschylus. In what follows many questions will be asked and a number of answers suggested, some old, some new. There will be much that is extremely speculative.

One or two things we know for certain. We know that the Danaids were taken as brides by the sons of Aegyptus; that they killed their bridegrooms on the wedding night; all except Hypermestra, who spared Lynceus. There can be little doubt that this action or some part of it

---

[3] P. Oxy. 2255 fr. 14 adds nothing to our previous knowledge.

[4] Whether by Aeschylus or by another, on which matter see ch. 9 below. The relative dates of the two plays are discussed by Murray, App. A, 88–97.

[5] Cf. F. Stoessl, *Die Trilogie des Aischylos* (Baden b. Wien 1937) 84. A. J. Podlecki, *BICS* 22 (1975) 1–19, discusses the principles which should be followed in reconstructing an Aeschylean trilogy. So far as my own reconstruction is concerned, I would ask the reader to believe that, where I cite passages in *Supplices* to support a hypothesis, this was not the result of ransacking the extant play for clues: rather they leapt out to meet the logical possibilities of subsequent action. (See now also F. Stoessl, *Die Hiketiden des Aischylos als geistesgeschichtliches und theatergeschichtliches Phaenomen*, Vienna 1979.)

constituted the second play. And one broad line of Aeschylean interpretation seems fairly evident. The victims of violence in *Supplices* become violent agents in the sequel, for violence breeds violence, *hubris* breeds *hubris*. Even in *Supplices*, for all their claims to *sophrosune*, the Danaids showed a potentiality of violence. There they threatened to kill themselves rather than submit to wedlock: in the outcome they kill their bridegrooms. Thus the themes of *bia* and *hubris*, prominent in *Supplices*,[6] were carried over into the later plays.

But how did this action come about, as it certainly did? *Supplices* ends with the Danaids under the protection of Argos and its king, who are ready to fight on their behalf. It is commonly – and I think rightly – assumed that the battle which threatened at the end of the play actually took place; that the Argives were defeated, Pelasgus was killed, Danaus became king of Argos and negotiated the treacherous wedlock of his daughters. This cannot be proved with certainty, and some scholars have thought that war was averted by diplomacy.[7] Too much weight need not perhaps be attached to the words of the Egyptian herald at 934ff. which seem to rule out the possibility of a peaceful settlement. But surely it would be something of an anticlimax, if Argos escaped the war which she had so boldly risked in the cause of the suppliants (and an over-simplification of the mind of Zeus, if the innocent did not suffer).[8] More objectively, the economy of the trilogy would be embarrassed by the continued presence of a live Pelasgus: better that he should die and that Danaus should become king. That Danaus was at some time or other king of Argos is a solid feature in the tradition. He is not king when the trilogy begins. That a discredited Danaus was promoted to the kingship at the end of the trilogy is hard to believe. It will be shown below that there are considerable advantages to be derived from the hypothesis that he became king in *Aegyptii*.[9]

To the circumstances which may be supposed to have prevailed in that play and to have led up to the arrangement with the sons of Aegyptus we will return later. It is unlikely that the murder of the bridegrooms,

---

6 On ὕβρις, cf. H. G. Robertson, *CR* 50 (1936) 104–9: references in 107, n. 2.

7 Cf. Wilamowitz (1) 20f.

8 At 630ff. the Danaids, while calling down blessings on the people of Argos, return again and again to the name of Ares. Some writers have suggested – and it may well be true – that these references foreshadow the murderous actions of the singers (contr. 749). In any case I feel that the ironical effect is greatly enhanced if the Argives in fact suffer the miseries of war.

9 When Danaus receives a bodyguard in the *Supplices* (985ff., cf. esp. τίμιον γέρας), this might be regarded as a half-way stage to the kingship. One further point: if Danaus becomes king, his daughters presumably cease to be μέτοικοι (609) in need of a πρόξενος (491) and become full citizens.

involving the passage of a night, took place in the course of a play. It is more probable that, as *Supplices* ended at nightfall,[10] so did *Aegyptii*; and that the opening of *Danaides* revealed the murder of forty-nine bride-grooms and the sparing of the fiftieth. What happened then? One thing only we know for certain: that Aphrodite appeared and delivered a speech which proclaimed the universal power of sexual love. It is obvious that in this way she commended the action of Hypermestra. It has been assumed – perhaps too readily – that she spoke in Hypermestra's defence and that Hypermestra was on trial.

Fr. 125 M, from Aphrodite's speech, is the longest and most important of our fragments.[11] It is with this fragment that any serious attempt to recover what is lost should begin. In order to put the whole action in its proper frame, we must look to the end. For this passage must, surely, come near the end of the trilogy. It has a breadth and finality of argument which must settle once and for all whatever it was intended to settle. But does Aphrodite speak as an advocate at a trial? Like Apollo defending Orestes in the *Eumenides*? The analogy is seductive, but leads to difficulties. It is, for example, a one-sided trial in which one party only has divine support: yet no god or gods can have prosecuted Hypermestra. Perhaps a better counterpart to Aphrodite can be found in *Eumenides* – not Apollo, but Athena. Not Apollo defending Orestes, but Athena persuading the Furies. To the question of a trial I shall return. Nor do I wish to deny that Aphrodite had a function in relation to Hypermestra (she clearly had). But I suggest that she had an even more important function in relation to Hypermestra's sisters.

What happened to the Danaids (and for that matter to Danaus) at the end of the trilogy? Critics have tended to shrug off this awkward question and concentrate upon the destiny of Hypermestra and Lynceus, who of course lived happily ever after and were the progenitors of the Argive kings. But the question is fundamental and must be faced. Say Hypermestra was vindicated: something must have been done about her sisters. If Aeschylus could not, at *Eumenides* 778, leave a chorus of angry

10 Cf. 768–70.

11
  ἐρᾷ μὲν ἁγνὸς οὐρανὸς τρῶσαι χθόνα,
  ἔρως δὲ γαῖαν λαμβάνει γάμου τυχεῖν.
  ὄμβρος δ' ἀπ' εὐνάεντος οὐρανοῦ πεσὼν
  ἔκυσε γαῖαν · ἡ δὲ τίκτεται βροτοῖς
  μήλων τε βοσκὰς καὶ βίον Δημήτριον ·
  δενδρῶτις ὥρα δ' ἐκ νοτίζοντος γάμου
  τέλειός ἐστι · τῶνδ' ἐγὼ παραίτιος.

Furies 'in the air', no more could he leave in the air a chorus of Danaids,[12] blood-guilty as well as aggrieved. In point of dramatic structure, they must have had an *exodos*: whither and to what fate? Say Hypermestra was vindicated: were her sisters found guilty? And, if guilty, were they punished? And, if so, how and where and when? It has been suggested that the trilogy ended with the Danaids condemned to their famous punishment in Hades (and, admittedly, *Supplices* 230f. and 416 might look forward to such a conclusion). But that story has not been proved to be as old as Aeschylus.[13] Moreover, it may well be doubted whether an Aeschylean trilogy is likely to have come to a conclusion with the eternal punishment of a chorus. Nor should we forget that these were the wronged women of *Supplices* and that they were driven to murder by desperation and by the ill-judged counsels of their father and that their every emotion had been communicated to the audience with the lyric genius of Aeschylus. If not with their punishment, the trilogy can only end in one way: with their reconciliation. With their reconciliation to marriage. It was the function of Aphrodite to reconcile them, as it was the function of Athena to reconcile the Furies; and fr. 125 is then part of the persuasive speech – or one of the persuasive speeches – through which she carried out this function. If this view is correct, the trilogy ends as it began with the attitude of the Danaids to marriage, but with a change of attitude, with a conversion.

This view has been put forward with great cogency by Professor K. von Fritz, to whom I am much indebted at this point. Thanks to his article,[14] I can deal briefly with a complex question which can no longer be avoided. To what were the Danaids opposed? To marriage with cousins *qua* cousins? To a forced marriage? Or to marriage *qua* marriage? This question, which has been much debated, turns partly upon passages of disputed reading.[15] The Danaids regard the marriage as forbidden by *themis* (37), but there is

---

[12] It can safely be assumed that the Danaids formed the Chorus of this play, whatever may be true of *Aegyptii* (see p. 64 below).

[13] Cf. J. Vürtheim, *Aischylos' Schutzflehende* (Amsterdam 1928) 24ff.; Garvie (1) 234f.

[14] Von Fritz (2); cf. Lesky (2) 104f., Emily A. Wolff, *Eranos* 56 (1958) 119–39; 60 (1959) 6–34, esp. 136f. For a careful examination of the whole problem see now J. K. Mackinnon, 'The reason for the Danaids' flight', *CQ* 28 (1978) 74–82.

[15] 8–10; 335–9. In the former passage Bamberger's αὐτογενεῖ φυξανορίᾳ is the most popular and, I think, the correct solution (unless with Page and Johansen, we prefer αὐτογενῆ φυξανορίαν), since it brings out a suitable contrast with 6–7: their flight is spontaneous (αὐτογενεῖ), not enforced; it is flight from men (from husbands), not exile from a city. Cf. von Fritz (2) 123. The difficulties of 335ff. are complex, and I will only refer to Garvie's careful examination ((1) 219ff.), which leads him to the conclusion (with which I agree) that 'we must look for the Danaids' motivation purely in their own character, and not in any simple obedience to a supposed moral or social principle'. There is much to be said for the hypothesis of a lacuna or lacunae (Wilamowitz; now Johansen).

little or nothing in *Supplices* which suggests that they (unlike the Athenians) regarded a marriage with cousins as incestuous. Both at the end of the opening anapaests (37–39) and in the words of Danaus (227f.) the stress is on lack of consent: it is a marriage to which neither the women nor their father have agreed. The sons of Aegyptus, on the other hand, claim the Danaids as their property (38, 918ff.), but on what right their claim is based – and indeed all the circumstances which led up to the flight and the pursuit – are left obscure in *Supplices* and are perhaps unlikely to have been clarified in the sequel. This obscurity must be deliberate,[16] and it can hardly have any purpose except to concentrate attention upon the violence of the pursuit and the loathing which it engenders. The violence of the Egyptians puts them in the wrong; they are guilty of *hubris*, and their victims deserve the pity of the Argives, under the divine sanction of Zeus Hikesios.[17] The distinction between hatred of a forced marriage and hatred of marriage as such cannot be pressed too far, since, in the dramatic situation, force is the only guise under which marriage presents itself to the Danaids, as an act comparable to war or to the preying of bird on bird.[18] But there are passages in which the language of the Danaids suggests a horror of male contact in any form.[19] The Handmaidens sing of Kypris and of marriage in general terms,[20] and it is in terms of the broadest generality that Aphrodite speaks of her own powers. If we want a formula that will cover all the facts, we cannot do better than say that the violent approach of the sons of Aegyptus has warped the feminine instincts of the Danaids and turned them against marriage as such.[21] At the end of the

---

[16] Cf. W. Headlam, *CR* 14 (1900) 111–12; von Fritz (2) 125. The whole δίκη-theme is acutely discussed by Kaufmann-Bühler 38–50.

[17] Cf. 486ff., after 478f.; 639ff.

[18] War: 83, 335, 1064. Birds: esp. 223ff., 510. Cf. B. H. Fowler, *C et M* 28 (1967) 14f. (on beast metaphors in the play); Petrounias 76–82 ('Vogel jagt Vogel').

[19] Cf. 141ff.

[20] Von Fritz (2) 262: 'Die Abneigung gegen einen bestimmten Freier hat nie und nirgends als Beleidigung der Liebesgöttin gegolten.' The attribution of 1034ff. to a supplementary chorus of Handmaidens is denied by some, notably by Taplin 230ff., whose acute examination of the problems involved in the entry and movements of such a chorus deserves close study. He ends by putting forward 'with the utmost diffidence . . . the desperate remedy that the anapaests 966–79 might have been interpolated'. No Handmaidens, then! If there *were* Handmaidens, they must have had a significant dramatic role to play; and it is not difficult to see what it was. A division of opinion among the Danaids is inappropriate at this stage, before their common action in the sequel. Aphrodite is given due honour first by the Handmaidens, then by Hypermestra, then by all the Danaids? Taplin, however, adopts an earlier suggestion that the ὀπαδοί at 1022 are not the Handmaidens, but the Argive bodyguard (cf. 985) which has attended Danaus, now acting as a supplementary chorus and singing the praises of Aphrodite. Short of some indication of their identity, the suggestion is not enticing, but cannot be ruled out. Garvie is non-committal.

[21] Von Fritz (2) 262: 'Die Verletzung ihrer Weiblichkeit durch die Aigyptossöhne hat die Danaiden mit Abscheu erfüllt gegen jede Ehe und gegen jede Verbindung mit einem Mann.'

trilogy, then, they must be restored to normality and made freely to accept their destiny of marriage. It is Aphrodite's function to bring this about with her persuasions.

If the Danaids were converted to the idea of marriage at the end of the trilogy (which seems a reasonable hypothesis), were they actually married or were marriages arranged for them? This is far more speculative. But some arrangement must have been made for their future. There is little point in persuading women to marry, unless they are to be married; and it was in fact one part of the tradition that Danaus married off his homicidal daughters – with some difficulty, according to Pausanias.[22] The story of the foot-race goes back at least to Pindar's ninth Pythian ode (111ff.)[23] – the Danaids being ranged at the finishing-tape to be chosen in order of attractiveness by the swiftest runners. It seems to lack dignity, and one may prefer to think that Aeschylus did not use it. He need have done no more than indicate that they would be married in due course.[24] But the possibility cannot be ruled out that bridegrooms were actually produced for them upon the stage. This trilogy seems to have run to supplementary choruses. Was there, then, a chorus of bridegrooms (like the Propompoi in *Eumenides*)? By our standards this might seem rather ridiculous, but it is not certain that a parade of noble Argives, full of *aidos* towards their brides, would have struck the audience of Aeschylus in that light. The *exodos* would then have balanced that of *Aegyptii* (see below); and there would have been one other signal advantage. For this would have brought upon the stage for the closing scene representatives of the state of Argos, which had undoubtedly played an important role in the action, and the destinies of which will have been announced towards the end of the trilogy. The political theme is already prominent in *Supplices*, and it will be suggested that its importance increased in the later plays.

At this point we must return to *Aegyptii*. To attempt to recover its economy in every detail would be unprofitable, but, by careful attention to *Supplices*, it may be possible to determine certain situations which it certainly or probably contained.

(1) Reasons have already been given for supposing that a battle took place in which the Argives were defeated and Pelasgus was killed.[25] But

---

[22] 3.12.2.

[23] In *BICS* 16 (1969) 9–15 I explore the possibility of a relationship between this ode and the trilogy.

[24] Perhaps the marriage of Hypermestra and Lynceus alone was solemnized (or about to be solemnized) at the end of the trilogy: perhaps under new rites invoking the protection of Hera (see n. 53). (So Miss M. L. Cunningham, in correspondence.)

[25] It is a minor point whether sounds of battle were heard, as in *Septem*, before the outcome of the

the outcome must have been such that the state of Argos – and Danaus himself – were not deprived of all liberty of action (and so of dramatic interest). How could this be, if the Argives had been defeated? There is a simple explanation: the defeat was followed by a siege. Let us observe, then, *Supplices* 955f.: 'Go to the well-fenced city, locked within its deep device of towers' (στείχετ᾽ εὐερκῆ πόλιν | πύργων βαθείᾳ μηχανῇ κεκλημένην). The style of Aeschylus does not in general run to decorative amplifications, and I suggest that this looks forward to the sequel.

(2) That is the situation: Argos defeated and beleaguered. How does it lead to the surrender of the Danaids to their suitors? One thing is certain: the Argive people cannot simply have gone back on their word. The irrevocability of their decision is proclaimed by Pelasgus in the strongest terms at *Supplices* 944f.: 'Through this the bolt has been driven clean, for it to stay compact' (τῶνδ᾽ ἐφήλωται τορῶς | γόμφος διαμπὰξ ὡς μένειν ἀραρότως). This unanimous decision not to surrender the Danaids to *force* (βίᾳ) must govern Argive action also in *Aegyptii*. But if they are willing, if they are persuaded – that is another matter: (940f.) ταύτας δ᾽ ἑκούσας μὲν κατ᾽ εὔνοιαν φρενῶν | ἄγοις ἄν, εἴπερ εὐσεβὴς πίθοι λόγος. This is where Danaus must have played the leading role: a Danaus who now is or becomes king. Whether he was elected king simply in virtue of his descent from Io or whether his election was bound up with an offer to surrender willing daughters to the Egyptians is a matter of mere speculation. His motives too must remain hypothetical: perhaps he distrusted Argive powers of resistance; perhaps he saw a way, a plan, a μηχανή, not only to preserve his daughters' virginity, but also to retaliate upon his enemies. But the initiative must have come from him. He is in fact characterized in *Supplices* as the man who might devise such a plan. It is the only way in which he is characterized – and characterized from the beginning: he is βούλαρχος, πεσσονομῶν – planning his moves, playing his cards (11ff.). He is the planner, the calculator, the embodiment of worldly wisdom, the man who always knows best.[26] Whatever his motives, whatever the political situation, he has one essential function to perform: he must persuade his daughters. However the earlier part of the play was managed, we can envisage this as the central scene. A scene opening perhaps with utter despair on the part of the Danaids, who have placed their hopes in the

---

fighting was announced. It is perhaps worth saying that, because *Supplices* has no prologue, we cannot therefore assume that both the later plays opened with the *parodos*. Cf. n. 38 below.

[26] The impression of 11ff. is reinforced by the first words of Danaus (176ff., esp. προμηθίαν); they are echoed at 969f. (πρόνοον καὶ βούλαρχον, followed by μῆτις). Every reference in *Supplices* to his wisdom, forethought and planning must look forward to the disastrous device of *Aegyptii*.

gods and in men, who see themselves abandoned by the gods, abandoned by men, abandoned even by their own father. Then comes a stroke of Aeschylean irony. Their father has not failed them after all. He expounds his plan, appealing at once to their hatred of wedlock and to their sense of filial piety;[27] and they comply. 'If they choose freely and of good will, you may take them, should pious argument in fact persuade them.' Those words must have been significant for the future; and they are doubly significant. They look forward to the holy and persuasive words with which Aphrodite converted the Danaids to marriage. But they also look forward to the persuasions of Danaus, necessary to the plot of *Aegyptii*. A speech of persuasion indeed, but not εὐσεβής.[28]

(3) It was not εὐσεβής, because it involved, not merely deeds of murderous violence (which the Egyptians themselves had provoked), but also a breach of hospitality. Zeus figures in *Supplices* for the most part in his aspect as Hikesios, the protector of suppliants, but twice (627, 672) as Xenios, the protector of foreigners, of guests. This is appropriate enough, since the Danaids have found *proxenoi* in the Argive king and people: it may have been even more appropriate in the sequel. Indeed I suspect that, just as Zeus Hikesios presides over *Supplices*, so did Zeus Xenios over *Aegyptii*.[29] The murder of the Egyptians was a breach of hospitality, since, when peace had been made upon terms, it was not as *polemioi*, but as *xenoi* that they entered the city to claim their brides. They were not only *xenoi* to the city, but they were probably the personal *xenoi* of Danaus. Towards the end of *Supplices*, the question of the accommodation of the Danaids is raised. It is raised twice (957ff., 1009ff.), by the king and by Danaus. There are two sets of choices. The Danaids may share common quarters with

---

27 The filial obedience of the Danaids in *Supplices* (204ff., 968ff.) prepares for a more dramatic instance in *Aegyptii*? Von Fritz (2) (256f., 259 n. 1) criticizes A. Elisei (*Studi ital. di filologia classica*, n.s. 6 (1928) 197ff.), perhaps rightly, for overstressing the submissiveness of the Danaids, but I feel that he himself underestimates the role probably played by Danaus in the sequel. In the absence of the play, however, we cannot know what was the balance between the two factors of their decision.

28 Nor would the Danaids give themselves κατ᾽ εὔνοιαν φρενῶν (though the Argives were not to know this).

29 If this is right, it strengthens Miss Cunningham's case for attributing P. Oxy. 2251 to *Aegyptii* (*RhM* 96 (1953) 223–31). The attribution is criticized by H. Lloyd-Jones in the Loeb Aeschylus, vol. II (1957) 571f.; a rejoinder by Miss Cunningham appeared in *RhM* 105 (1962) 189f. I would point out (i) that the attribution is consistent with Snell's ν[ῦν δόμον, which would be particularly appropriate to the situation I envisage below, and that such an appeal to Zeus Xenios by the Chorus in the early part of the play would have a powerful irony in view of their future action; (ii) that ὁρᾶν, ἐφορᾶν are common of deities in *Supplices* (cf. O. Hiltbrunner, *Wiederholungs- und Motivtechnik bei Aischylos* (Berne 1950) 39) to a degree unparalleled in Aeschylus. For appeals with the imperative or optative of these verbs, mostly to Zeus: 1, 104, 145, 206, 210, 359, 811, 1030, cf. 531. See now Garvie (1) 200–2, who concludes: 'Tempting as it is to accept the fragment for the Αἰγύπτιοι, the evidence is just not strong enough, and we are not entitled to draw conclusions from it.'

other women or have rooms to themselves. It has long been recognized
that this may have had a relevance to the sequel, so as to facilitate the action
of the Danaids and the independent action of Hypermestra.[30] The other
choice too may be significant (and is the one repeated in the speech of
Danaus). Will they be the guests of the king or of the city? Now, where the
Danaids spend the night which follows *Supplices* is of no dramatic
moment: where they spend the night which follows *Aegyptii* may be of
crucial importance. If they choose – or rather Danaus chooses for
them[31] – the royal apartments, and if Danaus becomes king and inherits
the royal palace, then the murder of the sons of Aegyptus is the murder of
guests under his own roof. 'Heavy is the wrath of Zeus Hikesios', said the
Chorus-leader in *Supplices* (347). No less heavy is the wrath of Zeus
Xenios; and it is this wrath, together with an intolerable pollution, which
Danaus will have brought upon himself and upon his daughters. But he
will also have brought it upon the city of which he is now king. This surely
must be the religious background to *Danaides* and must affect whatever
action is there taken by the Argive state.

    These, then, seem to me the most probable hypotheses about *Aegyptii*.
Argos defeated and besieged; Pelasgus dead and Danaus king or becoming
king; a voluntary surrender of themselves by the Danaids, on the basis of
their father's murder-plot; a crime prepared against Zeus Xenios. Further
speculation on the economy of the play is not, perhaps, very profitable. It
has been assumed that, despite the title, the Danaids formed the chorus of
this play also. Try as one will, it is very hard to see how the play could have
been managed with a main chorus consisting of the sons of Aegyptus, and
there is no reason why it should not have been named after a
supplementary chorus.[32] This chorus entered, I suspect, late in the play,
and only to claim their brides, after negotiations had been completed. No
formalities of marriage would be required, since the Egyptians already
claim the Danaids as their property; and the cunning of Danaus might well
have avoided such formalities.[33] We can only guess at the tone of this
scene. Perhaps the bridegrooms entered the house of death with words of
ardour, proclaiming the passion which, as they think, is about to be
fulfilled. Naturally, we should like to know whether any indication was
given that Hypermestra would take a line of her own; whether she was

[30] Cf. Wilamowitz (1) 21; F. Stoessl, op. cit. 84.
[31] Cf. 970ff.
[32] Cf. Pohlenz I 51; Lesky (2) 107. This trilogy will have been extraordinarily closely knit, if it had
    unity of Chorus as well as approximate unity of time and place.
[33] Miss Cunningham's suggestion.

already distinguished from her sisters in this play and Lynceus from his brothers.[34] Here there seems little solid basis for speculation, and I confine myself to a single point. There was one way at least in which Lynceus could have been introduced with plausibility. The entry of the Egyptians must have been prepared by negotiations. It is not inconceivable, therefore, that Lynceus, as negotiator, was a character in the play. If he had a speaking part, it would have given him an opportunity to show a degree of *sophrosune* which merited salvation and a persuasiveness in his protestations of desire which awoke *himeros* in his destined bride.

Why did Hypermestra spare Lynceus? μίαν δὲ παίδων (so runs *P.V.* 865f.) ἵμερος θέλξει τὸ μὴ | κτεῖναι σύνευνον. Some critics have taken παίδων in dependence upon ἵμερος and believe that she spared her bedfellow out of a desire for children. In the context of *Prometheus* it is not perhaps easy to decide between this and the rival interpretation, namely that παίδων depends on μίαν ('one of the children') and that Hypermestra was charmed by sexual desire.[35] But, if (as I believe) this passage is related to the themes of the Danaid trilogy, there can be little doubt that the latter interpretation is correct. It is of course relevant that Hypermestra and Lynceus bred the race of Argive kings: the power of Aphrodite is the power of fertility. But the fertility is promoted by desire. ἐρᾷ μὲν ἁγνὸς οὐρανὸς τρῶσαι χθόνα, | ἔρως δὲ γαῖαν λαμβάνει γάμου τυχεῖν (fr. 125): 'Pure heaven is in love to penetrate the earth, and love of marriage seizes on the land.' I cannot separate ἵμερος θέλξει in *Prometheus* from the terms in which the Handmaidens of *Supplices* sang of the attendant train of Kypris (1039f.): Πόθος ⟨ᾱ⟩ τ' οὐδὲν ἄπαρνον τελέθει θελκτόρι Πειθοῖ. 'Yearning, and that magical Persuasion to which nothing is denied.' *Eros*; *pothos* and *himeros*; *peithein* and *thelgein* – these form a cluster of related words, all associated with the power of Kypris or Aphrodite. For that matter it was not the Handmaidens who first raised the theme of the persuasive magic of sexual attraction, but the dry, calculating, puritanical Danaus himself,[36] when he spoke of the passer-by, overcome with desire (ἱμέρου νικώμενος), 'darting a seductive arrow of the eye (ὄμματος

---

34 That both Hypermestra and Lynceus had speaking parts and that there was dialogue between them seems unlikely.

35 E. Harrison, *Proc. Cambr. Philol. Soc.* 160–2 (1935) 8 (oddly misreported by Murray 60 n. 6), argues that to take παίδων with ἵμερος 'is more consonant with the tragic poets' use of παῖς', but this argument has little force in view of γέννα πεντηκοντάπαις preceding (853), and I would rather ask whether it is consonant with ἵμερος θέλξει in a context of wedlock. The interpretation I reject is put in an extreme form, and given a historical setting, by A. Diamantopoulos, 'The Danaid tetralogy of Aeschylus', *JHS* 77 (1957) 222.

36 It is most unfortunate that 1001f., with their reference to Kypris, are so corrupt. Still, Kypris is mentioned – and doubtless made responsible for the phenomena that Danaus so deplores.

θελκτήριον τόξευμα) at the tender loveliness of virgins' (1003–5). The purpose of these lines is not to characterize Danaus (or the Danaids),[37] but to introduce a theme which will immediately be carried further by the Handmaidens and will receive its culmination in the speech of Aphrodite. This, surely, was the force which moved Hypermestra to disobey her father; and it was because sexual desire now presented itself to her, not as a brutal rape, but as a persuasive and enchanting courtship, that she was able to separate herself from her sisters. Aeschylus was renowned as the best of all writers of satyr-plays. The satyr-play which followed the Danaid trilogy was *Amymone*, about which we know little, but enough for our purposes. It told how another of the daughters of Danaus was saved from the brutal lust of a satyr by the god Poseidon, whose lover she then became. It can hardly be doubted that Aeschylus had taken up and translated into suitable satyric terms the theme of the contrast between rape and courtship which had already been developed in the trilogy.

What indications may have been given in *Aegyptii* to foreshadow the separate action of Hypermestra we can hardly know. The opening scenes of *Danaides* must have revealed that action and its motives. Again, we do not know how it was managed,[38] but it seems likely that the Chorus, when they entered, carried, not the olive-branches which they called ἐγχειρίδια in the *parodos* of *Supplices* (21), but real daggers this time. The defection of Hypermestra will have been disclosed. The situation confronts Danaus – and no less the state of Argos – with a problem. Did it lead to a trial? If so, of whom, and at whose instance? Where, and before what court? There was a trial in the tradition – or rather two trials. According to one account,[39] Hypermestra was brought to trial by Danaus and acquitted by the Argives; according to another,[40] there was a trial of Danaus (not the Danaids) at the instance of Aegyptus, who had come to Argos to avenge his sons. Aegyptus can have played no part in the Aeschylean trilogy. If any action was taken against Danaus and the Danaids, it must have been taken by the *polis*. But at the outset the initiative would seem to rest with Danaus, who would certainly have been anxious to punish Hypermestra. To him

---

[37] E. A. Wolff, *Eranos* 57 (1959) 31, on 991–1013: 'This eloquent plea would surely be superfluous if the Danaids had an inborn antipathy to men, or if they were devotees of Artemis.' Perhaps, though I should prefer to say that it throws light not on the Danaids as they are, but as first Hypermestra and then her sisters will become – susceptible to the charm of sexual desire.

[38] Danaus *may* have come to wake his daughters and have made a prologue-speech (see n. 25) of sinister irony. To such a speech fr. 124 M might have belonged; equally, or better, it may have come towards the end of the play in connection with the marriage of the Danaids: cf. von Fritz (2) 134f., 267. But both text and interpretation are doubtful.

[39] Pausanias 2.19.6; 21.1.

[40] Σ Eur. *Or.* 872.

the slaying of the forty-nine Egyptians was the triumphant outcome of his plot, the sparing of the fiftieth a treacherous act of disobedience and, since Lynceus was left alive, a threat to his security. But, if Danaus is concerned, so is the *polis* – for reasons which have already been suggested. In some way the Argive state must have given a decision upon the issues involved; something in the nature of a trial must have taken place. Did Danaus refer the case of Hypermestra to the sovereign people? Or did he seek to act under his own powers, and did the people intervene? The question is interesting, but perhaps unanswerable. To an even more interesting question some answer can be suggested. The case must have brought king and state into some kind of relationship. What relationship was that?

I have already referred to the principle that, if any feature in the extant play seems to receive emphasis disproportionate to its dramatic value there, it may well be relevant to the lost plays. In *Supplices* Pelasgus insists upon the sovereignty of the people; the Danaids are obstinate at first in their refusal to entertain the idea.[41] Since it is important that the city as well as the king should be committed to the protection of the suppliants, we cannot say that the theme lacks relevance. In this play, nevertheless, the dramatic action is unaffected by the constitutional position, since king and people take the same line. For this reason it may be thought that the theme is disproportionately stressed. There are, moreover, a number of passages[42] in *Supplices* in which Pelasgus or Danaus expresses apprehension – an apprehension not warranted by the events of this play – about the reactions of the Argive people. (To one of these passages I shall refer in detail below.) I suggest that in these ways the audience is being prepared for a situation later in the trilogy in which a king is repudiated by the people, and that this situation is to be found in *Danaides*.

On stage or off stage, Danaus had to put his case to the Argives. The subject of effective speech receives some prominence in *Supplices*. Pelasgus knew how to speak persuasively to his citizens (615, 623f., cf. 523), and he put the right words into the mouth of Danaus (519). But a time would come, when Danaus had to speak without the guidance of Pelasgus. Speak he will have done, full of confidence in his cleverness and in his eloquence (775).[43] What he was made to throw into his argument we do not know. He may have stressed the fact that Argos was now avenged upon a foreign foe who had humiliated her in battle. He may have gone back over the rival claims of himself and the Egyptians. He will have referred to the duty of

---

[41] Cf. 365ff., 397ff.

[42] 201, 398ff., 484f. (on which see p. 69 below).

[43] With 775 compare fr. 126 M.

obedience owed to a parent.[44] But one advantage which Pelasgus possessed
he lacked. Pelasgus had been able to persuade the Argives by speaking of
the wrath of Zeus Hikesios (616ff.) and of the pollution which threatened
the city. Weighing in the balance against Danaus are the wrath of Zeus
Xenios and a pollution already incurred. For this, if we are right, is the third
and last of three difficult situations with which the state of Argos has had to
deal. The second (in *Aegyptii*) is conjectural, but about the first we are fully
informed in *Supplices*. It involved a dilemma: on the one hand the danger
of an external war, on the other a religious obligation. A king took his
stand upon religion and was supported by the people. In *Danaides*, I submit,
a king is rejected by the people, rejected on religious grounds, rejected by
those of whom the Chorus in *Supplices* had sung (671f.) that they
worshipped Zeus above all in his capacity as Xenios. Pelasgus had spoken
to the people of pollution (619, cf. 473), but his first reference to *miasma* in
the play had a different context. It was not perhaps for nothing – or for
mere antiquarian interest[45] – that Aeschylus made Pelasgus tell the story
of Apis (262ff.), the prophet-healer who had cleansed the land of deadly
snakes, which the earth had sent up in wrath, when she was polluted by
ancient deeds of blood (παλαιῶν αἱμάτων μιάσμασι). The services of Apis
were not forgotten by the men of Argos (270), nor presumably the
occasion of them. This time it was for the Argive state itself to find the
cure. In the words of Pelasgus: 'If in its commonalty a city is defiled, then
let the people take common action to work out the cure' (τὸ κοινὸν δ' εἰ
μιαίνεται πόλις, | ξυνῇ μελέσθω λαὸς ἐκπονεῖν ἄκη, 366f., cf. 268).

It is of course possible that these proceedings took place – that Danaus
spoke and that representatives of the city of Argos reached their
decision – in face of the audience. But the trial in *Eumenides*, in so far as it is
analogous, may be a misleading analogy. There are dramaturgical
difficulties involved;[46] and I am inclined to believe that, as in *Supplices* and
probably in *Aegyptii*, an assembly was held off stage; that Danaus left, full
of confidence, to put his case; and that meanwhile the Chorus sang a song

---

[44] It will be observed that an injunction laid by Danaus on his daughters involved them, if I have read
the situation aright, in a (highly Aeschylean?) clash between two religious duties: they can honour
their father or their guests, but not both. These are two of the three duties to which reference is
made in 698–709 (on which see V. L. Ehrenberg, *Historia* 1 (1950) 522 n. 21 and Kaufmann-Bühler
22).

[45] Murray 81 makes the same point from a rather different angle. I am not concerned to deny that the
name of Apis was also intended to link Argos and Egypt: cf. J. T. Sheppard, *CQ* 5 (1911) 220–9,
Murray 24f.

[46] *Supplices* requires two actors only, and we have no reason to suppose that a third would have been
available in the later plays. But it would not have been easy to stage such a trial with only two
actors.

of suspense – or perhaps there was a *kommos* expressing the contrasted emotions of Hypermestra and her sisters (the former suppliant at an altar?).[47] After the ode someone – whether Danaus or Lynceus or a messenger – will have brought news of the decision. At the nature of that decision we can, I suggest, make a good guess.

That decision or those decisions. My basic hypothesis is that, asked to condemn Hypermestra, the people of Argos instead condemned Danaus and his other daughters. The condemnation of a king might well be prepared by passages to which I have already referred, and particularly by 480ff., where Pelasgus instructs Danaus in certain precautions: 'in order that reproaches be not levelled against me, for the people is given to accuse its rulers'.[48] A remark which is inapposite in the context of *Supplices*. The apprehensions expressed by Danaus in that play (492ff., esp. 499; 985ff.) may seem exaggerated, if not pointless, unless some real danger threatened him in the sequel; and I suspect that he may have been condemned to death, though, for obvious reasons, he can hardly have been executed.[49] We are on firmer ground in speculating about the verdict on the Danaids. These women had suffered cruel persecution, which had won the sympathy of the Argives, and they had acted on the instructions of a father: so far they were deserving of mercy. But creatures so grievously polluted could not safely be allowed to remain within the territory of Argos. Let us cast our minds back to the second sentence of *Supplices*: φεύγομεν οὔτιν' ἐφ' αἵματι δημηλασίαν ψήφῳ πόλεως γνωσθεῖσαι. 'We are in exile, but not condemned to banishment for bloodshed by vote of a city' (5–7). Where they stand, the words have a redundant fullness. But is it not Aeschylean that they should foreshadow the condition in which the Danaids actually find themselves towards the end of the trilogy?

The Danaids are in flight again, with both Egypt and Argos barred to them and perhaps without the protection of their father. What can they do, except sing a song of utter and final despair? There was one thing they could do, and perhaps they did it: take refuge at an altar,[50] suppliants to the gods again, and repeat their threat of suicide. If so – and I do not suggest

---

[47] Miss Cunningham's suggestion.

[48] It is an advantage, if we can dispense with Tucker's non-dramatic interpretation of these lines: 'a subtle reproof administered to "Demos"'. As to the text, there is much to be said for Headlam's punctuation after ἐμοῦ κάτ'.

[49] His death might have entailed the consequence to which he refers at 988. He was spared at the command of Aphrodite?

[50] *Supplices* 482, 494, 501 may suggest that altars within the city itself played a part in the sequel – in *Aegyptii* perhaps as well as in the *Danaides*. All three plays may have involved some movement of the Chorus between orchestra and altar.

that it is more than a possibility – the situation is beyond the scope of human wisdom, and the stage is set for the entrance of Aphrodite. In Euripides she might have arrived without warning. In Aeschylus her entry is more likely to have been prepared; and in the only comparable Aeschylean theophany Athena appears in answer to prayer. Hypermestra may have prayed to Aphrodite (for it is conceivable that she was still in danger from her sisters); or they in their extremity may have prayed to Artemis and been answered by the appearance of Aphrodite; or in a *kommos* both goddesses may have been invoked (cf. *Supplices* 1031ff.).

Whatever the mechanics of her entry, Aphrodite, as representative of the divine wisdom and the divine will, has more than one task to fulfil. She has to restore the Danaids to normality, to reconcile them to the destiny of marriage. About this something has already been said, and we shall return to it in a moment. One pressing matter must have received attention in this closing scene: the purification of the Danaids from their blood-guilt. According to one tradition, they were purified by Hermes and Athena at the command of Zeus;[51] and it certainly seems rather outside the province of Aphrodite, though she might well have announced the will of her father. It must probably remain uncertain how the purification was arranged and how timed in relation to the marriage of the Danaids (if there was such a marriage). But purification there must have been, and it must have been ordained by the offended Zeus.

Zeus must have ended the trilogy, as it began with him – began with Zeus Hikesios and continued with Zeus Xenios. Zeus is also *teleios*, ordaining the end, accomplishing everything 'to which his counselling mind may lead him' ($\tau \hat{\omega} \nu \ \beta o \acute{\nu} \lambda \iota o s \ \phi \acute{\epsilon} \rho \epsilon \iota \ \phi \rho \acute{\eta} \nu$, *Supplices* 599). But his mind is unfathomable: so at least it appeared to the chorus of Handmaidens (1057f.). Yet something of the mind of Zeus may have been revealed as the trilogy drew to its close.

Many issues had been raised: issues of religion and politics and society and individual decision, inextricably interwoven (as they always are in Aeschylus). The central thread is that of men, women and marriage. The Danaids reject the violent suit of their cousins and are pursued by them. It is an affair of the family, but the state becomes involved: the city of Argos protects the suppliants. Who can say that the Danaids were wrong to flee

---

[51] Apollodorus 2.1.4. Hermes would come in well as a link not only between the upper and nether worlds, but between Hellas and Egypt (cf. 220, 920). A silent appearance, as in *Eumenides*? This is of course quite speculative, and one could equally argue that Apollo had a role to play: in the light of 214–16 (for he had himself been banished for bloodshed, yet could be described as $\dot{\alpha} \gamma \nu \acute{o} s$ – was his $\sigma \upsilon \gamma \gamma \nu \acute{\omega} \mu \eta$ to extend beyond the context of *Supplices*?) and of 262ff. (he was the father of Apis).

from brutal lust, or the Argives wrong to be moved by pity for them and by fear of Zeus Hikesios? Yet marriage is the destined lot of women, and the institution of marriage a necessary part of the structure of society. It was not wrong in the eyes of Aeschylus that men should champion the cause of women and shed blood for them (476f.), but it was paradoxical, in a society where men must play the dominant role.[52] It was a paradox which resulted directly from the wrong relation between men and women exemplified by the sons of Aegyptus and the daughters of Danaus. Given this relationship, in which the men pursue the women like birds of prey, nothing can go right. It was not upon this basis that marriage could perform its function in society; and it must have been with a very different picture that Aphrodite turned the hearts of the Danaids. In some way, at the end of the trilogy, Aeschylus must have been concerned to dignify the status of women in marriage[53] in contrast with the ignominious plight of the Danaids in *Supplices*, when the Herald seeks to drag them screaming from the altar.

How, precisely, he dealt with marriage as an institution we cannot say. How he dealt with marriage as a relationship between the individual man and the individual woman emerges from the story of Hypermestra, if it has been rightly interpreted, and for that matter (making due allowance for the satyric) from the story of Amymone. In either case a woman who has rejected sexual desire under the mode of *bia*, of force and violence, comes to accept it under the mode of *peitho*, of persuasion and enchantment. She who would not be forced is successfully wooed. If one thing is more certain than any other in the interpretation of the trilogy, it is this. It is something that the Danaids in *Supplices* could not envisage, though their hand-maidens, not being themselves the objects of a brutal pursuit, were able to do so. The Danaids could not envisage it, for they were prevented by their fears from understanding the moral of the story of Io.[54]

It was a mysterious story, and much is left in mystery. But we know how it began and how it ended. It began with a lustful Zeus and a jealous

---

[52] For this theme, cf. also 643ff., 913, 1068. The right relation of men and women in society was a problem with which Aeschylus was exercised, and not only in this trilogy (see ch. 6 below).

[53] Cf. D. S. Robertson, 'The end of the Supplices trilogy of Aeschylus', *CR* 38 (1924) 51–3, who suggests that the trilogy ended with the inauguration of the Thesmophoria (cf. Herodotus 2.171) as a festival safeguarding the dignity of women in marriage. This suggestion, accepted broadly by Thomson (1) 308, criticized by Vürtheim, op. cit. 74f., is not without attraction. I should myself have expected that, if the cult of Demeter was to play such a part, there would have been some preparation in *Supplices*. It may have been sufficient for the purposes of Aeschylus that marriage was to be under the joint protection of Zeus and Hera: cf. *Eum.* 213f. Fr. 737 M might belong here?

[54] For Io in *P.V.* see ch. 9, pp. 194f. It may be that this theme deserves more prominence than I have given it here: see Murray's interesting study of the Io-theme and its related imagery, together with Garvie's remarks on pp. 70f., 224.

Hera; it began in violence and a bestial transformation, and continued in much suffering for Io. But it ended with an act of gentleness, and Epaphus was engendered 'by the laying on of the hands of Zeus and by the breathing of his spirit'. (ἐξ ἐπαφῆς κἀξ ἐπιπνοίας Διός, 17.) Most significant of all may be an expression which the Danaids use within a few lines of the close of *Supplices* (1067), when they sing in this connection of the *eumenēs bia* of Zeus.[55] Force has become kindly.

So also did the Erinyes, those agents of violence, become Eumenides. It is perhaps a misconception of the thought of Aeschylus to suppose that we must choose, once and for all, between a violent lustful Zeus and the begetter of Epaphus; between the Zeus that works vindictive justice through Erinyes in *Agamemnon* and *Choephori* and the Zeus that speaks persuasively through Athena in the closing scene of *Eumenides*. In each case both aspects are true of the working of Zeus in human affairs through the process of time. In each case the operation of the divine seems at first to be a matter of force alone; in each case there is a revelation that the divine works also as a persuasive agency.[56] That – and nothing more nor less – is the great religious insight of Aeschylus.

---

55 εὐμενεῖ βίαι M, εὐμενῆ βίαν Valckenaer. If the reading is uncertain, the combination of the notions of force and benevolence is not. A similar combination seems also to be found at 576ff., also in connection with the story of Io, but this passage too is unfortunately corrupt.

56 This is certain for *Oresteia* (see ch. 8 below), virtually certain for the Danaid trilogy, and (in my view) highly probable for the Prometheus-plays, though whether because they were written by Aeschylus or by another under the influence of his thought I leave for consideration in ch. 9.

CHAPTER FOUR

Oresteia: introductory

The superlatives which have been lavished on *Oresteia* need neither repetition nor modification. It is an astonishing work of art and structure of thought. The only surviving trilogy, it consists of three plays, each with its own prevailing character, its own situation and action, yet wrought into a single whole. The plays are surprisingly different in technique.

Agamemnon, much the longest of surviving Aeschylean tragedies, is in point of technique the most paradoxical. Its perspective is vast, since it envisages not only the whole history of the house of Atreus but also the whole history of the Trojan War. There is a brilliant variety of songs and scenes and speakers. Yet, on inspection, its economy appears austerely archaic, so that one critic could describe it as 'lyric tragedy raised to its highest pitch'.[1] Aeschylus now had three actors at his disposal: the third he uses only for a silent Cassandra. Not only so, but his use of the second actor is meagre, the play consisting largely of choruses and of scenes played between one actor and the Chorus. This is still true, when more actors than one are on stage together: Clytemnestra does not converse with the Herald; she addresses a silent Cassandra and, when Aegisthus enters, remains silent herself, until the very last lines of the play. Only one scene is fully played between two actors and that briefly (855–974). It is as though Aeschylus had reserved this elementary dramatic resource for the climax of the play, for the duel between wife and husband, to return, in the two great *kommoi* which follow, to the old lyric technique.

Technically, *Choephori* is more 'modern', as its action is more complex. The stage-action of *Agamemnon* could not be simpler: the king returns and is killed. 'The events are few, but their significance is so overwhelming that they require immense emotional preparation.'[2] To show them as the

[1] Lucas (1st ed.) 93ff. [2] Lucas (1st ed.) 95.

73

inevitable product of past events, to accumulate foreboding, right up to the striking of the blow, was well suited to the lyric mode which is employed. The central feature of *Choephori* is another stupendous *kommos*, this time with two actors joining forces with the Chorus. Otherwise the lyric element is far less prominent than in *Agamemnon*. The action includes two features which were to be staples of subsequent tragedy: a 'recognition' and an 'intrigue'. Two actors are fully employed, but the third is reserved for an all-but-silent Pylades. Of the scenes which mirror *Agamemnon*,[3] the duel between son and mother is a briefer counterpart to that between husband and wife; in the scene which follows the corresponding tableau, the Chorus plays little part. It is the unseen Furies that lead into the sequel.

The action may be varied, but the tone throughout is sombre, the interest narrowly concentrated upon the theme of vengeance through matricide – and upon the house. In *Eumenides* the horizons expand once more. We are at Delphi, and then at Athens. Scene follows vivid scene. Powerful as are the visual effects in the earlier plays, this play is spectacular. The Prophetis enters by a *parodos*, goes into the temple – to re-emerge, crawling.[4] Next Orestes is seen, with Apollo beside him (and perhaps Hermes). The ghost of Clytemnestra upbraids sleeping Furies, who then emerge one by one into the orchestra.[5] Apollo returns, threatening them with his bow. We move to Athens. Orestes enters, embraces the *bretas*; the Furies follow and dance round him, singing their Binding Song. Enter Athena. The Areopagus is empanelled. Enter Apollo;[6] and the trial takes place. The tension is visible, as the jurors cast their votes. Here only in the trilogy – in the trial-scene – does the third actor come into his own. Apollo and Orestes depart, and Athena is left alone with the Chorus. Here only in the play does the lyric mode return in a great final *kommos*. The play ends with a spectacular procession, as the Chorus are escorted to their new home; all is light and colour.

In this play every dramatic resource is deployed that was available to Aeschylus. It is almost as though, in the trilogy, he had taken us from primitive Argos to the neighbourhood of classical Athens, as he moved from an archaic to a modern dramaturgy.

Three plays, then, each with its own prevailing character, its own dramatic situation and problem, yet a single work of art. Each play can

---

[3] See ch. 7, p. 133.

[4] Apparently so, cf. Taplin 363. Taplin rightly criticizes some attempts to make the play out to be more spectacular than it obviously is.

[5] On the production here, see ch. 7, n. 50.

[6] See ch. 7, p. 148.

stand on its own, but only to a limited extent. It is not only that the first play and the second both demand sequels; that the crimes of Clytemnestra and Aegisthus must be avenged by an Orestes who already looms, that the close of *Choephori* leads straight to Delphi. The actions are linked, but so is the understanding of those actions. If each play has its own strategy, there is also a strategy of the trilogy as a whole, with themes and symbols carried from end to end. It is only in the light of the closing scene of *Eumenides* that *Agamemnon* can be understood. There is one great unifying theme; there is one great god. The theme is justice; and it runs from the first epithet given to the Atridae (*Agam.* 41) to culminate in an actual trial upon the stage. The trilogy can be seen as a vast dramatic exploration of justice, human and divine. One retributive act follows another, and it is the justice of Zeus as well as the justice of men. Dike is Zeus' daughter. But what is the character and quality of this justice? In the *parodos* of *Agamemnon* the Chorus sings its famous Hymn to Zeus, to whom they look to cast aside the burden of their anxiety; and they try, in difficult terms (which we must examine), to explain why this is so. But the Hymn is preceded by an omen of sinister ambiguity and followed by the sacrifice of Iphigenia which it portended. The placing could not be more challenging. The days are perhaps gone by, when Aeschylus could be likened to an Old Testament prophet delivering the messages of an unproblematic Jehovah. The perplexities of Job might be nearer the mark. For it is more and more realized that, for Aeschylus, Zeus and his justice and the divine world as a whole, their nature and their relationship to human life, were the end and not the beginning of an agonizing search.

Aristotle, who was interested in action rather than interpretation, distinguished the phases of plot as *desis* and *lusis* – complication and dénouement. This distinction is no less applicable to the development of moral and theological themes. What seems at the outset to be a simple vengeance, a simple punishment authorized by a simple Zeus, acquires, as the trilogy develops, aspects of greater and greater complication. *Agamemnon* and *Choephori* are plays of moral and theological *desis*, and the same is true of the first half of *Eumenides*. The *lusis* awaits Athens and Athena and the trilogy's closing scene. It will be our first task to examine some of the complications which develop. It is not an easy task, since it involves isolating issues and themes which, in the drama itself, are worked into a single fabric. The dramatic world of Aeschylus' masterpiece is a monistic world, every part of which relates to every part; and it is only a slight exaggeration to say that every feature of it was always present to the mind of its creator and should, in a greater or lesser degree, be present to us.

We begin with *Agamemnon* — with a hero who gives his name to a play in which he appears so briefly, and only, it would seem, to be murdered by the woman who has held the stage. Yet it is the doings of Agamemnon — not only the sacrifice of his daughter, but that war for the conduct of which the sacrifice was made — which loom over the first half of the play and in the light of which his one stage-action, when he treads the precious draperies to his death, must be understood. What does it mean that the agent of Zeus' just punishment of Troy turns out himself to be an offender to be punished?

Our first task is to consider Agamemnon. The fact remains, however, that, if the wider action beyond the stage is concentrated upon Agamemnon, the stage itself is held almost throughout by Clytemnestra. The agent of punishment is an adulterous wife, but one whose daughter had been cruelly sacrificed. Perhaps to our surprise, however, we find that the woman who confronts us from the outset is neither, primarily, the adulteress nor the mother, but an anomalous creature — a woman with the will and mind of a man, resentful of male domination. So at least it will be argued — and that, through his Clytemnestra, Aeschylus has raised a great social question, which is that of the right relationship between the sexes in society, a question which is carried through from *Agamemnon* into *Choephori*, from *Choephori* into *Eumenides*.

It is carried into *Choephori*, since the avenging son is at the same time restoring male domination, playing the return match in the struggle between the sexes. But at this point fresh complications emerge. And another great social issue comes into prominence, which is the problem of homicide and the scope of blood-vengeance. Blood for blood: and the proper avenger is the next of kin. The drama focuses upon the extreme case, where a parent can only be avenged by the killing of a parent. And this is an act which will be performed upon the direct command of a god. What light does this throw on Orestes — and on the god who commands? These are questions which continue into the final play, when Apollo first receives Orestes into his shrine and purifies him, then pleads his cause at Athens before the Areopagus under the presidency of Athena.

The prosecutors of Orestes are the Erinyes who have pursued him from Argos to Delphi and from Delphi to Athens. They represent the cause of the mother; and, if we look at this play alone, it is easy to see them in that light alone. But they do not suddenly erupt into the trilogy with the murder of Clytemnestra. From *Choephori* we learn that, if Orestes had failed to avenge his father, he would have been pursued by that father's wrathful hounds: that he was threatened with Erinyes either way. If this imports an ambiguity into the relationship between Apollo and the Erinyes, *Agamemnon* had already established an enigmatic relation between the Erinyes and a Zeus who sent the Atridae in an Erinys-role against Paris and his city. It will be suggested that Aeschylus used the Erinyes as a powerful emblem of tragic process and its apparently endless and inevitable horrors. What, then, do we make of the final scene of *Eumenides*? Of all beings we might suppose Erinyes to have the most ineluctable wrath, to be the least responsive to reasonable persuasion. Yet Athena persuades them, the daughter of Zeus persuades them. Is this not where we should find the *lusis* of the moral and theological issue, the necessary complement of the Hymn to Zeus, the coping-stone of a grand structure of dramatic thought and the chief contribution of Aeschylus to Greek thinking about the gods?

CHAPTER FIVE

Agamemnon and the Trojan War

We need not suppose that the ancient tragedians were constantly worrying, in principle, as to which character was central to their plays. Sometimes it was obvious, at other times it was not, in which case the debates of modern scholars tend to be rather arid. Agamemnon gives the name to his play, but Clytemnestra dominates the stage, appearing in scene after scene, whereas Agamemnon has only one scene. Clytemnestra's will to mastery[1] is a thread running throughout the play from the first speech to the last. Yet that will reacts to Agamemnon's male prerogative, and the central scene – his scene – is, though he does not know it, the clash between two rivals. Here at least the roles are twinned. And they are twinned in the central action of the play, which could not be simpler. There are two events: Agamemnon returns and is killed. It is Clytemnestra who acts: does Agamemnon, then, *not* act?

He acts – he takes a decision and acts – twice. Once upon the stage, when he agrees to enter the palace – and we see him enter – treading upon precious fabrics. But this action loses half its meaning, if we forget that, ten years before, at Aulis, in a scene which the poetry of Aeschylus has made hardly less visible, he had sacrificed his daughter. Neither of those actions, however, makes sense without the Trojan War. For there is a third action of Agamemnon's. Does Agamemnon *not* act? Did the man who initiated and conducted the Trojan War not act? We may say, if we like, that the stage action is simple and is primarily Clytemnestra's, but the total dramatic action is vast and includes the whole of that war, which is indeed a principal, if not *the* principal, interest of the earlier part of the play. A *parodos* of unexampled length is filled with its preliminaries; Clytemnestra has her speech about victors and vanquished; the first *stasimon* describes the

[1] See ch. 6 *passim*.

sufferings of the Greeks; the Herald comes back with tales of the war; in the second *stasimon* we hear of the Trojan side. And there is still Cassandra to come.

The Trojan War was a great historical event, the greatest in the mythological history of Greece. It was an event unparalleled until the Persian Wars in which Aeschylus and his audience had fought. Every reason, then, why it should rivet the attention of that audience. More than that, however, it was an affair of justice. It was the *first* affair of justice in this trilogy which constitutes a dramatic exploration of justice at the divine and human levels. The Atridae pursue their grievance against Paris and the Trojans; and they are sent by Zeus. It is the justice of Zeus. They are sent in the role of Erinyes to exact retribution. Everything we are told about the character of this war – and we are told a great deal – reflects upon the justice of Zeus and the operations of Erinyes.

The stage-action, by its nature, concentrates attention upon individuals: a Clytemnestra, an Agamemnon, and (in the sequel) an Orestes. The war has a wide perspective: it affects communities. In Troy the marriage-song becomes a dirge. In Greece there is the *boē* and the armada; and then we hear of the battles and hardships, of the urns and lamentations; but also there is the greeting of the conqueror. Greeks admired success, and Agamemnon returns triumphant.[2]

The focus is upon Agamemnon. The emotions which have accumulated about the war are focused upon the figure of the conqueror, when he enters (with his prize).[3] He is addressed as *ptoliporthos*: 'sacker of a city'. The Chorus retract their misgivings (799ff.). But misgivings they had had, when, for a time, they saw the condition of the conqueror undesirable as that of the captive, preferring for themselves such prosperity as brought no *phthonos* (471ff.). This followed money-changer Ares, the urns, the laments, and those mutterings which were equivalent to a public curse. This at the human level. But it also followed a striking statement about the gods. 'The gods,' sang the Chorus, 'are not regardless of those who have slain many.' They go on to sing of black Erinyes who annihilate those who prosper without justice; they sing of the stroke of Zeus.[4] Only then do they

---

[2] The trilogy which opens with the Trojan War ends with the Areopagus and the Athenian *polis*, and which opens with the Atridae sent in the role of Erinyes against Troy ends with the establishment in Athens of a public cult of the Erinyes. This is the true 'political' significance of the trilogy, on which see the admirable articles of the late Colin Macleod.

[3] And with visible booty? Perhaps, but see Taplin 304f. I cannot help feeling, however, that, when the notions of 'wealth and the wasting of it' are introduced, they would be enhanced by some visible reminder of the fabulous wealth of Troy. The question remains open.

[4] This is true however we read and interpret 469f. These lines echo 367 and are a clear case of

decry the status of the city-sacker, but so apprehensive have they become for Agamemnon that they change their tack. Perhaps after all the news is *not* true. Yet how can what they have sung apply to an Agamemnon who had been sent by Zeus like an Erinys to execute justice upon Troy and has returned successful from his mission?

One fact is clear. As a necessary means to the sack of Troy, Agamemnon had sacrificed his daughter Iphigenia and so provided Clytemnestra with a motive for killing him. At the level of human motivation, it is clear why Agamemnon will suffer. (And this is equally true, if we take into consideration her resentment of male superiority.) But why should his killing be a matter of that divine justice which the Chorus, rightly or wrongly, seems to fear? With what justification does he suffer?

One answer is given later in the play, when Clytemnestra claims to embody an *alastor* taking vengeance for the cruel feaster Atreus (1500ff.), what she had called 'the thrice-fattened *daimon* of this race' (1476f.). That the house had been haunted since the Thyestean banquet by victims seeking vengeance was made manifest through the visions of Cassandra: they are avenged by the death of Atreus' son. The natural avenger is Aegisthus, son of Thyestes and brother of the murdered children; and, when he enters, he speaks of justice and avenging gods (1577ff.). But by his part in the action, such as it was, he had won co-rule in Argos, an adulterer like his father whose own adultery was dynastically motivated (1585). So human motives are interlocked with the divine justice. Clytemnestra plays the greater part and makes the more contentious claim; and it is contested by the Chorus (1505ff.). They say she cannot disavow responsibility, that the *daimon* was only a collaborator; and it was in fact no part of her motivation to avenge the Thyestean banquet. Her motives were quite other and related to actions which Agamemnon had himself performed. If he pays for the offence of his father, he brings about his death by behaving in ways which prove disastrous to himself. Why? Where do we seek the reasons for his decisions? In his situation? In intelligible human motivation? Or elsewhere? There is one way to short-circuit speculation, if we say that, in order that earlier offences not his own should be punished in him, it was necessary that he should so act as to provoke his own killing; that he was compelled to act

---

ring-composition. One would prefer, therefore, that the passive βάλλεται should be of the thing struck rather than the thing hurled, in which case the emendation κάρανα (Tucker, Headlam) is inviting (cf. *Cho.* 396). ὅσσοις must at all costs be preserved, not simply because it is 'vivid' (Rose), but because of 947, where it is the jealous eye (ὀμμάτων . . . φθόνος) of heaven which may strike. Least of all should we read οἴκοις (Weil, Page), where the impersonal word is intrusive between the personal statements which precede and follow.

wrongly, or dangerously, by a superhuman force. This amounts to saying that some original offence was (presumably) deliberate and humanly motivated, whereas the events which flow from it are supernaturally determined, including the mental processes of subsequent actors. Which is not quite plausible. One might ask, further, there being two parties to these acts of divine justice, why the punishing agents (themselves incurring guilt) should be allowed their motives in human terms and the surrogate offender should not – or at least why his human motivation should be reduced to a subordinate role. Before adopting such a view, one should look carefully at those passages which involve decisions – and look at them in the context of the Trojan War. The theme of inherited guilt has its place, but it is worth noting that, apart from ambiguous hints,[5] it is excluded from the play until another train of causation has been fully developed, Iphigenia sacrificed, the war described, Agamemnon and Clytemnestra seen in confrontation, and Agamemnon has entered the palace to meet his death, his active role in the play terminated – until, that is to say, light has been thrown upon the character of his actions and the mind of the man.

Agamemnon's appearance upon the stage is brief (783–974), but it is elaborately prepared, notably in the 'Entrance Song' of the Chorus, in the course of which a scene is described. It is a song of unexampled length; it is a scene which, though not shown upon the stage, can rank as a scene in the play. Agamemnon is the leading figure, and he speaks. His words are given in *oratio recta*: it is his first speech in the play and should be evaluated as such. We have Agamemnon at Aulis on his way to Troy; we have Agamemnon at Argos on his triumphant return. How are the scenes related? In Aeschylus, should we not expect to find a close relation between them? In each scene Agamemnon takes a decision. At Aulis he decides to sacrifice Iphigenia, at Argos to enter the palace treading on scarlet draperies. What, if any, is the connection between the two decisions? We must take Aulis first and examine the poetry, which is deeply moving and closely wrought.

Aulis[6]

Confronted with a dilemma, Agamemnon sets it out. 'Which of these courses is without ills?' he asks. He chooses one course rather than the other.

[5] Cf. Peradotto 246; Lebeck 34f.; Edwards 23 and his n. 28. One is tempted to say that, in the close-wrought fabric of *Oresteia*, no relevant notion can be presumed absent at any point, nor are the ambiguities of Aeschylus ever to be disregarded. But the theme does not become *overt* till much later in the play.

[6] The discussion which immediately follows repeats in large measure what I have said in *BICS* 21 (1974) 3ff. Cf. Peradotto, esp. 249ff.

Why? The alternatives are set out in the first half of the stanza (205ff.), carefully balanced with *epanaphora* (βαρεῖα μέν . . . βαρεῖα δέ) and leading to the words already quoted. It might seem that up to this point the scales are even. But is this true of the balance of the poetry? The first alternative is given in a single noun-phrase: 'not to comply' (τὸ μὴ πιθέσθαι), the second in twelve words: εἰ τέκνον δαΐξω δόμων ἄγαλμα, μιαίνων παρθενοσφάγοισιν ῥείθροις πατρῴους χέρας, πέλας βωμοῦ. Untranslatable of course. 'If I kill [by cutting] my child, the delight of my house, defiling a father's hands with streams [of blood] from the cut throat of a virgin hard by the altar.' 'Harsh terms,' says Page, 'deliberately chosen.' This seems almost an understatement, so vivid and so revolting is the description, so discordant the clash between words of sacrifice and words of family relationship. It is revolting to us; to Greeks, accustomed to the sight of a sacrificial victim held above the altar, of the blood streaming down when its throat was cut, it must have been more revolting still.[7] Do we, then, react to the poetry by saying: 'Yes, a difficult choice indeed', or by asking ourselves what Agamemnon can possibly put in the balance to weigh against his own all too eloquent words?

A simple answer is that he puts words of war: ships and allies (to which we shall return). If the answer is too simple in itself, the fact remains that the horrifying effect of the scene which is about to be described derives largely from a contrast between the defenceless frightened child and the heroes who slaughter her. The arbiters who disregard her prayers, her cries of 'father' and her youth, are 'lovers of battle' (φιλόμαχοι, 230). The actual sacrifice should no doubt be envisaged as not unlike the well-known vase-painting which shows Neoptolemus cutting the throat of Polyxena in the presence of Nestor, Diomede and other heroes.[8] War prevails over the child – the war which so dominates the earlier phases of the play. Why does Agamemnon decide for war? And how did Aeschylus intend us to regard his decision? The second question at least is easily answered.

It was a mad decision and a primal source of woe. At the beginning of the next stanza (218ff.) the Chorus sings: ἐπεὶ δ' ἀνάγκας ἔδυ λέπαδνον . . . τόθεν τὸ παντότολμον φρονεῖν μετέγνω, which Fraenkel translates: 'And when he had slipped his neck through the strap of compulsion's yoke . . . from that moment he reversed his mind and turned

---

[7] I once read a description of the beheading of Lady Jane Grey, at which the onlookers were astounded that so much blood should flow from so small a body.

[8] Reproduced by Vickers, Pl. 1; J. D. Beazley, *Attic Black-figure vase-painters* (Oxford 1956) p. 97, no. 27.

to utter recklessness.'⁹ The temporal clause refers to the moment of decision and is picked up by τόθεν, the point of time being thus strongly marked.¹⁰ It is by his decision that he takes on the yoke-strap of necessity and loses his freedom. From that point onward his mind learns a new daring without limits; in effect, having chosen to sacrifice his daughter, the man who wept at 204 acquires the reckless cruelty needed to play his part in the scene which follows, when 'he brought himself to become the sacrificer of his daughter' (ἔτλα δ' οὖν θυτὴρ γενέσθαι θυγατρός, 224f.). This hardness in mortals, this *tolma* and *thrasos* (for so the Chorus sees it), springs from a madness or distraction (*parakopa*) which is qualified as 'base-coun-selling' (αἰσχρόμητις) and 'the beginning of woe' (πρωτοπήμων). The madness did not set in after the decision but showed itself in the decision: it was the decision and not the sacrifice which was the beginning of woe. The design which the madness counsels is *aischron*. A natural choice of words? As natural, perhaps, as to call the change of wind in Agamemnon's heart 'impious, impure, unholy' (219f.), because the act on which he is now bent disregards one of the most sacred of ties? And yet it is a striking word. One of the alternatives open to Agamemnon was the abandonment of his expedition, which would have meant forgoing vengeance, incurring the shame of desertion, losing the glory of conquest – some or all of these things, to all of which, by heroic standards, the adjective 'shameful' would be appropriate: it is applied to the alternative of child-sacrifice. We are now in the heart of the difficulties of the passage.

The study of Aeschylus is dogged by uncertainties of reading and interpretation, not least in crucial passages. 'How,' asks Agamemnon (212f.), 'am I to become [prove, show myself] *liponaus*, having failed [*or* failed of] my alliance?' The last expression (ξυμμαχίας ἁμαρτών) is most naturally taken to mean that he will have lost his alliance, his allies, and it is clear from the preceding narrative that, if the wind does not change, there

---

⁹ On the intervening words (φρενὸς πνέων δυσσεβῆ τροπαίαν ἄναγνον ἀνίερον), see p. 96 below.

¹⁰ Edwards, in his closely reasoned article, maintains that 218–24 do not continue, but repeat, the account of Agamemnon's thoughts and actions; that what he took upon himself was 'not the necessity of choosing one particular option, but *the necessity of making a choice between the two terrible alternatives*'. Later, in his n. 43, he speaks of a decision 'to accept the responsibility of making a choice'. But this decision to decide is exposed as a chimera, if we say that a sensible man (not infatuated or predestined to infatuation) would not have chosen either alternative! Edwards can hardly mean this. It is in the nature of a dilemma that a choice *must* be made (which was as true of Pelasgus as it is true of Agamemnon). Now such a situation could be described as *ananke* and Agamemnon as yoked to it, but it is not a yoke that he was free to take on or not to take on. Aeschylus has deliberately used an active verb, has linked the action (with a present participle) to a 'change of wind' and then stressed the point of time with a τόθεν. It is the point of time at which Agamemnon makes his decision, choosing war as against the child.

will soon be no fleet to sail.[11] Should we, then, take λιπόναυς to mean 'abandoned by my ships'? It can, however, be argued with great force that, in a context of war and on the analogy of λιποστρατία and similar words, λιπόναυς here connotes desertion.[12] Writers have laid great stress upon the heinousness of this crime and the horror with which it would strike a fifth-century audience; and, without putting undue emphasis upon the role of the allies, we may believe that heroic warriors bent on war might well have despised those who drew back.[13] The matter is important, if Agamemnon, in making his decision, makes it as a social being sensitive to the reactions of his fellows. To this issue we must recur.

If this dubiety were not enough, there is worse to follow, involving text as well as interpretation. Agamemnon goes on: 'For it is right and proper passionately to desire a sacrifice to stay the wind and a maiden's blood.'[14] But who is right to desire it? If the subject of the infinitive is unexpressed, it must surely include Agamemnon himself, and we must make what we can of it. But there is a difficulty. The main MS tradition has the words ὀργᾷ περιόργως, and scholars are not agreed whether this is tolerable Aeschylean Greek. If, as I incline to think,[15] it is not, then we must have

---

[11] This is brought out in the preceding stanza. The winds are unsparing of ships and tackle, so that the fleet will not much longer be seaworthy. The interpretation of βροτῶν ἄλαι (194) is debated: see most recently E. K. Borthwick, *JHS* 96 (1976) 1–7.

[12] Dover, *Dioniso* 48 (1977) 68f. gives other examples. Add that λιπο-compounds are generally active at this date. There are, however, one or two examples of a passive sense: Pindar fr. 94a 16 Sn³ (λιπότεκνος); Crates comicus fr. 22 (λιποπωγωνία).

[13] To withdraw the allies as a motivating factor would simplify the interpretation of the passage, but it would almost certainly be wrong to do so (see p. 97 below). We need not, however, go so far as Page. He insists on the role of 'the confederate chiefs' who will act, if Agamemnon does not, so that his refusal would not even save Iphigenia's life. We must not be misled by Euripides' *IA*, in which Agamemnon and Menelaus in succession consider abandoning the campaign, but dare not in view of the strong feeling of their allies, and in which Iphigenia accepts martyrdom in a crusade against the barbarians. In our play, however, it is not a crusade but a quarrel, in which the allied chieftains are present as supporters of the Atridae, their *stratiotis aroge*; and we have no reason to suppose that, if the aggrieved parties think the price of vengeance too high, their friends will prosecute the quarrel without them. (It is not infrequently the case that a Euripidean situation is virtual evidence that the situation envisaged by his predecessors was different.)

[14]
            παυσανέμου γὰρ
    θυσίας παρθενίου θ' αἵματος ὀργᾷ
    περιόργως ἐπιθυμεῖν
    θέμις . εὖ γὰρ εἴη.

[15] With Page as against Fraenkel (whose parallels are hardly cogent). The problem is complicated by a variant αὐδᾷ (for ὀργᾷ) which is found in the margin of M and in the text of Tr. If corrupt, no explanation can be given for the corruption; if correct, the subject must be (as M glosses) ὁ μάντις. It is defended by R. D. Dawe, *Eranos* 64 (1966) 16–18, who interprets as follows: 'Calchas says that it is right angrily to desire the blood of Iphigenia.' That the verb should look back to 201 is not inconceivable, but the prophet's job was to tell the Atridae what to do, not to dictate their emotions to them! θέμις (sc. ἐστί) is surely the main statement, used as δίκη ἐστί is often used, but perhaps

recourse to the simplest of emendations, adding one letter and reading (with Bamberger) περιόργῳ σφ'. To whom in that case does the pronoun refer? To the allies (implied in ξυμμαχίας)? That is the common – and tenably correct – view, in which case Agamemnon is showing himself under social pressure. But there is another candidate whose claims are not to be casually dismissed. The name of the goddess Artemis resounds at the end of the preceding stanza (202), and she who has created the situation is bound to be in Agamemnon's mind. The main argument in her favour I reserve for a footnote[16] and will merely state a growing conviction that the pressure he alleges in his closing sentence is one from the divine world.

Agamemnon had received from the goddess a contingent command, presenting him with alternatives between which he was free to choose: if he wishes to sail, he must sacrifice his daughter; if he refuses, the adverse wind will persist and the expedition will dissolve. What, however, if he had received an unqualified command from a greater god to sail against Troy? At 60ff., after the vultures and the Erinys sent to avenge them, the Coryphaeus intones: 'Thus does Zeus the master, the Zeus of Hospitality, send the sons of Atreus against Alexander.' Which has led some critics to assume that the Atridae had received a specific command from Zeus to go against Troy. This is a misconception which has done much harm. It is odd, in that case, that in the moment of decision, Agamemnon does not play this strongest of cards; it is odd that we hear nothing of this command. When was it given, and through whom? There is one spokesman of the divine

with an added religious overtone (cf. n. 16). How did the corruption arise? We cannot say, but in the transmission of texts, virtually anything can happen, though some things are more likely than others!

[16] The Triclinian gloss which gives Artemis as the subject of ἐπιθυμεῖν has generally been brushed aside and, on the basis of the received text (no subject being expressed), it is indeed incredible. With σφε, however, the case is not to be dismissed and is powerfully argued by M. Ewans, *Ramus* 4.1 (1975) 27f. As I see it, the language used is crucial. ἐπιθυμεῖν is itself strong: as Fraenkel says, 'that a virgin's blood should become the object of anyone's ἐπιθυμία is most unnatural'. Add the emphatic doubling of ὀργᾷ περιόργως) and we have an expression of fantastic strength. To whom is it appropriate? Everything turns now on the meaning of ὀργή. It can (from Hesiod onwards) have the weak sense of 'temperament' or 'mood', but that will obviously not do here. It can be used of a particular strong emotion, generally 'anger', but this was not the emotion felt by Agamemnon or by the allies in connection with the sacrifice. Unwelcome though it be in a play – and trilogy – so full of wrath human and (especially) divine, we must have recourse to the much rarer use of ὀργή of other emotions (cf. Soph. *OT* 1241). The whole expression, then, if we take it of Agamemnon or the allies, amounts to a powerful statement that they lusted passionately after the blood of Iphigenia. As for Agamemnon, is it conceivable that, so soon after 207ff., he could be made to describe his emotion in such terms? As for the allies, with their lesser commitment, φιλόμαχοι as they may be, is this not grossly inflated language? From these difficulties Artemis saves us. 'Anger' can be restored, divine anger: we know that she was angry (cf. the language of 131ff.), and we know that Greek gods were angry and ruthless when they were offended in their province. Even θέμις falls into place in a matter of divine right. 'For stopping the wind she has every right in her exceeding wrath to set her heart on the blood of a virgin shed in sacrifice.' For the role of Artemis see further on p. 99.

world, who is Calchas. He interprets the omen at 122ff.; at 198ff. 'the prophet', who is doubtless Calchas again, reveals the terms of Artemis. Are the commands of a greater god passed over in silence? It is essential to observe that the reference to a 'sending' by Zeus does not come until it has been firmly established (40ff.) that Agamemnon and Menelaus are pursuing a human quarrel (recalled at 62); and that it is led up to by the simile of the vultures. And how are the vultures avenged? By a special divine interposition? Did Aeschylus or his audience believe this? The vultures go after the robbers and avenge themselves, with the backing of divine powers.[17] So too the Atridae: they cry 'Havoc' and go after the offender. Zeus sends them, but no more than the angry vultures do they receive a command.

No, but they receive a message, which comes, as divine messages often do, in the form of an omen, sending them on their way. πέμπει (61) is picked up and explained by πέμπει (111), and then — and not till then — do we understand why the Coryphaeus said that the Atridae were sent, or sent on their way, by Zeus. They were sent by the bird of Zeus (112, 135). They were sent 'with avenging spear and hand' (ξὺν δορὶ καὶ χερὶ πράκτορι), vengeance their motive and retribution the divinely-approved consequence of their mission. There is a message, and it is interpreted by Calchas; and his resounding words include along with great benefits — for Troy will indeed be sacked — 'ill-fated things' (μόρσιμα). In the justice of Zeus evil is blended with good. 'Let the good prevail,' sings the Chorus; 'May it turn out well!', says Agamemnon (217). But it will be long before good prevails in the trilogy.

It was not for the sake of dispelling a misconception that I have dwelt so long on Zeus and his ominous dispatch of the Atridae. Omen and sacrifice go together, the one foreshadowing the other, both accepted by Agamemnon in prosecution of the war which is the context of his dramatic existence. It is a context of many dimensions; and events are seen from a multiplicity of angles. Not least is this true of the Rape of Helen, which was the proximate cause of the war, and to which we can distinguish three reactions (if not four).[18] To the Atridae it is an injury to be redressed; to Zeus it is a breach of hospitality to be punished. But the Coryphaeus' statement that the sons of Atreus were sent by Zeus Xenios is followed by a striking phrase: it was 'in the matter of an adulterous woman' (πολυάνορος

---

[17] I may be too positive about this: contrast Macleod (1) 133.

[18] The fourth reaction, which does not directly concern us here, is that of the Trojans who, out of pride of wealth, celebrated their prince's unlawful acquisition with a wedding-song, thus sharing in his guilt. See App. D (on the second *stasimon*).

ἀμφὶ γυναικός, 62). And this is itself followed by reference to the sufferings endured by Greeks and Trojans alike. There is no overt comment, though a tone of resentment may be felt, but later, when the Chorus sings of the Greek dead, the laments and the mutterings, we hear of the man who fell nobly in the slaughter 'because of another's wife' (ἀλλοτρίας διαὶ γυναικός, 447). On the entry of Agamemnon the Coryphaeus is frank (799ff.): when he set out to war for Helen, they had questioned his wisdom and 'drawn an ugly picture' of him in their minds, but success had changed all that and they greet the conqueror with sincere loyalty and affection. Naturally, one thinks of the sophisticated discussion in the early chapters of Herodotus I, the cynical view of the Egyptian. But there is no sophistication here. The resentment of the common people at this war for a woman is as natural as their change of attitude when the war has been won. It is as unheroic as the reaction of the Atridae – and their fellow-nobles – is heroic. For what greater insult could there be to a prince than the theft of his wife? Therefore the Atridae must march and their friends must rally round them as the *aroge*.[19] It is the Atridae's war.

But Aeschylus has handled the relationship of the Atridae with some care and subtlety.[20] They are introduced into the play as a pair, closely linked (40ff.), but in the course of the *parodos* they are separated, notably in the omen of the eagles. There are two kings, ruling jointly; corresponding to them are two birds. But, in a sentence of deliberate artificiality, Agamemnon's bird is singled out (θούριος ὄρνις . . . οἰωνῶν βασιλεύς, 113f.), his brother's bird trailing behind at the end of the sentence, disparaged in terms of militancy.[21] In the prophet's interpretation, however we take the text, a distinction between the two brothers is marked with great insistence (122ff.). That Agamemnon should henceforward take the lead, make the decision, perform the sacrifice, is natural, since he is Iphigenia's father. It is indeed a dramaturgical necessity; and we should make too much of a distinction between the Atridae, if it were not for the next passage in which we hear of Menelaus (410ff.). Helen has departed, and we listen to the 'spokesmen' of the house. The sensitive reaction of Menelaus which is now described is so congenial to modern feeling that we may not observe how astonishing it is in the context of a heroic world. In a corrupt sentence, σιγὰς ἀτίμους ('dishonourable silences') is fairly certain and either ἀλοιδόρους or ἀλοιδόρως ('without reviling'). Contrast the

---

[19] See n. 52 below.
[20] Discussed more fully at *BICS* 21 (1974) 8f.
[21] Cf. Fraenkel II p. 70 (on 115); Page p. 80 (on 122ff., *ad fin.*).

opening of the *parodos*, where the Atridae, injured in their Zeus-given τιμή
(43f.), raise the cry of war (48) and gather their friends about them to
avenge the injury. Now we see Menelaus sitting in a silence that aggravates
his loss of honour, without any expression of heroic resentment. He sees
Helen in a waking dream; and in his sleep she comes to him only to slip
insubstantial from his grasp.[22] It is a wonderful evocation of the power of
Helen's beauty, but it is also the final withdrawal of Menelaus as a factor, as
an impulse, in the play. Of course he took part in mustering the expedition,
went to Troy and played his Iliadic role, but so far as the *poetry* of this play
goes he remains in a waking and a sleeping dream. It is Agamemnon's war;
and he will enter, alone, as conqueror, as the great 'sacker of a city' (783ff.).
How is this victorious Agamemnon presented? From Aulis we move to
Argos.

Argos

The speeches and dialogue of this scene are as closely wrought as anything
in Aeschylus. First, let us consider the speech which Agamemnon makes
in response to the greeting of the Chorus. (It is most unlikely that
Clytemnestra, to whom he does not refer, is present on the stage.[23] The
duel of wills between wife and husband has not yet begun, the theme of
male domination has not been raised, though it has been amply prepared.)
The speech falls into two sections, the first (810–28) addressed to and about
the gods, the second (829–50) addressed to the Chorus and political in tone;
it is rounded off (851–4) by a return to the gods and the theme of victory. It
is at 830 that he turns to the Chorus with a disquisition on loyalty and a
recognition that in his success he is liable to *phthonos*, to envy (832f.). A
recognition, perhaps, of danger, though not from Clytemnestra, and he
might be thinking of Aegisthus. All may not be well in the community:
cautery or knife may be needed and will be used, in consultation with a
general assembly. All is quite conventional, but has sinister overtones for
those who know the situation.

The conqueror's address to the gods is more significant – and more
debatable. What is its tone? Fraenkel's 'great gentleman' can perhaps be
dismissed as the amiable eccentricity of a distinguished scholar. Do we
accept in its place the 'vanity and arrogance' which Page imputes to
Agamemnon? First, let us observe one obvious point of irony. The last

[22] On various points of detail, see *BICS* 21 (1974) 16f., nn. 35–9.
[23] See Taplin 306.

speech made upon the stage had been the Herald's (636–80), thanks to which we know that, if Agamemnon has returned, his fleet is lost or scattered. Hence the irony of 853, with its reference to gods 'who, having sent out, brought back' (no object expressed).[24] Odysseus? Agamemnon does not know whether he is alive or dead, but those who knew their *Odyssey* were aware how long his return was delayed. Menelaus? But his survival (as we learnt from the Herald) is no less conjectural. But 853 picks up a reference to the home-coming in Agamemnon's very first sentence (ring-composition), in which he attributes to the gods responsibility for two things, closely linked with a particle ($\tau\epsilon$): his return and his just vengeance (811ff.). To what have they brought him back? If he has been the instrument of the gods' justice upon Troy, he returns to fall victim himself to their justice, the instrument of which is Clytemnestra who now speaks. She speaks of Justice leading him to a home such as he had not thought to see ($\dot{\epsilon}s\ \delta\hat{\omega}\mu$' $\dot{a}\dot{\epsilon}\lambda\pi\tau o\nu$, 911). This is matter of fact, whatever it may imply about the nature of a divine justice which operates through human resentments and retaliations. But what light, if any, is thrown by this section of Agamemnon's speech upon his state of mind?

It used to be said that it was a sign of arrogance in Agamemnon when, in his first words, he attributes only part responsibility to the gods and (with the stressed personal pronoun) seems to place himself on an equality with them.[25] The point is dubious; we shall need — and shall perhaps find — better evidence of vanity than that. This evidence comes later, during the conflict with Clytemnestra. A victorious king may be allowed some pomp? The question is whether anything he says goes beyond convention — and so far beyond the requirements of the themes which are being deployed as to reveal a significant mental state; and judgement is here subjective. Naturally, the quasi-legal aspect of this punitive war is brought to the fore, the exaction of a penalty sanctioned by the gods. There is great stress on slaughter: the divine vote was for the deaths of men and cast in a bloody urn (814f.). All references to the sack must of course recall not only Clytemnestra's 320ff. but the Herald's 551ff. (with all its talk of Greek sufferings). Naturally, Agamemnon says nothing of the Greek dead. The only blood specified is in fact the blood of princes (828), licked by the ravening lion that overleapt the wall. A lion of the Pelopid house? I have

---

[24] For the return voyage, cf. 338ff., esp. 343f. In the Herald's last speech, if the metaphor at 659 ($\dot{a}\nu\theta o\hat{\upsilon}\nu$) seems to recall 197 ($\check{a}\nu\theta os$), this may simply indicate that Aeschylus, when he wrote about the return voyage, had that passage about the outward voyage at the back of his mind; it was not, perhaps, very likely to be spotted by an audience.

[25] Page has a good note *ad loc.*

suggested elsewhere[26] that Agamemnon may have come to see the war as a contest between dynasts. If so, he will be vulnerable to the temptations of Clytemnestra, to which from these possibly idle speculations we must now turn.

'Now descend from your chariot, but do not set your foot upon the ground – the foot that has sacked Ilium' (905ff.)[27]; and she bids her servants lay a path of scarlet draperies, over which Agamemnon will, with misgivings, enter the palace, led by the goddess Justice (911) to meet an unsuspected doom. Why does he, despite all the objections he raises, comply with his wife's request?

Few critics are content with a purely metaphysical answer. Fraenkel found reasons[28] – and they were bad ones – in the state of Agamemnon's mind, but they were not necessarily bad for that. Page too found a reason – which may be a better one – in his mental state: 'he is at the mercy of his own vanity and arrogance'. Lebeck, who believes that he was under compulsion, writes:[29] 'He acquiesces because he cannot do otherwise and, at the same time, because he wishes to.' 'Necessity and choice,' she says, 'interact in his yielding . . . The choice which he makes in the "carpet" scene is the direct result of a prior choice at Aulis.' But this last statement is perhaps a little out of focus.

What *was* necessitated by his choice at Aulis was his death at the hands of Clytemnestra. No doubt among the reasons for which she wished him to enter the palace in this invidious way (though not the only reason) was that he might incur the hostility of heaven (*phthonos*). But treading the draperies was not necessary to his death: he was not killed for that. If he had maintained his refusal – for that matter, if Aeschylus had never introduced this motif at all – he would still have met the bath and the sword. Indeed, remembering that we are dealing with a fiction, the question we should ask is this: What did Aeschylus gain by introducing this episode?[30] He gained a contest between husband and wife, man and woman, in which she wins a spiritual victory. But this, though vital to a major theme of the trilogy, is not our present concern. He gained – and Lebeck sees this well – a symbol of sacrilege, resumptive of all relevant acts of similar impiety. But why

[26] Cf. *BICS* 21 (1974) 15 n. 10.

[27]

$$\nu\hat{\upsilon}\nu\ \delta\acute{\epsilon}\ \mu o\iota,\ \phi\acute{\iota}\lambda o\nu\ \kappa\acute{a}\rho a,$$
$$\check{\epsilon}\kappa\beta a\iota\nu'\ \dot{a}\pi\acute{\eta}\nu\eta\varsigma\ \tau\hat{\eta}\sigma\delta\epsilon,\ \mu\grave{\eta}\ \chi a\mu a\grave{\iota}\ \tau\iota\theta\epsilon\grave{\iota}\varsigma$$
$$\tau\grave{o}\nu\ \sigma\grave{o}\nu\ \pi\acute{o}\delta',\ \hat{\omega}\nu a\xi,\ '\mathrm{I}\lambda\acute{\iota}o\upsilon\ \pi o\rho\theta\acute{\eta}\tau o\rho a.$$

[28] Fraenkel II pp. 441f.

[29] Lebeck 76f.

[30] For a good discussion see Taplin 308–16.

should a man be sacrilegious?[31] Why did Agamemnon slaughter Iphigenia at the altar? Why did he tread the draperies? Why did he want to tread the draperies? Between the answers to these questions, is there anything in common? Before we attempt to answer this last question, we must return to the scene between husband and wife. Agamemnon was tempted and fell. Why did he fall so easily? The temptation was put by Clytemnestra to the 'sacker of a city'. In the response of Agamemnon there are three phases.

First comes his speech of indignant rejection (914–30). It opens with a rebuke, expressed not so much with humour as with a kind of wit.[32] A long speech after a long absence! She is not in any case the right person to praise him. For that matter, she is inciting him to effeminacy and behaving towards him as though he were a barbarian. By strewing his path with draperies she is making it invidious (epiphthonos). Such valuable fabrics are an honour due to the gods; he knows that he is a mortal and therefore cannot tread them without fear. Honour him as a man, not as a god. Foot-mats are one thing, ornamental fabrics are another; they sound different (in the ears of men).[33] Good sense is the greatest gift of the gods. Call no man happy (olbios) until he has died prosperous. One proverbial truth follows another. Agamemnon knows all the reasons why he should not do as Clytemnestra says. And yet he does it. Why?

The answer may emerge as Clytemnestra turns from rhetoric to argument (931ff.). Agamemnon knows three things: (i) that the act is presumptuous and sacrilegious, an infringement of divine prerogative and so likely to attract the hostility of the gods; (ii) that there are modes of behaviour characteristic of barbarians, improper for a Greek; (iii) that phthonos is to be expected from men as well as gods. They are all true: it is for Clytemnestra to make them appear tolerable or inviting.

(i) 933f. are at first sight difficult.[34] 'Would you have vowed to the gods in fear that you would so act [or make this sacrifice]?' A strange question to ask! Yet the sense is vouched for at 963–5, when Clytemnestra says that she

---

[31] Why did Paris trample on the sacrosanct (371) and his fellow-countrymen condone – nay welcome – his actions? To this Aeschylus devotes part of the first, but most of the second, stasimon: it is not unconnected with the wealth and pride of Troy. See App. D.

[32] Contrast Méautis 180. See also A. N. Michelini, Hermes 102 (1974) 524–39.

[33] Despite Page's objections, I follow the Blass/Fraenkel interpretation of 926f. At 930 below Weil's εἶπον τάδ᾽ is palmary; and since what will give Agamemnon confidence is a course not of action but inaction, there is much to be said for Weyrauch's οὐ for ὡς (adopted by Mazon, with a reference to Suppl. 398).

[34] Here I am indebted to K. J. Dover's lucid examination of the passage in 'I tessuti rossi dell'Agamemnone', Dioniso 48 (1977) 55–69. For a totally different interpretation of the dialogue, wholly favourable to Agamemnon, see V. Di Benedetto (ibid. 179ff. and L'ideologia del potere e la tragedia greca: ricerche su Eschilo, Turin 1978, 148ff.), who believes that Agamemnon, brooding over the sacrifice of Iphigenia, has learnt wisdom by suffering.

'would have vowed much trampling of robes' to bring Agamemnon back, *if* an oracle had so commanded; and Agamemnon here replies: 'Yes, if an expert had prescribed this task [*or* rite]'. The notions which clarify the exchange are two: (a) damage by trampling (which is what so worries Agamemnon at 948), and (b) the idea that one might propitiate the gods by sacrificing some especially valuable possession (as when, in Herodotus' story, Polycrates tried to jettison his ring).[35] What Clytemnestra has done is to invest the action with a spurious air of religious propriety – spurious because the circumstances are totally different and there is no real analogy. What Aeschylus has done is to remind us that Agamemnon had already sacrificed a treasure (δόμων ἄγαλμα, 208) and done it on the unquestioned authority of a religious expert (186). To this we shall return.[36]

(ii) 'What,' asks Clytemnestra, 'do you think Priam would have done?' To which Agamemnon simply replies: 'I think he would certainly have walked upon embroideries.' That, and no more! Yet might one not have expected the speaker of 919 indignantly to reject what was for a Greek no legitimate analogy? That he secretly desired the pomp of a Priam is 'reading between the lines' – a subjective judgement and not demonstrable. If it is right, however, note that, whereas Clytemnestra's first question was directed towards the conventional Greek, her second is directed towards the *ptoliporthos* and peer of the great dynast he has conquered.

(iii) *Phthonos* was the prime difficulty, since Agamemnon has already shown himself sensitive on this score, aware that such an action might provoke hostility in gods and men (921, 926f.). Clytemnestra deals with it by an essay in semantics. Greek has two words descriptive of an attitude towards the success of others, the semantic fields of which overlapped.[37] There is *phthonos*, which is hostile and dangerous; there is *zelos*, which can connote envy, but often means little more than admiration (or emulation). Clytemnestra tells her husband that he cannot have the admiration which is his due and his desire without incurring *phthonos* from the envious. 'The man who is not envied (*aphthonetos*) is not admired (*epizelos*)' (939). Which is partly but not wholly true. From the successful man himself we have had already a disquisition (832ff.) on the psychology of *phthonos*, the natural human tendency to grudge success in others. It is true, but it is no less true that this tendency can be – and need not be – activated by gratuitous acts

[35] 3.40–3.
[36] See p. 95 below.
[37] Cf. P. Walcot, *Envy and the Greeks* (Warminster 1978) 2f.

of arrogant display. Still, the words of Clytemnestra have presented
phthonos in a more acceptable light.

A final appeal to masculine vanity – a danger of which Agamemnon
was unaware, an appeal which turns the scale – and he gives way, but not
without misgivings. At least he will take off his shoes[38] before treading
these 'purples' of the gods (946) and pray that no jealous eye may strike him
from afar. He is ashamed to waste the substance of his house, trampling
underfoot its wealth and fabrics bought with silver. Does this come oddly
from the conqueror of wealthy Troy who had gloated over the aromatic
ashes of Priam's wealth (820)? Is there a fascination here as well as a scruple,
leading to a pomp of language only surpassed in Clytemnestra's scornful
rejection of those scruples (958ff.)? Clearly, there are two Agamemnons
here. There is Agamemnon the conventional Greek who would be
aphthonetos, and Agamemnon the conqueror, the 'sacker of a city', who
would be *epizelos*. With the aid of the temptress, the conqueror wins the
day.

Let us now return to Aulis. Agamemnon makes two decisions, and they are
closely linked. They are linked by the whole structure of the play up to this
point: the war begins, the war ends; there is the outward journey, bought at
the price of Iphigenia, and the return journey which brings Agamemnon
back to his death; and, in between, the nature and quality of the war are
vividly portrayed.[39] Both his decisions are conditioned by war, and it is the
same war. Both confront us with a question. Why did he do it? How could
he bring himself to do it? Why did a man so well seized of conventional
propriety, aware of the probable reactions of gods and men, perform an
action which was *epiphthonon* – a sacrilegious action? One sacrilegious
action he had performed in gruesome fact: he had cut the throat of his own

---

[38] For this precautionary action there are two possible motives: to mitigate the damage and, by an
act of humility, to mitigate the sacrilege. In the latter case the precaution is futile (like other
similar formal acts in Aeschylus, cf. p. 140 below), but it is what Agamemnon seems to have in
mind, when he goes on to pray that no jealous eye may strike him from afar. In the following
sentence, however, there is great stress upon the value of the endangered objects
(δωματοφθορεῖν/πλοῦτον/ἀργυρωνήτους). What, then, is the force of γάρ in 948? And in relation
to whom does Agamemnon feel *aidos*? Fraenkel writes: 'Such waste of valuable property would be
regarded by the gods as wicked arrogance.' John Jones, *On Aristotle and Greek tragedy* (London 1962)
85ff., who otherwise puts great – too much? – emphasis upon the economic aspect (the destruction
of '*oikos*-substance'), speaks of 'the religious "shame" (*aidōs*) of the wealth-wasting'. But the last
time we met this notion (of *aidos*) was at 937: 'pay no regard to the blame of men', which was
followed by ἀφθόνητος (939). Surely, φθόνος at 948 is a hinge-word between the two kinds of
disapproval which Agamemnon fears. Fraenkel's note on 948 deserves careful reading. As he says,
truly, 'the reader's understanding of the whole play depends in great measure upon what he decides
here', but the views he quotes to criticize may be nearer the mark than his own.

[39] Cf. n. 24 above.

daughter at the altar. Here is our second question. How did it come about that this man of conventional virtue and normal affection 'brought himself to be the sacrificer of his daughter' (225), reaching a state of mind which struck the Chorus as 'impious, impure, unholy'? The answers to both questions are bound up with that war which dominates the first half of the play. For Agamemnon exists, acts and suffers, in the context of war. But how, precisely, did that context affect his decision at Aulis? We must now return to the text of the earlier passage, taking into consideration a phrase so far disregarded.

Following the omen, following the Hymn to Zeus, it is sung of Agamemnon that he blamed (or abused) no prophet (μάντιν οὔτινα ψέγων, 186). This is in fact the first statement of a reaction on his part. To what? Who is the *mantis*? Calchas of course, the *stratomantis* of 122, the interpreter of the omen, but it was the same Calchas who conveyed the ultimatum of Artemis. At 186 the audience has not yet heard, explicitly, of the sacrifice and may think first of the omen, but gradually it becomes clear, as the long anacoluthic sentence unfolds – temporal clause after temporal clause setting the scene – as we wait (as Aeschylus wished us to do) for the main statement, which does not come until 205ff., that the present participles of 186f. are contemporaneous with the dilemma and decision of Agamemnon.[40] And it was indeed the stark horror of the sacrifice which might have evoked a reaction against the prophet from the general who was also the father.

Line 186 has, on the whole, received less attention than it deserves, though Fraenkel has a good, if brief, note. Pointing out that οὔτινα generalizes the statement,[41] citing *Iliad* 1.106 and 12.230ff., he remarks that 'Agamemnon does not behave as others in corresponding circumstances usually behave towards the seer concerned.' M. L. West, who is interested in echoes of the Cycle, carries the matter a little further.[42] Is not Aulis the background to Agamemnon's outburst in *Iliad* 1? May it not be that, in the *Cypria*, he had greeted the prophet's ultimatum with a similar response?

---

[40] 184ff. First we have a subject, with twin present participles in agreement with it; then a temporal clause opening with εὖτε, which appears to break off (192ff.) without a main statement, only to be followed by another temporal clause opening with ἐπεί (198), still without a main statement. The sentence appears to have lost its way, until, at 205, we find ourselves back with the subject of 184. It is tempting with Stanley and Headlam to change τόδ' in 205 to τότ'.

[41] Fraenkel's categorical statement that 'the weakened use of *nullus*=*non* has no analogy in Greek' is challenged by S. L. Radt, *Mnem.* ser. IV 26 (1973) 116. Not all his references are equally cogent, and the fact remains that, if existent, this use is singularly rare. The generalizing force could perhaps be expressed by saying that Agamemnon did not give way to 'prophet-abuse'.

[42] *CQ* 29 (1979) 5.

Indeed, since heroes did not like seers to inhibit their activities with sinister prophecies, this might be regarded as a normal heroic reaction;[43] and it seems fair to ask why Aeschylus prefaced the Aulis-story not only with a statement, at 187, that Agamemnon bowed before the storm (though that, as we shall see, is not, strictly, what is said) but also with a hero's reaction which was perhaps recognizably untypical.

Of the answers which could be given some can be ruled out. For Fraenkel, Agamemnon is more moderate, more restrained, than his epic forerunners and so more admirable, but his view that the hero acts at Aulis with full understanding of the lesson of the Hymn to Zeus conflicts not only with the following line but with the whole tenor of the subsequent narrative.[44] No more can one believe in a pious man with a sense of mission who, so far from blaming the gods, will not even revile their authorized interpreter — a view which depends solely on the old illusion that Agamemnon felt himself to be carrying out the will of Zeus, having perhaps received the god's direct command.[45] Two better answers can be given. First, that it was in the nature of Agamemnon to accept the conventional authority of a prophet. Speak of the 'nature' of Agamemnon, and we seem to be back in the old slough of psychological interpretation (about which there will be more to say). Perhaps, however, we should recall his answer (at 934) to the subtle temptress in the matter of the fabrics: yes, he would have done it, if some expert had prescribed the rite. The second answer would be that what was offered ran with his desires. Does this appear far-fetched? It is fetched from no farther than the following line.

Three words have been omitted from our study (and for that matter three words in 219): a metaphor has been omitted, which is a serious matter in Aeschylus. Agamemnon is said to revile no prophet, bowing before the storm (ἐμπαίοις τύχαισι συμπνέων, 187). But this is wrongly put, though the metaphor is indeed that of storm-winds. Fraenkel translates as follows: 'letting his spirit go with the blasts of fortune that fell upon him'; and this comes close, but not close enough, to the Greek. *Sumpnein* is a striking verb, not found elsewhere before Plato. Those who, in Plato or Demos-

---

[43] An adverse reaction to unwelcome prophecies was not confined to the nobility, to judge by the words of the Chorus at 1132ff.

[44] Fraenkel II p. 119. It is interesting to note that two strong advocates of Agamemnon hold – both wrongly, in my view – that his attitudes were in conformity with that lesson, but for Fraenkel it was at Aulis, for Di Benedetto on his return to Argos (see n. 34 above). For Fraenkel's view it can be argued that it gives a clear logical connection of thought at 184, but I suspect that, like everything else about this enigmatic Hymn, it is left to be clarified as the trilogy unfolds.

[45] See p. 85 above.

thenes,[46] are said *sumpnein* or *sumphusan* (συμφυσᾶν) are active partners,
collaborators: to put it crudely, then, Agamemnon is not simply blown
upon, but joins in the blowing. It is the wind of his emotion which is said, at
the very moment of decision, to back (φρενὸς πνέων ... τροπαίαν, 219)
and blow 'impious, impure, unholy'.[47] That was the crucial blast, when his
emotions, in the end, lent their own force to the blasts of fortune, the man
collaborating with the gods to his own undoing; and the question we
should still be asking is what, precisely, those emotions were.[48]

This may sound deplorably psychological. 'Psychology' in this connection has become, with some justification, a dirty word; and readers may
have noted that I have so far avoided the word 'character' – a word which
invites a misconception which, in my view, renders beside the point much
that has been written about characterization in Aeschylus.[49] Speak of
'character', and it is thought to be implied that Aeschylus was writing – and we are interpreting – out of that kind of interest which a modern
writer might have in the 'psychology' of a Napoleon or a Hitler or some
fictitious dynast. It need imply nothing of the kind. There is a basic
principle of which one must keep firm hold, which is that 'character' enters
into Aeschylean tragedy in so far as there is an action to be performed that
needs such-and-such a person, acting from such-and-such motives, to
perform it. 'Character' is derivative from motive; and motive is bound up
with social values. It is not an individual as such, but an individual in
society, that is characterized. Clytemnestra kills her husband, a crime
which could have been committed by more than one kind of woman:
Aeschylus chose to present a woman of masterful will, resentful of male
domination, not because it interested him to explore her anomalous
psychology for its own sake, but because through such a woman he could
focus attention on a great – and potentially dramatic – social issue, which
was the relationship of the sexes in society.[50] Agamemnon kills his

---

[46] Plato, *Laws* 708d; Dem. 18.168. On our passage, cf. LSJ s.v. συμπνέω: '*going along with* the sudden
blasts of fortune, *yielding* or *bowing* to them' – a good example of the lexicographer telling us, not
what the word means, but what it *ought* to mean!

[47] Page is wrong not to relate the two passages and to limit the reference of 186f. to the hold-up at
Aulis (in which Agamemnon did *not*, finally, acquiesce). Those winds do indeed suggest the
metaphor. Fraenkel (on 187) puts it well: 'The thought goes back to the opposing winds which are
the bearers of the first, and causes of the later, ἔμπαιοι τύχαι.' This note and that on 219 (on mental
'winds') are particularly valuable.

[48] One might indeed suggest that, as at 933ff. Clytemnestra's two questions are addressed to
Agamemnon in two roles (see p. 92), so here the two lines 186 and 187 (with their parallel
participles) offer two contrasted but closely related explanations of Agamemnon's compliance.

[49] A subject well handled by P. E. Easterling, *G&R* 20 (1973) 3–19.

[50] See ch. 6 *passim*.

daughter, at the prospect of which action he and his brother struck the ground with their staves and wept. Yet he performed it, suffering a change of mind, of emotion, to which attention is specifically directed, but not because Aeschylus was primarily interested to present a particular individual in a particular poignant situation. I repeat that Agamemnon exists, acts and suffers, in a context of war. War is a social phenomenon; and the society was that of the heroic age.

The scheme of moral values which prevailed in the heroic age – and still survived into the classical period with strength enough to evoke a response in the audiences of tragedy – has been described as a 'shame-culture' and as a 'results-culture'.[51] It was a shame-culture in its preoccupation with status and prestige, which must be preserved at all costs and, if it has been infringed, restored at all costs. The Atridae have been grossly insulted in their *timē* by the rape of Helen, and therefore they must retaliate, therefore they must make war, which is the only form of redress available (and, despite the legal language, *talio* the only 'justice'). This is what Agamemnon desires and what his friends, his allies, his *aroge*, expect of him.[52] He desires it, ultimately, to the point of sacrificing Iphigenia. Scholars may continue to debate the meaning of *xummachias hamarton* and *liponaus*.[53] Does Agamemnon fear to lose his fleet or fear the censure of his peers? It is an interesting question, but one should not forget that the stigma of humiliation and the stigma of cowardice are equally characteristic of a shame-culture: to forgo his vengeance and to desert his fleet would be parts of the same disgrace. Is there more to it than that?

It was a 'results-culture', laying the main emphasis upon success and the acclaim which this wins from the social body. Wars must be won, at

---

[51] I have argued elsewhere (Winnington-Ingram 311f.) that the tragic character which serious drama took on, when it developed in Athens, derived largely from the nature of Greek morals and the consequences which the poets saw to follow therefrom – and that in two particular respects: (i) the over-valuation of success, leading to *hubris* and the exemplary fall of the hubristic man; (ii) the emotional demand for retaliation, for doing harm to your enemy as he would do or has done to you (a principle which meets us again and again in Greek literature of the classical period), leading to recurrent – and theoretically interminable – violence.

[52] On 47 Fraenkel rightly says that in ἀρωγά 'we have both the military conception and the idea of a lawsuit; the expedition is at the same time a demand for legal redress'. (Note the return of legal language at 810ff.) It may not be accidental that the word recurs, in the same grammatical construction, at 226. The righting of Menelaus' wrong needed the gathering of a host of warriors; it needed the sacrifice of a young girl by her father.

[53] Ambiguity is the last refuge of the indecisive critic. Ambiguity, however, is never far away in Aeschylus, and I toy with the idea that he has deliberately used language here which admits of different interpretations: allies who may disperse or blame Agamemnon for failing them; a fleet incapable of sailing or deserted by its admiral. At 155 τεκνόποινος suggests vengeance by a child as well as vengeance for a child. True, the language of 212f. is not oracular, but it *is* obscure, and I do not think it is merely the lapse of millennia which makes it so for us.

whatever cost; and glory attends the victor. (We have noted how the misgivings of the Chorus disappeared when Agamemnon returned victorious.) Is it too much to say that, when the die is cast, war takes over and generates its own values, including the ambitions and vanities of commanders? At Aulis, Aeschylus has given no clear indication that Agamemnon was motivated by a lust for military glory, but it was as the great 'sacker of a city' that he returned to Argos. And here the social factor takes on another aspect. The higher the value placed upon success, the more temptation to pursue it beyond bounds, to exploit it with an abuse of power. Which is *hubris*. All too familiar with this phenomenon, the Greeks developed, as a counterpoise, that ideal of salutary restraint to which they gave the name of *sophrosune*; and society became not only the fount of honour but also the critic of excess. And that is why Agamemnon fears the disapproval of his fellows for an act of arrogant display, anxious to be at the same time *epizelos* and *aphthonetos*. Does this sound schizophrenic? It is not a schizophrenic individual that Aeschylus depicts, but a schizophrenic society – a society which demands the restoration of honour by an act of retaliation and would despise the weakling, which applauds success but disapproves the arrogance which success engenders, fears it as it fears the jealousy of heaven towards human greatness.

If we have, for a time, lost sight of the divine world, it cannot for long be kept out of account. When, threatened by the abuse of power, they invented *sophrosune*, the Greeks invoked, as always, the aid of gods to support their own morality. The gods either grudge success to mortals (*phthonos*) or punish those who have won it unjustly. Which? The matter is explored in the play. Let us return to the first *stasimon*. From the grief of Menelaus the Chorus turns to the lamentations of every house in Greece, which is most understandable, since all wars lead to lamentations. But the singers do not stop there. They forebode something still cloaked in darkness (459f.), some intervention of gods who 'are not regardless of those who have slain many'. Even there they do not stop, but go on to sing of black Erinyes that annihilate the man who wins success without justice; and they associate his fate with the heavy burden of excessive praise (468ff.) and with the thunderbolt of Zeus. Justice in one breath, the danger of excessive prosperity in the next. They commend the middle state, rejecting the ambition to be *ptoliporthos*. That their fears are for Agamemnon is evident, and they begin to hope that the news may not be true after all.

There might seem to be some confusion of thought. The notion of excessive prosperity and praise exciting the hostility of divine powers is traditional, as is also the notion of the dead seeking vengeance through Erinyes. But there is a reference to success without justice. We wait for the second *stasimon*, in which, notoriously, the notions of divine jealousy and divine justice are distinguished. The theme is Troy and the Trojans, Paris and Helen, the marriage-song which becomes a dirge, by the work of Zeus Xenios and an Erinys (748f.). Yet it was not the fabulous wealth of Troy which in itself entailed its destruction, but an act of *hubris* breeding after its kind (750ff.), an old *hubris* breeding a new one, when the time is ripe (763ff.). In Troy wealth and prosperity had led to *hubris*, and the justice of its punishment is evident. But – and this has hardly been denied – the whole passage, while arising directly out of the tale of a wealthy and hubristic Troy, is relevant also to the coming doom of Agamemnon, whose entry it prepares. The last stanza tells of *Dike*, who has no respect for the power of wealth mispraised: enter an Agamemnon who has despoiled wealthy Troy. He enters with the claim to have executed justice upon that city. Where, then, was *his* injustice? Where was *his* hubris? What was the *dussebes ergon* that bred others after its kind (758ff.)? What was it that caused him to be reckoned among the 'evil of mortals' (765)? Whence came the defilement of hands (776)?

If a simple answer is sought, Iphigenia is that answer; and we remember the language in which the Chorus described the state of mind of the sacrificer (219f.). But it is Iphigenia in a context; and the context is that of war. Iphigenia and the war are inextricable: without her sacrifice it cannot be; without the war her sacrifice need not be; without the sacrifice of lives wars cannot be. Artemis asked for the sacrifice of Iphigenia, but it should be observed that the lavish bloodshed of the Trojan War would have taken place (and the gods have taken note of it), even if there had been no intervention on the part of Artemis, no sacrifice of Iphigenia. Artemis intervened. Why?[54] Because of the cruelty involved in the omen, the slaughter of the hare and her unborn young by the birds of Zeus. But an omen is nothing apart from that of which it is ominous, which is, in this case, the slaughter of the innocent in war. Artemis and Zeus are at odds? Yes, in a sense. Yet the Zeus-sent omen was itself frank enough. There was a price to pay. For what? For justice, for revenge, for whatever else might be sought. Omen, sacrifice, war-and-sack, are links in a chain, which is a chain of deaths.

There is a price to be paid for justice. The whole sequence illuminates the tragic outcome of a divinely-appointed system of justice when it operates,

[54] Cf. Peradotto 240ff.

not by plague or thunderbolt, but through the violent pursuit of human resentments. Hence the mystery of the Hymn to Zeus, which is not resolved until we come to the closing scene of *Eumenides*.[55] There is a price to be paid for a revenge which not only gratifies a human instinct but obeys a social code. There is a price to be paid for success, for the praise and glory which attend the leader in a martial enterprise, when war takes control and conquest becomes an end in itself. The price – for justice, for revenge, for conquest – Agamemnon was prepared to pay, even if it was the sacrifice of his own daughter.[56] We last see him alive marching to his death over blood-red fabrics, the great conqueror worsted by a woman, still fearing censure from the society whose praise he covets. We shall see him dead, wrapped in a blood-stained robe.

[55] See p. 169 below.
[56] 'He is nearly committed to this war which will destroy countless innocent lives; very well: if he must do this, let him first destroy an innocent of his own – and take the consequences' (Kitto (2) 4f.).

CHAPTER SIX

Clytemnestra and the vote of Athena[1]

It will not be disputed that the relationship between the sexes was a subject of great interest to Aeschylus. His *Supplices* turns on the question of marriage, willing or unwilling; and this is true, whether the Danaids were actuated by a passionate celibacy or by a horror of what they considered. incest. The loss of the succeeding plays renders the interpretation of the Danaid trilogy speculative.[2] But in *Oresteia*, Aeschylus returns to similar themes: marriage, wife and husband, the relative status of men and women. This last issue becomes explicit during the trial of Orestes, when Apollo proclaims the superiority of the male and Athena endorses his judgement with her vote. This scene, if variously interpreted, has been recognized to be important. Equally it has been recognized that Clytemnestra, for whose murder Orestes was on trial, is herself depicted as an anomaly: a woman with the mind and counsel of a man.[3] The connection between these two aspects of the trilogy deserves perhaps a further examination.

It is first necessary to consider the characterization of Clytemnestra. Quite apart from the issues raised in *Eumenides*, it is doubtful whether the accepted 'masculinity' of Clytemnestra has received attention commensurate with the stress which the poet has laid upon it, nor has it been fully considered in relation to the motives of her conduct. Some, indeed, will deprecate the psychological approach to an Aeschylean character.[4] But

---

[1] This chapter remains substantially as in *JHS* 88 (1949) 130–47. A few passages have been rewritten and the notes revised.

[2] See ch. 3 above; and, for a suggestion that a similar theme may have appeared in the Theban trilogy, ch. 2. pp. 45f.

[3] γυναικὸς ἀνδρόβουλον κέαρ (11): see n. 10 below. Stanford 92f., argues successfully that in ἀνδρόβουλος the second half of the compound is based upon βουλεύομαι and signifies 'deliberation, planning', the rational process of decision proper to man. The notion of will or determination in the pursuit of a clearly envisaged end is, however, not far away.

[4] See ch. 5 pp. 96f.

there are no a priori grounds on which we can decide up to what point the poet's interest in character developed, as develop it admittedly did. Clytemnestra is the test-case, and we must judge by what we find. The more austere, however, is the view taken of Aeschylean characterization, the more is it incumbent on the critic to give proper weight to this characteristic of Clytemnestra (largely irrelevant to the traditional story) in considering the general themes of the trilogy.

In any play – certainly in a Greek play – the first references to a character are likely to be revealing. The Watchman in his opening soliloquy does not at first refer to Clytemnestra directly: he speaks (11) of 'a woman's heart of manly counsel' which has set him at his post.[5] He is a servant in fear, and after this paradoxical phrase we know whom he fears. He is a servant in sorrow for his master's house, and hints at the adultery of his mistress (18f.). When the beacon shines out, he calls to Clytemnestra, but we do not yet hear her name. It is Agamemnon's wife (26) whom he bids leap from her bed (which should be Agamemnon's bed) and raise the ὀλολυγμός, the woman's cry of joy. But Agamemnon's wife has another consort; the woman has the mind of a man.[6]

Clytemnestra is not addressed by name till 84, during the anapaests of the Chorus, when she makes a silent appearance to supervise the sacrifices.[7] She is addressed as daughter of Tyndareus, which immediately associates her with her sister Helen, the γυνὴ πολυάνωρ; and as Helen was the bane first of Menelaus and then of Paris, so will Clytemnestra be of Agamemnon and later of Aegisthus.[8] Disdaining to reply to the Chorus, she enters the palace, not to reappear for 150 lines. The song of the Chorus is meantime concerned with the sacrifice of Iphigenia, and we wonder what effect that sacrifice has had upon this woman of manly counsel. Iphigenia, Aegisthus (hinted at only), the masculinity of Agamemnon's wife: the elements of the situation are now before us. It remains to see how they are combined.

The Chorus round off their ode with words intended for the ear of the approaching queen, when they call her 'sole bulwark of the Apian land'. The Chorus-leader speaks to her: 'I have come to pay homage, Clytemnestra, to your rule (258).' The word is κράτος and (with κρατεῖν)

---

5 See also n. 10. On the technique by which Clytemnestra's name is at first withheld, see Thomson (2) on *P.V.* 5.

6 Since γυνή means both 'woman' and 'wife,' ἀνήρ both 'man' and 'husband,' the sexual antithesis may be stressed even where the words are used in the latter meanings.

7 This is controversial, cf. Taplin 280–85. If one thing is certain, it is that, if Clytemnestra comes on at this point, she goes off again, to reappear about 255. On which passage, also controversial, cf. Taplin 285–88.

8 The relationship of Helen and Clytemnestra as women will be further developed (see p. 111).

is commonly used in the trilogy to denote authority, domestic or political. Indeed, to revert to the Watchman's speech, it is, in fact, from the verb κρατεῖ (10) that the audience derives its first impression of the queen.[9] 'I watch', said the Watchman, 'for so rules a woman's hoping heart of manly counsel'.[10] κράτος, κρατεῖν will be met again at salient points in the trilogy. Now Clytemnestra stands before us as a ruler, as sole ruler, but only in the absence of her husband. 'It is right,' says the Chorus-leader, 'to honour the wife of a reigning prince, when the male throne is left empty' (259f.).

The closing words of the Chorus-leader, the opening words of the queen, have intricate associations. For instance, when the queen speaks of the night as of a mother that has given birth to the day (265, 279), it is to remind us of her own motherhood, of Iphigenia, and of the theme of heredity which runs through the trilogy. The reference back to γυναικὸς ἀνδρόβουλον ἐλπίζον κέαρ is equally unmistakable. The Chorus-leader suggests (262) that Clytemnestra's messengers of good may be merely hopes. This suggestion she rejects (266), and announces the capture of Troy. What then *is* the evidence (272)?[11] A god. Is it a dream then (274)? Is it a rumour (276)? 'You make light indeed of my understanding, as though I were a young girl (παιδὸς νέας ὥς).' Clytemnestra does not forget these accusations which impute to her the psychology, not only of a child, but of a woman, given to irrational hopes and, where her emotions are involved, easily convinced.[12] When, in two brilliant speeches, her imagination has ranged over land and sea and over the scenes of siege and capture,[13] 'Here,' she says, 'you have my woman's words (348).' No wonder the Chorus-leader makes amends: 'Lady, you speak sensibly, like a wise man' (γύναι, κατ' ἄνδρα σώφρον' εὐφρόνως λέγεις, 351). It is a compliment which she has virtually demanded. On this note the scene ends, as it began.[14]

The Chorus sing their first *stasimon*. What begins as 'an exultant hymn

[9] κρατεῖ is a natural word for a house-slave to use, but obtains a broader significance as the play develops (see Daube 39ff.); it is closely associated with νικᾶν, etc. (see n. 35 below).

[10] Headlam's preference for Anon.'s ἐλπίζειν was ill-founded: it weakens κρατεῖ (a key-word), unduly stresses the notion of ἐλπίς and thus throws ἀνδρόβουλον out of gear. Since ἐλπίς is by convention a characteristic of women, the succession κρατεῖ, γυναικός, ἀνδρόβουλον, ἐλπίζον duplicates the paradox (male–female–male–female). Stanford and others argue that Clytemnestra is in very truth characterized by feminine ἐλπίς, in combination with masculine deliberation. The evidence for this is slight. She is indeed a victim of the tragic ἐλπίς (Headlam in *Cambridge Praelections*, Cambridge 1906, 115), but in the same way as any male sinner. See also n. 16 below.

[11] As punctuated by Prien, Page; contrast Fraenkel. Cf. App. E, n. 49.

[12] Cf. εὐπιθῆ (274), following ἀπιστίας (268), πιστόν (272).

[13] See also n. 49 below.

[14] Cf. also 352 (πιστά σου τεκμήρια) with 272.

for triumph over Troy' ends in 'apprehension for the conqueror'.[15] It is almost with relief that they remember the news may not be true and return to their former allegations.[16] Good tidings have been brought by fire (475). But are they true? To trust such a message is childish (cf. 277), witless (contr. 351). To believe too readily is just like a woman (483, 485, 487).[17] Better evidence, however, than the beacons is now at hand in Agamemnon's herald. Him they cannot disbelieve, and Clytemnestra (590ff.) refers contemptuously to such accusations as they had made:[18] ἦ κάρτα πρὸς γυναικὸς αἴρεσθαι κέαρ. 'How like a woman, to be carried away!' Clytemnestra herself has no need of a herald, except to carry a message to her husband; and in this message are reiterated the words – man, woman, husband, wife.[19] With irony and with a brazenness that deceives none of her listeners, she maintains the role of the conventional wife, the home-keeper, the watch-dog.[20] When she speaks of the faithful wife who has never tampered with any seal, we think of Aegisthus. She is as innocent of joys from another man as . . . of the tempering of bronze: and we are reminded that this is no ordinary woman, subject to feminine weakness.[21]

From this message we may pass rapidly to her greeting of Agamemnon.[22] The Chorus try to warn him on his entrance (808f.), but he does not understand. His mind is on war and politics (matters outside a woman's sphere), concerning which he will 'take counsel'.[23] He turns to enter his palace with the prayer that Victory, which has attended him, may remain still constant. On the word νίκη Clytemnestra enters.[24] The speech she

---

[15] Headlam, op. cit. 110. See also ch. 5 pp. 79f.

[16] Thus it is the male Chorus, not Clytemnestra, whose beliefs and disbeliefs are conditioned by their hopes and fears. This characteristic of the Chorus is put to brilliant use at 1346ff. in order to ease the difficulties of the dramatic situation: note especially 1366f., which gives them their excuse for not entering the palace. Cf. App. E.

[17] πρὸ τοῦ φανέντος χάριν ξυναινέσαι (484) precisely describes the mental process of the Chorus at 352ff. (repeated at 583 under the influence of the Herald's speech). αἰχμᾷ (483) is obscure; but, if ἄτολμον αἰχμάν at Cho. 630 is an oxymoron (Thomson (3)), then the word ('spirit, mettle') can be applied to Clytemnestra more appropriately than the Chorus realize. See n. 69. Fraenkel ad loc. prefers 'authority, rule', which may be right. Stinton 259 n. 30 is somewhat non-committal.

[18] Note πεισθεῖσα (591). She speaks as though she had heard 475ff. This may be something more than a dramatic convention: it conveys the impression that nothing can be hidden from her (cf. n. 20, n. 28).

[19] 600, 602, 603, 604, 606ff., 612.

[20] ἐράσμιον πόλει (605) is spoken as though she had heard 540, 544.

[21] On the double meaning of χαλκοῦ βαφάς see Thomson (3) (his 616–17) and the cautious remarks of Fraenkel II p. 305.

[22] The intervening stasimon bears on Clytemnestra through the theme of Helen, though their relationship is not yet fully brought out. On her entry, cf. Taplin 300 n. 4 and 'Silences', HSCP 76 (1972) 92f.

[23] βουλευσόμεθα (846), βουλευτέον (847): the male function which Clytemnestra has usurped (11).

[24] On the dramatic effect at this point see the excellent remarks of Taplin 306–8.

now makes, her longest in the play, is of outstanding importance. In it all the elements of her character and situation are combined.

To Iphigenia she does not refer openly, but when she speaks of a child who should have been present (877ff.), Iphigenia, as well as Orestes, is in her mind.[25] The references to Aegisthus are clear and extensive, as Headlam has shown.[26] But when Clytemnestra speaks of 'the fearful hardship for a woman without man to sit solitary at home' (861f.), issues are raised which transcend adultery and go back to the man-woman of the Prologue. To the sister of Helen physical celibacy may not have been congenial: but this is unimportant. That Clytemnestra had been, literally, ἄρσενος δίχα is an ironical lie; but that is not all. Where this woman had sat solitary during her husband's absence was upon his throne, as the Chorus pointed out on her first speaking entrance;[27] and this to her was no ἔκπαγλον κακόν. Now the royal man returns, and the glories of his state are described by Clytemnestra herself with fulsome rhetoric (896ff.). The whole passage, which at the beginning speaks the modest, loving wife and ends with a clear cross-reference to the ἀνδρόβουλον κέαρ,[28] is dominated, like Clytemnestra's address to the Herald, by the theme of the relationship between man and woman.

The thesis of this chapter – and it is supported by the continual emphasis which the dramatist places upon the sexual polarity and upon the anomalous personality of Clytemnestra – is that she hated Agamemnon, not simply because he had killed her child, not because she loved Aegisthus, but out of a jealousy that was not jealousy of Chryseis or Cassandra, but of Agamemnon himself and his status as a man. For she herself is of manly temper, and the dominance of a man is abhorrent to her. Thus, when she kills her husband, it is not only an act of vengeance, but also a blow struck for her personal liberty.[29] The same motive explains her choice of

---

[25] See Thomson (3) on 877 (his 868). κύριος (fem.) is found at Aesch. Suppl. 732. Note that this is Clytemnestra's first direct address to her husband. Not only may 886 refer to the trick which was played on her at the time of Iphigenia's death, but the πῆμα of 865 includes this first and worst news from the Trojan expedition; the tears of 887 which are now dry were tears for Iphigenia (cf. 1525), who is foremost among τὰ πρὶν κακά of 904.

[26] See Thomson (3) on 889–94 (his 880–5).

[27] 258–60 (see p. 102).

[28] φροντίς (912): cf. 1377. In fact, τὰ δ᾽ ἄλλα φροντίς κτλ. answers τὰ δ᾽ ἄλλα . . . βουλευσόμεσθα (844ff.) – again, as though Clytemnestra had actually heard the words. οὐχ ὕπνῳ νικωμένη may recall 854 (νίκη), as it looks forward to 941f.

[29] Cornford (Thucydides Mythistoricus, London 1907, p. 160) speaks of 'the proud and masterful princess, at the death-grip now with the principle of Agamemnon's lordship', and presents the issue in terms of a historical transition from matriarchy to patriarchy. Snell (Philologus, Supplb. 20.1 (Leipzig 1928) 122f.): 'Die Ermordung des Agamemnon ist also eine Befreiungstat der Klytaimestra.' But subsequent writers have not done justice to this aspect of the subject.

Aegisthus. Agamemnon, for all his weakness at Aulis and in the scene which follows, was a lion of the Pelopid house, a great warrior and conqueror. Aegisthus is seen in the vision of Cassandra as a lion indeed (a Pelopid), but a cowardly lion, and later as a wolf mating with this human lioness in the absence of the noble lion (1224, 1259). He is οἰκουρός (1626), 'keeping the home' while the Greeks were at Troy. This was the woman's part. Aegisthus is addressed as 'woman' by the Chorus at the end of the play (1625),[30] and Orestes in *Choephori* implies the same charge (304). This woman-man was chosen by the man-woman to be her mate. The return of her husband is a threat. Yet so great is she that she does not fear his return, but rather longs passionately for it, because it will give her the opportunity of avenging herself and of demonstrating her superiority. It is in the light of this situation that the next scene must be considered – the scene in which Clytemnestra induces Agamemnon to enter the palace treading on scarlet draperies.

Why is she at such pains that he should make his entrance so? Is it merely that the act is *epiphthonon* and that by putting him in the wrong before the gods she will facilitate her triumph? Why, for that matter, does an Agamemnon so sensitive to the danger of *phthonos* give way so easily? Because he is a doomed sinner blinded by *ate*? This vital confrontation raises problems of dramatic function and religious import which have already been discussed in the preceding chapter,[31] with special reference to the mental processes of Agamemnon; and what has been said there need not be repeated here. What must be stressed, however, is that this scene cannot be justly appreciated, unless we realize that it is a confrontation between two persons whose attitudes and decisions are intelligibly motivated upon the human level.

It is suggested above that, in the last analysis, Clytemnestra killed her husband because he was a man and in order to avenge herself upon his male supremacy. But to kill him was only half her victory. First she must prove herself the stronger.[32] Her physical victory is won, necessarily, by craft; the spiritual contest is on equal terms, and in the course of it Agamemnon will be compelled, as his own words reveal, to play the woman's part. 'Pamper me not so,' he says, 'as though I were a woman (γυναικὸς ἐν τρόποις); nor adore me as though I were a barbarian, with loud open-mouthed prostrations' (918ff.). The protests are complementary and significant. Just

---

[30] See p. 113.

[31] See ch. 5, *passim*.

[32] 'In the use of ἐγώ, ἐμοί, ἐμέ at the end of three successive lines we hear an undertone of strife between the two wills' (Headlam *ap.* Thomson (3) – his 922). Add ἐμοί in 943.

as the conqueror of Priam is to be reduced to barbarism, so the cuckold of Aegisthus is to be reduced to effeminacy. Out come the copy-book maxims. So Agamemnon will play safe and behave as a good conventional Greek? The temptress turns from rhetoric to argument, in that brief stichomythic dialogue[33] which is the crisis of the play, putting forward point after point which he ought to reject in specific terms but does not, ensuring that the vain conqueror who would be *epizelos* prevails over the cautious Greek who fears to be *epiphthonos*. For our present enquiry the closing lines are particularly revealing (940ff.). 'It is not for a woman to thirst for battle' underlines the reversal of the normal roles. Clytemnestra's reply is itself based upon a conventional conception of the relation of man to woman[34] and is thus irresistible to Agamemnon, who condescends to her: 'Do you too desire a victory in strife?' 'Be persuaded,' she replies, 'you are still the master if you make a voluntary concession to me.' Every word is significant.[35] πιθοῦ: and to be easily persuaded is the mark of the woman. κρατεῖς: yet the mastery at this very moment passes from him. ἑκών: for unless this is so, half the sweetness of her victory is lost. 'Well, if you will' (944) – and the victory is won.

After the victory of *peitho*, the victory of *bia*. But this is delayed by the master-stroke of the Cassandra scene, which serves manifold purposes, most of them irrelevant to the present investigation. One aspect, however, is relevant, for Cassandra also has her place in what may be termed the sexual pattern of the play. The last words of Agamemnon proclaim his own subjection (κατέστραμμαι, 956). A few lines earlier, commending his concubine to the queen, he had said: 'No one submits willingly to the yoke of slavery (953).' Yet this is a precise description of his own behaviour and condition.[36] Thus at the outset a point of comparison is established between Cassandra and Agamemnon in respect of bonds and freedom. The scene in which Clytemnestra bids her come down from the chariot and enter the palace is parallel to the scene between husband and wife which has just been examined. As an ingredient of her triumph, Clytemnestra means to kill Cassandra, as she means to kill Agamemnon; but in this instance also she wills to win a victory of persuasion, even where she could command.

---

[33] See pp. 91ff. above.

[34] 'The business of men is war, and women are for their recreation. Sure of their own superiority, they find pleasure in condescending to humour feminine caprice' (Thomson (3), 1, 26).

[35] Reading κρατεῖς (Weil) μέντοι παρείς (Bothe; γ' del. Wecklein). For parallels see Thomson (3) (his 934). κρατεῖς, heavily ironical, recalls 10 and 258. The κράτος and νίκη themes are closely associated.

[36] At 945 πρόδουλον is, therefore, no superfluous ornament, but puts the idea of slavery into circulation. At 951 the masculine τὸν κρατοῦντα has a shade of irony.

πείθω νιν λόγῳ (1052), she says; but Cassandra makes no move and the queen admits defeat (1055, 1068). This slave has not yet learnt, like Agamemnon, to bear the yoke (1066).[37] Her enslavement is of the body only.[38] When she has finished her prophesying, she faces her fate, recoils from it, but goes to meet it bravely, entering the palace a free soul.[39] Thus the slave proves herself superior to the conqueror, the barbarian to the Greek, the woman to the man.

After the murder of Agamemnon, the play falls into three parts: the speeches in which Clytemnestra justifies herself to the Chorus, the *kommos* in which her anapaests alternate with their lyrical laments, and the Aegisthus-scene. It is during the first two of these only, out of the whole play, that she can discard ironical pretence and stand revealed in her true colours. Compare and contrast her opening sentence (οὐκ ἐπαισχυνθήσομαι, 1373) with her first address on Agamemnon's entrance (οὐκ αἰσχυνοῦμαι, 856).[40] The same assertion of frankness introduces, there, the pretence of wifely affection, here, the true account of her mind and motives. It is the speech of the 'woman of manly counsel', who could both plan (οὐκ ἀφρόντιστος, 1377) and carry out (ἐξειργασμένοις, ἔπραξα, 1379f.).[41] The Chorus are amazed that she can use such language . . . ἐπ' ἀνδρί.[42] She replies without irony: 'You make trial of me as though I were a thoughtless woman.'[43] But their praise or blame is all one to her. 'Here is Agamemnon; my husband; a corpse; the work of my right hand, a just craftsman.' The word πόσις receives great emphasis; its juxtaposition to νεκρός suggests perhaps a causal connection between those

---

37   The parallel between the two scenes is perhaps brought out by the repetition of ἔκβαιν' ἀπήνης τῆσδε (906, 1039). Persuasion: πείθω νιν λόγῳ (1052) is reinforced by the πιθοῦ (1054) of the Chorus, whose 1049 has already called attention to this theme and hinted at the outcome of the encounter (ἀπειθοίης). Enslavement: 1038, 1041, 1042, 1045, 1066, 1071.

38   Hence the irony of 1084 (δουλίᾳ περ ἐν φρενί).

39   Cf. Pohlenz I 101; E. Fraenkel, *Die Kassandraszene der Orestie* (Stuttgart 1937) 9. The key-note is τλήσομαι τὸ κατθανεῖν (1289), which is followed by εὐτόλμως (1298), τλήμων . . . ἀπ' εὐτόλμου φρενός (1302). εὐτόλμως: because this is the *right kind* of τόλμα – a hint, one might say, of that ambivalence of qualities, etc., which is a pervading theme of the closing scene of *Eumenides*. (A study of εὖ and εὐ-compounds in *Oresteia* would be illuminating.)

40   Similarly 1393 (πρέσβος Ἀργείων τόδε) might recall 855.

41   As the inspired Cassandra knew: 1102 (μήδεται), 1107 (τελεῖν). For Clytemnestra is τέλειος, like a man (cf. 972). The text of 1378 is disputed. Page mentions Karsten's νίκης τελείας with some approval; Thomson accepts Wilamowitz' νίκη τέλειος (with ἀγῶνος οὐκ ἀφροντίστου in the preceding line). If there are two themes which we might expect to find somewhere in this speech, they are νικᾶν and τελεῖν. The matter remains doubtful, however.

42   It is perhaps characteristic of them that, after what she has done, they are still so shocked by what she says (γλῶσσαν, -στομος, λόγον in two lines). In 1407ff. they are still preoccupied with the fact that a woman (ὦ γύναι) has done it – a phenomenon which they can only ascribe to drugs.

43   γυναικὸς ὡς ἀφράσμονος (1401): cf. 1377, 351, 11.

two conditions. But Clytemnestra has claimed that the deed of her hand was just. In her next two speeches she advances her justification.

The theme of the first speech is Iphigenia. The Chorus wish to proceed against Clytemnestra for the murder of her husband. But what opposition did they make when Agamemnon sacrificed his own daughter[44] – her daughter – at Aulis 'to charm the winds from Thrace'? The point is unanswerable, and is not answered by the Chorus. μεγαλόμητις εἶ, is their comment – 'proud is your spirit' – for at the end of her speech the queen had spoken not as mother, but as competitor for power who has gained one victory of force and is prepared to gain another.[45]

Her second speech is more complex. From Iphigenia it moves to Aegisthus; from Aegisthus to the infidelities of Agamemnon, to Chryseis and Cassandra. The sequence of thought is subtle and will, it is to be hoped, continue to defy the transpositions of editors. Clytemnestra swears 'by Justice fully taken for my child, by Ate and Erinys', that she has no fear – 'so long as Aegisthus lights fire upon my hearth'. Thus the ground of her confidence is not only Justice, not only Iphigenia, but Aegisthus.[46] Now, as we have seen, the significance of Aegisthus lies in his function as a substitute for Agamemnon. As a person he is effeminate and she can dominate him; but as a male he can command force and so is a necessary tool for her masculine will. Thus, the opening half of the second speech picks up both aspects of the first: Iphigenia and the ἀνδρόβουλον κέαρ.[47] More must be said about the relationship of these two factors, but meantime the mention of Aegisthus leads Clytemnestra to accuse Agamemnon of sexual infidelity.

Is this simply a parry to the similar charge which has been brought, and will continue to be brought, against her? If so, the charges cancel out,[48] and the amours of Agamemnon are not valid to justify Clytemnestra. Yet she reverts to this theme again in *Choephori* (918). Was sexual jealousy then among her motives? But if Clytemnestra was jealous, she was jealous

---

[44] See also n. 52 below.

[45] She speaks κατ' ἄνδρα σώφρονα (351), prepared to teach her male opponents a lesson in σωφροσύνη (1425). On the detailed interpretation of 1421–24, which is vexed, see the editors.

[46] Further, it is δίκη τέλειος which really destroys her ground of confidence, for the same principle which operated through her to kill Agamemnon will operate through Orestes to kill her (and Aegisthus cannot save her in the end). It is partly for this reason that the conception of δίκη is amplified in 1433 by Ate and Erinys to show the type of justice which is involved. Note that the very powers by which she swears will in fact be the ground of her fear (revealed in *Choephori*).

[47] The mention of Aegisthus is also prepared by στερομέναν φίλων (1429).

[48] Daube (182) points out that, unlike Aegisthus, Agamemnon is not culpable in Attic law. But the Chorus does not attempt to defend him on this score, any more than in his treatment of Iphigenia. For Aeschylus he was guilty on both counts of an offence against marriage (see p. 111 below).

primarily of Agamemnon himself, who went to Troy and came back a
conqueror, while she, knowing herself to be the stronger, was left to keep
the home. If she was jealous of the Chryseids and Cassandra, perhaps it was
not simply that they had shared his bed, but that Chryseis had shared his
hut beneath the walls of Troy (1439), and Cassandra his life on board the
ship (1442).[49] But the significance of the charge is still not exhausted, for
there is a link of primary importance between the first speech dealing with
Iphigenia and the second speech dealing with sexual infidelity.

Agamemnon died justly, because he had killed Iphigenia; Agamemnon's death was 'not undeserved' (ἄτιμα, 1443), because he had insulted
Clytemnestra in her status as a wife (1438). To the latter charge, when it is
repeated in Choephori, Orestes replies by quoting, in effect, a 'double
standard' of morality (Cho. 919), which is a symbol of that inferiority
against which Clytemnestra chafed. No less, however, did the act of
Agamemnon in sacrificing his daughter strike at the relationship of
husband and wife and emphasize the inferior status of the wife. In
considering the dramatic function of Iphigenia, we need not over-simplify
or suppose that, if Clytemnestra's deed was an act of self-liberation,
vengeance for her daughter was a mere pretext. Doubtless she had loved
her daughter; doubtless that love had turned into hatred of her husband.[50]
It is not merely, however, that two separate motives had combined to
make her kill her husband. For the motives are inextricably connected.
Clytemnestra describes her daughter as φιλτάτη ὠδίς (1417); later as ἔρνος,
a shoot or branch (1525). The terms insist upon the intimate physical
connection between mother and child.[51] In each case the phrase is
completed by words expressive of the father's share in the child. 'His own
child, my dearest birth-pang' (1417f.). 'My branch raised up by him'
(1525). It has already been noted that when, in her first speech to
Agamemnon, Clytemnestra referred to the absent Orestes, she did so in
terms which could apply to Iphigenia. 'Wherefore there stands not by our
side, as should have stood, the child, the ratification of my faith and
yours, . . .' Such was the value that Agamemnon placed upon the pledge of

---

49   The two spheres over which her imagination had ranged commandingly in her first great speeches
     to the Chorus (see p. 103). It is of the second of those speeches that Wilamowitz (1) could say: 'dass
     Klytaimestra, die Frau, die zu Hause sass, die eroberte Stadt schildert . . . ist wirklich ungehörig.
     Nirgend sonst gibt es so naive Dramaturgie, denn nur weil die Königin zu Stelle ist, bekommt sie
     das zu sagen, was wir hören sollen'. When Wilamowitz erred, his errors were upon the same lordly
     scale as his successes! In 1443 ἰστοτριβής is indefensible. Despite Fraenkel's objections, the
     conjectural ἰσοτριβής may well be right and, as interpreted above, gives a perfectly good sense.
50   When the fountains of her tears had dried up (887f., cf. 1526).
51   And may, therefore, be relevant to the argument about parentage in Eumenides (see p. 123 below).

their mutual love, claiming full rights of disposal in a child that was hers no less than his.[52] Thus both the offences of which Clytemnestra accuses her husband are sins against marriage and strike at the status of the woman in marriage.[53]

On neither score can a defence be made by the Chorus for all their loyalty to the dead. They pray for death themselves. This is not the place for a full analysis of the ensuing *kommos*, in which the traditional form of lamentation is complicated by a divergence of sympathy between the participants, by argument and counter-argument, and by reference to the deepest philosophical issues of the trilogy. In one aspect, however, the *kommos* continues the debate upon the responsibility of Clytemnestra. The Chorus pray for death, now that their protector is dead, 'that endured many things in a woman's cause, and by a woman's hand lost his life' (1453f.). They ascribe the blame for all the loss of life at Troy, and (apparently, though the text is corrupt) for Agamemnon's death, to Helen. They apostrophize the *daimon*, 'that falls upon the house and the double line of Tantalus and wields a like-souled mastery from women – to wring my heart' (1468ff.). κράτος τ' ἰσόψυχον ἐκ γυναικῶν κρατύνεις. The very difficulty of the Greek is a sign of the ambiguous effect which the poet intends.[54] To the Chorus, reminded as they have been of Aegisthus, the thought of Helen and the comparison of the two sisters is easy, both instruments to secure the victory of a malign fate. But κράτος has associations: with Clytemnestra and her desire for dominance. Now it is used of two women; for while Clytemnestra gains the mastery through her

[52] In 1417 the possessive αὑτοῦ expresses primarily the horror of killing one's own child. It is, therefore, perhaps far-fetched to see in it the notion of possessiveness and (in contrast with ἐμοί) the implication that, while Clytemnestra had the birth-pangs, Agamemnon owned the child. At 1524ff., however, if Thomson (3) is right to translate 'whom he consented to rear for me' (referring to the husband's option of acknowledging or exposing the child), the phrase is even more expressive of the marriage-relationship: later, by an equally arbitrary act, Agamemnon revokes his first decision. Contrast Fraenkel, Page.

[53] Since Apollo stands forth as the champion of marriage (*Eum.* 211ff.), it is interesting to note a parallel between his argument there and Clytemnestra's here (1412ff.). Where Apollo says to the Furies, in effect: 'You pursue an offence by a child, but not an offence by a wife against her husband', Clytemnestra says to the Chorus: 'You pursue an offence by a wife against her husband, but not an offence against a child.' Since ἀνδρηλατεῖν occurs in both passages, I am inclined to think the first part of the compound significant (see also n. 60 on 1586). Apollo says (221): 'You do not ἀνδρηλατεῖν (pursue your man) with justice'; Clytemnestra says (1419); 'You did not ἀνδρηλατεῖν, as in justice you should have done.' The offence of Agamemnon against Iphigenia, and so against Clytemnestra, is by no means forgotten in *Eumenides* (see pp. 121f.), and it would not be surprising if, when Aeschylus wrote πιστώματα at *Eum.* 214, he had *Agam.* 878 (ἐμῶν τε καὶ σῶν κύριος πιστωμάτων) in mind. Yet Apollo can appeal to the sanctity of marriage in upholding Agamemnon's cause.

[54] On the interpretation of ἰσόψυχον see Daube 25; also Fraenkel (who makes rather heavy weather) and Page.

male characteristics, Helen gains it by ways traditional to women.[55] The pattern by which Aeschylus expresses his theme of the relationship of the sexes is thus further complicated.[56] It may well be that the poet returns at this point to the basic motive of Clytemnestra in order to illuminate the debate which follows.

For Clytemnestra, who had exultantly claimed full responsibility (1406), now changes her ground, with the mention of the Daimon. She sees herself, or would have the Chorus see her, not as the wife of Agamemnon, but as the embodiment of an ancestral curse (1497ff.). The instrument of the curse indeed she is, but personal responsibility Aeschylus will not allow her to disclaim (1505ff.); the less so, perhaps, in that she is actuated by motives extraneous to the bloody history of the house of Atreus.[57] It is at this point that she returns (1521ff.) to the theme of Iphigenia, with that phrase which links her and Agamemnon as parents of the murdered child, and thus relates her vengeance as a mother to her status as a wife. Yet again she returns (1555ff.) to Iphigenia, and it is the climax of bitterness when she tells how the daughter will meet her father at the rapid Ford of Sorrows, will fling her arms about his neck and kiss him.[58] Yet when she has played this her strongest card, she reverts to the Daimon. For she knows, without the Chorus's ominous suggestions of further bloodshed, that the matter is not ended by appeal to the memory of Iphigenia; that she cannot claim to be the embodiment of the Daimon and deny its implications. It is a change of mood indeed when she tries to strike a bargain with the ancestral curse and so rid the palace of 'the madness of mutual slaughter' (1567ff.). But such compromise is futile; and Aegisthus is a symbol of its futility.

The entry of Aegisthus is an effective piece of bathos. The stage, which has held only Clytemnestra and her victims, now fills with soldiers. The

[55] It is partly for the sake of this contrast that the femininity of Helen is so eloquently evoked at 737ff. διφυίοισι (1468) may, of course, simply mean 'two'; since, however, a distinction between the two brothers has already been implied at 115, the word may rather mean 'of two natures', the uxorious defeatist Menelaus (410ff.) being the proper victim of Helen, the ambitious warrior Agamemnon of Clytemnestra.

[56] N.B. γυναικός (1453), γυναικός (1454), ἀνδρός (1461), ἀνδρολέτειρα (1464), ἀνδρῶν (1465). Why is Clytemnestra's retort (1462ff.) so vehement? 'Do not blame Helen, blame Agamemnon for the deaths of many men (and of Iphigenia).' Clytemnestra herself is not responsible for destroying πολλῶν ἀνδρῶν ψυχάς. But she is ἀνδρολέτειρα in a special sense, and it may be (cf. Méautis 203) that she is still anxious to claim for herself the full responsibility for this death (contrast 1497ff.).

[57] If the δαίμων represents, as in a sense it does, an evil heredity, Clytemnestra does not share in this heredity. It is hardly to the point to suggest (Daube 192) that she had acquired the family curse by marriage. Helen and Clytemnestra (whose own heredity is ἔξω τοῦ δράματος) are both extraneous factors used by the δαίμων to effect its purposes.

[58] ὡς χρή (1556) may recall ὡς χρῆν (879).

queen stands silent while Aegisthus, who has had no share in the emotional tension of the preceding scene, makes a forensic speech. A crude character, he prides himself on his cunning, his worldly wisdom, his clear-sightedness (1623).[59] He advances the male interpretation of the death of Agamemnon, in terms of fathers, sons and brothers, and of the competition for power.[60] For this death he takes full credit to himself, claiming the male prerogative of planning and decision;[61] he claims full authority in the state (1638ff.). But which is the ruler? Which is the man? The Chorus-leader calls him 'woman' and taunts him with his home-keeping (1625 ff.);[62] and the audience will draw the correct conclusion. Yet this is the person that Clytemnestra has hailed as her shield of confidence (1437). For it is part of her predicament that she cannot dispense with the formal protection of a man and of the armed force which a man alone can command. Between the death of Agamemnon and the entry of Aegisthus Clytemnestra spoke without pose or dissimulation. Now she enters upon her new role, the consort of Aegisthus as formerly of Agamemnon. She listens with contempt to the altercations of the men; and when these threaten to lead to bloodshed, she intervenes with good counsel, but closes with her old irony: 'Such is a woman's word, if it is worth hearing' (1661). The quarrel continues to reverberate until she ends it and the play with two significant lines. 'Pay no regard to these idle yelpings; I and thou, as masters of this house, will make good order' (1672f.).[63] Mastery in the dual number ($\kappa\rho\alpha\tauο\hat{υ}\nu\tau\epsilon$); but the first person singular ($\dot{\epsilon}\gamma\dot{\omega}$), from word-order and

---

[59] Note especially 1623. This characteristic reappears in *Choephori* (see n. 75). Note also the specious lucidity ($\tau\omega\rho\hat{\omega}s$, 1584) of 1583–6, which omit the one point damaging to his case, yet already known to the audience from 1193.

[60] Note the male words in 1580–5: $\mathring{\alpha}\nu\delta\rho\alpha, \pi\alpha\tau\rho\dot{\omega}\alpha s, \pi\alpha\tau\dot{\eta}\rho, \pi\alpha\tau\dot{\epsilon}\rho\alpha, \mathring{\alpha}\delta\epsilon\lambda\phi\dot{ο}\nu$; even $\mathring{\eta}\nu\delta\rho\eta\lambda\dot{\alpha}\tau\eta\sigma\epsilon\nu$ (1586) may contribute to the effect (see n. 53). Aegisthus is, in one aspect, the $\mathring{\alpha}\lambda\dot{\alpha}\sigma\tau\omega\rho$ embodied (and truly $\pi\alpha\tau\rho\dot{ο}\theta\epsilon\nu$), taking vengeance as a son on the son of Atreus $\chi\alpha\lambda\epsilon\pio\hat{υ}\ \theta\omega\nu\alpha\tau\hat{\eta}\rho\omega s$. In another aspect, he is an ambitious prince, a candidate for power, renewing with Agamemnon the rivalry of their fathers: cf. 1583–5 ($\mathring{\alpha}\rho\chi\epsilon\iota\nu$). Thus he, like Clytemnestra, has a motive (and essentially the same motive) beyond the desire and duty of vengeance.

[61] Cf. 1609 ($\delta\upsilon\sigma\beta\omicron\upsilon\lambda\dot{\iota}\alpha s$), picked up by the Chorus at 1614, 1627, 1634. There are two points; (i) Aegisthus is guilty as instigator to wilful murder (see Mazon's edition, p. 69, n. 1) and will pay the penalty; (ii) his claims are exaggerated ($\pi\hat{\alpha}\sigma\alpha\nu$, 1609, picked up by $\mu\dot{ο}\nu\omicron s$, 1614). For, to the audience, $\beta\omicron\upsilon\lambda\epsilon\dot{\upsilon}\epsilon\iota\nu$ must (as at 846f. and at *Cho.* 672) recall the $\mathring{\alpha}\nu\delta\rho\dot{ο}\beta\omicron\upsilon\lambda\omicron\nu\ \kappa\dot{\epsilon}\alpha\rho$ of Clytemnestra. The Chorus, invincibly reluctant to face the true nature of the queen, may accept his claim to be the arch-plotter: what they hold against him (1635, 1644) is that he allowed a woman to do the killing; but the reversal of roles goes farther than they know.

[62] 1625–7 are, without doubt, addressed to Aegisthus (see Fraenkel). The sexual theme is further emphasized at 1639 (where $\pi\epsilon\iota\theta\dot{\alpha}\nu\omicron\rho\alpha$ is a carefully selected word), at 1643f., and at 1671 (the conventional view).

[63] $\dot{\epsilon}\gamma\dot{\omega}$ and $\kappa\alpha\lambda\hat{\omega}s$ are supplied from schol. vet. Tr. So Page's OCT, despite the objections of Fraenkel and the qualms expressed in Denniston–Page. For intransitive $\epsilon\mathring{υ}\ \tau\iota\theta\dot{\epsilon}\nu\alpha\iota$, cf. Eur. *Med.* 926.

rhythm, receives great emphasis. It is Clytemnestra who will, in fact, be master, and it was for this mastery that she killed her husband.

κρατεῖ (10) was the first indication of the character of Clytemnestra; κράτος (258) greeted her first speaking appearance; the ironical κρατεῖς (943) marked the climax of her struggle with Agamemnon; and with κρατοῦντε (1673) the first play ended. *Choephori* opens with κράτη – with Orestes appealing to Hermes Chthonios: 'who watchest over my father's powers (πατρῷα κράτη)'.[64] For the son has now returned to claim his birthright and to retrieve the defeat, the loss of mastery, which his father had suffered.[65] Here, as elsewhere in this play, the reference is primarily 'political'; but, since Orestes is to renew with Clytemnestra the duel between man and woman, it is personal also. It is both personal and political, for she is now the real master of house and state, whose harsh government is revealed by the Chorus of female slaves who enter with Electra – servants in fear, as the Watchman of *Agamemnon* was a servant in fear. If Clytemnestra does not dominate the second play as she dominated the first, her near presence is always felt; and, though her part is short, the scenes where she confronts her son are the peaks of dramatic interest in the play. It is worth examining how her first entry is prepared.

In the broadest sense, it is, of course, prepared by the whole of the preceding portion of the play, during which the children meet, recognize one another and concert their terrible plan. Clytemnestra is spoken of as mother, even as murderess (189), though there is a tendency at first to use vague plural expressions.[66] Not till the later stages of the *kommos* is she spoken of as victim, for then the work of the Chorus is accomplished; Electra has become a wolf,[67] and Orestes is ready to accept the role of snake which he had played in Clytemnestra's dream. But after his blunt statement: ἐκδρακοντωθεὶς ἐγὼ κτείνω νιν (549f.) – 'turned to snake, I am her killer' – there is a regression away from Clytemnestra, through the plurals of 556–8, to Aegisthus. For it is part of the preparation for her entry that Orestes speculates in detail upon the way in which he will

---

[64] On this controversial phrase, see Garvie's important article in *BICS* 17 (1970) 79–91. I accept his view that πατρῷα κράτη here refers to Agamemnon's status in the infernal world, from which he is implored to help in the restoration of an earthly sovereignty.

[65] Cf. 499 (εἴπερ κρατηθείς γ᾽ ἀντινικῆσαι θέλεις).

[66] E.g. 117, 142, 144, 273, 367, 377.

[67] 421f.: a wolf, like Aegisthus (*Agam.* 1259).

find – Aegisthus.[68] Yet, if dialogue leads us to expect the man, lyric leaves
no doubt that the woman will appear. For in the interval, while Orestes
and Pylades disguise themselves as Phocian travellers, the Chorus sing of
unnatural crimes, of women who had steeled their hearts to kill a son, a
father, even (the Lemnian crime of crimes) their husbands. The ode
contains phrases which may recall the scheming nature of Clytemnestra
and her love of mastery.[69] But her unnatural crime is to be avenged by a
son who kills his mother (as Althaea killed her son, as Scylla killed her
father); and the avenger will be introduced into the house by Clytemnestra
herself – κλυτὰ βυσσόφρων Ἐρινύς.[70]

The immediate preparation for her entry is a striking theatrical effect.
For Orestes, in his role of Phocian messenger, bids the servant summon one
in authority (τελεσφόρος); a woman – or better a man: 'man speaks to

---

68 Why these speculations? Not, certainly, because it interested Aeschylus to introduce, by a
side-wind, other versions of the legend. Whether we should explain the retreat from Clytemnestra
in terms of the mental state of Orestes is more doubtful. (See ch. 7, p. 141.)

69 The ode demands a fuller analysis than it can receive here. Briefly, however, Str. 1 (585–93) is full
of vague suggestions and echoes. The monsters which infest land and sea may recall *Agam.* 1231ff.,
which is related to the general theme of this ode by τολμᾷ (1231), παντότολμος (1237), θῆλυς
ἄρσενος φονεύς (1231). Sinister lights (λαμπάδες) are a constant feature from *Agam.* 8 onwards.
Ant. 1 (594–601). The passage from these frightful phenomena of nature to the πάντολμοι
ἔρωτες of women is through ὑπέρτολμον ἀνδρὸς φρόνημα; and the succeeding examples
illustrate, by implication, the crimes of men as well as those of women (see below). ἔρωτας, ἔρως:
for this Chorus, like that of *Agamemnon* and like Orestes, accounts for Clytemnestra's conduct in
terms of Aegisthus. But θηλυκρατὴς . . . ἔρως is perhaps ambiguous, and 'female love of mastery'
touches her true motive (θηλυκτόνῳ in *P.V.* 860 is a parallel for subjective θηλυ-). παρανικᾷ
recalls the battle between Agamemnon and Clytemnestra, now resumed between mother and son.
Str. 2, Ant. 2 (602–22): Althaea and Scylla. Note the following points. (i) In neither case (nor
really in that of Clytemnestra) is the motive ἔρως in the ordinary sense. (ii) The case of a mother
killing a son (Althaea) suggests a father who killed a daughter *and*, no less, a son who will kill a
mother (cf. μολὼν ματρόθεν κελάδησε). (iii) The case of a daughter killing a father (Scylla)
suggests a son who will kill a mother *and* a father who killed a daughter. (iv) Thus both stanzas hint
at both the male crimes of the trilogy, while applying primarily to Clytemnestra (cf. μήσατο,
πρόνοιαν). In 620 we should read, with Porson, νοσφίσασα προβούλως: she deliberately chose the
time when he was sleeping – ἁ κυνόφρων. The tone is that of *Eum.* 625ff.
Str. 3 (623–30). The text and the precise connection of thought are uncertain. In any case,
however, the stanza refers to Clytemnestra and probably hints (ἀθέρμαντον, 629) at the erotic
motive absent from the preceding stanzas. The man–woman contrast is strongly marked, and the
ἀνδρόβουλον κέαρ is recalled by γυναικοβούλους (-ων) μήτιδας φρενῶν, followed by ἐπ' ἀνδρί.
γυναικείαν ἄτολμον αἰχμάν is probably, like ἀθέρμαντον ἑστίαν, an oxymoron (see Thomson (3)
ad loc. and n. 17 above): but Clytemnestra displays both τόλμα and αἰχμά (if that means a keen,
restless spirit).
Ant. 3 (631–8). The strictly parallel crime of the Lemnian women. What was their motive?
Sexual jealousy of the foreign women imported by their husbands, according to one version of the
story: then compare Cassandra? But the effect of their crime was to leave the island under the
control of women (see Apollodorus, 1. 9. 17).
τί τῶνδ' οὐκ ἐνδίκως ἀγείρω (638); indeed they all have their appropriateness.
For a careful examination of this ode, see now Stinton 252–62, who presents a powerful case for
transposing Str. 3 and Ant. 3. See also J. P. Gould, *JHS* 100 (1980) 55.

70 See Tucker (2) *ad loc.*; Stanford 93.

man with confidence and makes plain his evidence' (663ff.). ἄνδρα, ἀνήρ, ἄνδρα: and it is Clytemnestra who enters. What does she say? She behaves with formal propriety as the lady of a house. She offers the hospitable services for which a woman is responsible – the bath and the bed; 'but if anything needs be done requiring counsel, that is the work of men' – to whom she will communicate. But βουλιώτερον and ἀνδρῶν in juxtaposition must (particularly after the preceding ode) recall the ἀνδρόβουλον κέαρ; and there is significance even in the hospitality she offers. For, using the functions of a woman to carry out her manly counsel, she had killed her husband in a bath.[71] She dissimulates, as in *Agamemnon*; but when, after the false news,[72] she rounds off the scene by saying that she will communicate these things to the masters of the house and will take counsel, we know who is the master and who the counsellor.[73]

The expected catastrophe is postponed, as in *Agamemnon* by the Cassandra-scene, so here by the entry of Orestes' Nurse. This simple soul takes us back to the past, and in so doing illuminates the immediate future. Soon mother and son will face one another, and she will plead with him by her motherhood. So the poet reminds us of the infancy of Clytemnestra's child. At the same time he makes the Nurse, and not Clytemnestra, display a mother's affection and a mother's grief.[74] He achieves two purposes which may conflict upon the level of prosaic logic, but combine poetically to enhance the scene between unnatural mother and unnatural child; and it is to this scene that the Chorus now look forward (827ff.), when Clytemnestra will cry τέκνον, and Orestes will harden his heart.

The reference to Clytemnestra prepares the entry of Aegisthus, as hers was prepared by expectation of him. He cannot enter the trilogy without bathos, and his very inferiority is a commentary upon her predicament. Hypocritical, pompous, and with a good conceit that he cannot be imposed upon,[75] he is now to be the vehicle of subtle irony. For, like the Elders in *Agamemnon*, he doubts that the news is true; and he uses the same metaphor of fire to express his doubt: ἢ πρὸς γυναικῶν δειματούμενοι λόγοι | πεδάρσιοι θρῴσκουσι θνῄσκοντες μάτην;[76] 'The words of women's fears leap heavenwards only to die in vain.' Thus for the last time

---

[71] The circumstances of his death were mentioned as recently as 491ff.

[72] On the ascription of 691–9 to Electra, see ch. 7, n. 34 and App. F.

[73] βουλευσόμεσθα (718), after τοῖς κρατοῦσι (716), hints at the reality.

[74] Cf. 749f. See Méautis 233f.; Vickers 404f.

[75] N.B. βλέποντα (844), ἰδεῖν (851), ὠμματωμένην (854): see n. 59.

[76] 845f. θνῄσκοντος (Portus) is supported by the schol., by a number of parallels (see Thomson (3) *ad loc.*), and perhaps by 852. It may be right, but I feel that something is needed to describe the sinking of the flame, corresponding to καμεῖν and ὄλλυται in the *Agamemnon* passage (482, 487).

Clytemnestra is accused – and by one who should have known better – of a woman's weak credulity. Yet this time the accusation is justified. For Clytemnestra no longer controls the situation. She is numbered among the deaf and the sleepers (881); she asks, not answers, questions (885). Nevertheless, it is the circumstances that have changed, not the fibre of the woman. This is clear in the contest which follows.

The death-cry of Aegisthus is heard, and the Chorus-leader says that the issue of the battle is now decided (874). But this is not true: the real battle has not yet begun – the contest between mother and son which resumes the contest between husband and wife and which, like that earlier battle, is fought with the twin weapons of *peitho* and of *bia*. 'The dead the living slay,' cries the Servant to Clytemnestra (886); and she reads the silly riddle with characteristic speed. 'By craft we shall perish as we slew.' She demands a 'man-slaying axe',[77] to decide the issue of victory or defeat. It is her instinct to do battle as a man. She does not realize that Aegisthus is dead; the words of the Servant did not imply it. But the sight of Orestes and Pylades with drawn swords reveals to her the true situation and her own ignominious weakness. The 'might' of Aegisthus (her 'shield' of *Agamemnon*) has perished;[78] for a woman force, unprepared by cunning, was futile, and on this occasion the cunning had been used against her. The weapon of persuasion remains. With a swift efficiency she turns to wheedle her son as she had wheedled her husband; and the scene which follows is parallel to the scene in which she persuaded Agamemnon to tread the scarlet draperies. At the word τέκνον, at the sight of the breast, Orestes hesitates. Will Clytemnestra win yet another victory? But Apollo speaks, with the voice of Pylades. 'I count thee victor (903),' replies Orestes; for the victory in the contest belongs neither to the son nor to the mother, but to the god of Delphi.

Clytemnestra, however, does not easily accept defeat; and in the following thrust and parry we are taken back to the fundamental issues. For Orestes now threatens her life, as Agamemnon had threatened her liberty. To Orestes, indeed (as to the Choruses in both plays), the explanation of her conduct lies in her passion for Aegisthus (894f.), whom she had preferred to Agamemnon in life, with whom she must sleep in death (904ff.). Clytemnestra replies with an appeal which misses the reality by an equal margin: 'I nursed you and would grow old beside you' (908). Not

---

[77] It matters little whether, or in what version of the story, she killed her husband with an axe. The stress is on the epithet and on the first half of it.

[78] βία is significant and the periphrasis should not be emended away (as by Thomson, *CR* 56 (1942) 71).

only is this appeal already somewhat prejudiced by the Nurse's speech: it is inherently absurd, for Clytemnestra no more needs a son in her old age than she needed a husband in her prime; and the reply of Orestes means more than he knows: 'Could you who killed my father live with me?' The dialogue as it proceeds is packed with meanings that do not relate to our present theme. But, when Orestes charges his mother with selling him into slavery, the climax is approaching. 'Where,' she asks, 'is the price which I received in exchange (916)?' It is a price which Orestes is ashamed to put into words. To such a simple charge, she makes a simple reply: she advances, as she had advanced in *Agamemnon*, the infidelities of her husband. The lines which follow are the very core and centre of the dialogue.[79]

'Do not criticize him who works, you who sit within.' 'It is grief for women to be parted from their man, my child.' 'Yes, but the man's work supports them while they sit within' (919–21). The two lines spoken by Orestes are straightforward statements of male superiority. The husband supports the wife with his labour, with his valour, and in return demands that he be free from her criticism. ἔσω καθημένη (919) is reiterated and re-emphasized by ἡμένας ἔσω (921). For this was Clytemnestra's situation, while Agamemnon was at Troy; and her own intervening comment carries us back to the entry of Agamemnon and her speech of greeting (*Agam.* 861ff.). Then, when she deprecated solitude, it was an ironical lie, which yet hinted at the real meaning for her of the presence or absence of her husband.[80] Here the reply accepts the crude assumptions of Orestes. Yet in reducing her to the level of her paramour, it is such an over-simplification of the relationship between man and woman as the rest of the trilogy repudiates. It is corrected by that twofold reference to the woman who sits at home, which implies the collision of the powers and gifts of Clytemnestra with the conditions of her life as a woman.[81] The price which she received for the murder of her husband and for the banishment of her son was indeed Aegisthus, whose outward protection it was part of her humiliation to need, but whose weak character allowed her to continue the male role. Her predicament and its sorry solution lead as directly to the

---

[79] Thus 924f. return to 912; 927 to 910f.; 928 to 908 – leaving the discussion of motive and the man–woman theme in the centre of the design.

[80] See p. 103 above.

[81] And by expressing those conditions in economic terms offers a fundamental generalization about men and women. For while πονοῦντα and μόχθος might relate to the man as warrior (cf. *Agam.* 330, 555, 567), τρέφει implies his function as breadwinner.

matricide (922) as the husbandhood of Agamemnon led to his murder (*Agam.* 1405).[82]

Clytemnestra has a speaking part in *Eumenides* also, but the short scene in which her ghost upbraids the sleeping Furies[83] tells us little about Clytemnestra living. The woman who in *Agamemnon* despised the 'plausible visions of a dream' (*Agam.* 274f.), but in *Choephori* allowed her action to be governed by a dream (*Cho.* 32ff.), is now herself a dream in the minds of her avengers (116). This is in itself a symbol of that decline in personal interest which the broad design of the trilogy imposed upon the dramatist. In *Eumenides*, the divine powers and the general issues hold the stage; and it is through the utterances of gods that the special case of Clytemnestra is set against a wider background. But amid the debates of the gods we shall do well to remember the woman of the earlier plays.

These debates turn largely upon the relative status of man and woman. The Furies are the champions of Clytemnestra – of Clytemnestra as mother. But Apollo, in defending Orestes, speaks for Agamemnon, not only as husband, but as man (625ff.); he disparages the motherhood of Clytemnestra, denying the right of the female to be regarded, in the full sense, as parent of the child (658ff.). Athena casts her vote for Orestes frankly on grounds of preference for the male (737). But these pronouncements come at the end of a long process of argument, which must now be examined.

The scene between Apollo and the Furies at Delphi (179–234) is a kind of preliminary, in the absence of the defendant, to the later trial before the Areopagus. It serves to present in a vivid form the direct clash, in interest and point of view, between the two parties. 'Your oracle bade that he should kill his mother.' 'My oracle bade that he should bring vengeance for his father' (202f.). To the Furies it seems inconsistent – and perhaps it is – that the god who accepts the polluted man should hurl abuse at his 'escort'.[84] There may, in fact, be more in common between the two parties than either could willingly admit. 'We drive matricides from their homes.' 'When a woman kills her husband, what then?' (210f.). The answer, as Apollo should know, is that, according to his own code, the son must

---

[82] See p. 108 above.

[83] I hope it will not irritate the reader, if in the remainder of this chapter I call the Chorus of *Eumenides* Furies and not, as in the subsequent chapters, Erinyes, which is strictly preferable.

[84] This is perhaps brought out by the repetition πέμψαι (203), προπομπούς (206). Both Orestes and the Furies were performing their proper functions in accordance with codes which placed the onus of avenging homicide upon the blood-relations of the victim. Aeschylus' treatment of Apollo is discussed at length in the following chapter.

avenge the father or suffer persecution by Furies. But it is a good point to make against his opponents. When they reply that in such a case no kindred blood is shed (212), the narrowness of their interests is revealed; and Apollo retorts effectively that they dishonour the institution of marriage, pledged by Zeus and Hera – they dishonour Kypris and the love of man and woman (213ff.). This solemn reference to marriage is clearly of the first importance, and, whether Apollo is fully entitled to his argument or not,[85] he gets on the whole the better of the first exchange, despite the arrogant violence of his partisanship. But this is only a preliminary contest. We must now pass to the trial itself. And there are two things to bear in mind: that this *is* a trial conducted before an audience who were no doubt already connoisseurs of advocacy, and that the arguments of Apollo convinced only half the jury.

The entry of Apollo to witness and to plead, is dramatic,[86] but his wrangle with the Furies is not immediately resumed. Instead, the Furies address to Orestes questions which are intended to elicit facts, but which soon lead to controversy. The rival claims of the dead are starkly juxtaposed (598f.). Orestes bases his case upon the crimes of his mother, who had killed a man, a husband and a father.[87] He asks, as Apollo had in effect asked (211), why the Furies did not pursue Clytemnestra when she was alive (604), and he receives the same answer: 'She was no kin of the man she slew.' We are back to the issue of the earlier scene. But, where Apollo's rejoinder had referred to the institution of marriage, Orestes asks, bitterly, whether he was, in fact, of his mother's blood (606). 'A false step,' observes Professor Thomson; and so it is, for Orestes bases his reply on the weakness, not (like Apollo) on the strength of his case. Yet it is in this kinship of blood that the horror of matricide resides. 'How then,' say the Furies, 'did she nurture thee beneath her girdle? Dost thou abjure thy mother's blood?'[88] They appeal to the apparent fact and to the universal sentiment of mankind: and at this point the reaction of the audience is bound to be sympathetic. The position is beyond Orestes, who invokes the aid of Apollo. The god will return to the question of kinship between mother and son, but his earlier arguments also must be carefully examined.

Apollo makes four speeches, in the first of which he seeks to dispose of

---

85 See n. 53 above.

86 On which see ch. 7, p. 148 below.

87 ἀνδροκτονοῦσα (602) is virtually itself a double charge (see n. 6).

88 Which is φίλτατον – 'nearest and dearest'. Compare and contrast, therefore, Apollo's commentary on marriage (216): ὅθεν βροτοῖσι γίγνεται τὰ φίλτατα. But has either of these bonds the priority over the other? If 605f. insist on the horror of matricide, perhaps they also imply the question: is the bond between mother and son any closer than that between husband and wife?

the matter on the basis of authority.[89] He is the prophet who never lies (615);[90] he is the mouthpiece of Zeus. But not only are 'appeals to authority useless when there is a conflict of authority':[91] this appeal is subtly prejudiced for an Athenian audience: 'Never yet,' says Apollo, 'have I spoken on my throne of prophecy, concerning man, woman, or city, what was not ordered by Zeus, father of the Olympians' (616ff.). οὐ πόλεως πέρι: from the god who medized.[92] And if he could be wrong about politics, he is not necessarily right about man and woman. The appeal was to Zeus, but for Aeschylus the will of Zeus is something to be anxiously explored, not accepted upon the authority of an Apollo. Did Zeus say: 'Avenge a father's death and pay no honour to a mother'? This is the reply of the Furies (622–4), and Apollo must now argue the point.

His argument is a simple one.[93] The death of a man is different (οὐ . . . τι ταὐτόν, 625) – different, that is, from the death of a woman. This particular man is qualified as noble and as a king, by divine right.[94] His death is rendered the more shocking by the fact that a woman killed him, not in open fight but by treachery: the method is described in detail. The speech must be read in the light of the earlier plays. Craft (which it is perhaps not for Apollo to disparage)[95] was imposed upon Clytemnestra, since in the circumstances of her life it was impossible for her to fight as an Amazon (or as a goddess).[96] Yet with the weapons at her command she fought, and reversed the roles, so that Agamemnon became the woman, she the man. We cannot judge Apollo's argument out of all relation to the portraits of man and woman in *Agamemnon*, and Aeschylus has ensured that we shall not do so in two ways: by reference to the generalship of Agamemnon (631f.), and by reference to the manner of his death. Agamemnon was killed on his return 'from warfare, where he had, for the most part, won success'. There had, as Headlam says, been 'unfortunate

---

[89] But τῇ σῇ φρενὶ δοκεῖ (612f.) already suggests a personal opinion (cf. 640, τῷ σῷ λόγῳ). Nor is it for Apollo to decide (κρῖνον), but for the human jurors, whose votes will be divided.

[90] Cf. μάντις ἀψευδὴς τὸ πρίν (*Cho.* 559).

[91] Thomson (3) 1, 62.

[92] Moreover, as Thomson (1) points out (278), the more advanced democrats, at least, would not willingly admit the infallibility in political matters of an oracle which had such close connections with the Dorian aristocracies.

[93] Note that he does not this time invoke the sanctity of marriage. That point against the Furies has already been made, so that we can compare with μητρὸς τιμάς (624) the ἄτιμα and ἄτιμος of 213 ff. Apollo now deals with the relative standing, not of blood-tie and marriage-tie, but of man and woman (N.B. τιμαλφούμενον, 626).

[94] For an analysis of the roles of Agamemnon – (i) man and husband (ii) lord of the house (iii) victorious general (iv) king – see Macleod (1) 142ff.

[95] Which his own agents employed in *Choephori* (*q.v.*: 557, 726, 888).

[96] See p. 126 below.

incidents'.[97] Then why refer to them? In order to remind the audience of Iphigenia, of Clytemnestra's justification (such as it was), of Agamemnon's weakness at Aulis – and at Argos. For when Apollo speaks of the robe, the embroidered garment with which Clytemnestra fettered her husband (πεδήσασ' ἄνδρα δαιδάλῳ πέπλῳ, 635), we are meant to think not only of the material, but of the spiritual entanglement; not only of the robe, but of the 'carpet' (the ποίκιλα κάλλη of *Agam*. 923), by means of which she had subjected his will to hers and forced him to accept the feminine role.[98] There is thus a certain irony in justifying the matricide on the grounds that Clytemnestra the woman had killed Agamemnon the man, and this is further brought out by the description of Agamemnon (637) as 'all-worshipful' (παντόσεμνος), when he had been so humiliated, and as an 'admiral of the fleet' (στρατηλάτης νεῶν). An *argumentum ad homines* when addressed to the seafaring men of Athens? No doubt; but its effect is surely blunted by that recent reminder of the ill-omened history of the Argive ships.

Apollo's argument does not impress the Furies. They return to Zeus. Does Zeus, who bound his father Cronos, give greater honour to a father's fate (640ff.)? A debating-point which causes Apollo to lose his temper.[99] By making the obvious retort that bonds are not to be compared with death, which is irrevocable,[100] he plays into the hands of his opponents. For, as they are quick to remark, this is the very charge against Orestes – that he had shed a 'mother's kindred blood'. Thus Apollo is forced back to the point at which Orestes had handed over his defence (606). Unless he can dispose of it, the matricide stands condemned.

Apollo puts forward (658ff.) the famous 'physiological' argument, which has been so much discussed. The mother, while she has the function of nourishing the child in the womb, is not the true parent or τοκεύς, but a stranger who gives safe keeping to another's plant.[101] The purpose of this argument is to defend matricide from the charge that it violates the relation

---

[97] See Thomson (3) *ad loc*.

[98] *Agam*. 918 (see p. 106).

[99] He loses his temper because the charge of inconsistency which they make, and to which the attention of the jury is specially called (642f.), is true. His abusive language (644) recalls 68ff. and 185ff., and it is this abuse of the beings with whom he is really so closely involved that gives the clue to his inconsistency. See ch. 7, p. 137.

[100] A constant theme: e.g. *Agam*. 1018ff. (with Fraenkel's note), *Cho*. 71ff., 520f., *Eum*. 261ff.

[101] The mother (ξένη) cherishes the embryo for the father (ξένῳ). This certainly suggests a relationship between husband and wife very different from that implied at 213ff. But is this really the sense required: that husband and wife are strangers? Is it not possible that we should read ξένον (Pearson) for ξένῳ? Mother and child are strangers; and this has an ironical application to the scene in which Orestes – apparent ξένος, real kinsman – confronts his mother. See also Lebeck 126.

of kinship, and the god has been driven to the position at which it is the only argument which can do so. Such a doctrine, perhaps already known in Athens,[102] might be welcomed in a masculine society as a counterpoise to the manifest uncertainty of fatherhood. For, if one thing is sure, it is that the mother carries and bears the child, and the intimacy of this relationship is confirmed by instinct and emotion. When Orestes first questioned the tie of blood between himself and Clytemnestra, the audience was bound to share in the indignation of the Furies. Did Aeschylus intend that they should now accept, upon the authority of Apollo, a theory which deprived the mother of real kinship with her child?

Two extreme interpretations are possible,[103] but neither is satisfactory. It is not plausible to say that it was introduced as a frigid and unconvincing argument, though the only one which will meet Apollo's case. How can we say this, when it is backed by the analogy and endorsement of Athena? (These are an essential factor to which we must return.) But is it more sensible to see it as a conclusive and completely valid argument, the final stage in a progressive undercutting of Clytemnestra's stance?[104] The trouble here is that, if it undercuts her case, it also undercuts, retrospectively, so much of the poetry and dramatic force of what has preceded in the trilogy.[105] It is reduced to absurdity, if we put it like this: 'So Clytemnestra was not in the full sense Orestes' parent (*tokeus*) after all, had no right to call him *teknon*; he need not have worried, nor need we'! Nor for that matter should half the jury have voted to condemn.

We should perhaps consider the character of the argument and what, if valid, it proves. A combination of physiology and semantics, it is highly sophisticated and intellectual; it provides, at the intellectual level, a means of distinguishing the two cases – the killing of a husband, the killing of a mother; more than that, it leads through the analogy of Athena to the goddess's own statement of male priority with its sociological implications (to which we shall return). But, if it solves an intellectual problem, does it not leave an emotional problem unsolved? If the mother is not *tokeus*, she is still *trophos*. It will be noted how often this root is found in earlier stages of the debate. 'Am I of my mother's blood?'[106] asks Orestes (606). 'How then

---

[102] Thomson (3), *ad loc.*; Aly, *Philologus*, Supplb. 21.3 (Leipzig 1929) 40 (who argues that Aeschylus introduced the doctrine from Sicily).

[103] See the useful discussions of Lebeck at 124ff., 135ff.   [104] See Vickers 404f. 413f.

[105] We have been made to feel that the matricide is not just another crime, but the very climax of horror, cf. *Agam.* 1283, *Cho.* 932 and discussion in ch. 7, p. 133.

[106]   Ορ. ἐγὼ δὲ μητρὸς τῆς ἐμῆς ἐν αἵματι;
                         Χο. πῶς γὰρ σ' ἔθρεψεν ἐντός, ὦ μιαιφόνε,
                         ζώνης;

did she nurture you beneath her girdle?' replies the Coryphaeus. Apollo gives an answer, but leaves the fact untouched. In *Choephori*, in the related passages which deal first with Clytemnestra's dream and then with the showing of her breast, the theme of nurture is insistently repeated (545, 898, 908, 928). Sympathy with Clytemnestra may be reduced by the Nurse's speech (750, 754, 760), but the fact remains. The mother carries the child, nourishes it in the womb, gives birth to it in pain, suckles it at the breast: all these things remain untouched by Apollo's argument, and it is upon them that rests the universal sentiment of mankind which is outraged by matricide. The motherhood of her who bore not only Orestes but Iphigenia cannot be so easily disparaged.[107]

Apollo's bolts are now all shot (676).[108] His opponents are no less ready for the verdict to be pronounced. If the audience at this stage makes its own summing-up, it may feel that the balance has been held steady between the adversaries. When the votes are counted, they are found to be equally divided; and this verdict not only corresponds to the balance of argument, but is a sign that Orestes had been confronted with an intolerable dilemma, subjected to contradictory claims *both* based upon the blood-tie and backed by the law of the vendetta. It has been well said that 'Aeschylus was not interested in the solution of an insoluble conundrum.'[109] But he *was* interested in the acquittal of the matricidal son and in making that given fact of legend an intelligible and significant part of his dramatic whole. The acquittal is brought about by the 'vote' of Athena, given for a specific reason. Apollo is so treated in the trilogy that we can to a considerable extent discount his *ex cathedra* pronouncements. Athena, with her dignity and courtesy, is far more impressive; as the protectress of the men of Athens and foundress of the Areopagus she carries more weight.

The reason which she gives for her support of Orestes is already hinted at in the closing speech of Apollo, who quotes her as evidence in favour of his theory of parentage (662ff.). For Athena, daughter of Olympian Zeus, was

---

[107] There is a possible reminiscence of Iphigenia in this very speech of Apollo's, where the word ἔρνος, which had been used by Clytemnestra of her daughter in a striking passage (*Agam.* 1525, cf. p. 110 above), occurs twice (661, 666). This might in itself signify little, but it is not all. The mother, says Apollo, 'like a stranger keeps safe the plant (ἔρνος) – provided a god blast it not (οἷσι μὴ βλάψῃ θεός, 661)'. Why make this qualification, which is as unnecessary, and therefore as significant, as the reference to the 'unfortunate incidents' at 632? To remind us of the pregnant hare in the omen and her offspring (βλαβέντα λοισθίων δρόμων, *Agam.* 120), of the offence against motherhood which called down the wrath of Artemis and led to the sacrifice of Iphigenia. 'The young hare in the womb on which they feast . . . is the child of Clytemnestra' (J. T. Sheppard, *CR* 36 (1922) 8).

[108] On the ascription of 676f. to Apollo see App. G. Apollo adds a piece of testimony in favour of his contention (662–6: see below), and an appeal to the self-interest of the jurors (667–73).

[109] Thomson (1) 289.

not nurtured in the darkness of the womb (665). As evidence, the analogy has little weight, for all human beings are so nurtured, nor can Apollo's physiology abolish this physical fact. But if his case is not strengthened thereby, the audience is prepared for the partisanship of the goddess. When the time comes, Athena could not give her reason more explicitly. She votes,[110] not out of pity, not out of respect for the suppliant, not in order to gain advantage for her city, but on these grounds. 'No mother bore me. The male I commend in all things – except for marriage – with all my heart, and am strongly on the father's side. Thus I will not pay more regard to (οὐ προτιμήσω) the death of a woman who killed a man, the master of a house.' This is the climax of the man–woman theme.[111] 'Zeus,' said the Furies to Apollo (640) 'pays more regard to (προτιμᾷ) a father's fate, by your account'; and Apollo's view is now ratified by Athena. How is this to be explained? We may fall into error if we attempt to answer this question without reference to Clytemnestra.

For there is a sense in which Athena is the counterpart of Clytemnestra and serves as the poet's final comment upon her character and motives. When Orestes reached Athens, he prayed to Athena, wherever she might be, whether in Libya or 'whether, like a bold captain (θρασὺς ταγοῦχος ὡς ἀνήρ, 296), she surveys the plain of Phlegra'. For Athena fights like a man.[112] In fact, she was neither in Libya nor at Phlegra, but in the Troad,

[110] It does not matter greatly, though perhaps a little, to the argument of this chapter to decide whether Athena casts a vote in addition to laying down the principle of 'acquittal if the votes are equally divided' (as argued by e.g. Gagarin, *AJP* 96 (1975) 121–7). On this question there may never be agreement among critics. If, after much hesitation, I have come to believe that she does *not* vote along with the jury, it is mainly for the following reasons. (i) The last thing Aeschylus should be doing is to encourage the audience to make calculations and observe that, if she votes, then there was a majority of the human jury for condemnation. If that was a point, it should have been made openly. And as a point it would disparage the vital effect of equal division. (Talk of Athena voting alongside her people is a sentimental distraction.) The goddess is not a member of the jury and it is not proper for her to vote on the main issue (cf. 471f. and the whole of that speech): what is proper for her as presiding officer is to lay down a principle of procedure. (ii) It is doubtful whether a different view would have been taken, if it were not for the language of 734–41. Even here, it is strange that this vital principle should be laid down in a one-line afterthought (741). ('And, by the way, . . .') What should be observed, I suggest, is that 741 returns to the legal language of the opening lines of Athena's speech. It is a kind of ring-composition enclosing her statement of preference for the male. Do we then say that 741 *is* her ψῆφος, in accordance with that preference? Hardly, for, whatever the truth about her vote, her words must have been matched with some visual effect. If she votes with the jury, she places a voting-pebble (ψῆφον . . . τήνδε) in the urn. (Before or after 736–40?) If not, I would suggest that at 735 she holds up a pebble but does not place it: she waits until the votes have been counted and then, at 752f., adds her pebble to the heap of acquitting votes (the ψῆφον . . . μίαν of 751?). [This note was written before I had seen D. A. Hester, *AJP* 102 (1981) 265–74, who argues the same case in greater detail and with full bibliography (to which should be added Vernant 25 n. 1, who upholds the opposite view).]

[111] 739f.: γυναικός is woman-wife, ἄνδρα is man-husband (see n. 6).

[112] ταγοῦχος ἀνήρ go together in syntax, but ὡς ἀνήρ makes its effect separately.

as she tells in her first words (397ff.), taking possession of the land which the leaders and princes of the Achaeans had given her as the prize of war. For she had fought at Troy; and Orestes (454ff.) can refer to her comradeship-in-arms with Agamemnon. Athena fought at Troy; Clytemnestra, left to keep the home, hated the very Chryseis who had shared Agamemnon's hut and the Cassandra who had sailed with him on his homeward voyage. When he returned, she could kill him not in fair fight ('like an Amazon, with far-shot arrows'), but with craft and traps. Everything, then, that Clytemnestra's nature demanded and her sex forbade or hampered, Athena is free to do, by virtue of her godhead. She is god-goddess to Clytemnestra's man-woman; and her masculinity wins her praise and worship, while that of Clytemnestra leads to disaster for herself and others. There is thus a bitter irony, when the goddess, who in all things commends the male and is free to exercise her preference in action, condemns the woman of manly counsel for seeking the domination which her nature demanded.

Yet it is altogether natural that Athena should vote as she does. Herself in authority, she respects the status of the master.[113] Daughter of Zeus, she can sympathize with the relationship of child to father, and so votes for Orestes. But the issue of the trial had come to turn upon two other relationships, in which she had no part. The argument was between Apollo, who stood (at least at 213ff.) for the marriage-tie, and the Furies, who stood for the bond between child and mother. Upon this issue Athena, who was born of no mother, the virgin-goddess who eschewed wedlock, gives her vote; and since there can be no question upon which side it will be cast, we should at least ask how much validity and what precise significance attaches to this vote. The matter must be considered in two ways: in terms of theology and in terms of society.[114]

Theologically, Athena has importance, for Aeschylus, only as a potential spokesman of the will of Zeus. Apollo, with considerable pomp, had claimed to speak for his father, but this claim was prejudiced in various ways. Athena also is a child of Zeus, and, as her bearing is more dignified, so her solutions are clearly better than Apollo's. At the voting, she speaks for herself and makes no claim to higher authority, but later, when she

---

[113] ἐπίσκοπον (740): cf. 296 (ἐπισκοπεῖ).

[114] Not in terms of the psychology of Orestes, which is of comparatively little importance in *Choephori*, and of less in *Eumenides* (see ch. 7, p. 141 n. 34). What is relevant, perhaps, is the absence of personal relationship between him and Clytemnestra. The bond between mother and son is here as tenuous and abstract as it could very well be. This, of course, has the effect of emphasizing the general sociological issue, but it also helps to make the acquittal of the matricidal son morally tolerable.

brings her divine persuasion to bear upon the Furies, she makes reference to her father's will.[115] 'Bright testimony,' she tells them, 'came from Zeus; and he who gave evidence was he himself who prophesied that Orestes for this deed should not come to harm' (797ff.). This must, of course, be read in the light of her preceding remarks: that the Furies were not defeated, that the outcome of the trial was an equally divided vote, which was an honest one (ἀληθῶς, 796). It may be noteworthy that the wording of the oracle is negative. Orestes – and this is the will of Zeus – was to suffer no harm for what he did (799). For the main responsibility rested upon Apollo, who gave the oracle[116] – that is to say, upon the social code under which Orestes acted. This code was imperfect and embodied 'justice' to a limited degree. We see it in the process of supersession. This is the significance of the reference to Zeus in the next speech of Athena. Tactfully, yet firmly, she reminds the Furies of the thunderbolt of Zeus, which had already been employed against recalcitrant divinities of an older generation.[117] The will of Zeus for the evolution of human society is not to be frustrated. But there is no need of the thunderbolt in this case (829), for the Furies recognize Zeus as all-powerful (παγκρατής, 918) and accept their place in the new order which his daughter has established in Athens.[118]

It is generally recognized that a great part of the interest in the trilogy, and particularly in *Eumenides*, is sociological, in the sense that Aeschylus has dramatized a signal advance in the organization of human society – from the vendetta to the court of law. The point need not be laboured. Athena succeeds where Apollo failed, because his code was still tied to the obsolete blood-feud. The dilemma which faced Orestes could only be escaped by the establishment of a court of law to try cases of homicide. The divided vote seems to recognize this fact; and the jurors who returned this verdict were, in fact, those Athenians who are represented as at once the pioneers and beneficiaries of the new order. But their goddess did not give the vote which acquitted Orestes on the ground that he had been placed in an impossible position: she gave it out of preference for the male. Has this fact, too, a sociological significance?

So Thomson argues. 'If we ask why the dramatist has made the outcome of the trial turn on the social relations of the sexes, the answer is that he regarded the subordination of women, quite correctly, as an indispensable

---

[115] See also ch. 7, p. 147 n. 60.
[116] This may be the point of the repeated αὐτός (798). Cf. 200 (παναίτιος), 579f.
[117] The threat should not be over-stressed, cf. Taplin 408 n. 2.
[118] Cf. 850 (φρονεῖν δὲ κἀμοὶ Ζεὺς ἔδωκεν οὐ κακῶς). The relationship between Zeus and the Furies, which is the basic metaphysical problem of the trilogy, is discussed in ch. 8 below.

condition of democracy . . . a necessary consequence of the development of private property.'[119] That Aeschylus has, in fact, made the outcome of the trial depend upon the relationship between the sexes cannot be denied; and it is the less possible to disregard the emphatic pronouncement of Athena because it is not only the trial but, if the foregoing analysis has been correct, the whole trilogy which turns upon this relationship. One may doubt, however, whether the simple statement (made by Professor Thomson in a different context)[120] that to Aeschylus 'the subjection of women was not only just but preferable to the liberty which they had formerly enjoyed' is an adequate description of the dramatist's views.

It might, for instance, be considered that Aeschylus adopted a strange method of proclaiming the natural superiority and rightful dominance of the male, when he opened his trilogy with a play in which the man – husband, king, and general – is routed upon every plane by the woman. And not by one woman only, if the superiority of Cassandra to her conqueror is admitted.[121] It is, indeed, striking how interest and sympathy are concentrated upon the women in *Agamemnon*, where, to set against Iphigenia, Clytemnestra, and Cassandra, we have the humiliated Agamemnon and the ignominious Aegisthus.[122]

---

[119]   Thomson (1) 288: cf. 289 ('the principle of male precedence, now formally ratified as the basis of democracy . . .'); 291 ('the matricide is acquitted by an appeal to historical expediency'). Professor Thomson's treatment of the whole subject raises many questions upon which anthropologists are far from agreed. For the purposes of the present argument, it can be granted that Aeschylus was consciously envisaging the change from a tribal to a democratic society, in the former of which women enjoyed a greater freedom than in the latter. The actual setting of the story is, of course, the aristocratic half-way stage, in which the institution of marriage is firmly established and male supremacy strongly marked, and in which the blood-feud is seen operating within the family and not the clan. Nor is it necessary to examine the hypothesis that the Erinyes were – and were thought by Aeschylus to be – originally associated with matrilineal descent. In the trilogy they have, in theory, an equal interest in both parents (cf. *Eum.* 512). The dramatic situation forces them, however, to be bitter partisans of the mother (cf. *Eum.* 210), though they do not – and could not logically – disparage the man-father in the way that Apollo disparages the woman-mother.

[120]   Thomson (1) 306.

[121]   See p. 108 above.

[122]   And the Watchman, the Herald, and the Elders – all dominated by the queen's superior personality. The Elders, in particular, play the feminine role to her, as is pointed out in n. 16. It is largely for this reason that, with some hesitation, I retain the closing pages of my article, though they have been criticized by scholars otherwise in sympathy with its main tenor: by Vickers 432 n. 33, and by Macleod (1) n. 82 (who describes them as 'an aberration'). To suggest, as I have done, that Aeschylus may not have been entirely happy about the humiliating status of women in Athenian society perhaps goes beyond the evidence. What should be abundantly clear is that, not content to present his audience with a wicked and a dangerous woman, he showed himself aware of the tragic predicament of a woman possessed of outstanding gifts of intelligence and will-power living in a male-dominated society. No doubt, in company with his male contemporaries, he accepted as a necessary feature of society that men must lead. But the female population of Athens will have included women with every variety of gifts – the potential Artemisia, the actual Aspasia, the imaginable Lysistrata. Aware of this (as Aeschylus presumably was), did he regard the social

But Clytemnestra, it will be said, is an abnormal woman, in that she has the mental characteristics of a man. This is true, and it is the cause of a personal tragedy which is almost Sophoclean. This tragedy, given its final touch of irony by the words of Athena, is absolute, since it was impossible in Clytemnestra's own society, and equally impossible in democratic Athens, for a woman of dominating will and intelligence to exploit her gifts to her own satisfaction and for the advantage of the community. The underlying social problem is one which has only been solved partially and intermittently in human history. If Aeschylus, who had fought against Artemisia at Salamis,[123] realized the normal predicament of such a woman in a predominantly male society, this does not mean that he saw how it could be avoided, or that, when he made Athena proclaim the primacy of the male, he did not share the view of his contemporaries that it was a necessary basis of society, to which the very existence of such a woman as Clytemnestra was a menace. The words of Athena, at that solemn moment, were not vain; nor could they be. Yet, even so, we have not perhaps exhausted the significance of the theme.

The trilogy treats of the relationship between man and woman and of the institution of marriage. Against this institution Clytemnestra rebels, partly because it is ill adapted to such as her, partly because, in the matter of Iphigenia, her husband had violated the basis of mutual respect upon which marriage should stand. Clytemnestra is not only the tragic exception, over whom the general rule rides roughshod: she is a symbol of all wives and mothers who suffer from the inferior status of the woman in marriage. It is for this reason, if for no other, that the dramatist has taken pains that Iphigenia shall not be forgotten in *Eumenides*.[124] The foundation of the Areopagus solved, triumphantly, the social problem of homicide. Did Athena's proclamation of male superiority solve the social problem of the relationship of the sexes in marriage? Did democratic Athens in the fifth century solve this problem, or did Aeschylus think that it had done so?

Athens did not. We need not indeed suppose that the most extreme statements of feminine subjection tell the whole truth, or that no respectable woman in Athens had any scope for the development of her personality, or that there was no equality, no mutual respect, in any

structure with complacency? Perhaps he did. I repeat, however, that the men in *Agamemnon* cut a poor figure by comparison with the women – nor does the 'male chauvinist' god have the *beau rôle* in *Eumenides*! See also n. 125 below.

[123] See Herodotus 8 *passim* esp. ch. 93. Her high status among Xerxes' commanders, in counsel and in fight, will have been known to Aeschylus and may well have impressed him.

[124] See p. 122 above and n. 107.

Athenian marriage. There is evidence to the contrary.[125] But the impression remains that in this field of social life the Athenians had, on the whole, failed to achieve a harmonious balance and, in degrading the status of women, had committed an injustice which damaged their society. Euripides was very conscious of this, and his Medea speaks for her sex. But did not Clytemnestra do the like? It is hard to believe that Aeschylus, whose women have such powers and courage, regarded with complacency a state of affairs which can have changed but little in the generation which separates Oresteia from Medea.

For the interest which Aeschylus shows in the social relationship of the sexes it may not be easy to account, since (unlike the problem of political homicide) we have no reason to suppose that it was a burning issue in Athenian politics. The fact remains, testified in more than one trilogy. At this point we badly miss the end of the Danaid trilogy, which Aeschylus may have been able to take for granted, when in the closing scene of Eumenides he passes to other themes. For the earlier trilogy also dealt with the institution of marriage; and, if it led to the conclusion that the married lot must be accepted by women, it is not unlikely that it was also concerned with their dignity in marriage.[126] Oresteia makes by implication the same claim on behalf of women – a claim which was, broadly, not met by Athenian society. Aeschylus, who regarded, and rightly regarded, the Athenian democracy as a new peak in social achievement (to which the closing scenes of Eumenides are, in one aspect, a triumphant hymn) was not necessarily its blind propagandist.[127] Athena, who inaugurates the new order with dignity and patience, does not necessarily speak the final word

---

[125] Cf. A. W. Gomme, CPh 20 (1925) 1–25 = Essays in Greek history and literature (Oxford 1937) 89–115. His article was salutary and stimulating, but rather tendentious. Of the subsequent literature on the 'social position of women in classical Athens', which is large and increasing, I will only mention J. P. Gould's masterly survey in JHS 100 (1980) 38–59, which must be the starting-point for future work. He examines law and custom, which are relatively objective, but also evidence from the rich corpus of mythology bearing upon the complex emotional attitudes of Greek men towards the sexual duality. For it is male attitudes that meet us wherever we look, and female reactions are a matter of hazardous inference. We learn that a woman might on occasion discuss politics with a man (Gould, op. cit. 50), but only in the home! Did intelligent women resent this restriction? We do not know. Was the relative freedom of the demi-monde widely envied? We do not know. Did they *feel* that they were, in Marxist terms, 'an exploited class'?

[126] See ch. 3 above.

[127] The sensibility of the artist is bound to detect and likely to reveal the flaws that inevitably mar the harmony of any social or political system. It is this, in part, which gives him his social importance; and the more deeply he is 'committed' to some creed the less likely he is to perform this vital function. I see no reason why Aeschylus should not have praised the just achievements of Athenian democracy without being blind to its actual or potential defects.

of the wisdom of Zeus, when she gives her vote to Orestes with such an explicit absence of sympathy for the opposite cause. To achieve her ends she employs the sovereign democratic virtue of Persuasion; yet $\Pi\epsilon\iota\theta\acute{\omega}$ had work still to do, in creating a just social order, which was beyond the imagination of this masculine goddess, but not perhaps beyond the poet's.

CHAPTER SEVEN

Orestes and Apollo

To take apart the intricate fabric of *Oresteia* is a hazardous business. In *Agamemnon*, it is not too unsatisfactory to handle separately the motivation of a hero whose actions have a public character determined by a war which has reached its conclusion; and with his death interest in him as a person, though not as a force and a cause, wanes, if it does not disappear. Clytemnestra, however, remains to play her role in *Choephori* and even, as a ghost, in *Eumenides* – a Clytemnestra whose concerns might at first sight appear domestic, but which on examination prove to have an important public aspect.[1] The theme of male domination is taken up and developed; and it is in this context that we have already been introduced to Orestes and Apollo and the conflict of powers in *Eumenides*. There is a great social issue, which is that of the right relation of men and women in society. But there is another, which is homicide, shed blood crying out for vengeance, blood-vengeance by the next of kin, the shedding of fresh blood which itself cries out for vengeance. This too is a concern of Aeschylus, but focused, as tragedy often is, on the extreme case, where the killing of a husband by his wife demands the killing of a mother by her son. Vengeance through matricide: on this twofold theme *Choephori*, in its narrow setting of palace and tomb, with its Chorus of household-slaves, insists relentlessly.[2]

What sort of a play is it? How do its action and structure compare with those of its predecessor? A man returns home and is killed by a woman: a

---

[1] Gagarin 87ff. has an interesting chapter on 'sexual and political conflict in the *Oresteia*,' which he sees as being, in an important aspect, a conflict between male and female values, the former being essentially military (and ruthless) and preoccupied with prowess and success, the latter being more concerned with the effects of action upon individuals and the *oikos* (and the home community), with pollution and formal religious observances. He finds the same conflict in *Septem* (his 151ff.) and a parallel between Agamemnon and Eteocles.

[2] The main stress is on the *oikos*, though the *polis* is not lost to sight, cf. 302ff., 431, 864.

man returns home and kills a woman; it is the same woman, the men are father and son. There is a remarkable parallelism of structure, most striking on the visual plane, for in each play there is disclosed a tableau, the killer standing above his two victims, one male, one female, and a blood-stained fabric is seen. The killer makes speeches justifying the act. The murders are preceded in both plays by a confrontation of killer and victim, a tense dialogue which has the character of a contest of wills. These parallels have often been remarked: less obvious, but no less significant, is a parallelism in the first half of the plays. Has Troy fallen? Can the evidence be trusted? Has Orestes returned? Can the evidence be trusted?[3] That the evidence shall not be overwhelmingly convincing is in each case essential to the irony. For the news, in *Choephori* as in *Agamemnon*, is of a longed-for return; and it is true. True, but disastrous. The fall of Troy means the death of Agamemnon; the return of Orestes means matricide.

The purpose of all these parallels must be to compare the actions, to bring out between them a similarity – or it might be a difference. Is the act of vengeance represented as better or worse, more or less tolerable, than the crime avenged? What difference does it make to the case of Orestes that he has been sent by Apollo? Orestes will ultimately be acquitted: in what way, if any, does he show himself to deserve acquittal? How easily, and by what stages, did he come to matricide? Finally, there is that nagging question which haunts the criticism of Aeschylus: how interested are we invited to become in Orestes as a person? All these questions arise, and, if they interlock, they can to some extent be considered separately.

Is it the similarity which is being brought out by the structural parallels or is it also a difference? In the disastrous history, is the second phase in some way less terrible than the first? Or is it a culmination of horror? At this point we must beware of introducing arguments from *Eumenides* which the audience has not yet heard. What they *have* heard is the words of Cassandra (*Agam.* 1280ff.). The exile will return – 'the mother-killing child, avenger of his father' – to put the coping-stone ($\theta\rho\iota\gamma\kappa\dot{\omega}\sigma\omega\nu$) for his kin upon these disasters ($\ddot{\alpha}\tau\alpha\varsigma$).[4] What they will hear at the end of this play is words of the Coryphaeus (*Ch.* 1065ff.) telling of a third storm-wind which has struck the royal house, how a third agent has come as saviour – or as *moros* (should she say?): saviour because he seemed to be liberating the house from tyranny, fatal because the outcome of the matricide threatens its

---

[3] The psychology of *elpis* varies according to the situation. In *Agamemnon* it is not until the Chorus wish to disbelieve that they seriously question the evidence (475ff.); in *Choephori* Electra is longing to believe, but in an agony of suspense (211).

[4] Cf. *Cho.* 932 ($\dot{\epsilon}\pi\dot{\eta}\kappa\rho\iota\sigma\epsilon\nu$).

extinction.[5] *Oresteia* is a drama in which things get worse before they get better!

The point is arguable: what should be beyond argument is the similarity – the avenging son like the mother who was herself an avenger. And there is another question we should not forget to ask. How does he, the son who kills his mother, compare with the father who killed his daughter? While we are on parallels, we should note two passages which, on the plane of imagery, may be felt to relate the two plays. The first is in the recognition-scene – the last place, it might be thought, where, amid the joy of reunion, sinister suggestions of an evil heredity could be introduced. And yet here are to be found, without strain or jar, one explicit and two unmistakable symbolic references to the sacrifice of Iphigenia. Electra greets Orestes (238–43) as one who has a fourfold claim on her affection, not brother only, but father and mother and sister, for to him returns the love owing to 'her who was sacrificed without pity' (τυθείσης νηλεῶς). We cannot suppose Electra to be criticizing her father, but those who had heard the earlier play were bound to recall how Aeschylus represented the sacrifice as a cruel and sacrilegious act. The second reference is made by means of a leading metaphor from *Agamemnon*. Orestes compares the two of them to the young of a dead eagle, orphaned and starving: 'for they are powerless to bring the paternal prey to their dwelling-place' (250f.).[6] Agamemnon was an eagle and his prey was Troy, but, as the omen foreshadowed, Troy at the cost of Iphigenia.[7] In the third instance, the notion of sacrifice returns in a fresh context. Orestes prays to Zeus to save the children of his sacrificial priest (θυτῆρος, 255). Those who can believe that, after *tutheises* above, the word *thuter* does not echo a phrase in *Agamemnon* (ἔτλα δ'οὖν θυτὴρ γενέσθαι θυγατρός, 224) are welcome to their faith, which is stronger than mine! Orestes continues: 'Whence will you have from a like hand the tribute of a fine repast?'[8] What is the point of all these references? Surely that these are children of Agamemnon, that the young eagles will soon show their power to bring home to the eyrie prey

---

[5] Cf. 855ff. The Chorus, always particularly concerned with the fortunes of the house, think that the issue hangs on the ensuing conflict between Orestes and Aegisthus (cf. ἀνδροδαΐκτων, 860) which will either bring destruction or salvation to it. The death-cry of Aegisthus follows, but so does the entry of Clytemnestra. Kill her, and the alternative (ἤ . . . ἤ) is false, the extinction of the house will be threatened as much by the success as by the failure of Orestes, its survival only secured by the outcome of the trial at Athens (*Eum.* 754ff.).

[6]   οὐ γὰρ ἐντελεῖς
θήραν πατρῴαν προσφέρειν σκηνήμασιν.

[7] See ch. 5, *passim*.

[8]   πόθεν
ἕξεις ὁμοίας χειρὸς εὔθοινον γέρας;

such as their father brought, that the hand that prepares *this* sacrifice will be *homoia*.[9] There follows immediately the account of Apollo's oracle.

From the eagle-metaphor and Agamemnon we turn to the snake-metaphor and Clytemnestra. It is prepared in the passage we have just been considering. Agamemnon was an eagle, who had died in the coils of a viper, who was Clytemnestra (249). In due course we learn of her dream. She had dreamt of a snake that was her own child and drew blood from her breast (527–33). When Orestes hears of this, he eagerly accepts the omen and in plain terms announces that, turned to snake (ἐκδρακοντωθείς, 549), he will kill his mother. He will be a snake as Clytemnestra was a snake; and, as she killed by craft, so shall she be taken in the same snare she used: so ran Apollo's oracle (558). Thus, not only is Orestes the young eagle who will carry back to the nest prey like his father's, but he is also the child of a snake who will use against his mother craft like hers. Each of these equations is immediately followed by a reference to Apollo. The similarity between children and parents is disconcerting; the mention of the god should be reassuring — and is so to the actors. Should it also reassure the audience? Is the similarity between the actions brought out by the general structure of the plays and by these particular parallels fallacious — fallacious because it discounts the intervention of Apollo? What difference does it make to the case of Orestes that he had been sent by Apollo to avenge his father?

Since Apollo is a bright god and his opponents so repulsive, since the prestige of his oracle was so great (and its pronouncements often so enlightened), since he claims to be the spokesman of Zeus (and was commonly so regarded), since in the outcome Orestes goes free, the view has frequently been taken that the Apollonian command in some way simplifies the issue, distinguishing Orestes' act from other killings in the house of Atreus, absolving him, so that we only wait for the ultimate triumph of the god. Such a view may indeed have been held at Delphi.[10] I would suggest, however, that Apollo is used by Aeschylus not to simplify, but to complicate the issue.

We must not read Greek dramas backwards; we must not read *Agamemnon* and *Choephori* in the light of a play which the audience had not yet seen and heard. The Aeschylean Apollo is a mysterious and ambivalent figure. The allusions to him in *Agamemnon* are tantalizing. Briefly, in men's hopes he is the Healer (146, 512), in his actions the Destroyer — of the

---

[9] Contrast 141 (χείρά τ' εὐσεβεστέραν).

[10] Cf. *CR* 47 (1933) 98. In this chapter I have incorporated material from that article written many years ago (and too much under the influence of Wilamowitz). The basic argument remains unchanged.

Greeks before Troy (510f.) and, in more than one sense, of Cassandra; he is
Paean and Apollon.[11] In *Choephori* his oracle looms over the action. It is
likely to have been mentioned in the *prologos*;[12] it is reported by Orestes at
269ff.; absent from the *kommos*, it returns at 555ff.; the Delphic Apollo is
sung, among other gods, at 783ff. and, with special emphasis, at 935ff.;[13]
between those choruses comes the climax of action and the intervention of
Pylades (900ff.); after the action, at 1029ff., three times we have from
Orestes the oracular name of Loxias; almost immediately he sees the
Erinyes; encouraged by the Chorus, he leaves for Delphi as his one
recourse. Orestes is impelled towards matricide by Apollo.

But not by Apollo alone. Whereas *Eumenides* (till near the end) is
marked by a divergence of divine powers, *Choephori* is marked by a
convergence of powers all driving Orestes towards the same act. Of major
gods there is Zeus (of whom more must be said), and Hermes (link between
two worlds),[14] and Apollo. But the great *kommos*, from which Apollo is
absent (though Zeus is not), is directed towards the chthonian world and
the powers that there belong. Among them are those Erinyes who preside
over blood-vengeance (400ff.). It is not, however, in the *kommos* that we
first, in this play, hear of Erinyes. At 269 Orestes speaks of the oracle of
Loxias and continues to speak of it for nearly thirty lines. We shall return to
this passage, merely noting here the extraordinary fact that, barring the
first line, it is wholly taken up with the penalties which threaten Orestes, if
he fails to pursue those guilty of his father's death, fails, that is to say, to 'kill
in return' (ἀνταποκτεῖναι, 274); and that these penalties are chthonian in
origin and character.[15] He will suffer grievous plagues arising from the

---

[11] Cf. *Agam.* 1082. The god's relationship to Cassandra is veiled in a sinister mystery: note the horrified
question of the Coryphaeus at 1204. The twofold aspect of the god is brought out at 1072ff. in terms
of a contrast of songs (cf. Haldane 38f.). Cf. *Cho.* 340ff., on which see n. 23 below.

[12] A trace of this may have survived in Aristoph. *Frogs* 1141–3, which is paratragedic, largely, in style
and metre and could have come from a passage corresponding to *Cho.* 556ff.

[13] On these two choruses, see App. H.

[14] For a valuable discussion of Hermes' role, see Garvie (2) 84ff. Cf. also ch. 8, p. 162 (and n. 25).

[15] 275 is still a puzzle – a three-word line in which no word can be interpreted with certainty
(ἀποχρημάτοισι ζημίαις ταυρούμενον). 'Maddened to fury at the deprivation of my substance'
(Headlam). But the personal motives of Orestes wait for 298ff. and are intrusive here, where all the
stress is on the command and threats of Apollo. ζημίαις should refer to penalties exacted whether
by or from Orestes. But which? Mazon translates: 'En écartant, farouche, les peines qui ne privent
que d'argent': a refusal, that is, to accept monetary compensation (thus amplifying τρόπον τὸν
αὐτόν). This interpretation is popular (cf. Tucker, Rose) and is perhaps the best bet, though there is
no other hint of 'blood-price' in the trilogy and ταυρούμενον is unduly strong. Accepting
Hartung's transference of 275 to follow 277, one could wish to take ζημίαις of the penalties about
to be described and ταυρούμενον of the state of the victim (cf. Soph. *OT* 478 and Wilamowitz (2)
182), but in that case one can (*pace* Wilamowitz) make no good sense of ἀποχρημάτοισι, since
Orestes' *economic* situation, already deplorable, will not be significantly worsened if he fails to
avenge.

earth; he will be attacked by Erinyes brought to fulfilment by his father's blood. If this passage stood alone, it would still be significant, but it does not. The warning or threat comes back with epigrammatic clarity at the climax of the play, in the stichomythic dialogue between mother and son (924f.). 'Watch out,' says Clytemnestra, 'for the wrathful hounds of a mother.' 'But how,' replies Orestes, 'if I let this pass, am I to escape a father's hounds?'[16] The dilemma is absolute; and it is Apollonian. Later still, when Orestes feels his sanity wavering, he asserts that he killed his mother 'not without justice' and cites as his chief ground of confidence 'the Pythian prophet Loxias who proclaimed that, having done this deed, I should be free of an evil charge but, having left it undone – I will not speak the penalty' (1029ff.).[17] The aposiopesis is all the more effective that within twenty lines he cries out at the sight of Erinyes. (If we must not read *Choephori* with foreknowledge of *Eumenides*, it may be that we should not forget these passages of the earlier play when we read the opening scene of the later.)[18]

Orestes was impelled towards matricide by Apollo – but an Apollo who appears to stand in a strange association, if not alliance, with the chthonian world. But our study of 269ff. has not yet taken us to the close of the speech. At the end of his grisly recital, Orestes asks a question. 'Are those such oracles as one should trust?' ($\tau o\iota o\hat{\iota}\sigma\delta\epsilon$ $\chi\rho\eta\sigma\mu o\hat{\iota}s$ $\hat{a}\rho a$ $\chi\rho\dot{\eta}$ $\pi\epsilon\pi o\iota\theta\acute{\epsilon}\nu a\iota$; 297) And he goes on to say that, even if he trusts them not, he has his motives. So translated into English, the question might seem to imply scepticism or a reluctance to accept the oracular pronouncement. Nowhere else in the play, however, is there a trace of such a reaction on his part. Nor is it likely that the words look back simply to the opening statement that Loxias' oracle will not betray him (269f.). The plural noun and its qualification ($\tau o\iota o\hat{\iota}\sigma\delta\epsilon$) can only refer to the long catalogue of horrors. We must remember that, in Greek, a question with $\hat{a}\rho a$ can be neutral, it can also imply the answer 'Yes' or the answer 'No'.[19] What, then, does Orestes mean? What reaction could the recital evoke? Not, surely, mistrust of the oracle, but quite the reverse. Backed by such threats as these, how can it fail to carry conviction? When he continues: 'Even if I

---

[16]   Κλ. ὅρα, φύλαξαι μητρὸς ἐγκότους κύνας.
                 Ορ. τὰς τοῦ πατρὸς δὲ πῶς φύγω, παρεὶς τάδε;

[17]   καὶ φίλτρα τόλμης τῆσδε πλειστηρίζομαι
                 τὸν πυθόμαντιν Λοξίαν, χρήσαντ' ἐμοὶ
                 πράξαντα μὲν ταῦτ' ἐκτὸς αἰτίας κακῆς
                 εἶναι, παρέντα δ' – οὐκ ἐρῶ τὴν ζημίαν.

[18] See p. 152 below.
[19] Denniston, *The Greek particles* (Oxford 1934) 46f. On a possible ambiguity here see n. 48.

trust them not, the deed must be done' and lists the human motives which drive him on, he is adding, not substituting: oracle or no oracle, there are many convergent reasons for his action — not only a god's commands, but grief for a father, the poverty of exile, the usurpation of his city now under the rule of 'two women'.[20] His thoughts turn to Aegisthus.[21]

Immediately there follows that *kommos* which is, technically and poetically, the most striking feature of the play. It is a lyric of great length, complexity and power; and any interpretation which does not attempt to do it justice stands self-condemned. It has indeed engaged the attention of distinguished scholars and evoked outstanding works of scholarship.[22] Yet it remains a problem, and that not only because the text, where it is not patently corrupt, is often hard to interpret. Of this lyric, from which Apollo is absent,[23] but which is yet deeply concerned with the impulse towards matricide, the tendency and purpose are often debatable. Some things, however, can be said with reasonable confidence.

Its traffic is with the infernal world (so recently brought to our attention in the preceding speech). It is addressed, largely, to the dead Agamemnon and to the powers of that world to which he now belongs. It is the *goos*, the ritual lamentation that he has never properly had, but it is also an incantation to secure his aid towards vengeance and culminates in an *epoide*. In both capacities it is full of ritual motifs and language. It is lyric, and (though this has, strangely, been denied) in it the role of the Chorus is of primary importance and in some degree governs its complex structure.[24]

---

[20] 299–304. One can feel no confidence that we have the words as Aeschylus wrote them. θεοῦ ἐφετμαί is surprising after 298, since it is not plausible to distinguish (with Rose, II, 147) between the commands and the threats. We must fall back on the explanation that the force of τε is here 'not only' (cf. Denniston, op. cit. 515, though his illustrations are not encouraging). Even so, the commands (as distinguished from a desire to obey those commands) are oddly described as a ἵμερος. Yet πολλοί . . . ἵμεροι must refer to the whole cluster of motives. Last and worst, the construction of 302f. is hardly tolerable as it stands, since τὸ μὴ . . . πέλειν is not a consequence, still less a purpose, of the pressure of poverty. Something has gone seriously wrong, whether we are to athetize 299–301 with the earlier Wilamowitz or simply shake our heads with the later, whose formula should be restated as follows: *ut minime laudanda, ita vix toleranda*. Orestes' mind has not yet begun to totter and, when it does, it totters in lucid Greek.

[21] For the stress on Aegisthus, cf. e.g. ch. 6, p. 114.

[22] Wilamowitz (2) 186ff.; W. Schadewaldt, *Hermes* 67 (1932) 312–54; A. Lesky, *Sitzungsberichte Wiener Akademie Phil.-hist. Klasse* 221 (1943) 1–127 (who reviews earlier interpretations on pp. 4–9). See also Lebeck 93–5, 110–30. To all of these works I am indebted in ways which need not be specified in detail.

[23] We need not suppose the audience to *forget* Apollo — and the striking speech which has immediately preceded — as they listen to the *kommos*. Those who retained some memory of *Agamemnon*, when they heard *Cho.* 341ff. with its contrast of θρῆνος and παιών, might well have recalled *Agam.* 1072ff. *paion/paian* is in any case a contaminated word, cf. *Agam.* 645, *Cho.* 151.

[24] The structure of the *kommos* is unusually complicated. After the introductory anapaests (306–14), it can be considered in three (if not four) sections. (i) 315–422. Four triads, or groups of three stanzas,

Their positive role is indicated at the outset by the introductory anapaests of the Coryphaeus (306–14) which state the *lex talionis* – a theme which is then dropped to be picked up later at the appropriate moment. What is it, then, that the Chorus actually does by its lyric stanzas and, in the first section of the song, by the anapaests of the Coryphaeus which separate the triads? (i) It encourages the children to have confidence in their ability to reach the dead and the ability of the dead to help them (324ff., 354ff.).[25] (ii) When the children retreat into fantasy, the Chorus confronts them with reality, including the real fact that there is a woman to be killed (388). There is a reference to children (in a corrupt text, 379) and, from Orestes, to parents (in one which is ambiguous and obscure, 385).[26] (iii) Orestes and Electra appeal to a Zeus who seems at one moment to belong to the infernal, at the next to the supernal, world;[27] Electra appeals to Earth and the 'honours of the chthonians'. The time has come for the Coryphaeus to recall the *lex talionis*, in the specific form of blood for blood, and to associate it with an Erinys (400ff.). The first occurrence of that dreadful name since Orestes gave his account of Apollo's oracle will have been marked by an audience which knew that, by tradition, Orestes was himself to be pursued by Erinyes. Now he calls upon the 'mighty Curses of the dead' to look upon the plight and dishonour of the Atridae (405–7); he calls

sung in order by Orestes, Chorus, Electra. Orestes leads and Electra follows, taking her subject-matter from him; and their stanzas are in strophic correspondence. The stanzas of the Chorus correspond, the first with the second triad, the third with the fourth. The triads are separated by anapaests intoned by the Coryphaeus. The scheme is thus: α β α (anap.) γ β γ (anap.) δ ε δ (anap.) ζ ε ζ. (ii) 423–55. The scheme is as follows: η (Ch.) θ (El.) ι (Or.) ι (Ch.) η (El.) θ (Ch.). This is surprising (see n. 29 below) – slightly less so perhaps if we take the first two stanzas together, and the last two, as corresponding metrical units and regard the arrangement as chiastic (though the outside elements are divided differently between the singers). The phenomenon is unparalleled. (iii) 456–65. A pair of stanzas including the formal invocation, each consisting of a line from Orestes, a line from Electra, and three lines from the Chorus. (iv) A short pair of stanzas from the Chorus, followed by closing anapaests.

25 354ff. are rightly interpreted by Lesky, op. cit. The Chorus correct the pessimistic implications of Orestes' 345ff.: Agamemnon is still powerful in the world below.

26 The received text of 378f. is clearly corrupt. The preceding lines, while sound, are already ambiguous in their bearing. For, if (i) Agamemnon is dead and (ii) the murderers are in power (which seems to be the surface meaning of the 'double lash'), the two points are made in such a way as to remind us that (i) help *will* come from the world below (cf. 476ff.) and (ii) impurity of hand is bound to be punished. The stimulus to action is thus a guarantee of success. As for 378f., it is hardly worth sorting out the less probable of the remedies which have been suggested. One may suspect that here also there is ambiguity, that the hands of the children are destined to a greater impurity. But this is highly speculative (and hardly comports with the perfect γεγένηται). The interpretation of 385 (τοκεῦσι δ' ὅμως τελεῖται) has been much debated. The web of parent–child relationships throughout the trilogy invites ambiguities from *Agam.* 155 (τεκνόποινος) onwards; and one may suspect that three notions may be present: (i) payment for a father's death; (ii) payment rendered by a mother; (iii) payment for a mother's death. On both passages cf. Lebeck 116–19.

27 See also ch. 8, pp. 163f.

on Zeus in desperation, but says nothing of his own role. More is needed. Electra comes to the fore; and with her reference to 'all that we have suffered at the hands of parents' (418f.) the *kommos* passes into a new phase, which is one of narrative. (iv) The Chorus now joins her in narrating the *atimia* of Agamemnon's burial and his mutilation by Clytemnestra;[28] and this leads up to the formal invocation, but first to the first clear statement by Orestes that he will kill his mother.[29]

It would, surely, be perverse to deny that there is a sequence of emotions here, a progression through lack of confidence and retreat from reality to that firm resolution to act which the Chorus commends towards the end of the *kommos* (452, 455).[30] Does this mean, however, that the pressures of the *kommos* were necessary to bring a hesitant Orestes to the point of action? That its purpose should be interpreted, significantly, in terms of his mind? The matter has been much debated and is not easily settled. But it brings us back to questions which have already been posed:[31] how easily and by what stages did he come to matricide? in what way, if any, does he show himself to deserve acquittal?

An oblique approach may be useful. There is a third party to the *kommos*: not only the Chorus, not only Orestes, but Electra. Electra we have already seen: indeed she is the centre of interest from the end of the *parodos* to the moment of recognition. Bidden to take offerings to her father's grave, she asks the Chorus in what terms she should pray. Prompted by the Coryphaeus, she makes a prayer which, combining all its elements, implies the matricide, but, though she speaks of mother and of father, she uses of the enemy generalized plurals and a verb of dying, not of killing (ἀντικατθανεῖν, 144).[32] Is this a shrinking from the implications of her prayer? Is it part of a characterization? Her courtesy to the Chorus – her all but deference – is appealing; she is womanly and would be chaste and pious (140f.), asking if a retaliatory killing is a pious request to make of the

---

[28] *Maschalismos* (cf. Soph. *El.* 444–6): a gruesome – and futile – precaution against vengeance from the dead, the hands and feet being cut off and tied under the armpits of the corpse.

[29] Transpose 434–8 to follow 455 (Weil, Wilamowitz, Lesky), and this statement of resolve comes as the climax to this whole section of the *kommos* ('Dieses τείσει wirkt wie ein Blitz', Lesky, op. cit. 93); in addition a more normal arrangement of corresponding stanzas is produced. Despite Lesky's powerful advocacy, however, the temptation to transpose should probably be resisted, cf. Schadewaldt, op cit. in n. 22. (See also Groeneboom's judicious note *ad loc.*) Nor need we tamper with the received text of the stanza, despite the neatness of Herwerden/Page. There is, however, a case for punctuating, with Headlam: τὸ πᾶν ἀτίμως ἔλεξας; οἴμοι, πατρὸς δ' ἀτίμωσιν κτλ.

[30] 455: πρέπει δ' ἀκάμπτῳ μένει καθήκειν. Cf. 512 (ἐπειδὴ δρᾶν κατώρθωσαι φρενί).

[31] See p. 133 above.

[32] A small point not to be pressed, but perhaps deliberate.

gods (122).[33] Turn to the *kommos*. In the first phases she is at one with Orestes, but at 418ff. it is she who steers the song on to a new course. 'What should we say to hit the mark?' Whether the mark is the dead father or (more probably) the living brother, the answer is clear: it is the griefs they have suffered at the hands of 'parents'. They are griefs that cannot be assuaged, and her wrath is like a ravening wolf (421). She goes on to join the Chorus in the whole horrible story of her father's burial, which she and they know and Orestes does not. Shrinking woman into ravening wolf: is this a psychological progression? Or is it rather the unfolding of implications?

Perhaps Electra does not matter: she is going to be jettisoned.[34] Perhaps it is different with Orestes, who must strike the blow, who will be pursued by Furies. Does *he* shrink? In the *prologos*, such of it as we possess, his determination to avenge is firmly stated. Is there sign thereafter that resolution is lacking? There is a tendency, often noted and clearly deliberate on the part of the writer, for generalized plurals to be used of the prospective victims, but it is shared by Orestes not only with Electra but with the bloodthirsty Chorus.[35] Divergence from matricide in the direction of Aegisthus admits of a different explanation.[36] Still, one must be fair. However limited an interest Aeschylus may have had in individual psychology, it remains true that, in a general way, he depicts real people acting plausibly in a real situation – acting within the moral code of a real society.[37] Orestes is to act within a society for which the parent is a supreme object of *aidos*. At the moment of crisis he will ask whether he is to respect his mother's breast (896ff.). To be a matricide in principle is one thing, to strike the blow perhaps another; even to *say* that one will strike

---

[33] No question could be more central to the tragedy.

[34] To be picked up in their different ways by Sophocles and Euripides. 'This uncompromising abandonment of a named character is remarkable . . . She has played her part and so she is dispensed with' (Taplin 340). Having no part in the sexual pattern, she would have been an embarrassment to the development of a major theme. There was even a dramaturgical necessity for the interest in personality, so marked in the case of Clytemnestra, to be diminished as the trilogy went on. The final play was to be a play of gods, and in it Orestes will have a strictly subordinate role (cf. Macleod (1) 140). No more in *Choephori*, despite his major role, does his individuality matter as does that of Clytemnestra in *Agamemnon*. Whether Electra is jettisoned before or after 691ff. is another matter. 'She does not of course say 691ff' (Taplin). Despite the advocacy of Headlam, one should no doubt regard the ascription of that speech to her as a lost cause; and I should be happy to do so, could I find the lines really pointed in the mouth of Clytemnestra, and were I not reluctant to abandon the subtle double irony, if they are spoken by Electra. As it is, I print a revised version of *CR* 60 (1946) 58ff. as App. F.

[35] 117, 144, 273, 367, 377. Cf. Lebeck 116. (The list includes the oracle as quoted by Orestes!)

[36] See ch. 6, p. 114.

[37] On the importance of social values for an understanding of Aeschylean characterization: see ch. 5, pp. 96ff.

the blow is a stage. And Orestes says it, but not until a certain point has been reached in the mental progress of the *kommos*. It seems pedantic to deny that, in some way, it has served as a necessary preparation for his task. What is important is to observe what turns the scale.

Orestes was impelled towards matricide by the oracle of Apollo, by a Chorus which urges the claims of the infernal world and sets out the *lex talionis*, but also by motives on the human plane, personal to himself, yet intimately bound up with the house to which he belongs. It is important to observe how this theme runs through the play. Among those precious lines from the opening of the play preserved for us in Aristophanes' *Frogs* is one which runs as follows: ἥκω γὰρ ἐς γῆν τήνδε καὶ κατέρχομαι, 'I am come to this land – I am come back'. The comic poet, as in duty bound, makes fun of it as pleonastic, but it is nothing of the kind. κατέρχεσθαι is a technical term for return from exile, and so this note is struck at the very outset.[38] What else Orestes may have said in this context we do not know, but in the recognition-scene there is strong emphasis upon the plight and destitution of the children, first from Electra (132–7) and then in a speech of Orestes which has already been examined (246ff.). The scene ends, after the account of the oracle, with a statement of human motives which are in themselves sufficient to require the action (which is matricide). They include deprivation of property and usurpation of authority. In the last, crucial and decisive phase of the *kommos* the emphasis is upon *atimia*, upon insult and outrage and the loss of honour which, if unrequited, they entail. It is the dishonour suffered by the dead Agamemnon, which rebounds upon his children, one an exile and the other a virtual slave, that turns the scale and evokes the direct threat of Orestes to his mother's life (434–8).[39] After a brief lyric invocation (456–65), the Chorus, who have pressed and won their point, but who understand far better than the actors the implications of what is happening, react with horror as they contemplate the intolerable griefs, the cruel bloody strife, of a fatal family. And yet they pray to the *makares chthonioi* for the victory of the children. After this miniature *stasimon* in two short stanzas the Chorus drops out and the song ends. There follows a second invocation in spoken trimeters.[40] Apart from two lines (to Gaia and Persephassa), all is addressed to the father, the vocative *pater* being repeated insistently. The tone is largely secular.[41] The

---

[38] Note that it closely follows the word κράτη in the first line, on which see ch. 6, p. 114.

[39] See n. 29 above.

[40] Cf. W. Schadewaldt, *Monolog und Selbstgespräch* (Berlin 1926) 144, on non-lyric 'doublets' following a lyrical scene.

[41] The prayer of Orestes at 497–9 is rather strangely expressed in the form of a strong alternative: *either*

themes especially picked up from the *kommos* are the destitution of the children and the dishonour of the father. There is much stress on the house; there is stress on *kratos* (480, 490, 499). 'Father, . . . to my prayer grant mastery of your house.' 'Send Justice . . . if, once mastered, you wish to be victorious in your turn.'[42] It is the masterful woman who stands in the way.

It might seem that there are three distinct and separable directions from which Orestes is impelled towards matricide.[43] There is Apollo's oracular command; there is the infernal world crying out for vengeance and lending its powers to secure it; there are human resentments at work in the mind of the avenger. Now one, now another, is highlighted in the economy of the play; and it is futile and superfluous to try to relate them in terms of the psychology of Orestes. It is superfluous because they are in essence one and the same or, at the least, aspects of the same homogeneous tragic justice which has met us at every point in the drama: retaliation based upon human resentments, yet leading to the punishment of offenders and so a law upheld by Zeus, but operated by Erinyes. It meets us in *Agamemnon*, and it meets us in *Choephori*: Zeus and the Erinys meet in the *kommos* (but this is a subject which must wait for a later chapter). Where, then, does Apollo's oracle stand? Does it stand in some significant way apart from the other two forces? This is a matter to which we must return later in the chapter, when we examine his role in *Eumenides*. For the present let it be noted that he too stands for retaliation by the next of kin nor is he innocent of association with the infernal world and its Erinyes. Perhaps his absence from the *kommos* is more apparent than real.

The closer the links between the impelling forces the more hazardous it may be to account for the mental processes of Orestes in terms of one or the other. When Dodds writes:[44] 'The divine purpose, of which both

---

send Dike (a personification) to fight alongside your friends *or* grant that they may get the same grip in return (upon their foes). For ὁμοίας, cf. 257, 274, 556f. (which explains what is meant here, i.e. craft). The alternative is illusory, since, in terms of the trilogy, human resentments are the means employed to effect the divine justice.

[42] εὔμορφον κράτος (490). 'His shining might' (Thomson (3)); 'la brillante victoire' (Mazon) – neither of them very close, and Wilamowitz's explanation of the epithet is rather laboured (Wilamowitz (2) 206). Groeneboom has a good parallel in Soph. *OT* 189 (εὐῶπα ἀλκάν). A matter of *bona verba* in a prayer? But more suited to the hymn-style of the Sophoclean chorus? One may suspect that here, as with some other εὐ-compounds in the trilogy, the epithet is related to the ubiquitous polarity of good and evil. A deity with infernal connections is asked to grant victory (or mastery) 'in a good form (or guise)', a prayer which cannot and will not be answered.

[43] Cf. Garvie (2) 82.

[44] Dodds (3) 30. This view of a 'humble' Orestes is one which I should be only too happy to accept, if I could find real evidence for it in the text. For a similar *plaidoyer*, cf. Peradotto 258–61; and Macleod (1) expresses some sympathy at p.140.

Agamemnon and Clytemnestra were unconscious and guilty agents, is for Orestes something consciously known and humbly, though not easily, accepted', Apollo's command is no doubt in mind. 'He is aware,' Dodds continues, 'that his act is a crime, even before he has committed it; but receiving it as a duty, he stands as a type of all those who take upon themselves "the necessary guilt of human action".' His quotation does not perhaps inspire confidence; and it is striking that from the play itself, to support his view, he cites a single line (930) coming at the close of a battle of wits which is not otherwise marked by a sense of criminality on the part of Orestes.[45] Dodds did not seek evidence in the *kommos*, though others might be inclined to do so. Indeed it is cardinal to Lesky's interpretation of that feature that an Orestes who has so far appeared as the agent of an external divine power now takes upon himself personal responsibility in full knowledge of what he is doing. But is it Orestes who learns or we, the audience? The *kommos* is fraught with ironical ambiguities, in the Aeschylean manner. When Electra sings (338): 'What of these things is well, what without evils?', she means that their situation is wholly bad, but uses much the same words as Agamemnon used at Aulis of his dilemma (*Agam.* 211). When, at 398, she demands 'justice out of unjust things' ($\delta\iota\kappa\alpha\nu$ δ' $\dot{\epsilon}\xi$ $\dot{\alpha}\delta\iota\kappa\omega\nu$ $\dot{\alpha}\pi\alpha\iota\tau\hat{\omega}$), she means, by a common Greek idiom, justice in place of injustice, but her words can equally suggest a justice resulting from unrighteous acts. No more, when Orestes, having declared that at his own hands Clytemnestra will pay the penalty, adds: 'Then may I perish!' (438), is he envisaging the threat of his own destruction which will follow, but merely using a cliché of familiar type.[46] When in the lyric invocation he sings (461): 'Ares will join battle with Ares, Dika with Dika', he does not envisage the coming conflict of rival causes so evenly poised in the matter of his own life and death. These things are for the audience, but not as revealing the minds of the singers.

'Orestes has not merely suffered his situation,' writes Dodds, 'but he has understood and in a sense mastered it.' How true is this? Let us look rapidly at the closing scenes. Clytemnestra uncovers her breast and bids Orestes reverence it ($\alpha\check{\iota}\delta\epsilon\sigma\alpha\iota$ 896ff.), whereupon he turns to Pylades with a question: 'Am I to shrink ($\alpha\check{\iota}\delta\epsilon\sigma\theta\hat{\omega}$) from killing my mother?' The breast is

---

[45] Dodds (3) adds: 'cf. 1016–17 and 1029', neither of which is striking evidence for a sense of criminality before the act.

[46] Cf. Groeneboom *ad loc.*, R. Hölzle, *Zum Aufbau der lyrischen Partien bei Aischylos* (diss., Freiburg i. Br. 1934) p. 55 n. 123, for examples of this *topos*. On Polynices' reported prayer at *Sept.* 636, see ch. 2, p. 50 n. 87. Is there not the same kind of irony here? Lebeck 200–1 ends a fair-minded paragraph with the words: 'This phrase is more than a stereotyped formula. It is a premonition of future torment.' But is it Orestes that has the premonition?

the supreme symbol of motherhood, the parent a supreme object of *aidos*. Pylades then speaks for Loxias; and his third line is most significant. 'Count as enemies any rather than the gods' (ἅπαντας ἐχθροὺς τῶν θεῶν ἡγοῦ πλέον, 902). If Orestes neglects the oracle, he will earn the enmity of Loxias, backed by all the pains the oracle foretold (269ff.). He kills his mother: he *dare* not do otherwise. What, though, if there are other hostile gods?[47] So far from 'mastering' his situation, he has not 'understood' it, until, first, he sees his mother's breast, then hears her threat of avenging hounds and, giving his answer, realizes the intolerable dilemma with which he is faced. He does *not* understand, until this late hour, that in responding to the threats of Apollo he lays himself open to precisely the same dangers from another quarter.[48] At last he understands his situation, but cannot master it without the aid of the god who has brought it about. No wonder he appears after the murder in the guise of a suppliant[49] and bound for Delphi, towards which we, with him, now move, Orestes pursued by Erinyes, we (it might be hoped) with a clear recollection of *Choephori*.

Apollo plays a prominent role in *Eumenides*. We see him first in his own oracular home: we see him twice. We see him with Orestes, whom he promises to guard and sends to Athens under escort of Hermes.[50] Later, after the Erinyes have been aroused by the ghost of Clytemnestra and have deployed into the orchestra, he reappears, bow in hand, and threatens to drive them from his precinct. In both scenes he expresses the utmost detestation of them. Apart from their hideous aspect (which the audience can now see), he has two points against them: that they are old (68f.), and that they are barbarous. That, he says, is where they properly belong, not in the temple, but in that barbarian world of castrations and impalements with which we are familiar from Herodotus (186ff.). He speaks, that is to say, for a younger generation of gods and for Hellenic civilization. To the

---

[47] Cf. *Eum.* 66.

[48] At this point we might return, tentatively, to 297. Is it so certain that this line does *not* relate to the opening words of the speech? A question introduced by ἆρα has a built-in possibility of ambiguity which can be exploited. Orestes means that he *must* trust the oracle, believe its threats and confide in its protection; by the 'danger' of 270, he – and the oracle – mean the obvious hazards of the enterprise. But the real danger is the pursuit by the Erinyes of his mother which it entails and which obedience to the god's command involves. Is such an oracle to be trusted? It will be long before we know the answer to that question.

[49] His role in the final play is essentially that of a suppliant (cf. Macleod (1) 140), which he plays appropriately. But too much stress can be laid upon this (and the approving adverb of the Prophetis at 44); and I should hesitate to say, with Macleod, that he shows the spirit of enlightened fear praised by the Furies.

[50] On the staging here and at 140ff. see Taplin 369ff. I am, however, reluctant to abandon the eccyclema and the tableau and am inclined to stick to the account I gave in 'The Delphic temple in Greek tragedy', *Miscellanea tragica: in honorem J. C. Kamerbeek* (Amsterdam 1976) 485–7.

violence of his language corresponds the physical threat of his bow (179ff.).
Before the Chorus leaves, there is a brief preliminary debate which, as we
have seen in an earlier chapter, lays out a basic issue of the trial-scene to
come, the Erinyes disregarding the tie of marriage, Apollo disregarding the
tie of blood.[51]

At *Cho.* 269f. Orestes said: 'The great-powered oracle of Loxias which
bids me go through with this danger will be no traitor.'[52] Noting duly that
this was immediately followed by the god's chthonian threats, we pass to
the end of the play, where Orestes prays to Apollo, and the Chorus sees the
only hope of purification in Loxias (1057ff.).[53] When, at *Eum.* 64, Apollo
speaks his first words, 'I will not betray' (οὔτοι προδώσω), they seem to
echo the words of Orestes in *Choephori.* At this point we should consider
what, actually, in the course of the play, Apollo does for Orestes. (i) He
accepts him as a suppliant (*hiketes, prostropaios*) and gives him sanctuary.[54]
This, however, is only a temporary refuge, and even in Apollo's temple he
is surrounded by his enemies. (ii) He purifies him, a prospect stressed in
Choephori. Yet this act of purification seems to have only a limited validity,
and the Erinyes continue to track him by the scent of blood. When he
reaches Athens, he claims to be free of pollution, but not in respect of
Apollo's ceremony alone. The theme seems to be handled with a deliberate
vagueness.[55] (iii) He sends him to the city of Pallas. 'There,' he says, 'with
judges of the case and with persuasive words, we shall find means to secure
that you are free once for all of these troubles' (81ff.). (iv) His last and
principal service was to bear witness at the trial and, virtually, conduct the
defence as, virtually, a co-defendant (579f.).

A jury, speeches and a verdict: the words of Apollo adumbrate the trial
to come, and by 'persuasive words' (θελκτηρίους μύθους) no doubt he
means his own advocacy (though the expression will look forward also to
the persuasions of Athena). About the word for means (μηχανάς) there can
be a certain ambivalence. If it can be used of the designs of a Zeus (*Suppl.*
1073, *Agam.* 677), it could also suggest the dodges of an advocate. The
process of argument has been examined in an earlier chapter, and we have
seen how an Apollo who disparages the tie of blood is driven by these
partisans of the mother into a position where he can only defend the

---

51 See ch. 6, pp. 119f.
52   οὔτοι προδώσει Λοξίου μεγασθενὴς
                          χρησμὸς κελεύων τόνδε κίνδυνον περᾶν
53 εἰς σοι (Erfurdt, followed by Mazon and Page) seems the best remedy for the opening of 1059.
54 On Greek supplication in general see the admirable article of J. P. Gould in *JHS* 93 (1973) 74–103.
55 This complicated matter is well discussed by Taplin 381ff. See now A. L. Brown, *JHS* 102 (1982)
30ff.

matricide by establishing a distinction, in point of parenthood, between father and mother to the disadvantage of the latter.[56] He cites the anomalous parentage of Athena and with that closes his case, having thereby set the argument upon a new track. The verdict follows in due course, and it is twofold. The votes are equal, which is surely an indication that the dilemma of Orestes was absolute, the conundrum insoluble.[57] It is the 'vote' of Athena, who commends the male in all things, which ensures that Orestes shall go free and his house be saved from extinction. Behind the preferences of a masculine goddess lies a sociological principle surely accepted by Aeschylus and his audience, a belief in the superiority of the male and, despite all the tragedy and irony that has gathered around this theme in the course of the trilogy, in the necessity that men should play the dominant role in society.[58] Apollo's plea is upheld.

Nevertheless, there is more to be said about Apollo's role in the trial – more than the fact that he is hard pressed by the Erinyes and fails to win a clear majority of the votes (a fact stressed by Athena in the closing scene). His entry and exit are both, if the text is sound, highly unusual: the former unheralded, the latter unremarked. It is convenient to take the latter first. One might have expected at least an exchange of courtesies between the sibling-gods, but no such is found nor any clear indication when Apollo leaves the stage. His last words are at 748ff. (if he speaks those lines, which is not certain); the last occurrence of his name is in the thanksgiving speech of Orestes, as one of a trio of gods responsible for his salvation, but no part of that speech is addressed to him. Has a speech (or speeches) dropped out? Where from? Not after the announcement of the verdict (752f.), which must be immediately followed by Orestes' joyous address to his saviour-goddess. A speech from a god after the departure of Orestes at 777 would seem equally intrusive, when we eagerly await the reaction of the Chorus. No, Apollo leaves, unobtrusively, his departure covered by the strong emotional tension of Orestes' speech, at 753; and, since at 676f.[59] the god had announced that he would wait for the verdict, the audience may be prepared to see him go once that verdict has been given. Apollo is faded out, as the play moves towards a new issue with which he is little concerned.[60] But we must also look at his entrance, which is, admittedly, remarkable.

---

[56] For a full discussion of his argument, see ch. 6, pp. 122ff.

[57] Cf. p. 124 above.

[58] See ch. 6, pp. 127ff.

[59] For the ascription of these lines to Apollo, see App. G.

[60] Orestes does not address Apollo, but gives thanks to him (obliquely) at 758–60 as one of a trio of

The one fixed point is the couplet addressed to him at 574f.; and there can be little doubt that it is spoken by Athena.[61] Why should the Erinyes ask a question (575) to which they know the answer? But Athena does not know and has every right to ask, which she does severely in the tones of a trial judge. This is her province, what is Apollo doing here? What concern has he in the trial? He answers that he has come as witness and as advocate; he tells her to start the trial, which she does. As the text stands, we can only suppose that he enters by a side passage, covered perhaps by the stage movements implied in 566ff., not seen by the audience, it may be, until skilful production discloses him in all his majesty in centre-stage, and certainly not seen by Athena, until just before she addresses him.[62] But is the text sound? Of the difficulties which have been raised some are not very material, but there is one surprising feature which needs discussion.

As the text stands, Athena is about to deliver an address – to announce, to the city as a whole and to the jurors who must try the case, *thesmoi* valid for all future time (570ff.). Her purpose is interrupted by the appearance of Apollo, and she starts the trial (582) without giving the address, which is in fact postponed until the arguments are concluded and both sides are ready for the verdict (674ff.). Then, and not till then, in words which recall 571, Athena delivers her long and important speech. It cannot be said that it is inappropriately placed, coming as it does immediately before the solemn casting of the votes. Still, the whole affair is remarkable – not only the postponement of a declared intention, but the interruption of a speech by the unheralded arrival of a fresh character who is then addressed. The view has, therefore, been advanced that our text is faulty, that the speech of Athena about the *thesmoi* originally preceded the entry of Apollo, which was more conventionally introduced.[63] This hypothesis may raise more difficulties than it solves, but, while we should not underestimate the boldness and originality of Aeschylus, we should certainly ask what dramatic purpose, if any, was served by this unparalleled phenomenon.

Let us return to the words which Athena addresses to Apollo – and they

divinities, between Pallas and Zeus 'the third *soter*', to whom his restoration is due. The stress is on Zeus (cf. 760f.), so again at 797ff., where Apollo is not named. It is Zeus and not Apollo that is important in the closing scene.

61 Cf. Taplin 396.

62 On the staging at 566ff., see Taplin 392–5. 'We have, then, a crowded stage movement'; and that is true without the stage crowd of citizens which has sometimes been assumed. Taplin is almost certainly right that the only representatives of the citizen body to appear on stage are the Areopagites, to whom the *stratos* of 566, the *Attikos leos* of 681, and all the other references to citizens refer (cf. Macleod (1) 127). At 570 note the present participle ($\pi\lambda\eta\rho ου\mu\acute\epsilon νου$): the movement is going on while Athena speaks?

63 Argued at length by Taplin 395ff.

are the only words of hers in the whole scene which acknowledge his presence in court and in the whole play, apart from 798f., which refer to him at all. Their tone is severe. That there should be some recognition of one another on the part of the two gods was necessary (and is one of the good reasons for attributing the lines to Athena): that it should not be too close was equally necessary. Athena is the presiding judge, Apollo a party to the dispute, her impartiality in which is a cardinal point. It was essential to avoid an impression that the two of them were hand in glove in opposition to the older gods, all the more since Athena is going to sustain an argument of Apollo's. That is the complaint of the Chorus, when the case has been decided against them; that is how all too many modern interpreters have been inclined to view the situation. The insulation of Athena from Apollo is deliberate and significant.

The whole strategy of the play is based upon a contrast between the two gods, both confronted with the Erinyes, each faced with a problem. The action has two settings: Delphi and Athens. Apollo, who finds Erinyes at the very heart of his sanctuary, must save his suppliant from a fate in which his own command has involved him.[64] This he cannot – or does not – do himself, but sends his client to Athens; the Erinyes he drives from his temple with violent words and the threat of violent action – to continue their pursuit. Athena then receives, with equal courtesy, pursued and pursuers. She sets up a court to try this difficult case. Before it Chorus and Apollo set out their arguments. The votes are equal; and Athena has laid down that equal votes mean acquittal.[65] Orestes leaves the court a free man for a house which has been saved from extinction. The Erinyes rage and threaten, now not Orestes, but Athena's city. It is her task, not to drive them away casting their venom upon her soil, but to induce them to stay – to stay with honour. By patient persuasion she induces them to accept a new home and cult.

To this difference of tone and method, this contrast of *bia* and *peitho*, we shall return in the following chapter. Athena succeeds where Apollo fails, and this may have profound significance at more than one level, not least at the level of social order. As we have already noted,[66] the trilogy raises two great social issues. Upon one of them, which is the right relationship of the sexes in society, the god and the goddess see eye to eye: Apollo's argument is upheld and his client acquitted, when the patron-goddess of Athens gives her vote through preference for the male. But there is another – and wider – issue. We have already asked what, exactly, Apollo did for

[64] See p. 145 above.   [65] On the 'vote' of Athena, see ch. 6, p. 125 n. 110   [66] See p. 132.

Orestes. What did Athena do? She gave her preference to the male, but first she had set up a court-of-law to try cases of homicide, she had replaced the vendetta. In this respect there was a fatal flaw in the position of Apollo which appears already in *Choephori*, though attention is not focused on it until late in the play. It need not surprise us that the man who has been sent by Apollo to exact vengeance should also seek the support of infernal powers. It is perhaps more surprising to learn that the oracle had foretold infernal penalties, if Orestes failed in his vengeful duty. It is not, however, until the closing scenes that first the threat and then the reality of his mother's pursuing hounds bring out the fact that he is himself liable under the *lex talionis* to a vengeful pursuit. The flaw in Apollo's position is exactly this: that his justice is bound up with kin-vengeance, with the ethic of the blood-feud and its interminable consequences. Apollo claims to break the chain by his fiat and his purification, but this he cannot do and the pursuit by Erinyes continues. He cannot do it because his own unrecognized connections with the pursuers are so close. What he cannot do Athena accomplishes by the establishment of a court-of-law which eliminates the blood-feud.

In the light of this we can perhaps see a reason why Aeschylus handled the *thesmoi* as he did. They are new *thesmoi* (490),[67] inaugurating a new and more highly civilized order for which the credit goes to Athena and her Athenians. She is about to expound its virtues when Apollo enters. Do we not then slip back into an older world, as both parties wrangle inconclusively in terms of the blood-feud and their argumentation only serves to bring out the inherent disadvantages of the old system? It is the court and the verdict which are new, salutary and hopeful. Perhaps, then, Athena's proclamation is appropriately placed after all, preceding the verdict, preceding that transformation of the Erinyes to which it leads up.[68]

A fuller consideration of the closing scene will follow in the next chapter. Meanwhile let us return briefly to the beginning of the play. For the flaw in Apollo's position is evident even in the speech of his Prophetis. It deserves careful study: not a word is wasted. Key in hand, she approaches the central door, but first addresses herself in prayer to a number of deities. 'I give first place to Gaia, first prophetess; and after her I pray to Themis,

---

[67] The interpretation of 490ff. has been settled once and for all by Dover 230ff.

[68] Athena's 696ff. echo the Chorus' 517ff. (on which see p. 165 below), showing that there is common ground between them. It is no doubt a subjective judgement that 696ff. stand better immediately preceding the final solution than preceding the trial in which the Chorus slips back into its narrow partisan role.

her daughter and successor. Third holder in peaceful succession was
another Titanid, another child of Earth ($\chi\theta ov\acute{o}\varsigma$), Phoebe; and it was from
her that Apollo received the seat of prophecy as a birthday gift and took the
name of Phoebus.' (1ff.) Prayer has given place to a brief history of the
Delphic oracle – and one which rejects the common version that Apollo
had seized the oracle by force. This is the prelude of her prayers (20). Pallas
follows, and the Nymphs, and Bromios; the springs of Pleistos, Poseidon,
and Zeus most lofty, the accomplisher. She goes in to do her duty.
Thirty-three lines have been spoken before she enters the shrine, to find the
suppliant Orestes surrounded by sleeping Erinyes, and emerges in a state of
shock. On the most natural interpretation of the text, she comes out on all
fours, which has been thought below the dignity of tragedy. But we should
be wrong to deny that there is some humour in this scene – humour in the
contrast between the hieratic language of the priestess with its emphasis
upon the peace and concord that have always reigned at Delphi and then
her incoherent horror and her more or less ludicrous descriptions of these
hideous beings who have invaded the sanctuary. Women? No, Gorgons.
But they are the wrong shape. Harpies? But they have no wings. She goes
on to describe them in a detail with which stage-production cannot
compete.

There is a touch of humour:[69] there is far more than that. The presence
of Erinyes in the shrine of Apollo, so paradoxical, so shocking to the
Prophetis, raises more than one question. They are asleep. But what right
have Furies to sleep? None, according to Clytemnestra's ghost who
upbraids them. But may there not be a hopeful omen for Orestes in the
mere fact that their pursuit has flagged? There is a far more fundamental
question. What right have they to be there at all? The incongruity of their
presence appals and baffles the Prophetis. It is too much for her: let Apollo
see to it (a final touch of humour?). He is the healer-prophet, the expert in
monstrosities; he purifies the houses of others, let him, the master, take care

[69] Humour is not entirely lacking in the speeches of the Watchman and the Herald (in *Agamemnon*), of
the Nurse (in *Choephori*). It was no doubt through the minor personages of Aeschylus that Greek
tragedy felt its way towards a greater realism in the depiction of character. The speech of the
Prophetis is in effect an exquisite miniature drama in itself. It is the easier for humour to bulk large in
the introduction in that the play it introduces does not, on the whole, evoke poignant human
emotions. Clytemnestra expresses her resentment, but she is a ghost. Orestes, though desperately
afraid as he tries to keep a few yards ahead of Furies who would suck his blood, is not racked with
guilt. The gods who dominate the play evoke a different order of response; and, if there is strong
emotion in *Eumenides*, it awaits the closing scene. Some critics have found satire in the trial scene at
the expense of Athenian legal procedure, which I find distracting, though it is of course true that we
should approach the arguments with an awareness of the connoisseurship of the audience (see p. 120
above).

of his own (6off.).[70] And away she goes. But are the Erinyes, in view of
Apollo's cruel threats to Orestes, his association with the avenging hounds
of Agamemnon, so incongruously situated after all? Physician, heal thyself!
When he appears in person and drives the Furies away, saying that they
have no right to touch his civilized abode (185),[71] unless we have forgotten
Choephori so soon, we can but feel that the god might himself take to heart
the first of all Delphic precepts: *gnothi sauton*.

Finally, we return to the opening lines of the play. It was historical fact
that Apollo's oracle had replaced an earlier – and chthonian – oracular
cult.[72] This is the theme of the Prophetis' brief history of Delphi – this
transition from the chthonian to the Apollonian which – and this is
stressed – had taken place with good will and without any violence.
Looking back, when we hear of Gaia and a child of Chthon, surely we can
not forget those infernal powers that were so prominent in *Choephori*.
Looking forward, we shall hear Apollo abusing the Erinyes for their mere
antiquity, we shall find that he and his adversaries (though not Athena)
regard their struggle as one between two generations of gods. Yet Apollo
had inherited his oracle from the older generation and a chthonian power.
For Aeschylus the relationship between chthonian and Olympian gods was
a religious issue crucial to his tragedy;[73] and it raised a problem which
could not be solved by a god whose own relationship to the chthonian
world was so ambiguous, nor could it be solved by his violent speech and
gesture. That is why Orestes had to go to Athens – and not only Orestes
but the Erinyes themselves in order that they might find their rightful place
in a civilized community. If the peaceful transitions of the opening lines are
mirrored in the harmonious close of the play,[74] a role for Athens is already
foreshadowed, when the Prophetis tells how 'the sons of Hephaestus' (that
is, the Athenians) once sent Apollo on his way from Delos to Delphi (9ff.).
No reference to Athens or Athenians in a tragedy needs excuse, but the
terms of this one are worth noting. They are 'makers of roads'
(κελευθοποιοί), and it is a new way which they will pioneer; they civilize a
land which was uncivilized (12–14).[75] This was to aid Apollo in his

---

70   τἀντεῦθεν ἤδη τῶνδε δεσπότῃ δόμων
                            αὐτῷ μελέσθω Λοξίᾳ μεγασθενεῖ.
                            ἰατρόμαντις δ' ἐστὶ καὶ τερασκόπος
                            καὶ τοῖσιν ἄλλοις δωμάτων καθάρσιος.
71   οὔτοι δόμοισι τοῖσδε χρίμπτεσθαι πρέπει
72 On *Cho.* 935ff., see App. H.
73 See ch. 8, pp. 155–6.
74 Cf. Lebeck 142.
75 χθόνα | ἀνήμερον τιθέντες ἡμερωμένην (13f.). On the civilizing role of Athens, cf. Macleod (1)
    135.

progress from east to west. But there was a journey to be made in the opposite direction. If on that earlier occasion they escort Apollo and honour him greatly (πέμπουσι . . . καὶ σεβίζουσιν μέγα), the play ends with Athenian Propompoi escorting to a new and rightful home goddesses whose name in Athens was that of Semnai (1041).

CHAPTER EIGHT

Zeus and the Erinyes[1]

In *Eumenides* Apollo claims authority from Zeus. Not so the Erinyes. Apollo may be accounted great, says the Coryphaeus (229–31), at the court of Zeus, but they will nevertheless continue their just persecution of Orestes. They sing that Zeus shuns their blood-stained and loathly company (365f.), but seem to claim that, pursuing a function allotted to them not by Zeus but by Moira (334ff.), they are doing a service to the gods by relieving them of a distasteful task (360ff.).[2] An audience which made its first acquaintance with these infernal powers in the opening scenes of *Eumenides* – hideous in aspect, cruel in method, truculent in speech, narrowly intent upon avenging a wicked woman – might incline to share the simple detestation of a civilized Apollo for these barbarous creatures and, later, might wonder by what sleight-of-hand the dramatist transforms them into worshipful and benevolent divinities.

But we do not so make their acquaintance. The transformation is dramatic and designed, but designed to do more than resolve a situation proper only to the closing scene of *Eumenides*. We have already seen how unwise it is to 'read the trilogy backwards' and not in the forward movement which presents itself to an audience. It is unwise to observe the conflict between Apollo and the Erinyes in *Eumenides* heedless of that enigmatic relationship between him and the infernal world which was disclosed in *Choephori*.[3] It is no less unwise to take at its face value the detachment of the Chorus in *Eumenides* from the government of Zeus – and for that matter the whole theme of a conflict between older and

---

[1] This chapter incorporates material from *JHS* 74 (1954) 16–24.
[2] The text of 360–2 is uncertain, but this must be the general purport. εἰς ἄγκρισιν ἐλθεῖν: note that is precisely what Athena will do, ἀνάκρισις being a technical term for the preliminary examination by a magistrate before a case comes up for trial.
[3] See ch. 7, pp. 136f.

younger gods – without recalling the intimate association in the earlier
plays of Erinyes with the justice of Zeus. Zeus sends Erinyes.

Few would deny the paramount religious interest in all extant
Aeschylean tragedy. The drama, as the religion, of Aeschylus – and the
two are hardly separable the one from the other – is centred in a Zeus who
is conceived as the upholder of a just moral order. Aeschylus has been called
the prophet of Zeus. But when we ask what was his distinctive
contribution to Greek 'theology' (if the term may be used), the question is
not easily answered.[4] Was it that he gave Zeus an unchallengeable
supremacy among the gods? But this Zeus already has in Homer. That he
insisted upon the justice of Zeus? But Hesiod so insists. That he displayed
that justice as working slowly but surely throughout the generations? But
that conception we find in Solon. Neither can we find the contribution of
Aeschylus in proverbs such as 'excess breeds outrage' or even 'we learn by
suffering': Aeschylus is no Herodotus. Does his greatness then reside not so
much in originality of thought as in the intensity with which he felt and the
poetic power with which he expressed notions derived from traditional
beliefs or earlier thinkers? It is true of course that his thinking is deeply
rooted in tradition. I would suggest, however, that he faced problems
inherent in the theology which he found and worked to solve them with
rare and original insight, creating for this purpose symbols which he
bequeathed to Sophocles – and which we may still find valid.

I would suggest that a problem which exercised him, and which arose
directly out of the subject-matter of tragedy, concerned the relationship
between the supernal and infernal worlds, between Zeus (and along with
Zeus the other bright gods of the heavenly Olympus) and, on the other
hand, the dark primitive powers that dwell in the earth. It was all very well
for an Isocrates, glibly, to divide the gods into two classes: 'those who are
the cause of good things for us and are called Olympians, and those who are
set in charge of disasters and punishments and bear less agreeable names'.[5]
There was indeed a distinction between the chthonians (χθόνιοι) and the
ouranioi (οὐράνιοι, Ὀλύμπιοι), often blurred (as all students of Greek
religion know), but marked broadly by differences of cult and, above all,
by the emotional attitude of the worshippers, who worshipped the
Olympians, for the most part cheerfully, in the hope of good and the
chthonians, gloomily, in the fear of evil. Isocrates is good evidence for

---

[4] It is the great value of F. Solmsen's *Hesiod and Aeschylus* (Ithaca, N.Y. 1949) – which also deals with
Solon – that it enables us to isolate the distinctive contribution of Aeschylus. Cf. *Gnomon* 23 (1951)
414ff.

[5] v. 117.

popular views, but the most ordinary Greek was well aware that Olympus too might be a source of evil, the earth of benefits as well as plagues. No doubt, however, it was to an association with the dead that the terror which often attended the worship of the *chthonioi* was due. The earth was the dwelling-place of the dead; the powers of the earth were the representatives of their interests and influence. And there was one class of dead particularly to be feared, which was those who, having died by violence, did not rest in the earth but demanded satisfaction.

Along with the bright figures of a Zeus, an Apollo, an Athena – along with an ambivalent Hermes or Demeter – the divine world of Greek belief contained many bogies, *daimones* who deserve the name of 'demons'. There were those Gorgons and Harpies whom the Prophetis called to mind,[6] and many others, including the Erinyes. Now, if the Erinyes alone seem to have attained a position of serious importance in Greek 'theology', there could be more than one reason for this. And one reason is of course the work of Aeschylus himself, who may well have been the first to impose clarity of form and conception upon them.[7] The previous history of their cults and functions is notoriously obscure, but the very controversies to which it has given rise are significant, if we wish to understand the use which Aeschylus made of them. A view was once popular that saw these goddesses as in effect the vengeful dead themselves within the earth making their power felt to retaliate upon the killer. If *Arai* is one of their names, are they not embodiments of a dying curse? This view has now been generally abandoned, largely because it does not fit the Homeric evidence, where, among a dozen references to an Erinys, very few are connected with death, still fewer with deliberate murder. The range covered is wide, including a mother's curse (four times), a father's curse, the breaking of an oath, disregard of primogeniture, and a breach of natural law. The last example – the horse Xanthus, who spoke – is bizarre, but perhaps significant, since it points towards the not infrequent association of Erinyes with *moira* or Moirai, the notion that it is their role to punish some breach of divinely-appointed order.

On these matters we cannot be too precise – and need not be, since it is clear that Aeschylus had inherited a variety of notions which were at his disposal, and which we can see him, to a certain degree, manipulate at his dramatic convenience. His Erinyes are at their narrowest – and it is perhaps characteristic of them at any given moment to be narrow – in the early

---

[6] *Eum.* 48ff., on which see p. 151 above.
[7] Cf. Winnington-Ingram 206ff. (some of which is repeated here).

stages of *Eumenides*. A mother's 'wrathful hounds', they have a vision limited to the cause they serve and, in the circumstances, espouse the case of the female against a 'male chauvinist' Apollo. But Orestes had good cause to fear the 'wrathful hounds' of a father, if he neglected his task; and indeed, when the Chorus of *Eumenides* turn to theory, they claim that their function had been one to protect parents without distinction of sex (513ff.). Nor is there any distinction of sex – or reference to parents – when the Chorus of *Agamemnon* sing (*Agam.* 462ff.) of black Erinyes who annihilate the man who prospers without justice. And, if this follows a reference to the concern of gods with those who have slain many, we shall find, as we look back in the play, that this slaughter arose in the course of an action springing, not from homicide, but from a breach of hospitality, punished by Zeus Xenios by the sending of Erinyes. These are the first Erinyes in the trilogy; and this is the first full mention of Zeus.[8] If we ask what Olympian Zeus has to do with these fearsome powers of the nether world, we must answer with other questions. Where there is punitive justice, is there not also fear? Is there not also force? What is the place of fear and force in the moral governance of Zeus?

Later in the *parodos* of *Agamemnon* – a little later, but significantly postponed – the Chorus make their famous affirmation of faith in Zeus (160ff.). Naming him in terms which in themselves invite a question – 'Zeus whoever [of whatever sort] he be' (Ζεὺς ὅστις ποτ᾽ ἐστιν), they go on to say that, weighing all things in the balance, they can find nothing like Zeus, 'if one is to cast away the vain burden of care from the mind in very truth'.[9] But do their cares diminish, as the play proceeds? No, foreboding, which is the very keynote of the play, increases steadily up to the murder of Agamemnon. Up to, and beyond. With the confident assertion of the 'Hymn to Zeus' compare the cry of the Chorus during their lyric scene with Clytemnestra (1485ff.). 'Woe, woe, it is on account of Zeus, who is responsible for all, doer of all. For what is accomplished for mortals without Zeus? Which of these things is not god-ratified?'[10] Very different is the tone. For the thought of Zeus, which was then proclaimed as

---

[8] Previously we have Διόθεν at 43. The Atridae derive their throne and sceptre from Zeus – a Homeric notion which suits their typically 'heroic' reaction to a derogation from their τιμή.

[9] At 160f., if προσεικάζειν means 'liken' (as it does elsewhere in Aeschylus), the construction is slightly anacoluthic, as explained by Page. Is it possible, however, that, on the analogy of προσέοικα, τὰ προσεικότα ('what meets the situation'), the sense is something like this: 'weighing up everything, I cannot make < anything > suit [fit the bill] except Zeus, if etc.'?

[10]   ἰὼ ἰὴ διαὶ Διὸς
   παναιτίου πανεργέτα·
   τί γὰρ βροτοῖς ἄνευ Διὸς τελεῖται;
   τί τῶνδ᾽ οὐ θεόκραντόν ἐστιν;

the ground of confidence, is now a source of terror. Why? Because the accomplishment of Zeus' will has led to the death of Agamemnon and is leading, as they begin to see, to the matricide of Orestes.

But already in the Hymn – in its phrasing and its placing – there is complication. After the words quoted, the Chorus go on to sing that Zeus has led mankind upon the path of understanding by his ordinance that learning shall come *by suffering* ($\pi\acute{a}\theta\epsilon\iota$ $\mu\acute{a}\theta os$); and they suggest that this suffering may be a grace or favour ($\chi\acute{a}\rho\iota s$) conferred by divinities who exercise their awful authority by means of force or violence ($\beta\iota\alpha\acute{\iota}\omega s$).[11] Between the notions of grace and violence there is a clash: it is virtually a paradox. It is not, however, more inharmonious than the context within which it lies.[12] The stanzas of the Hymn to Zeus (as it is convenient, loosely, to call it) interrupt the narrative of the events which preceded the sailing of the armada against Troy: they lie between the omen of the eagles devouring the hare with her unborn young and the sacrifice of Iphigenia, which that omen portended. This was a bold and significant stroke of construction. Significant, because the sacrifice, no less than the fall of Troy, can now be seen in the light of the Hymn, but significant also, because the Hymn, with its affirmation of faith, must now be interpreted in the light of the sacrifice. The context is inharmonious; and the disharmony resides in the contrast between the unholy crime committed against Iphigenia and the dispatch of the Atridae to execute justice upon Troy. And so we are taken back to the anapaests of the Coryphaeus (60 ff.).

The action of *Oresteia* – the stage-action along with its explicit antecedents – consists in a series of acts of retributive justice which have one thing in common: they emanate from Zeus and are expressions of his will. They have another thing in common: they are carried out by

---

[11] 182f. $\delta a\iota\mu\acute{o}\nu\omega\nu$ $\delta\acute{e}$ πov: (FTr: $\delta\acute{e}$ $\pi o\hat{v}$ MV) $\chi\acute{a}\rho\iota s$ $\beta\iota a\acute{\iota}\omega s$ ($\beta\acute{\iota}a\iota os$ Turnebus) $\sigma\acute{e}\lambda\mu a$ $\sigma\epsilon\mu\nu\grave{o}\nu$ $\mathring{\eta}\mu\acute{e}\nu\omega\nu$. The differences involved are palaeographically insignificant. The text has been much discussed. Recently, M. Pope, *JHS* 94 (1974) 100–13, has argued for accepting M's reading in both cases; he is answered by N. B. Booth, *CQ* 26 (1976) 220–8, who rejects it in both cases. I return to the fairly common view represented by e.g. W. Kranz, *Hermes* 54 (1919) 305 and Fraenkel II 108ff. that $\pi o\hat{v}$ is wrong and $\beta\iota a\acute{\iota}\omega s$ right. The tone of the Chorus is not questioning, but tentative: hence the enclitic is to be preferred. As for $\beta\iota a\acute{\iota}\omega s/\beta\acute{\iota}a\iota os$, whichever is read, the paradox remains. The adverb is only objectionable in so far as it does not comport with $\sigma\acute{e}\lambda\mu a$ $\sigma\epsilon\mu\nu\grave{o}\nu$ $\mathring{\eta}\mu\acute{e}\nu\omega\nu$, the metaphorical force of which (on which see Fraenkel *ad loc.*) it might seem to diminish. On the other hand, it gives a better sentence-structure, $\delta a\iota\mu\acute{o}\nu\omega\nu$ gaining a significant complement which justifies its stressed position and the notion of *bia* the stress which it deserves, whereas, with the emendation, the participial phrase becomes an appendage, a quasi-decorative epithet, not at all in the Aeschylean manner. This seems to me the more serious objection. The adverb might seem less inappropriate to the nautical metaphor if we knew more of the ways in which discipline and efficiency were maintained on board an Athenian trireme.

[12] The disharmonies of the *parodos* are well brought out by Fraenkel II 111ff., 146f. See also Reinhardt 20ff.

Erinyes – the final vindictive pursuit of Orestes by the goddesses themselves, the earlier vengeances by human beings acting as their surrogates[13] – and to this agency owe their peculiar character. Clearly, this twofold statement demands some substantiation. Let us first take the Trojan War. Aeschylus' handling of this theme has been examined in an earlier chapter, and we saw how closely Agamemnon's fate is bound up with a war by which his desires, his duties and his crimes, are all conditioned.[14] This alone might justify the length at which it is treated, the resources the dramatist has lavished upon it. More than that, it illustrates the functioning of Erinyes and characterizes the justice of Zeus when he sends Erinyes to execute it. If the treatment is lavish, so is the suffering which falls upon the Trojans – upon the guiltless young as upon the guilty old. For the great net which was cast over Troy (355–63) caught not only the great but the young (Aeschylus did not use *megas* four times in seven lines through inadvertence), whose plight had already been described in Clytemnestra's second 'beacon' speech.[15] No less lavish was the suffering of the Greek avengers, on the battlefield (60–7, 555–74) and in their desolate homes (429–55). We have Clytemnestra's speech to tell us about these things, and the 'money-changer' chorus, and Agamemnon's Herald, a messenger of good who cannot keep away from themes of suffering and death and ends by telling us of the disastrous homeward voyage. And all this had been foreshadowed and symbolized by the sacrifice of an innocent child without which the expedition could not sail. Thus we come to know what the justice of Zeus upon Troy involved by way of indiscriminate suffering and new wickedness. When the Coryphaeus says to Clytemnestra (354) that a grace (χάρις) not unworthy of the toils has been wrought, when the Herald says (581f.) that the grace of Zeus which has brought these things about is to be honoured, we must surely recall the mystery of those *daimones* whose grace is bound up with violence.[16]

For this 'grace' Agamemnon is prepared to pay the price, which is the deaths of many. But for this he must suffer. 'Of those who slay many the

---

[13] Cf. esp. *Agam.* 60–2, after 58f.

[14] Cf. ch. 5, *passim*.

[15] At 327f. it is best to keep the reading of the codd.: φυταλμίων παῖδες γερόντων. It is true that the untimely death of the young is a common theme, but the stress is here on the survivors left to mourning and slavery. οἱ μὲν stands for Trojans in general, hence the masculine πεπτωκότες, but ἀνδρῶν (and κασιγνήτων) make us think of the women, these being their natural protectors, then come the children. γέροντες would be quite inappropriate to what immediately follows: the older men are not enslaved, but killed, like Priam. Cf. Fraenkel *ad loc.*

[16] *Agam.* 354 (χάρις γὰρ οὐκ ἄτιμος εἴργασται πόνων), 581f. (καὶ χάρις τιμήσεται Διὸς τάδ' ἐκπράξασα).

gods are not unwatchful; and black Erinyes in time, when a man prospers
without justice, reverse his fortune and annihilate him' (461ff.).[17]
Immediately there follows a reference to the thunderbolt of Zeus.[18]
Agamemnon is prepared to pay the price, which is also the death of one in
particular. But for that he must suffer at the hands of Clytemnestra, who
prays to Zeus a prayer (973f.) which is answered, but later, proclaiming an
act of justice (1406), will swear by Ate and Erinys 'to whom I sacrificed this
man' (1433). This is in her scene with the Chorus after the murder. Later in
that same scene she will claim to embody the *drimus alastor*, the *daimon* that
had haunted the house of Atreus since the Thyestean banquet. For there
was a second train of causation leading to the death of Agamemnon, who
pays for his father's offence as well as his own. What right have we to see
this *daimon* as part of the Fury-connection? Every right, since it was as a riot
of 'kindred Erinyes' that Cassandra's prophetic vision (1186ff.) saw the
dead children of Thyestes. Alastor and Daimon, Arai and Erinyes: they are
all expressions of the same power working through Clytemnestra and
Aegisthus to punish Agamemnon for deeds which he did and which he did
not do. Working through Aegisthus, who, as he contemplates the work of
his accomplice, cries out: 'Now can I say that avenging gods look down
from above the earth upon the griefs of mortals, now that I see this man
lying in the woven net of the Erinyes' (1578–81).[19] Vengeance comes from
above, rises up from below.

One is tempted to say, with only slight exaggeration, that, in
Agamemnon, from 60ff. onward, every reference to Erinyes is associated,
textually, with Zeus, every reference to Zeus with Erinyes.[20] Instances
have been given already. But turn back to 973. Clytemnestra calls on Zeus

---

[17] See ch. 5, p. 98.
[18] On the interpretation of 469f. see ch. 5, n. 4.
[19]

ὦ φέγγος εὖφρον ἡμέρας δικηφόρου.
φαίην ἂν ἤδη νῦν βροτῶν τιμαόρους
θεοὺς ἄνωθεν γῆς ἐποπτεύειν ἄχη,
ἰδὼν ὑφαντοῖς ἐν πέπλοις Ἐρινύων
τὸν ἄνδρα τόνδε κείμενον, φίλως ἐμοί,
χερὸς πατρῴας ἐκτίνοντα μηχανάς.

In my translation I take γῆς with ἄνωθεν, with some hesitation in view of Fraenkel's argument. At
1580, Page shows sympathy with Nauck's πάγαις for πέπλοις which gives 'a much better phrase
than the text offers' – and much more Aeschylean (one might add), since straightforward
descriptive epithets are notably rare in *Oresteia*. (Cf. F. R. Earp, *The style of Aeschylus*, Cambridge
1948, pp. 54ff.) In the light of 1611, one might invoke ring-composition in support of the
emendation.

[20] I am encouraged by Lebeck's sensitive examination (her p. 64) of 355ff. to see a deeper significance
in the collaboration there of Zeus with a Night whom we shall learn to be mother of the Erinyes.
The contrast of day and night, light and darkness, is of course a dominant feature in the imagery of
the trilogy (cf. Petrounias 244ff.).

Teleios to accomplish her prayer, and at once the hearts of the Chorus chant 'self-taught the lyre-less dirge of an Erinys' (990ff.). If not Erinyes, it is a *daimon*, it is curses, it is a spirit of Wrath. Menis (*Μῆνις*) is an important word (and deserves its capital). It is Menis (or a Menis) which Calchas saw to threaten the Atridae (155) in a passage which immediately precedes the opening of the Hymn to Zeus; and on that passage Fraenkel[21] rightly observes that '*Μῆνις* and *Ἐρινύες* belong closely together.' In the second *stasimon*, it is Menis which is said (699ff.)[22] to exact an account for the dishonouring of the guest-table and of Zeus 'of the common hearth' (*Ξυνεστίου*)'. Later (748f.), at the end of the 'Trojan' section of the *stasimon*, by a kind of ring-composition, it is an Erinys, sent (as at 61) by Zeus Xenios, that ordains a bitter ending to the marriage (just as Menis transformed one kind of *kedos* into another). In the final *kommos*, in one of two important passages concerned with Zeus, the notion of wrath returns (1485ff.). The agonized cry of the Chorus already quoted proceeds from their own apostrophe to the *daimon* that falls upon the house, which is picked up by Clytemnestra with her 'thrice-fattened *daimon*' and her reference to bloodshed after bloodshed. 'It is indeed a great *daimon* and heavy of wrath (*βαρύμηνις*) of which you speak', sings the Chorus, but they end their stanza by attributing all responsibility to Zeus. Finally, we come to 1563ff., which is the climax of all choral utterance in the play.[23] 'It abides, while Zeus abides upon his throne, for the doer to suffer – it is divine law (*θέσμιον γάρ*)'. There follows the question: 'Who can expel the seed of curse (*γονὰν ἀραῖον*) from the house? The race is glued to disaster.'[24]

In *Agamemnon* the divine world is represented above all by Zeus, but also by the Erinyes he sends. In so far as they belong to antithetical areas of that world, their relationship is problematic, but it is not, exactly, presented as a problem. Apart from the first 'sending', the notions are juxtaposed rather than explicitly related to one another. It is in *Choephori*, where divine powers converge to impel Orestes towards matricide, that their relationship becomes an issue, as the infernal world moves into the centre of interest. And this is indicated at the outset, in the very first line of the play,

---

[21] II 93 and, on the epithet μνήμων, 94. See also n. 59 below.

[22] τελεσσίφρων (cf. Zeus τέλειος); ὑστέρῳ χρόνῳ (like the ὑστερόποινος Ἐρινύς of *Agam.* 58f.).

[23]   μίμνει δὲ μίμνοντος ἐν θρόνῳ Διὸς
                  παθεῖν τὸν ἔρξαντα· θέσμιον γάρ.
                  τίς ἂν γονὰν ἀραῖον ἐκβάλοι δόμων;
                  κεκόλληται γένος πρὸς ἄτᾳ.

[24] Cf. *Eum.* 417 (for Ἀραί as a Fury-name).

by a prayer to Hermes, a god who belongs to *both* worlds, but is here addressed as *chthonios*. He is implored to be saviour (σωτήρ) and ally (σύμμαχος). But the god who is pre-eminently *soter* is Zeus; and the prologue-speech ends with a prayer to Zeus also to be *summachos*. Ring-composition, one might say, at its purest and most effective. Whether there intervened in the missing section of the speech references to the nether world or hints of other chthonian powers we cannot say. Nor can we say for certain, though it is highly probable, that Orestes told of Apollo's oracle and its instruction to use that craft of which Hermes *dolios* is to be the patron.[25]

It is Apollo who is the new factor in *Choephori*; and, since the most striking single feature in the play is a *kommos* directed towards the infernal world, one might expect to find a strong polarization between Olympian and chthonian gods, between the bright light of Olympus and the nether gloom. What we find is something both different and surprising, when the play discloses an enigmatic relationship between Apollo and the Erinyes with whom his oracle threatens Orestes, when we discover that, threatened with persecution if he does not act, he suffers persecution when he does, and in both cases by the same infernal powers. In this matter, where does Zeus stand? Not vaguely in the background. Zeus is hardly less prominent in *Choephori* than in *Agamemnon*.

Where does Zeus stand in relation to Apollo? The audience will have been familiar with the notion that the latter through his oracle was the spokesman of Zeus, but this claim, though made in *Eumenides*, is not to be found in *Choephori*.[26] Orestes' first extant reference to Apollo (269) follows prayer to Zeus (246f.), but the two are not brought into relation. In those late choral odes which address a variety of gods both Zeus and Apollo are found, but not in special relationship. It is the relationship between Zeus and the infernal world which becomes the matter of interest. I quote Lebeck:[27] 'Throughout the play prayers to the infernal gods alternate with appeals to Zeus. This alternation . . . reaches a climax in the commos and re-echoes in the hymns that follow it.' The text of those hymns is in a deplorable state, which is something of a disaster, since they are clearly full of links (and ironies) closely related to our themes. Rather than burden my own text with hypotheses, however seductive, I prefer to deal with these

---

[25] On Hermes, see Garvie (2) 84ff. and App. H below. The principal passages are 726ff. (following the appeal to πότνια χθών), 812ff. and (perhaps) 946ff.

[26] One must always make the following proviso: unless such a claim was made in the missing section of the *prologos*.

[27] Lebeck 96 (with n. 2 on p. 193).

odes in an appendix[28] and concentrate attention on a passage in the *kommos* which is most illuminating.

It comes at that point where addresses to the father are replaced by appeals to divinities. First Orestes calls upon Zeus to 'send up from below a late-punishing doom (ὑστερόποινον ἄταν)'.[29] An audience would not need actually to recall *Agam.* 58f. in order to grasp the implications of this phrase, which are in any case clarified within a few moments in a passage of striking symmetry.[30] 'When,' sings Electra, 'will Zeus lay on his hand?' It is a Zeus who shatters the peaks. Then, with a demand for justice, she calls on Earth and 'the honours of the chthonians' (Γᾶ χθονίων τε τιμαί). In the next sung stanza (405ff.) Orestes calls first to the sovereignties of the nether world, the powerful Curses of the dead, to end with a despairing question: 'Where, O Zeus, should one turn?' Between the two sung stanzas, in the mid-point of this chiastic formation, lie the anapaests of the Coryphaeus, proclaiming the law (νόμος) that blood demands blood, 'for murder summons an Erinys . . . bringing doom upon doom (ἄτην ἑτέραν . . . ἐπ' ἄτῃ).' There are two things to be said. In a song whose whole weight and emphasis are upon the nether world and its regent powers Zeus is summoned and questioned; not only so, but the appeals to those powers are embraced between two arresting cries to Zeus. What Zeus is this? A nether Zeus (Ζεὺς χθόνιος)[31] was not unknown to cult and was sometimes equated with Hades or Pluto, ruling the realm of the dead as his namesake ruled the world of light. The Chorus of *Supplices* threaten that, if they do not win the Olympian gods to their side, they will hang themselves and so transfer their suppliance to 'him of the earth, the host of many guests, the Zeus of the dead' (156ff.); and Danaus later will speak of 'another Zeus, of whom they say that there among the dead he judges a final judgement of offences' (230f.). Hence the splendid blasphemy of Clytemnestra (*Agam.* 1385ff.), when she dedicates the third wound of her fallen husband as a prayer-gift to the Zeus 'beneath the earth' who 'keeps corpses safe' (τοῦ κατὰ χθονὸς Διὸς νεκρῶν σωτῆρος). Zeus *soter* indeed! Such a nether Zeus we might suppose it to be that sends up from below (κάτωθεν) ate to punish late in time (382f.).[32] But a Zeus who shatters the peaks (394ff.) can

---

[28] See App. H.

[29] 382f., reading ἀμπέμπειν (Headlam), with an imperative sense.

[30] Attention is called to the chiastic order by Lebeck 193.

[31] The main evidence about Zeus Chthonios is usefully summarized by M. L. West in his note on Hesiod, *Works and Days* 465. This Zeus is ambivalent: 'he can be conceived as an extension of Zeus, or as a chthonic counterpart of Zeus'.

[32] Strictly, perhaps, κάτωθεν ἀμπέμπειν need not imply anything about the whereabouts of the 'sender'.

be none other than the cloud-gathering wielder of the thunderbolt. A thoughtful Greek might well be perplexed by Zeus *chthonios*. Was he really another god, Zeus only by analogy? Or was it the one and only and supreme Zeus, but operating within the nether world? Certainly Aeschylus could not tolerate a bifurcated Zeus or a bifurcated world: neither cult nor legend for all their efforts could keep the upper and nether worlds apart, as Sophocles knew no less than Aeschylus.[33] And they knew it as tragic poets. The two worlds cannot be kept apart, when an Olympian god, in the execution of his justice, insists upon blood for blood. And that is the second thing to say.

There is a problem to be solved in *Eumenides* which lies deeper than the mere fate of Orestes. From the conjunction of Zeus and Erinyes certain consequences flow, dramatically. In the earlier plays associations of violence and cruelty gather about Erinyes, until, when we see their hideous aspect and hear their truculent speech, we feel that this is indeed how Furies should look and speak. But, since at point after point the poet has insisted that Erinyes are ministers of the justice of Zeus, it follows that our conception of that justice and that god must be correspondingly affected. It follows that, when, after the acquittal of Orestes, the Chorus still rage and threaten, Aeschylus could not leave them so, unless he was prepared to admit that the faith which the Argive elders had expressed in Zeus was one that contained as much despair as hope. It is in terms of this problem that we should consider the closing scene of the play.

Critics are less perturbed today than they once were by the fact that the play has a quarter of its length to run after its ostensible subject – the fate of Orestes, personally, and of the house of Atreus – has been determined by the verdict of a court; less inclined to apologize for the closing scene or regard it as an addendum of mainly local interest gratifying to local pride. The Athenian aspect, which is vital, is better understood. Not only is a threat averted, but Athena wins a triumph which has its moral, social and religious connotations. As for the Erinyes, their *timē* is restored;[34] they acquire a home, a cult and a new name; they are in some sense and degree transformed, taking on a role in the new order Athena has established in her Athens. But what does this *mean*? The trilogy ends with joy, with a triumph of good over evil. What does this mean? Has the poet of Iphigenia turned sentimental optimist? Has the sleight of hand of a consummate

---

[33] See Winnington-Ingram 211, n. 21.
[34] On this theme, much stressed (e.g. 780, 792, 796, 807, 810, 822, 824, 833, 838, 845, 854, 868, 891), see Macleod (1) 139.

dramatist played a brilliant trick on us? When the Chorus promise fertility to their hosts, has he dealt from his pack – or produced from his sleeve – a known aspect of the chthonian world which has hitherto been concealed, in order to send his audience home happy?

I say, the trilogy ends. If we are to understand the last phase of *Eumenides*, we must never forget that it brings not merely a play but a vast and complex trilogy to completion.[35] A word must be said at this point about the strategy of Aeschylus, the way in which (as has been suggested above) he manipulates the concept and presentation of Erinyes. They are at their narrowest in the first half of *Eumenides*, where he causes the convergent powers of *Choephori* to diverge, separates – or seems to separate – the two worlds which there refused to stay apart. There is – or appears to be – a sharp contrast and conflict between Olympians and chthonians, old gods and younger gods, focused on the clash of interest between Apollo and Erinyes; and to sharpen this contrast, to enhance the dramatic tension, and to prepare the sequel, these Erinyes are (one might say) narrowly departmentalized, interested in shed blood only (by which they track their victim), in the blood of a kinsman only, and, from the nature of this particular case, partisans of the woman against the man. They are narrow, and they are cruel; their words are ferocious, and much stress is laid on their hideous methods. Half-way through the play there is a change of tone; and the choral ode at 490ff. is something of a turning-point.[36] The Chorus has responded to the courtesy of Athena. Instead of rejecting the jurisdiction of her new court, they issue, not a threat, but a warning. They sing, not in the passionate vindictive tones of their earlier songs, but with reasonable argument and broad generalization. The song looks forward, and it looks back. When they assert the necessary role of fear in a just community, it is a position which will be accepted by Athena: no less so, when they commend a middle course between anarchy and despotism.[37] What may be equally significant is the presence in the language of this ode of unmistakable echoes from the great choruses of *Agamemnon* which deal with the justice of Zeus.[38] The concept and presentation of Erinyes has broadened out in preparation for the closing scene.

[35] On this essential function of *Eumenides* see, especially, Macleod (1) *passim*, whose notable contribution deserves the closest study.

[36] Lebeck 145ff. argues that wider aspects of the Erinyes are to be found earlier in the play, especially in their 'binding song', but I agree with Taplin (391 n. 4) that 'her overemphasis detracts from the full impact of the new insights revealed by the later song 490ff.'.

[37] With 517ff. compare 696ff.

[38] Compare 520f. with *Agam.* 180, 533ff. with *Agam.* 757ff., 539ff. with *Agam.* 381ff., 558 with *Agam.* 396. Cf. Solmsen, *Hesiod and Aeschylus* 197ff., Lebeck 160ff.

It narrows again in the trial-scene, under the renewed influence of a narrow Apollo; and of course, when they have lost their case, indignation and threats return, directed now against Athens. Athena must intervene to save her city. Courteous and patient, she reasons with them, and in the end they are reconciled; they accept her gifts and promise their rewards. Wanderers, they accept a home; disgraced (as they think) by a *repulsa*, they accept a cult. They will be Semnai; they will be Eumenides.[39] The keynote of the scene is a transformation of evil into good; and this is brought out in many ways, both subtle and spectacular.[40] Words, themes and symbols formerly associated with crime and disaster now appear with a new connotation, free from contamination, like the *ololugmos* with which the trilogy ends, celebrating the victory won by a good strife, by a good persuasion. The trilogy is haunted by polarities – light and darkness, day and night, good and evil, hope and fear, paean and *threnos*. But the polar opposites refuse to be kept apart (any more than the two worlds of gods): always the worse encroaches on the better – always until the closing scene. 'Say woe, woe,' sang the Elders in *Agamemnon*, 'but let the good prevail.' The good *has* prevailed.

But what has really happened? We come back to the question: is this more than a dramatic trick or a facile optimism? Two things have

[39] It is a standing puzzle that the latter name does not occur in our text of the play; and Hermann's suggestion has been widely accepted that a reference to Athena's giving the Chorus this name (cf. the Argument and Harpocration) has fallen out in the lacuna he posited after 1027. Macleod (2) 201 makes two points. (i) Athena ought not to be giving them this name, when their cult-title at Athens was Semnai (Paus. 2.11.29), cf. 1041. (ii) The title of the play refers generally to their change of role and specifically to 992 (on the mutual good-will between city and goddesses, with the adjective εὔφρων twice). Both points carry weight, but do not dispose of the problem. For it remains very odd that Aeschylus – or anyone else for that matter – should have named the play with a word not used in the play, but a known title elsewhere of the goddesses. (Odder still, of course, if it was *not* a known title!) Known in Athens in 458? Not from Sikyon, perhaps (Paus., loc. cit.), but from Colonus (cf. Soph. *OC* 42, 486). Sophocles, while giving the goddesses their Colonus-name, hints several times at their Athenian title (e.g. *OC* 41, 90, 100): is it not possible that Aeschylus made Athena hint in some way at the Colonus-name? But, if so, it must have been done more clearly than just by the adjective εὔφρων. Suspicion falls on 1040. εὐθύφρονες makes sense, but it is not the sense required: we do not want at this point the combination of mercy and justice (and it is no good referring to εὐθυδίκαοι, 312). Nor, one might have thought, would Aeschylus have wished to blunt the effect of his accumulation of εὐ-compounds (not merely 992, but 1019, 1026, 1030f., 1034, 1035, 1038) by using the syllable from a different root. Wecklein's Appendix and Dawe's *Repertory of conjectures on Aeschylus* (Leiden 1965) record various unconvincing attempts to replace the word with εὔφρονες *uel sim*. εὐμενίδες as a feminine adjective will hardly do. Headlam boldly prints εὐμενέες. Whatever was written was glossed with εὔφρονες, which was then expanded *metri causa* to εὐφύφρονες? (I take this opportunity of pointing out the curious – though probably irrelevant – fact that, in Euripides, the Furies are anonymous in *Electra*, always Erinyes in *IT*, always Eumenides in *Orestes*.)

[40] References could be multiplied. Cf. e.g. Thomson (3) I, 69; R. F. Goheen, *AJP* 76 (1955) 122–32; Lebeck 131ff.; (on light and darkness) J. Peradotto, *AJP* 85 (1964) 388ff.; (on colour) Macleod (1), esp. n. 73; (on *ololugmos*) Haldane 37f.

happened. Or rather one has happened and one is happening, to justify the faith of Aeschylus – for this closing scene is in essence an expression of faith. Athena, by instituting the court of the Areopagus, has shown a way of dealing with homicide which avoids the recurrent bloodshed of the vendetta. It is a better way than that of the Erinyes demanding blood for blood, a better way than that of Apollo, who may accuse his adversaries of barbarity, but cannot himself solve the problem, because his own code is tied to a barbarous vengeance by the next of kin. Now the first thing we are told about the Athenians in this play (12f.) is that they were road-builders who made a wild land civilized;[41] and what we see in the play, as it proceeds, is a new development in civilization taking place in Athens under the guidance of a daughter of Zeus. What actually has happened? We might put it this way: the Erinyes have transferred their sphere of operation from the clan or the family to the city-state. For what is now revealed of their nature is by way of addition rather than subtraction. They will still dwell underground, but will send up the benefits of earth and not its plagues. They will send them to those who deserve it, but they are still ministers of punishment. 'Great is the power,' says Athena, 'of the sovereign Erinys . . . To some they bring songs, but to others a life blinded with tears' (950ff.).[42] In their unreconciled state they thought that it was only through blood-vengeance that the sanctity of life could be protected. But Athena saw – and made them see – that a less frightful means was possible within the framework of the state. The Areopagus, the court of law, has taken the place of the blood-avenger, but the parties to a case of homicide will swear an oath by the Erinyes.[43] A divine sanction behind the human court, they have come to represent that element of force and fear without which no society yet known to men can be maintained. 'From these fearful visages,' says Athena, 'I see great gain for these citizens' (990f.).[44]

[41] See ch. 7, n. 75.

[42]
μέγα γὰρ δύναται πότνι' Ἐρινὺς
παρά τ' ἀθανάτοις τοῖς θ' ὑπὸ γαῖαν,
περί τ' ἀνθρώπων φανέρ' ὡς τελέως
διαπράσσουσιν, τοῖς μὲν ἀοιδάς,
τοῖς δ' αὖ δακρύων
βίον ἀμβλωπὸν παρέχουσαι.

[43] Cf. E. Rohde, Psyche (Eng. transl., London 1925) 178, 212 n. 156.

[44]
ἐκ τῶν φοβερῶν τῶνδε προσώπων
μέγα κέρδος ὁρῶ τοῖσδε πολίταις·
τάσδε γὰρ εὔφρονας εὔφρονες ἀεὶ
μέγα τιμῶντες καὶ γῆν καὶ πόλιν
ὀρθοδίκαιον
πρέψετε πάντως διάγοντες.

Fear is not banished; retribution is not banished. 'While Zeus abides upon the throne, it abides that the doer must suffer.' So the Chorus of *Agamemnon*. 'It is for the doer to suffer: this is the voice of a thrice-ancient word.' So the Coryphaeus of *Choephori*; and by the antiquity of the law no disparagement is implied. Justice it was, and the justice of Zeus. Under the old order the doer suffers and the sufferer retaliates and a kind of justice is done, but violence breeds violence and evil is perpetuated in the process of its punishment. If Zeus were in the old order only, then the prospect for mankind would indeed be grim, the Hymn to Zeus would offer little reassurance. But Zeus is also in the wisdom of Athena, who says: 'To me also has Zeus given the gift of a good understanding' (850).[45] In Zeus she places her trust (826); and, after she has reconciled the Erinyes by her persuasions, she ascribes the victory to Zeus Agoraios (973).

When Zeus was worshipped at Athens, as in some other states, under the title of Agoraios,[46] it was as presiding over the civic life of the city; and it is in the context of a city-state that Zeus' daughter finds her solution to the problem of homicide. But what, specifically, is the victory which has been won, and which she ascribes to Zeus under this title? Not, surely, as Farnell thought, the victorious ending of the trial of Orestes. The lines refer rather to Athena's 'strife for good' (974f.) which has won a victory over the angry Furies. 'I love,' she has just said (970f.), 'the eyes of Persuasion, for they have looked upon my voice and tongue.'[47] Zeus – the political Zeus – is the ultimate authority, Peitho the minor divinity who carries out his purposes.[48] Zeus wills the development of a democratic Athens; Peitho is the power which should make it work in a community that speaks, reasons and persuades, as Athena has persuaded the Erinyes. It is a structural feature of the play that, whereas Apollo abuses them, threatens them with violence, and achieves nothing, Athena treats them from the first with tact and courtesy, and ends by persuading them to accept a place in her regime. This business of *persuading* Erinyes is indeed remarkable.[49]

---

[45]   φρονεῖν δὲ κἀμοὶ Ζεὺς ἔδωκεν οὐ κακῶς.

[46] Cf. Farnell, *The cults of the Greek states* I (Oxford 1896) 58f.

[47]   στέργω δ' ὄμματα Πειθοῦς,
ὅτι μοι γλῶσσαν καὶ στόμ' ἐπωπᾷ
πρὸς τάσδ' ἀγρίως ἀπανηναμένας·
ἀλλ' ἐκράτησε Ζεὺς ἀγοραῖος·
νικᾷ δ' ἀγαθῶν
ἔρις ἡμετέρα διὰ παντός.

[48] See below, p. 169.

[49] At 383f., amid a cluster of significant epithets, they describe themselves as σεμναὶ καὶ δυσπαρήγοροι βροτοῖς: in the outcome they will be persuaded to be Semnai! For a similar paradox – Furies who can pity – cf. Soph. *O.C.* 84ff., on which see Winnington-Ingram 265.

The antithesis between force and persuasion is natural and obvious; as a tool of Greek thought it was inherited by Aeschylus from the common stock of proverbial wisdom. Do we say, then, force is evil and persuasion good? No such simple categorization fits the facts of the case or comes up to the level of Aeschylean thought. In Aeschylus, neither power is absolutely good or absolutely evil. Clytemnestra, the temptress, persuades her husband to his undoing; and there persuasion and force converge to the same evil end.[50] We may remember the striking paradox in the first *stasimon* of *Agamemnon*, where the Chorus, thinking of Paris and the persuasive power of sexual attraction, sing that the 'bad' Peitho works violence.[51] There she is a spirit attendant upon Ate, but in *Eumenides* she serves Zeus Agoraios through the *thelkterioi muthoi* of Athena, working beneficially even upon the very embodiments of *bia*. Nor, for that matter, is *bia* less ambivalent than *peitho*, being itself a potential minister of good. That is surely the mystery of those stanzas about Zeus in the *parodos* of *Agamemnon*, the law of learning by suffering, the paradoxical grace or favour (*charis*) of divinities (*daimones*) who exercise their awful (*semnon*) authority by violence (*biaiōs*). These things are hard to understand in the context of *Agamemnon* and *Choephori*, where the lesson is never learnt until it is too late, the *charis* is victory in a bloody conflict that corrupts the victor's *sophrosune*, the justice of Zeus is conditioned by the violence of its Fury-agents. Surely, Aeschylus has chosen language at the end of this stanza which suggests those ministers of Zeus who haunt the succeeding phases of the trilogy.[52] Surely, it is not until the closing phase that the Hymn to Zeus acquires its full meaning. How can *bia* be beneficent? When it is exercised within the framework of a city-state. That is one question and its answer. There is another. How can Erinyes become Eumenides? And the answer is: through the persuasions of an Athena. For, in *Eumenides*, not only does she teach mankind how to solve a specific social problem: she teaches us how to deal with Furies. This is that second thing which justifies the faith of Aeschylus in the triumph of good over evil.

Erinyes meet us in the trilogy primarily in the context of the blood-feud. For this Athena substitutes legal process, with rational argument and consideration of circumstances before a court. The court represents a citizen body for which the control of homicide is a vital political interest. Immediately following the goddess's reference to Zeus Agoraios, the

[50] For the role of Peitho in the 'return-match' cf. *Cho.* 726, where she is given the epithet δολία and associated with chthonian Hermes.

[51] *Agam.* 385f., on which see App. B.

[52] See p. 158 above.

Chorus prays that Stasis may never raise its ugly noise in the city nor the dust drink the black blood of citizens, be angry and exact a swift penalty of blood for blood (976ff.).[53] The murder of Ephialtes was still fresh in the memory of the audience; the fear of clan feuds was not an empty one nor the control of private vengeance a matter of remote social history.[54] Nevertheless, one may doubt whether the significance of the Aeschylean Erinyes is exhausted by a narrow, if vital, social theme.

The last statement about the divine world made in the trilogy is striking and perhaps surprising. Before the final *ololugmos*, it is sung by the Chorus of Propompoi that all-seeing Zeus and Moira have 'joined forces' (συγκατέβα, 1045f.).[55] The words need not perhaps imply that they have been at variance, but they are distinguished as powers. Within this play a distinction is already to be seen in the second *stasimon*. The Erinyes claim no authority from a Zeus who shuns their company: it was Moira (or a Moira) that spun the thread which from their very birth gave them their function to perform; the law which they proclaim is *moirokrantos*.[56] Turn back to *Choephori*, to the anapaests which introduce the *kommos* (306ff.). They tell of the great cry raised by Dike as she exacts her debt: 'For a word of hate let a word of hate be accomplished (τελείσθω); for a bloody blow let him pay a bloody blow. He has done, he must suffer.' Dike, we know, is daughter of Zeus; Zeus, we know, is *teleios*; the cry echoes the words of the Chorus at *Agam.* 1563f., when they sing that 'it abides, while Zeus abides upon the throne, for the doer to suffer'. But the prayer for accomplishment, if it is to be *Diothen* – emanating from Zeus, is yet addressed to the 'great Moirai'.

It seems that this is one form which the religious and philosophical problem of the trilogy takes on for Aeschylus: the relationship of Moira (or Moirai) to Zeus, of an ineluctable fate to a god who is spoken of as *teleios*, as

---

53   τὰν δ' ἄπληστον κακῶν
μήποτ' ἐν πόλει στάσιν
τᾷδ' ἐπεύχομαι βρέμειν.
μηδὲ πιοῦσα κόνις μέλαν αἷμα πολιτᾶν
δι' ὀργὰν ποινᾶς
ἀντιφόνους ἄτας
ἁρπαλίσαι πόλεως.

54   Cf. Dover 234f. Macleod (1) 130, is right to remark that 'to pray for a city that it should be free of faction is natural and normal at any time', but the thoughts of the audience in 458 B.C. might well go back to the assassination of Ephialtes.

55   The best clue to the metaphorical force of συγκαταβαίνω (on which see Groeneboom *ad loc.*) is perhaps to be found in *Cho.* 727. Zeus and Moira have 'joined forces', they are 'on the same side', the stress being more on their present convergence than on a past divergence.

56   *Eum.* 391–3 (θεσμὸν τὸν μοιρόκραντον ἐκ θεῶν δοθέντα τέλεον). The wording is perhaps deliberately obscure. The *thesmos* is 'granted by the gods', with the suggestion that this province has been willingly surrendered by them, but ratified by *moira*; and this the Chorus regard as the end of the matter.

all-powerful, the doer and cause of all.[57] It is an old problem not to be resolved by ransacking Homer or questioning the common man who will at one moment be overcome with a feeling of inevitable and inscrutable destiny and at another situate his hopes and fears in a more or less anthropomorphic deity. What one can say, in a general way, is that *moira* (in whatever degree of personification, singular or plural) – and indeed the whole wide vocabulary of fatality – connotes the rigid, the intractable, the violent, the blind, the primitive, aspect of divine operation. The question may be that of an arbitrary and unintelligible destiny decreed at birth, but this is not the most characteristic Aeschylean view, least of all in *Oresteia*. When Orestes says (*Cho.* 911) that Moira has brought about his mother's death, it is not meant that a mysterious dispensation has singled her out of all people to meet this of all fates but rather that she is involved in a process which leads inevitably to the matricide. At the same time it is ironically true of Orestes himself, not that he has been chosen by a malign fate to murder his mother (as Oedipus to lie with his), but that the course on which he is set will inevitably result in his pursuit by Erinyes. Moira stands in fact for the rigidity of the law of *talio*, an inexorable power with which you could not plead or reason. The Furies who carry out the decrees of Fate have the same characteristics. They are rigid, like the operations of cause and effect (which in part they represent); they are blind (and so are well called daughters of Night)[58] and, being blind, tend also to be indiscriminately cruel. They are said to be mindful (*mnemones*),[59] because through them the past lives in the present repeating its patterns, as bloodshed evokes bloodshed in the vendetta.

How, then, are the world and man and human society to be liberated from the bondage of an automatic Necessity, with self-repeating patterns of evil and destruction? The Chorus of *Agamemnon* put their confidence in Zeus. But the justice of Zeus – of a Zeus who sends Erinyes – appears no less rigid. The Chorus of *Choephori* couple Zeus and Moirai (and Erinyes)

---

[57] τέλειος (*Agam.* 973); παναίτιος, πανεργέτας (*Agam.* 1485f.); παγκρατής (*Eum.* 918). The issue is clearly raised in *Prometheus Vinctus*, which may not be the work of Aeschylus, but is in many respects highly Aeschylean. At 515 the Coryphaeus asks: 'Who is the helmsman of necessity (ἀνάγκης)?', and Prometheus replies: 'The tri-formed Moirai and the mindful (μνήμονες) Erinyes'. 'Is Zeus then weaker than they?' 'Yes, he could not escape from what is fated (τὴν πεπρωμένην).' The passage is well discussed by Fraenkel III 729. See also Winnington-Ingram, App. C, 334f., with particular reference to some difficulties in the language of 511f. Winnington-Ingram ch. 7 ('Fate in Sophocles') has a discussion of fate in Aeschylus (pp. 155–9), some of which is repeated below.

[58] Here Aeschylus departs from the Hesiodic version of their parentage. It is much stressed (321, 745, 791f., 844, 1034); and they are thus, on the mother's side, sisters of the Moirai (961).

[59] 383, cf. *PV* 516, Soph. *Aj.* 1390; and we should not forget the μνάμων Μῆνις of *Agam.* 155 (on which see n. 21 above).

as the divine authorities behind *talio*. We revert once more to the strategy of the trilogy. *Eumenides* sorts things out which have been fused in the earlier plays, only that they may be harmonized at a higher level. The rigid justice of Zeus is presented visibly and audibly at its most horrible, without mention of Zeus except to say that he shuns the company of its executors; claiming to derive their function from Moira, they find themselves in conflict first with one and then with another child of Zeus. The solution is found by Zeus' daughter, relying on Zeus' wisdom and Zeus' power. The last statement in the trilogy about the divine world is that Moira and all-seeing Zeus have 'come down together'. The solution involves a transformation of the Furies. What does this mean?

Note then, first, that the Furies, whatever they represent, are divine. That is why they must not only be recognized, they must be worshipped. They are *semnai* (awful or worshipful), and we do right to stand in awe of them. This is particularly true in the moral sphere, since they represent the inexorable consequences of our actions. But they must also be subjected to the influence of that other great power which is creative of events – the power of Peitho or Persuasion. Athena shows the way to deal with them, which is not to deny them (respect for fact being the beginning of wisdom), not to abuse and threaten them (as Apollo did and only made them rage the more furiously), but to reason, persuade and reconcile, to make them Eumenides, and so bring about, not only a reconciliation, but a collaboration of Force and Persuasion towards good ends. Athena shows how to do it, and that it can be done, and that it is the ultimate will of Zeus that it shall be done. For Athena represents a higher level of the divine purpose than the Furies (or Apollo), being a goddess of wisdom, the patron-goddess of Athens, with its social progress, its intellectual activity, and its creation of harmony in many forms. Among those forms is that of tragedy.

At this point it might be wiser to stop, reflecting merely how strange it is that philosophers and theologians have not in general taken more interest in tragedy[60] – strange that, in their debates about the problem of evil, they have neglected the evidence of those experts in evil, the tragedians, who have consorted with it intimately and, what is more, have done something with it of a most extraordinary kind. But what is it that they have done?

[60] There are of course important exceptions, e.g. Hegel, Schopenhauer, of whom by far the most interesting, influential – and controversial – is Nietzsche. His *Birth of tragedy* has recently been subjected to an exhaustive examination by M. S. Silk and J. P. Stern (*Nietzsche on tragedy*, Cambridge 1981), to which the reader is referred.

Why is it that, instead of shrinking away in horror, we greet their work as one of the heights of man's creative achievement? Aristotle's 'pleasure' may be the wrong word for an experience which, particularly on the clean palate of youth, can be appalling and heart-rending: why do we welcome and seek to repeat it? Many and various and too often unconvincing are the answers which have been given.[61] Is any better than to say that we value the great tragedies for the truth and honesty and insight with which they illuminate dark areas of human experience in a flawed world? For, if we are to find a formula, it must fit a Sophocles who rejects the consolations tragedy is sometimes thought to offer, and must fit an Aeschylus who, with equal or greater power to evoke the horror and pathos of events, could end his later trilogies with the prospect of a brighter future – a Sophocles who so often depicts a failure to persuade, an Aeschylus who hymns the triumphs of persuasion.[62]

By way of epilogue, I should like to refer to two systematic philosophers, one ancient and the other modern, whose thought seems to have significant points of contact with that of Aeschylus. The ancient philosopher is – oddly enough – that Plato who banished the tragedians from his ideal state, because they attributed evil to the gods. There is a remarkable passage in *Timaeus* where he states that 'the generation of this universe was a mixed result of the combination of Necessity and Reason'.[63] He goes on: 'Reason over-ruled Necessity by persuading her to guide the greatest part of the things that become towards what is best; in that way and on that principle this universe was fashioned in the beginning by the victory of reasonable persuasion over Necessity.' The significant point is, of course, the conception of a Necessity that can be 'persuaded' – a notion which commentators find perplexing. In making the link with Aeschylus, I am encouraged by F. M. Cornford who, casually as it were, in an Epilogue to *Plato's cosmology*,[64] threw out this suggestion and made a valuable contribution to the interpretation of the closing scene of *Eumenides*. Whether Plato would have been prepared to carry this conception into the moral world we cannot say. Nor is it very likely that he derived it from Aeschylus. (Would he have looked for – or condescended to recognize

---

[61] See Silk and Stern, op. cit. 265–80 (for a subtle analysis of N.'s conception of the tragic, with particular reference to modern discussions by F. R. Leavis, *The common pursuit*, London 1952, and A. M. Quinton, *Proc. of the Aristotelian Society*, 1960); 312–26 (on Hegel); 326–31 (on Schopenhauer).

[62] For such a view of Sophocles, see Winnington-Ingram, esp. ch. 11.

[63] *Timaeus* 48a 2ff.

[64] *Plato's cosmology* (London 1937) 361ff.

– philosophic truth in a tragic poet?) A. N. Whitehead, one of the few
modern philosophers to have paid adequate attention to tragedy, knew
Plato and also knew Aeschylus. The important role of 'persuasion' in the
creative process as he envisages it will be familiar to those who still pay
serious attention to this seminal thinker. There is a passage in *Adventures of
ideas*[65] where he speaks of Plato's 'final conviction . . . that the divine
element in the world is to be conceived as a persuasive agency and not as a
coercive agency'. 'This doctrine,' he says, 'should be looked upon as one of
the greatest discoveries in the history of religion.' As a comment on Plato,
it may be too narrowly founded upon that one passage in *Timaeus*. As a
comment on Aeschylus, it might well stand, with one modification (which
Whitehead might have accepted). That the Greek gods of power, with all
their record of forceful action, might in the outcome be not only coercive
but persuasive agencies – that, surely, was the great contribution of
Aeschylus to Greek religious, and for that matter philosophical, thought.
That is the final lesson of *Oresteia*; and, so far as we can divine the outcome
of the Danaid trilogy, it is likely to have been the lesson there also; and
there are indications that in the development of the Prometheus story the
author of *Prometheus Vinctus* – whether Aeschylus or another writing
under the influence of Aeschylean thought – found the solution to a
cosmic problem in the triumph of persuasion over violence.[66]

[65] *Adventures of ideas* (Cambridge 1933) 213.
[66] On *peitho*, see now R. G. A. Buxton, *Persuasion in Greek Tragedy* (Cambridge 1983).

CHAPTER NINE

Towards an interpretation of
Prometheus Bound

He who writes on Aeschylus is here confronted with a difficult problem. Ancient scholarship regarded *PV*[1] as a genuine play, but in modern times serious doubt has been thrown upon its authenticity. To omit it entirely from consideration would be arrogant, possibly premature, and indeed (for reasons which may appear) unhelpful to the study of Aeschylus: to treat it as without question Aeschylean is no longer sensible.

W. Schmid's famous attack upon the authenticity was treated with unmerited scorn, for which, however, there was some excuse in the arbitrary and perverse character of much of his argumentation. A decade ago the evidence was re-examined by C. J. Herington, who, without reliance upon the Sicilian hypothesis, found himself able to defend the play as authentic Aeschylus. More recently, Mark Griffith, who entered on his research with some confidence that he would reach a similar conclusion, after a fair-minded and infinitely careful examination accumulated evidence which bears against the Aeschylean authorship: devising relatively objective tests, he has added substantially to the already acknowledged anomalies and built up a powerful case, all the more telling for the modesty with which it is presented.[2] For un-Aeschylean features it

---

[1] The play is commonly referred to as *Prometheus Vinctus*. For Λυόμενος there is no Latin equivalent, the language having no present participle passive: *solutus* is incorrect and could even be misleading. Since I have to refer constantly to the two plays in association, it has seemed better to distinguish them as *Desmotes* and *Luomenos*, but I have used the convenient abbreviation *PV* in references and occasionally elsewhere.

[2] W. Schmid, *Untersuchungen zum Gefesselten Prometheus* (Stuttgart 1929); C. J. Herington, *The author of the Prometheus Bound* (Austin, Texas 1970); Griffith (1). See also Taplin 240–75 (who finds many dramatic techniques which are 'unlike Aeschylus as we know him from the other plays') and App. D, 460–9 (where he reviews 'the accepted and assumed defences against attack' on the authenticity of the play). The 'Sicilian hypothesis' has taken various forms but is, basically, that the play was influenced, and some of its peculiarities are to be explained, by Aeschylus' visit or visits to Sicily; and by some it is thought to have been written in Sicily towards the end of the poet's life for

is often possible to think up explanations: as they multiply, the question arises in the mind how many special hypotheses one should allow oneself![3]

The surprising role of Zeus is no great difficulty, once the problematic character of the Oresteian Zeus is understood. Given a charming but ineffectual chorus, a diminished role for its songs perhaps followed. Given a static hero, long expository speeches perhaps followed. Given a largely divine cast, greater simplicity of style perhaps followed to redress the balance (and we need not posit a Sicilian audience of Dorian speech). And so on. These are major features bound to have been under conscious control: it is the relatively minor – even trivial – differences which have the greater evidential value. Metrical matters are not exactly trivial, but this type of evidence is an impressive part of Griffith's case. Here again we must be careful. It is not the absence of characteristic Aeschylean metrical schemes that impresses: Aeschylus might well have thought that the heavily syncopated iambics so prominent in *Oresteia* (in theological and tensely emotional contexts) – and for that matter the slow trochaics or iambo-trochaics – were inappropriate to a simple-minded chorus of young females. What should disconcert the orthodox is relatively trivial features in the handling of iambic trimeters, trochaic lyrics and recitative anapaests.[4]

Uneasy in mind, some critics have fallen back on a rhetorical question. Is it conceivable that there were two poets, one of them to us anonymous, capable of the grand conception of this work, capable of writing such a scene as the entry of Io? But perhaps, under the influence of Aristophanes and Aristotle, we assume too easily that there were only three tragedians in the fifth century who were any good. There were others who, to our knowledge, won prizes defeating the great names of Sophocles and Euripides. Should we assume that verdicts of this kind were simply perverse? Among the tragedians were sons of Aeschylus. There remains the possibility that Aeschylus did have a hand in the composition of this piece, that he left a scenario and perhaps written passages. No ground, however, could be less secure than that. The fact remains that no honest scholar can still retain a simple faith in the Aeschylean authorship of the play: so many indications converge to distinguish it from the extant plays.

The matter is complicated, however, by the question of a sequel: there are *two* plays to be considered, one extant and the other lost. Those who

performance there. The hypothesis has recently been critically examined by Griffith (2). Full bibliography in Griffith (1) and (2).

[3] Cf. Taplin, App. D (see n. 2 above).

[4] Summarized by Griffith (1) on pp. 66, 74f., 101f.

have accepted the unauthenticity of *PV* have generally considered it to be a *monodrama*, an isolated play; to the older orthodoxy it formed part of a trilogy, a *Prometheia*, though there has been much dispute as to that trilogy's constitution. It has been argued that *Desmotes* needs no sequel. But can this be true? Can it be true of a play which deals with an apparently irreconcilable conflict, yet with mysterious hints of a final resolution; which builds up towards the revelation of a secret of cosmic significance; which foreshadows the ultimate loosing of Prometheus from his bonds – and his loosing by Heracles? The play demands a sequel no less than *Supplices* and *Agamemnon* demand sequels. Not only so, but it demands a sequel like the lost *Luomenos* (about which we know or can plausibly conjecture more than we had any right to expect).[5] To the details we will come later, here mentioning only that in it Prometheus suffers the intensification of his torture foretold in *Desmotes*, that Heracles was a character and shot the gluttonous eagle of Zeus. As for the notion that some later poet looked at a genuine *Luomenos*, itself presumably a *monodrama*, and exercised his wits by writing precisely that play which might have preceded it, if it had had a predecessor, that is a theoretical possibility which will only commend itself to those who are desperately anxious to uphold a position. No, *Desmotes* and *Luomenos* stand or fall together as genuine works of Aeschylus. To the sequel and the trilogy, if trilogy there was, we must return, when we have sought to interpret the extant play. For it is a notable play, whether by Aeschylus or by another. It could be that the attempt to understand what we possess may throw some light upon what we have lost.

PV presents a conflict. What happens when an irresistible force meets an immovable object? The tiro in logic can solve the problem: the dramatist's task is more difficult. Zeus and Prometheus are both characterized by *authadia* or self-willed obstinacy.[6] Zeus is a tyrant, presented visibly through his minions Kratos and Bia, depicted as unpersuadable; Prometheus is no less stubborn. It is a main function of the Oceanus-scene to bring out the apparently insoluble nature of the conflict. The dramatic movement is towards an intensification of the resistance of Prometheus, leading to an intensification of his punishment. Yet the situation *must* have been resolved. The human race *did* survive, despite the hostility of Zeus; Prometheus *did* become an effective deity with a cult in Athens. The

---

[5] Cf. R. Unterberger, *Der gefesselte Prometheus des Aischylos* (Stuttgart 1968) 9 and *passim*. See also the review by H. Lloyd-Jones, *CR* 20 (1970) 241f.

[6] For αὐθαδία cf. 907 (Zeus); 964, 1012, 1034 (Prometheus).

situation has an Aeschylean potential. Known trilogies of Aeschylus end
with solutions of some kind to problems of some kind: *Oresteia* certainly,
the Danaid trilogy probably. There are hints of an ultimate solution in
PV.[7] One hint comes early: the reluctance and sympathy of the first
tormentor – and an Athenian audience knew that Hephaestus was to share
an altar with Prometheus in Athens. The Io-story is ambivalent; and if her
sufferings seem to intensify the hero's hatred for Zeus, he knows that a
happier destiny awaits her. There is a hint – indeed a statement – that he
will be released by a descendant of Io's, though in circumstances which
cannot yet be imagined. And there is the 'secret weapon' of Prometheus,
who knows that Zeus will contemplate a 'marriage' leading to his
downfall; *he* knows to whom, but will not reveal it. *We* know – and the
audience knew – that Zeus will be in danger through his lust for Thetis: we
also know that the 'marriage' did *not* take place, that Zeus did *not* fall.
Therefore, the secret *was* revealed, but in what circumstances we – and
they – do not yet know. (Is it conceivable that any competent dramatist
could have left a single play in such a state as this? For that matter, is it
conceivable that *Luomenos*, as known to us, did *not* have a predecessor
something like *Desmotes*?)

A solution could have been reached on various levels. There could have
been a simple bargain: Zeus agrees to the release of Prometheus in return
for the revelation of the secret. And such a bargain there may well have
been. But a simple piece of horse-trading seems beneath the level not only
of Aeschylean tragedy but also of *PV*, whoever wrote it. The writer has in
fact handled the theme with skill to engage the curiosity of the audience
and also (it would seem) to relate the forward-looking utterances to the
mental states of the hero. The first revelation comes in the *parodos*.
Prometheus tells the Chorus (167ff.) that Zeus will come to need him, to
reveal the new design which threatens his power, but that he, Prometheus,
will not be persuaded to reveal it until he is released and compensated.
Zeus, harsh though he is, will some day be *malakognomon* and seek his
friendship – and Prometheus will meet him (σπεύδων σπεύδοντι, 192). As
the play proceeds, the unlikelihood of this development increases. Still, at
257f., when the Chorus asks whether any term is set to his ordeal, he
replies: 'None other, except when it seems good to him' (which implies a
decision or an agreement on Zeus' part). At 511, after the Oceanus-scene, a

---

[7] Accepting the authenticity of *PV*, C. J. Herington (*Arion* 4, 1965, 387–403) argued that a 'last phase'
of Aeschylean drama was characterized by movements of this kind. The argument is weakened, but
not necessarily invalidated, if *PV* is attributed to another poet and a post-Aeschylean date.

new theme is introduced with great emphasis – the joint theme of destiny (Moira) and necessity (*ananke*). Prometheus is destined to escape his bonds, but only after much torture. Not even Zeus can evade a fated destiny (518). To the question 'What is fated for Zeus except to rule for ever?' no answer is yet given.[8] The next development is in the Io-scene. Io is mortal, Prometheus not fated to die. Death would have been the riddance of his woes. 'As it is, no term is set to my toils until Zeus falls from his tyranny' (755f.). Which is not what he said at 257f. Surely, this is no oversight on the part of the poet. The hero now assumes that Zeus *will* make the fatal marriage (764), that he himself will withhold the saving knowledge, since Zeus will not loose him (770), and thus that Zeus will fall. It is that situation which is eloquently presented by Prometheus at 907ff.: the curse of Kronos fulfilled, a fallen Zeus suffering worse torments than Prometheus now endures. Why this change? Surely, because his hatred for Zeus has been intensified by the plight of Io. He longs for Zeus to fall.

One might be reminded of Philoctetes, who cannot bring himself to benefit the Atridae, even to his own advantage.[9] But there is a difference. Prometheus knows that he is destined to be loosed, and by a descendant of Io (769–72). The four lines are vital, but ambiguous. 'And is there,' asks Io, 'no escape for him from this fortune?' 'No,' replies Prometheus, 'except for me only, if I were released from bonds.' 'Who then will be your liberator when Zeus is unwilling?'[10] 'It is destined to be one of your descendants.' The words are consistent with three possibilities. (i) There are limits to Prometheus' knowledge of a future which is, after all, contingent on a decision he has yet to take: he only knows that some day he will be loosed. Sure that Zeus will not loose him, determined not to reveal his secret, he believes that Zeus will fall, whereupon his enemy's writ no longer runs, his will no longer counts. This is what Prometheus may well have in mind. (ii) The words can, however, be taken to imply (though this will not be what Prometheus means) that the liberator will act in defiance of a still-powerful Zeus. (iii) There is a third possibility. He can be taken to be answering the question: 'Who will be the liberator?', disregarding the last two words of Io's sentence and thus leaving it open that Heracles acts with the consent of Zeus. Of the three possibilities the audience knows – and we know – that (i) is excluded by the facts. The audience has no sure ground for choosing between (ii) and (iii), and modern scholars are rash to use this passage,

---

[8] On this passage and its relation to Aeschylean thought, see Winnington-Ingram 334f.
[9] Cf. Winnington-Ingram 295ff.
[10] In 771, there seems little to be said for Pauw's ἄρχοντος – a possible but superfluous emendation, if indeed it is not damaging.

confidently, in reconstructing the sequel. In short, the extant play hints at a solution but gives no clear indication of how that solution was reached – a surprising feature, surely, in a *monodrama* written by a competent dramatist. Zeus changes his mind, or Prometheus changes his mind, or there is a change of mind in both parties, but why this or that or both these things happen does not emerge. At this point we should consider what Zeus stands for, and what Prometheus, bearing in mind that there is a third party involved, which is the human race.

First, then, for Zeus.[11] What is abundantly clear – and has always surprised – is that the picture of Zeus corresponds at point after point with the traditional Greek picture of the tyrant.[12] Zeus is almost, but not quite, a character in the play. He does not appear, but is represented by his servants, Kratos and Bia,[13] and, at the end of the play, by his 'lackey' (941) Hermes. It can be said that all the minor characters are figures to be found in a tyrant's court: Hephaestus, the unwilling accomplice; Oceanus, the man of would-be influence, careful of his own skin; Hermes, the willing agent. There is much stress on Zeus as the *new* ruler[14] – and the arbitrary ruler. Clearly, if Zeus comes to an accommodation with Prometheus (as he *must* have done), there has been a development. In the situation? No longer the new ruler, he can afford to relax his severity? Or is it just that he sees a threat to his rule and, wisely, evades it? Or does his nature change, develop, evolve? This is a controversial conception, on which it is not too easy to form a sensible view.[15] For Reinhardt two aspects of divinity are set side by side in Aeschylus, both valid. This is an important insight: but is the order in which they appear a matter of indifference? The Erinyes in *Oresteia* could be a helpful analogy, not least because they are ministers of the justice of Zeus. For the greater part of the trilogy, they stand for a harsh law of retaliation violently applied; in the outcome they add to this function a benevolence – a fructifying not a withering power – but without losing their harsh penal function. It could be that, in the development of the

[11] G. Grossmann, *Promethie und Orestie* (Heidelberg 1970), who accepts *PV* as authentic, discusses the relationship between the two pictures of Zeus on pp. 272–90.

[12] The evidence is conveniently assembled by Thomson (2) 6–12. (I am much indebted to his edition throughout.)

[13] It has not always been observed that Bia will have been a female figure. We know that female police agents were employed in Syracuse in the fifth century, and support has been found in these facts for the 'Sicilian hypothesis' (see n. 2 above). See, however, Griffith (2) 124.

[14] New ruler: cf. 35, 148ff.

[15] The notion of a developing Zeus has been defended, as against e.g. L. R. Farnell (*JHS* 53, 1933, 47), H. Lloyd-Jones (*JHS* 76, 1956, 56f.), by e.g. A. D. Fitton-Brown (*JHS* 79, 1959, 52ff.) and Dodds (2) 41ff. (with additional references to modern work). 'Common sense . . . would suggest that a god who wears one aspect at one time and an opposite one thirteen generations later might reasonably be supposed to have changed in the meantime' (Lucas (2nd ed.) 106).

Prometheus-situation (by Aeschylus or by a poet working under his influence), Zeus adds without subtracting. Indeed it has been suggested, on the evidence of Plato's *Protagoras*,[16] that, as part of the settlement, a Zeus who now accepts the survival of humanity gives his own social gifts to man, showing himself in a new aspect. Are we back with the embarrassing concept of an evolving Zeus? Or are we perhaps asking the wrong question? Perhaps we should turn to the third party and ask ourselves in what light primitive man could possibly see the powers governing his universe except one of harshness and force. Has Zeus evolved? That question may be beyond our comprehension to answer. But human society has evolved. Let us turn to Prometheus.

Prometheus is punished for the theft and gift of fire, which is stressed at the outset. A cardinal feature of the play, however, is the couple of long expository speeches from the hero which begin with a picture of man in the Hobbesian state of nature, his life poor, nasty and brutish, and ends with the proud claim: 'All arts (*technai*) for mortals come from Prometheus' (506). Dodds[17] has warned us that we should not talk too glibly of technology. Fire leads to metallurgy and ceramics, but of these metallurgy is barely mentioned (714) by this craftsmen's god and ceramics (and the potter's wheel) not at all. The stress throughout is rather on applied intelligence. Still, technology or no technology, it is a remarkable product of anthropological insight (to whomsoever the writer may have been indebted).[18] The human race is confronted with a situation calculated to destroy it, which is represented as the intention of Zeus; and it would have been destroyed, if it were not for Prometheus with his gift of fire – and his gift of hope. It might seem surprising that this is prior to the gift of fire, yet without it men would have despaired and could have made no use of his later gifts.[19] This spiritual, if dangerous, gift was necessary to the whole

---

[16] Plato, *Prot.* 321d 3: τὴν μὲν οὖν περὶ τὸν βίον σοφίαν ἄνθρωπος ταύτῃ ἔσχεν, τὴν δὲ πολιτικὴν οὐκ εἶχεν· ἦν γὰρ παρὰ τῷ Διί (which may recall *PV* 186f.); 322c 1–5 (where Zeus sends Hermes with the gift of αἰδώς and δίκη to men). Cf. H. Lloyd-Jones 99.

[17] Dodds (2) 5, 32 n. 1.

[18] It could well be Protagoras? Cf. West 147 (with references).

[19] After 247 we expect the gift of fire: what we get instead is therefore likely to be important. Greek poets had for long been thinking about the nature of hope and its role in human life, which was ambivalent, as Sophocles was to say clearly at *Ant.* 615ff. (on which see Winnington-Ingram 171f.). Hesiod, *WD* 96ff., has been much discussed. Why was Elpis left behind in Pandora's Box? As a good thing or a bad? Probably the former (cf. West *ad loc.*), though the implications are far from clear. For Solon, fr. 1.36, hope is a deceptive thing, and this is a notion which might be suggested by the epithet τυφλὰς applied to ἐλπίδας by Prometheus, yet it is described by the Coryphaeus (presumably without irony) as a gift of great benefit. What then, precisely, was it that Prometheus gave? 'I stopped mortals,' he says, 'from προδέρκεσθαι μόρον.' Plato, *Gorg.* 523d (where the point is obscure and it is not clear if it derives from the passage in *PV* – see Dodds *ad loc.*) says that

process of applying intelligence to the amelioration of life. There follows a broad view of the development of human society.

I have spoken of development. Yet it might appear that *PV* could not be more closely circumscribed in point of place and time. Prometheus is the loneliest hero in the history of drama (prior to Beckett) – and the most inactive. Pinned to the rock by Hephaestus on the remote frontiers of the world, far from the mortals he has benefited,[20] he is left alone by his torturers. Alone with nature, which he apostrophizes. But he is visited, the action of the play consisting in a series of visits. He is visited by the Oceanids. Sympathetic (like Hephaestus), they can tell him of the sympathy of mankind; and they provide an audience for the story of his quarrel with Zeus and his services to man. He is visited, from the court of Zeus, by Oceanus and Hermes. Above all, he is visited by Io, the human victim; and, when he tells of her wanderings, past and future, the horizons expand to embrace half the human world (and it seems likely that they were complemented by the wanderings of Heracles in *Luomenos*). So much for place: from this remote spot is surveyed the whole world of gods and men. As for time, the dramatic time is short, and its shortness – between the crucifixion of Prometheus and the intensification of his punishment at the end of the play – seems to be guaranteed by the continuous presence of the Chorus. If we look more closely, however, we shall see that, unobtrusively, the poet has expanded the time-scale within the play.

In the *prologos* the sole emphasis is on the theft of fire; and one is led to suppose that the punishment closely followed the crime. But when Prometheus tells the story of his gifts to mankind, of a progress from primitive cave-dwellers living like beasts to the possessors of all those practical arts of life, all those intellectual techniques (including the art of writing),[21] we have before us the picture of a long process of evolution. It

Prometheus had already been instructed to stop men from foreknowledge of death (προειδότας τὸν θάνατον). What then did Prometheus do? Clearly, the hope of living for ever was not among the blind hopes he implanted, but, if the hour of death was known, the forward gaze (προδέρκεσθαι) would be on it, the brevity of life would be insistent, the certainty of death would inhibit ambition and enterprise. Free of this knowledge, men would be in a fit state of mind to use the gift of fire and derive civilization from it.

20 At 2 the reading ἄβροτον (derived from scholia) is rightly preferred by Page to M's ἄβατον. Cf. 11 (ring-composition).

21 The lines (46of.) are among the most intriguing in the play. 'I discovered for them . . . combinations of letters [to be] the memory of all things (μνήμην ἁπάντων).' The contribution of written record to the development of civilization is obvious enough. He then adds the words μουσομήτορ' ἐργάνην: 'Muse-mother work-woman'. ('Εργάνη is known as a title of Athena.) Memory (Μνημοσύνη) was mother of the Muses (Hesiod, *Theog.* 54, on which see West *ad loc.*). 'The importance of memory to the oral poet needs no stressing' (West), but with Prometheus' invention writing now does her work for her. It is tempting to associate with these lines a group of vases on which Muses carry book-rolls and appear to be singing from them. The group was studied by E.

is a feat of the historical imagination, introduced (do we say?) without much regard for logical consistency – a set-piece on its own. But it does not stand alone in this regard. The story of the theft of fire is a primitive and essentially pre-historical myth, but with Io, primitive as some features in her story may be, we approach history. She is ancestress of the Argive kings and one can count the generations back as they fade from history into a quasi-historical myth. Io's story, moreover, as she recounts it, is not that of primitive cave-dwellers but of a settled monarchy, of a king consulting established oracles. (Inachus may be a river-god, but there is no stress on that.) The passage of time has escaped our notice as we listen to Prometheus on his rock.[22] In *Luomenos*, with Heracles, we are close to Greek history as the Greeks conceived it.[23] He fought in the first Trojan War, and the Heraclidae were closely associated in legend with the foundation of Sparta. But Prometheus is still on his rock, the problem still unsolved. How it was solved in the sequel, what future for the human race was there secured or foretold, we may never be able to establish. Is there not, however, a certain likelihood that, just as in *Oresteia* we pass from the heroic monarchy of Argos to the semblance of democratic Athens, to an Athena who addresses herself not only to the first Areopagites but also to the fifth-century audience, so at the end of the Promethean drama the final settlement was relevant not only to the dramatic setting but also to the poet's own world of city-states? If Zeus gave civic gifts to man, they were gifts to an Athens in which Prometheus was worshipped.

Zeus and the primitive world, Zeus and the civilization of the city-state: so different in aspect. Dare we say, need we say, that Zeus has developed? For Aeschylus Zeus is not a datum, but a mystery to be investigated; not a

Pöhlmann, *Griechische Musikfragmente* (Nuremberg 1960) 10 and Anhang II (who, however, confuses the issue by arguing that the rolls contained musical notation) and later by H. R. Immerwahr, 'Book rolls on Attic vases', *Classical, medieval and renaissance studies in honor of Berthold Louis Ullman* (Storia e letteratura 93, Rome 1964) I 17–48, esp. 28–33. How odd that the daughters of Memory, of all people, should use, should need, libretti! One cannot help wondering whether vase-paintings and *PV* 460f. share the nature of a manifesto in favour of written composition. Of the sixteen vases listed by Immerwahr, the earliest is dated 'about 450 (or little later)' (Beazley) and may have led the way. Five more are attributed to 440–430 or 430, the remainder mostly to the last quarter of the fifth century. It would of course be rash to use this coincidence, intriguing though it is, as evidence for dating *PV*.

[22] Cf. E. T. Owen, *The harmony of Aeschylus* (Toronto 1952) 57.

[23] The time-gap between *Desmotes* and *Luomenos* is specific, if not much emphasized: thirteen generations (*PV* 774). But to Prometheus on the rock it will seem interminable (94). On that line a scholiast states that in *Purphoros* he says he has been bound for three myriads of years; and this has given rise to much rather unprofitable discussion, being used as an argument for placing that play third (because of the perfect tense) or (with or without the emendation δεθήσεσθαι) for placing it first. Without the actual text the matter cannot be settled, but it is likely that, as in *PV* 94, psychology is more in question than chronology.

solution to problems, but himself a problem to be solved. That is why it would not have been impossible for Aeschylus to use myths so diverse for the exploration of the same problem – not impossible for a poet under the influence of Aeschylus to present in *PV* a Zeus apparently so inconsistent with the Zeus of *Persae* or *Oresteia*. As though there were no apparent contradictions in the Oresteian Zeus, who had won a victory of force over his predecessors (*Agam.* 167ff.), but teaches men wisdom, by force (176ff.), who sends those Erinyes that seem to perpetuate evil in the process of punishing it. The Promethean problem may be not dissimilar, though worked out in terms of a different story. Above all, the role of Prometheus constitutes a primary difference. What are we to make of it? That is something far more difficult to understand.

Prometheus is a rebel. A romantic rebel? But there is no 'romance' in Greek tragedy. He is a resister, counterpart of the powerful tyrant whom he resists: equally self-willed, equally stubborn, equally impervious to persuasion. This is well brought out in the scene with Oceanus. And his stubbornness intensifies in the course of the play, as does the force of Zeus. The only prospect for him is continued torture until one of two things happens: Zeus *either* weakens and makes amends *or* by his own folly meets a violent end to his rule – a fate from which Prometheus may or may not save him. Remembering that the drama is played before an audience of human beings, we can disregard the strange view that Prometheus is a meddler, a tiresome sophist, who is rightly punished until he learns to submit. Zeus is depicted – and indeed behaves – as a tyrant; and, however respectful Greeks thought it right to be of lawful authority, it was right to resist tyrants. Is there any sense, then, in which Prometheus can be said to be in the wrong? 'Wittingly I erred' (266).[24] He accepts the term of the Coryphaeus (*hemartes, hemarton*). This action in helping mortals was not only from the point of view of the Zeus-party an offence but, since he was acting against his own interests, it was in terms of Greek prudential morality a folly. The Chorus make their point again at 1036ff. He must learn to be sensible, which is what people demand in vain of Sophoclean heroes.[25] Yet, given Zeus as he is presented, what else *can* a Prometheus do except resist? Resistance to tyranny is resistance, whenever we find it in human history, and it is heroic; and no generation more than ours has had cause to recognize its heroism, familiar as we have become with resisters

---

[24] It is impossible not to think of the Socratic paradox, but rash to draw any inference therefrom.
[25] Knox in an acute passage (45–50) draws attention to Sophoclean features in *Prometheus Bound*.

and 'freedom-fighters'. The stubbornness of Prometheus is determined by the harshness of Zeus.

Yet, in the sequel, Prometheus does concede. For the Oceanids he lacks *euboulia* (1038); to Hermes, after the extravagant language of his response (1040ff.), he seems positively mad (1054ff.).[26] Yet, sooner or later, he will reach that accommodation with Zeus foreshadowed at 190–2. How does this come about? At this point we must consider what we know of *Luomenos*. We know that Prometheus, who sank into Tartarus[27] at the end of *Desmotes*, has been restored to the light of day, still bound to the rock and now tortured by Zeus' eagle that feasts upon his liver. We know that the Chorus consisted of his fellow-Titans, who came to visit him, as the Oceanids visited him in *Desmotes*; and we have two anapaestic fragments which clearly come from their entrance. By a happy stroke of fortune (rare for the student of Greek drama) Cicero was led to translate – and to include in his *Tusculan Disputations* (II 23–25) – a substantial portion of a speech addressed to the Titans by Prometheus. He tells them of his torture by the eagle and of his wish for death. 'What should I fear,' he said at *PV* 933, 'who am not fated to die?' Now[28] he regards death as a boon withheld. Is the hero becoming less heroic, the resister weakening in his resistance, the torturer winning the day, as he so often does? But there is one other significance in the scene and situation. Since the Titans are free to come to him, they have been released from their imprisonment in Tartarus; and the presumption is that Kronos also has been released and established in the Island of the Blessed.[29] The release of his enemies must signify at least a new temper in Zeus, of which Prometheus should take note. One question we should be asking is what kinds of persuasion may have been brought to bear on him during the sequel. The Chorus of Titans might well have carried more weight than the Oceanids. Is any other source of persuasion known to us?

---

[26]
> τοιάδε μέντοι τῶν φρενοπλήκτων
> βουλεύματ' ἔπη τ' ἔστιν ἀκοῦσαι.
> τί γὰρ ἐλλείπει μὴ ⟨οὐ⟩ παραπαίειν
> ἡ τοῦδ' εὐχή; τί χαλᾷ μανιῶν;

[27] Descent into Tartarus, as such, is not part of Hermes' threat at 1016–19 (as Taplin points out, 272), but, in the light of 1029 and 1051, an audience will surely assume that this is where Prometheus is going: 1029, in particular, could be taken to imply that a period in Tartarus was to be part of his πόνοι. (On 1026ff. see n. 52 below). Not too much importance should be attached to this, the main purpose of which is to provide somewhere to put the hero between the two plays.

[28] Fr. 324 M (his page 119, line 11). If Cicero's translation is reliable (*a leto numine aspellor Iouis*), Zeus was given a function attributed at *PV* 933 to fate; and Thomson (2) (19 and n. on *PV* 530–4) draws a tentative conclusion from this about the relation between the two powers.

[29] And the curse of Kronos (910–2) has, presumably, been revoked – an unusual experience for a curse in Greek tragedy.

It is certain that Heracles played a role in *Luomenos* for which there is evidence quite apart from the fact that his name has wandered into the dramatis personae of *Desmotes*. Along with his (and preceding his) we find the name of Ge. Now it is not impossible to think of explanations for her intrusive presence there, but the most likely hypothesis is that she, like him, was a character in *Luomenos*.[30] The mere fact that she is Prometheus' mother might give her right of entry to the play, but this would count for little and give us little inkling of her role, had she not been introduced, with some prominence, in *PV*, where (at 199ff.) he tells his own story of the war in heaven, the internecine struggle between Zeus and the Titans. Then, so he tells us, he gave good counsel to his fellow-Titans, but was unable to persuade them (204ff.); they scorned his crafty devices and relied on force alone (on *kratos* and *bia*, 207f.). Now it was from his mother, whose names were both Themis and Gaia, and from her prophetic foreknowledge that he learnt that victory would lie with guile and not with force (209ff.); and when his counsel was rejected, it seemed best to him in the circumstances to take his mother with him and of his own free will take sides with Zeus; and it was through his counsels that Kronos and all his allies found themselves in Tartarus.

Prometheus tried to persuade but failed. The main antithesis here, however, is between *force* and *guile*.[31] It is by guile that he teaches Zeus how to defeat his violent adversaries; and guile is a form of intelligence. But Zeus goes on to rule with the aid of Kratos and Bia, against which powers all the intelligence of Prometheus seems vain. What is needed to resolve the situation is genuine persuasion; and at turn after turn the vocabulary of persuasion meets us in *PV*. Most striking perhaps is a brief interchange between Prometheus and Oceanus. 'Do you not recognize,' asks the latter, 'that for a sick wrathful temper words are doctors?' Prometheus' reply continues the medical metaphor: 'Yes, if at the right time one assuages the heart and does not try to reduce its swollen state by force' (377ff.).[32] The subject is Zeus' choler, but what is said applies to the mental state of both contestants: the time is not yet ripe for the application of soothing remedies. But the words must look forward to such a time of 'election' – and in *Luomenos* it must be close. One cannot but suspect that, if 'right-counselling Themis' (18) had a role in the play, it was to counsel

---

[30] West's alternative hypothesis (141f.) is ingenious and quite plausible. For those who believe *Luomenos* to be the final play it has the advantage of reducing the clutter, which is all the more desirable for any who wish to find room for Thetis (see n. 34).

[31] On force, guile and persuasion in Soph. *Phil.* see Winnington-Ingram 280f.

[32] On 377ff. see Thomson (2) *ad loc.* (his 393–6).

and persuade; that, in a play which we know in some respects to have mirrored the structure of *Desmotes* (as *Choephori* mirrors *Agamemnon*),[33] a scene with Gaia–Themis mirrored the scene with Oceanus; that she gave advice in circumstances which admitted of success as his did not; that the would-be go-between was followed by one who could effectively intercede between the antagonists. Some coming and going there must have been; someone must have told Prometheus that the threat to Zeus' reign long prophesied was now imminent, that Zeus was in pursuit of Thetis. It should be someone conversant with the affairs of Olympus (as we cannot suppose the Titans to have been), with a motive for telling Prometheus (which is hard to see in Hermes).[34] The goddess whom he himself had brought to the court of Zeus would seem ideal for this role. What else might she have told him calculated to persuade? That Zeus' attitude towards the human race has changed? Was it she who brought Prometheus to see that a more forcible son of Zeus might be worse not better for that race? We are reduced to mere speculation.[35] At this point we can no longer evade the vexed problem of the trilogy, if there was a trilogy.

Three play-titles which include the name of Prometheus are found in the catalogue which has come down in our MSS of Aeschylus: *P. Desmotes*, *P. Purphoros*, *P. Luomenos* (in that order). A fourth is *P. Purkaeus*, which we know from a didascalic notice to have been the satyr-play appended to the three tragedies of 472 B.C. (one of which was *Persae*). A case can be made for equating it with *Purphoros*. Duplicate titles are not uncommon in the tradition of the dramatists: there are four examples in the Aeschylean catalogue alone. But omission is no less probable and could easily have been caused by the similarity of names: for instance, the catalogue contains *Glaukos Pontios*, but not *Glaukos Potnieus*, *Sisuphos Drapetes* but not *Sisuphos Petrokulistes*. The fragments attributed to *Purphoros* are not conclusive either way.

---

[33] See ch. 7, p. 133 above.

[34] Hermes, making that second journey at which 950f. might hint; and it is not unlikely that he appeared in the sequel. Another candidate for a part is Thetis, favoured by Fitton-Brown and West. Her case depends entirely on schol. PV 167, where it is stated that an amorous Zeus pursued her on Mt Caucasus to have intercourse with her, but was stopped by Prometheus revealing the secret. Zeus himself cannot have appeared, but a scene with Thetis, corresponding to the Io-scene in *Desmotes*, has its attractions. The trouble is that that scene is, to our knowledge, already mirrored in *Luomenos* by the scene with Heracles.

[35] Nor can we say at what point in the play a scene between Prometheus and Gaia–Themis, if there was one, was introduced. The fact that her name precedes that of Heracles in the dramatis personae could be indicative, but is far from conclusive.

If *Purphoros* belonged to a trilogy along with *Desmotes* and *Luomenos*,[36] a further question arises. Was it the first play or the third? (It cannot have been the second.) The matter has been much debated. The natural assumption, at first sight, is that the title 'Fire-bringer' refers to the bringing of fire to men by Prometheus: add that his loosing seems to be the end of the story, and the case for making *Purphoros* first seems obvious.[37] It could hardly have been set on earth with a human chorus; it is not too difficult, however, to envisage an action set in some no doubt unspecified region of heaven, dealing with the aftermath of the divine war, the determination of Zeus to destroy men, the decision of Prometheus to save them with the gift of fire, his detection and the announcement of his punishment. As for the Chorus, we need not suppose that the dramatist had less resource and boldness than a modern interpreter.[38]

This hypothesis, however, suffers from twin objections which some will find insuperable. I do not refer to the fact that, in the narrative of Prometheus to the Oceanids, the poet will have been recapitulating the story of the war in heaven which he had dramatized (or narrated) in the earlier play. The real objection is not that this one speech covered old ground, but that the whole technique of exposition – and the first half of the play is largely expository – is appropriate only to the first play of a trilogy, being spacious, gradual and cumulative, like the expositions of *Supplices* and *Agamemnon*, assuming that the audience knows nothing.[39] There is a further, but related point. If there was a first play dealing with the war in heaven (or its aftermath), Zeus must have been portrayed in it. How? In our *Prometheus* he is the new ruler; then he must have been newer than new. In our *Prometheus* he is violent and tyrannical. If he had been so portrayed in an earlier play, the effect of *Desmotes* would be blunted: yet in what other way could he have been seen? The *prologos* of the later play, in particular, would lose its effect. There Zeus is first revealed through his

---

[36] Taplin's argument (*JHS* 95, 1975, 184–6) that the use of *epikleseis* in the titles – *Desmotes*, *Luomenos* – is in itself an indication that the plays did not belong together in a trilogy is answered by West 131. It cannot of course be asserted that our titles go back to the poet and/or the original *didaskalia*, but it may be observed that the poet (or the clerk) was in difficulties when two or more plays of a trilogy were dominated by the same character and (in this case) might have been reluctant to use such titles as *Oceanides* or *Titanes*.

[37] Cf. Pohlenz I 77f., West 131.

[38] West suggests that a Chorus of Meliai, tree-nymphs, acted as intermediaries between Prometheus and mankind.

[39] Prometheus is not named until line 66, 'not as early as we might expect if he had not been seen before' (West). The argument is double-edged. What of Clytemnestra? It is only on the third reference that she is named (*Agam.* 10f., 26, 83f.): so too with Prometheus (*PV* 4ff., 18, 66). 'Diese kunstvolle Steigerung . . . ist nur sinnvoll im *Eingangs*stück einer Trilogie' (Unterberger, op. cit. 23).

servants Kratos and Bia, which is the extreme presentation of his tyranny, establishing the problem which the dramatist has set out to handle. Zeus – or the view of Zeus – can move from this point, but towards it there can have been no movement. Is it conceivable that any competent dramatist could have written our play as he has written it to be the sequel to any imaginable *Purphoros?*

If, however, *Purphoros* was the third play, how did it come by its title (its *epiklesis*), and what can its dramatic content have been? The first question is easy to answer, the second more difficult. Prometheus was honoured with a torch-race, a *lampadephoria*; and, when Sophocles (*OC* 55) describes the Titan Prometheus who was worshipped in the vicinity of Colonus as the *purphoros*, it is probable that he had this ritual in mind.[40] Now the fact that Prometheus had a cult in Athens as a patron of smiths and potters may well have affected the poet's whole conception of this figure whom he has promoted from the trickster of folklore to become the founder of civilization, from the thief of fire to be the inventor of all arts. The cult of Prometheus seems to have been closely associated with that of Hephaestus, himself honoured with a *lampadephoria*; and, if that gave a poignancy to the opening scene of *Desmotes*, it would have given the trilogy an 'Aeschylean' symmetry for it to close with Prometheus taking his place alongside Hephaestus in Athenian cult. Such a close gives symmetry and edification, but not a dramatic action for a final play. For such a cult to have been ordained and prophesied is the ending for a play, and not a play. For that matter, could it not have been the ending of *Luomenos*, as can well be admitted by those who regard *Luomenos* as the final play of a trilogy (and no less by those of another school of thought, for which *Purphoros* is a mirage, a mere doublet of *Purkaeus*, and there were never more than two linked Prometheus plays – as it were a dilogy)?[41]

The crucial question then arises: could the play, the dilogy, the trilogy, have been brought to an end within the compass of such a play as we know – or can reasonably conjecture – *Luomenos* to have been? And it is complicated by two imponderables, one of which concerns the likely

[40] Cf. e.g. Thomson (2) 32–4, West 148 (for an interesting suggestion about the dating of the trilogy). Prometheus *was* πυρφόρος (literally carrying fire to men), and he *was* πυρφόρος (in cult). The latter commemorated the former; and there is little doubt, on any sensible reconstruction of the trilogy, that he appeared, in retrospect or prospect, in both roles. The argument is not that the play-title *could* not refer to the former, but that it could as well, if not better, refer to the latter.

[41] The protagonist of the dilogy-theory is F. Focke, 'Aischylos' Prometheus', *Hermes* 65 (1930) 259–304. Lloyd-Jones 95–103, suggests that the third play in the *didaskalia* was not a Prometheus-play at all but *Aitnaiai*. Ingenious and closely reasoned, the hypothesis is admittedly speculative and has not won much acceptance (cf. e.g. Taplin 464f.).

length of the play, the other the competence of the dramatist.[42] As for the former, *Desmotes* is a short play, roughly the same length as the surviving plays of Aeschylus other than *Agamemnon*, which is much longer. Since *Choephori*, which mirrors *Agamemnon* in several ways, is much the shorter play, it is not inconceivable that a play mirroring *Desmotes* might have been much longer – though one might prefer it not to be *too* long. The real trouble has always been that so many questions are so amply raised in *Desmotes* (including one which has not yet been mentioned) and so much of what we know about *Luomenos* seems to carry that play so far without resolving them (and indeed adds to them) that it becomes hard to see how, in a play of normal length, they could have been resolved. Which brings us to the question of competence. When it was confidently assumed that the dramatist was Aeschylus himself, a high degree of competence worthy of the author of *Oresteia* had also to be assumed. Aeschylus, in his one surviving trilogy, did not allow himself to be hurried or deny himself room for the development of his themes. Can we make the same assumption about an unknown dramatist or may we suppose that he followed a leisurely *Desmotes* with a crowded and perfunctory *Luomenos*? For what do we need to find room between the end of *Desmotes* and the final close of the entire drama?

Luomenos opened (as we know from Procopius) with a Chorus of Titans entering to anapaests. (Thus no *prologos*.) This must have been followed by a lyric entrance-song (or a *kommos*). They are addressed by Prometheus in an expository speech, and no doubt there was dialogue between him and the Coryphaeus. At some point came the entry of Heracles – probably unprepared, like that of Io. Heracles shoots the eagle, but will hardly have done so before he has been told what the bird is after.[43] There followed a scene – and to judge by its counterpart in *Desmotes* it must have been of some length – in which Prometheus foretells the journeying of Heracles. Perhaps there was a scene with Gaia–Themis, but this is hypothetical. If so – and if, though this too is hypothetical, it corresponded to the Oceanus-scene in *Desmotes* – it is unlikely to have been very short.

[42] The stagecraft of *Desmotes* is subjected to a critical, not to say hostile, examination by Taplin. Often, I think, he goes too far, but I am inclined to agree that there are features in the play which fall short of Aeschylean standards – the standards of 458 B.C. But such judgements tend to be subjective. I would add a more objective, if minor, point. Thomson (2) points out that, in the dialogue between Kratos and Hephaestus at 36–51, the retorts of the former reiterate the closing words of the latter's speeches. This kind of 'picking-up' – between speakers or indeed between sentences of the same speaker or writer – is a common feature of Greek style. Here it is constant and tedious, a trick of style, a mannerism which it would be hard to parallel in extant Aeschylus. (See also Taplin 242).

[43] Thomson suggests that a whirring of wings was heard as at *PV* 125ff. on the approach of the Oceanids.

Gaia–Themis or no, if Prometheus was loosed during the course of the play (which is virtually certain),[44] and if this was the last play, it was done with the prior consent or subsequent acceptance of Zeus and followed by suitable ordinances or predictions; and towards this end there must have been some coming and going, something in the nature of negotiation.[45]

The features mentioned in the last paragraph could no doubt have been embraced within the compass of a single play of reasonable length (if longer than *Desmotes*), though one may feel that the negotiation, however prepared by the Titan-*parodos* and (possibly) by an early scene with Gaia–Themis, might have been rather perfunctory, not quite on the scale and in the tone of *Desmotes* (and certainly not up to Aeschylus at his best). The main difficulties, however, are not concerned with a Prometheus who can only talk and listen and take one vital decision but with the role and movements of Heracles, to whom we must now turn back. There are three phases, two of which are relatively well documented.

(i) It is certain that Heracles shot the eagle with his bow. We have a line, probably from this play (fr. 332 Mette), in which he prays to Apollo, the hunter-god, to direct his shaft; and we have a line (fr. 333) in which Prometheus 'saved by him' addresses (or refers to) him as 'dearest son of a hated father'.[46] There is no difficulty in supposing that Heracles on stage shot the bird off stage.[47] The order of events is not quite certain, but it is reasonable to suppose that he did it out of a spontaneous impulse of pity. Now for the son of Zeus to kill the bird of Zeus and so frustrate the willed torture of Prometheus was surely a remarkable event, one of which Zeus must take note and could hardly notice favourably; and those scholars are likely to be right who believe that Heracles at this point incurs the wrath of his father.

---

44 Those who postpone the actual loosing to the third play must assume a restricted sense for the participle Λυόμενος, which is present and not perfect – not Prometheus loosed, but Prometheus in the process of being loosed or 'The loosing of Prometheus'. Is it really conceivable, though, that such a title would have been given (by whoever gave it) to a play in which he was not actually loosed? And there is the specific statement of the scholiast on *PV* 511 (fr. 320 M): ἐν γὰρ τῷ ἐξῆς δράματι λύεται, ὅπερ ἐμφαίνει Αἰσχύλος.

45 On the possibility of a scene with Thetis see n. 34 above.

46 Was this line spoken after the shooting (as I incline to believe) or after the loosing? The latter only if Prometheus and Zeus were still at variance when the loosing took place, which may or may not have been the case. Plutarch's use of σωθείς rather than λυθείς may offer some (weak) support to the view I have taken.

47 Contrast West 142. Of course a producer who had five cranes at his disposal might have spared one for a stuffed eagle who will tumble to earth and lie as if waiting for the retriever. Judgement here will depend somewhat on the view taken of the well-known production-problems of *Desmotes*, which are horrendous, and from which I shrink, referring the reader to West's own discussion and the more cautious survey of Taplin (ch. 5, *passim*).

(ii) We have fragments of a long speech (or speeches) in which Prometheus foretells the journeyings of Heracles in the West, as he foretold those of Io to the East and South.[48] This is likely to have followed the shooting of the eagle, for which it was a return of gratitude.[49] The whole scene must have been of some considerable length. Heracles will have told his story, as Io told hers; the story of his birth, of the jealousy of Hera, and of his labours. If so, Prometheus will have learnt that these, or many of them, were beneficial to the human race, clearing the earth of monsters; that this son of Zeus had been the friend of man (and friendship is a leitmotif of *Desmotes*). Whether this struck Prometheus as a paradox (cf. fr. 333) – and indeed how the theme was handled in the scene between them – we cannot know. The prophetic account of Heracles' journeyings would naturally have been upon a scale comparable to the account of Io's and, like that account, may have included a retrospect. Our meagre fragments contain one tantalizing piece of information (fr. 326a, 6, cf. 326c), which is that, when Heracles is in desperate straits, Zeus will take pity on him and lend his aid. Without the full context we cannot know what significance is to be attached to this. If Heracles left under the wrath of Zeus, it could be a sign that his father is relenting towards him – it could be a sign, like the ultimate destiny of Io, the full implication of which Prometheus does not yet see. I say 'if Heracles left': for if one thing is certain it is that the man who has received detailed prophecies about his journey must leave (like Io) to face the hazards therein foretold. Which brings us to the crucial question: when, and in what circumstances, did the loosing of Prometheus take place?

(iii) This is the other act, along with the shooting of the eagle, that we know Heracles to have performed. Now, since the god Hephaestus had bound Prometheus with expert skill, the loosing was indeed, for a mortal, a 'Herculean' task; and every word in the *prologos* of *Desmotes* which stresses the fastness of the bonds (e.g. 6, 19) is a prospective tribute to the superhuman strength of Heracles.[50] There seems no good reason to suppose that this task was not carried out in face of the audience: if the binding could be 'produced', so could the loosing. So great is the stress upon this theme in *Desmotes*, so crucial is the act in relation to the

---

[48] See West 144–6 for a valuable discussion of 'Heracles' travels and how the poet's idea of them relates to tradition'.

[49] Contrast Thomson (2), who regards the prophecies as a thank-offering for the release, which he places early.

[50] West's nonchalant Heracles breaks the shackles 'with two or three resounding blows' of his club, which seems a studied insult to the god.

great quarrel, to the destiny of Prometheus – and, it may well be, of Heracles – that one could wish to find it at some grand climax of the drama. Wherever one looks, however, there are uncertainties, difficulties and problems, which must now be rehearsed.

For the loosing of Prometheus the third play seems to be ruled out, not so much by a scholiast who might have made a mistake as by the title of the second. Where, then, in *Luomenos* do we place it? Subsequent, of course, to the shooting of the bird and (probably) to the prophecies, prior to the departure of Heracles (unless we suppose him to have returned successful after a time-lag, which is not quite inconceivable but surely most unlikely). Does this mean that it took place in the middle of the play? To such an arrangement there are grave objections. The drama goes off at half-cock: a long awaited and crucial event happens too soon, and what follows must be an anticlimax. Moreover, the hero, unbound and stretching his legs (*lelumenos* with half *Luomenos* yet to come), finds himself with nowhere to go, no possibility of an entrance or an exit – a predicament most unwelcome to a character in Greek tragedy. No, the loosing must come, as a climax, towards the end of the play, after which Heracles may proceed on his journey, Prometheus can exit on foot to whatever destination may be indicated.

For we do not know quite where we are. We do not know – and never shall know – what progress is made in *Luomenos* by way of negotiation between Prometheus and the ruler of the universe, and through what intermediaries (for they cannot meet). For Prometheus to reveal his secret what is necessary is not simply release – or the promise of release – but a realization that the regime of Zeus has changed and, perhaps above all, that the replacement of Zeus by a more violent son would not be in the interests of the human race. Such a realization may have been a gradual process, if beginning with the release of the Titans from Tartarus. It is not impossible, though it makes a crowded play, that things had reached such a point, before the departure of Heracles, that the loosing of Prometheus took place with the approval of Zeus.[51] What, though, if we take *PV* 771f. in the most obvious way, and suppose that Heracles acted in defiance of Zeus'

---

[51] Reference should be made at this point to Probus and Philodemus. Probus on Virg. *Ecl.* 6.42 writes as follows: *hunc quidem uolturem [sic] Hercules interemit, Prometheum tamen liberare ne offenderet patrem timuit. sed postea Prometheus Iouem a Thetidis concubitu deterruit . . . ob hoc beneficium Iuppiter eum soluit.* A coherent and plausible story, but how closely Probus is following Aeschylus we cannot tell. Philodemus περὶ εὐσεβείας p. 41 G. is better evidence, since he refers to Aeschylus (fr. 321 M) as authority for the statement that Prometheus was freed 'because he revealed the prophecy about Thetis' (Gomperz' supplements are certain).

will? Then he will leave the stage in trouble with the ruler of the universe on two scores.

If so, they are scores which must be settled in a closing play. The trouble is that, subsequent to *Desmotes*, there seems too much action to be accommodated in one play, too little for two. Let us now turn to another complication which may await resolution, first remarking that, when a hero has proved himself capable of undoing the work of a god, there is nothing to be done with him except to make a god of him, which is indeed what happened to Heracles.[52] More than that, he was given a goddess – an appropriate if minor goddess – to wife, he was given Hebe. An eminently suitable match – as suitable as that of Prometheus and Hesione to which the Oceanids refer. The reference is perhaps surprising, but it leads up to the entrance of Io;[53] and to Io we must now turn.

The introduction of Io serves more than one purpose, quite apart from

---

[52] There is no positive evidence that the deification of Heracles was a theme of the trilogy, but it is likely enough. Nor need we worry too much about the time-table in relation to his labours and other events (of which there was more than one version), since our author may well have treated the legend freely. There is, however, one further point to be dealt with. The reader may be surprised that I have said nothing so far about Chiron, contrary to a general view that a substitute was required as a condition of Prometheus' release and was found to be available in the Centaur, grievously wounded by Heracles and longing for death. The evidence consists of (i) *PV* 1026–9 (ii) Apollodorus, *Bibliotheca* II 5.4 and 5.11: none of it is free of difficulty. (i) Prometheus is told by Zeus' messenger that he must not expect an end to this μόχθος (torture by the eagle has just been described) until some god (θεῶν τις) is found to take over his πόνοι and is willing to go to dark Hades and the gloomy depths of Tartarus. It is this role which Chiron is supposed to have played. But what inducement would there be for Chiron, who longs for death to free him from the torment of his wound, to take over the πόνοι of Prometheus? Go down to Hades, yes, but Tartarus is not the ordinary residence of the dead but a place of punishment for notable offenders, in general and specifically in our plays (where, at *PV* 152ff., a distinction is drawn between Hades νεκροδέγμων and that lower region which is Tartarus). It sounds, then, like an impossible condition which is set, and in fact it is. (ii) The Apollodorus passages (both of which have been subjected to emendation) have been taken to mean that Chiron was offered to Zeus (whether by Heracles or by Prometheus) as a substitute, surrendering his own immortality to Prometheus. The difficulty is obvious. Prometheus is already an immortal god – a fact which is much stressed in the plays. He has never died or can die: how, then, can he exchange mortality for immortality with another? To say that he was threatened with loss of immortality by Zeus lacks all foundation (and conflicts with *Luomenos* fr. 324). To say that he must find a substitute before resuming his life as an immortal comes near to cheating. A substitute where? In Hades? But, although (for dramatic reasons) he seems to have had a spell in Tartarus (like his fellow-Titans), it is in the world of the living that he is tormented in the plays and will be liberated in due course. In the story only one mortal is a candidate for immortality, and that is Heracles. In *JHS* 71 (1951) 150–5 D. S. Robertson makes a strong case for holding that in the Apollodorus passages (the textual difficulties of which are closely examined) it is for Heracles and not for Prometheus that Chiron is offered as a substitute (the Olympian quota being, as it were, full). What, then, of *PV* 1026–9? We can only suppose that the message of Hermes, which was in any case misleading (one way or another) turns out to have a different application, but still within the context of Prometheus' liberation. *Non liquet*: but the uncertainties are such as to excuse the critic from paying too much attention to this theme.

[53] This indeed is the sole purpose of the reference (552ff.). The word πιθών (560) is deliberately chosen to contrast with the forcible pursuit of Io.

the value of her unprepared entry – and her grotesque mask – as a sensational and spectacular effect. She is, like Prometheus, a victim of Zeus, and her sufferings help to intensify his obstinate resistance. It is immediately following her departure that Prometheus makes that half-revelation of his secret which leads to the appearance of Hermes. If Io is a victim, she is – or appears to be – the victim of Zeus' lustful designs. The speech in which she tells her story (640ff.) is one of disconcerting power and subtle overtones: even the facts are at first unclear. Her sufferings stem in the first instance from Zeus' demand that she be sent out from her father's home to satisfy his desire (654); and such a demand is part of the portrait of a tyrant. The father at first refuses, but is then compelled by divine authority – compelled to a violent act.[54] He drives her out. Then, however, as we come to see, her sufferings are due to the jealousy of Hera: her physical transformation, the watchful eyes of Argus, the lash of the *oistros* which drives her from land to land. But this is not the end of the story. Prometheus knows – though he may not grasp its full significance – that she is destined to become 'the glorious bride of Zeus' (834) and that in the end she will be impregnated by him, not by violence, but by the mere touch of an unfrightening hand (849). This is immediately followed (853ff.) by a reference to the Danaids, to the husband-murders ('may Kypris come in such kind to my enemies', 864) and to the sparing of Lynceus by Hypermestra under the enchanting influence of *himeros* (865ff.).[55]

This passage looks like a cross-reference to the Aeschylean trilogy and, if so, implies a familiarity on the part of the poet of *Desmotes* with Aeschylus' handling of the story. Despite a strong political factor, the broad general context of the Danaid trilogy is that of the sexual relationship between men and women, the place of marriage in society; and a strong antithesis is brought out between the violent approach of the Egyptians to their cousins, a kind of rape of the bride, and the persuasive enchantment of mutual desire upon which those relations should be based, which caused Hypermestra to spare her husband, and which Aphrodite will have commended when she appeared in the final play. Such a set of ideas, then,

[54] 671f. πρὸς βίαν should be taken with πράσσειν. At 659f. he asks τί χρὴ δρῶντ᾽ ἢ λέγοντα δαίμοσιν πράσσειν φίλα; the answer which comes is πρὸς βίαν πράσσειν. For it is a violent act, though performed reluctantly. ἄκουσαν ἄκων: cf. 19 (ἄκοντά σ᾽ ἄκων). The parallel is exact: both Hephaestus and Inachus are forced by a command of Zeus to act with cruel violence (cf. 15, 74) against their will and natural instincts. With ἐπηνάγκαζε (671), cf. 16, 72. All this is clear enough. I suggest, with some hesitation, that there is a sociological insight here, expulsion from the father's house being in some degree the fate of all virgins at marriage, and (misled perhaps by a modern use of *oestrus*) that there is a psychological insight also, the sexuality of Io being in the background of the narrative.

[55] See ch. 3, pp. 65f.

may well stand behind the story of Io as told in *Desmotes*, involving that contrast between force and persuasion which we see to be otherwise essential to the development of the drama. All this might have stood by itself without bearing on the sequel – or so we might have believed if we knew nothing of that sequel. But we know two things: we know about the secret, and we know about Heracles. The secret which Prometheus held as his weapon against Zeus was that some day he would contemplate a fatal 'marriage': in fact that he would lust after Thetis, lie with her (adding her to his numerous immortal and mortal loves) and beget a greater son. He did not lie with her. One can say that, on the revelation of the secret, this was purely precautionary: still, it was a victory of intelligence over blind desire. It is hard to believe that the themes associated with the pursuit of Io were not taken up in connection with the revelation of the secret. It is no less hard to believe that the antecedents and career of Heracles do not belong to the same pattern of thought. For Heracles was the product of one of Zeus' amours and for this, like Io, suffered from the hostility of Hera. Hera may of course have dropped out of consideration entirely in the last phase of the story, or she may have come to accept Io and her progeny (she was the patron goddess of Argos) and, no less, Alcmena's son, the demigod who becomes a god and to whom her daughter is given in marriage. One may even remember some Aeschylean passages – the Handmaidens[56] in *Supplices* singing in one breath of Kypris, Zeus and Hera (*Suppl.* 1035), Apollo in *Eumenides* (213–15) speaking of the pledges of Hera Teleia and Zeus and, simultaneously, of Kypris as dishonoured by the Erinyes' disregard of the marriage-tie – and may wonder whether in the final settlement of the Prometheus-situation Zeus and Hera, at variance over Io and Alcmena, were seen ultimately as the joint guardians of marriage, in close association with a Kypris in her persuasive rather than her violent aspect.[57]

These observations are not offered as the solution of a problem. Their purpose has been to show, by a careful consideration of *Desmotes* and what we know or can reasonably conjecture about *Luomenos*, that there seems to be more thematic material than can comfortably be accommodated in the latter play, enough perhaps to occupy two plays subsequent to the former. Enough *thematic material*, but that is not the same thing as a dramatic action. Assuming Prometheus to have been loosed towards the end of *Luomenos*, he was loosed either with or without the prior consent or subsequent

---

[56] In whom (*pace* Taplin) I still believe.
[57] On this theme I find the discussion in Thomson (2) 36f. most valuable.

acceptance of Zeus. In the former case the total drama is virtually at an end, *if* we can suppose all loose ends to have been tied up within a brief compass of time and dramatic action, and *if* we suppose *Purphoros* to be either the first play or a mirage. If he was loosed without that consent, or acceptance, there must have been a third play. But a play must have a local setting and (what comes to the same thing) a Prometheus loosed must have somewhere to go. It is a dilemma. One may toy with the idea that the third play was set in Athens (with a human chorus)[58] and find a role for Athena. One could, with enough ingenuity, write a scenario for a final play which the unknown poet, if not Aeschylus, might have written. But the exercise would be pointless, since the kind of indications which help us with *Luomenos* are totally lacking. Better admit that this is one of the most intriguing problems in the history of literature, but one which is, on our evidence, insoluble and, barring some extraordinary piece of luck, likely to remain unsolved.

[58] If so, it is another inaccuracy in the *Vita* (cf. West 132).

APPENDIXES

APPENDIX A

A word in *Persae*[1]

Aeschylus, for some reason which we cannot determine, opened his *Persae* with a reminiscence of the first line of Phrynichus' *Phoenissae*. In doing so, he changed $\tau\hat{\omega}\nu$ $\pi\acute{\alpha}\lambda\alpha\iota$ $\beta\epsilon\beta\eta\kappa\acute{o}\tau\omega\nu$ to $\tau\hat{\omega}\nu$ $o\grave{\iota}\chi o\mu\acute{e}\nu\omega\nu$ – a change for which the difference of metre could sufficiently account. It has, however, been suggested[2] that $o\grave{\iota}\chi o\mu\acute{e}\nu\omega\nu$ was 'chosen instead of the colourless $\beta\epsilon\beta\eta\kappa\acute{o}\tau\omega\nu$ . . . in order to sound the first note of disaster heard so clearly in $o\check{\iota}\chi\omega\kappa\epsilon$ at line 13'. That the perfect of $\beta\alpha\acute{\iota}\nu\omega$ could itself convey a sinister sense is shown by *Persae* 1002f.: add the adverb $\pi\acute{\alpha}\lambda\alpha\iota$ to it, with Phrynichus, and it certainly does not. But is the $\tau\hat{\omega}\nu$ $o\grave{\iota}\chi o\mu\acute{e}\nu\omega\nu$ of Aeschylus sinister? The case for believing so must stand on its own Aeschylean legs without help from Phrynichus. It may not be enough to say with Broadhead[3] that 'the opening sentence is purely factual, so that it would be out of place to anticipate there the forebodings expressed in lines 8–11'. The occurrences of this word must be considered together and in order; and light may be thrown on the verbal art of Aeschylus.

1. The hint, if it is seizable at all, is of the vaguest description: it would go for nothing, if it were not followed up.

12–13. $\pi\hat{\alpha}\sigma\alpha$ $\gamma\grave{\alpha}\rho$ $\grave{\iota}\sigma\chi\grave{\upsilon}s$ $\text{'}A\sigma\iota\alpha\tau o\gamma\epsilon\nu\grave{\eta}s$ $o\check{\iota}\chi\omega\kappa\epsilon$. The hint is slightly stronger, just by reason of the fact that the subject is not plural, but a singular abstract noun (used collectively). To say that strength has gone suggests that it has perished rather more strongly than to say that men have gone suggests that they are dead.

59ff. $\tau o\iota\acute{o}\nu\delta\text{'}$ $\check{\alpha}\nu\theta os$ $\Pi\epsilon\rho\sigma\acute{\iota}\delta os$ $\alpha\check{\iota}\alpha s$ $o\check{\iota}\chi\epsilon\tau\alpha\iota$ $\grave{\alpha}\nu\delta\rho\hat{\omega}\nu$. With characteristic ring-composition, Aeschylus rounds off the anapaests with a return to the subject-matter and language of line 1, $\Pi\epsilon\rho\sigma\acute{\iota}\delta os$ $\alpha\check{\iota}\alpha s$ corresponding to $\Pi\epsilon\rho\sigma\hat{\omega}\nu$, $o\check{\iota}\chi\epsilon\tau\alpha\iota$ to $o\grave{\iota}\chi o\mu\acute{e}\nu\omega\nu$. As in 12–13, the subject of the verb is a singular abstract noun; and what was said on that passage applies here also. But there is more to follow. $o\grave{\upsilon}s$ $\pi\acute{e}\rho\iota$ $\pi\hat{\alpha}\sigma\alpha$ $\chi\theta\grave{\omega}\nu$ $\text{'}A\sigma\iota\hat{\alpha}\tau\iota s$ $\theta\rho\acute{e}\psi\alpha\sigma\alpha$ $\pi\acute{o}\theta\omega$ $\sigma\tau\acute{e}\nu\epsilon\tau\alpha\iota$ $\mu\alpha\lambda\epsilon\rho\hat{\omega}$. Of these words $\pi\acute{o}\theta os$ is neutral as between absence and death, though it is used, with its cognates, about the dead; $\sigma\tau\acute{e}\nu\omega$, $\sigma\tau\acute{e}\nu o\mu\alpha\iota$, are extremely common in tragedy of lamenting the dead (cf. 548, to which we shall return). The ensuing use of words proper to lamentation thus strengthens the potential suggestive force of $o\check{\iota}\chi\epsilon\tau\alpha\iota$.

[1] Reprinted from *BICS* 20 (1973) 37f.　　[2] J. T. Sheppard, *CR* 29 (1915) 34.
[3] Broadhead, n. on 1–2.

Taking these passages by themselves and together, we can, I think, say with some plausibility that the use of οἴχεσθαι in 1 is hardly a hint at death, in 13 a faint hint, in 60 a clear hint. But we must look at other occurrences also. In 252 τὸ Περσῶν δ' ἄνθος οἴχεται πεσόν (which is the first tidings of the loss of life) would seem to recall 59, but now the word πεσόν puts the meaning of οἴχεται beyond ambiguity.[4] At 916 τῶν οἰχομένων is clearly sinister. There are many reminiscences in the closing scene of themes and words from the earlier part of the play,[5] and this may be one of them, deliberately recalling 1, 13, and 60. But the most interesting – and to my mind the conclusive – passage is 546ff. Here, in a context of lamentation – the lamentations which round off the first half of the play – τῶν οἰχομένων is immediately followed by νῦν δὴ πρόπασα μὲν στένει γαῖ' Ἀσὶς ἐκκενουμένα.[6] It is surely hard to believe that this was not written with 59–62 in mind.

If this line of interpretation is correct, Aeschylus has gradually – and deliberately – unfolded the implications of οἴχεσθαι. One might compare a similar but less elaborate instance of the same technique in this play.[7] Περσῶν (1, 15, 23) and Περσίδος (59) are followed by περσέπτολις (65), on which I quote from Broadhead's note: 'That Aeschylus . . . hints at a connexion between Πέρσαι and πέρθω, is not unlikely. Here, at the beginning of the play, the Persians are the "destroyers of cities" (*das Zerstörervolk*), but they end by destroying themselves (Pohlenz, p. 47; cf. διαπεπόρθηται τὰ Περσῶν πράγματα, 714).'

That proper nouns may be significant and that events may disclose the implications of a name is a familiar Greek notion.[8] It seems that something of the sort may be true of any word. The word has a life and a potency of its own; and it could well be this power of the word as such that accounts, partly, for that repetitive verbal technique in Aeschylus which is so alien to our mental habits that some critics have been reluctant to acknowledge its importance.

APPENDIX B

Agamemnon 385f.[9]

(i) I should be the last to deny that Aeschylus saw a parallel between the situations of Paris and Agamemnon (to whom the thoughts of the Chorus work round in the course of the *stasimon*) or that language used of Paris in the earlier

[4] Cf. E. B. Holtsmark, *SO* 45 (1970) 15.

[5] I give some examples in ch. 1, n. 37.

[6] There are some uncertainties about the text (see Broadhead *ad loc.*) which do not affect the point.

[7] Simpler still, at 73 θούριος, of Xerxes, is 'a common epithet of "dashing", "impetuous" warriors' (Broadhead); when it recurs in 718 and 754, 'the context suggests something of Xerxes' rash impetuosity'.

[8] Cf. Fraenkel II 331 (with references); W. J. Verdenius, *Maia* 15 (1963) 125.

[9] Reprinted from *BICS* 21 (1974) 6–8.

stanzas may have relevance also to the history and state of Agamemnon.[10] The fact remains that, in these opening stanzas (up to 402), the subject is Paris and the language used must be understood primarily of Paris, must make sense in relation to him.

(ii) βιᾶται δ' ἁ τάλαινα Πειθώ. An oxymoron, obviously (comparable to Pindar's μάστιξ Πειθοῦς at *Pyth.* 4.219). Both Fraenkel and Page are obsessed with the notion that Peitho here must have something to do with persuasive speech. 'Peitho overpowers a man . . . and at the same time talks him out of his resistance' (Fraenkel). 'Persuasion *compels* him: he talks himself, or is talked by others, into action against his better judgement' (Page). Persuasive speech is indeed one of the earliest connotations of the word.[11] But Pindar did not call the temple prostitutes at Corinth ἀμφίπολοι Πειθοῦς (fr. 122, 1 f. Sn³), because they were good at chatting up their clients; nor for that matter did he say that wise Peitho held the keys of holy love-makings (*Pyth.* 9.39) because of anything the bridegroom said to the bride or the bride to the bridegroom. I take my examples from Pindar rather than Aeschylus, not wishing to assume an interpretation of the Danaid trilogy which I have advanced elsewhere.[12] Note, however, that at *Suppl.* 1038–40 Peitho, who like Pothos is the child of Cypris, is given the epithet θέλκτωρ: 'enchanting'. It is the persuasive, the enchanting, power of sexual attraction of which we should think in our passage. Nothing could be more relevant to the case of Paris, on whom the beauty of Helen (so strikingly evoked below)[13] worked with the force of violence towards violent consequences.

(iii) If Πειθώ is the power of sexual attraction embodied in Helen, why then is it described as προβούλου παῖς ἄφερτος "Ατας? For 'the powers of evil genealogically connected' Fraenkel cites a number of parallels from Solon, Aeschylus and others. He also refers to *Persae* 97ff., which describes the process – essentially seductive – by which Ate 'carries out her acts of παρασαίνειν and παράγειν on man'. One can, then, say that, if Cypris, who works seductively, is the 'mother' of Peitho, no less may be true of a seductive Ate. This could well be the correct explanation – that Peitho is an attendant spirit presented poetically as child of the major force which it serves, but perhaps it is not totally satisfactory. In

---

[10] Cf. Lebeck 37ff., who goes too far, however, in saying (p. 38) that, in between 366 and 399, 'there flow one from another a series of reflections having little to do with Troy and Paris, everything to do with the destiny of Agamemnon'.

[11] And of course persuasive *speech* plays its role in the Aeschylean exploitation of the *peitho–bia* antithesis: Clytemnestra persuading Agamemnon, failing to persuade Cassandra; Athena persuading the Furies, etc., etc. It can indeed enter into the sexual context (cf. J. de Romilly, *JHS* 93 (1973) 161 n. 35). At Homer, *Il.* 14.216f., the armoury of attractions which Aphrodite lends to Hera, in the form of a girdle, includes, along with φιλότης and ἵμερος, ὀαριστὺς πάρφασις κτλ. At h. Aphrod. 7, however, πεπιθεῖν does not imply speech; and it may be noted that, at Hesiod, *WD* 70ff., cunning words were given to Pandora by Hermes, whereas the gifts of the Charites and of πότνια Πειθώ were golden necklaces.

[12] Ch. 3 above, cf. *BICS* 16 (1969) 9–15. In Pindar, *Pyth.* 4.184ff. is an example of non-verbal persuasion associated with a non-erotic emotion: τὸν δὲ παμπειθῆ γλυκὺν . . . πόθον . . . ναὸς Ἀργοῦς. *Pyth.* 4.219 (cited above) is more complex: it was desire for Hellas that struck the burning heart of Medea μάστιγι Πειθοῦς, but she longs for Hellas because it is the home of Jason. Verbal persuasion enters in here, because her emotion results partly from the λιταὶ ἐπαοιδαί taught to Jason by the Cyprus-born.

[13] *Agam.* 737ff.

what did the ἄτη of Paris consist? In his capitulation to the attractions of Helen? Then it was not until the persuasive force of those attractions was brought to bear upon him that his infatuation arose. But, if Peitho is the child of Ate, Ate should be not only logically but temporally prior to Peitho. Page, in a long note (on 386ff.), faces this problem more frankly than any other critic and works out a solution of characteristic clarity. Paris is not himself responsible; the wrath of heaven has been aroused by the earlier sins of a Troy grown too wealthy and too proud; his sin is not a cause but an effect; he is 'the symbol and scapegoat' of the corruption of his fathers; the fault is that of 'the society which produced him'. Page refers, naturally, to the preceding stanza; and one should indeed seek to find a relationship between the process described in 385f. and the references to wealth which precede. Wealth for Aeschylus is dangerous but, as we learn later, not necessarily fatal. It is dangerous, because – and this is traditional morality – excess of wealth tends to lead men into outrageous behaviour.[14]

Page's argument contains an important truth, but he presses it a little too hard, and the picture of Paris as a more or less innocent victim driven 'against [his] will and judgement' to commit a sin is overdrawn. If Trojan society was corrupt, Paris was a corrupt member of it. Page speaks of 'certain wretched victims, who are no more responsible than anyone else – perhaps not responsible at all'. But is this Aeschylean? Is there any clear instance in which an Aeschylean sinner, whatever the influence of a fatal past may be, does not collaborate with this fatality by reason of his own impulses and motives? One thing Paris did, in the story as widely known: he chose between three goddesses, and he chose Aphrodite.

(iv) 'It must be regarded', writes Fraenkel (II 97), 'as an established and indeed a guiding principle for any interpretation of Aeschylus that the poet does not want us to take into account any feature of a tradition which he does not mention.' But, like most general principles, this needs to be applied with a judicious consideration of the individual case. Fraenkel was not in fact writing about this particular issue; and later, on 698 (p. 334), he writes as follows. 'The idea of the goddess of Strife standing behind the rape of Helen . . ., and therefore also facilitating her landing in Troas,[15] is natural in itself and may have made the stronger appeal to Aeschylus because it was Ἔρις in the *Cypria* . . . who caused the quarrel of the goddesses and consequently the judgement of Paris.' With this possible exception, there is no reference in *Agamemnon* to the story. How likely was it that it would come into a spectator's mind at this point?[16]

The story was certainly known in the mid-seventh century, though whether the works of art which show it antedate the *Cypria* is not clear. The *Cypria*, which will have been familiar to Aeschylus and to some of his audience, contained it, but also contained a number of features which Aeschylus did exclude or modify. Was the story known to Homer? The *ate* of Paris was so known: Ἀλεξάνδρου ἕνεκ' ἄτης occurs three times in the *Iliad* and can perhaps rate as a formula,[17] but at 3.100 and 6.356 it is naturally taken to refer to nothing other than Paris' infatuated act in

---

[14] Cf. *Agam.* 381ff.   [15] See p. 204 below.

[16] In what immediately follows I am much indebted to T. C. W. Stinton, *Euripides and the Judgement of Paris* (London 1965) 1–4.

[17] I take the variant ἀρχῆς to be an aberration.

seducing Helen. *Il.* 24.27ff. is more interesting, since the same formula is used, but followed by: ὃς νείκεσσε θεάς, ὅτε οἱ μέσσαυλον ἵκοντο, | τὴν δ' ἤνησ' ἥ οἱ πόρε μαχλοσύνην ἀλεγεινήν. The whole passage (23–30) was athetized by Aristarchus, wrongly according to Reinhardt,[18] who held that the *Iliad* presupposes the story of the Judgement. The question has been much debated, but Stinton is probably right to claim that the burden of proof now lies on those who say Homer did not know the story. It might be rash either to deny or to take for granted that these lines formed part of the *Iliad* which was known to Aeschylus and his audience. But if they did know these lines, light could perhaps be thrown on the thought of *Agam.* 385f.

(v) The advantage of assuming a reference to the Judgement here is that it makes the initial *ate* of Paris prior to the Rape of Helen – and it makes it consist in a wrong decision. Of course, in a sense, Paris had to 'decide' whether he would or would not 'rape' Helen: in the Judgement he had to decide between the gifts offered by the three goddesses, between power, wisdom and sexual prowess. And he chose sex, perhaps because his wealthy background made him prone to luxury. (We shall see the 'values' of Trojan society in a later ode.[19]) This choice once made (whether or not the goddess had made the specific offer of Helen), his capitulation to her sexual attraction is inevitable. Ate is in full control, her child Peitho is irresistible (ἄφερτος). Finally, why is Ate πρόβουλος? The word is rare in classical Greek literature, and this is its first occurrence.[20] Fraenkel thought it obvious that this 'political' word carried the suggestion of a προβούλευμα, a first or preliminary decision which needs carrying into effect: 'the προβούλευμα which [Ate] authorizes is then passed on to Peitho, who in her turn takes the necessary measures for its execution.' Thus on the divine level; at the level of Paris' infatuated mind, the wrong decision in principle is ratified in action.

APPENDIX C

Agamemnon 637[21]

χωρὶς ἡ τιμὴ θεῶν. A minor but fascinating problem. There are, essentially, three interpretations in the field. (i) E.g. Stanley, Verrall. 'The religious province is distinct' (in the two cases). The phrase ἡ τιμὴ θεῶν is taken together, despite the absence of an article with θεῶν (on which see below). Quite apart from this

---

[18] 'Das Parisurteil', *Tradition und Geist* (Göttingen 1960) 16ff. One of the objections raised against the passage has been that νείκεσσε implies an abuse of Hera and Athena by Paris which does not form part of any known version of the story. This objection seems satisfactorily disposed of by A. W. H. Adkins, *JHS* 89 (1969) 20 (who is not, however, maintaining the authenticity of the lines). It is unnecessary to suppose that (in Stinton's words) there may have been a version in which Paris added insult to injury. Failing this supposition, it seems rather unlikely that an interpolator of late date would have used νείκεσσε in what Adkins shows to be a truly Homeric sense. Not a great deal of weight need perhaps be placed on the fact that μαχλοσύνη is normally used of female lust.

[19] See p. 205 below.

[20] For the facts see Fraenkel *ad loc.*

[21] Reprinted from *BICS* 21 (1974) 10.

difficulty, the mode of expression seems impossibly obscure, τιμή referring to two contrasted τιμαί θεῶν embracing two contrasted sets of gods. It is not surprising that Headlam and Fraenkel prefer a radically different interpretation.

(ii) θεῶν is taken with χωρίς, the whole sentence being equivalent to χωρὶς θεῶν ἐστιν ἡ τιμή. The normal position of the article is preserved, but, as Page remarks, the expression remains obscure, 'especially in respect of the sense assigned to ἡ τιμή'. (That is of course the objection, not to the idea of upper and nether gods having separate τιμαί.) How can the phrase κακαγγέλῳ γλώσσῃ μιαίνειν imply a τιμή? For that matter, when the Herald speaks of τιμή and θεοί in the same breath, what can he mean by τιμή other than the honours which are being paid to the gods for the good news, the grace (χάρις) of the victory over Troy? We should bear in mind 581: χάρις τιμήσεται Διὸς τόδ' ἐκπράξασα. Is the Herald *at this point* associating the bad news with gods at all, let alone drawing a clear-headed and sophisticated distinction between two sets of gods? It was the Coryphaeus that said δαιμόνων κότῳ (635).

(iii) So we are forced round to Page's view. 'The honour of the gods stands aloof from, is kept distinct from, inauspicious utterance of the kind.' (The reaction of the Chorus to Cassandra's cries is very similar, cf. 1074f., 1078f.) The position of the article in relation to the dependent genitive is rare, but not quite unparalleled. We must suppose that τιμὴ θεῶν coalesces into a single notion for which one article suffices.

But this is not quite the end of the matter. The Coryphaeus *has* just said δαιμόνων κότῳ (without specific gods in mind?), the Herald *does* say τιμὴ θεῶν; and this might suggest to an audience a δαίμονες/θεοί contrast. When the Herald gets to 644f., having given us his vivid characterization of his bad news, then – and not till then – he comes out with the 'blasphemous paradox' of παιᾶν' Ἐρινύων (645, cf. *Cho.* 151: παιᾶνα τοῦ θανόντος). *That* is the sort of paean they must expect, if they insist on hearing his bad news: in fact not a paean but a dirge. (Again, compare the opening of the Cassandra-scene.)[22] He then echoes their δαιμόνων κότῳ with οὐκ ἀμήνιτον θεῶν (or whatever the right text may be at 649).[23] The separation of upper and nether gods, of gods and demons, is as artificial as the separation of songs. If there is any insistent theme in the earlier part of the trilogy, it is this, despite the desperate efforts of Chorus and characters to establish such a separation.[24]

APPENDIX D

Agamemnon 681ff. (the second *stasimon*)[25]

It has always been recognized that much of the play is taken up with the exposition

---

[22] On paean and dirge (and other musical themes in *Oresteia*) see Haldane 37ff.
[23] Which I can only regard, with Page, as an unsolved problem. The line must, however, contain the notions of 'gods' and 'wrath' in some combination.
[24] Cf. ch. 8, *passim*.
[25] Reprinted from *BICS* 21 (1974) 10–14.

of past happenings given largely but not exclusively in choral odes. Taking one passage with another, it would be possible to compile a narrative in strict chronological order, though this was the last thing Aeschylus wished to do. The earlier Argos-story is given partly by Cassandra, partly by Aegisthus: apart from certain hints,[26] Aeschylus reserves inherited guilt until he has firmly established the personal responsibility of Agamemnon. Chorus, Clytemnestra and Herald all contribute to convey not the incidents so much as the character of the Trojan War, its quality as an act of retaliatory justice, involving the innocent with the guilty.[27] Particularly obvious and striking is the use of the *parodos* to narrate the departure of the expedition, briefly at 45–8, then the omen which sent the Atridae on their way,[28] then Aulis and the sacrifice of Iphigenia (104ff., 184ff.). But the story is amplified in later choruses. Paris came to the house of the Atridae and seduced Helen (399–402), prior to which we hear of the wealth of Troy (with a possible hint at the Judgement of Paris).[29] Then we are taken to the moment of Helen's flight and told of its immediate effects in Argos, of the unheroic reaction of a sensitive Menelaus.[30] Thus we are taken back behind the *parodos*, behind the στρατιῶτις ἀρωγά, the omen and the sacrifice of Iphigenia.

The first *stasimon*, after the first two stanzas, after the flight of Helen, is concerned with Argos; of Troy it is merely said that she brought to Ilium destruction as her dowry (406). But there is a story of Helen's coming to Troy, which is reserved for the second *stasimon*. We revert to 403ff., to make a fresh start with a Helen whose very name is ominous of the destruction she causes. Now we have her sailing eastward across the Aegean: ζεφύρου γίγαντος αὔρᾳ (693). Can we fail to remember that this was the wind denied to the Greeks by Artemis and that pursuit by the huntsmen (694f.) was long delayed? Helen and Paris were well away; there was time. Time for them to make landfall on the leafy banks of Simois; time for marriage and a marriage-song.[31]

---

[26] Cf. Lebeck 33f.

[27] 63–67 (briefly), 320–47, 429–55, 551–79, 636–80.

[28] Where did the omen appear? It is generally supposed that, like the corresponding but distinct omen mentioned at *Il.* 2.301ff., it appeared at Aulis: there have been references to the fleet and to 'the youth of Hellas', and the στρατόμαντις is already in post. But, as Fraenkel points out, Aeschylus does not 'place' the incident by precise topographical detail, whereas the sequel to the omen is specifically located (190f.) at Aulis. He also points out that the μέλαθρα of 116 could, as in the *IA* of Euripides, refer to the quarters of the Atridae at Aulis. I should be inclined to suggest, however, that, by his very vagueness, Aeschylus has left it open to the hearer to take μελάθρων (which is followed by οἴκοις βασιλείοις at 157) of the actual palace so central to the drama and to believe that the omen which, unlike the Homeric omen, so intimately concerned the persons of the Atridae was given to them as they were, with their own forces, leaving their own house. There should be a time-gap between the omen and the first stage in the fulfilment of the prophet's interpretation of it. This is secured, in dramatic time, by the interposition of the Hymn to Zeus. Could it not also represent the transition from Argos to Aulis?

[29] See p. 201.

[30] See p. 87.

[31] It is always welcome if an interpretation can help with a textual problem. Looked at in this way, in terms of two eastward voyages separated by a long interval of time, it is clear that at 696 κελσάντων (codd.) is to be preferred. The Greeks are on the track, but of those who had long made their landfall. It makes little difference whether we take κελσάντων as a genitive absolute or as dependent on ἴχνος. Since there is a parallelism between the two voyages, it is not too difficult to understand ἔπλευσαν out of ἔπλευσεν: Helen sailed, so did the Greek trackers, but their prey had already

We are told something we have not heard before – how Paris and Helen were received by the Trojans. They were welcomed with a marriage-song, sung 'loudly' (or perhaps 'in words of good')[32] by the 'bridegroom's' kinsmen. Note the sequence: ἀτίμωσιν, νυμφότιμον, τίοντας – which is deliberate. We can now look back to the first stanza of the first *stasimon*, in which the offence of Paris is related to the wealth of Troy. I have already referred[33] to Page's suggestion that Paris was the representative of a society corrupted by wealth. Now we see the values of that society. To them the dishonouring of the guest-table protected by Zeus is nothing in comparison with the acquisition by their young prince of the most beautiful woman in the world, whom they honour in a marriage-song.

The arrival of the couple at the banks of Simois is, like everything connected with Helen, given a touch of beauty by the epithet ἀεξιφύλλους, which is immediately blasted by that astonishing δι' Ἔριν αἱματόεσσαν (698). It was an evil spirit, personified Strife (perhaps the spirit that presided over the Judgement of Paris), that brought them there. It was an evil spirit, personified Wrath, that brought bride and bridegroom to Ilium. The word for marriage-tie is as ill-omened as the name of Helen; the marriage-song must be re-learnt in the form of a dirge.

On the fable which follows, despite certain difficulties, I propose to say nothing,[34] but turn instead to the much-debated stanza (737–49) in which it is applied. On this stanza there are two things which can be said without fear of contradiction: that it must be descriptive of the Helen/Troy relationship, and that it must contain two phases – joy and destruction. And there are two particular problems: the structure and reference of 737–43, the identity of the Erinys. Most interpreters have assumed that 737–43 are descriptive of Helen (which, directly or indirectly, they certainly are), and that Helen in the end is equated with an Erinys. That is the crucial problem.

Page,[35] finding the equation illogical, argues that the connection between fable and application is looser than has been supposed and states flatly that 'it is certain that the Erinys here is the Erinys', i.e. the Fiend of Wrath, who was sent by Zeus

landed. Is it merely a subjective impression that, if we read κέλσαν τὰς, the Greeks are made to land prematurely? Is it not Helen's landing that is due to Eris, as her wedlock with Paris is due to Menis?

32   At 706 ἐκφάτως, though unexampled, makes sense. But in view of the constant (and one might say structural) use of εὖ and εὐ- compounds in the trilogy one cannot but be attracted by Karsten's εὐφάτως. It is characteristic of marriage-songs to use *bona uerba*, of which εὔλεκτρος might be an example. When the marriage-song turns into a dirge, we find Paris described as αἰνόλεκτρος (712).

33   See above, p. 201.

34   Nor do I wish to go into the question whether, and how far, the details of this elaborate set-piece refer beyond the immediate context of Helen and Troy. Cf. B. M. W. Knox, 'The lion in the house', *CPh* 47 (1952) 17ff., who points out the self-contained character of the passage (marked by the repetition ἔθρεψεν, προσεθρέφθη), the stress on the notions of τροφή and οἶκος, the likelihood that lions were a badge or symbol of the Pelopidae. It seems not improbable that there is a chain of suggestions and cross-references linking the passage to the horrors of the house of Atreus, and perhaps especially to the child Orestes. (Cf. also Lebeck 50f.). Just as the theological reflections to which the Chorus is led by the Troy-story at 750ff. become a preparation for Agamemnon's entry, so the Erinys-aspect of Helen (see below), pictured through the fable, may be a preparation for the act of Clytemnestra.

35   On 744ff.

Xenios in pursuit of Helen, not a personification of her. Lloyd-Jones,[36] in an ingenious and at first sight attractive interpretation, argues that 741–3 are descriptive of Eros rather than of Helen herself, and that Eros, first acting as *numpheutria* and putting the lovers to bed (παρακλίνασα), then proves to be an Erinys and brings about a bitter end to the wedding.

We should perhaps concentrate on three points. And first on πομπᾷ Διὸς ξενίου . . . Ἐρινύς (747f.), which clearly recalls the statement at 60–62 that Zeus Xenios sent the sons of Atreus against Alexandros. This followed the passage which tells how a god sends a ὑστερόποινον Ἐρινύν against those who robbed the vultures' nest. Whether we say that the Atridae embody an Erinys or perform the function of an Erinys, the association is inescapable. Can the Erinys at 749 be, in effect, the Atridae and their expedition? Yes, so far as the expression συμένα Πριαμίδαισιν goes, since they were a hostile attacking power. But this Erinys is called δύσεδρος καὶ δυσόμιλος; and these terms are inappropriate to the Atridae, but closely linked to the fable, where it is an inmate of the house (such as Helen has become) that changes from a source of pleasure into a priest of ruin (ἱερεύς τις ἄτας).

Next for παρακλίνασα. Lloyd-Jones's interpretation suffers not so much from the fact that parallels for παρακλίνειν in this sense are rather late as from the difficulty of understanding the word in that sense without an object expressed or clearly implied (and 737ff. do not clearly imply the twofold object required). And can one be wrong to feel that παρακλίνασα is a hinge-word (like μεταμανθάνουσα at 709), marking the transition from delight to disaster?[37] Something or somebody has changed direction.[38] But what or who? Surely we must ask ourselves what a nominative feminine participle at this point was likely to have suggested to a hearer of the ode. What would he have expected the subject to be? There is no feminine noun in the preceding lines to which it could refer. Did the hearer say: 'I am sure Aeschylus has a suitable noun up his sleeve; I must be patient, even if I have to wait for half-a-dozen lines'? He has just heard of something or somebody that came to Troy; and, whether the lines specifically describe Helen or not, Helen's beauty has been evoked. Is he not likely to think of Helen as the subject, as so many readers have done? But then he begins to be puzzled. The language is that of an authority (ἐπέκρανεν) and of a hostile power (συμένα). He waits and discovers an Erinys, but Helen is still in the forefront of his mind.

Finally, συμένα. An aorist participle. When did it happen? When did the Erinys move to the attack, sent by Zeus Xenios? Perhaps one should not try to be too precise about the time-reference of an aorist participle. It could be contemporaneous with the other participle, παρακλίνασα, in which case the assault awaits the Argive forces. But, equally, it could be prior, referring to the time when Helen first came to Troy, when this disastrous force, so rightly named, sailed across the

---

[36] *HSCP* 73 (1969) 99–104.

[37] At the corresponding place in the antistrophe, after a strong stop there is a strong contrary movement of thought.

[38] There is no clear parallel for intransitive παρακλίνειν, but verbs of physical movement run to intransitive uses (cf. Kühner–Gerth I 91). If ἀποκλίνειν (cf. e.g. Soph. *OT* 1192), why not παρακλίνειν?

Aegean with a west wind, only to be pursued by the Argive hunters. The two voyages are parallel and complementary.

Is it not, however, illogical – and even ridiculous – to suppose that the voyage of Paris and Helen was made πομπᾷ Διὸς ξενίου: 'by the sending or escorting of the deity most offended by her going thither' (Page on 744ff.)? We seem to be confronted with a dilemma, because, in view of δύσεδρος καὶ δυσόμιλος and what I can only regard as a clear reference back to the fable in these words (and for that matter in παρακλίνασα), it seems equally inappropriate to associate πομπᾷ Διὸς ξενίου here, specifically, with the voyage of the avengers. Yet, in interpreting an ode so much concerned with the two voyages, it is unwelcome, to say the least, to separate the Zeus-sending of the Erinys from both of them. It is perhaps ridiculous to say that Paris *qua* offender was sent across the Aegean by Zeus: is it so ridiculous to say that Helen was?

We come back to the fundamental question. Is it or is it not admissible to regard Helen as being, if not the embodiment of an Erinys, so closely associated with one as to make no matter? To regard Helen as daemonic? Later in the play (1455ff.), the Chorus sing of Helen as having destroyed many lives beneath the walls of Troy: they sing of a spirit of Strife. Clytemnestra is indignant that they should turn their wrath against Helen as the sole slayer of many men; and they go on to sing of the *daimon* who attacks the house and the twin-natured Tantalids – a *daimon* that wields power through women.[39] At that stage in the play the emphasis is upon the inherited curse of the house working upon the two brothers through their wives. The brothers differ in character, and so do their wives: the ambitious warrior Agamemnon is victimized by the man-woman Clytemnestra, the uxorious Menelaus by a Helen who is the quintessence of femininity, both serving the triumph of the *daimon*. In the earlier phase of the play, however, Helen brings ruin on Paris and his fellow-Trojans; and it is through her and her attraction, the ostensible reward of their crime, that the crime is punished. The initial crime was committed at Argos. Can it not be said that, by taking Helen (ἑλέπτολις) with them, Paris and his friends were taking their own destruction, since she was bound to be pursued and the crime avenged? (Helen herself was never punished!) Paris and Helen made their landfall on the banks of Simois, and it was because of Eris; a bridal ceremony took place, and it was brought about by Menis; an Erinys was sent with them on the voyage by Zeus Xenios. The Erinys is hardly distinguishable from the seductions of Helen's beauty. An Erinys can take the form not only of armed force but also of the seductions of love. βιᾶται πειθώ.

Let us return briefly to 737–43. What came to Troy? Helen came: the Chorus has sung about her coming and the joy with which she was received. On any showing this passage is a wonderful evocation of Helen's charm and beauty,[40] but its grammatical structure and the precise reference of its evocative phrases is far from certain. There are four phrases, the last three in asyndeton, but in 741 we must, for the sake of metre, read τ' or δ'. This is in itself a serious objection to taking all four phrases on the same grammatical level as descriptive of Helen. First,

[39] On this passage see ch. 6, pp. 111f. Cf. Fraenkel II 347 (on 749) for the daemonic character of both Helen and Clytemnestra.

[40] Cf. the eloquent words of Fraenkel on his p. 357.

then, what does φρόνημα νηνέμου γαλάνας mean? 'Spirit of windless calm' sounds good in English, but 'spirit' is misleading. φρόνημα means a state of mind. Whose mind? Helen's? Does it refer to her own insouciance? (We might compare 407). But I think Lloyd-Jones is probably right to see it as the state of mind of the Trojans when they received her (which has been an important feature of the ode). Then read δ', answering the μέν of 739, answering it with three figures which I should take to be descriptive of Helen. It was precisely as an ἄγαλμα πλούτου that the wealthy Trojans saw and welcomed her. (She is an ἄγαλμα for their wealthy city just as the virgin Iphigenia was an ἄγαλμα for the house of Agamemnon.) The first Helen-phrase thus looks back to, and (with the help of ἀκασκαῖον) links up with, the preceding μέν-clause. It is followed by a double chiastic paradox: μαλθακὸν ὀμμάτων βέλος, δηξίθυμον ἔρωτος ἄνθος. 'Love is darted from the eyes of the beloved to those of the lover.' So Lloyd-Jones, rightly (citing Barrett on Euripides *Hipp.* 525f. and 530–34). The eyes are those of Helen: the glance is soft, but it is a weapon. It is Helen that is the flower (ἔρωτος being not a defining but a possessive or associative genitive), but a flower that wounds. βέλος and δηξίθυμον look forward to – and prepare – the devastating change at 744.[41]

APPENDIX E

Agamemnon 1343–71[42]

When the death-cry of Agamemnon is heard, the Chorus talks, but does nothing. This is the *locus classicus* of a Chorus which, in a situation that seems to demand effective intervention, is debarred from intervening by the necessity of remaining a Chorus. Did Aeschylus and his audience feel a difficulty here? No, says Professor G. Thomson; it is merely that modern taste is influenced by 'the crude realism of the Elizabethan drama'. But this will not do, for it is Aeschylus himself, through the Chorus, who raises the issue of their entering or not entering the palace, which

---

[41] νυμφόκλαυτος (749) is as difficult to interpret as any epithet in Aeschylus. Fraenkel in his careful note maintains that a verbal adjective of this type could only be understood in the sense of 'wept for by a bride (or brides)' or 'weeping for a bride (or brides)'. (He phrases it slightly differently.) He therefore favours Blomfield's 'sponsis deflenda' or Headlam's 'bringing tears to brides'. Since brides did lose their husbands through the operation of the Erinys, this cannot be said to be grossly inappropriate. But, as Fraenkel says, 'it at first seems strange that "bride" here does not refer to Helen'; and his first instinct to relate νυμφόκλαυτος here to νυμφότιμον at 705 is one which many must share. Could we look at it this way? When the bride is seen in all her beauty and charm, she is honoured; later she is bewailed as a source of disaster. There is a reversion to the theme of dirge following marriage-song (see n. 32 above). The weeping is not, however, done by the Erinys or by Helen herself. We can only say, then, that this may be one of those cases in which Aeschylus has put a considerable strain upon language, calling the Erinys 'one of bride-bewailing'. The matter remains very doubtful.

[42] Reprinted from *CQ* 4 (1954) 23–30. The substance of that article was read as a paper to the London Classical Society in January 1948, under the title of 'The characterization and role of the Chorus in the *Agamemnon*'. Since then Professor Ed. Fraenkel's important edition appeared, and I dealt with a number of points arising out of it.

they discuss in the most realistic way.[43] Assuming that a technical difficulty exists, with what skill and success did the dramatist handle it? Criticism has on the whole been adverse.

One means of easing the difficulty would be to prepare the audience during the earlier part of the play for the way in which the Chorus was bound to behave at this crisis. It has been suggested,[44] for instance, that the passage (72ff.) in which they dwell upon their age and feebleness was designed to excuse their later inactivity. Had they pleaded their age and feebleness, the audience would no doubt have been reminded of the earlier passage. But they do not. Instead, they advance, at noticeable length, cogent reasons for the action they do not take. They debate, perhaps because they are old, perhaps because they are a Boule,[45] perhaps just because they are Greeks, but the outcome of the debate is not determined by any of these factors. It is (I suggest) governed by mental characteristics which have already been established in previous scenes. The Chorus behaves in character; and this character has been revealed, particularly, (i) in that part of the play which falls between the entry of Clytemnestra and the entry of the Herald; (ii) in their scene with Cassandra.

The parallelism of *Agamemnon* and *Choephori* extends beyond the symmetry of the double murders and involves the earlier phases of the two plays.[46] In each an event is hoped for, longed for: in *Agamemnon* the fall of Troy, in *Choephori* the return of Orestes. Both events are attested at first by dubious evidence: the fall of Troy by the beacons, the return of Orestes by the lock of hair.[47] It is essential to the irony that the evidence should be dubious. For both events are proved true – but lamentable: the fall of Troy leads directly to the death of Agamemnon, the return of Orestes to the matricide. In *Agamemnon* it is the Chorus (as in *Choephori* it is Electra and the Chorus) which is subjected to conflicting emotions by the news and the uncertainty. Let us turn to the entry of Clytemnestra.

'Have you good news', they ask (261f.), 'or are your messengers of good merely

---

[43] Thomson (3) II 136 ascribes the modern reader's difficulties to two other causes also. (i) The employment of proverbs and quasi-proverbial expressions is strange to us. But, as elsewhere in Aeschylus, it is not the employment of proverbs that matters so much as the end to which they are employed. (ii) The dialogue appears prolix in a literal rendering, because of the explicit nature of Greek idiom. Yet Aeschylus could be brief when he wished – witness any of the brilliant passages of *stichomythia* in this trilogy. I would suggest that the length of the debate is due in part to the need for interposing (as it were) an insulator between Cassandra and Clytemnestra. This is the kind of function which a choral ode often performs, but in this case Aeschylus was, for obvious reasons, unwilling to separate the exit of Cassandra from the death-cry of Agamemnon by more than a few lines of anapaests.

[44] By Headlam *ap.* Thomson (3), loc. cit.

[45] If indeed they are, 'A council of regency' they certainly are not (see Fraenkel II 144f., 398ff.). A consultative council they might be – had the regent queen cared to consult them. But at 844ff. Agamemnon states that he will take counsel, not with the elders, but κοινοὺς ἀγῶνας θέντες ἐν πανηγύρει. Nowhere is there a clear indication that they have a constitutional status. What is more to the point, then, is that here are men exercising their male function of taking counsel – with complete futility in face of the woman with the ἀνδρόβουλον κέαρ (see below). (Note that they are less futile in face of Aegisthus.)

[46] See also ch. 7, p. 133.

[47] Since, unlike the lock (194), the footprints are not associated textually with the theme of hope, we need not go into the question of the genuineness of *Cho.* 205ff. (see Fraenkel III 815ff.).

hopes?' For this is the effect of their interrogation (σὺ δ᾽ εἴτε κεδνὸν εἴτε μὴ πεπυσμένη | εὐαγγέλοισιν ἐλπίσιν θυηπολεῖς).[48] She replies, in effect: 'Your εὐαγγέλοισιν I accept, your ἐλπίσιν I reject: πεύσῃ δὲ χάρμα μεῖζον ἐλπίδος κλύειν' (266). The Argives have taken Troy. The keynote of the ensuing stichomythia is the incredulity of the Chorus. πέφευγε τοὖπος ἐξ ἀπιστίας (268). ἦ γάρ τι πιστόν ἐστι τῶνδέ σοι τέκμαρ; (272).[49] Has she convincing proof? 'Yes,' replies the queen, 'if a god has not played false.' A dream, does she mean (ὀνείρων φάσματ᾽ εὐπειθῆ, 274)?[50] If not a dream, then a rumour (276)?[51] In short, they accuse Clytemnestra of being the victim of ἐλπίς and prone to persuasion – the characteristics not only of a child (παιδὸς νέας ὥς, 277) but, according to convention, of a woman.

Clytemnestra does not forget. At the close of the scene we find her saying: τοιαῦτά τοι γυναικὸς ἐξ ἐμοῦ κλύεις (348), and the Chorus retracting the accusations of the stichomythia. Not only do they say: γύναι, κατ᾽ ἄνδρα σώφρον᾽ εὐφρόνως λέγεις, but describe the evidence as convincing (πιστὰ . . . τεκμήρια, 352). They do this, not out of mere politeness, but because they really are convinced. What has convinced them? The sheer force of the evidence? Hardly; because, coldly considered, it is a tall story, though in fact true.[52] Their conviction derives partly from the dominance of her personality (witness their comment at 318f.), partly from their wish to believe that the news is true. This becomes clear when we turn to their remarks before the entry of the Herald.

In the meantime they have sung a choral ode, in which they are led to explore the implications of the news of victory. If Troy had been destroyed as an act of justice, as a punishment for sin, is there not the danger that the conqueror himself, who has sinned in the process of conquering Troy, will fall victim to a similar act of justice? Thus, what appeared to them at 354 as a χάρις (a joyous and successful event for which to thank the gods) is now sinister; the return of Agamemnon has become something to be dreaded. They now wish to believe that the news is not

---

[48] εὐαγγέλοισιν ἐλπίσιν is of course far more vivid than ἐλπίδι εὐαγγελίας (Schütz) would have been, since εὐάγγελος is the epithet essentially of the messenger (cf. 21, 264, 475, 646). As to the sentence as a whole, the intention of the speaker seems to be rightly explained by Fraenkel *ad loc.* I cannot help thinking, however, that Aeschylus has cast the sentence in this rather strange form in order to suggest a further alternative, not in the speaker's mind. There *is* news: but is it really good or bad?

[49] It is not easy to choose between Karsten's emendation (printed above) and Prien's punctuation of the traditional text. H. L. Ahrens's objection to the latter (see Fraenkel *ad loc.*) is hardly decisive: πιστὰ τεκμήρια (352) clearly does refer to this line, but might, surely, refer as easily to τὸ πιστόν and τέκμαρ taken in separation as to πιστὸν τέκμαρ taken together.

[50] εὐπειθῆ, the third word of this root, means primarily 'persuasive, convincing'. In view of the preceding εὐάγγελος and of what is said below about the use of εὖ and εὐ-compounds in the trilogy (see p. 214 n. 67) I suspect that it also carries the sense of 'persuading of good' (here and also at 982). In any case there is the implication that the queen is too easily persuaded to believe what she wishes to be true.

[51] Unless the speaker has forgotten μὴ δολώσαντος θεοῦ, it must be implied that a φάτις, like a dream, might have a divine origin (though the sensible man would not too readily put his trust in either).

[52] Fraenkel (II 183f.) well describes the function of the queen's second speech in carrying conviction to the elders.

true, so their doubts about its truth return.[53] These are expressed in terms which remind the hearer of the earlier scene. For instance, θεῖον ψύθος (478) corresponds to μὴ δολώσαντος θεοῦ (273); παιδνός (479) to παιδὸς νέας ὥς (277); πιθανός (485) to ἀπιστίας, πιστόν, εὐπειθῆ (268, 272, 274).[54] Once again, by implication, they accuse Clytemnestra, the woman, of the traditional weakness of her sex. Yet it is not against Clytemnestra that the accusation lies, but against themselves. γυναικὸς αἰχμᾷ πρέπει πρὸ τοῦ φανέντος χάριν ξυναινέσαι (483f.).[55] But this is precisely what the Chorus, under the influence of Clytemnestra and their own desires, had done at 354, when they said: χάρις γὰρ οὐκ ἄτιμος εἴργασται πόνων. πρὸ τοῦ φανέντος means, in effect, before the real quality of the event has been revealed. Since their own song has now revealed something of that reality, they retreat into unbelief. Which of the parties, then, has beliefs and opinions which are at the mercy of emotion? Clytemnestra or the Chorus? The woman or the men?

At this point a word must be said upon a wider theme. If Aeschylus characterized the Chorus in this particular way, it was not because the personal or collective characteristics of these elderly gentlemen of Argos were interesting *per se*. Whether in choruses or principals, Aeschylus portrays character with strict relevance to his tragic themes and purposes. As I have tried to show elsewhere,[56] one of the tragic themes of *Oresteia* is the relationship of the sexes. The theme is developed in *Agamemnon* through the characterization and motivation of Clytemnestra, as it is developed in *Eumenides* through the arguments of Apollo and the vote of Athena. The primary characteristic of Clytemnestra is masculinity. At

---

53 Fraenkel discusses this passage at length in II 245–9. It is good that he rejects the view of the Chorus as 'merely an accompanying instrument' and finds their doubts 'based on true psychology'. I suggest that the psychology is both simpler and more precisely related to the context than he makes out.

54 So too εὐαγγέλου (475) recalls 262, 264; and φρενῶν κεκομμένος (479) is a retractation of their εὐφρόνως (351; cf. 275, 277). 485–7 (πιθανὸς . . . κλέος) are very difficult. Is πιθανός active or passive in sense? Fraenkel has shown that only the active sense 'accords with the bulk of the evidence from the earlier period'. Is ὅρος genuine? If so, what does it mean? These are the principal questions, but we must also ask of ἐπινέμεται ταχύπορος: Where does the 'fire' spread? Whither does it travel so fast? If we read ἔρος (which in some other respects has its attractions), it is the fire of desire spreading in the woman's soul, perhaps with the further suggestion of desire-kindled belief outrunning the evidence: there can be no idea of the topographical dissemination of rumour and belief. Yet nothing is more characteristic of Aeschylus than to repeat at the end of some self-contained section (e.g. a speech, an ode, or a scene) a theme or words from the beginning. When, therefore, we find θοὰ βάξις at the beginning of this epode and ταχύπορος at the end, πόλιν διήκει at the beginning and ἐπινέμεται at the end, it is virtually impossible to resist the conclusion that πιθανὸς . . . ταχύπορος also refers to the swift spreading of the rumour through the city. But it is not so easy to obtain the required sense from ὅρος either by interpretation or by emendation. Fraenkel defends ὅρος in the sense of decree or ordinance, but there are serious objections. 'A woman can easily talk men round.' Yes, but not by issuing orders; nor could the speeches of Pericles, when Persuasion sat upon his lips, be described as ὅροι. A woman's ordinance, *qua* ordinance, is not more persuasive or swifter-travelling than a man's. Further, this meaning is at once too close to κλέος and too remote from it. 'A woman's ordinance travels fast, but a woman's rumour dies fast' is not good writing. τί τῶνδ' ἄνευ κακῶν; We must admit that the problem is not yet solved. This means we cannot be sure whether πιθανός refers to persuasion exercised *on* or *by* Clytemnestra. Both are relevant to our theme. See also Page *ad loc.*

55 The point is not affected by the doubtful interpretation of αἰχμᾷ. On χάρις in *Oresteia* see *Gnomon* 23 (1951) 419 n. 1.

56 Cf. ch. 6 *passim*.

the climax of the play there is a contest of wills between her and her husband, in the course of which she compels him to play the feminine role. Agamemnon's own words are the evidence for this: μὴ γυναικὸς ἐν τρόποις ἐμέ | ἅβρυνε (918f.); yet he ends by treading, luxuriously, the scarlet draperies. The relationship between Clytemnestra and the Chorus is a subordinate element in the same pattern. The Watchman had described his mistress by the phrase γυναικὸς ἀνδρόβουλον ἐλπίζον κέαρ (11), where ἐλπίζον implied that, along with her manly counsel, she entertained the irrational hopes of a woman. But *her* hopes are seen to be well founded; the accusations of the Chorus are disproved and recoil upon themselves. Since they, not she, allow their beliefs to be dictated by their hopes and fears, they (like Agamemnon) play the feminine role to her male lead.[57]

It is in the scene with Cassandra that the Chorus are again significantly characterized. The situation being different, the characterization of the Chorus, though consistent with that which we have been studying, is aimed at a different effect. Broadly speaking, what they display in this scene is a reluctance, amounting to refusal, to face facts. This characteristic also is relevant to a general theme of fundamental importance, about which a few words must first be said.

There is a line three times heard in the Parodos, which greatly strikes the imagination: αἴλινον αἴλινον εἰπέ, τὸ δ' εὖ νικάτω (121, 139, 159). This line is descriptive of the trilogy as a whole, since the development of the action involves a tale of woe, yet good prevails in the end.[58] But, if it is descriptive of the trilogy, *Agamemnon* and *Choephori* are built to that formula in exact reverse, for in them people are always saying εὖ and it is always the evil which prevails. The persistence with which the personages of the drama express hopes for the best, even when they fear the worst, needs no illustration. Nor is this the place to demonstrate how intricately Aeschylus has employed the polarity (as it might be called) of εὖ and αἴλινον in shaping not only the trilogy and its component plays but also individual scenes, speeches, and odes.[59]

In *Agamemnon* it is the function of the Chorus (though not of the Chorus alone) to attempt, often desperately, to preserve a façade of good before the reality of evil. So, as the Herald approaches, their leader says: ἀλλ' ἢ τὸ χαίρειν μᾶλλον ἐκβάξει λέγων· | τὸν ἄντιον δὲ τοῖσδ' ἀποστέργω λόγον· εὖ γὰρ πρὸς εὖ φανεῖσι προσθήκη πέλοι (498ff.). It might seem strange that he should use the expression πρὸς εὖ φανεῖσι so soon after his fellows had said: γυναικὸς αἰχμᾷ πρέπει πρὸ τοῦ φανέντος χάριν ξυναινέσαι (483f.). It is not really strange, for the appearance of the Herald is evidence of actual news, good or bad, and the thought of bad news they cannot tolerate.[60] The Chorus are believers once again; and their response to

---

[57] Cf. p. 104 n. 16.

[58] It is perhaps not fanciful to find in it a formula for the tragic art itself.

[59] One illustration may serve. The first half of the Watchman's speech is dominated by evil (culminating in 18f.: κλαίω . . . διαπονουμένου), but closes with a prayer for good (20f.: note εὐτυχής, εὐαγγέλου). The theme of the second half is good (εὐφημοῦντα, 28; εὖ πεσόντα, 32), but it reverts to evil at the end (τὰ δ' ἄλλα σιγῶ, 36; λήθομαι, 39). The silence of the Watchman is later paralleled by the concealments of the Chorus and the Herald.

[60] I can see nothing in 500 to suggest that the elders are 'still distrustful and full of sinister forebodings' (Fraenkel II 252), except in so far as there is always an undertone of foreboding. But the form of their

the Herald's tale (551ff.) is as emotional and as complete as was their response to Clytemnestra.[61] He begins his speech with the words εὖ γὰρ πέπρακται (551); and, though he is forced back to the theme of death,[62] he makes himself and his hearers believe that the gain outweighs the sorrow (νικᾷ τὸ κέρδος, πῆμα δ᾽ οὐκ ἀντιρρέπει, 574). Like them in the earlier scene, he greets the fall of Troy as a χάρις (581) for which to thank the gods, knowing all the time that he is concealing the appalling losses of the Greeks on the return journey,[63] just as the Chorus on their part are concealing all those sinister reflections which had developed during the first *stasimon*.

But it is in the scene with Cassandra that evasion reaches its climax. Here the dramatist exhibits an ingenious economy. Cassandra is the prophetess doomed to carry no conviction with her prophecies; and, as Professor Gilbert Murray has pointed out,[64] we see 'the curse of disbelief working on the elders, without their knowledge. At first they do not understand; when forced to understand they do not believe, and quickly forget.' This is well said; yet, in disbelieving things which are so unwelcome, they are merely acting in a character already established.

A certain obtuseness we must allow to the Chorus of a Greek tragedy. οὐ κομπάσαιμ᾽ ἂν θεσφάτων γνώμων ἄκρος | εἶναι, κακῷ δέ τῳ προσεικάζω τάδε (1130f.). Such a remark, which invites the sneer of the philistine and the parody of a Housman, could be paralleled in many plays. But in *Agamemnon* it forms part of a pattern, being a reluctant and tentative admission of the evil trend of Cassandra's prophecy. In the lyrical utterances of the Chorus from 1121 onwards we can perhaps trace the following sequence of emotions. The sheer horror which they express at 1121ff. (ἐπὶ δὲ καρδίαν κτλ.) is countered by an almost abusive comment upon the prophetic art (1132ff.): ἀπὸ δὲ θεσφάτων τίς ἀγαθὰ φάτις βροτοῖς τέλλεται; κακῶν γὰρ διαὶ πολυεπεῖς τέχναι θεσπιῳδῶν φόβον φέρουσιν μαθεῖν.[65] Once again the antithesis of εὖ and αἴλινον will be noticed, and the resistance of the Chorus to the latter. Then Cassandra's theme shifts from Agamemnon to herself, and their mood to one of pity (1140ff.). But at the harsh σχισμὸς ἀμφήκει δορί (1149) they revert to a kind of resentment at the alarm her prophecies inspire, the evil content of which is again underlined in their expressions (1150ff.). In particular, δύσφατος is the opposite of εὔφημος, which we shall meet below. The Chorus, who stigmatize her agonies as μάταιοι, still wish to believe in good or at least to speak of it. But this Cassandra makes very

prayer, with its repeated εὖ, is intended to convey the opposite impression. εὖ φανεῖσι is both confident and inconsistent with the tone of 484.

[61] νικώμενος λόγοισιν (583) describes equally well their reaction to Clytemnestra's speeches. In 584, though the primary sense of εὐμαθεῖν is 'ease of learning', I strongly suspect that the idea of 'learning good news' is present also (see n. 67 below).

[62] 568ff.; note especially τοῖς λοιποῖσιν Ἀργείων στρατοῦ, the full significance of which does not appear until he makes his final speech. It means more and worse than στρατὸν . . . τὸν λελειμμένον δορός (517).

[63] Thus πάντ᾽ ἔχεις λόγον (582) is a lie; and, since he has just mentioned the generals (in the plural) he must know it. Why did the truth have to be dragged out of him? Because εὔφημον ἦμαρ οὐ πρέπει κακαγγέλῳ | γλώσσῃ μιαίνειν (636f.). (Cf. App. C.)

[64] *Aeschylus: the creator of tragedy* (Oxford 1940) 221.

[65] πολυεπεῖς: whatever the precise meaning, 'the context points to something depreciatory' (Fraenkel).

difficult. Her following lines (1156ff.), with their explicit τότε μέν . . . νῦν δέ (what Greek could resist the cogency of μέν and δέ?), seem all too clear (τορὸν ἄγαν, 1162), and the lyrical section ends in a spirit of poignant compassion.

Cassandra's first speech in trimeters deals, like her earlier lyric stanzas, with the children of Thyestes (χορὸς | ξύμφθογγος οὐκ εὔφωνος· οὐ γὰρ εὖ λέγει, 1186f.). This fact about the past the Chorus is bound to admit; no oath of ignorance can remedy it.[66] When the prophetess speaks (1212) of the curse of unbelief, they reply ἡμῖν γε μὲν δὴ πιστὰ θεσπίζειν δοκεῖς. But past events are no real test of their faith. In a fresh bout of inspiration, she prophesies (1214ff.), now in clearer images, the murder of Agamemnon; and the response of the Chorus shows how little they are prepared to understand: τὰ δ' ἄλλ' ἀκούσας ἐκ δρόμου πεσὼν τρέχω (1245). Cassandra is provoked into a plain statement: Ἀγαμέμνονός σέ φημ' ἐπόψεσθαι μόρον (1246). How will the Chorus react to this? εὔφημον, they say – εὔφημον, ὦ τάλαινα, κοίμησον στόμα (1247). From θῆλυς ἄρσενος φονεύς (1231) and from other phrases they must have gained some inkling of the truth; and the fear that grips them (1243) is that such hints may prove as true, as factual, as the Thyestean banquet. They recognize the tendency of the prophecy, but they cannot bear to have it *said*. If εὔφημον is primarily a prescription of silence, the literal meaning of the word is that of using good, or well-omened, expressions.[67] These are the two degrees of evasion: to say well of what is not well, or (at the worst) to keep silence; both are exemplified again and again throughout the play. But, as Cassandra says, οὔτι παιὼν τῷδ' ἐπιστατεῖ λόγῳ (1248).[68] To which the Chorus-leader replies: οὔκ, εἴπερ ἔσται γ'· ἀλλὰ μὴ γένοιτό πως. That futile πως is the last – or almost the last – weak effort of the spirit of evasion.

---

[66] In 1196 τὸ μὴ εἰδέναι can be regarded as certain (see Fraenkel *ad loc.*).

[67] The employment of εὖ and εὖ-compounds in the trilogy deserves a separate study. A good example of a slight shift between two meanings of εὖ is to be found in 1187 (quoted above). In other cases there seems to be a deliberate ambiguity (see p. 210 n. 50 and p. 213 n. 61 above). So insistent is this small syllable that εὔφημος, εὐφημεῖν come very close in places to meaning the saying of εὖ. This kind of literal 'euphemism' characterizes the closing lines of the *Eumenides*, where the syllable can at last be reiterated without fear of sinister disclosures, for good has unequivocally prevailed.

[68] 'There can be no doubt that . . . the word [παιών] means "healer, physician"' (Fraenkel *ad loc.*); nor that there is a reference to Apollo, who is here represented as exercising in person the function he delegates at 1202 (ἐπέστησεν). Apollo was invoked by Calchas (146) and by the Herald (512) in his capacity of healer. But it is not in that capacity that he directs Cassandra's prophecies. He is, rather, the destroyer; ἀπόλλων (1081) and Λύκειος (1257) – a title associated with violence and destruction, though obscure in its precise relevance. (That the function of Apollo should be in debate prepares for the *Choephori*.) This explanation does not, however, by itself provide a link with the preceding words of the Chorus-leader. The link is perhaps twofold. (i) The Chorus, which had referred with distaste to the evil terms in which prophecy is couched (1132ff., 1154f.), now demands a εὐφημία that would make prophecy impossible. (ii) εὐφημία is characteristic of the paean (see references in Fraenkel), a song closely associated with Apollo as healer and averter of misfortune. But that is not the song appropriate to this occasion. The connection of thought is subtle, but it is made easier to follow by the opening of the Cassandra-scene, which has already raised the issue of what type of song and cry is appropriate to Apollo. Cassandra invoked him with ὀτοτοτοῖ, to the astonishment of the Chorus, who use the term δυσφημοῦσα (1078). When they say (1075, 1079) that he has no concern with θρῆνος and γόοι, they imply that his proper invocation is ἰὴ παιάν (cf. 146), his proper song the paean. Out of this contrast of songs Aeschylus makes a grim paradox at 645 (παιᾶνα τόνδ' Ἐρινύων) and, very explicitly, at *Cho.* 150f. (See Haldane, *passim*.)

The end of the Cassandra-scene is mainly concerned with the fate of the prophetess herself. The approach of this fate, which does not run counter to the presuppositions and hopes of the Chorus (for they will have regarded it as an intelligible, if deplorable, act of jealousy), is accepted by them, and they can pass over such references to the major crime as Ἀγαμέμνονος μοῖραν (1314) and ἀνὴρ δυσδάμαρτος ἀντ' ἀνδρός (1319). But, when Cassandra has entered the palace, they show quite clearly that they have grasped the possibility or likelihood of Agamemnon's death (1338ff.).[69]

The cry, when it comes, is certainly Agamemnon's. βασιλέως οἰμώγμασιν accepts the fact, as τοὔργον perhaps implies that it was not unexpected (1346). The Chorus-leader summons his fellows to take counsel.[70] There are twelve speakers.[71] The first five are all in favour of action. The first (1348f.), with a certain caution, would rouse the citizens. The second and third (1350–3), more impetuous, are for entering the palace at once. The fourth (1354f.), a clear-sighted man,[72] sees the prelude to a tyranny. All the more reason against delay, says the fifth (1356f.). The sixth and seventh speakers are 'realists', the sixth (1358f.) recognizing that the initiative rests with the 'doer', the seventh (1360f.) that mere words cannot raise the dead.[73] Yet something must be done, for it is better to die than tamely to submit to tyranny: the eighth and ninth speakers (1362–5) revert to the policy of action. It remains for the tenth speaker (1366f.) to propound an ingenious solution for their difficulties: ἢ γὰρ τεκμηρίοισιν ἐξ οἰμωγμάτων | μαντευσόμεσθα τἀνδρὸς ὡς ὀλωλότος; The speakers at 1346, 1359, and 1361 had frankly accepted the obvious fact of Agamemnon's death. But this Chorus has already shown a propensity for believing or disbelieving what it wishes to believe or disbelieve. So now: is Agamemnon really dead? The speaker questions the evidence of groans just as, in an earlier scene, the Chorus had questioned the evidence of fire. His τεκμηρίοισιν recalls 352 (πιστά σου τεκμήρια) and 272 (τέκμαρ) and the related passage at 475ff. But, if τεκμηρίοισιν recalls that earlier sequence of belief and disbelief, μαντευσόμεσθα cannot but recall the recent scene with Cassandra, her explicit prophecies and their refusal to accept them. The eleventh speaker (1368f.) seizes eagerly on this way out. The twelfth (1370f.), the Chorus-leader, who is perhaps taking the sense of the meeting,[74] repeats that they must know with certainty how fares the son of Atreus. They do not have long to wait.

[69] Though we may no longer be able to recover what precisely they said at 1338ff.

[70] In 1347 ἄν πως has not been emended with certainty. Headlam adopted Donaldson's εὖ for ἄν (pointing to the converse error at 552), and it has its attractions: the weak πως recalls the μὴ γένοιτό πως of 1249, while to say εὖ after the admitted death of Agamemnon is the *reductio ad absurdum* of evasion and thus prepares us for the course which the debate will follow.

[71] 'Fortunately unanimity has been reached on this point, a rare phenomenon in these studies' (Fraenkel III 633).

[72] ὁρᾶν πάρεστι (1353): a tiny point, perhaps, of individual characterization. No doubt, like Aegisthus (*Cho.* 854), he prides himself upon this quality.

[73] He underestimates his companions!

[74] It may not be certain, but it is surely probable, that the last speaker is the Chorus-leader. If so, what he says may carry special weight. The sense of πληθύνομαι is obscure: it is very doubtful whether it could mean (not so much 'I follow' as) 'I am supported by' a πλῆθος or majority. That is not to say, however, that a majority of the Chorus is still in favour of action. Just as the effect of 1358–61 is

Thus the debate falls into shape. First the demand for action; then the realistic objections to action; then the demand for action renewed; then the acceptable compromise based upon evasion. Aeschylus, in order to meet a technical difficulty, has made brilliant use of a characterization of the Chorus already established to serve more fundamental dramatic purposes. Surely there is no need to apologize for this scene.

APPENDIX F

Choephori 691–9[75]

The lines are attributed to Clytemnestra by M (for what that is worth, which is little), to Electra by the Aldine edition (for what that is worth, which is less), by Turnebus and some later editors. The case for Electra was argued at length by Headlam, cf. Thomson (3) II 214ff. (and *JHS* 61, 1941, 40). By recent writers it has been rejected with little short of contumely, cf. e.g. Rose 187 'one of the numerous oddities of criticism', Fraenkel II 305 n. 5, Taplin 340. The main reason for this is of course that Electra appears to be dismissed once and for all at 579 (σὺ μὲν φύλασσε τὰν οἴκῳ καλῶς), following 554 (τήνδε μὲν στείχειν ἔσω): it is the Chorus (who must remain) that is enjoined σιγᾶν θ' ὅπου δεῖ καὶ λέγειν τὰ καίρια (which they do in the scene with the Nurse). For her to be silently re-introduced would breach what Fraenkel calls the 'grammar of dramatic technique'. At best we must suppose that Electra attends Clytemnestra in her domestic (and servile?) role and herself takes the opportunity of 'timely speech'. If she is present, it is she that is addressed at 712ff., and the peremptory tone of 715 will then be bearing out the statement at 135 that she is ἀντίδουλος. A nice point, if true, and a stroke of irony that Orestes should be introduced into the house by his accomplice. One cannot, however, say that 715 is pointless if addressed to a *real* slave, when the *parodos* has pictured a household in fear.

The negative argument is strong and many will find it conclusive, to be countered only by special pleading. It may, nevertheless, still be worth putting the other case. There are difficulties, if we ascribe the lines to Clytemnestra. The apparent contradiction between 695 (φίλων ἀποψιλοῖς με τὴν παναθλίαν) and 717 (οὐ σπανίζοντες φίλων) can be explained, if with a rather unwelcome reliance on 'psychology': Clytemnestra has gone too far, she recollects Aegisthus and corrects herself. (Give the lines to Electra, and 717 becomes a contemptuous retort.) But this brings us to the principal difficulty, which is to decide Clytemnestra's tone, if it is Clytemnestra: is she sincere or insincere? If insincere (and we know that dissimulation is part of the man-woman's role), why such a

counteracted by 1362–5, so the final and decisive impression upon the audience is made by the unanimity of the last three speakers. It would have been easy in production to convey by gestures the acceptance by the Chorus as a whole of this temporizing policy; and, though it cannot be proved, I think it very likely that this was done.

[75] Reprinted from *CR* 60 (1946) 58ff. (revised).

violent contrast between the extravagant terms of 691ff. and the cold propriety of 707ff.? If sincere (cf. e.g. Rose, and J. C. Lawson, *PCPS* 1934, 9ff.), and if we discount the Nurse (e.g. 738) as a hostile witness (which is a dubious proceeding), what are the movements of her mind? Maternal tenderness is still alive? Or do we say that she now realizes her hope of compromise with the *daimon* (*Agam.* 1568ff.) is vain, that the Curse is still alive? Does the death of Orestes mean for her the extinction of hope (rather than the disappearance of a threat)? Is it not the survival of Aegisthus which matters to her?

Too many questions altogether. Too many questions which nothing else in the play, where the 'psychology' of Clytemnestra is simple, helps us to answer.[76] Perhaps this is one of those cases, not infrequent in Aeschylus, in which the word is more important than the man (or woman). These lines contain words and themes which have connections up and down the trilogy: it may be worth looking at one or two of them.

(i) ἐλπίς. However we read and interpret the text of 698f., it is clear that the speaker speaks of Orestes as of a hope that has failed.[77] The theme of hope is prominent in both *Agamemnon* and *Choephori*. There is indeed a correspondence of moods between the earlier scenes of the two plays.[78] Just as the fall of Troy (which means the return of Agamemnon) is good news which comes first on the doubtful evidence of the beacons but is finally confirmed by the arrival of the Herald, so the home-coming of Orestes is first a matter of dubious evidence and wild surmise. σαίνομαι δ' ὑπ' ἐλπίδος, says Electra (194), when she sees the lock of hair; and at 236 Orestes is greeted as δακρυτὸς ἐλπὶς σπέρματος σωτηρίου.[79] In both plays, however, the long-hoped-for event merely precipitates a fresh catastrophe in the house of Atreus. It is Electra who, like the Nurse (776), has placed her hopes in Orestes.[80]

(ii) The hope is a hope of cure (cf. ἰατρός, 699), another theme which runs through the trilogy. It is particularly associated with Apollo, the healer god (cf. e.g. *Agam.* 146, 512). But Apollo is also a destroyer. It is a fundamental issue of *Choephori* (explored in ch. 7 above) whether the intervention of Apollo will save or destroy, will cure or aggravate the troubles of the house. These troubles are

---

[76] On the reaction of the Sophoclean Clytemnestra (*El.* 766ff.) see Winnington-Ingram 232f. No doubt Sophocles had *Choephori* in mind and there are echoes of language, but too much weight should not be placed upon the later play in deciding the attribution of *Cho.* 691ff. Note, however, that it is only if we ascribe the lines to Clytemnestra that we are caught in the net of Sophoclean psychology.

[77] Headlam's defence of the received text is far-fetched and Thomson's μὴ παροῦσαν not wholly convincing. Mazon and Rose adopt Orelli's ἐκγράφει, Page chooses Pauw's προδοῦσαν.

[78] See ch. 7, p. 133.

[79] δακρυτὸς ἐλπίς is itself an ambiguity with which we can compare *Agam.* 270 (tears of joy, a joy that will ultimately evoke tears). Transpose 235–7 and attribute them to the Chorus (with Rossbach and Thomson (3)), and the hope is still that of the partisans of Agamemnon.

[80] To play fair, one should perhaps point out that, in *Agamemnon*, Clytemnestra was accused, wrongly, of falling victim to irrational hopes (cf. ch. 6, pp. 103f.), and that there might, therefore, be some irony to be extracted from our passage. What sticks in the gullet, however, is the notion that the Clytemnestra of *Choephori* could ever have entertained 'hopes' of Orestes – hopes of cure. What she did hope (539), vainly, was that her offerings at the grave would be ἄκος τομαῖον . . . πημάτων (the epithet is sinister).

described as βακχεία κακή (a certain reading), a metaphor which seems to look back to the χορός, the κῶμος, which the inspired vision of Cassandra saw in the house of Atreus (*Agam.* 1186, 1189), and forward to the Furies of *Eumenides*, who describe themselves as μαινάδες (*Eum.* 500). Will Apollo, with his enigmatic relationship to the Furies, rid the house of ravening spirits? For Clytemnestra to use, in innocence, words which suggest Apollo, might have a certain irony, but it is Electra that knows by whom Orestes has been sent, and if she speaks the lines she has Apollo in mind.

(iii) When the speaker uses the metaphor of the bow (τόξοις, 694), I find it hard to believe that, in this play, it does not recall Apollo – in his destructive aspect, as ἰατρός recalls the healer. But it is used of the Curse, the 'Αρά. The breeding curse which haunts the house of Atreus (*Agam.* 1565) in *Choephori* naturally takes the form of the curse (or Curses) of the dead Agamemnon, and in the *kommos* (Cho. 406) Orestes calls on the πολυκρατεῖς 'Αραὶ τεθυμένων to see the plight of the Atridae. It is this invocation that will be in the mind of Electra (if she speaks the lines). But the action of Orestes merely summons up the γενεθλίους ἀράς of Clytemnestra (912), which are embodied in the Furies, the 'Αραί of the following play (*Eum.* 417).[81]

In short, some of these associations might have some ironical force if the lines are spoken by Clytemnestra, but if Electra speaks them the effect is one of a sustained double irony. She thinks that what she says is in every particular untrue (or not true of Orestes and herself): that so far from being ruined they are saved; that the curse of the house has been turned successfully and finally against her enemies, who will be struck down by the well-aimed bolts of Apollo from afar; that she has found and not lost a dear one; that Orestes was well advised to return to Argos; that the cure for the βακχεία κακή (by which she may mean no more than the riotous behaviour of Clytemnestra and Aegisthus)[82] has been found through the healer god; that her hope is fulfilled. In fact, what she says is in every particular only too true: the return and act of Orestes are but a further stage in the ruin of the house and involve a regeneration of the curse; the intervention of Apollo is calamitous and provides no cure but merely an aggravation of the disease; she has found Orestes, who had better have stayed away, merely to lose him; and the hope she has in him is illusory. Is this not Aeschylean? And should not the speech be given to Electra?

---

[81] In my original article I attempted to relate the use of ἐπωπᾶν here with the frequent use in the trilogy of ἐποπτεύειν of supervising powers, but this now seems to me far-fetched.

[82] Cf. Headlam, *ap.* Thomson (3) II 216, citing *Cho.* 942–4.

APPENDIX G

Eumenides 674–80[83]

```
      ΑΘ.  ἤδη κελεύω τούσδ᾽ ἀπὸ γνώμης φέρειν
675        ψῆφον δικαίαν, ὡς ἅλις λελεγμένων;
      ΧΟ.  ἡμῖν μὲν ἤδη πᾶν τετόξευται βέλος·
           μένω δ᾽ ἀκοῦσαι πῶς ἀγὼν κριθήσεται.
      ΑΘ.  τί γάρ; πρὸς ὑμῶν πῶς τιθεῖσ᾽ ἄμομφος ὦ;
      ΧΟ.  ἠκούσαθ᾽ ὧν ἠκούσατ᾽, ἐν δὲ καρδίᾳ
680        ψῆφον φέροντες ὅρκον αἰδεῖσθε, ξένοι.
```

So the parts are distributed in the MSS. But clearly either 676–77 or 679–80 belong to Apollo. Karsten gave him the latter couplet, and the majority of recent editors has followed him.[84] Weil in 1861 did likewise, but transposed the couplets. In his Teubner text however (1907) he reverted to the traditional order of lines and attributed 676–77 to Apollo. This attribution seems to have all the internal evidence in its favour. The following points are not all equally cogent, but their cumulative weight is considerable.

(i) Apollo has been presenting 'the case for the defence' and has just finished the last of several speeches of fair length. It is more natural that he, in answer to Athena's question, should state that he has finished his case, that she should then turn to his opponents and ask if they have anything further to say.

(ii) The plural is used of both sides: ἡμῖν 676, ὑμῶν 678. But in the former couplet there is a change from plural to singular in the second line. If it is given to the Furies, this change has no motive except metrical convenience. Further, it is harsh, if not impossibly harsh, to make their leader speak in one line for the whole Chorus, in the next in her own person, particularly in view of the fact that *she* has done the talking, while they are *all* doing the waiting! But Apollo can quite naturally speak in the first line as advocate for Orestes, then announce his personal intention of waiting to see how the verdict goes. Which in fact he does, and presumably leaves the stage soon after it is given, though there is no certain indication when.[85]

(iii) The metaphor in πᾶν τετόξευται βέλος is appropriate to Apollo. When he appeared to the Furies in his temple, he was armed with the bow (181ff.). Then he threatened them with actual arrows; now it is a natural figure with which to describe his arguments.[86]

---

[83] Reprinted from *CR* 49 (1935) 7f.

[84] E.g. Campbell, Headlam, Mazon, Sidgwick, Verrall, Wecklein, Wilamowitz.

[85] Orestes has already said (243): ἀμμενῶ τέλος δίκης. And once he has been besieged by the Furies he cannot but wait in any case. That the Chorus make use of a similar expression at 732 does not affect the argument either way.

[86] The arrows of Apollo occur elsewhere in the trilogy, e.g. *Agam.* 510. At *Cho.* 1033 the metaphor (τόξῳ κτλ.) is suggested by the mention of Apollo. At *Eum.* 628 we find that the archer god can sympathize with the far-darting Amazons, but not with the crafty murderess Clytemnestra.

(iv) No doubt the reason why Karsten's attribution was made and accepted is that the solemn appeal to the jurors to respect their oath seemed more appropriate in the mouth of the Delphic god than in that of a Fury. I do not wish to discuss here the part played by Apollo in this play and in the trilogy as a whole, which I take to have been not altogether creditable.[87] But an earlier reference that he has made to the juror's oath must be taken into consideration. Lines 619–21 are difficult, but can hardly bear any meaning other than the following. He has answered Orestes' question (εἰ δικαίως εἴτε μή: 612–13) with a resonant δικαίως, and has claimed to speak with the authority of Zeus. He continues: 'Consider how great is the force of this claim to justice (τὸ δίκαιον τοῦτο); I bid you follow the will of my father.' By μέν and δέ this is given the form of an antithesis between τὸ δίκαιον and βουλὴ πατρός. No doubt the distinction implied is to the confident Apollo purely formal and rhetorical. But the following line still postulates it. He gives as a reason why they should follow the will of Zeus that Zeus is stronger than an oath. What other oath can this be than their juror's oath, which was, as we learn from 674–75, ἀπὸ γνώμης φέρειν ψῆφον δικαίαν – to decide the case on its merits according to the best of their judgement?[88] In effect, they must do as they are told, should a paradoxical conflict arise between τὸ δίκαιον and Apollo's interpretation of the will of Zeus. It is an attempt to browbeat with which we can compare 713–14. Now for Aeschylus such a conflict is at least conceivable (there could hardly otherwise have been a divided verdict); and I believe that in the τῇ σῇ φρενί of 612 he has put us on our guard against the subjectivity of Apollo's coming pronouncement.[89] However this may be, Apollo has, in form at any rate, incited them to perjury, in what is perhaps a threat, as 667ff. is a bribe. Now to make him say in our passage ὅρκον αἰδεῖσθε might after this be an intended effect of irony. But it is surely easier to ascribe this couplet to the Furies, who have already displayed their interest in oaths and the weight which they put upon them. I refer to 429ff., where they wish to make the issue depend on a contest of oaths between themselves and Orestes upon the simple question of fact, and are rebuked by Athena for this undue simplification. Further, it is appropriate for the Furies to reinforce Athena's words and remind the jury that they must return a just verdict according to their consciences, uninfluenced by the bolts of cajolery, threatening and (as I believe) sophistry that have come from Apollo's bow.

(v) 678 might well be addressed by Athena to Apollo and Orestes, though it is perhaps doubtful whether a goddess would so lump together a fellow-deity and a mortal. To both sides she is polite, for she desires the favour of both Apollo and the Eumenides for her beloved citizens. Indeed the idea in ἄμομφος is one of the leading notions of this play, which is to end to the satisfaction of all parties. It is the wish of Athena that offence shall be neither given nor taken by any. Thus ἄμομφος here of Orestes would be complementary to the point of the same adjective at 475: there she says that she regards the city as having no claim to resentment against him, here she would be anxious that he should have no fault to find with Athens.

[87] Cf. ch. 7, *passim.*

[88] Cf. Mazon II 151 n. The Athenian dicast swore in cases for which the laws did not provide to give his verdict γνώμῃ τῇ δικαιοτάτῃ (Dem. xxxix 40). Aeschylus probably had the terms of this oath in mind.

[89] The tone of τοὺς ἐμούς τε καὶ Διός (713) is a similar warning signal.

But it is no less appropriate to the Furies. Taking it together with the occurrence of the word in her first address to them (413), we find the same suggestion of reciprocity. There she was on the point of referring disparagingly to their outward appearance, but checked herself on the grounds that they had done her no offence. So here she wishes to avoid giving offence to them – by cutting short the presentation of their case. On either interpretation it is not surprising to find a cognate word occurring towards the end of the play, when the Furies, now the Σεμναί, sing that the inhabitants of Athens will find nothing to complain of in their lot under the new régime, protected alike by Pallas and by themselves (1019: οὔτι μέμψεσθε συμφορὰς βίου[90]).

If the Medicean manuscript had given 679–80 to Apollo, the strength of these considerations might well have justified us in altering the attributions of these two couplets. As it is, the tradition is neutral; and against a number of reasons for giving 676–77 to Apollo and leaving the Furies with 679–80 there appears not to be one for the course taken by the great majority of editors.

APPENDIX H

Choephori 783ff., 935ff.

783ff. The ode consists of three pairs of corresponding stanzas, each pair being separated by a mesode not in correspondence. There is little reason to suppose (with some editors) that these stanzas should be repeated at the end of the antistrophes as ephymnia. The text is in a deplorable state.

The ode follows the departure of the Nurse to summon Aegisthus and is sung in anticipation of his entry; it consists largely of appeals to deities to aid Orestes in the coming struggle. The closing stanzas (819–37) are particularly corrupt (*plura corrupta quam sana*, Page), but, if one thing is clear, it is that, while the closing words (τὸν αἴτιον) point to the Aegisthus who now enters, the mesode (827–30) envisages a confrontation of Orestes with a Clytemnestra who will call him τέκνον. The matricide will be in the minds of the audience throughout.

The earlier part of the ode consists of a series of prayers. (i) First to Zeus, addressed as 'father of the Olympian gods' and thus associated firmly with the supernal world, who is implored to protect Orestes. The prayer continues in terms which seem to recall Orestes' prayer at 246ff. (with μέγαν ἄρας, 791, compare 262). The closing reference to penalties (or rewards) is obscure and possibly ambiguous. (ii) Household gods (see below). (iii) Apollo (without much doubt). The bright god (who dwells in the στόμιον, cf. 954) is implored to grant the light of freedom to one who is veiled in darkness. (iv) Apollo is immediately followed by Hermes, his rightful collaborator. Text and interpretation are obscure, but this

[90] The οὐ μέμφομαι of Orestes at 596 hardly belongs to the pattern, but reminds us that the final solution will be satisfactory to him as well as to the Athenians – and the Furies (cf. 836: ἐπαινέσεις).

is a god who works in darkness, by night and by day alike. Clearly this is the Hermes – χθόνιος and νύχιος – of 727f.

Of these prayers, (ii) is perhaps the most intriguing. Who are these gods that dwell in the deep interior of the house? *Di Penates*, say the commentators, and point to the appropriateness of the epithet in πλουτογαθῆ μυχόν [for μυχός as store-cupboard, cf. *Agam.* 96]. Actually, there is no close equivalent in Greek to the Latin term, and we wait until Dion. Hal. 1.67.3 for an explicit equation of θεοὶ μύχιοι with *di Penates*. House-cult, in our evidence, is generally associated, not with such a collective, but with specific gods, e.g. Zeus ἑρκεῖος or Hestia or the ἀγαθὸς δαίμων. Aeschylus prefers the generalized expression for reasons which are well explained by Wilamowitz (2) 225f. This divine collective embodies the total experience of a house which we know to have embraced recurrent bloodshed. It is this which makes it appropriate – and vain – for the Chorus to pray for an absolution of blood by new acts of justice (i.e. new acts of revenge), and that the aged *phonos* may no longer breed in the house. Moreover, it invites the audience to remember that among the spirits which haunt the house are a *daimon* of heavy wrath and the Erinyes of the children of Thyestes. No doubt much more could be relevantly said about the connections of house-gods with the chthonian world.

935ff. Another deeply corrupted text. The ode consists of two pairs of stanzas, each separated by a mesode. (The case for repeating the mesodes as ephymnia is slightly strengthened by the repetition in M of the opening words of 961ff. after 971.)

Clytemnestra has gone in to her death; the Chorus sing a song of triumph – the triumph of Justice, which has come to the house of Agamemnon, in the guise of lions, in the guise of Ares, as it came to the sons of Priam, a penalty heavy with justice (βαρύδικος ποινά). It was brought about by the exile sent from Pytho, sped on his way by good counsels from the gods. The main stress is upon Apollo, in preparation for the closing scene and the following play. We may note the following points.

(i) In the mesodes (942–45, 961–64) much emphasis is laid upon the house, no longer bridled (962), no longer wasted in its substance by the two polluters (943f.), and thus on the 'political' motivation of Orestes.

(ii) In the first antistrophe comes the sole reference to Zeus – to Zeus as father of Dike (948–51). Dike is said to have touched a hand in the battle. Whose hand? The preceding sentence reads: ἔμολε δ᾽ ᾧ μέλει κρυπταδίου μάχας δολιόφρων ποινά, the interpretation of which is much disputed. Reading ᾧ, does it refer to Orestes or, better, to Hermes (cf. 726ff.)? In either case, ποινά (which should not be tampered with) is the subject of μέλει and lacks personification. Read ᾇ (with Auratus), and everything falls into line. μέλει has its common construction with dative and genitive; Ποινά is a personified spirit, akin to, if not identical with, an Erinys (cf. *Eum.* 321ff.); and with it the daughter of Zeus, breathing destructive wrath among the enemy, links hands. The battle is κρυπτάδιος, the spirit δολιόφρων.

(iii) After the δολιόφρων Ποινά comes an Apollo who had commanded craft – but (according to the Chorus) a craft which was no craft: the sense is clear, however we deal with the ἀδόλως δολίας of M. Much of the stanza is badly corrupted, but the opening and the close are not and are worth noting. I quote Dodds (1) 91 n. 66: 'At *Cho.* 953, Aeschylus' Chorus address [*sic*] Apollo as μέγαν ἔχων μυχὸν χθονός, and the corresponding phrase at 807, ὦ μέγα ναίων στόμιον must also in my judgement refer to Apollo. This seems an unnatural way of speaking if the poet has in mind merely the Pleistos gorge; the temple is not in the gorge, but above it. It looks more like a traditional phraseology going back to the days of the Earth-oracle.' If this is right (as I think it is), it provides a good reason for *not* changing M's Παρνάσσιος to Παρνασσίας (with Paley). Aeschylus is deliberately associating Apollo with the Earth *as such*. Not only does this match his close involvement with Erinyes in this play, but it looks forward to the opening lines of the Prophetis in *Eum.* (on which see ch. 7, pp. 150f.). But, if the stanza opens with a 'chthonian' Apollo, it ends with a reference to the rule of supernal gods (οὐρανοῦχον ἀρχὰν σέβειν).

(iv) The Chorus sing (965ff.) of μύσος and καθαρμοί. Sometimes they show themselves more aware than the actors of the implications of what is being done, cf. 466ff., and it is conceivable that they realize that, despite the divine sanctions, there is guilt to be absolved. More likely, however, they are thinking of the pollution of the house by the criminal usurpers, the μιάστορε of 944. In either case this is preparation for the closing scene in which Orestes is pursued by Erinyes on the scent of blood, his only recourse the purification of Apollo (1059). Time will indeed do its work, but it will not be through the rites of Apollo, but by the verdict of a court, that Orestes and his house are saved.

SELECT INDEX

PRAISE FOR *WRITE-A-THON*

Like the best coaches, Rochelle Y. Melander will strengthen your creative muscles, get your writerly heart pounding, and show you you're capable of way more than you've ever imagined. *Write-A-Thon* will help you go the distance with your book.

> —Gayle Brandeis, teacher, activist, and author of *My Life with the Lincolns and Delta Girls*

Write-A-Thon: Write Your Book in 26 Days (and Live to Tell About It) gives you the information, inspiration and tools you need to write a good book in less than a month. Want to know the secret to writing successfully? You're holding it.

> —Donna Gephart, award-winning children's book author, wrote *Olivia Bean, Trivia Queen* in twenty-nine days

Melander is a friendly, entertaining, fully engaged, and smart guide to hold your hand and lead you through twenty-six days toward completion of the first draft of your masterpiece.

> —Sue William Silverman, author of *Fearless Confessions: A Writer's Guide to Memoir*

Write-A-Thon is your no-excuses guide to getting that dream book finished. Each lesson builds upon the last, helping you to grow as a writer. *Write-A-Thon* is like having your own personal coach sitting on your shoulder, guiding you through the process of writing a book. I wish I had a book like this when I first embarked on my writing journey.

> —Kimberly Llewellyn, author of *The Quest for the Holy Veil*

Loaded with exercises, motivational quotes, and real-life examples, her book doesn't just explain how she is so productive—she shows you how to do it, too. As a runner, I especially enjoyed the marathon analogy she employs throughout the book. Sure, a marathon sounds insurmountable at first, even for seasoned runners—but with preparation, training, and practice, most runners can complete one. The same is true of would-be authors—whether you've been writing for years or are just getting started, you can write a book in a month with Melander's *Write-A-Thon* as your guide. Motivating, insightful, and fun to read, this book is one you'll keep handy for years.

> —Kelly James-Enger, author *Goodbye Byline, Hello Big Bucks: The Writer's Guide to Making Money Ghostwriting and Coauthoring Books*

Write-A-Thon is wise, user-friendly, witty, breathtakingly thorough, and fun.

> —Robert McDowell, author of the bestselling *Poetry as Spiritual Practice: Reading, Writing, and Using Poetry in Your Daily Rituals, Aspirations, and Intentions*

A life coach as well as writing teacher, Melander infuses the text with so many ideas, and exercises, as well as energy that you'll never again look at writing the same way. I know I won't. If you're serious about the craft, you need this book.

—Libby Fischer Hellmann, author of *Set the Night on Fire*

Write-A-Thon is the tool every writer has been waiting for. Whether a professional or a wanna-be writer, you will find the practical help, the inspiration, and the kick in the pants to get writing. This book is more than a book—it's a whole a new life built out of words.

—Jane Rubietta, international speaker and award-winning author of *Come Along: Journey to a More Intimate Faith*

In *Write-A-Thon*, Rochelle Melander knocks down excuses for not writing and sets out a detailed plan for turning your idea into a book. The key is that she shows how to do it in less than a month—not the years that so many writers seem to think it will take. You can bet that *Write-A-Thon* is going to be on my required reading list for new writers!

—Jennifer Lawler, author of *Dojo Wisdom for Writers*

This book is filled with the energy, knowledge, and tips from an established author who has not only written a book in a month, she held me accountable to write a book in a month, too! I couldn't have written or published *Creating Your Best Life* in record time without her prodding, accountability, and good humor in a difficult situation. This book will help everyone to finally write that book that is lurking in their brain and trying to get out!

—Caroline Adams Miller, MAPP, author of *Creating Your Best Life*

If you have been waiting for the perfect moment to begin your writing project, this book will help you stop chasing excuses and start putting words on the page.

—Jennifer Manske Fenske, author of *The Wide Smiles of Girls*

[Not sure] where to start? No worries. She offers easy-to-understand tips and tools to get you rolling. If you've ever dreamed of starting (and completing) a writing project, this is the time to do it. Buy this book and get going!

—Kathy Cano-Murillo, founder of CraftyChica.com and author of *Waking Up in the Land of Glitter* and *Miss Scarlet's School of Patternless Sewing*

WRITE-A-THON

Write your book in 26 days
(and live to tell about it)

ROCHELLE MELANDER

WRITER'S DIGEST
BOOKS

WritersDigest.com
Cincinnati, Ohio

For more resources for writers, visit www.writersdigest.com/books.

To receive a free weekly e-mail newsletter delivering tips and updates about writing and about Writer's Digest products, register directly at www.writersdigest.com/enews.

15 14 13 12 11   5 4 3 2 1

Distributed in Canada by Fraser Direct
100 Armstrong Avenue
Georgetown, Ontario, Canada L7G 5S4
Tel: (905) 877-4411

Distributed in the U.K and Europe by F&W Media International
Brunel House, Newton Abbot, Devon, TQ12 4PU, England
Tel: (+44) 1626-323200, Fax: (+44) 1626-323319
E-mail: postmaster@davidandcharles.co.uk

Distributed in Australia by Capricorn Link
P.O. Box 704, Windsor, NSW 2756 Australia
Tel: (02) 4577-3555

PE
1408
.M45
2011

Edited by Melissa Wuske
Designed by Terri Woesner
media   Production Coordinated by Debbie Thomas

DEDICATION

Work hard, play harder.
—GRETCHEN WILSON

For my parents, who taught me to work hard.
And for Harold, who reminds me to play.

ACKNOWLEDGMENTS

*Sometimes it's just surreal out there, while you're
running a marathon. People just standing out in the cold,
even the rain, cheering for you, blasting music for you.
It's an awesome show of camaraderie and community.*
—JOHN ROBERTS

I've always said it takes a village to raise a book, and *Write-A-Thon* was no different. *Write-A-Thon* is here because of the concerted effort of many people. I owe heaps of gratitude to those who shared wisdom, provided support, and supplied treats:

Without the diligence and encouragement of my agent, Ivor Whitson, *Write-A-Thon* would still be little more than a dream. Thanks for calmly encouraging me to keep moving forward.

The team at Writer's Digest Books has put their heart and soul into launching *Write-A-Thon*. Kelly Messerly enthusiastically welcomed the proposal and offered her wisdom to help shape the book. My amazing editor, Melissa Wuske, has been a writer's dream: patient, insightful, and encouraging. At the end, Cynthia Laufenberg brought her gentle editorial touch to the manuscript.

Write-A-Thon was inspired by the nine-day *Write-A-Thon* I completed with Susan Lang and the many books I was privileged to write fast with my husband, Harold Eppley. In 2006, I shared the idea of *Write-A-Thon* with my friend and critique partner Debra Brenegan, and she urged me to write the book. The former Schwartz Bookstore and Boswell Book Company generously provided space for my first National Novel Writing Month workshops, where I got to test-market these ideas with real people. In addition, Boswell Book Company owner, Daniel Goldin, and my bookseller friends were a constant source of cheer and books during the writing and rewriting of this book. Ron Klug, Sharon Nagel, and Jeannée Sacken offered resources, suggestions, and support throughout the writing journey. My National Novel Writing Month buddies, both online and in person, have made every *Write-A-Thon* fun. I have gained gobs of wisdom about the art and discipline of writing from my guests at the Write Now! Mastermind class and on the Always Write! podcast. The young people I am privileged to teach through Dream Keepers have taught me persistence, courage, and how to write outside the lines. My brave, dedicated clients inspired me every moment I was writing. I am deeply grateful for this amazing community of writers who surround me. Thank you for sharing your stories, strategies, and ideas with me. I could not have written this book without you.

Karen Natterstad nudged me to court my inner athlete and try running. Catherine Alexander provided wine and an ear when I hit the wall. My mastermind partner, Marjorie Treu, kept me accountable and reminded me to dream bigger. At various stages of the writing process, Jan Ewing and Mitch Mitchell provided conversation, food, and a place for me to write away from the noise of my life.

My children have been joyful companions as I worked on this book. Sam blasted his music and offered bits of wisdom from rock stars. Elly shared her best writing ideas and always remembered to put chocolate and magazines on the grocery list. Our dog, Muffin, kept my feet warm while I read through a whole library of books on writing. Of course, none of this would have been possible without my dear husband, Harold, who took the children on errands, stocked up on snacks, and cooked every single day so that I could lock myself in my office and write. Your love and assurance mean the world to me.

TABLE OF CONTENTS

PART TWO: THE WRITE-A-THON

PART THREE: RECOVERY

PREFACE:
WHY WRITE A BOOK?

A [person] must do three things in life:
Write a book, plant a tree, have a [child].
— José Martí

So you want to write a book. You've been contemplating the task for years. Or maybe you have an urgent desire to write a book to increase your credibility. You're right about that. A book adds instant clout and can bring in extra cash. Either way, you're in good company: More than 80 percent of Americans say they want to write a book. Here are twelve reasons to write a book. See if one or more fits you:

1. YOU HAVE SOMETHING TO SAY. You are constantly thinking about how you could change the world and, more specifically, the lives of those you love, if only you could tell them what you know about nutrition, exercise, dog training, or high finance. Maybe you've tried to tell people what you know—either in person or in long e-mails explaining your point of view. Perhaps you've even started a website or a newsletter where you can write about your ideas. You have a lot to teach the world. You need to write a book so your friends won't avoid you because all you do is give advice. Stop giving advice and e-mailing your ideas to friends. Write a book instead.

2. YOU MAKE UP STORIES. Some people—like your boss, parents, or significant other—might call it lying, but you know the truth. You have been making up stories since you were old enough to talk. Your beloved grandfather with the twirly mustache was secretly a spy. The woman who sat in front of you on the subway yesterday—the one who was crying and rubbing the tattoo on her arm that said *Arnold*—you spent the whole ride debating whether Arnold broke up with her or died in a tragic accident. And today, when you stopped at the coffee shop, you wondered what was going on between the old homeless man and the young handsome businessman at the back table. Stop wondering aimlessly. Put your stories into a book we all can enjoy!

3. YOU HAVE A UNIQUE POINT OF VIEW. You have been in your business or profession for a long time. You have developed tools and techniques that you believe could support your colleagues or clients in doing something better, faster, and for more profit.

You probably have some idea that your point of view works—you get clients easily and your colleagues keep asking how you do it (whatever *it* is). You have some choices to make. You can use your unique point of view to be the best at what you do. Or you can teach others what you know and become known for being the expert on a topic or process. On top of that, writing a book will save you time and maybe earn you some money. When people ask how you do it, you won't have to say, "Buy me dinner, and I'll give you the short version." Instead, you'll be able to sell them your book.

4. YOU NEED TO BUILD CREDIBILITY. Maybe you have a unique point of view or a great process but no one knows it. You do good work but you're bound by confidentiality not to talk about what you do. You don't have the same credentials—or as many credentials—as your colleagues. Nothing screams credibility like being the author of a great book. When you tell people you're an author, they'll be a bit more impressed. Your credibility will increase. It might not even matter what your book is about. People often respect those who took the time to write a book (instead of just reading one or watching the CliffsNotes version on television).

5. YOU COLLECT CHARACTERS. Every odd and intriguing person you meet is a potential character for a story. You don't ruminate over bad exes or nasty bosses because they will serve a higher purpose—as villains in your stories. You hear voices in your head, but you don't worry that you're crazy. The voices are your characters talking to you. People who collect dolls or salt-and-pepper shakers need glass cabinets to house them. But you collect characters. You need a novel to hold them. Short stories are fine, but a novel will give them plenty of space to demonstrate all the unique qualities that piqued your curiosity when you first met them.

6. YOU WANT TO TEACH PEOPLE WHO YOU ARE. You have business cards, but—let's face it—you can't get many words on one of those little things without it looking sloppy. You also have a website—but you can't exactly hand it out when you speak. You need something more portable to help people get to know you and your work. Your goal is to get people to work with your company, buy your product, or hire you to consult, coach, or speak to them. You need a way for them to know you and your product. A book that offers your customers real value can teach them about you and help them see the worth of buying your products or services.

7. YOU WANT TO BUILD A BIGGER PLATFORM. Peeps make your world go round. No, not the colorful sugary kind the Easter bunny brings. Peeps as your people, who listen to you, buy your stuff, and hire you. These are your raving fans—and a good portion of what the publishing world calls your platform. Here's the rub: You need a platform to get a book published by a traditional publisher. But a book can be a great tool in building your platform because people who read it often become part of your fan base. Note that I said *bigger platform*. Hopefully, if you are thinking about writing a book, you already have a platform that you've put together through speaking, tweeting, and good old-fashioned networking. You can now grow and strengthen your platform by giving your peeps a book.

8. YOU CAN'T AFFORD THERAPY. Writing a book can be a beneficial therapeutic endeavor. In fact, psychologists have done hundreds of studies that prove that writing makes you healthier, happier, and better able to achieve your goals. Why spend oodles of money complaining about your past to a total stranger when you can write about it (or the lessons you learned from living it), sell the story, and make oodles of money for yourself? Duh! Forget therapy! Write a book. (Besides, it can be great fun to cast your best frenemy as the villain of your novel.)

9. YOU HAVE THE INFORMATION. Once upon a time, you gathered a bunch of information on a topic. You always meant to turn it into a book, but now it's gathering dust on a shelf in your bedroom closet. Maybe you wrote about your family history as bootleggers for your grandparent's anniversary and think others might be interested in reading it. Perhaps your Ph.D. dissertation has some appeal beyond academic circles. Or maybe you've collected information for years on a topic that fascinates you—beer making, beading, or porch gardening. If you've got the material, why not take a few weeks to rework it into a book? What do you have to lose, except your free time?

10. YOU THINK LIKE A WRITER. Everything that happens to you is material. (Heck, everything that happens to anyone you remotely know or whose conversation you've overheard is material!) You write stuff down on random pieces of paper and napkins. When someone tells you a wrenching story, you say, "That might make a good novel." When life goes wrong, you write about it. When things go well, you write about it. You write. That's what you do. So, sooner or later, you are going to write a book. It's inevitable. Why not do it now—in the next twenty-six days?

11. YOU WANT TO MAKE MONEY. If this is your reason for writing a book, you better have one kick-ass idea and marketing plan. Writers don't make a ton of money. I once read that if you took the salaries of all the writers in the United States—the Stephen Kings along with the peons like me and you—and divided the total by the number of writers, each writer would make about fifty dollars a year. Some years, for some books, my royalty statements come, and it appears I owe the publisher money. Hah! Other books earn me coffee money. Making money isn't a good reason to write a book. Why? Because you will be disappointed. I'm not saying you can't make money writing. You can. You just can't count on a book being your ticket to the easy life.

12. YOU HAVE YOUR REASONS. Maybe you can't articulate them right now or you're too embarrassed to share them with others, but you know you want to write a book. You have always known this, or you woke up this morning with the idea, and you are ready to begin. Good. All you need is the passion and dedication to see the process through to the end. Let's go!

INTRODUCTION

How do you do it?

I hear that question frequently. Usually the questioner means, "How do you manage your life and still get your books written?" For me, managing life means managing a marriage, parenting two school-age children, coaching writers, speaking, editing books and a quarterly periodical, connecting with friends, volunteering as a writing educator in the inner city, exercising, and—of course—writing books.

I started writing books fast because I was blessed with unreasonable deadlines from publishers at the age and stage in my career when I was willing to do just about anything to get a book in print. So, I did. In the past fifteen years, I've written and published ten books, more than a hundred articles, and many other resources. Nearly every book I wrote with my husband was completed in less than three months, often in as little time as six weeks. In the fall of 2004, my friend Susan Lang and I wrote the book *Welcome Forward* in nine days. I wrote my first solo book, *A Generous Presence* (all five hundred pages of it), in just over five months. In 2007, I wrote my as-yet-unpublished two-hundred-page memoir in just two months. The first draft of this book, *Write-A-Thon*, was written during National Novel Writing Month in 2009. In each of these experiences, I learned what all writers learn: Deadlines work.

How do you do it? When people ask me that, they get this starry look in their eyes—like I must be a magician, capable of being in two places at once. I know that look; I used to have it. Before I actually wrote a book, in my wannabe writer days, I'd pay obeisance to anyone who had written a book. I thought these writers must have some secret trick that I didn't know about. Maybe it was a special pen, the right plot-development formula, or a password-protected muse. I believed these people knew something I didn't. I wanted to stop being a wannabe writer and join the club of real authors.

Now that I've written books, I know something that most wannabe writers do not know (that I did not know). But it's not magic and it isn't much of a secret. Chances are, you probably know the one thing you need to do (and do repeatedly) to be a successful writer, but you don't know that you know it!

That's how it was with me. By the time I wrote my first real book, I had already written a master's thesis in one year, while taking all the coursework for the degree, teaching, babysitting, cleaning houses, and trying to have a life. I'd completed many writing projects for publishing houses. I'd written articles and speeches. I had all the skills necessary to write books fast. But I still sat in the audience at book signings sighing over Molly McAuthor and wondering what I needed to do to be *just like her.*

Now I know what it takes to be an author. And you can, too. Do you want to know the *real* difference between writers and wannabe writers? Showing up. That's it—the big secret. Those who write, write. Wannabe writers wait for inspiration to move them into action. It rarely does. As Peter De Vries once said, "I only write when I'm inspired, and I make sure I'm inspired every morning at 9 A.M." I will teach you the life skills and writing tools you need to show up often enough to write your own book fast.

WHY A WRITING *MARATHON*?

A few years ago, a friend planned and completed a marathon bike ride to celebrate her fortieth birthday. A few months before the bike ride, she planned the course—a five-hundred-mile ride across Wisconsin and back. Then she put together a training schedule that would prepare her for the trip. By following the training schedule, she was able to complete the marathon ride without difficulty.

As my friend described the process she used to train for and complete her marathon bike ride, I thought, "That's how I write books!" After years of writing and editing books at a breakneck pace, I've discovered that I like marathon writing. Although I can and have taken longer to write a book, I appreciate the focus that emerges when time is tight. In a deadline-bound writing marathon, all the crap of daily life falls away and the essential emerges. Plus, it's just easier to clear out one's schedule for a month or a series of weekends and work like crazy than to try to fit writing into everyday life.

Plenty of people have written books marathon style. Chris Baty, founder of National Novel Writing Month, believes that what stands between most writers and a finished book is a deadline. He created NaNoWriMo (www.nanowrimo.org) to provide wannabe writers with the deadline they needed to complete a book. It worked. Every November, writers across the country participate in NaNoWriMo by writing a 50,000-word novel in thirty days. In 2010, 200,500 writers participated and 37,500 finished writing a 50,000-word or 175-page novel. Since 1977, writers have competed to write the best novel over Labor Day weekend, a mere seventy-two hours (www.3daynovel.com).

But what about people who want to write a *nonfiction* book in thirty days? One writer and journalist, Nina Amir, has declared November National Writing Month, hoping to include nonfiction writers who want to finish anything (a book proposal, an article, or a book) during the month. For the past several years, I've issued the same challenge to the readers of my e-zine, *Write Now! Weekly Writing Tips*. I recently coached a busy urban pastor through the first draft of her doctoral dissertation. She'd struggled for months to get a word on paper. A month after we began to work together, the pastor had finished writing the draft (while working full time)!

But for all of us—and you—the challenge remains the same: How? This guide is designed to provide you with everything you need to write your book—fiction *or* nonfiction—in twenty-six days. I've done it more than once. You can, too!

HOW TO USE THIS BOOK

The write-a-thon program is a collection of short essays and exercises that will provide you with the life skills, performance techniques, and writing tools you need to get your book done fast. Like many programs, the write-a-thon works best when done as designed, from beginning to end. The tools introduced in each section build on the work you have done in the previous one. Some of you will be able to use the book just like that.

If you're a big-picture thinker—someone who likes concepts better than details—you may need a sense of the whole course before you begin. Skim the book from beginning to end. Then, go back to the beginning and work through the book.

If you believe you don't need the whole program to get *your* book done fast, use the book as a tool for encouragement or problem solving. This book is packed full of practical tools and ideas to help you write faster and without angst.

NO EXCUSES

Remember the big secret from above? Showing up. That's the key to writing books fast. The only way to get the big things done in life—and writing a book *is* a big thing—is by doing them. You have to do the work: no excuses. You have to write even if you:

- don't know how
- work a full-time job
- didn't sleep last night
- are sick
- don't feel like it
- can't afford the time
- have a sick child, spouse, or friend
- feel terrified
- think it's impossible
- believe that no one cares
- know that others will criticize you

You have to do the work. Tired, angry, worried, or overwhelmed: You need to write. You have to work in the midst of your complicated daily life. There will never be a perfect time to write the book bubbling inside you. Sometimes you just have to work at the big things while the little ones pile up around you.

But how? Turn the page and get started! And remember: The pain is temporary, the book is forever.

A marathon runner will tell you that training is everything. I recently spoke with a client who is participating in a marathon in the heat of August. When I marveled at her courage, she said, "I can do it. I've been training."

When I was in my senior year of college, I agonized about graduate school. Could I do the work? Was I smart enough? Would I succeed? One of my trusted mentors assured me that I would. "Look at it this way," she said. "You're like a marathon runner who's been training hard for nineteen years. You've been studying since you were three. You can do this."

If you're going to write a book and you've never written a word, you need to train your writing muscles to support you in writing this book. If you want to write that book in twenty-six days and you haven't mastered your crazy schedule, you're going to have to train your life to support a writing marathon. This section of the book will teach you how to train for the twenty-six-day writing marathon. Don't skip it. Your success at the marathon depends on your success at training.

The amount of time it takes you to train your life depends on you—how long you've been writing, what your life looks like, and how quickly you can adapt your life and learn new skills. Marathon runners often train as much as twenty to twenty-six weeks to prepare for the twenty-six-mile race. This training program (hopefully) won't take that long. Plan to spend two weeks to a month in training. You'll need that much lead time to clear your schedule for your twenty-six-day writing marathon anyway!

Most marathon runners have a variety of tools to help them train for their big race: sneakers, running clothes, maps, a heart-rate monitor, and training charts. Your tools will be much more simple and are available in low-tech or high-tech versions. Choose the format that works for you and your life:

- A journal. If you want a lower-tech version, choose a paper journal that's easy to use—one that opens easily, lies flat when you write, and isn't too bulky to take with you on an excursion. I prefer unlined journals because they are more adaptable to a variety of uses, including making charts, creating collages, and doing other nonlinear exercises. If you work better with electronic devices—laptop, smartphone, iPad, and so forth—explore applications that allow you to record your ideas and create charts and collages.

- A write-a-thon binder or story bible. If you want a physical story bible, purchase a three-ring binder in your favorite color, at least 2½ inches wide. Choose a binder with a plastic sleeve on the cover. Get one or two packets of pocket page dividers—which you will label as you move through the training process. This will be the container for your book's notes or ideas. If you prefer to keep all your notes and ideas on your computer, the application Scrivener works well for both managing project items and doing word processing. If you want to keep your electronic binder simple, create a new folder for your book and organize your documents inside it.

- A stack of index cards or sticky notepaper to carry with you and jot down ideas or take notes. Most smartphones have a built-in notes feature that you can use as well. If not, you can always send yourself an e-mail or a text message. Online applications like Google Docs and Evernote allow the user to record, save, search, and access information from anywhere.

- Your calendar, paper or electronic.

- Other tools will be introduced during the training process.

This part of the book is organized into four smaller sections:

- Attitude Training: Get rid of the excuses
- Writing Training: Learn the basics
- Course Training:
    - Plan your novel
    - Plan your nonfiction book
- Life Training: Schedule the marathon

Each section has essays and exercises geared to get you ready for the twenty-six-day marathon. Do them in order or do the ones that make the most sense to you right now.

When marathon runner John Bingham decided to run, he was an overweight forty-three-year-old who had learned how to live without exerting physical energy. On his first day, outfitted in shorts and brand-new running shoes, he ran from his garage to the bottom of the driveway. It wasn't much of a start. But it was a start. That's all I'm asking of you. Get your stuff. Get into your chair. Ready, set, WRITE!

ATTITUDE TRAINING

GET RID OF THE EXCUSES

MOVE FROM WANNABE
TO WRITER

*Training for a marathon is an act of
faith. Actually running the marathon is an
act of courage. With faith and courage, ordinary
humans can accomplish great things!*
—RANDY ESSEX

When I was in graduate school, we'd often finish classes with a need to attend an attitude adjustment hour at the local bar. Consider this section—and especially this chapter—your attitude adjustment tool.

The biggest difference between the wannabe writer and Molly McAuthor is attitude. The wannabe writers have a million excuses—"if onlys" and "maybe somedays"—taking up valuable space in their brains. Molly McAuthor has learned to challenge and overcome her excuses, taking on the attitude that she can and will write. And she does. Most authors have faced their doubts and excuses and written anyway. Here's what they have to say about the most common "if onlys" and "maybe somedays" uttered by wannabe writers.

INSPIRATION

The wannabe writer says, "If only I was inspired" or "Maybe someday the big idea will hit me and I will write." Here's what Madeleine L'Engle said about waiting for inspiration: "... lots of people, ages varying from fifteenish to seventyish, talk to me about the books they could write, if only ... The reason they don't ever get around to writing the books is usually, in the young, that they have to wait for inspiration, and you know perfectly well that if an artist of any kind sits around waiting for inspiration he'll have a very small body of work. Inspiration usually comes during work rather than before it." Jack London said, "You can't wait for inspiration. You have to go after it with a club." Don't wait for inspiration. Waiters wait. Writers write.

TIME

The wannabe writer says, "If only I had more time to write" or "Maybe someday I'll retire and have enough time to write my memoir." We have the time and energy to do what we choose to do. Pulitzer Prize-winning novelist Carol Shields wrote her last novel while sick with stage-four breast cancer. She wrote an hour a day. In fact, when her children were young, she wrote only two pages a day. She would drop off her five kids at school, come home and clean up the house, write for the hour before lunch, and then edit the two pages in the hour before they came home from school or just before bed. Shields wrote her first novel in longhand while sitting in bed each night. She'd write two pages fast and then shut off the light. At the end of the year, she had a novel. Anthony Trollope wrote only three hours a day yet was quite prolific. He tried to write 250 words every fifteen minutes. He shared his writing life with a job at the post office. "Too busy" is just another excuse not to write. Procrastinators are too busy. Writers write.

MATERIALS

The wannabe writer says, "If only I had the right materials" or "Maybe someday, when I get the ultimate writer's computer, I'll get that magnum opus together." Joanna Trollope has written every one of her novels in pen on a legal pad. Toni Morrison writes her books in pencil on a legal pad. Gertrude Stein scribbled her poems on odd scraps of paper. Most of my last book was planned on the back of old envelopes. What more could you need? If you're looking for the perfect pen, get a job as a buyer at an office store. Consumers consume. Writers write—with any little stub of a pencil and scrap of paper they find!

EDUCATION

Wannabe writers say, "If only I had the right education" or "Maybe someday I'll know enough to write this book." Anne Lamott, a best-selling writer, dropped out of college to write. J.A. Jance writes every one of her best-selling mystery novels not knowing what will happen next. She writes to find out the answer! Education and knowledge help, but you don't need them, to be successful. Students study. Writers write.

TALENT

The wannabe writer says, "If only I had more talent" or "Maybe someday I'll have the confidence to try to write." Novelist Gail Godwin said, "I work continuously within the shadow of failure. For every novel that makes it to my publisher's desk, there are at least five or six that died on the way." Erica Jong said it this way: "Everyone has talent.

What is rare is the courage to follow that talent to the dark place it leads." Don't worry about having enough talent. Hard work trumps talent. Always.

AGE

The wannabe writer says, "I used to dream of writing a book, but now I'm too old to do something like that" or "I'm not old enough to write something worthwhile. I need to wait until I have more life experience." Best-selling author Billie Letts published her first novel at age fifty-six, *Where the Heart Is*. Novelist Harriet Doerr won the National Book Award at seventy-three for her novel *Stones for Ibarra*. On the other end of the age spectrum, author Christopher Paolini began writing his novel *Eragon* when he was fifteen. As Madeleine L'Engle said, "I am every age I have ever been." Don't let your age (or other people's negative comments about your age) keep you from writing. Write anyway.

SPACE

Virginia Woolf believed that every woman needed a room of her own. Many wannabe writers use this as their excuse for not writing, putting off their work until they have their own space or the perfect desk. Mystery novelist Sheldon Rusch wrote his first novel at his local Starbucks. A friend of mine recently claimed a small corner of her basement—cordoned off by bookshelves—as her studio, requiring that her family use a password to enter. One of my clients takes regular weekends away to write her books. All of us crave and need space to write. What separates the wannabe from the writer is the courage to claim it—no matter what.

We all have our private list of "if onlys" and "maybe somedays." If only I were healthier, younger, older, more poetic, smarter, better connected, or ready. In the end, the ability to move from being a wannabe to a writer takes one thing: putting your butt in the chair and words on the paper no matter what excuse or reason or person tries to prevent you.

Cynthia Ozick calls writing an act of courage. E.B. White called it an act of faith. It is both. Stop excusing yourself. Start writing.

WRITE NOW

In your journal, write your own list of "if onlys" and "maybe somedays" for writing. List every excuse you have used to avoid writing, no matter how inconsequential or crazy it may sound ("I can't write because today I planned to trim my nose hair"). Save this. You will need it for the next chapter's exercise.

NO EXCUSES

*Laziness is nothing more than the habit of
resting before you get tired.*
—JULES RENARD

Most writers use excuses to avoid writing from time to time. Excuses allow us to evade facing or telling the truth. Excuses are really little white lies. Most of them are not true—but they usually point to a truth or pertinent information that we need to face (and sometimes fix). The writers who daily put their butt into the chair have figured out how to do an end run around their excuses, taking on the attitude that they can and will write. And they do!

Here are some common truths and bits of information that hide inside excuses:

- **LACK OF VISION.** We make excuses about how we don't have time to get to our writing because we need to fulfill our commitments to our family, friends, or a community organization. We do this because we have not taken the time to think through our life's vision. We have a vague sense that we want to write but we have not visioned what that might look like. Or, if we have a picture of our writing life, we don't let that vision guide our lives. We allow external demands to set our schedule.

- **LACK OF A PLAN.** We have plenty of ideas but no idea how to write a book (or this particular book). We don't have an outline. We don't have a goal. We don't even have the next step in the process. So we make excuses about not having the background to write this book or it not being the right time for this project.

- **SELF-DOUBT.** We have read the statistics about the difficulty of getting published or we've heard the stories about how damn hard it can be to write a book, so we use excuses to protect ourselves from facing our fears. We worry that we don't have enough knowledge, courage, or talent to write a book. We come up with pretty good reasons for not even trying—like having to take care of our families or make a living.

- **A REAL ISSUE.** We get to work early every single morning, intent on writing. And every morning, this or that colleague manages to use up our precious time chatting about American Idol, the football pool, or a new diet. When our writing friends say, "Why haven't you written?" we think we have a legitimate excuse. What we have is information we are using as an excuse: We cannot write at work. When we stop whining, we see that this is a fixable problem.

In order to learn from our excuses, we need to become BS detectors. We need to sift through the excuses to find the kernel of truth or information that drives them. We nose around in our excuses, figure out what's BS, and then discover what that BS can teach us. How can this BS help us to move beyond excuses to solutions?

WRITE NOW

1. **List the excuses you use to avoid writing.** If you did the exercise in the last chapter, use that list.
2. **For each excuse:**
   - Ask, "Is this true?" If your excuse was that you could not write because you needed to trim your nose hair, you might answer: "Okay, my nose hair has gotten out of control lately but it's not like it is hanging down to my lips or anything. So, no, it's not true."
   - For each excuse that *is not* true, ask, "What is true?" You might write something like: "What is true is that I'd rather spend the day trimming my nose hair and plucking my eyebrows because I know how to do that. I don't know how to write this book. I am afraid of writing."
   - For each excuse that *is* true and for the truths behind your excuses, ask, "What do I need to do to fix this?" Mr. Nosehair might discover that he is less afraid of writing for an hour than writing for a whole day. So he might set a short time limit—like ten or twenty minutes. Or, he might simply do a writing exercise each morning. Once he gets good at that, he can expand his writing time and scope.
   - Fix the problems that are fixable!

Do this exercise now and every time you find your excuses getting in the way of your writing plan. It will help you ferret out the truth about your excuses—and support you in finding the problems that really need to be fixed.

VISION YOUR WRITING LIFE

Some men see things the way they are and ask, "Why?"
I dream things that never were, and ask, "Why not?"
—George Bernard Shaw

I was a little girl when I first knew that I wanted to be a writer. I spent my days writing and performing plays, piecing together poems, jotting down my fierce wonderings in a journal. When I wasn't writing or performing, I was soaking up the words of other writers.

Despite this early vision, I've taken many detours: ordained ministry, teaching, and life coaching. Each of these detours—and the people on those journeys—provided their own vision for my life. Inside them was a host of external demands that pulled me away from my early vision of writing books. But in the midst of every other thing that planted itself in my life, the vision of being a writer kept popping up, like bright daffodils.

Recently, I came across an exercise that has helped me and my writing-coaching clients fully imagine their writing lives. In recent studies, psychologists had people visualize their best possible self (BPS) for twenty minutes on four consecutive days. They instructed participants to write a vision of their lives five years in the future, imagining that they had worked as hard as possible and everything had gone as well as possible. The results of these studies showed that writing about one's BPS "was associated with a significant immediate increase in positive mood, with an increase in subjective well-being three weeks subsequent to the intervention, and with decreased illness five months later." In addition, the participants did better at regulating their behavior so they achieved their goals.

In my work with clients, the BPS exercise has supported them in taking the step from wannabe to writer. I invite my writing-coaching clients to do the BPS exercise, slanted specifically to their writing life. I instruct them to:

> Imagine yourself five years from now. Everything has gone as well
> as it possibly could. You have worked hard and succeeded at ac-
> complishing all of your writing goals. Write about your accomplish-
> ments—what degrees you have earned, what articles and books you
> have written, what talk shows you have appeared on, the awards

you have won. Write about your daily writing practice. What does it look like? Where and when do you write? How much are you able to accomplish each day? Envision your writing community—who do you connect with, who buys your books, who reviews them, who is interested in the ideas you are sharing and the stories you are telling? Write about anything else that is relevant: where you live, what other work you do, or how your day unfolds in addition to the writing. Use as much sensory detail as possible.

In the original experiment, psychologists had participants repeat this exercise four times in the space of a week. In my experience, both as a participant and a coach, the BPS exercise accesses more of our deepest desires with each consecutive try. At first, participants vision a future that's contained within the box they are living in. It is only with repeated writing and the encouragement of a coach or buddy that the person visioning can be truly visionary.

WRITE NOW

Set aside time this week to do the BPS exercise four times. It's best to do it by hand. Some writers and psychologists suggest that we get closest to our heart's desires when we write with hand to paper instead of on the computer. As you write, don't worry about spelling, grammar, or logic. Don't think about what is literally possible. Allow yourself to dream wildly.

The first time you do this exercise, stick to the instructions I have provided above. As you repeat the exercise, one of the following alternatives can help you in freeing your imagination. Again, use as much detail as possible:

- Write book jacket copy about yourself.

- Write an acceptance speech for a major literary award.

- Imagine you have won a prestigious literary fellowship. Write your fellowship profile.

- Write an introduction for yourself and tell what sort of an event it is for.

- Write an article about yourself and the writing work you do. Imagine where it will be published.

- Write about a day in your new life, five years from now. What are you doing with each minute of the day?

- Write the story of your life five years from now from the point of view of someone you have mentored or inspired through your writing.

- Interview your future self about your future writing career.

- Create a visual representation of your vision using pictures from magazines and mock-ups of books you will write. Do this on a piece of paper that can fit inside or in the outside sleeve of the write-a-thon binder or in your journal.

As you work on this vision, you will get excited and want to share your ideas with others. Think of this vision as a precious and beautiful butterfly, just forming inside the cocoon. Open up a real cocoon at this point, and all you'll see is a goopy mess. Your butterfly is too fragile to be in the company of other people. It is not fully formed and cannot withstand the scrutiny of other people. Keep this vision to yourself for now. Don't show it to family members or friends.

MAKE AFFIRMATIONS

*You already have everything you need to be
a long-distance athlete. It's mind-set—not miles—
that separates those who do from those who dream.*
—JOHN BINGHAM AND JENNY HADFIELD

When I think about the practice of making affirmations, I get this vision of myself saying goofy things into the mirror: You can write. You will write. You are a wonderful and capable writer, worthy of the Nobel Prize for literature. Then I want to puke.

Nearly every writer I've met has been tormented by negative inner voices. Anne Lamott calls it radio station KFKD, while others have labeled the voices the inner editor or gremlins. No matter what name you give your inner voice, if it isn't saying something good, you are in trouble. Though the idea of making affirmations still makes me gag a bit, I have regularly used and taught two affirmation exercises to my clients. They are absolutely necessary for claiming the attitude of a writer.

PRACTICE GRATITUDE

So you've already got KFKD playing in your head. Chances are school taught you how to examine situations for problems. In addition, psychologists have discovered that most of us have a negativity bias. That means we are more likely to notice and remember the events and experiences that produced negative emotions. No doubt, you are an expert at noticing pathology (the bad stuff) in your own life. I know I am. If there's a half-empty glass in any room, I'll see it. If I've had an amazing day, getting lots of great writing done, I'll obsess about the one task I didn't get to or could not complete.

To counter this obsession with my own faults and failures, I've begun to practice gratitude. Each night before I go to bed, I find three events to be thankful for or three blessings. Here are some ways to modify the exercise:

- Each night, name three (or more) things you are grateful for about your writing work. Name what was good or positive about each item. Finally, ask yourself why it happened. Did you have something to do with it or was it random?

- Invite a writing buddy to exchange daily gratitudes with you. Each night, write down one reason you are grateful that this person is writing or is your writing buddy and e-mail it to her.

- Write a letter of gratitude to a writing mentor.

- When you are having an especially difficult time with a project, make a long list of everything you appreciate or are grateful for about the project.

CHALLENGE AND REFRAME YOUR ASSUMPTIONS

On a recent plane trip from San Diego to Milwaukee, I chatted with my seatmate about my desire to move to San Diego. He said to me, "Well, you could never afford to live in San Diego. No one can." I looked out the window, down at the bustling city filled with people who were clearly living here. But I didn't challenge his assumption. I let it fester inside of me and began to believe it as truth. When my daughter was five, she assumed she could do anything. Our days were filled with her mantra, "I can do it! I can do it!" about actions as varied as completing homework sheets to opening large, heavy doors to being able to fly on a broom.

For every book project I've undertaken, there's been some person who has voiced his assumption that I cannot do it. It will be too hard or too long. I am too busy. My children require too much attention. When these voices threaten to become my assumptions, more fodder for KFKD, it's time to challenge them. This exercise will support you in challenging your unhealthy assumptions and adopting the assumptions that will make this marathon a breeze!

1. Write down every assumption you have about the twenty-six-day writing marathon—helpful or unhelpful.

2. Underline the ones that will not be helpful to you. Unhelpful assumptions are any idea—no matter how logical or statistically accurate—that says you cannot accomplish your goals. While it may be logical to assume that most people cannot write a book in twenty-six days, that assumption will hinder you from completing this task. It's time to dump it!

3. Challenge your negative assumptions!
   - Write down the assumption you want to challenge ("No one can write a good book in twenty-six days").
   - Write every argument you have against the assumption ("In October, many people write books in a weekend. The write-a-thon gives me WAY more time than that!).

- At the bottom of the paper, rewrite the assumption so it says the exact opposite ("Everyone is capable of writing a great book in twenty-six days").
- Rewrite it again in the first person ("I am capable of writing a great book in twenty-six days!").
- When you have challenged each negative assumption, make a list of your opposite assumptions—including the helpful assumptions from the first list—and put it in your write-a-thon binder or journal.

Look at these assumptions daily. Repeat them to yourself. Remember—those who finish the twenty-six-day writing marathon are those people who assume they can do it! And you can!

Choose one of the above exercises and complete it.

TAKE YOURSELF SERIOUSLY

Glad deadlines make you feel needed because you are.
I may knit you a sweater with some embroidery
saying LOUISE FITZHUGH'S WORK IS NEEDED—
but you'd have to have a chest as vast as god forbid mine
to give enough room for such a long statement.
—URSULA NORDSTROM IN A LETTER TO NOVELIST
LOUISE FITZHUGH

When I started Dream Keepers, my program of mentoring young writers, a colleague suggested that the time I spent with young people was more valuable than the writing instruction. She said, "Well, you could just as well be playing tiddlywinks with them." Her comment hurt; she didn't seem to value my work as a writing teacher. Still, I knew the importance of teaching young people to use writing as a tool for self-expression.

I wanted to show her how wrong she was. I began to take the work more seriously than before. I gave my group a name, listed my goals for how this work would change lives, wrote out my vision for our progress in the next ten years, listed the reasons I was the person to lead this project, and began to implement a plan to achieve my goals. By simply taking myself more seriously and then treating my work that way, I respected my program and my role as a mentor. I no longer cared what my colleagues and friends thought about the work. I knew it was important, and that was what mattered.

You've already written your vision. List ten ways your writing work will help other people and change lives. Then list ten reasons why you are the person to do this work.

WRITE IT DOWN

I recently met a woman at a writing conference who had a stack of business cards with her name and new occupation on it: writer. Of course, she had not published a thing. But, as she said, "These cards legitimize my dream." You don't need cards to be legit, but they may help. So will any sign or clue in your world that you are a writer. Psychologists have discovered that our environments prime us or prepare us to behave in certain ways. When our environment is filled with signs that we are writers, we are more likely to both believe it and act on it. Here are some ideas:

- business cards
- letterhead
- an e-mail signature
- a title on your social media profile
- a room of your own
- books about writing
- writing materials
- an inspirational saying
- a talisman
- a T-shirt or tote bag with the label, "Writer"
- a nameplate with your title, "Writer"
- a license plate or bumper sticker that proclaims your new profession
- a file or shelf of materials about your writing topic

IF YOU'RE REALLY BOLD

Claim your author title right now. Include the phrase, "Author of the forthcoming book, *Life Lessons From the Edge* (or whatever book you are writing), in your e-mail signature, social media information, and elevator speech. No one needs to know that the only phrase you've written so far is the title!

TELL OTHERS

When I began to write seriously, I would pinch myself while I told potential employers, "I can't work in the morning because that's my writing time." Of course in those days, I was usually not really writing; I was staring into space and worrying about writing and pounding my head against the table because I couldn't get the words out. Still, I am convinced that saying that over and over and over helped me envision myself as a writer. Before long, my walk matched my talk. I was writing when I said I was, and I had the product to prove it.

Make a commitment to work your new occupation into the conversation at least once a day. You don't need to announce your goal or talk about your project. Just let people know you will be writing. Here are some examples:

- "Yes, I am fascinated by zoning regulations in our neighborhood but this year I don't have time to research for the association. I am spending my mornings writing."

- "While a lecture on the mating habits of squids sounds riveting, I will need to decline. I am spending Thursday night writing."

- "I'd usually love the opportunity to run the PTA, but this year I'm using evenings and weekends to write."

WRITE NOW

Choose one of the actions described above and do it! Know that you might feel awkward or like an imposter as you announce your new career, hand out business cards, or claim the title of your as-yet-unpublished (and perhaps unwritten) book. Take a deep breath and press on. Claiming you are a writer before you are an established author is what psychologists call "fake it until you make it" or acting "as if." By acting as if you are already an author whose work is in great demand, you will learn to take your work seriously. Do that for a few weeks—or twenty-six days—and soon you will have written that book!

WHY WRITE?
HOW WRITING HEALS

The pen is mightier than the sword.
— Edward Bulwer-Lytton

You've no doubt heard the famous quote above. What you may not know is that the pen can also trump medication and the therapist's couch. The practice of writing can heal you both physically and emotionally. So while you think you have been working on a book that will make you rich or famous or both, you have also been healing yourself. Whether you are at the point where you are so exhausted you cannot write one more word, or you are so geeked you could write another book, take a deep breath and read about how what you are doing is not only good for your work, it's also good for your health.

WRITING HEALS YOUR BODY. In a study conducted with asthma patients at the State University of New York at Stony Brook, School of Medicine, study participants wrote about their most stressful experiences. The control group wrote about their daily activities. According to the book *Asthma Free in 21 Days*, 47 percent of the patients who wrote about their challenging life experiences showed improvement in lung function that could not be attributed to medication or other factors. Twenty-four percent of the control group showed improvement as well. Notice this: Both groups improved their lung function through writing.

WRITING HEALS YOUR HEART. Research by psychologist James Pennebaker has shown that people who used writing to make sense of their traumatic life experiences had the long-lasting effect of feeling happier and less anxious. He asked his subjects to write for fifteen minutes a day on four consecutive days. Half of the group members wrote about a difficult or traumatic event in their lives. The other half of the group, the control group, was asked to write about their day or to describe their living environment. A year later, he examined the subject's medical records. The people who wrote about their difficult experiences were healthier than the others. What made the difference? According to Pennebaker, it was the meaning-making that mattered. The people who showed increased insight into their difficult situation during the four days stayed healthier than those who simply wrote about their daily routine or the color of the carpet.

WRITING HELPS YOU ACHIEVE YOUR GOALS. In a study we looked at earlier in this book by psychologist Laura King, people who wrote about their best possible future selves showed an immediate increase in mood and, after five months, a decrease in illness. In addition, this writing work improved their ability to take control of behavior and make positive changes. Writers were better able to set and achieve their goals.

WRITE NOW

How do you tap into the healing power of writing? You write—just like you will do for the write-a-thon. All of the studies suggest that any kind of writing will improve your health and sense of well-being. Write now, get healthy!

WRITING TRAINING
LEARN THE BASICS

PRACTICE

We are what we repeatedly do. Excellence,
then, is not an act but a habit.
—ARISTOTLE

You've heard the old joke about how to get to Carnegie Hall: practice, practice, practice! My teenage son told me he wanted to be a rich and famous guitarist. "How do you think that will happen?" I asked. We had a long conversation about how guitarists like Eric Clapton and Joe Satriani had become famous. Same answer: practice. Musicians practice. Marathon runners train. What about writers?

Truth is, anyone who graduated from high school and college has practiced writing. If you've had a job that required you to write, you've had more writing practice. But studies suggest that the stars of their fields—like cellist Yo-Yo Ma and tennis players Venus and Serena Williams—have put in about ten thousand hours of practice. To put that in numbers we understand, if you practiced writing forty hours a week, it would take you 250 weeks to get in your 10,000 hours. That's nearly five years of full-time writing. If you write part time—say twenty hours a week—you'd need to nearly double that time to get to professional or genius status.

But you have a book to write now. How do you speed up your practice time? You write every time you have a free minute. You write as much as you can in the months leading up to your twenty-six-day writing marathon. I've provided several writing practice tools below that will help you get ready. Take whatever time you have between now and your twenty-six-day marathon to practice writing.

That said, do not by any means put off the twenty-six-day marathon because you don't think you are good enough. Too many people postpone their writing dreams because of self-doubt. Yes, you need to practice. The more you practice, the easier the writing will be for you. But remember: Every book gets revised and edited. Whatever you write can be perfected. For now, you need to get ready to get that book out of your head and onto the paper. So put in your month or six weeks of practice now. By the time the writing marathon starts, you'll feel ready to write a book. The practice will prepare you to knock this book out of the ballpark!

1. THE DAILY DUMP. Julia Cameron calls these morning pages. Natalie Goldberg refers to the work as writing practice. I call these daily pages "the daily dump" and liken it to throwing up on paper. Whatever the name, it's a vital part of strengthening your writing muscles—just as scales are essential to playing the piano or stretching is integral to running. In the daily dump exercise, we write one to three pages each day about absolutely anything—dreams from the night before, angst about the writing ahead, or lists of things to do with our day.

As a writer and coach, I've discovered that the more you write, the more you write. In other words, journaling can increase your productivity. But the daily dump does more than improve your writing skills, increase your confidence, and boost your productivity. The daily dump also supports you in accessing your ideas and feelings. As you write, you will come up with solid ideas and stories for your book. The more you write, the more those ideas will become clearer and deeper. In time, the daily dump will help you catch those coveted aha moments.

To do your daily dump, write one to three pages a day. Write the pages quickly and without overthinking the content. You can write them in any form you'd like—in your project journal, a spiral notebook, or a separate document on your computer.

Commit to doing daily pages throughout the training process. I encourage my clients to continue this habit while writing their books, as well. The daily pages are a good place to map out your daily writing schedule and explore the ideas in the scene or chapter you are currently writing.

2. WRITE BREAKS. If you work or parent full time, take a write break several times during the day. A write break is a short break from daily life—one to ten minutes—for writing. Use the time to complete a brief writing exercise. You can find some at oneword (www.oneword.com) or Language Is a Virus (http://languageisavirus.com) or create your own.

3. PRACTICE PIECES. Writing short articles or blog posts can provide helpful practice for the writing marathon. One website offers a program that challenges participants to write ninety articles in ninety days. Another encourages writers to write a blog post every day for a month. In the first week in May, many children's book writers commit to writing a picture book a day for seven days. Not bad projects for the book writer in training. Choose one or more types of short pieces to write—articles, blog posts, picture books, or poems. Choose a time period—five or ten or fifteen days. Now commit to writing one piece each day for the duration. This practice will get you in the habit of writing daily. This will help you when you get to the marathon. You won't have to wonder what it is like to write daily because you will already have done it.

PREWRITING

A Mind Map always radiates from a central image. Every word and image becomes in itself a subcentre of association, the whole proceeding in a potentially infinite chain of branching patterns away from or towards the common centre.
—TONY BUZAN

When I face a challenging chapter or article, I mind map. I write the topic in the center of a large piece of paper. Radiating from the word, like spokes on a bicycle wheel, I write categories of thought: stories, images, themes, examples, facts, statistics, and so forth. By the time I get all of my ideas on paper, I have my answer. The chapter structure emerges organically from the mind map.

I used this process when I was working on my website. I used it to outline every chapter of my book, *A Generous Presence*. It works because the process mirrors our thinking process—radiant instead of linear. It also takes away the fear of the blank page because we start writing after we have already generated ideas for the mind map.

Mind mapping is one way to do prewriting, or writing that prepares you for working on your story or book. Prewriting removes anxiety from writing. Most teachers provide prewriting tools for their students because prewriting is a low-stakes way of putting ideas onto paper. During the prewriting process, you don't have to worry about word choice, grammar, or continuity. Your only job is to release your ideas from your brain.

During the training period for the marathon, try the following techniques as you do your daily dump or begin brainstorming for your book. By the time you get to the twenty-six-day marathon, you will have several tools to support you in dealing with the blank page. Return to these pages when you are writing your write-a-thon book. Prewriting removes the anxiety from both planning and writing your book.

WRITE NOW

1. MIND MAP. The mind map helps you record all of your ideas for a particular piece or scene. Use a sketchbook or piece of typing paper. You can use a regular pen or pencil, or colored markers and pencils. Use the directions in the first paragraph of this chapter to create your own mind map.

2. BRAINSTORMING. Use this tool when you need to generate ideas. Write a list of everything you think might be helpful for writing about this topic or scene. Write as fast as you can and in no particular order. Don't edit yourself. You may not understand what and idea has to do with your book, but your brain has an idea. Set free your brain to dream.

3. FREEWRITE. When you need to release ideas from your subconscious mind, the free write can be a helpful tool. Set a timer for twenty minutes and write as fast as you can about your ideas for the piece you are writing. Don't analyze or judge anything you write. Don't think about this writing in connection with the finished piece, just write.

4. DIRECTED QUESTIONS. This tool helps you get clear about your ideas for the chapter or piece of writing. It can also help you narrow your focus. Interview yourself about the idea you are working on. For a nonfiction chapter or article, ask and answer questions such as:

- What is my main point?
- What do I really want to say?
- What effect do I want to have on my readers?
- What points do I need to include to make this clear?

If you are working on a fiction scene or chapter, ask questions like:

- What does each character want?
- What does each character feel?
- How does the action convey the desires and emotions of each character?
- What mood am I creating in this scene?
- What needs to happen in this scene to move the story forward?
- What elements of setting contribute to the scene?

5. PLAY JOURNALIST. If you are stuck about where to start a piece, it can be helpful to list the basic facts that any journalist would start with in a piece. Who? What? When? Where? Why? How? Then ask yourself, what's the most interesting angle?

6. MAP IT. If you are writing a novel or a memoir, it can be helpful to create a visual map of each location you are writing about. If you are writing a memoir, when you create the map of a house and the landmarks nearby, you will remember stories you can use in your work. Either way, keep the map near you when you write so you can refer to it.

7. TALK IT OUT. I've noticed that my writing-coaching clients who are speakers and teachers get their best ideas when they have an audience. If this is you, think about talking through your ideas with a friend or a small group of colleagues. Record the conversation and transcribe your words of wisdom as a first step toward gathering your ideas together for a book.

DISCOVER WRITING STRENGTHS

*In discovering these giftings, former Gallup Organization
researchers Marcus Buckingham and Donald Clifton
ask us to "isolate the tense" we are thinking of when
performing a particular task. Am I thinking, "When will this
be over?" or am I thinking, "When can I do this again?" If I
am asking the former, then I am probably operating outside
of my giftings. If I am asking the later, it is a good sign
that I am operating in my giftings.*
—Marcus Buckingham and Donald O. Clifton

Every writer has strengths and weaknesses in the process of converting the ideas into words on a page. Some writers excel at research, others love doing the rough draft, and some revel in the rewrite. Even professionals struggle with stages of the writing process. For the purposes of the twenty-six-day writing marathon, we are looking at strengths and weaknesses in the five stages of the writing process: research, prewriting, writing the rough draft, revising, and proofreading. Note that most writers don't move through the five steps in order. Most writers repeat the steps during the writing process, sometimes multiple times.

RESEARCH. Finding the information you need to support the ideas, create the characters, inform the plot, or design the setting in your book. This step in the process might include reading information in books, articles, and on websites or interviewing people. Research might also mean taking field trips to locations important to your book's topic, characters, or setting.

PREWRITING. Getting your ideas onto paper for the very first time. Prewriting may include brainstorming, mind mapping, taking notes, or making lists. The previous chapter on prewriting can help you find a method that works for you. This step is focused primarily on getting the content or ideas onto the paper in a format that you can later access as you write the rough draft.

WRITING THE ROUGH DRAFT. In this phase, you take the content you developed through research and prewriting and write it! Whether you are putting together scenes or paragraphs, when you're done with the draft, you'll have a rough copy of your book.

REVISING. You add words and sentences, eliminate awkward phrases, and reorganize sentences and paragraphs in order to create a good product. If you are writing nonfiction, you focus on ideas, organization, chronology, word choice, and sentence fluency. If you are writing fiction, you consider criteria such as plot, character, dialogue, setting, pace, and consistency. In this stage, you might get support from a trusted writing buddy or critique group who will read your work and suggest ways you can make it better.

PROOFREADING. In this step, you make a final check for mechanical, grammatical, and spelling errors.

EVALUATING STRENGTHS AND WEAKNESSES

When you're writing a book in twenty-six days, the one thing you don't have to waste is time. For that reason, it's important to know the steps in the process that challenge you and plan extra time to get those done. That might mean taking one or more of the book tasks and doing them either before or after the write-a-thon. Some writers choose to do all of the research before the write-a-thon and most of the editing afterward so they can write like crazy during the twenty-six-day event.

One of my clients, who is not a native English speaker, struggled with the details of grammar—and keeping the whole piece in the same voice. He hired an editor to help him clean up the grammatical pieces that he struggled with *after* finishing his project. That way he could concentrate on getting his book written without worrying about grammar. Another client knew she was great at writing dialogue but not so good at the necessary narrative between the dialogue. She decided to write most of her entire first draft in dialogue. Whenever she knew there needed to be a narrative introduction or transition, she wrote "narrative transition" in the manuscript as well as a bit about what she planned to write. Then she highlighted it in yellow and kept writing dialogue. She gave herself extra time in the rewriting phase to add the narrative. Knowing these challenges gave the writers the information they needed to craft their writing plan to fit with their strengths and weaknesses.

In order to develop a plan for the writing marathon, you need to know what you are good at and what you struggle with. After even a week of daily pages and writing practice pieces, you can evaluate your strengths and weaknesses. Use the process described below to evaluate your writing process.

1. ASSESS STRENGTHS. A strength is something you are good at doing that you also like to do. I like prewriting. That is one of my strengths in the writing process. I am also good at understanding the internal structure of a piece of writing. Knowing this helps me design an approach to writing that works for me. Take a look at the five categories above. Think back to the last week of writing practice and your past writing experiences. Using those experiences as a guide, put a star next to the tasks you are good at doing.

2. IDENTIFY CHALLENGES. A challenge is something you struggle with in the writing process. It might also be a task that you find boring or difficult, like formatting foot-notes or creating character names. It is perfectly normal not to be good at everything in the writing process.

3. GET HELP. Look at the lists again, paying special attention to the items you did not star. Which of these do you need help with? Make a list. The next chapter will help you make a plan for getting the support you need to write the book.

GET SUPPORT

It's not 26.2 miles. It's 10 water stops.
—MARATHON SIGN

Running may look like a solitary sport, but it's not. Smart runners receive support from the day they decide to run a marathon until the glorious moment when they cross the finish line. During the training period, runners need help purchasing the proper shoe, designing a training program, addressing strains and injuries, and getting outfitted for the big day. On race day, runners depend on the support of their running friends, water stations, and even the cheering of the crowd. No one crosses the finish line on her efforts alone. A whole host of people support and strengthen the marathon runner.

It's the same with writing. A writer may spend hours alone, but no one finishes a book without the support and assistance of many people. Even professional writers who have written multiple books need help with researching, staying accountable, and editing. You are no different.

In the last chapter, you made a list of your strengths and challenges. In this chapter, you will use this list to create your plan for addressing your individual writing challenges. To create that plan, we will look at when you might need help and who can help you at various stages of the writing process.

WHEN DO YOU NEED HELP?

You've made your lists. You already know what you need help with as you work on your book. Take a look at the following write-a-thon schedule and match it up with your own list of challenges. When will you need help?

- **BEFORE THE WRITE-A-THON.** You may need help testing out the viability of your project, researching, talking through ideas, and structuring the book. If you are writing a novel, you might need help with a specific element of your story—plot, point of view, or character.

- **DURING THE WRITE-A-THON.** You may have done most of the research before you begin to write. If not, you may need to have help available to assist you in researching the book. You may also need help writing dialogue, organizing a chapter, establishing voice, or staying accountable.

- **AFTER THE MARATHON.** This is when everyone needs help! Most writers hire outside help to guide the revision process or to edit the book.

WHO CAN HELP YOU FINISH THE WRITE-A-THON?

There are many forms of writing help available to you. This is a list of a few of the people you can enlist or hire to support you in getting your project done and done right. Look at the list below and star those you need to support you in doing the twenty-six-day writing marathon:

- A writing buddy can help you talk through ideas, structure your book, and keep you accountable. If you trust this buddy, he can also read drafts and offer suggestions for revision. This person doesn't need to be a professional writer but does need to be someone who is actively writing. It's best if you can enlist a buddy who will do the write-a-thon with you. Then you can keep each other accountable through daily e-mail or social media check-ins.

- Members of a writing group can help you talk through ideas, keep you accountable, and read your work and offer suggestions for revision. If you decide to do the write-a-thon together, you can hold each other accountable and even have write-ins.

- A writing coach can talk through ideas with you, help you structure your work, and support you in creating a write-a-thon schedule that works for you. A writing coach can also help teach you tools for accountability or even be a partner in the accountability process.

- An editor can help you clean up the manuscript at the end of the process. See Why Hire an Editor? in Part Three for more information.
  - A development editor will work with you as you create a book project. A development editor primarily works with the structure and content of your book, supporting you in creating material that is readable, consistent, and interesting.
  - A copy editor can review the manuscript for errors in grammar and other conventions as well as checking for redundancies or consistency.
  - A proofreader can review the manuscript at the end for typographical errors and any other mistakes.

Create a list of the people you need to help you write this book. Place it where you can see it and begin the search for the perfect writing team.

GET THE GEAR

*There's nothing to writing. All you do is
sit down at a typewriter and open a vein.*
—Walter Wellesley "Red" Smith

You might be wondering, "What tools do real writers use to get their books written?" You may imagine that legal thriller author John Grisham has access to special plot-building software or that marketing guru Seth Godin uses a dictionary of snappy idioms. Maybe so—but you don't need any snazzy tools to be a real writer.

Children's writer and illustrator Kevin Henkes writes the first drafts of his novels in spiral notebooks and types the final draft on an old typewriter. He doesn't own a computer. Turkish novelist Orhan Pamuk writes by hand on graph paper notebooks, filling one page with words and leaving the opposite page blank for revisions. Edwidge Danticat writes her first draft on blue exam notebooks she buys in bulk. Other writers swear by their computer word-processing programs. But rest assured, you don't need much more than pen and paper to start a writing project.

If you're serious about doing this writing marathon, you probably want the staples of twenty-first-century technology: a computer with a word-processing program (most publishers like Microsoft Word), a printer, Internet access, and e-mail. You'll also need a project journal and notebook, which we'll get to in the next section. If you plan to do at least some of your writing at a coffee shop, hotel, or vacation home, create a portable writing kit. This can be as simple as a tote bag with notebook and pen, or as complex as a small suitcase complete with computer, travel printer, and extra paper.

If you're a techno-geek, you can explore writing software and smartphone applications. Fancy computer programs for writers like Scrivener exist and are getting better all the time. But you don't need any fancy programs to write your book. All you need is pen, paper, and a free moment. (Oh yeah, and that vein!)

 WRITE NOW

Collect your writing gear—either in a specific place in your home or as a portable writing kit.

THE PROJECT JOURNAL

[I begin] every day by writing in a journal, sometimes about the writing I'm doing, sometimes about what's on my mind at the moment. So for each novel I now write, I create a new journal entry, but before I do that, I read a day in the last Journal of a Novel for the previous novel. This allows me to see that, whatever I might be experiencing at the moment, I have experienced it and survived it before.
—ELIZABETH GEORGE

Writer Debra Farrington uses a project journal. John Steinbeck kept a journal when he wrote *East of Eden*. I kept a project journal for the last book I wrote—and found it essential to the writing process. The project journal is a small notebook, capable of being carried around, that provides the writer with a container for ideas, questions, meanderings, insights, and phrases.

When I wrote my book *A Generous Presence*, my last task at the end of each writing session was to put notes about the next chapters in my project journal. Sometimes I just recorded the next chapter's topic. I carried the notebook with me as I drove to client meetings or ferried children to lessons, and scribbled down ideas as they came to me. The notebook rested on my bedside table at night, in case I woke up with an idea. The next morning, I'd take the journal to the Y and jot down notes as I rode the exercise bike. That journal entry (and the previous day's notes) became my guide for the morning's writing.

At a recent reading, memoirist Wade Rouse spoke of his practice of recording each day's events in a journal. Children's writer Michael Morpurgo said, "Ted Hughes gave me this advice and it worked wonders: Record moments, fleeting impressions, overheard dialogue, your own sadnesses and bewilderments and joys." For the writer, everything is material. Once you begin a project, ideas for the book swirl around you like flies to honey. The project journal becomes a place where you can record and explore these ideas.

Purchase or find a small notebook. I encourage you to find something that's durable but not fancy. You don't want to mind scribbling in it! I'm a big fan of the Moleskine journals. I use the large, plain reporter for most projects. But for smaller projects, I like the pocket journal. Some of my writing-coaching clients use the plain spiral-bound notebooks you can get for about a dime each at the beginning of the school year. Other clients choose to use Google Docs or Evernote so they can record and access their project notes from anywhere. It doesn't matter what kind of notebook or electronic application you use. Just get something to record your project ideas. You'll need it.

Write in your project journal. Record your project title or describe how you feel at this point in the process. Start carrying the journal around with you and practice jotting down ideas.

TAKE NOTE

*I keep a small sheath of 3 × 5 cards in my billfold.
If I think a good sentence, I'll write it down. …
Occasionally, there's one that sings so perfectly the
first time that it stays, like "My boy has stopped speaking
to me and I don't think I can bear it." I wrote that down on
a 3 × 5 card, perhaps on a bus, or after walking the dog.*
—Joseph Heller

M ost of us don't get our best writing ideas when we're sitting in front of the computer or staring at a blank piece of paper. Our ideas come to us while we're walking or drifting off too sleep or riding the bus to work. We tell ourselves we'll remember. But we don't.

Heller, quoted above, is not the only writer who takes his notes with him. Novelist Dan Chaon, author of *You Remind Me of Me*, carries a pocket full of color-coded note cards and jots down notes wherever he goes. Once he gets a stack of note cards, he transcribes them into the computer and "writes furiously from 11 P.M. to 4 A.M." Novelist Bernard MacLaverty, author of *Grace Notes*, also swears by his playing-card sized note cards. He says, " … at night I might be sitting with a dram and would always have a pad beside me for scribbling, most of the time it turns out to be nonsense, but sometimes you get something."

Okay marathoners, this tip might just save this project for you! Take on his practice of carrying blank 3 × 5 cards (or an electronic equivalent). You'll no doubt get your best ideas when you are running errands, having lunch with your buddies, or driving to work. Make sure you have a place to put these ideas. Otherwise some other writer will grab those brilliant thoughts out of the air and put them in her book!

WRITE NOW

Tuck a few blank sticky notes, index cards, or even your project journal in your pocket or purse. Take a pen along, too. If you have a smartphone, you can use the notes feature to record your thoughts. Just make sure you record those stray ideas. When you get to the blank piece of paper, you'll have a place to start.

STOCK YOUR LIBRARY

Inside every fat book is a thin book trying to get out.
—UNKNOWN

You don't need a lot of stuff for the marathon. But you will need a few writing-related resources. Here are the resources I cannot live without.

MERRIAM-WEBSTER'S COLLEGIATE DICTIONARY. Yes, I know that most word-processing programs have dictionaries. They can be enormously helpful in a pinch. But I depend on a real dictionary to look up words I don't know and to make sure I am using the right words. Get the latest edition of whatever dictionary you like as words change all the time. Merriam-Webster has a helpful online resource for those of you who write in coffee shops and libraries: www.merriam-webster.com.

THE BABY NAMES ALMANAC BY EMILY LARSON (OR A SIMILAR BOOK). If you're like some writers, the hardest task in writing your novel will be naming the characters. After you've used up the names of all your heroes and enemies, where do you find the perfect name? Do what parents have done for generations—pick up a baby-naming guide, preferably one that tells you a lot about the names such as origin, meaning, regional use, and when it was popular. You'd hate to give an Amish girl a name popularized by twenty-first-century television. And if you're writing nonfiction, don't think you can escape owning this book. Most nonfiction writers have to change names to protect the innocent, and a baby-naming guide can make that task easier.

THESAURUS. A thesaurus allows you to vary your words. Let's say you're writing a book about coffee. When you get to the chapter on brewing the perfect cup of java, you might want to use a word other than brew. A thesaurus gives you access to synonyms, antonyms, and other related words. *Roget's International Thesaurus* is organized by subject. *Webster's New World Roget's A-Z Thesaurus* is organized alphabetically. ThinkMap Visual Thesaurus offers the related words in a visual format (www.visualthesaurus.com). Get the tool that works for you.

THE CHICAGO MANUAL OF STYLE. This resource will let you know what grammatical rules have changed since you were in school. You can also check on how to format bibliography items, place a comma or hyphen, and properly refer to a president, reverend, or queen. Because grammar changes daily, subscribe to the online version for the most up-to-date information. This is something you can do at the end of the marathon, when you edit the book. During the marathon, you will be too busy writing to think about when to use a semicolon (www.chicagomanualofstyle.org).

WRITE NOW

Think about what resources you will need for your particular project. When I am writing for children, I keep the *Children's Writer's Word Book* by Alijandra Mogilner nearby so I don't confuse my readers with words they haven't learned yet. If you're a mystery writer, you might need a book on forensic medicine or poisons. Stock your library. Then take time to familiarize yourself with each of the resources. That way, when you need them, you'll know exactly how to use them.

COURSE TRAINING

PLAN YOUR NOVEL

THE TWENTY-SIX-DAY NOVEL

Most beginning writers (and I was the same) are like chefs
trying to cook great dishes that they've never tasted themselves.
How can you make a great (or even an adequate) bouillabaisse
if you've never had any? If you don't really understand why
people read mysteries (or romances or literary novels or
thrillers or whatever), then there's no way in the world you're
going to write one that anyone wants to publish.
—Daniel Quinn

Many philosophers have wondered what it would be like to be God. For the next month, you get a stab at the job. Well, sort of. You get to decide on and design your novel's world. Do you want to be chasing demons in a parallel universe or taking tea in nineteenth-century London? Are your characters falling in love or hunting down a brutal murderer? Will you be setting the stage for an epic disaster or a major discovery? You will begin your godly duties by choosing a genre.

UNDERSTANDING GENRE

If planning a book is like mapping out a marathon, choosing the genre is a bit like choosing what kind of a marathon this will be. Will it be a full marathon or a half? Will we be running or walking? Is there a theme or a cause? Once we know the kind of marathon we're planning, we can make the rest of the decisions—like where to place the rest stops. It's the same with book planning: Once we know the genre, we will have an easier time choosing an appropriate setting and creating a plot.

Perhaps you already know what kind of book you are writing. You woke up in the middle of the night with a mystery novel fully formed in your head. All that's left is the writing of it. Or maybe you have no idea what genre your book fits into. Instead you have a few characters in mind and perhaps a setting. Finding the right genre for your book will help you write it. Most novels have the same elements—characters set loose in a setting to achieve some goal. But each genre also has its own set of conventions. Mystery novels tend to be plot driven, while literary fiction focuses on the characters. Knowing the genre you are writing for will help you structure and write your book.

Here is a list of some of the most common novel categories and genres. As you read the list, jot down a few titles of the books you've read in each category.

MIDDLE-GRADE FICTION. The middle-grade fiction novel is designed for readers between eight and twelve years old. The novels can take the form of a variety of genres including mystery, science fiction, fantasy, issue driven, or historical stories. These novels run from 10,000 to 40,000 words, with an average of 35,000 words.

YOUNG ADULT FICTION. Young adult fiction is geared toward readers age twelve and older. The story can take the shape of a number of genres including romance, mystery, science fiction, fantasy, historical, or issue-based novels. Young adult fiction runs from 45,000 to 85,000 words, with some fantasy stories running as long as 120,000 words.

LITERARY FICTION. Think of literary fiction or serious fiction, as it's sometimes called, as a novel that focuses on style, setting, and the character's motivations and emotions.

COMMERCIAL FICTION. This is a broad category that refers to books with mass commercial appeal. The books are often plot driven and may contain some cultural or issue hook, like shopping or terrorism. The books can be further categorized into more specific categories or genres like chick lit, women's fiction, thrillers, and true crime.

MYSTERIES. This category refers to plot-driven stories that involve some sort of a mystery, often a murder, but also missing persons, art fraud, and theft. The mystery and crime fiction genre has exploded in past years and includes police procedurals, paranormal mysteries, hobby mysteries, spy novels, historical mysteries, thrillers, cozies (where the murder happens offstage), and more. Mystery novel series often follow an interesting professional or amateur sleuth.

ROMANCE. In the romance novel, characters pursue, find, avoid, lose, and rediscover love. The stories must balance interesting, likable characters and plenty of conflict to keep them apart until the last delicious moment of the book.

SCIENCE FICTION AND FANTASY. These two genres ask, "What if?" Science fiction looks at scientific facts and wonders what would happen if we could use them to, for example, create a colony on Mars. The fantasy writer pushes that "What if?" question even further and creates entire universes. While the science fiction writer must pay attention to the laws of the universe, the fantasy author creates his own laws of reality.

HORROR. This genre lights up the dark parts of humanity in order to scare the reader. A horror novel might focus on anything from serial killers to the supernatural.

HISTORICAL FICTION. This genre takes the plots and characters and plunks them down in a historical setting, hopefully with an accurate representation of the time and place.

WHAT GENRE DO YOU READ?

I cannot keep myself away from a mystery novel any more than my dog can pass by a fire hydrant. I've tried. I'm always buying the latest one-thousand-page literary tome only to find that before I've read one hundred pages, a fast-paced mystery has tempted me away from it.

When choosing your genre, think about what you love to read. Plenty of writers have come to me with an idea for a novel in a genre they've never read. After an enthusiastic start, they get stuck or lost and wonder how to proceed. Writers who know and love the genre they are writing in also get lost, but they have a better sense of how to find their way again. Because these writers know their genre, they know eight or ten clever ways popular mystery or romance writers move their characters from point A to point B. The moral of the story: Choose a genre you love to read and know well.

When you read the above list of genres, you jotted down examples from your own reading history. Now take the list and look through your bookshelves and reading log. For each book you've read, add a tick mark next to the category it belongs to. For example, *The Girl With the Dragon Tattoo* by Stieg Larsson will give you a tick mark in mystery while *Gone With the Wind* gets you a tick mark in historical fiction. Be honest and count only the books you have actually read. If your bookshelf is filled with classics to impress visitors while you read trashy romance novels or old westerns under the covers at night, make sure you skip the unopened volumes. When you're done, look to see what categories have the most tick marks. Choose your genre from this category.

WRITE NOW

You've chosen your genre. Before you plan the characters, setting, and plot, reflect further on what you love and hate about the books you have read. Use these lists as a guide for planning your novel:

1. Make a list of everything you love to read and read about in a book. Include characters, setting, plot, professions, style, themes, and anything else you can think of. Be as specific as possible. Your list might include professions that interest you (I like to read about professors and archeologists), a style you prefer (short, snappy chapters or long descriptive paragraphs), or what people eat (lots of foreign foods or home baked comfort foods). Include it all!

2. Make a list of everything you loathe in a book, including all of the categories listed above and anything else you can think of. Your list might include characters that annoy you (maybe you don't like talking dogs), topics you find boring (historical novels put you to sleep), or a style that puts you over the edge (chirpy chick lit gives you the heebie-jeebies). Get it all down.

THE STORY BIBLE

---

*In writing a series of stories about the same characters,
plan the whole series in advance in some detail, to avoid
contradictions and inconsistencies.*
—L. Sprague de Camp

Writers who want to pitch a TV series create a show bible. The bible contains the concept, location, bios of the characters, full episodes, synopses of potential episodes, and possibly even a pilot episode. Once the TV series is launched, the show bible is used to keep track of details about the setting and characters to preserve continuity. The show bible reminds writers about pertinent but minute facts. No doubt the writers for the TV show *Buffy the Vampire Slayer* needed to know the characteristics of each demon that Buffy fought as well as the names of her high school classmates who turned out to be vampires. It would be confusing if a student who was supposedly a vampire one season were suddenly able to see her reflection during the next season. As novelists, we can borrow the show bible tool and create a story bible for our project.

A story bible is a place to hold all of our planning for the novel. Everything we create for the book can go into the story bible: concept, setting, character descriptions, potential plot conflicts, and developing scenes. The story bible can hold all of the tiny pieces of information we want to include in our novel such as dialogue fragments, phrases, and cultural references. Man Booker Prize-winning novelist Kazuo Ishiguro "compiles folders of notes and flowcharts that lay out not just the plot but also more subtle aspects of the narrative, such as a characters emotions or memories. ... He collects his notes in binders and writes a first draft by hand." During the write-a-thon, the story bible can be a helpful tool for recording and remembering information. What color and model of car did our protagonist drive in chapter one? How did she take her coffee? And what was the name of that dead pet hamster she buried in chapter three? When we want the protagonist to get into her car, we don't have to skim through one hundred pages of text to find out what kind of a car it was. We can turn to our story bible.

During the editing process, the story bible helps us add depth and texture to the book. If we have collected pieces of dialogue, we can weave them into the narrative.

If we have been gathering descriptive bits, we can drop those in to create mood. We can also use the story bible to check our book for continuity. What may seem like meaningless details to us—who cares if the protagonist takes her coffee black in the beginning of the book and with sugar at the end?—can annoy readers.

CHOOSING A FORMAT

A story bible can take many forms. Some writers prefer their story bible to be an electronic file on their computer. New services allow writers to store and share their work online, so they can access their story bible from any computer or wireless device. Writers can leave the story bible open while they work on their novel and fill it in as they write.

Other writers like the feel and security of a physical story bible. A three-ring binder with pocket page dividers for each section works well for this. Writers can develop and add visual collages for their setting and character, mind maps of scene development, and ideas on sticky notes and index cards. The bible can be kept at the writer's desk for easy reference and transported just about anywhere for brainstorming sessions.

A third option takes the information for the story bible and lays it out on white-boards, walls, and bulletin boards. Novelist Hilary Mantel takes her notes and tacks them to a "seven-foot-tall bulletin board in her kitchen; they remain there until Ms. Mantel finds a place for them in her narrative." Another writer works with a long piece of butcher-block paper taped up along one wall of her office. On it she includes the timeline for her books and index cards filled with specific characters and their traits. These visual tools allow the writer to have everything visible while writing. The writer doesn't need to wonder if the protagonist has blue eyes or brown eyes. She can look up at the wall and see her character sketch.

If none of these options seems quite right, feel free to combine them. While my story bible is in a three-ring binder, I also use an open document on my computer to jot down ideas and information while I am writing. That way I stay focused on the story and continue writing while also honoring the ideas that are flying rapidly into my brain. You will find your own magic combination of electronic, print, and posted story bible.

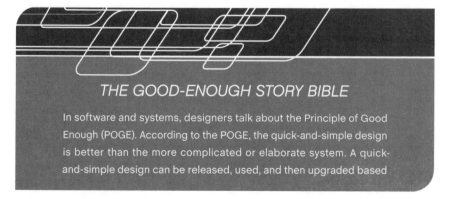

THE GOOD-ENOUGH STORY BIBLE

In software and systems, designers talk about the Principle of Good Enough (POGE). According to the POGE, the quick-and-simple design is better than the more complicated or elaborate system. A quick-and-simple design can be released, used, and then upgraded based on the experience and needs of consumers. Apply the principle of good enough to your story bible. Creating the story bible should never become more important than writing your book. Create your story bible and plan your novel as quickly and simply as you can. As you work on your novel, you will adapt and expand the story bible according to your needs and not someone else's idea of what your preparation should look like. Do what works for you.

WRITE NOW

Decide which format you will use for your story bible and create it. Know that you will be filling in the details of your story bible throughout the novel-planning process. As you work through the next chapters, you will create characters, describe their setting, and develop a plot. All of this work will go into your story bible.

WHERE DO YOU GET YOUR IDEAS?

Write what you know.
—WRITING ADAGE

Forget the boring old dictum "write about what you know."
Instead, seek out an unknown yet knowable area of
experience that's going to enhance your understanding of
the world and write about that.
—ROSE TREMAIN

Where do you get your ideas? Neil Gaiman calls it the question authors fear most. Certainly this question annoys many authors. Maybe the question bugs us because we really don't know where our ideas come from. Speculative fiction author Harlan Ellison once replied to the question, "Poughkeepsie." Science fiction writer Chris Fox has said, "I just take photographs as they fly overhead." Over the years, Gaiman has answered the question in many ways, including "From the Idea-of-the-Month Club" or "From a little ideas shop in Bognor Regis." Now Gaiman tells the truth about his ideas: He makes them up.

Where do you get your ideas? It's actually a worthy question to consider. All books begin with a nugget of an idea. For each author and perhaps even for each book, the nugget comes in different forms. Some books begin with a character. Mystery writer Val McDermid spent years developing her series character, lesbian journalist Lindsay Gordon, before she wrote any books featuring her. Other books begin with a snippet of a plot, maybe a news story found online or on television. Thriller writer Gabrielle Lord based her book *Fortress* on a news story about a group of children and their teacher who had been abducted and held hostage. The idea for a novel can also start with a setting or an issue the author wants to explore. Some writers start with bits of all of the above, developing the character, plot, and setting in tandem.

START WITH WHAT YOU KNOW

Speculative fiction writer Darrell Schweitzer echoed the famous adage "Write what you know" when he said, "If you don't know it, don't write it." As you search for ideas, take inventory of what you already know. Your own collection of experiences, education, and interests can become a rich source for plot, setting, and character. Grab your project journal or a large sheet of paper and create a series of lists or mind maps about what you know in the following categories.

EXPERIENCE. Include the ordinary, daily experiences (marriage, parenting, corporate life) and the extraordinary one-time experiences (skydiving, surgery, or an African safari). Any experience is fair game, including the ones you've only lived vicariously through friends and family.

KNOWLEDGE AND TRAINING. List the areas you studied in your formal education, even if you weren't paying all that much attention, as well as the informal training you've had. Maybe you've taken yoga or automobile repair classes. This might lead to a character who is a yoga teacher or marries a mechanic.

HOBBIES AND INTERESTS. What do you do for fun? What do your children and friends do for fun? Did you collect stamps or comic books when you were a kid? Maybe your children are devoted to geocaching, the modern treasure-hunting game that uses a GPS. Or perhaps you have a lifelong interest in the history of tools. Make a list of all the hobbies and interests you know well enough to incorporate into a book.

FAMILY SECRETS. One of my great-grandfathers had two families, one here and one in Sweden. What secrets are hiding in your family tree? Make a list of stories and rumors you have been overhearing for years. Who knows, maybe the nugget for your novel was planted in a hundred-year-old scandal!

WHAT DO YOU WONDER ABOUT?

Novelist W.P. Kinsella said, "Use your imagination. Trust me, your lives are not interesting. Don't write them down." If you're going to write a great novel, you will need more than our own life stories to add to the mix. You'll need to broaden your search and consider what piques your interest and stirs your imagination. Start by making lists of what interests you in each of the following categories.

PEOPLE. Who are you curious about? What kinds of people get you thinking, "What if?"

PLACES. What places would you like to explore? Where would you travel if you had the time and money?

PROFESSIONS. What professions intrigue you? Have you always wondered about the private lives of astrophysicists or zookeepers?

EVENTS. Do you wish you knew what it was like to be part of a protest? Maybe you wonder what victims of disaster experience. Think about the events that have captured your interest in the past and list them.

FACTS AND IDEAS. What facts and ideas do you wonder about at idle moments? Madeleine L'Engle took her curiosity about mitochondria and turned it into the fantasy novel for children, *A Wind in the Door.* What facts or ideas might become your next story?

ISSUES. Novelists like Jodi Picoult (*Sing You Home, House Rules*) and Khaled Hosseini (*The Kite Runner*) have used their novels to explore popular issues. What issues have enough steam to drive your next book?

TRUE STORIES. Many novelists get their ideas from a snippet of a story found in a magazine or on television. Take a look at your daily paper or monthly magazine in a new way—as a novelist searching for the seeds of a new character or tale. Start a list of true stories that might become fodder for your next book.

EVERYTHING AND THE KITCHEN SINK. Evolutionary biologist Stephen Jay Gould collected sandals made from recycled automobile tires that he purchased in developing countries around the world. He saw these sandals as examples of innovation. What might you collect that will inspire your writing? Round out your collection of lists by creating a list of everything else that has fascinated you in your life. This might include websites, art pieces, jokes, anecdotes, poems, riddles, conversations, books, movies, plays, TV shows, analogies, metaphors, processes, methods, sneakers, and kitchen sinks.

ASK THE QUESTIONS

The same questions that cause anxiety can be gold for the novelist. "What if the plane crashes?" becomes the opening conflict of our novel. The worry "I wonder if I can trust her?" becomes a tool we use to understand our antagonist. Characters and plots live inside our questions. Take the lists you have created above and ask questions:

- What if …?
- I wonder …?
- Wouldn't it be interesting if …?
- If only …?
- Why?
- Why not?

WRITE NOW

No doubt the above work generated a lot of ideas. Most writers and wannabe writers have a million good ideas floating around in their brains. We jot them in our notebooks and on our to-do lists, but often juggling too many good ideas and potential projects prevents us from following through on them.

For the write-a-thon, choose one idea. If you're not sure which one to choose, think about which project has the most energy for you. Which story will wake you long before dawn and keep you up hours beyond your bedtime? Which story will you want to skip work, dates, and even dinner to write about? Choose that one. The rest can wait.

In the next chapters, you will develop characters, create a setting, and design your plot. The above lists will come in handy as you plan your book. Start with what you know, consider what you are curious about, and ask a lot of questions! Keep the rest of your idea jottings safe for future projects.

THE WHO

If a character isn't alive for you,
he will never live for your readers.
—MARGARET MARON

What fictional characters would you invite to a dinner party? I'd love to spend an evening with the poet detective Adam Dalgliesh from P.D. James's literary mystery series. My daughter would choose to spend the meal with Ivy and Bean, the young creations of author Annie Barrows. My friends added their own suggestions—the hunky Ranger from Janet Evanovich's Stephanie Plum series and the wise-beyond-her-years Anne of Greene Gables, created by Lucy Maud Montgomery. For the twenty-six-day write-a-thon, you get to create a cast of fictional characters you will work, eat, and sleep with for the next month or so. This chapter is designed to help you create characters your readers will want to invite to dinner. (Well, some of them at least.)

WHAT MAKES A GOOD CHARACTER?

Like the perfect loaf of French bread, crusty on the outside and tender on the inside, it's much easier to spot a good character than to create one. My bread tends to fall flat or get soggy on the inside, making it a poor dinner companion. Good characters are round and surprising. The first look, be it crusty or tender, is never all there is. As the story unfolds, we get to know the unpredictable and delicious nuances of the character. Flat characters are like mass-produced white bread—no depth or texture. No matter how you squish them, they are what they are—sufficient but not filling or memorable. The flat characters will show up in the scene and do their duty to move the plot forward, but we won't get attached to them. They won't be coming to dinner or haunting our dreams for years. Round characters have a voice that we hear long after we've closed the book.

So how do you create a round character? Well-developed characters have three defining elements:

1. THEY WANT SOMETHING. The character's wants can change throughout the novel, but the author must be able to articulate the wants for each character in one sentence. Mystery writer Michael Connelly says, "All persons are defined by their wants and needs. Their desires. Attaining the things we want creates conflict within ourselves and in our relations to the world. This natural human condition must be embedded in the people you write about. It helps define their characters. It makes them real." Or as Ray Bradbury said, "Find out what your hero wants. Then just follow him."

2. THEY HAVE A UNIQUE POINT OF VIEW. The character sees the world in a unique way. Screenwriter Syd Field says, "Point of view is an individual and independent belief system." The characters you create will have their own unique set of values, beliefs, ideologies, and feelings. They will each express their point of view through their attitudes, habits, appearance, actions, and speech. You will know the adages they tack up on their walls, the experts they pay attention to, and the events that throw them into a tizzy. You will have a list of their attitudes toward everything from white bread to red wine.

3. THEY CHANGE. Round characters are transformed by the events in their lives. They are not static beings, expressing the same point of view from beginning to end. Something will change for each character in the course of a story, even if the change is hardly noticeable.

WHERE DO YOU FIND YOUR CHARACTERS?

A friend of mine puts composites of ex-boyfriends in her books. Another takes tidbits from people he observes at coffee shops and in bookstores. I like to create my protagonists based on people I admire, putting qualities in my characters that I wish I possessed. When it comes to finding characters, we have to dig into our own experience and exercise our imagination to create a group of people we're going to want to spend the next twenty-six days with. Here are places to discover characters.

START WITH YOURSELF. Psychologist and mystery author Stephen White writes about psychologist Dr. Alan Gregory, no doubt mining his own psychologist persona. Perhaps Jane Smiley used her own experience as a professor in Iowa when she wrote her satiric academic novel *Moo*. You are the sum of your parts—all of the ages you've been, the roles you've had, and the experiences you've gathered. These various parts can become the embryos of your characters, the small beings from which fully formed characters grow. As Gore Vidal has said, "Each writer is born with a repertory company in his head and as you get older, you become more skillful at casting them." In the last chapter, Where Do You Get Your Ideas?, you listed your experiences, education, and interests. Look back at that list and add to it. How might your experiences become the seed of a new character?

CONSIDER WHO YOU KNOW. No doubt you've encountered some pretty unique people in your years on the planet. Make a list of everyone you've known who might make a good character, whether you loved them, despised them, or only admired them from a distance. Feel free to put anyone and everyone in your notes. Remember, you won't be lifting them from your life and dumping them in your book without changing a few identifiable characteristics.

THINK ABOUT WHOM YOU'D LIKE TO KNOW. Do you wonder what a conversation with your barista would be like? Do you pour over photos of celebrities in magazines, wondering what their private lives are like? Do you peruse the websites of rocket scientists, trying to find out what exactly they do every day? Make a list of the people you are curious about. Start with real people you've wondered about—like your mail carrier or the guy who built your deck. Branch out into professions and types of people you find intriguing, like jewel thieves or rare book collectors. Round out your lists with your wonderings about people who think or believe in certain ways. What would it be like to have a character who opposes breastfeeding? How about a character who hoards plastic bags? Who do you wonder about?

MIX AND MATCH. Many an author has faced curious friends or acquaintances, demanding to know if the author based the details of this or that character on them or people they know. Friends will sidle up to an author at a party and ask, "That angry boss in chapter four—that's really old Mr. Crumpet, right?" or "Is that librarian me?" The smart writer will deny any likeness to persons living or dead.

One way to protect yourself is to mix and match your characters. Remember those flap books from childhood? Each page was divided into three separate flaps—head, body, and feet. The reader could mix and match the physical characteristics of each person, giving a baseball player a ballerina's outfit and rain boots, or dressing up a ballerina in a pirate's costume and baseball cleats. Take that mix-and-match idea and apply it to the characters you've noted above. When it comes to putting the characters together, grab the physical qualities from someone on the bus, add the attitude of your best friend, mix in a little life philosophy from your mother, maybe even an outfit from the latest fashion magazine, and *abracadabra*, you'll have a round character that no one (or everyone) will recognize.

GETTING SPECIFIC

Once you've put down the broad strokes of your characters, it's time to get specific. In order to develop round characters who have a complicated history of desires, ideas, and attitudes, we need to know them as well as we know ourselves. Here are a few tools to help you create rich, interesting characters.

CHARACTER QUESTIONNAIRE. In the TV show *Dragnet*, Detective Joe Friday—played by actor Jack Webb—made famous the phrase, "Just the facts, Ma'am." When it comes to building a character, use a character questionnaire to develop a list of basic facts about each character. Many versions of character questionnaires are readily available online. Usually it includes some of the following characteristics: name, age, height, weight, ethnicity, hair color, eye color, skin color, physical appearance, education, profession, beliefs, health issues, hobbies and interests, family, friends, home (where does he live, what kind of a home does he have, how is it decorated, is it messy or clean, and so forth), and favorites (food, clothes, music, books, activities, TV shows, sports teams, etc.).

PROUST QUESTIONNAIRE. In the late nineteenth century, it was popular for English families to answer questionnaires. French writer Marcel Proust answered a list of questions in a confession album of a friend. Several times throughout his life, Proust answered this or a similar list of questions. Two of these lists survive and have become known as the Proust Questionnaire; both can be found online. Several modern-day magazines have taken up this tradition, most notably Vanity Fair. Search online for a version of the Proust Questionnaire and answer the questions for each of your characters.

TWENTY-FIVE RANDOM THINGS ABOUT ME. A few years ago, lists of twenty-five random personal facts began popping up on Facebook. People posted lists of trivial and substantial personal facts and then tagged their closest friends and family members, inviting them to do the same. Read through a number of these and each list takes on the personality of its creator. Funny, intelligent, poignant, or totally random, these lists reveal the nuances of a person's character. Compose your own list of random facts for each of your major characters. What would they include? How would they write it? Who would they tag? Who would they block from seeing their list?

GENOGRAM. Family therapists create genograms—a visual display of an individual's family relationships and medical and psychological history—to better record and see family patterns. For years, I've used genograms as a tool for creating and visualizing a character's family history. While software exists to aid individuals in creating genograms, you can easily draw one with pen and paper. For each character, include name; current age; birth date; death date (if relevant); marriages, divorces, and significant partnerings; pregnancies, miscarriages, stillbirths, and abortions; birth, adopted, or foster children; significant medical and emotional history; places of residence; occupations; and educational levels.

The following symbols tell you how to depict the basic information on the genogram. Other symbols can be found online by searching for "genogram" or "genogram symbols."

> Female: circle
> Male: square
> Age: Place the number inside the circle or square.
> Marriage: Join circle and square with a solid line.
> Unmarried couple: Join two people with a dashed line.
> Divorce: Put a double slash mark on the solid marriage line.

Cinderella's Genogram

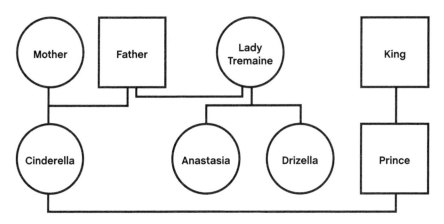

COLLAGE. Writers who need a break from their desks and relentlessly pounding their keyboards might choose to create a collage for each of their characters. Using photos of people, clothes, and settings clipped from magazines, newspapers, and old books, the collage can portray characters as the author sees them. Sayings and other odds and ends, like postcards, trinkets, and mocked-up business cards, can further depict the personalities of the main characters.

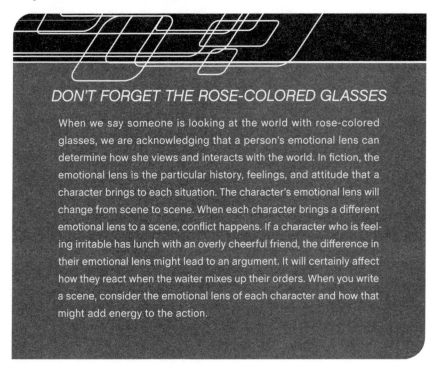

DON'T FORGET THE ROSE-COLORED GLASSES

When we say someone is looking at the world with rose-colored glasses, we are acknowledging that a person's emotional lens can determine how she views and interacts with the world. In fiction, the emotional lens is the particular history, feelings, and attitude that a character brings to each situation. The character's emotional lens will change from scene to scene. When each character brings a different emotional lens to a scene, conflict happens. If a character who is feeling irritable has lunch with an overly cheerful friend, the difference in their emotional lens might lead to an argument. It will certainly affect how they react when the waiter mixes up their orders. When you write a scene, consider the emotional lens of each character and how that might add energy to the action.

HOW TO PORTRAY CHARACTER

Now that you have a story bible stuffed with information about your character, and you know everything from what color socks she wears to the kind of music she listens to while running, you need to think about what pieces to reveal and how. As mystery author Michael Connelly said, "One telling detail will take you further than a page of description."

Here are several ways authors can show who their characters are:

1. DESCRIPTION. Despite novelist Michael Connelly's warning about description, many authors utilize straight description to depict the character's values, temperament, passions, and conflicts. In Abraham Verghese's novel *Cutting for Stone*, the narrator explains the typical behavior of one of the main characters, Dr. Thomas Stone: "As a surgeon, Stone was famous for his speed, his courage, his daring, his boldness, his inventiveness, the economy of his movements, and his calmness under duress. These were skills that he'd honed on a trusting and uncomplaining population, briefly in India, and then in Ethiopia. But when Sister Mary Joseph Praise, his assistant for seven years, went into labor, all these qualities vanished."

2. SELF-PORTRAIT. In a self-portrait, we learn about the character from the character's own description. In Janet Evanovich's mystery series featuring Stephanie Plum, Plum provides a brief self-portrait in every book. This can be as simple as Stephanie's statement about her appearance in *Two For the Dough*: "I, on the other hand, was the blue-eyed, fair-skinned, product of a Hungarian-Italian union ..." Another example of self-portrait can be found in Sandra Cisneros's novel *The House on Mango Street*. In a short chapter titled "My Name," the main character, Esperanza, describes herself by explaining the origin of her name, its meaning, and how it has affected her life.

3. APPEARANCE. The author tells the reader what the character looks like, either through her own words, as in the Stephanie Plum example above, or from the viewpoint of another character. In Jacqueline Winspear's mystery novel *Maisie Dobbs*, we meet Maisie through the eyes of the corner newspaper salesman, Jack Barker: "Even if she hadn't been the last person to walk through the turnstile at Warren Street tube station, Jack Barker would have noticed the tall, slender woman in the navy blue, thigh-length jacket with a matching pleated skirt short enough to reveal a well-turned ankle. She had what his old mother would have called 'bearing.'"

4. ACTIONS, BEHAVIORS, AND HABITS. The author can use what a character does, including small habits, behaviors, and preferences, to reveal character traits. How a character approaches a challenging situation, the kind of handbag she carries, and what color tie he wears—these large and small details give a character depth. In Jennifer Egan's Pulitzer Prize-winning novel *A Visit From the Goon Squad*, the first character the reader meets is Sasha. She is in the restroom of a hotel restaurant, looking in the mirror, "adjusting her yellow eye shadow," when she spies a handbag on the floor. The owner is in the stall. Sasha steals the wallet out of the handbag. As the story continues, the reader learns that stealing is a habit for Sasha. We get to know more about her through the list of items she has stolen in the last year: "Five sets of keys, fourteen pairs of sunglasses, a child's striped scarf, binoculars, a cheese grater, a pocketknife, twenty-eight bars of soap, and eighty-five pens, ranging from cheap ballpoints she'd used to sign debit card slips to the aubergine Visconti that cost $260 online, which she'd lifted from her former boss's lawyer during a contracts meeting."

5. REACTIONS TO PEOPLE AND EVENTS. You can develop characters by showing how they react to the people they encounter and the events in their lives. In *Catherine, Called Birdy*, author Karen Cushman reveals Catherine's moral code and her sense of independence and humor in this description of treating her father's clerk: "My father's clerk suffers today from an inflammation of his eyes, caused, no doubt, by his spying on our serving maids as they wash under their arms at the millpond. I did not have the mother's milk necessary for an ointment for the eyes, so I used garlic and goose fat left from doctoring Morwenna's boils yesterweek. No matter how he bellowed, it will do him no harm."

6. OTHER CHARACTERS' REACTIONS TO THEM. A character's traits are also exposed through the facial expressions, body language, and actions of other characters in the book. In Louis Sachar's novel *Holes*, we learn about Stanley Yelnats's appearance and social status from the reaction of his teachers to his physical size: "He was overweight and the kids at his middle school often teased him about his size. Even his teachers sometimes made cruel comments without realizing it. On his last day of school, his math teacher, Mrs. Bell, taught ratios. As an example, she chose the heaviest kid in the class and the lightest kid in the class, and had them weigh themselves. Stanley weighed three times as much as the other boy. Mrs. Bell wrote the ratio on the board, 3:1, unaware of how much embarrassment she had caused both of them."

7. DIALOGUE. How a character speaks and what she says to a variety of people tells us much about who she is. In Jennifer Egan's *A Visit From the Goon Squad*, Sasha stole the wallet from a woman we do not see at first. A bit later in the chapter, we learn more about the woman when she appears before Sasha and her date, Alex, in the lobby of the hotel and says, "You haven't seen—I'm desperate." She is so desperate, in fact, that she does not even complete the sentence. Two paragraphs later, the woman says a bit more, "Someone stole my wallet. My ID is gone, and I have to catch a plane tomorrow morning. I'm just desperate!" Though this woman has uttered only two very similar lines, we know she is a frazzled out-of-town visitor to New York.

8. THOUGHTS. A character's thoughts often reveal as much or more than his dialogue. A character's musings can help the reader understand his actions as well as how and why an experience was meaningful to him. In Louise Penny's mystery *The Cruelest Month*, the author uses a character's thoughts to help the reader understand the inner conflict that bubbles beneath his spoken words. Peter and Clara are married artists. When Clara discovers that Peter has secretly peeked at her new painting, she asks, "Tell me what you think." Before Peter answers Clara, he thinks: "It was so beautiful it hurt. Yes. That was it. The pain he felt came from outside himself. Not inside. No." Peter then says, "It's astonishing, Clara." A few lines later he asks, "But are the colors quite right?"

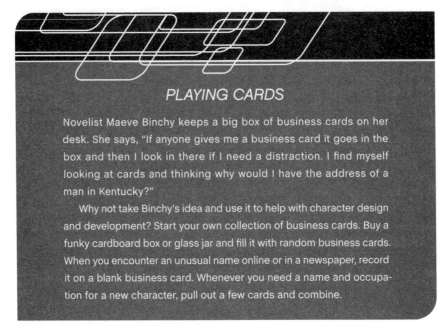

PLAYING CARDS

Novelist Maeve Binchy keeps a big box of business cards on her desk. She says, "If anyone gives me a business card it goes in the box and then I look in there if I need a distraction. I find myself looking at cards and thinking why would I have the address of a man in Kentucky?"

Why not take Binchy's idea and use it to help with character design and development? Start your own collection of business cards. Buy a funky cardboard box or glass jar and fill it with random business cards. When you encounter an unusual name online or in a newspaper, record it on a blank business card. Whenever you need a name and occupation for a new character, pull out a few cards and combine.

A FINAL WORD

Mystery writer Elizabeth George offers a perfect summary for creating characters in her book, *Write Away*: "Give them flaws, allow them to doubt themselves about something, see to it that they grow and change, and make certain you are putting them into conflict." If we follow George's advice, not only we will create characters we want to get to know better, we will also design characters our readers might take to dinner, to bed, or the beach!

THE WHERE

---

*... I will put up with almost anything if a book has
a strong sense of place. The place doesn't have to be glamorous,
but it does have to be colorful, both in the way it looks,
and the people who live there.*

—ANNE WILSON

Every story needs to happen somewhere. When an author creates a distinct and interesting somewhere, it leaves an imprint on the reader. Once the book is closed, we might imagine that on a free Saturday we could talk over tea with Jane Eyre at Thornfield Hall or settle in for a story in front of the fire at Laura's *Little House in the Big Woods*. As writers, our job is to create this memorable setting—not only so readers can enter fully into our world, but also so we enjoy our daily visits there.

In his book, *No Plot? No Problem! A Low-Stress, High-Velocity Guide to Writing a Novel in 30 Days*, National Novel Writing Month founder Chris Baty suggests that writers set their novels where they live or, at the very least, in a place they know. A participant in my National Novel Writing Month workshop disagreed with Baty's advice, choosing instead to set her novel in a futuristic world she created. She defended her choice by saying it freed her to add anything she wanted to the setting, a definite plus when writing a book quickly. Whether you choose to set your book in your backyard or on Mars, your characters are going to need to be somewhere for the next twenty-six days.

WHAT SETTING IS

A novel gives the reader a world to visit for the duration of the story, complete with all the sights, sounds, smells, textures, and tastes of reality. In order for this complete world to come together, the author needs to be aware of creating a setting on three levels: landscape, location, and props. Let's look at each in turn.

LANDSCAPE. The landscape provides the backdrop for the story, the events and emotions that surround the novel's action. *Maisie Dobbs*, the first book in Jacqueline Winspear's mystery series featuring the character of the same name, is set against the backdrop of World War I England. Whether Maisie is eating a meal with her widowed father or working as a nurse at a makeshift hospital at the war front, the landscape of war is present, informing the description of the specific location and creating a pervasive atmosphere and mood.

LOCATION. Within the larger landscape, the setting contains specific locations, places where the writer sets the action. In these places, we watch the characters do their jobs, shop for groceries, fight with their children, make love, and sleep. If the locations are done well, they tell us something about the characters. We see the places the characters have chosen to live and work, and that tells us who they are. When a character describes a street or a room, we learn about who they are through their descriptions. In Steig Larsson's *The Girl With the Dragon Tattoo*, we learn little about Lisbeth Sanders from her own words about her apartment—just that it's a place to crash, make sandwiches, and work on her worn-out sofa. We learn much more about Lisbeth and her home when we see the apartment through the eyes of journalist Mikael Blomkvist: "All her furniture seemed to be strays. She had a state-of-the-art PowerBook on an apology for a desk in the living room. She had a CD player on a shelf. Her CD collection was a pitiful total of ten CDs by groups he had never heard of, and the musicians on the covers looked like vampires from outer space. Music was probably not her big interest."

PROPS. Props are the details that give the setting its flavor and reveal character traits. A prop might be the type of pet the protagonist owns or the books she keeps on her bedside table. These smaller pieces hold specific meaning for the character or not—but in both cases, they tell us something about who we are meeting on the page. Who can forget the sandwiches at the beginning of *A Wrinkle in Time*—liverwurst and cream cheese for Mrs. Murry, bread and jam for Charles Wallace, lettuce and tomato for Meg, and tuna salad for their guest, Mrs. Whatsit? The sandwich-making props give the characters something to do while they talk, but they provide more than that for the reader. The middle-of-the-night sandwich-making details create a warm family atmosphere and portray the tastes of each character.

WHAT SETTING DOES

Setting is more than the location for the story's action. The setting depicts character attributes, propels the plot forward, and more. Here are just some of the functions of setting:

- **PROVIDES THE WHERE AND WHEN OF THE ACTION.** From the imaginary Hogwarts (the wizard school in the Harry Potter novels) to Civil War and reconstruction Tara (the plantation in *Gone With the Wind*), setting gives us a time and place to locate our story.

- **CREATES ATMOSPHERE AND MOOD.** Who can imagine *Wuthering Heights* without the moors or *Death Comes for the Archbishop* without the New

Mexican desert? Spooky, cheery, depressing, or dull—the setting sets the mood for the action of the story.

- **SUPPORTS AND CREATES PLOT.** Consider what Russian playwright Anton Chekhov wrote: "If in the first act you have hung a pistol on the wall, then in the following one it should be fired." When setting supports plot, it becomes more than a mere backdrop, dumped into the book just for show. Instead, the abandoned mansion or art museum is transformed into turning points for the story.

- **REVEALS CHARACTER.** In Jennifer Weiner's chick-lit novel *In Her Shoes*, we learn a lot about both Rose and her sister, Maggie, when Maggie looks into Rose's closet: "Rose, fat, lazy, unfashionable Rose, Rose who couldn't be bothered to exfoliate or moisturize or polish her fingernails, had somehow managed to acquire dozens of pairs of the absolutely most perfect shoes in the world."

- **FUNCTIONS AS A CHARACTER.** The setting can take on many roles, including that of an antagonist for the protagonist to fight against. Think Mount Everest and the storm in the book *Into Thin Air*.

RESEARCHING SETTING

Every writer approaches the research and creation of setting differently. Some need to see the actual locale, walk around in it, and breathe in the details. Others draw from their own memory of past travels or photos from books and the Internet.

Elizabeth George, who lives in California and sets her novels in her homeland of Great Britain, takes a trip to England before writing each book. She walks through potential settings, taking photos and copious notes. When she gets home, she uses these photos and notes to add details to her rich narratives. Edwidge Danticat, author of *Breath, Eyes, Memory*, uses her own travel photos and pictures from magazines to create a collage on a bulletin board in her office. When novelist Liam Callanan wrote *The Cloud Atlas*, his story of a missionary sent to Alaska to dispose of Japanese balloon bombs, he couldn't take the time to travel to Alaska. Instead, he used maps, books, and Google Earth to create the setting for his novel.

For the purposes of the twenty-six-day novel, Baty's advice of setting the novel where you live has its benefits. When blocked, you can take a field trip to the actual setting, seeing the park where the murder takes place or the hotel that houses the wedding reception. After soaking up actual details, you might return to the novel with a fresh take on the setting. On the other hand, creating a setting out of thin air, so to speak, gives you the freedom to make stuff up.

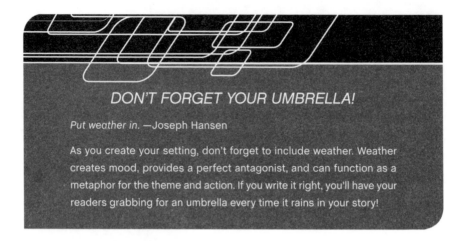

Put weather in. —Joseph Hansen

As you create your setting, don't forget to include weather. Weather creates mood, provides a perfect antagonist, and can function as a metaphor for the theme and action. If you write it right, you'll have your readers grabbing for an umbrella every time it rains in your story!

WRITE NOW

Before you begin the twenty-six-day write-a-thon, create a section of your story bible for setting. Choose the landscape, locations, and props that will be important for your story. Think abut how you want setting to create mood or generate plot. If possible, collect photographs or draw maps that will help you describe the setting while you write. You may even choose to write up some preliminary descriptions of places where your action will take place. Some writers compile a playlist of music for the time and place of their novel, playing it while they write. Others create an electronic collage they can leave open while they write, adding to their creation of place. No doubt both help the writer create a place the reader will remember.

THE PLOT

The plot is just a bribe to keep them reading.
–KURT VONNEGUT

A ristotle said that every book needs a beginning, middle, and an end. According to Chris Baty, plot is "the movement of characters through time and over the course of your book." Jane Yolen defines plot as the "sequence of events showing characters in action." However you define plot, the characters you created and crafted a setting for now need something to do. They can't just sit on the page gazing at their belly buttons. Well, they could navel gaze throughout the next twenty-six days, but that would be boring both for you and your readers! This chapter will examine various types of plots and consider how to outline a novel for the twenty-six-day marathon.

TYPES OF PLOTS

A novel plot can evolve in three basic directions. First, a character wants something but encounters opposition. This is your classic novel plot: Conflict happens. In the second type of plot, the character gets to explore his wants without a bunch of overt opposition. Instead, the character seeks something and the reader follows his journey to find it. The third direction combines both types of plots. Here's a menu of options for creating a plot.

CONFLICT PLOTS. The protagonist wants something but roadblocks keep appearing to thwart her desires. Here are the seven classic ways this plot plays out. Of course, in the best books, the protagonist fights multiple antagonists:

- Man against Man
- Man against Self
- Man against Nature
- Man against Society
- Man against Machine
- Man against God
- God against Everybody

A KINDER, GENTLER PLOT. Some books avoid outright conflict and instead focus on:

- a slice of life
- a personal revelation or discovery
- a journey
- creation

THE COMBO PLATTER. As a writer, you don't have to choose just one type of plot. The kinder, gentler plot gets more interesting when the protagonist who is searching for inner peace meets a monster on the road to enlightenment. Most protagonists get to bump up against their fair share of demons, including their own internal conflicts. Choose one major conflict as the big question or challenge of the book and then make a list of all of the little conflicts your protagonist will face.

HOW TO BUILD A PLOT

With billions of books in the world, there's no pressure to create a brand-new plot. All books—romance, mystery, literary, or horror—fit into one of the basic types of plots. Since it all has been done before, beg, borrow, or steal one of the many basic plot structures out there. In fact, crime writer Robert Campbell recommends it: "… I suggest that you occasionally spend some time studying the anatomy of books you admire, breaking them apart into [an] outline …" Take a book you love and sketch out the basic plot twists and turns. Use that as a worksheet for developing your own plot.

If that doesn't work, try fitting your plot into the classic plot structure described below.

Situation

Inciting event. Something happens to set the action in motion. Cinderella's beloved father marries a wicked woman. Poor Cinderella, who had been happily living with her father after her mother's death, suddenly gets a stepmother and two nasty stepsisters.

Complication

The plot thickens as the conflict set up in the situation intensifies. This part of the book can go on quite some time, depending on how much opposition the protagonist encounters. Cinderella's stepmother and wicked stepsisters turn her into a house servant. Then Cinderella discovers that the handsome prince will hold a ball to find a bride. The stepsisters say that Cinderella can attend, but only after she cleans the house and gets them ready. By then it would be too late. Plus, the poor girl has nothing to wear. What ever will she do? But wait! The fairy godmother shows up and fixes everything. She gives Cinderella a dress, fancy glass slippers, a magical carriage, and the warning: You must be home by midnight!

Climax

All this plot thickening leads to boiling over as the movement of the plot reaches its climax. For Cinderella, the climax happens as she dances with her handsome prince, only to hear the clock chime midnight. She rushes out of the dance, hoping to escape the castle before her beautiful clothing returns to rags (and her poor carriage men turn back into mice).

Denouement and Resolution

The plot thickened, boiled over, and now life changes for the characters. The prince has Cinderella's glass slipper, and his men search far and wide for the woman whose feet fit into the tiny shoes. At last, they arrive at Cinderella's house. The stepsisters try to prevent Cinderella from trying on the shoe but do not succeed. Cinderella slips her foot into the shoe. The prince has found his bride! In the resolution, the story wraps up the loose ends. The characters go on to live a new life, transformed by the events of the story. Cinderella marries the prince and lives happily ever after.

TO OUTLINE OR NOT?

Thriller author Jeffrey Deaver says, "I spend eight months outlining and researching the novel before I begin to write a single word of prose." But author Andre Dubus III does not outline. He simply follows the good sentences, one after another. So what's best? Both have advantages.

DETAILED OUTLINING GIVES YOU A ROAD MAP FOR WRITING. The detailed outline includes everything you need to write the book—what happens when, who it involves, historical timelines and calendars, and any additional research that adds to the plot. When mystery writer Laura Lippman plans her books, she creates "elaborate, color-coded plot charts, using index cards, sketchbook pages, colored ribbon, and magic markers."

SKELETON OUTLINING GIVES YOU THE BROAD STROKES OF PLOT OR CONTENTS. You may not know everything about what will happen to the characters but you do know where they start, how the story ends up, and the general movements the characters take to get from beginning to end. Robert Campbell creates a series of documents that help him keep track of the plot: chronology, cast of characters, timeline of history, and an agenda for each character. Some of the documents get filled out before he begins writing, but he fills out most of them as he writes. Each time he adds a new character or event, he records it in the appropriate document. The documents then become a resource for writing and revising.

I CALL THE THIRD METHOD *FLYING BY THE SEAT OF YOUR PANTS*. In this process, you start with some interesting characters and a problem or maybe just an idea. Then you write your way into a story. As Stephen King says, "I try to create sympathy for my characters, then turn the monsters loose." Or in the words of William Faulkner, "I set my characters on the road and walk beside them, listening to what they have to say."

Here is my sage advice: No one can tell you which way is best. None are best for everyone. But one is best for you. Do what works.

PLAYING WITH PLOT

Whether you fly by the seat of your pants or schedule every single breath your characters will take during the course of the novel, it's good to take a few plot tricks into the month with you. From the silly to the practical, these tools will help you create winning scenes for your write-a-thon novel.

LET'S PLAY CARDS! An old writing exercise invites writers to create three stacks of index cards: character, place, and action. Writers select one card from each stack and write a scene based on what they have chosen. Make this exercise work for your book by creating cards that relate to your characters, setting, and plot. To add more interest, invite friends to add their own ideas for each of the three categories. Throw those cards into your stacks without looking at them. Whenever you wonder what happens next, draw three cards and write.

ASK QUESTIONS. Mystery writer Jean Bedford uses a series of questions to help her keep her plot going in the right direction. Create your own questions that you can use to move your story forward each day. Here's a place to start:

- What is the main story?
- Where are the characters going?
- How will they get there?
- What obstacles will they encounter?
- How can they overcome these obstacles?
- What happens next?

THE SCENESTORM. I don't like to create long, detailed plot outlines. By the time I'm done, I feel like I've already written the book, and the fun disappears. But I do like to have a loose idea of what might happen in the book. Early in the process, I try to schedule a big old scenestorm—a brainstorm for possible scenes. Lay out your list of characters and settings in front of you. Ask the magic questions that we talked about in the ideas chapter:

- What if …?
- I wonder …?
- Wouldn't it be interesting if …?
- If only …?
- Why?
- Why not?

Write down everything you can think of, the crazier the better. What if Cinderella decides to bag the dance and go on an adventure? Where would she go? Who would she take? What if she met the prince on the way, only he had traded places with an ordinary person to avoid having to get married? What if the prince was gay? What if Cinderella was? Let your imagination soar. Once you have a list of potential scenes, use it as a guide or simply as an inspiration while you write.

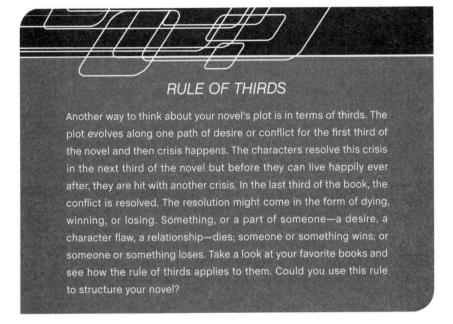

RULE OF THIRDS

Another way to think about your novel's plot is in terms of thirds. The plot evolves along one path of desire or conflict for the first third of the novel and then crisis happens. The characters resolve this crisis in the next third of the novel but before they can live happily ever after, they are hit with another crisis. In the last third of the book, the conflict is resolved. The resolution might come in the form of dying, winning, or losing. Something, or a part of someone—a desire, a character flaw, a relationship—dies; someone or something wins; or someone or something loses. Take a look at your favorite books and see how the rule of thirds applies to them. Could you use this rule to structure your novel?

WRITE AND LEARN

I've long taken comfort in Theodore Roethke's words, "I learn by going where I have to go." Whether you are a seasoned novelist or a beginning writer, you learn about plotting by writing a novel. Don't worry about the right way or the best way to plot your novel. Just write it.

POINT OF VIEW

*To put this most simply, point of view is merely
a decision the writer makes that will determine through
whose eyes the story is going to be told.*
—Elizabeth George

You've created characters, designed a setting, and mapped out a plot. Now comes the big decision: Who gets to tell this story? Will you tell the tale from the eyes of a single character or many? Will you play God and get into the heads of every person? Or will you step back and let the characters hash out their conflicts on their own?

No doubt you have a vague memory of what your high school or college English teachers said about point of view. Point of view can be categorized and combined in multiple ways. I've narrowed the field to the most popular points of view. Know that you can always do something different or combine these choices in any way that makes sense to you. Here's a quick guide to point of view.

CHARACTER VIEWPOINTS

Several different viewpoints get the author inside the heads of the characters. Mystery writer Elizabeth George groups these together under the heading "character viewpoints."

FIRST PERSON. The writer tells the story from inside the head of one person, using the pronoun *I.* Think Herman Melville's *Moby-Dick*: "Call me Ishmael" or Lisa Lutz's mystery novel *The Spellman Files*: "I duck into the parking garage, hoping to escape." In first person, the novelist has complete access to the protagonist and easily establishes his voice. The novelist can use syntax, diction, attitude, tone, and style of the protagonist's narration to show voice. The challenge: The novelist must figure out how to reveal events or information that the main character doesn't participate in or know about. Character-driven books are often written in the first person.

THIRD PERSON. The writer is still inside one character's head, but this time tells the story using *he, she,* or *they.* This is also called third-person limited or third-person subjective. The benefits and challenges are similar to the first-person point of view. But in the third person, the writer must convey the protagonist's voice without using the self-revelatory *I.*

Here are two different but equally compelling examples. In the mystery *The Daughter of Time*, Josephine Tey portrays the recuperating Inspector Alan Grant: "Grant lay on his high white cot and stared at the ceiling. Stared at it with loathing. He knew by heart every last minute crack on its nice clean surface." In just a few sentences, we know that Grant is in some sort of a hospital or care center. We can feel his frustrated impatience. Middle-grade author Megan McDonald also uses third-person subjective for her Judy Moody series. The first book, *Judy Moody*, begins: "Judy Moody did not want to give up summer. She did not feel like brushing her hair every day. She did not feel like memorizing spelling words. And she did not want to sit next to Frank Pearl, who ate paste, in class. Judy Moody was in a mood." Judy Moody might not be speaking, but we clearly hear her voice in these opening sentences. Judy emerges from the page as a round and cantankerous character.

SHIFTING FIRST PERSON. The writer tells the story through the voices of multiple characters, each speaking in the first person. Each character must have her own distinct voice or the reader can get confused. The advantage, of course, is that the author is no longer limited to what one person thinks, does, or sees. The author can tell the story from inside the head of several people. Perhaps the best example of this is the middle-grade novel *Seedfolks* by Paul Fleischman. The novel is set in an inner-city neighborhood and tells the story of a community of neighbors who transform a vacant lot into a community garden. Each chapter bears the name of a neighbor and tells a slice of the story in his or her own words. In chapter one, Kim tells her story: "I stood before the family altar. It was dawn. No one else in the apartment was awake." In chapter two, Ana says, "I do love to sit and look out the window. Why do I need a TV when I have forty-eight apartment windows to watch across the vacant lot, and a sliver of Lake Erie?" Each chapter tells a portion of the story in the distinct voice of a new character. In many ways, the method becomes the message: The story about a community garden is told by the members of the community.

SHIFTING THIRD PERSON. The writer tells the story from multiple points of view in the third person. The goal for this is to present each chapter in a tone unique to each character, even though the narration is written in the third person. Mystery writer Elizabeth George is the master of the shifting third-person point of view. In chapter one of her novel *With No One as Witness*, we are in the head of detective Barbara Havers: "Detective Constable Barbara Havers considered herself one lucky bird: The drive was empty." In chapter two, we are inside the head of Detective Inspector Lynley: "Despite the early hour at which he rose the next morning, Lynley found that his wife was already up." In these brief first sentences, the reader is introduced to the informal cadence of Detective Constable Barbara Havers, who is "one lucky bird," and the more formal tones of Detective Inspector Lynley, "despite the early hour at which he rose." Third person and shifting third person lend themselves well to plot-driven books.

OMNISCIENT

The author puts on the narrator's hat and plays God. The narrator knows, sees, and hears everything that happens and chooses what, when, and how to reveal it. Beyond the details of action and dialogue, the narrator comments on historical events, cultural norms, and the values of the characters. The narrator, like a fine storyteller, becomes the central character in the book. Charles Dickens expertly used omniscient point of view. Here are the opening lines of his novel *A Tale of Two Cities*:

> It was the best of times, it was the worst of times, it was the age of wisdom, it was the age of foolishness, it was the epoch of belief, it was the epoch of incredulity, it was the season of Light, it was the season of Darkness, it was the spring of hope, it was the winter of despair, we had everything before us, we had nothing before us, we were all going direct to Heaven, we were all going direct the other way—in short, the period was so far like the present period, that some of its noisiest authorities insisted on its being received, for good or for evil, in the superlative degree of comparison only.

OBJECTIVE

The objective point of view doesn't enter into anyone's head but simply tells the story through action and dialogue. A novel from an objective point of view reads much like a movie script or a play. The narrator is like a movie camera, relaying what can be seen through its lens. The advantage: The action and dialogue tell the story, without the messy interference of a narrator. The disadvantage: The reader may not connect with the characters. Reading the story may be more like overhearing a conversation at a restaurant—interesting but minimalist. Ernest Hemingway's short story "Hills Like White Elephants" is told from the objective point of view:

> The American and the girl with him sat at a table in the shade, outside the building. It was very hot and the express from Barcelona would come in forty minutes. It stopped at this junction for two minutes and went to Madrid.
>
> "What should we drink?" the girl asked. She had taken off her hat and put it on the table.
>
> "It's pretty hot," the man said.
>
> "Let's drink beer."
>
> "Dos cervezas," the man said into the curtain.
>
> "Big ones?" a woman asked from the doorway.
>
> "Yes. Two big ones."

CHOOSING POINT OF VIEW

Just reading a few books on point of view made my head swim. How do you decide which one to use for your novel? Each point of view decision has pros and cons. Here are some guidelines to help you decide what will work best for your novel.

START WITH WHAT YOU KNOW AND LOVE. As readers, we prefer certain points of view to others. Make a quick list of your ten favorite books of all time. What point of view does each author use? Which do you like best? Start with what you know and love.

CONSIDER YOUR STORY. As a writer, you know your story best. You know the characters, the setting, and how the plot unfolds. You know who can handle the responsibility of telling this story and who cannot. Look at your story bible and ask yourself these questions.

- Who can tell the story best?
- Who would be a reliable narrator? Do I want a reliable narrator?
- Who would be an unreliable narrator? How would that help the narrative unfold?
- Which point of view will work best for this particular story?
- Which point of view best portrays the themes of this story?
- Which point of view will readers related to best?
- When I hear the story in my head, what point of view is it in?

THINK ABOUT YOUR STRENGTHS. Every writer has his own set of strengths. Think about your work as a writer thus far. Which point of view feels most comfortable to you as a writer? Which point of view do you do best?

PLAY WITH POINT OF VIEW. Man Booker Prize-winning novelist Kazuo Ishiguro auditions narrators for his novels by writing a few chapters from various characters' points of view. Maybe the best way to decide what point of view works best for your story is to try writing a scene from different points of view. Try it in first person. Then try third-person subjective. Or try your hand at omniscient. Both during and after this writing practice, consider these questions:

- Which felt most natural?
- Which was easiest?
- Which presented the fewest problems?
- Which reads best?
- Which is most conducive to this particular story?
- Which allowed the protagonist's voice to unfold most clearly?

WRITE NOW

Once you have a sense of which point of view will work best for your novel, write a few more scenes. Pay attention to and make a note of:

- how long each scene is in terms of word count or pages, depending on how you want to track your progress
- how long it takes you to write each scene

In the upcoming section, Life Training: Schedule the Marathon, you will plan your marathon schedule. You will decide how much time you need to write each day and how many words you will need to accumulate in order to finish the write-a-thon in twenty-six days. Knowing how long it takes you to write each scene will help you plan your write-a-thon.

THREE MORE *W* QUESTIONS

*The body does not want you to do this. As you run, it
tells you to stop but the mind must be strong. You always go
too far for your body. You must handle the pain with strategy …
It is not age; it is not diet. It is the will to succeed.*
—Jacqueline Gareau, 1980 Boston Marathon champ

Most writers agree: Drafting a novel is hard work. Drafting a novel in twenty-six days, much like running a 26.2-mile marathon, borders on the insane. As marathon champion Gareau says in the above quote, the runner succeeds through will and strategy. The novelist must do the same. In the midst of the write-a-thon, when you think you've hit a wall, knowing the answer to these three questions might be the strategy that saves you: 1) What am I writing? 2) Who am I writing for? 3) Why am I writing this book?

WHAT AM I WRITING?

One of the best writing assignments I got came from my web designer. She asked me to write a short introduction—less than one hundred words—to my website. That assignment helped me focus both my work as a coach and my website writing. Whenever I got lost in writing a specific page, I would look back at the one hundred words and ask, "What does this page have to do with the main story of the site?"

At some point in the middle of writing the novel, you will get lost. You will wonder what your characters are doing and where they need to go next. The protagonist will be stuck in a swamp of a mess—literally or figuratively—and you will be banging your head against the desk. In these moments, it would help if someone would throw us a line and pull us (and our story) to safety. Luckily, we don't need someone else. We can create our own safety line.

Screenwriters create loglines for their scripts as a sales tool. The logline is designed to tantalize potential directors and producers into buying the script. For the novelist, the logline becomes our lifeline. It reminds us what the story is about and where it is going. In a sense, the logline can pull us out of the muck and put us back on solid ground. Here's a logline for *The Wizard of Oz*:

A Kansas farm girl, lost in the magical land because of a twister, must take a dangerous journey to see the wizard of Oz while being pursued by the wicked witch of the west and her evil helpers, in order to find her way home.

Take a moment to write a logline for your story. Make sure your logline answers these three questions: 1) Who is the story about? 2) What does the protagonist want? 3) What does the protagonist need to overcome?

When you have finished writing, copy your logline on a real or virtual sticky note and keep it near you during the twenty-six-day write-a-thon. Whenever you hit a speed bump, take a look at the logline. Review the above questions. Consider how the scene you are writing relates to the big picture of your story. Then write.

WHO AM I WRITING FOR?

During the 2010 National Novel Writing Month, I completed a series of children's novels for young readers. Many times during the month, the only thing that kept me going was the picture of one of my potential readers on my desktop—my daughter. When I started the series a year earlier, I read a few pages for her. She loved it. "When can I read your book?" she asked. Whenever I felt my attention drifting from the project, I looked at her picture and heard her words in my head, "When can I read your book?"

Having a potential reader in mind as we write can increase our chances of finishing our novel. We are no longer writing just for ourselves. We have an audience who is waiting for the book, who needs to read this story to gain insight or be encouraged. Maybe the potential reader is you. Maybe it is someone you know, a friend or a family member. Maybe it is someone you have to create the same way you conjured up your protagonist. Take a moment to define or create your ideal reader. If you have a picture of this person, put it on your desk. If you need a picture, find one in a magazine, throw it in a frame, and put it where you can see it every day.

Here are questions to help you define your ideal reader:

- Who is your ideal reader?
- Name your ideal reader's gender, age, and socioeconomic class.
- Who are your ideal reader's favorite authors?

- How does your ideal reader read books—in one big gulp or slowly?
- What else does your ideal reader buy?
- Where does your ideal reader shop?
- What does your ideal reader need?
- What does your ideal reader want?
- What does your ideal reader eat?
- What does your ideal reader do professionally?
- What else interests your ideal reader?
- How will your book help your ideal reader get through his day or night?

When you get to the place where you don't think you can write another word, take a look at your reader. What will she think if you quit? What will he do with his free time if you don't finish this book? Can you live with that pressure? If you can, you need to find a reader who looks a bit more pitiful and needy, and whose guilty stare will get you to put your butt in the chair and those fingers on the keyboard.

WHY AM I WRITING THIS BOOK?

Why do writers write? Someone said, "Because it isn't there." I heard another published novelist claim that she wrote to overcome boredom. I write for very selfish reasons. Writing books helps me work through the difficult questions and experiences life throws at me. When I don't understand an event or cannot overcome a loss, I give a similar challenge to a character and watch her struggle with it, hoping to learn something I can use in my own life. On days when my focus wavers and I don't know what to write next, I remind myself why I am doing this. Connecting to my purpose for writing the book gives me the energy and enthusiasm to keep going for one more day.

WRITE NOW

In the first section of this book, you wrote your vision for the ideal writing life. This book will become a part of that vision. Take a moment to consider why you are writing this book. Use the following questions to help you sketch out your writing purpose in your project journal:

- What purpose will this book serve?
- What personal questions or passions led you to write this story?
- What about these characters interests you?
- How will this story make the world a better place?
- What are you passionate about in this story?
- If you could summarize your reason for writing this book in one sentence, what would you say?

RESEARCHING THE NOVEL

When you step away from the "write what you know"
rule, research becomes inevitable, and it can add
a lot to your story. Just don't end up with the tail wagging
the dog; remember that you are writing a novel, not a
research project. The story always comes first.
—Stephen King

Novelists get paid to make up stuff. Still, well-placed research can make a novel's characters, setting, and period come alive. Whether a character is performing surgery at the war front or buying a pair of Manolo Blahniks, rich details garnered from research add depth to the story. But writer beware: Too much information, spewed out by a character or narrator in museum docent style, can read like a guidebook instead of a novel. Plus, you're writing this book in twenty-six days. How much research do you have time for?

WHERE TO LOOK FOR THE 411

You need to research your novel quickly in order to complete it during the twenty-six-day marathon. That means that big trips to Japan to find out what real Japanese food tastes like is probably out of the question. So how does the writer find information before and during the twenty-six-day write-a-thon?

START WITH YOUR EXPERIENCE. Several years ago I had an allergy attack at a writers conference. At the hospital, one of my writer friends said to me, "Look at it this way: The allergic reaction, the ambulance ride, this emergency room stuff—it's all research."

Your life experience holds treasure troves of information for your novel. Everything you do can become fodder for your book. Take copious notes about the basic experiences of your life, from shopping to child care. Next, start making life plans based on information you want to include in your twenty-six-day novel. Thinking about setting your write-a-thon story in an amusement park? Take a day trip. Need to know how police process criminals? Find out if you can take part in a citizen's academy at your local sheriff's department. Want some basic information about beer making? Tour a brewery.

When your book needs an information infusion, look back at your own experience or schedule a new one. Remember—it's all research!

CONSIDER WHO YOU KNOW. Maybe your life is pretty dull. You spend most of your days schlepping between work and home, hoping for a few extra minutes to work on your book before you fall asleep at night. Your biggest excursion in the last few months was a trip to Costco. Instead of having big adventures, you live vicariously through the wild excursions of your friends.

What kind of information do you need to fill out your novel? Are any of your family members, friends, neighbors, friends of friends, or other acquaintances having these experiences? As you plan your book, schedule interviews with anyone you know who can give you inside information from their personal experiences.

GET CONNECTED VIA SOCIAL MEDIA. A writer colleague of mine needed specialized information for a mystery novel she was writing. She put out a request on Twitter and within a day had connected with an expert in the field. Before the end of the week, she was interviewing her expert through Skype. While writing this book, I would do random surveys of friends and strangers on both Facebook and Twitter. No matter what I asked (What character would you like to have over for dinner? How do you research? Where do you write?), people were willing to answer. Because social media connects you not only with your friends but also with acquaintances and strangers who share similar interests, it can be a rich resource.

FIND IT ONLINE. If you cannot find your source after running through the people you know through six degrees of separation, you will be able to find either information or a source online.

- Information. Trying to find out what a marijuana plant looks like or who founded the Boy Scouts of America? Any old search engine should help you locate this information in a few clicks. A quick Google Blog search will let you know if someone blogs about a topic. You can also set up a Google Alert to e-mail you when information pops up online about a topic you are researching.

- Geography. Need to describe what central Africa looks like? Looking for a map of the route between Nashville and Los Angeles? The Internet is rich with maps and photos of the places you want to write about. From Google Earth to a wide array of photo websites, you can find detailed pictures of the places you want to describe in your book.

- Sources. Most trades and professions have their own associations, complete with a website, online directory, and other resources. In addition, most topics have groups of experts and hobbyists who gather online and in person. Several sites collect the names of trade, professional, and hobby associations, making searching for them amazingly easy.

BOOKS. There's nothing that says, "I'm writing a book" like a trip to the library or used bookstore. While most information can be found easily online, a book can provide reliable, detailed information for the writer. Decide what kind of books you will need during the twenty-six-day write-a-thon and load up before the writing begins. That way, you'll have everything you need at your fingertips.

WHEN TO RESEARCH

Thanks to the Internet, we can research our novels twenty-four hours a day. But should we? While you will do most of your novel's research before you begin writing, you'll also do some research during and after writing your book.

BEFORE. Do any heavy research before the twenty-six-day write-a-thon and put it into your story bible. If you can, create a bookmark folder of sites that you think might be helpful while you are writing. You might also purchase or rent any movies, books, or magazines you think you will need for the write-a-thon. But don't over-research. I've seen many novel projects die because the author was so committed to research that he never started writing. Don't fall into that trap. Research enough to start the project and then write. You can fill in the holes later.

DURING. Research during the novel can be another big trap. The author of a period novel wonders how eighteenth-century corsets were made and searches online. Three hours later, the author knows minute details about corsets but has lost her writing time for the day. Chris Baty recommends that writers stick to the five-click rule—learn what you can in five clicks online or forget about it. Because I lose track of clicks, I set a timer for my research. I give myself five or ten minutes to find something online or in a book. If I can't find it, I write the scene the best I can, highlight it in yellow with a note to myself to come back and fix the research, and move on. If this is information I absolutely must know, I schedule research time (apart from writing time) to do it.

AFTER. Novel research can always be filled in or fixed during the editing process. After the write-a-thon is over, do the research you didn't have time to do during the write-a-thon. Fill in all of those big blank spaces you left when you were too busy to find out what the first lumberjacks ate.

BE NICE, BUY LUNCH, AND SAY THANK YOU!

Mystery novelists Faye and Jonathan Kellerman have said, "All the information is out there. Footwork, a forthright manner, and a nice smile help to reel it in."

"Be nice and say thank you" may seem like something your mother would say, but so be it. Most people who might serve as experts for your novel will be willing to take time to talk to you. But they'll be happier and more willing if you are nice to them, buy them lunch, and say thank you. Acknowledging them in your book doesn't hurt, either!

COURSE TRAINING

PLAN YOUR NONFICTION BOOK

THE TWENTY-SIX-DAY BOOK

*Anyone who thinks this sounds boring doesn't have
a runner's mind set or hasn't chosen the courses well.
To a runner in just the right place, each repetition there has
a comfortable sameness to it. And each run there also
is a little different from any other.*

—Joe Henderson

As writers, the topic and type of books we choose become our course. For the duration of the time we are working on this book—be it twenty-six days or two years—we live and breathe these ideas. You need to figure out what kind of book you are going to write. And you need to know what type of book you could finish in twenty-six days.

The best kind of book to write in a month is a short one. (Duh!) The National Novel Writing Month goal is to write a 50,000-word book in a month. This is a pretty good length for a first nonfiction book. In fact, many nonfiction bestsellers come in at well under the 50,000-word mark. *The Secret* by Rhonda Byrne is only 35,793 words, while *The Prayer of Jabez: Breaking Through to the Blessed Life* by Bruce Wilkinson comes in at a mere 14,984 words. You'll need to think about how many words you'll need to make your book work. We'll get to that later. First, let's think about genre.

For years, I've heard people say that the reason people do National Novel Writing Month instead of National Nonfiction Writing Month is that it's too hard to write nonfiction in a month. Jabberwocky! Of course you can write a nonfiction book in a month. You might not be able to research *and* write your dissertation in a month, but you can certainly write a nonfiction book in a month. This section explores the types of books that are especially suitable to the twenty-six-day writing marathon. It's not that other types of books won't work for the write-a-thon—it's just that these work best:

1. MEMOIR. Having lived it is the next best thing to making it up! In the memoir, you tell your life story. Or, as you might want to call it, "Just a few episodes from my life story." If you're 103, you're not going to be able to tell a story from every single year of your life and do it in twenty-six days. (Or maybe you can, as long as they are six-word stories or poems.) If you've got a compelling story to tell from your life, a twenty-six-day writing marathon might just help you get it on paper.

2. THE BIG IDEA BOOK. A big idea book takes a single big idea and spins it into a short book that explores or explains the idea through anecdotes and evidence. Examples include Seth Godin's *Tribes: We Need You to Lead Us* and *Made to Stick: Why Some Ideas Survive and Others Die* by Chip Heath and Dan Heath. Big idea books are not complex. They simply present one groundbreaking idea in a way that helps the reader get excited by the idea and pass it on. That's why these books become runaway bestsellers—they are both revolutionary and accessible.

3. THE HOW-TO BOOK. The how-to book takes something you, the author, know how to do and teaches others how to do it, too. Chris Baty's *No Plot? No Problem!* (34,642 words) does this well. *No Plot? No Problem!* unpacks the novel-writing process and shows readers how to do it on their own in a short time frame. Another example is Brooke Siler's *The Pilates Body*, which teaches exercises for readers to do to achieve the look and fitness level of an expert Pilates student. The book *Fish! A Remarkable Way to Boost Morale and Improve Results* by Stephen C. Lundin, Harry Paul, and John Christensen teaches readers how to motivate employees (17,401 words).

4. THE PROCESS BOOK. The process book gives readers a process to follow and the tools they need to do the process for a time period between 21 and 365 days, or simply to use the process repeatedly. This might include a book of retreats, exercise routines, or menus. The book I wrote with my husband, Harold Eppley, *Growing Together: Spiritual Exercises for Church Committees*, takes a process we developed for committees to do together that includes prayer, questions, and Bible study. We created the process and then used it to develop fifty exercises on a variety of topics. Another example is coach Cheryl Richardson's self-coaching guide, *Life Makeovers: 52 Practical and Inspiring Ways to Improve Your Life One Week at a Time* (45,538 words). Each of her weeks includes an essay, challenge, and resources.

5. ESSAYS. A book of essays collects short writings around a subject or theme. Rachel Naomi Remen's *Kitchen Table Wisdom* (75,976 words) is a collection of inspiring stories about Remen's work with people who are dying of cancer. Richard Carlson wrote several books of short essays such as his best-selling *Don't Sweat the Small Stuff ... and It's All Small Stuff* (36,509 words). Many spiritual writers compile books of devotions, short essays based on biblical passages or spiritual themes. These books are often created to appeal to a specific market—such as businesspeople, parents, or people in recovery.

6. THE LIST BOOK. The list book is a variation on the book of essays. The writer develops a list of ten or twelve or ninety-nine things you need to know on a subject and spins out a series of essays or information for each item on the list. Kent M. Keith did this with his book *Anyway: The Paradoxical Commandments: Finding Personal Meaning in a Crazy World* (13,485 words). Chérie Carter-Scott took ten of her own ideas about life and wrote the book *If Life Is a Game, These Are the Rules: Ten Rules for Being Human* (31,822 words). Of course, your book doesn't have to be a serious, let's-change-the-world tome. You could write a humorous list book. Or you could write a list book that is nothing more than a list—no essays involved.

Barbara Ann Kipfer did this with her book *14,000 Things to Be Happy About*. The author started compiling the list of happy things in sixth grade and it grew to be a superlong list and megabestseller.

7. A BOOK OF QUOTES, PRAYERS, OR INSPIRATION. Find a theme that rocks your world (and your market). Then write your own wisdom or borrow from the great minds of history and collect the sayings in a book. These books can be wildly popular because they are easy to read and great for nabbing quotes for speeches, reports, and dinner party conversation. John Lloyd and John Mitchinson put together a clever book of quotes titled, *If Ignorance Is Bliss, Why Aren't There More Happy People?: Smart Quotes for Dumb Times*. Amy Gash collected quotes from children's books for *What the Dormouse Said: Lessons for Grown-Ups From Children's Books*. Barbara Bartocci has created a whole series of short prayer books under the title *Grace on the Go*. Each brief book of prayers is geared toward a different market—dieters, financial worriers, or people in grief. Kim McMillen created her own book of life lessons, *When I Loved Myself Enough*. Each page records some small lesson she learned in her life such as, "When I loved myself enough, I quit answering the telephone when I don't want to talk."

8. THE PARABLE. The parable book includes one very short story that teaches the idea of the book. The idea embedded in the story solves a problem that readers have in an innovative and inspiring way. Popular books in this category include *Who Moved My Cheese?* by Spencer Johnson (11,112 words), *The One Minute Manager* by Kenneth Blanchard and Spencer Johnson (15,553 words), and *Raving Fans: A Revolutionary Approach to Customer Service* by Ken Blanchard (20,799 words). Yeah, it kind of looks like Blanchard and Johnson own this market. Not true. But they're good at this kind of book.

So there you have it: eight types of books you could write in a month. No doubt there are others I have missed or failed to mention. Add them to the list. Now comes the tough part: deciding which book to write.

WRITE NOW

How do you decide what kind of book to write? In a moment, we'll think about topics, passions, purpose, and all that good stuff. First, review the list of types of books. Recall the books you have read and loved in the past—what categories do they fit into? Take a look at your bookshelves and count the books in each category. In your project notebook, make a list of the ten books you have appreciated the most in your life. What type were they? What features did they have that you liked (short sentences, good stories, great ideas, etc.)? You will want to incorporate some of these features into your book. Next, list all of the features you don't like in nonfiction books. Keep these lists. They will help you build a book that you'd go out of your way to buy.

THE PROJECT BINDER

*I collect lines and snippets of things somebody might say—
things I overhear, things I see in the newspaper, things I think
up, dream up, wake up with in the middle of the night. I write
a line down in my notebook.*

—RICHARD FORD

You need to have a place to hold your ideas and manage your projects. I know that people use many things for this—from canning jars to filing cabinets to computer files. I read about a guy who had just finished a novel. During the year of writing, he had put lots of cute, quirky, and poignant thoughts onto scraps of paper. He knew he'd eventually work these into the book—so he kept them handy in a paper grocery bag near his desk. The day before he sat down to type them into the computer, his wife—thinking this precious package was a bag of trash—tossed a year's worth of notes into the garbage can. Fortunately he got home before the garbage collector mistook his treasure for trash. The writer was able to rescue his year's worth of brilliant ideas. Learn from his mistake: Don't store your precious ideas in anything that might be mistaken for a garbage bag.

Instead, think about using a project binder. You already have a project journal. That's a great first step. It holds your initial plans and ideas. It's portable. And it's a great place to think in writing. But it doesn't hold research real well. The project binder can hold additional information. Get a three-ring binder and a set of tabbed dividers with pockets. Each tabbed divider can represent a section or a chapter. Put your ideas and research here. Clip articles and photos. Put in research notes and random thoughts. When ideas come your way, write them down on that index card or notebook you carry with you *at all times* and put that in the notebook.

When my husband and I wrote *The Spiritual Leader's Guide to Self-Care*, we started writing in March and turned it in December 1. I was pregnant when we began, had a baby in August, took a month off with her, and we still met the deadline. What saved us? The project binder. *The Spiritual Leader's Guide to Self-Care* is a fifty-two-week guide to wellness, complete with exercises and resources. I gave each section of our book a section in the notebook and filed away random thoughts and references all year. Each time I watched a movie that I thought could go in the book, I filled out an index card and stuffed it in there. When it came time to put together the resource list, it was all in the notebook! All I had to do was type it up. Since then, I've used a project binder (or two) for every book I've written.

Some of my clients use an electronic project notebook. That works well for a nonfiction book project, because electronic documents and files are searchable. Just remember to back up your files!

Create your project binder.

WHAT DO YOU KNOW?

Actually, I'm an overnight success. But it took twenty years.
—MONTY HALL

O vernight successes happen to people who put in years of preparation and training. As I mentioned earlier, some researchers believe that people who become stars in their field usually put in ten thousand hours of practice. (Yeah, you heard that right!) You only have 624 hours in the next 26 days, and you should use at least 208 of those hours to sleep. That leaves 416 hours for working, writing, and pleasure. Here's my philosophy: When it comes to writing, we all bring 10,000 hours of expertise (416 days) to the table. Most of us have been preparing to write some book our entire life—we just don't know which book that is! This section is designed to help you figure out the book you are meant to write.

WHAT DO YOU KNOW?

This exercise will help you gather your experiences and training together. You will discover your hidden areas of expertise. Write each of the following four topics on a separate page in your project journal. Then list everything you can think of in each category.

EDUCATION AND TRAINING. This is formal or informal training you have had. It could be anything from your bachelor's degree in physics to your regular yoga class to the team-building training they made you take at work.

EXPERIENCE. What experiences have built who you are today? List experiences from all areas of your life—home, business, and community. Did you play drums in your church band or raise a child with special needs? Put it down. Have you spent twenty years in therapy? Put it down. Parenting, marriage, and that crazy talk you had with the pharmacist all fit in this category.

SPECIALIZED KNOWLEDGE. What types of information do people come to you to learn? Are you good at directions, cooking, or crochet? Have you been forced to learn something due to necessity, like needing to care for an ill family member? Make a list of everything you have specialized knowledge in, even if it wasn't something you asked to learn about.

INTERESTS. What ideas, topics, and people are you curious about? Think about the kinds of magazines and books you buy, what headlines pull you into an article, what TV shows you tend to watch. Start detecting your interests by observing your own life. What compels you to look or listen? What do you pay attention to?

You may want to take a few days to compile this list. Ideas will come to you as you move on to other exercises. That's okay. We will come back to this list in one of the next sessions.Here's an example

EDUCATION	EXPERIENCE	SPECIALIZED KNOWLEDGE	INTERESTS
BA Theater	parent	clergy mysteries	gardening
BA Religion	minister	Greek	children
MDiv Theology	rural life	seizures	yoga
MA Literature	parenting	feeding tubes	
National Writing Project			

THE POWER OF PASSION

*Write something to suit yourself and many people will like it;
write something to suit everybody and scarcely anyone
will care for it.*
—JESSE STUART

I've met many writers who are searching for their million-dollar idea—the book thateveryone will love, that will make money and change the world. It rarely happns that way. Instead of looking for the ideas that other people might be passionate about, consider what stirs you. Think about the ideas that have changed your life. The books or blogs that end up being successful often come from the writer's own passion. And a good thing, too! The road to publication can be perilous. It takes passion to get there.

Here are some real-life examples from the world of books:

- Irving Stone's first book was about Vincent van Gogh. It was rejected sixteen times. *Lust for Life* was finally published in 1934 and has sold twenty-five million copies.

- Dr. Laurence J. Peter's manuscript *The Peter Principle: Why Things Always Go Wrong* was rejected thirty times. A publisher said, "I can foresee no commercial possibilities for such a book." When the book was published, it sold more than 200,000 copies in its first year and was translated into thirty-eight languages.

- After multiple rejections, author and illustrator Beatrix Potter self-published *The Tale of Peter Rabbit*. It sold so well that a publisher eventually picked it up. Nearly one hundred years later, Peter Rabbit is still selling well!

How do you find your passion? Children's writer and poet Ralph Fletcher asks his readers to consider their *fierce wonderings* and *bottomless questions*. I ask clients to consider what they would talk about, buy, attend, or seek out no matter the time or cost involved. Think about it, readers. What are you passionate about? Follow your passion and you may write a book that changes lives.

WRITE NOW

Take a few minutes to answer these questions in your project journal:

- What topics on your previous list are you absolutely passionate about?
- What topics do you find yourself lecturing about at parties?
- What problems or worries do you wish your book could solve?
- What questions or ideas keep you up in the middle of the night?
- What would you buy, attend, or seek no matter the time or cost involved?

FIND YOUR PURPOSE

The unread story is not a story; it is little black marks on wood pulp. The reader, reading it, makes it live: a live thing, a story.
—Ursula K. Le Guin

The writing that *works* (inspires, entertains, or educates a reader) often *serves a purpose*. Sometimes it serves a *greater purpose*. According to the authors of *The Power of Full Engagement: Managing Energy, Not Time, Is the Key to High Performance and Personal Renewal*, purpose "fuels focus, direction, passion, and perseverance." These authors define healthy purpose as something that is a challenge, internally motivated, and serves a greater purpose.

Writing that serves a purpose supports the reader in some way. It might be writing that entertains, informs, helps, humors, inspires, consoles, connects, gives hope, provides direction, or engages! Writing that serves a *greater purpose* does something to better a life, a family, or the world. This writing might raise money for a cause, raise awareness for an important political or cultural issue, or educate readers about a danger or an opportunity.

Whatever topic you are writing about, having a purpose will help you gather the energy you need to finish the twenty-six-day writing marathon. You might be willing to give up television, regular meals, and date night for something that matters to you. You won't be able to give up anything if the project is a piece of fluff that doesn't matter to anyone—you included. So choose something that matters—at least to you.

WRITE NOW

To consider the purpose of your writing, look back at your lists of experiences and passions. Ask yourself, if I chose this project:

- What purposes will this writing serve?
- Who will it serve?
- In what ways will it support the readers?
- In what ways does the work support a greater purpose? Is that important to me?
- Which one of these projects inspires or energizes me?

DETERMINE YOUR WRITING PROJECT

I hate writing. I love having written.
—Dorothy Parker

I meet a lot of people who want to write. Many never finish anything. Why? They have too many ideas. Because the possibilities are endless, they produce nothing. Instead they wander from idea to idea, not finishing anything. The only way to start and finish the writing marathon is to choose your project and stick with it.

You've done a lot of self-examination over the past few chapters. You've asked yourself about your experiences, education, passion, and purpose. You probably have one or two projects in mind. This chapter will help you choose one project. Start by answering this question: What do you want to have written a month from now?

Got it? Not quite? Then take a look at the questions in the Write Now section below. As you read each one, jot down or speak aloud the project that comes to your mind. Don't think too much—just answer.

WRITE NOW

- What project am I passionate about?
- What project will help other people the most?
- What project will be the most fun?
- What project best fits into my life right now?
- What is the one project I want to finish before I die?

Now you know which project you need to do, right? Good. In the next chapter, we will talk about understanding your book's market.

DISCOVER YOUR MARKET

*Understand that you need to sell you and your ideas
in order to advance your career, gain more respect, and
increase your success, influence, and income.*
—JAY ABRAHAM

Stephen Covey says, "Begin with the end in mind." You now have lists of your experiences, passions, and purposes. You know what book project you will complete during the write-a-thon. The final thing to think about is this: What do you want to do with the book? Some writers write only for themselves or their immediate family—to find healing or pass on a story to a future generation. Other writers want to have their work published. Still others will want to use their work as a tool to make money or increase business. Knowing what you want to do with the book and then understanding your market will help you write a book that works for your readers. This chapter will take you through a process that helps you define your book's market.

We begin a book project with a clear sense of our message. We rarely think about the living, breathing people who might read the book. (Unless we are really angry with those people and want to write the book to get back at them or show them how smart we are!) Big mistake! We need to write our book with the reader in mind. That way, we will create a product that people actually want to purchase.

Earlier in the book, I talked about the reasons people write a book. Let's take a second look at the reasons we want to write this book. This time we will also consider our audience. Review the list of reasons you may be writing this book. For each reason that fits you, determine the audience. For example, if you check number one you might add, "As a child safety advocate, I have something to say to parents and teachers about how to keep children safe."

1. You have something to say to _____.
2. You have a unique point of view that will interest _____.
3. You need to build credibility with _____.
4. You want to teach _____ who you are.
5. You want to build a bigger platform among _____.

6. You can't afford therapy. Working things out in print will help _____.
7. You think like a writer, and _____ will want to hear what you have to say.
8. You make up stories for _____.
9. You have material that will help _____.
10. You want to make money from _____.

If your answer to any of the above questions is *everybody*, go back and do the assignment again. If you think everybody wants to read your book, chances are good it won't appeal to anyone. The more clear you are about who is in your market, the better chance you will have of selling your book or using it to attract business. In the next section, you will get über-specific about who is your ideal reader.

GETTING SPECIFIC

In this section, you will compile a description of your ideal reader, what types of books he buys, what sort of content she wants. You can do this work in the project journal or create a mind map or collage for your project binder.

Who is your ideal reader?

- Is your idea reader male or female?
- How old is your ideal reader?
- Where does your ideal reader live? (e.g., West Coast, city dweller, etc.)
- What is your ideal reader's specific life status? (e.g., married, mother)
- What is your ideal reader's specific experience? (e.g., runner, cancer survivor, atheist)
- Does your ideal reader belong to a specific profession (e.g., nursing) or type of profession (e.g., technical)?
- Do your ideal readers gather in groups (e.g., Society of Actuaries)?
- Do your ideal readers get together online?
- What does your ideal reader want?

What types of books does your reader buy?

You can get a sense of your ideal reader's tastes by checking out the professional and hobby associations that cater to your reader. Most associations have bookstores on their websites stocked with the kinds of books that appeal to their members. Check out where these books are shelved in your local bookstores. You can also look at the trade or retail periodicals geared toward your ideal reader. The style and content of the articles as well as the ads will give you some idea of what your reader wants. For example, a beading magazine usually has multiple projects in it. That might mean that the beading hobbyist would be more interested in a book of ideas and projects than a tome on the history of beading. Most periodicals also have a book review section, which will give you more ideas about what your reader is interested in.

What kind of content does your reader want?

This is the step where you get to put your detective hat on. Scour the blogs and search through Twitter and LinkedIn groups to find out what your potential reader is clamoring for. Write down anything that might be relevant. Maybe some blogger is out there saying, "I wish someone would write a funny book about surviving chemotherapy," or "I wish I had a book of fun things to do in Milwaukee."

Now that you have a more complete picture of your ideal reader, think about your project. Do you think your project will help you achieve your goal? Will it help you make money or build a bigger platform? If not, what could you add to the project or how could you tweak it so it is more marketable? You will be thinking about these ideas in the next chapter, when you design your book.

Write a paragraph or two about your ideal reader, including the places where she hangs out and groups she hangs out with. You might even want to create a picture of her. Keep this near you when you write. Writing to the needs and hopes of your ideal reader will support you in overcoming writer's block.

And don't forget to save all your work from this chapter for your book proposal. An agent or editor will want you to define the market for your book.

DESIGN BOOK STRUCTURE

Many races have been won and lost because of course knowledge.
—Patti and Warren Finke

n a real marathon, someone else plans the course. The runner chooses the course based on any number of criteria—difficulty, timing, location, and so forth. A runner friend of mine selects her marathons based on how beautiful the terrain is. She wants to run on courses that give her visual pleasure.

In the months before the race, marathon runners try to learn as much as they can about the climate, course, and terrain. They want to know about the running surface, obstacles, bathroom and water stops, and any tight turns that might prove challenging. They make a race plan, crafting a strategy that includes everything from what they will wear to how fast or slow they will run each section of the course.

In this marathon, you get to plan the course. Your course is your book—and the structure that supports it. This chapter provides ideas for creating a book structure to go with your topic and book type.

The book structure is like the foundation and framing that you build the house on and around. Without both foundation and framing, a house cannot stand. Neither can a book. The proper framing will make your book easier to write. And, just like with a house, the framing for your book must match your content. You wouldn't put up a huge frame for a small Cape Cod home. In the same way, you wouldn't want to design a book that had twelve 8,000-word chapters if you wanted to write short, inspiring tips on marketing or exercise. This chapter will lead you through a series of steps to help you determine your book's structure.

STEP ONE: CHOOSE BOOK TYPE. No doubt you have already chosen your topic and the type of book you are going to write. Each of the book types lends itself to specific structures, as discussed above. As a reminder, the types of books that work well for the writing marathon are:

1. Memoir
2. The Big Idea Book

3. The How-To Book
4. The Process Book
5. Essays
6. The List Book
7. A Book of Quotes, Prayers, or Inspiration
8. The Parable

STEP TWO: DEFINE YOUR READER. Before you can determine your book's structure, you need to get a sense of who is going to read this book. Revisiting the home metaphor, we wouldn't want to build a three-story house for an elderly couple who could not manage climbing stairs. In the same way, we won't want to write a book using a structure that doesn't work for our reader. A book of long essays won't work for the harried manager who is desperate for some quick ideas on how to build her team's spirit. On the other hand, a book of quick quips and advice might frustrate the college professor who wants solid evidence. You defined your ideal reader in the last chapter. Now consider what kind of a book your ideal reader wants to read. List the features of this reader's favorite books including length, type of content, style of presentation, and more. Save the information you gather here for your book proposal.

STEP THREE: DEFINE YOUR CHUNKS. In a sense, every book is a collection of small chunks. Your chunks can be anything you want them to be, including a series of processes, essays, lists, quotes, prayers, or inspiration. You might even decide that your book needs a variety of chunks. In the book *What Would You Do if You Ran the World?: Everyday Ideas From Women Who Want to Make the World a Better Place*, Shelly Rachanow collected stories, ideas in action, statistics, quotes, inspiration, and pledge forms into a book designed to help women change their world.

When you think about defining your chunks, remember the various kinds of pieces you might include:

- preface
- introduction
- resource section
- callouts
- quotes
- lists
- exercises
- ideas
- conclusion
- appendixes
- sidebars
- essays
- statistics
- questions

Now it's your turn to define your chunks:

- Looking at your major topic, what information do you want to cover in this book? It might help you to create a mind map. Put the central topic of your book in the center of a large piece of blank paper. Surrounding it, put your ideas for what information you will cover in the book. You might want to write down information in categories such as statistics, stories, research, history, culture, and anecdotes.

- What kinds of chunks do you need to communicate the important points of your topic to your reader? Maybe you know that the majority of your book will be essays, but to help your reader understand the process you are describing, you might want to add exercises or questions. Add that to your list.

- What kinds of chunks are your readers looking for? Go back to your research from step two. What types of chunks do your readers want and need for this book to be effective for them? This isn't what you would like to put in or what you think the reader needs; this is what you see the reader clamoring for.

- What kinds of chunks do you like to read and write? Don't leave out your opinion. Most writers write first and foremost to solve a problem they have. No doubt you are also your most important audience. Think about what kinds of text you will and will not read.

- How long are your chunks? Your chunks can be anywhere from 100 to 8,000 words long. Once you have a list of kinds of chunks, estimate how many of each you will need and how long they will be.

STEP FOUR: ORGANIZE THE CHUNKS. At this point in the process, you're a little like the home builder who has a pile of lumber, nails, and some tools. Just like a stack of lumber looks nothing like a house, your stack of pieces doesn't resemble a book. In this step, you figure out how the chunks get put together:

- When you look at the chunks, do they fit into major themes? You might look back at the mind map you created in step three. It might give you some ideas of the big themes.

- Do you have an organizing theme you want to use? Some books use the calendar as their theme: twelve months of recipes or fifty-two weeks of decorating tips. Other books use themes such as seasons, chronology, or geographical areas to organize information.

- Will you organize your material into sections and chapters, sections, or simply chapters? What title will you give each chapter or section?

Chunks can be put together in myriad ways. Take a look at the books you have collected on your theme for additional ideas. Also look at your favorite books. Here are a few examples from the books on my desk right now:

- Many of the parable books are simply stories told in short chapters. Each chapter also has callout quotes or lessons that help the reader know what to take away from the story.

- *What Would You Do if You Ran the World?* is divided into four sections: What Would You Do for Yourself, Your Loved Ones, the Community, and the World.

- In the book, *Beyond Buzz: The Next Generation of Word-of-Mouth Marketing*, author Lois Kelly has nine main points she wants to communicate to the reader. She gave each point a chapter.

- In the inspirational book *Highlighted in Yellow: A Short Course in Living Well*, authors H. Jackson Brown Jr. and Rochelle Pennington collected their wisdom in six thematic chapters with titles like Kindness and Generosity.

- In the book *Adaptability: How to Survive Change You Didn't Ask For*, author M.J. Ryan has five sections of chunks: Introduction, Seven Truths About Change, The Actions of Change Master (the process of accepting change), Tips for Surviving Change, and Resources.

There is no wrong way to structure a book. But there are good ways and there are better ways. Don't do what you think you have to do or what others expect of you. Structure the book in the way that works for you, the writer, and your readers. Don't be afraid to change the book's structure. If you start writing the book and discover that it needs to be structured in a different way, make it happen. The book you are holding went through many structural changes in the process of writing it. Each reorganization made the book a better product. Your changes will do the same for your book.

STEP FIVE: CREATE AN OUTLINE. You have the big chunks and the little chunks and the themes and topics that go with them. Now create an outline and topic list. You don't have to make this an annotated outline—simply get down the bare bones of how the book will look. When you are done, you should have a list of topics organized by chapters or sections. This will be your map for the writing marathon.

STEP SIX: WRITE A SAMPLE CHAPTER. It's a good idea to get a sense of how the chapters are going to work before you begin the marathon. The one sure way of doing this is to write a sample chapter. If your book has a variety of types of chunks—exercises, essays, and lists—you might want to write a few sample chapters. It will also help you later on if you can time your writing. (You don't need to be exact, but it is good to know if writing a 1,000-word chapter takes you an hour or ten hours to complete.) When you are done with the chapter, save it on your computer. Then make a note of how long did it took you to write it and how long the chapter is.

Whew! You did it! You have done the hardest part of the process—creating a chapter structure and topic list. With this information, you will be able to plan your course and write your book.

CREATE YOUR RESEARCH AND DEVELOPMENT TEAM

Half of being smart is knowing what you're dumb at.
—David Gerrold

"You can't research and write a nonfiction book in a month! There's not enough time!" said my client.

I disagree. Not only have I written several nonfiction books in a month or less (such as the one you are holding now), I've done the research while writing. It's doable. Sure, you're not going to be able to write the definitive guide to horse breeds in North America in a month (unless you have the research done or really know your stuff). But you will be able to create a book.

After working with writers for many years, I've noticed that we tend to expand our work to fill the amount of time we have. If we have a month to research and write a book, we do it. If we have six months or six years, we stretch our work to fit the time period. For many writers, research becomes the excuse to never write or finish the book. Instead, we perpetually research. The twenty-six-day writing marathon is designed to get you comfortable with good enough research. Yeah, it won't get you a Ph.D., but it will get you a pretty good book. Don't worry about any holes in your research. You can fill in missing information during the revision process. Instead, take note of it and keep writing. I use the highlight function in my word processing program to mark sections that might need additional research. That way, I can write instead of agonizing over what I don't have time to do at the moment.

You've already sketched out the structure of the book. You've put together a list of topics or chapter titles you will be writing about. Print a clean copy of your book structure, complete with topic list. Put a check by any piece of the book you can write right now—without doing any more research. Circle anything you think you need to do research on before you can write it.

Good. Now you know what you don't know! The next step is to gather what you need to write the book—your research and development team. Whether your research and development team is made up of living and breathing human beings or a collection of websites and books, you need their support to get this book written! Besides—doesn't it sound cool to say you have to meet with your research and development team?

THE REAL DEAL

When my colleague Susan Lang and I wrote the book *Welcome Forward: A Field Guide for Global Travelers*, we had a living research and development team. And a good thing, too! Susan had never been outside the country, and I had never been to an economically underdeveloped country, where the most of the travelers who read the book would visit.

Our project manager gathered together fifteen global travelers for a weekend conference in Chicago. Through two and a half days of conversations—all of them captured on a digital recorder—we were able to develop a book structure and topic list. The conversations were filled with firsthand stories of travel that we could use to illustrate the chapters. After the weekend, we were able to use the digital recordings to access those stories. The weekend participants were also available to us via phone and e-mail for further information when we got stuck.

If you have a project that will benefit by the shared wisdom of others (and what project wouldn't?), consider holding a research and development brainstorming session. You can do this in an evening, a Saturday, or over a weekend. Find a comfortable space—your living room, a community center, or the community room at the library. Provide beverages and plenty of food to nosh on. (People think better when they are eating.) Invite people you think can contribute ideas, information, or stories to your project. Create a set of questions that will help your team help you. Here are some ideas for gathering the information:

1. After you share your questions, invite participants to write down their suggestions for the book on large index cards or pieces of paper.

2. Post your questions on large pieces of newsprint and hang them around the room. Invite participants to write their answers or ideas on sticky notes and place them on the paper.

3. Post your questions one at a time and invite participants to tell stories or give information on the specific topics you are curious about. Record these.

You can also do this process in the much slower and more laborious form of interviewing team members one by one, in separate locations. This certainly has its advantages, but speed isn't one of them.

It's also good to have a team of experts who will be available by phone or e-mail during your writing process. Ask your team members if they are willing to be available for the duration of your marathon for short interactions. Don't forget to thank them in the acknowledgments when the book is done.

THE VIRTUAL R&D TEAM

Let's say you don't know anyone who can be on your team. Maybe you're shy or just hate to ask people for help. That's okay. Here's the virtual answer to the R&D team:

1. GET BOOKS. Collect the books, periodicals, and other materials that will help you during the month. No doubt you've already begun to gather some resources for your project binder. Add to that. Pile all of your research together on a shelf, in a big box, or in a stack near your writing desk. You won't want to have to wander around the house searching for the book you need while you are doing the write-a-thon.

2. GET ACCESS. Sign up for access to journals or other periodicals you might need during the writing phase of your book. And make sure that your library card is up to date! The library is a great place to get what you need to write your book. (It's also a great place to work. But that's another chapter.)

3. BOOKMARK IT. Create a bookmark folder on your browser just for this book. Keep it separate from your bookmarks for social networking and gaming sites. You're not going to have time to play games during the marathon!

4. GET AN EXPERT. You may not realize it, but you may need some real-life expert information at some point during your writing process. You might need a story about someone losing a job or a most embarrassing moment. What do you do if you don't know anyone to ask? This is the time to put your social networking skills together. At LinkedIn, members can ask questions of anyone on the whole site. Pretty cool, eh? When you get to the site, look at the toolbar across the very top. Click on *More*, then *Answers*. When you get to the Answers page, there's a little box where you can type in your question. Go for it. As a writer, you can also use the Help a Reporter Out service to request information from thousands of potential sources (www.helpareporter.com)

5. GET A SEARCH ENGINE. You're going to need to research a few things online every day. Choose a search engine you like that works for you. You can also set up Google Alerts to e-mail you when information in your area of interest pops up online. In order to keep your writing momentum, don't spend more than five or ten minutes researching at a time. Get in, get your info, and get back to writing! Online research during the write-a-thon is much like consuming a fast-food dinner. The food isn't perfect, but it does the job for now.

LIFE TRAINING
SCHEDULE THE MARATHON

CREATE YOUR
LIFE PRIORITY LIST

*I placed the highest priority on the sort of life
that lets me focus on writing, not associating
with all the people around me.*
—HARUKI MURAKAMI

I've heard life coaches say, "You *can* do it all. You just cannot do it all *at one time*." True. Choosing to do the twenty-six-day writing marathon will mean choosing not to do some of the other activities you appreciate. Still, if you are part of the 80 percent of Americans who want to write a book before they die, there is no better time to write than now.

For years, I have made use of a life priority list—a list that names the five people and activities I will always make a priority. My list is: Self, Writing, Family, Friends, and my Coaching business. Any invitation that fits within this list frequently gets a yes. Any activity not on the list needs to prove its worth before I can say yes. The life priority list tool comes from coach Cheryl Richardson's book *Take Time for Your Life: A Personal Coach's 7-Step Program for Creating the Life You Want.* She calls the tool "an absolute yes list"—the five to ten people and activities you will always say yes to.

After years of coaching people who delayed their dreams because they put other people's dreams first, I came up with a list of reasons to do the life priority list. This is why I think having a list like this is a must:

- How you live today is how you live your life.
- When you say *yes* to that which matters least, you are saying *no* to what matters most. When you say yes to doing a million little inconsequential tasks, you are saying no to being a writer.
- The things that matter *most* must never be at the mercy of the things that matter *least*. A simple example: The hundreds of junk e-mails that jam up your in-box should never be more important than your work.
- What matters most to others might not matter most to you.

- In the book *The Incredible Shrinking Critic*, author Jami Bernard says most people think that women who say no mean yes when most of the time women (and men) who say yes really mean no. The life priority list gives you permission to say yes when you mean yes and no when you mean no.

The life priority list gives you the opportunity to do what you want to do with your life and time and not to just say yes to a million little things you feel obligated to do. Before you start the writing marathon, you need to choose what you will say yes to during the month and what you can say no to.

WRITE NOW

Using your project journal and your calendar, create a list of five things you will say yes to in the midst of the writing marathon. That means you will be saying no to everything else that comes your way. There is only one nonnegotiable on the list: writing. What are the additional yeses? What five people or activities are most important to you? During the marathon, you will orient your days around this list. You will eliminate anything that doesn't fit your plan.

MAP ENERGY FLOW

*What works for one writer
becomes paralyzing for the next.*
—Karen E. Peterson

"I'm not a morning person."
"I'm a midnight writer."
"I can't function after five."

No doubt you've said (or thought) one of the above about yourself. Each of us has genius times—the points during the day when we do our best thinking and getting those thoughts on paper. I'm a morning writer. I get up, get coffee, and write—before I do just about anything else, especially talking to people and checking e-mail. But several of my clients prefer other times of day. One client writes late at night and into the wee hours of the morning, when her husband and children are tucked safely in bed. Another starts her writing around noon, after reading the paper, answering e-mail, and taking a walk. Each of us has learned when we do our best writing and honors it.

Our ability to write, just like our energy for social, creative, and physical activities, shifts throughout the day. The only way to discover what works for you is to map your energy flow for a week. You will record your daily activities, what kind of task it was (social, intellectual, creative, or physical), and whether you had energy for it or not. By the end of the week, you will have a better sense of the times of day you write best. When it comes to scheduling your writing times, stick to the times of day you have energy for intellectual or creative tasks.

WRITE NOW

1. Map your energy.
   - Make copies of the sample chart below. For each time period, record your tasks.
   - Next to each task, record the type of task it is: physical (P), intellectual (I), creative (C), or social (S).

- Next to each task, put a plus when you had energy for the task and a minus when you didn't have energy for the task.

2. When you have finished recording your task and energy flow for a week, ask yourself:
   - When do I write best?
   - When do I like to do the other things that writers do: edit, research, submit, connect with other writers?
   - Am I doing the rest of my work, errands, and taking care of other responsibilities at the time of day that is most effective for me?
   - Is it possible to rearrange my schedule so I follow my natural patterns of energy?

Don't waste the best writing time of your day doing nonwriting things. In the next chapters, we will work on creating a schedule that works.

3. Find the holes. After you've gone through your schedule to map your energy, take a look at it again. This time, underline any activities you could let go of for a month. These are times when you are doing less essential activities (like watching television), when you have a chunk of quiet time (it might be 4:30 A.M.), or when you can sneak away from your work for a little writing.

TIME	TASK
6 A.M.—9 A.M.	
9 A.M.—12 P.M.	
12 P.M.—3 P.M.	
3 P.M.—6 P.M.	
6 P.M.—9 P.M.	
9 P.M.—12 A.M.	

PLAN YOUR
SCHEDULE

One hasn't become a writer until one has distilled writing into a habit, and that habit has been forced into an obsession. Writing has to be an obsession. It has to be something as organic, physiological, and psychological as speaking or sleeping or eating.
—Niyi Osundare

When theologian Eugene Peterson wanted to find time to read, he made appointments in his calendar with Flaubert and Dostoyevsky. One writer renamed her workshop Raleigh so when someone would call, her spouse would say, "Sorry, she's in Raleigh." I take my calendar at the beginning of every month and highlight the times of day I am writing in green colored pencil. I don't see clients or meet friends for coffee at that time. I encourage clients to schedule writing like it is a shift at work or an appointment with a physician they waited a year to see. No one would think of canceling that appointment to get their hair done or because they were tired and overwhelmed. Don't cancel this one!

That said, there are some tricks to scheduling that give you an advantage and make it much more likely that you will achieve your goal.

TRICK 1: BE SPECIFIC. Don't just say, "I am going to write 1,600 words a day." You need to also point out when, where, and what you will write. Studies show that people who write down when, where, and how a behavior will occur have a better chance of getting things done. In one study, women were asked to perform a breast self-exam during the subsequent month. One group was asked to write down when and where they would do so, while the other was not. Both groups were narrowed down to the women who expressed a strong intention to complete the task. Nearly 100 percent of those who designated when and where they would do the exam completed it. Only 53 percent of the second group did so, despite equally strong intentions to conduct the exam. In order to be 100 percent successful at finishing the writing marathon, specify the when and where of each day's writing task.

TRICK 2: MAKE WRITING AUTOMATIC. According to studies, automatic thoughts are stronger than rational ones—so if our automatic action in the morning is to turn on the e-mail before writing, we do it even if we rationally know that this is not going to benefit us. But we also have the capacity to automate the good things in our lives. In psychology, this is called a *good constraint.* Good constraints are those limits that keep us safe or healthy like always wearing a seatbelt or brushing our teeth before bed. We don't have to think about doing these behaviors because they are automatic.

You can make writing automatic by creating a when-then phrase. A when-then phrase uses environmental cues to help us take a goal-directed action. As a writer, you can link your daily writing time to any regular environmental cue that works for you. Note that you will make your when-then statement more effective if you link writing to something pleasurable—like drinking coffee or listening to favorite music. Here are some examples:

- When I sit down at the computer in the morning, I will write 1,600 words so I can achieve my goal of finishing a book in twenty-six days.

- When I have my afternoon tea at the kitchen table, I will write about three kinds of birds so I can achieve my goal of finishing my bird book in twenty-six days.

- When I get to the library at 5:00 P.M., I will write my chapter on planning casino parties so I can achieve my goal of finishing my party-planning book in twenty-six days.

TRICK 3: OVERCOME OBSTACLES. I guarantee you that the minute you start scheduling your writing time in writing, your kids will get sick, your best friend will break up with her boyfriend and will want you to rescue her from sure and certain despair, your spouse will suddenly have the desire for a deep conversation, the local cancer society will need you to be their block captain, your sister or cousin will have one teensy-weensy little favor to ask of you, and probably something in the house—like the plumbing—will get clogged up and need to be fixed.

Obstacles happen—whether we are working toward our goals or not. They're just more apparent when we have a goal we really want to achieve. We will be better able to overcome these obstacles if we plan ahead. Make a list of obstacles or distractions you expect to encounter during the twenty-six-day writing marathon. Here are some of mine:

- A child will get sick.
- I have books to read for work.
- The laundry will need to be washed.
- I have a project to edit this month.

Once you have a list, plan how to overcome the obstacles. One of my obstacles to getting this book written during National Novel Writing Month was the work I had already committed to doing. I was able to work around that obstacle by scheduling time for both writing projects during the day. That way, when I wrote my NaNo project, I didn't worry about getting my other project done because I knew I had time scheduled to do it.

You can also use the when-then statement to overcome obstacles. I created a when-then statement to help me overcome the distractions and stick with my writing schedule:

- When my child gets sick, I will put on a favorite video for her, take my laptop to the couch and write there so I can achieve my goal of finishing the twenty-six day writing marathon.

- When I see the stack of books to read, I will use the stack as a reminder that I have a book writing project to do. I will put in my writing time and then read the books so I can achieve my goal of writing my own book.

- When I see the piles of laundry, I will remember that I need to write 1,600 words on this project so I can achieve my goal of finishing this book.

In the end, the only thing standing between you and doing the work is you. If someone asks you to take time away from your writing, tell them you have to take a meeting with God, you have an appointment with Oprah, or the President is on line one. Tell them anything—just keep your appointment to write.

 WRITE NOW

Some of these exercises you will do now, some you will do when you get closer to the write-a-thon.

1. Make a writing schedule, specifying the when, where, and how of each day's writing.

2. Now that you know when and where you will write each day, you can do two things to make it more automatic and pleasurable.
   - What enjoyable activity do you already do that you can link your writing to each day? Activities might include drinking coffee or tea, sitting near a window with a view, or stopping at the coffee shop for an afternoon treat.
   - Create a when-then statement for your daily writing. Use this formula: When I encounter [external cue], then I will [goal-directed action] in order to reach my goal of [state your specific goal].

3. No doubt you have already generated a mental list of your obstacles to doing the twenty-six-day writing marathon. They might include: I'm not

ready, I'm too busy at work, who will cook dinner?, and so forth. Make a list of the specific obstacles you expect to face during the twenty-six-day marathon. For each obstacle:

- Make a plan for overcoming the obstacle. Perhaps one of your obstacles is that you always cook dinner. If you are going to write this book, you may need that time to write. A plan to overcome it might be enlisting your partner or a child to help with dinner, cooking meals ahead, or making simpler suppers.
- Create a when-then statement for each obstacle. One way to make obstacles work for you is to use them as a cue to take an action toward your goal. Taking the dinner example, you might write: "When I see my daughter warming up dinner, I will work on my project so I can reach my goal of finishing this book."

MANAGE YOUR ENERGY

*So remember the optimal formula for success: Work hard, rest,
work hard, rest. Also keep in mind the optimal formula for
disaster: Work hard, work hard, work hard.*
—John Bingham and Jenny Hadfield

I've always been a big proponent of the plow-straight-through-until-you-finish method of working. Growing up, my parents gave us the message that certain behaviors were lazy. (We learned to never admit to being bored, because the word *bored* would cause my parents to spout long lists of chores the way waiters list available beverages.) Many of my writing and editing projects have come with such tight deadlines that I've had to let go of pretty much everything but eating and sleeping to finish them on time.

According to Jim Loehr and Tony Schwartz, the authors of *The Power of Full Engagement*, the method I grew up with and sharpened in early adulthood was plain stupidity. According to the authors, spending an intense amount of energy on our work will not cause burnout. Burnout is caused by working constantly and not taking a break to rest and renew ourselves.

Runners build strength and endurance by challenging their muscles beyond their current levels and then resting. According to the authors of *The Power of Full Engagement*, "Faced with a demand that exceeds the muscles' current capacity, the body responds by building more muscle fibers in anticipation of the next stimulus." The authors have found this to be true of muscles at all levels—emotional, spiritual, and mental. Once we have pushed ourselves beyond our current limits, we need to rest and recover.

John Bingham talks about this in his book about running, *The Courage to Start*:

> ... resting is not doing nothing. Resting is giving the body a chance to recoup, to renew itself, and ultimately to rebuild itself into a body that will move faster or farther. The rest phase is the only time that the body has to bring itself up to your expectations. The training effect that we all want, the changes in our body's ability to handle the stress of running, occur during the rest phase not the activity phase. The adaptation process takes place while you are resting. The days

> when you don't run are the days when your body incorporates the
> new strength needed for the next run.

The authors of *The Power of Full Engagement* encourage readers to balance stress and recovery. They believe:

- When we spend too much of our energy without either resting or renewing, we will either break down or experience burnout. (Overuse it and lose it.)

- On the other hand, if we become couch potatoes and don't do anything, we will experience weakness and perhaps atrophy. (Use it or lose it.)

Since reading this book, I have adopted a stress and recovery model for writing. It works during twenty-six-day writing marathons, weekend writing retreats, and regular daily writing. You're going to stress the heck out of your writing muscles this month. I also expect you to take recovery breaks. Here's how one writer did it.

In *The Power of Full Engagement*, the authors speak about a writer who was used to putting in long continuous hours at his word processor to finish his books. Unfortunately, the writer could not maintain his concentration as the day wore on. Faced with a highly challenging book deadline, the author sought the help of the trainers who wrote this book. They suggested writing in ninety-minute blocks with thirty-minute breaks in between. The writer reported that the four and a half hours of daily writing with energizing breaks delivered more work than his previous eight-hour days.

Why did this work? Because the author used energy boosts during his breaks to help him recover his mental, physical, and emotional strength. Part of the key to this writing schedule is adding good recovery rituals. These include:

EXERCISE. I heard a story on NPR about inventor Trevor Baylis, who has created a battery charger that collects energy while you walk. The device can be used to power a cell phone. If moderate physical activity can recharge our cell phones, imagine what it can recharge in us. In fact, moderate physical activity can increase cognitive capacity by driving more blood and oxygen to the brain. At the University of Illinois, a research team tested the thinking of twenty-four women age sixty to seventy-five who never or rarely exercised. All of the women were put on a three-day-a-week program that included either a brisk one-hour walk or an hour of gentle stretching. In effect, the walkers were asked to push past their comfort zones physically, while the stretchers were not. After just six months, they gave the participants a series of cognitive tests and the walkers demonstrated 25 percent higher scores than the stretchers.

How will you use walking to jump-start your writing career?

- If you're already walking or exercising, plan to write for twenty to thirty minutes right after your exercise time.
- Take a ten-minute walk before you write.
- Take a ten-minute walk every time you experience writer's block.

- Take a ten-minute walk as a transition between scenes, sections, or writing projects.

Once you make walking a part of your daily writing practice, you'll discover that you write faster and more efficiently, come up with ideas more quickly, and easily solve your writing challenges. I've been combining the magic formula of walking and writing for years—to great success. Walking and writing have supported me in completing ten books and countless articles fast. Plus, the walking helps me burn off the chocolate treats I consume while working!

NAPS. Naps are not just for kindergarten students! NASA's Fatigue Countermeasures Program has found that a short nap of just forty minutes improved performance by an average of 34 percent and alertness by 100 percent. In a Harvard University study, subjects were able to recover their peak performance by taking a one-hour nap. In his book *What I Talk About When I Talk About Running*, novelist Haruki Murakami writes about taking a thirty-minute nap every day to keep healthy and improve his thinking.

A WALK IN THE PARK

In the 1980s, Association for Psychological Science Fellows Rachel and Stephen Kaplan proposed attention restoration theory—the idea that our voluntary or directed attention can be restored when our involuntary attention is highly engaged. The Kaplans discovered that being in nature boosts our involuntary engagement, helping us recover more quickly from directed attention fatigue. That's a good thing—directed attention fatigue makes us irritable and unable to write. In order for a walk in the park to restore one's energy, four factors need to be in place:

- Away. We need to be away from ordinary lives. That means that a walk in the park is better if your cell phone is off and you leave your computer at home.

- Fascination. We need to be in an environment that is conducive to effortless attention. That means that rock climbing or running an obstacle course, while fun activities, might not help us recover from directed attention fatigue.

- Extent. We need to view the environment as rich enough to be restorative. That means walking by one or two trees on a city sidewalk might not be enough. You may need to splurge and walk the extra few blocks to the park.

- Compatibility. We need to be able to get there and get around once we are there.

The bottom line? Get out of your office and walk in nature. Take different paths in the most natural spaces you can find in order to get the most out of the experience.

CONNECTING WITH FRIENDS AND HIGH ACHIEVERS. UCLA researchers discovered that women respond to stress with a cascade of brain chemicals that cause them to make and maintain friendships with other women. The researchers called their work the "tend and befriend" study. When women get stressed, their bodies release the hormone oxytocin—the breastfeeding hormone—that buffers the fight-or-flight response and encourages them to tend children and gather with other women instead. When women tend and befriend, more oxytocin is released, which further counters stress and produces a calming effect. The results were so significant, the researchers concluded, that not having close friends or confidants was as detrimental to a woman's health as smoking or carrying extra weight. Men, you need friends, too! A similar study found that friendship also reduced stress in men

Add to that another recent study on social contagion and obesity that found that people who had just one overweight friend—even if that friend lived across the country—were more likely to be overweight themselves. It follows that if you have one friend who is writing and finishing books, you will be more likely to do the same. No wonder National Novel Writing Month has become such a powerful force. The energy of more than 200,000 writers completing a big, hairy, audacious goal at once is compelling and can stir you to achieve more. When you feel stuck in your project, connect with another high-achieving writer. You'll get more done.

HEALTHY SNACKS. Marathon runners consume foods that help them maximize their energy throughout the course of the run. As a participant in the twenty-six-day writing marathon, you are no different. You need foods that will boost your brain's power. According to a study from Lund University in Sweden, eating low-glycemic index foods will improve concentration and short-term memory. Foods with a low-glycemic index include:

- fruits: grapefruit, apples, cherries, grapes, and oranges
- cereals and grains: oatmeal, bran, spaghetti, and rice

- legumes: soybeans, chickpeas, kidney beans, and lentils
- dairy products: milk and plain yogurt
- any foods that contain little or no carbohydrates including meat, fish, eggs, avocados, and most vegetables

Make a list of meals and snacks that boost your energy level. You can discover what foods boost and deplete your energy by keeping a food and energy diary. In the chapter Map Energy Flow, you tracked your energy for a week. If you can recall what foods you ate that week, record those on your chart. If not, record both your food intake and your energy levels for several days. When you are done, evaluate your chart. What foods provided enough energy for you to work for several hours? What foods depleted your energy? For example, I experience a brief energy boost from coffee and chocolate. Unfortunately, the boost doesn't last and before long, I'm ready for a nap! I have more energy for longer periods of time when I munch on healthier snacks—like grapes or a small bowl of oatmeal. Once you have a list of foods that seem to improve your energy, try them out. Observe how your energy level responds to each food. After a few days of experimenting, you will know what foods keep you energized and writing.

Before the writing marathon begins, make sure you stock up on these healthy foods. If you know what you are going to eat before the marathon, you won't have to think about it during the marathon. It will be there for you when you need it.

REPETITIVE, MINDLESS ACTIVITIES SUCH AS KNITTING, COOKING, DOING DISHES, SWEEPING THE FLOOR, OR BEADING A NECKLACE CAN BE HELPFUL. In the book *The Breakout Principle* by Herbert Benson and William Proctor, the authors suggest that breakout solutions appear when we walk away from our work and do something that is both mindless and repetitive. This practice creates the aha moment. Make a list of your favorite repetitive, mindless activities and keep it by your computer. When you are stuck, choose an activity on the list, take a break, and do it. You just might experience your own aha moment!

CORRALLING ENERGY

You have learned to manage your energy through alternating spurts of writing with energy recovery rituals. There's one last trick to managing energy: corralling and eliminating energy drains. Whenever we got a new puppy, we corralled the pup in the kitchen so her ability to chew up shoes and pee on carpets was strongly limited. That saved us from having to clean up too many messes.

During the course of the writing marathon, you need to cluster the stimuli and energy drains. Corral activities such as checking e-mail, answering the telephone, looking at the mail, and connecting with print and online media as well as social media. I am a big believer in clustering tasks. I don't answer e-mail as it comes in. Instead, I do it at a certain time each day. I don't answer the phone all the time—I return all the calls at a time that works for me. In the exercises below, you will list your energy drains and figure out how to contain them.

Finally, you will probably need to dump a few energy drains during the writing marathon. Some writers take the month off of Facebook and other social media. Others let go of emotionally costly friendships for the month. Taking a break from the people and activities that drain your energy will give you more energy to complete the writing marathon.

1. Look at the writing schedule you have been creating. Have you left time for energy recovery rituals? How can you do that?

2. Make a list of energy recovery rituals that work for you. Keep it near your writing space as a reminder.

3. Create a list of energy-boosting meals and snacks. Stock up!

4. Make a list of all of the energy drains that come at you during the day.
   • Cross off any energy drain you can dump for the month.
   • How can you cluster the remaining activities so they don't steal energy from your writing time?
   • Now that you've looked at letting go of and clustering activities and connections, are there any additional ones you need to take a sabbatical from for the month?

PRIME YOUR
ENVIRONMENT

I type in one place,
but I write all over the house.
—Toni Morrison

Our environments prepare us to behave in certain ways. Because I work at home, my environment is full of mixed cues. Everything I see reminds me of something I have to do: Dishes! Dinner! Clients! Editing! Laundry! The multiple demands for my time and energy often swallow up my writing thoughts. Before I can get to my computer to put anything on paper, I am tired and ready to give up for the day.

Clearly, this doesn't work when you are trying to complete the twenty-six-day writing marathon. In order to be successful at the writing marathon, we need to set up an environment that prepares us to write. When we live and work in an environment that shouts, "Write!" we are more likely to actually do it.

A few years ago, I took up beading. I kept my beading supplies on a shelf in my home office. Every so often, I would clear off my work desk and take out my beading supplies. Every time I did that, I enjoyed it. I loved the process of beading as well as the product. But because my beading supplies were hidden from me in a closet, I rarely beaded. A year ago, I set up a beading table in the corner of our library. My beading supplies sit on a shelf next to the table, and my current project is on the table. Every time I walk by the beading table, I see my work and think, "I could bead today." The environment cues me to bead. We need to take the same tactic for our writing environments.

So how do you create an environment that is conducive to writing? I encourage writers to discover where they write best and write there. In the book *How to Think Like Leonardo da Vinci*, author Michael J. Gelb posed the question: "Where are you when you get your best ideas?" Gelb has asked this question to thousands of people and the most popular answers included:

- in the shower
- resting in bed

- walking in nature
- listening to music

Notice that no one said that they get their best ideas at work or in front of the television. In fact, in a new study, researchers walked children through an outdoor environment before taking a test. The children who walked through a park instead of a city street scored higher.

Here are some places that famous and not-so-famous writers have found to be inspiring:

- Sir Walter Scott had an enormous desk with two working surfaces. Because Scott was driven, he always had multiple projects going at once. The dual working surfaces gave him the space to separate them.

- Mark Twain wrote on a typewriter in a gazebo.

- Daniel Silva, who writes spy novels, works in a basement office, with the lights turned low—where he can better imagine the dark things that will happen in his novels.

Here are some suggestions for preparing your environment for success:

1. CLEAR YOUR WORK SPACE. Start by committing yourself to a clean desktop. You cannot think about big ideas if your desktop is full of action items—sticky notes, unfilled forms, and long to-do lists. Try this:

- Move (or move out) keepsakes. Keepsakes can be just as distracting as stacks of work—and they need to be dusted. Move half of your keepsakes out of your office. Put the rest of your trinkets on shelves or on the wall.

- Move the tools. What else do you keep on your desk—an electronic pencil sharpener, paper clips, and a stapler? If you don't use these tools every single day, find a drawer or a closet to stow them in.

- Create a project shelf for your twenty-six-day writing marathon project. Use it to hold your project journal, project notebook, or story bible, and all of your resources, notes, and files.

2. SHUT OFF THE THINGS THAT SHOUT: "DEAL WITH ME!" University of Calgary professor Piers Steel found that 26 percent of the American public are chronic procrastinators, up from 5 percent in 1978. Steel said, "And why not? There are so many fun ways to kill time …. At work, e-mail, the Internet and games are just a click away, making procrastination effortless." In order to be successful this month, we need to turn off anything that tempts us to procrastinate. That means turning off the phone, cell phone, and e-mail. Sign off of Internet list serves. Turn off your Twitter and Facebook feeds. Write in a corner where you cannot see the gathering dust bunnies or the accumulating laundry. If you live in a noisy neighborhood, plug headphones into your computer and listen to music or soothing sounds.

3. INSPIRE YOURSELF. Once you've taken away the things that distract you from writing, it is important to leave behind a few things that inspire you to write. Here are some ideas:

- Quotes. One issue of *Writer's Digest* had an article called "The Tao of Sticky-note Quotes." It was a collection of inspirational quotes from working writers. I put the quotes that inspire me on my bulletin board in my office to remind me of who I am and what I am called to do. Here is one of my favorites by writer Natalie Goldberg: "Just write, just write, just write. In the middle of the world make one positive step. In the center of chaos, make one definitive act. Just write. Say yes, stay alive, be awake. Just write, just write, just write."

- Book cover. Every time I work on a book that doesn't have a contract, I make a mock book cover and post it near my computer. Seeing the cover reminds me to work on the book, to keep my promise to myself to work on my dream.

- Wear it! One writer I spoke to put on a big purple hat whenever she was working on her book. I've been known to wear a sparkling tiara when I am writing. Another client of mine wears a meaningful pin that reminds her to speak her truth.

WRITE NOW

Take a look at your environment and the suggestions above. Do what it takes to ready your work space for the twenty-six-day writing marathon.

If you don't have a home work space, create a writing bag and a plan for taking your work on the road. Block off weekends or days or whatever it takes to get writing. Go to a hotel, a hovel, or a coffee shop—just get out of the house.

And no mater what your situation, remember that you can write successfully anywhere. Young adult author Nancy Werlin writes at a favorite bread store. Madeleine L'Engle wrote her first books backstage at the theater, between the scenes she was performing in as a young actress. Dostoyevsky wrote *Notes From Underground* while his wife was sick and dying in the next room. My husband and I finished one of our books in the hazy days after our second child was born, often holding her with one hand and typing with the other. Do your best to create the perfect environment, but know you can write anywhere you have pen and paper.

TAKE TINY STEPS

What's all this business of being a writer?
It's just putting one word after another.
—IRVING THALBERG

W e're almost ready to make the final plans for the twenty-six-day marathon. There's just one last tool to learn: the art of taking small steps. Small steps make big goals doable. According to psychologist Robert Maurer, innovation or drastic change is very difficult. An example of innovation might be quitting an addiction cold turkey, cutting out all of your favorite foods at once, or writing a book in twenty-six days (yikes!).

Maurer says that when we anticipate taking big steps—like writing a book or a whole chapter—our brains can actually panic and our bodies go into a fight-or-flight response. This comes in handy when you're being chased by a lion or mugged. Unfortunately, the amygdala can also set off alarm bells whenever we want to depart from our usual safe routines. Every new opportunity can trigger a little fear. In his book *One Small Step Can Change Your Life: The Kaizen Way*, Maurer advocates taking absurdly small steps. These small steps bypass the fear center of the brain and we succeed.

Want to become a regular exerciser? Maurer encouraged a client to march in front of the television for one minute a day. After a month, she added another minute and then another until she felt ready to tackle an aerobics class. Want to improve your self-esteem? Maurer asked clients to name one thing they liked about themselves each day. Want to spend less money? Maurer suggested taking one item out of the shopping cart before checking out.

For years I've used the small-step method to write books and articles. When I have a tough writing assignment, I break it into small, doable steps. I take a step, break to eat or exercise, then take another step, repeating the process until the project gets done. As mentioned earlier, a colleague and I once wrote a guidebook on global travel in two weeks. We divided the sixty chapter topics by two and then did the math to figure out how many each of us had to write each day to get done and still have time to self-edit and look at each other's work and turn the book in on time.

When a client is stuck with a project, I will encourage him to divide it up into as many small steps as possible. After he has a list of small steps, I ask him to set a small-step goal for each day. For example, when one of my clients was stuck in the middle of writing a particularly difficult chapter of her memoir, I advised her to think about the chapter as a series of small scenes instead of as a whole unit. I encouraged her to write a scene, take a break, and write another scene. She reported that these small steps made this large task doable.

Anne Lamott, in her book *Bird by Bird: Some Instructions on Writing and Life*, described the small step in this way: " ... all I have to do is to write down as much as I can see through a one-inch picture frame." Then she goes on to tell the story that gives the book its title. Her brother was writing a report on birds. Lamott wrote, "[He was] immobilized by the hugeness of the task ahead. Then my father sat down beside him put his arm around my brother's shoulder, and said, 'Bird by bird, buddy. Just take it bird by bird.'"

I once worked with a student who was having a difficult time completing papers. When she got stuck, she would abandon the project and surf the Internet. We worked out a strategy that supported her in making progress toward finishing the paper when she couldn't write what she had set out to write that day. She looked over her list of small steps that needed to happen before the project could be completed and highlighted all of the steps that were different from writing: research, creating a bibliography, conducting an interview, and fact-checking. She agreed that the next time she got stuck with writing, she would work on one of these other tasks. Doing that gave her the comfort of knowing she was still working on getting the project done. It also relieved her writing anxiety and when she came back to the writing several hours later, she was able to do the work. She finished the next paper without problems.

Small steps really do make big goals doable.

WRITE NOW

You've already got a list of topics or scenes for your book. Now create a list of other small steps: research, phone calls, anything you need to do to finish this book in a month. Keep this list handy. You'll need it as you design your schedule. Here are some examples of small steps:

- Create a topic list.
- Write one section.
- Write half of a section.
- Take notes or collect ideas on a single topic.
- Write a scene.
- Collect reference books.
- Set up an interview.
- Visit two websites to gather additional information.

Divide your writing project into as many small steps as possible. When you are doing the writing marathon, you will set a small-step goal for each day. Remember, the turtle beat the hare one small step at a time!

DESIGN MARATHON SCHEDULE

Your first decision: Can you commit the time to training?
—JOHN BINGHAM AND JENNY HADFIELD

A s I've said before, writing doesn't just happen. You have to schedule it. The twenty-six-day writing marathon can take several forms, including fitting it into a thirty-day month, a long weekend, a series of long weekends, or twenty-six Sundays. In order to succeed, you will need to determine the length of your marathon, decide how you will do it, set your deadline, and schedule the writing time in your calendar. In this chapter, you will take everything you have learned about your book, your strengths, and your working style, and design the marathon that works for you. You will start by considering your manuscript length.

MANUSCRIPT LENGTH

For a runner, every marathon is the same length: 26 miles and 385 yards or 42.195 kilometers. With that fixed goal, runners can then compete against their own record by trying to run each marathon faster than the previous one.

Books vary in length. Many nonfiction books come in well under 50,000 words. Short novels happen, too. There's no reason a novel has to be humongous to provide the reader with a worthy read. In fact, most agents and publishers don't want to see a first novel that's much over 80,000 words. Here's a list of famous novels that come in under or around the 50,000-word mark:

> *The Lion, the Witch and the Wardrobe* by C.S. Lewis: 36,363
> *Fahrenheit 451* by Ray Bradbury: 46,118
> *The Red Badge of Courage* by Stephen Crane: 47,180
> *The Outsiders* by S.E. Hinton: 48,523
> *Slaughterhouse-Five* by Kurt Vonnegut: 49,459
> *A Separate Peace* by John Knowles: 56,787 words

For the National Novel Writing Month challenge, the goal is to write a 50,000-word book in thirty days. That means writers try to come up with 1,666 words or 6½ pages of double-spaced text every day. Novelists who complete the three-day writing contest typically turn in 100-page novels (that's 25,000 words). In the end, your book will be as long as it needs to be for you to tell the story. For the purposes of the write-a-thon, use the NaNoWriMo word-count goal of 50,000 words. I have no doubt that you can write the whole book, beginning to end, in twenty-six days.

You can figure out the length of your book using your book outline and a sample scene or chapter. Go back and check the word count of that scene or chapter. Multiply the single piece by the amount of scenes or chapters you expect to have in your book. Then add in any additional pieces you might have in your book, such as a resource list, an appendix, or sidebars. Add it all together, and you will have a general idea of your book's length.

So now you have your estimated book length. Next you need to consider how much time you will need to put it together.

ARE YOU A TURTLE OR A HARE?

How fast do you write? Are you a churn-it-out-in-an-hour kind of person? Or are you one of those people who must weigh every single word before you put it on paper? As the nineteenth-century writer Gustave Flaubert said, "You don't know what it is to stay a whole day with your head in your hands trying to squeeze your unfortunate brain so as to find a word."

We typically think of the hare as the writer who can finish a twenty-six-day writing marathon. (Twenty-six days? No contest! The hare can do a book in a weekend!) On the other hand, the turtle is the writer who plods away at a book for years until she finishes it. For the twenty-six-day writing marathon, you will need to call on both of your inner beasts—the turtle and the hare. The determination of the turtle will help you take one or more small steps daily, while the urgency of the hare will support you in getting your words on paper as quickly as possible each day.

Hopefully, you have already written a sample chapter or section of the book and timed yourself writing it. Now you know about how much time it takes for you to complete one small chunk of the book. About how many of these small chunks do you think you can do in a day? And how many days of small chunks will you need to complete your book?

Your answer tells you how long your marathon will need to be. And worry not. The more you write, the easier it will become. You may be more tired by day twenty of the marathon, but you will also be a faster writer than you were when you began.

SET THE DEADLINE

As I mentioned in an earlier chapter, Chris Baty started National Novel Writing Month because he believed that the only thing that stood in the way of a writer finishing a project was a deadline. Now you get to set your deadline.

Begin by figuring out when you are going to do your marathon. This program is designed to be done in twenty-six days, much like the National Novel Writing Month marathon in November or Script Frenzy in April. I appreciated the month-long marathon because it gave me a definite beginning and end. Having the full marathon in a month also helped me build momentum with my project. As Newton's theory of motion goes, objects in motion stay in motion. Finally, because I did my marathon during National Novel Writing Month, I had the support of other writers who were at the same task. If you have a month you can set aside to write the marathon, do it now. The end of the month, or your twenty-six days, is your deadline for finishing the project.

That said, your life circumstances might make it necessary for you to do the marathon in different ways. You can set up your twenty-six-day marathon in any way you want: twenty-six days within a two-month period, a series of weekends, or a day a week for twenty-six weeks. One writer who doubled as a college student knew she would be too busy in November to finish a book. She started in October so she would have a head start on word count and be able to take a week off during exams. You may need to work around professional projects or family obligations. Take account of those situations now and set aside your twenty-six days in a way that works for you. Once you've done that, you will know your deadline, too.

FINAL TIPS

The last thing you will do is schedule your marathon writing—blocking out time each day for the twenty-six days of writing so you can finish your book by the deadline. As you do this, here are some random tips:

- Schedule more time for yourself at the beginning and the end of your marathon. Doing so gives you a good start and allows you extra timein case you are behind when you get to the deadline.

- Chris Baty discouraged his NaNoWriMo writers from taking off more than two days of writing in a row. It's that momentum thing again.

- Even when you are busy, write for at least twenty minutes a day.

- Plan for time off. During my writing month—when I wrote this book—I took every weekend off. That meant putting in a 5,000-word day on Friday or adding a few extra words each day of the week.

- If you get behind, take time to reassess. Can you crank out 6,000 or 9,000 words this weekend so you can catch up? Do you need to give yourself a bit more time each day? Do you need more idea-gathering time so you have something to say when you write? Make adjustments.

The only thing left is to make the marks on your calendar. (Oh yeah, and write the book!) Do that.

Then take a deep breath and say, "I am a writer." This month you get to pretend you are a world-famous writer who cannot shift her schedule for anyone. I don't care if your children are vomiting. Give them a bucket, rub their sweet little heads, and write with your other hand!

Finally, dear readers: Have fun with the marathon! Writing a book fast is a wild, wonderful adventure. Buckle your seatbelts, hold on tight, and let the ride begin!

MEASURE YOUR PROGRESS

This mile marker is farther than most people will ever reach.
—MARATHON MILE MARKER SIGN

Anthony Trollope wrote every morning from 5:30 to 8:30 A.M. During that three-hour period, he aimed to write 250 words every fifteen minutes. He worked with a weekly page goal—usually forty pages a week. The prolific John Grisham writes a page a day. Stephen King writes ten pages each day, even on holidays. Ernest Hemingway stuck to a strict schedule of writing 500 to 1,000 words a day, starting early in the morning, before he started drinking. He kept track of his word count by writing it on the side of a cardboard packing case. Some days, he'd put in extra time so he could take the next day off to fish.

You now know *how much* you to need write each day to complete the twenty-six-day marathon. You have what scientists call, "a measurable goal." Goal-setting researchers and theorists Edwin Locke and Gary Latham coined the phrase, "That which cannot be measured cannot be achieved." You also have subgoals—daily word counts you must meet in order to finish the marathon. Now you need a method to track your progress toward your goal and keep you accountable.

If you were training for a marathon race, you would have a training schedule. You'd probably have a running buddy to keep you accountable. You might even have a website or chart where you could mark your progress. You'd keep track of information like the number of miles you had run, how long it took you, and how many calories you burned. When I started exercising seriously, I recorded my daily progress on an exercise calendar next to my desk. I never needed to wonder about my progress—I could see it.

For National Novel Writing Month, the more than two hundred thousand participants track their progress by entering their daily word count on the site counter. At the end of the month, they paste their entire manuscript in the word-count program so they can be declared winners.

If you're writing this book on your own, you may not have the same kinds of social support that runners or NaNoWriMo participants have—but you can still create a helpful measurement system to keep you accountable and on track. In fact, creating that system will make you more likely to achieve your goal. Here are some ideas:

- **CHOOSE HOW YOU WANT TO MARK YOUR PROGRESS.** You might want to write a certain number of pages a day, an amount of words per day, or a "chunk" of your book.

- **CREATE A CHART OR CALENDAR TO TRACK YOUR DAILY PROGRESS.** If you choose to use word count to mark your progress, your Microsoft Word program will track your word count for you. The program also allows you to select and count specific sections of your work. Make use of that to know how many new words you have written. Then record your daily output on a chart or calendar.

- **USE ONE OF THE FREE COMPUTER OR SMARTPHONE APPLICATIONS AVAILABLE TO TRACK YOUR DAILY WORD COUNT.** During National Novel Writing Month, you can register and track your word count via computer or smartphone at the NaNoWriMo site (www.nanowrimo.org). The write-a-thon section of my website, www.writenowcoach.com, offers a free write-a-thon word count tracker. WriteChain is a free word-count tracking application compatible with iPhone, iPod, and iPad.

- **PURCHASE OR CREATE A SEPARATE CALENDAR FOR YOUR TWENTY-SIX-DAY PROJECT.** Give yourself a colorful sticker every time you complete your daily writing goal.

- **ASK A FRIEND, FELLOW WRITER, OR WRITING COACH TO BE YOUR AC-COUNTABILITY PARTNER.** Agree to send them an e-mail once a week to let them know you are on track for finishing your writing marathon.

Finally, be sure you also give yourself rewards along the way. Every time you achieve a major subgoal—finishing a section of the book or completing a week of writing—do something to celebrate. I usually reward my daily writing with a trip to the gym or a walk around the neighborhood. One client of mine rewards his daily writing with a round of his favorite video game. After Jack London wrote his 1,000 words each day, he'd reward himself by getting drunk with his friends. Anthony Burgess, author of *A Clockwork Orange*, rewarded his daily output of 1,000 words with a dry martini. I prefer a good latte, but do what works for you. Burgess was a wildly prolific author. His method clearly worked for him.

PART TWO
THE WRITE-A-THON

I've been a fan of the TV show *The Biggest Loser* since the series began. On the show, two trainers work intensely with their obese clients to support them in creating and maintaining an exercise program that works for them. Throughout the contestants' duration on the show, the trainers stick to them like a burr on exercise fleece. Clearly, the method works. In the same way, I've seen my coaching clients make great strides simply because they finally have a goal, a plan, and an accountability partner.

A few years ago, one of my clients had a challenging writing assignment. She needed to write her research-heavy book in less than three months while coaching and parenting. When she got to the last part of the race, she had to cancel her clients and hole up in a house at the shore to finish. We spoke every single morning about what she would do. At the end of the day, she e-mailed me about her progress. I wish I could talk to each one of you every day of your book-writing marathon, too. I can't. But I have a good solution. Just after my last book was published, a coaching client said, "Reading this was like having you in my back pocket for a few weeks."

This section is designed to give you the benefit of having a writing coach at your side during the write-a-thon. These short essays will encourage and sustain you when you feel like giving in or giving up. You don't have to read them straight through. Read what you need when you need it. Or, do what I used to do with the Bible when I was a superstitious ten-year-old: Close your eyes, flip open the book, and point to a sentence. That just may be wisdom designed specifically for you at the moment you need it!

PUT YOUR BUTT
IN THE CHAIR

*One thousand hours of lap time reading before the
age of five helps your child learn to love to read and learn.
(That's about half an hour a day!)*
—New Futures School, Albuquerque, NM

*The way you define yourself as a writer is that
you write every time you have a free minute. If you didn't
behave that way you would never do anything.*
—John Irving

Want to run a marathon? You have to train. You need to put in the time running each week to be able to run the race and avoid injury. In order for babies to learn how to read, they need to put in the lap time—thirty minutes a day of lap time reading. It's no different with writing. If you want to finish your book, you are going to have to put in the time.

But how do you do it? How do you make sure you can stay in your chair and get the work done? Scientists call this self-regulation—the ability to discipline yourself, to do what you promised to do. Over the years, writers have had some pretty creative ways of avoiding distractions and keeping their butts in their chairs. Here are a few of them:

- Victor Hugo had his valet keep his clothes until he finished his writing.

- Novelist Liam Callanan wrote one of his books in a Panera Bread café. The fear of someone stealing his laptop kept his butt in the chair.

- Novelist Junot Díaz avoids distractions by listening to orchestra music and writing in his bathroom, sitting on the edge of his tub.

- Novelist John Wray wrote *Lowboy*, which takes place on a New York City subway, on trains. He rode throughout the city with his headphones on, typing away at his laptop. His initial reason? Writing on a train cut out distractions like e-mail and telephone calls.

- Nicholson Baker wrote his first novel on his daily commute. He dictated chapters of *The Mezzanine* into a voice recorder.

- Keith Donahue, author of *The Stolen Child* and *Angels of Destruction*, wrote both novels by hand on his subway commute to and from work.

- Best-selling novelist Danielle Steel writes until she gets hold of an idea that works. Once that happens, she says: "I sit at my typewriter and type until I ache so badly I can't get up. After twelve or fourteen hours, you feel as if your whole body is going to break in half."

The only way to write a book is to write it. Put your butt in the chair, on the edge of the bathtub, or on a commuter train and scribble or speak or type until it's is done.

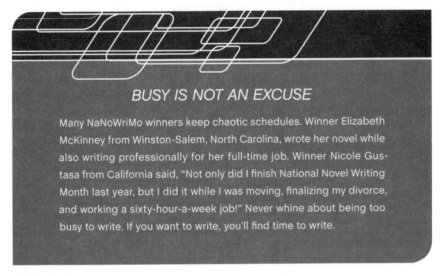

BUSY IS NOT AN EXCUSE

Many NaNoWriMo winners keep chaotic schedules. Winner Elizabeth McKinney from Winston-Salem, North Carolina, wrote her novel while also writing professionally for her full-time job. Winner Nicole Gustasa from California said, "Not only did I finish National Novel Writing Month last year, but I did it while I was moving, finalizing my divorce, and working a sixty-hour-a-week job!" Never whine about being too busy to write. If you want to write, you'll find time to write.

NO PAIN, NO GAIN

According to research by Ryan Howell of San Francisco State University, when we exert effort and experience some amount of stress in order to learn something or gain competency, we tend to feel better at the end of the day and throughout our lives. So fear not, weary writers! If you leave your writing time with an aching butt or a sore brain, trust that it is good for you. You'll feel better at the end of the day and much better by the end of the twenty-six-day writing marathon.

GET A CHEERING SECTION

---

*We can't all be heroes because someone has to sit
on the curb and clap as they go by.*
—WILL ROGERS

We write more when we connect with others who are writing productively. As I mentioned in an earlier chapter, a recent study on friendship and obesity suggested that having just one overweight friend increases our chances of being overweight. Other recent studies suggest that happiness is also contagious. It just makes sense that having one friend who writes like mad increases our chances of doing the same. The success of NaNoWriMo suggests that writers get more done when they're connecting with other writers. Other writers offer valuable support. You are who you connect with.

GET A CHEERING SECTION

If you've ever watched a real marathon, you know that cheering crowds buoy the spirits of marathon runners. Writers also need people who cheer us as we complete this wild and crazy write-a-thon. Make a list of everyone who has been a cheerleader for you in the past. If you can, create a visual representation of them to keep near you during the writing marathon. Also, create a list of current cheerers who can offer encouragement during the writing marathon. Ask these cheerleaders if they'd be willing to send cards, food, and encouragement during the write-a-thon. Tell these friends that you are doing a write-a-thon and, while they'd be bored (and distracting) sitting next to you on the sofa and cheering you on as you write, you could use some virtual cheering during the month. Ask if they would be willing to send you a card or an encouraging e-mail in the middle of your marathon (or whenever you think you will most need encouragement). It will help them (and you) if you can be specific about what kind of cheering you need. If hot food is what you need, friends are often willing to do a trade—feed them a few times now in exchange for them delivering meals during the write-a-thon.

FIND A WRITING BUDDY

Writing buddies hold each other accountable to writing goals. When you meet with a potential writing buddy, begin by defining and sharing your writing goals. Then discuss what you need from the writing buddy relationship. Some people want to be challenged while others need encouragement. Some writers want a friend to look at their work. Once you decide your purpose, there are multiple ways to stay connected. Choose the method that works best for your lifestyle. Some writers eschew social media and want to hear a friendly voice on the phone at the end of the day, while other writers don't like to be bothered with the phone but connect with hundreds of people on social media sites each day. In addition, some tools will be better suited to your goal. If you want your writing buddy to review your work, e-mail might be better than a phone call. On the other hand, if you just want to do a quick check-in, sending a text message might be your preferred method of communication. Here are some suggestions for connecting with a writing buddy:

TEXT MESSAGE. Exchange text messages as a way of staying accountable to your writing and to report your daily progress.

E-MAIL. Write a brief e-mail at the end of a daily writing session or the end of a writing week to report your progress and state your next goal. You can also use e-mail to exchange burning questions, paragraphs, or chapters.

SOCIAL MEDIA. Connect on Facebook or Twitter. On Facebook, you can commit to posting what you achieved each day for the marathon. Or, you can create a private group for those who are taking part in the write-a-thon. Either way, ask your buddies to give you a "like" for your progress. On Twitter, you can create a group using an application like TweetWorks. Or, you can set up a Twitter Chat to connect around your writing project at a specific time each day or each week.

PHONE CALLS. Hold a weekly mastermind phone call to brainstorm suggestions for overcoming obstacles and moving forward. Better it by using a video conferencing tool like Skype.

WRITE-IN. Spend a morning at a coffee shop, an afternoon at a local bookstore, or a weekend at a hotel and write. Sometimes hearing a friend type away can motivate you to do the same. In addition, writers can take brainstorming breaks to help each other overcome writer's block.

I meet regularly with a mastermind partner and with friends who write. At least once a month I attend an author reading at a local bookstore, hoping some of their wisdom, discipline, and good luck will rub off on me. When I speak with other writers about writing, I get more focused. I write more. They write more. Everyone benefits.

GET A LIFE!

If you have other things in your life—family, friends,
good productive day work—these can interact with your
writing and the sum will be all the richer.
—DAVID BRIN

Want to write better? Get a day job. Or sign up for a volunteer gig. Just get out of the house and do something! I'm not kidding.

Having all day to write seems to be every writer's dream. When I speak, writers tell me they would be more productive if only they didn't have to go to work, take care of their kids, or do the laundry. Phooey! Writers who have all day to write simply have more time to procrastinate and less stuff to write about.

Having a life can make you a better writer. Listen to what dentist and novelist Alaa al Aswany has to say about why he still practices dentistry:

> Society is a living organism and you must keep up. That's why I still
> practice, though for only two days a week. I will never close the clinic.
> The clinic is my window. I open it to see what is happening in the
> street. You can't get disconnected from the street, as a writer; that's a
> common mistake. You can be too easily welcomed every night by the
> richest people and the most influential. It is very dangerous because
> it is that relationship with the street that made you successful in the
> first place.

History proves that some of our best and most prolific writers also had day jobs. William Carlos Williams was a physician. Anthony Trollope was a post office inspector. Carol Shields raised five children. John Dunning is a bookseller. The poet William Stafford worked as a professor at Lewis & Clark College.

So there you have it, writers! Don't worry if you don't have all the time in the world to write. Your interaction with the world matters, too. The time you spend away from your writing just might fuel some of your most brilliant work!

WRITING AND PARENTING

"I get up at 5:00 A.M., walk three miles with girlfriends, come back and get the kids ready for school. When they leave, I pull up whatever file I was working on yesterday, edit my way through, and then keep going wherever I left off. I continue till about 3:15 P.M., when I magically turn into a mom again." —Jodi Picoult

DUMP THE GREMLINS

Send your judgment Gremlins out on the patio or lock them in the trunk of your car, or send them on a field trip. Be sure to thank them for caring as you wave good-bye.
—B. Lynn Goodwin

If you're a writer, you've encountered the gremlins. You have nasty little voices in your head telling you that your ideas are stupid or your writing stinks. Know this: You're not crazy. It's just that over the years, you've taken in all of the advice—nasty and kind—that your teachers, critics, and friends have given you. When you start to write, the advising voices rush in like the plague. You can't get a word on the page before you're hearing your second grade teacher say, "Make sure you spell it right!" You've got a brilliant phrase bursting out of your brain, but you can't get rid of the voice of that editor saying, "You're just not literary enough for us." You hit your writing stride and you remember what a critique group colleague said, "I just don't know if you got what it takes to write. No offense. I'm just sayin'." Before you even get started, the voices in your head defeat you.

I like author B. Lynn Goodwin's advice: Send the gremlins on a field trip or lock them in the trunk of your car while you are writing. Anne Lamott suggested locking up the critical voices in little glass canning jars and setting them on a shelf, out of sight of your work space. I don't care what you do with the little voices in your head, as long as you send them away until you are done with your writing time. You cannot write with that kind of nasty stuff floating around in your head. Kick them out. Now.

While you're kicking out the voices in your head, distance yourself from the living, breathing gremlins in your life. The one thing writers don't need is people who belittle them. A year or so ago, I was doing a writing project that required a bit of research. I called on colleagues for books that I needed to complete my work. When I borrowed a book from one colleague, a Ph.D. student, she said, "I suppose most of your work doesn't require many scholarly books." Zing!

I have been in several toxic writing groups. They didn't help—they just allowed other people to feel superior at the expense of others. One of my friends got so beat up after one of our critique groups that she considered stopping. She didn't. She now has finished and sold her novel as well as completed a Ph.D. in creative writing. The critical group members who were so hard on her have not published a thing.

All of us have naysayers and critics who are more than willing to belittle or dismiss us. You don't need this kind of help at any time, but especially when you are trying to do the twenty-six-day writing marathon. Release these critics from your life for the duration of the marathon.

When you start editing your work, you can invite in the gremlins—or your inner editor—to do the work of cleaning up the manuscript. You'll still want to keep the gremlins on a short leash; you want their constructive critique, not insults. They'll remind you to avoid using run-on sentences or too many adverbs. But for now, when you are trying to write, send them packing. Trust me, it works!

AVOID MONKEY MIND

You can only run one race at a time.
—ROCHELLE MELANDER

Religion professor and scholar Huston Smith wrote the following about meditation. He could have been talking about writing. See what you think:

> The motions of the average mind, ... are about as orderly as those of a monkey cavorting about its cage. Or rather a drunken crazed monkey. Nay, more, like the prancings of a drunk, crazed monkey. Even so we have not conveyed its restlessness; ... The mind is like a drunken crazed monkey with St. Vitus's dance who has just been stung by a wasp. Few who have seriously tried to meditate will find this metaphor extreme.

What happens in your brain when you try to write? My clients report a number of distractions and doubts. Listen in:

- I need to do more research.
- I'm not a real writer. I should quit.
- Maybe I could create a product for ...?
- I wonder if I could find those shoes online?
- I need a blog.
- I need to update my status on Facebook.
- Oh, oh, oh! I have a great idea for a book.
- Did I ever answer that e-mail to ...?
- Maybe I should work on that other writing project.
- I wonder what's happening on Twitter?

Take the distracting thoughts, add in a ringing phone, the buzz of your cell phone every time you have a text, the ping of e-mail arriving, kids or co-workers stopping by with questions—and be amazed that anyone writes anything. We are distracted, frenzied, impatient, and disorganized. We have difficulty managing our thoughts or our time.

Psychiatrist Edward Hallowell calls this *attention deficit trait.* He says, "It's a condition induced by modern life, in which you've become so busy attending to so many inputs and outputs that you become increasingly distracted, irritable, impulsive, restless and, over the long term, underachieving. In other words, it costs you efficiency because you're doing so much or trying to do so much, it's as if you're juggling one more ball than you possibly can."

Fortunately, the fix is easy:

1. SCHEDULE TIME TO THINK. Anyone who creates needs quiet time to mull over ideas and organize their thoughts. It's tough to do that when machines and people are vying for your attention. Commit to giving yourself at least thirty minutes of quiet time each day to think about your project. Don't use this time to read, write, or talk on the phone. Just be. Go for a walk, take a drive, or simply sit in a chair and stare out the window.

2. DIFFERENTIATE. When we spend 90 percent of our computer time responding to the ping of our e-mail or playing games on Facebook, it can be difficult to use the same space to write a sales letter or a poem. Find ways to make writing time different from work or play time. For example:

- Shut the door of your office and turn off your phones.
- Turn off all Internet access and close your e-mail.
- Set aside or clear away the rest of your work from the space.
- Change your desktop's wallpaper for your writing time.
- Use music or lighting to help define your writing time.

3. CHANGE YOUR ENVIRONMENT. I'm beginning to believe that mothers have to leave home in order to write (or write while the rest of the family sleeps). I've had too many of those "oh-I-think-I've-solved-it" moments interrupted by my daughter screaming, "Mom, come wipe my butt!" By the time I get back to the computer, I've lost the idea. But children are not the only distraction for writers. Everyone's home is packed with tantalizing and duty-filled diversions: a queue of on-demand movies, stacks of interesting books, piles of unpaid bills, and a long list of chores. Block off weekends or days away from your life and then leave the house and those temptations behind.

4. KEEP A MONKEY MIND FILE. When you write, keep open a separate document to record the thoughts of your monkey mind. That's where you can jot your wild ideas for new projects, possible future careers, reminders to get gifts for your in-laws, and anything else your brain throws at you. At the end of your writing time, review the monkey mind file and transfer information to the appropriate place (your to-do list or another project file).

5. REMEMBER, YOU CAN ONLY RUN ONE RACE AT A TIME. I once worked with a marathon runner who got so inspired during her morning run that she developed a long list of book ideas. Given her full-time job and her running schedule, she didn't know which project to squeeze into the remaining daylight hours. For several months she tried to juggle three book-writing projects, a writing assignment for a client, and her full-time job. One day I said to her, "You can only run one marathon at a time." Something clicked for her; she made a decision to work on one book. The rest she put into her someday file, knowing that some day she would be choosing those races.

Readers, take heart. Everyone who writes needs to learn how to tame the monkey mind. Don't believe that some writers are immune to this. They're not. They're just more experienced at getting their minds to quiet down for a few minutes a day. Learning these skills takes time and effort. But guess what? The more you write, the easier it gets!

AVOID OVERWHELM

Being a poet is one of the unhealthier jobs—
no regular hours, so many temptations!
—ELIZABETH BISHOP

I n a study on choice, students reported better satisfaction with their work and wrote better essays when they chose from six rather than thirty essay topics. As writers and wannabes, we can avoid feeling overwhelmed by limiting our choices of what to work on each day.

I've written a series of books with many short chapters. If I began each writing day looking at the list of more than fifty topics, I would not have finished a book. I'd have spent every day in bed, hiding under the covers, eating a big bag of chocolate.

To save myself from death by chocolate, I end each writing session by choosing three topics I want to work on the next day. I put those in my writing journal and jot down ideas throughout the day. This way, I limit the possibility of having too many choices. I am able to focus on the few topics in front of me. When other ideas float up (and they will), I jot them down in an idea file.

For years, I have kept small turtle trinkets next to my computer to remind me of the power of taking small, focused steps toward my goals. When I heard about the family pet tortoise Willy, who made a break for it, I was even more inspired. Running away at a breakneck speed of an estimated .005 miles an hour, Willy managed to travel nearly five miles from home in a month before being spotted by a local EMT and returned home. Talk about small steps adding up to great progress!

Small, focused steps have helped me write and publish ten books and hundreds of articles (and complete a master's degree with a 136-page thesis in one year). Focus made it possible for Helen Hooven Santmyer to spend her retirement years writing her 1,300-page epic novel, … *And Ladies of the Club.* Cory Doctorow finishes more than a novel a year by focusing solely on the novel for twenty minutes a day.

Focus will make it possible for you to finish this book in twenty-six days. Choose your topic for today or tomorrow and get writing!

VISION DAILY

Visualize this thing that you want, see it, feel it, believe in it.
Make your mental blueprint, and begin to build.
—Robert Collier

I've heard many writers say they love the writing product but loathe the process. According to William Saroyan, "Writing is the hardest way of earning a living with the possible exception of wrestling alligators." Shirley Hazzard said this about writing: "It's nervous work. The state you need to write in is the state that others are paying large sums to get rid of." In this way, writing can be much like exercise. We dread it but do it regularly because it is good for us and will produce results over time.

Olympic athletes who visualize running their events in their mind experience the same physical benefits as when they actually run the race. Injured athletes have used visualization to remain fit during recovery. Olympians have claimed that mental management accounts for 90 percent of their success. Athletic coaches suggest that those who succeed in visualizing also succeed at the actual event.

As an exerciser, I've noticed that the practice of visualization has improved how I feel about working out. Each night as I fall asleep, I rehearse the next morning's workout. I see myself running on the treadmill or elliptical glider, lifting weights, and stretching. The next morning, my workout feels familiar and comfortable—even when I am pushing myself past my current level of expertise. Denis Waitley, a performance enhancement coach in the 1980s and 1990s Olympic Program, has spoken about the power of Visual Motor Rehearsal. He says this in the book *The Secret*:

> When you visualize, then you materialize. Here's an interesting thing about the mind: We took Olympic athletes and had them run their event only in their mind, and then hooked them up to sophisticated biofeedback equipment. Incredibly, the same muscles fired in the same sequence when they were running the race in their mind as when they were running it on the track. How could this be? Because the mind can't distinguish whether you're really doing it or whether it's just a practice. If you've been there in the mind you'll go there in the body.

As a writer, you can use the same technique to achieve success in your writing. Writing doesn't have to be an anxious and painful activity. Be the director of your vision. Each evening, visualize yourself arriving to the next day's writing task with energy and enthusiasm. See yourself writing easily, the ideas flowing quickly. Vision yourself accumulating words and then get up the next day and do it!

GET REWARDS

Before the reward there must be labor.
You plant before you harvest.
—RALPH RANSOM

redit card companies and airlines reward you with prizes for frequent use. Why shouldn't you get a reward for amassing an embarrassing amount of words? Over the years, I've noticed that writers reward themselves in different ways. Here are some popular reward types in the writing world:

THE "I GET THE REWARD, THEN I WRITE" WRITER. This writer loads up on treats—anything from fancy food to a hot bath—to prepare for a writing session. Think of it as shoring yourself up for a speaking gig or preparing for a hot date. If you find yourself saying something like this, you might be this kind of a writer: "If I get the triple shot mocha caramel latte with whipped cream, I'll be sure to get the chapter written."

THE "I NEED SOMETHING TO MOTIVATE ME WHILE I WRITE" WRITER. Like a child clinging to a teddy bear, this writer needs some sort of comfort to keep writing. Some choose food, others choose music, and a few want a real-live friend in the room. This writer says things like, "I'll munch on this popcorn, then that chocolate bar, then drink that pot of coffee while I write, and the words will come faster."

THE "I'M GOING TO STICK IT OUT AND FINISH THE WORD COUNT BEFORE I HAVE FUN" WRITER. This writer knows how to both work hard and play hard. Sure, she will give up a morning coffee date or surfing social media sites to get the word count in, but when it is done, she is ready for fun. She says, "When I finish this scene, I will play a computer game. Or buy a book. Or both."

THE "WHAT? REWARD MYSELF? YOU HAVE TO BE KIDDING? WRITING IS REWARD ITSELF" writer. This is the person you hated in high school or college. He would study for hours, stopping only to run a marathon, and claim it was a blast. This writer finishes today's word count and decides to write more.

No doubt, all of the reward techniques work. But one works better than the others. Can you guess which one?

Years ago, psychologists did a research study with children and marshmallows. They put four-year-old children alone in a room with a marshmallow. They told them that they could eat one marshmallow right away or they could wait a few minutes and get two marshmallows. The psychologists left the room. So what happened? Some kids ate the single marshmallow. Some waited for the double dose. Here's the cool thing: Years later, the psychologists learned that the children who had waited for the double dose outpaced their peers in school achievement and test scores.

What does this mean for you? Delayed gratification works. You'll write more if you reward yourself after you finish your daily word count. Create a list of rewards that work for you. Keep it near the place you write. When you have met your daily writing goal, reward yourself. It's that simple!

PAY YOURSELF FIRST

You have to pay yourself first.
You can't let other things get in your way.
—James O'Shaughnessy

Nine days and less than 15,000 words away from finishing the National Novel Writing Month Challenge, I woke startled. In the passion of the race, I had totally forgotten about two editing projects I needed to finish by the end of the month. And, oh yeah, there was Thanksgiving thrown in there, too. How would I write 15,000 words and edit nearly 40,000 more words in a week? I sighed, shrugged off the covers, and slunk downstairs for coffee.

In the midst of my morning coffee, I remembered the famous financial wisdom I'd been repeating to writing and life coaching clients for years: "Pay yourself first." Financial gurus encourage us to sock away a bit of money in savings and retirement accounts before paying the bills. Fitness trainers teach that exercising first thing in the morning insures that exercise won't succumb to the demands of a busy schedule. The only way I would succeed at National Novel Writing Month was to follow this wise advice: Pay myself first. I would give my first or best moments of each day to writing.

The poet William Stafford was known to be an early morning writer. He would write each day between 4:00 A.M. and 7:00 A.M., when the world was quiet. Stafford began this practice when he lived in Civilian Public Service camps as a conscientious objector, where the workday began at 7:30 A.M. Stafford's daughter Barbara once told about getting up early to spend time with her father. The poet didn't discourage her but got up earlier and earlier to preserve his writing time. Stafford's commitment to writing daily worked. He accumulated 20,000 days of manuscript writing in his lifetime (that's a page a day, every day, for 54.7 years).

Stafford said this about his morning practice in his essay, "A Way of Writing":

> When I write, I like to have an interval before me when I am not
> likely to be interrupted. For me, this means usually the early morn-
> ing, before others are awake. I get pen and paper, take a glance out
> of the window (often it is dark out there), and wait. It is like fishing.
> But I do not wait very long, for there is always a nibble—and this is

where receptivity comes in. To get started I will accept anything that
occurs to me.

I have also found that the first hours of the day lend themselves best to writing. Before I check e-mail or phone messages, before my children tug at my sleeve for food and lunch money, before the demands of the day come calling, I am at my desk writing. Once I have my time in, I can go about the day without angst. Without that early morning writing time, I am angry and frustrated, always feeling like my day is missing something.

No matter where you are in your twenty-six-day writing marathon, you will have a day or a week when your writing project seems like a burden. Your dream of finishing a book in a month will seem like folly. Your to-do list will be long and the complaints of others against you will be longer. Why don't you answer your phone? When will I see you again? What are you doing that is so important you can't check e-mail until noon?

All I can say to you is this: Do not give up. Keep at it. Yes, this book of yours may be folly, but it is your folly. It is what you have dreamed of doing and now you are doing it. Don't let it go. Hold onto your dream, and pay yourself first. You don't have to write for many hours each day. Just give your first or your best minutes of the day to this project.

DROP EVERYTHING

---

*I would love for you to learn how to drop everything
and go create. ... dropping everything just as you would
drop your parcels if your child got hurt or you would
drop your clothes for spontaneous sex.*
—Eric Maisel

No matter where you are in the writing marathon, chances are it has become easier to drop the writing for life tasks than to drop life commitments for writing.

You know what I mean. You are busy working on the writing and your friend invites you out for drinks and although you don't have your daily quota in, you think, "Well, social connections are important, and I can get back to this tomorrow." Or, your kid gets sick, and you feel almost giddy with the relief that you can drop the project for a day.

But what if it were the other way around, as Maisel suggested? What if you were to say to yourself, "Oh, the laundry can wait, I need to write"? What if you left your steaming dinner on the table or the bed half made because you had an idea for your book and you dropped everything to write it down? What if you ran to your writing the way you run to meet your lover?

The benefit of a twenty-six-day marathon is this: It gives you permission to try tools like this one because it is only for twenty-six days. So try it. For the rest of the marathon, try dropping everything to write. Don't let your schedule limit your writing. Give in to writing at any moment that you feel inspired. One writer I know was so jazzed by National Novel Writing Month that she finished ten days early. She mastered the technique of dropping everything to write.

And here's the beauty of this: When you drop everything to write, you have the focus and passion of a new lover. You don't worry about word count or time or what you are missing outside of this one, true passion. Instead, you write with abandon, knowing that the world will still be there when you are done.

MAKE MISTAKES

*You can't create without making messes and
generating chaos and blundering down blind alleys
and crawling back up again—you can't create
without those efforts which end in disaster, because it's
the disasters which show you how to get things right.*
—SUSAN HOWATCH

*Ever tried? Ever failed. No matter.
Try again. Fail again. Fail better.*
—SAMUEL BECKETT

My daughter just started taking skating lessons at the Pettit National Ice Center. Can you guess what the instructors teach first at this Olympic training center? They teach the students *how to get up.*

I love this. We all fall. What separates those who succeed from those who don't? Getting up. Those who succeed get up over and over again. The rest sit on the ice and whine:

- "It's too hard."
- "No one supports me."
- "Why do I keep falling?"
- "My butt hurts!"

One thing I've noticed is this: No matter the medium, creating is hard work. It might look easy for writers to birth an epic novel in the movies, but in reality, it's bloody difficult. Like a real birth, the process of birthing a book can be chaotic and unpredictable business. We get stuck and discouraged. We make mistakes and leave behind messes. We fear failure. In the face of these experiences, we may be tempted to give up.

In Sir Ken Robinson's TED talk he said, "If you're not prepared to be wrong, you'll never come up with anything original." We need to make mistakes because the mistakes point us to the better path. Most creative artists know it is the mistakes that teach us the most. Whether you are creating a book or the perfect room, the disasters deliver the greatest lessons and eventually propel you to success. As a professional writer, I've never made a mistake that has not produced more fruit than my successes—in the long run. In a sense, knowing that mistakes happen and have a purpose can help us jump head first into the creative process without worry. We have nothing to lose.

Mistakes happen. If you're lucky, mistakes will also lead you to something better. Sticky notes exist because Spencer Silver created a weak glue for 3M instead of the supersticky glue he had tried to make. Four years later, another scientist, Arthur Fry, thought the superweak glue, applied to a small piece of paper, just might work to help him mark his place in his hymnal. Chocolate chip cookies exist because Ruth Wakefield ran out of baker's chocolate. She broke up some sweet chocolate into small pieces, stirred it into her cookie batter, and hoped the cookies would turn out. They did. But they weren't the chocolate cookies she had hoped for. Instead she had invented chocolate chip cookies. And what about you? What will your mistakes lead to? It's time to find out.

When you get to a point in your book where you feel stuck and frustrated, get connected to your mistakes. Figure out what's not working and look at those things thoughtfully. Use your journal to reflect on these prompts:

- What does this disaster, mistake, or mess teach me?
- If I were to coach a friend about this situation, I would say …
- If I could try something wild and off the wall, not caring about the result, I would …
- If this mistake had a purpose, it would be …
- This mistake would work if I …

With any luck, you'll leave this exercise with more ideas about how to keep writing. If not, go out and do something else badly: Play a song on the piano, paint a pot, or whip up a batch of cookies. It doesn't matter if you succeed. Making a mess of things might just give you an idea of how to go back and fix the mess in your book! And remember this: No matter how or how many times you fail, get up and try again. Like the old proverb says, "Fall seven times. Stand up eight."

CONQUER SABOTAGE

*You can't say, I won't write today because that excuse
will extend into several days, then several months, then …
you are not a writer anymore, just someone who
dreams about being a writer.*
—DOROTHY C. FONTANA

I n her book *Traveling Mercies*, Anne Lamott wrote about shopping for clothes with her terminally ill friend Pammy. At one point, Lamott asked her friend if the dress made her look "big in the hips." Pammy answered, "Annie? You don't really have that kind of time." People who are terminally ill face that reality every day. We do, too. We're just in denial.

In a lecture on her book *Defy Gravity*, author and teacher Caroline Myss said to the audience, and I am paraphrasing, "I would hate to have you get to the end of your life and discover that you have wasted it." Marianne Williamson said something similar, and again, I am paraphrasing: "The era of ditzy and data collection are over. You forgot who you are. Remember now. You have work to do."

We fail to do what we know we have been put on this earth to do for many reasons—because we are afraid, busy, or just too steeped in denial to realize we don't have that kind of time. After years of working to live out my calling and help others do the same, I've noticed some patterns. Whenever someone claims his big hairy audacious goal, anxiety happens. You get sick. Your children need extra help with homework. Work falls apart. The inner doubts creep out and bite you in the butt. If you are not careful, the drama can halt the writing process.

Worry not; the way you and your family react to your goal is normal. It's what happens in a system when someone stops doing what she has always done and behaves differently. The system—be it a body or a family or a group of friends—freaks out. Few will reward the person who bucks the system. Instead, the members of the system—and this includes you—practice the fine old art of sabotage to keep or restore order.

Know this: For the most part, the people who try to sabotage your progress don't intend to hurt you. They may not even realize they are getting between you and your goal. Heck, *you* may not even realize you are getting in the way of your own goals. Your excuses will sound so reasonable: *I needed to rest. It was too big of a project for me. My friends need me to be available.* Stop. Take a deep breath. Realize this: You don't have all the time in the world. If you are going to go after your big hairy audacious goal and reach it, expect sabotage. In fact, plan for it. When you acknowledge that sabotage happens, you can create a plan for overcoming it. In fact, it's essential that you make a plan. Why? Because if you dreamed up this project, the world needs this book. You have something to say. The sabotage is a sign that you are on the right track. Don't derail your dream.

So now the trick is to overcome the saboteur, recognizing that we might be our own worst enemy. Make a list of all of the ways you or others have tried to sabotage the project during the writing marathon thus far. Put it all down—from the reasonable excuses to the real emergencies to the outright plans to overtake your process.

Got it? Good. Now it is time to figure out how to overcome this sabotage.

The first and maybe easiest way to overcome the saboteur is to recognize her as your noble friend. The saboteur is present to remind you that what you are doing is important. Every time the saboteur appears, say thank you. Then put your head down and keep working.

Next, take a look back at our old friend, the when-then statement. Remember? A when-then statement connects an external cue with a goal-directed action. In our earlier chapter, we talked about creating when-then plans to help us use ordinary environmental cues to help us meet our daily writing goals. We also used them to help us overcome obstacles. Now that we are in the process, we look at the sabotage as new obstacles and create when-then statements to help us overcome them. Because—as we've said before—we don't have time for sabotage!

Finally, it's important to have at least one ally in your court to help you recognize and fight sabotage. The spouse who tells you the project is too hard, and you should just rest and take care of yourself, may not have your best interest at heart. He might be jealous that your work is taking you away from the relationship. Your best friend who calls every morning as you begin your writing time even though she knows better may not be forgetful. And don't forget to look in the mirror. Your own excuses may be your biggest obstacles. Take a look at your support list. Who on that list can help you recognize sabotage and fight it? Who can help you tell the truth? Find that person. Next time you suspect sabotage, ask for his support.

You can do this. You have to do it right now. Remember, you don't have all the time in the world.

CHALLENGE YOUR EXCUSES

Go ahead and make your excuses. Then challenge them! That's right:
Give your excuses a hard time. Try this:

- You think, "I don't have time to write!" Ask, "How much time
  do I have?" Dedicate an absurdly small about of time to write
  each day. Two minutes. Five minutes. I'll bet that in time you'll
  find you have more time than you thought you had.

- You think, "I don't know what to write about!" Ask, "What do I
  know?" Quickly write down five things you know a lot about or
  five ideas for this project.

- You think, "I'm not inspired." Tell yourself, "So what. Inspiration
  comes WHILE writing and not before."

Talk to yourself about your excuses the way you'd talk to a child making excuses for not doing homework or taking out the trash. Then
get writing!

OVERCOME
PERFECTIONISM

Don't get it right. Just get it written.
—JAMES THURBER

I'm a psychiatrist and author. I never get writer's block, because I was at a writing conference years ago where a writer said, "Writer's block is the fear of writing crap. So just write crap." That's exactly what I do, then either rework the crap later or throw it out.
—DOREEN ORION

The tyranny of perfection halts most writing careers before they begin. The prose that seemed perfect in our heads disappears when we try to put it on paper. We imagine that professional, best-selling writers write perfect first drafts. We think we are failures. So we stop writing. Or we never begin.

Know this: Everyone writes what Anne Lamott called "shitty first drafts." (Even the professionals.) If someone says he doesn't, he's probably lying. First drafts are just that—drafts. Your next draft will be better. After several stabs at getting the writing right, you will. With time, effort, and a little magic dust, your work will shine.

Don't sit there with your head in your hands, trying to come up with the perfect first sentence. Instead, write what you are thinking. Write what you dreamed last night. Write what you overheard at the coffee shop. Write down anything and go from there. Mike Ness of the band Social Distortion said, "If I'm writing, I have a trash can full of crumpled-up paper. It's like you've got to write shit first, then the good stuff starts to come."

When I started my first career as a minister, I struggled to write my weekly sermon. (Just thinking about that time gives me an anxious stomachache.) This was before the era of the Internet and online sermon services. I would search for the perfect idea—the one that would make the congregation say, "Wow, that will change our lives!" When I could not come up with the perfect idea, I would scour my books and magazines for any idea that would work. When that failed, I would start with the only thing that was there: the biblical text. This became my fail-safe method of sermon preparation. I would start by retelling the biblical story. Somewhere in that retelling, I would come up with a nugget of an idea and be able to write the rest of the sermon. Once I had a draft, I could move the pieces around and get a pretty good sermon to preach.

Find your own fail-safe plan. What can you write about that will lead to more writing? Do you have journal entries you can mine? Could you start by describing what the character is wearing? Could you pretend you are giving a lecture on your topic to your employees? Instead of worrying over a first sentence that is not perfect, find a place to start and write until your hand gets tired. Once you start, do everything in your power to hold on to that momentum.

You have my permission to write nothing but garbage. Just get it down on paper. You are not writing the perfect book. You are writing the good enough book. Before long, you'll get into your groove. Next month, you can cut out the pieces that don't work and rewrite the rest. You'll end up with a piece of writing that is better than you could have imagined.

It's the process that has worked for hundreds and thousands of award-winning writers throughout the centuries. Why shouldn't it work for you? Leave your quest for perfect prose behind and write away! That is the only way to finish a book in twenty-six days.

CONSERVE ENERGY

Marathon running is a terrible experience:
monotonous, heavy, and exhausting.
—Veikko Karvonen, 1954 European and
Boston Marathon Champ

Writing is the hardest work in the world. I have been a
bricklayer and a truck driver, and I tell you—as if you
haven't been told a million times already—that writing is
harder. Lonelier. And nobler and more enriching.
—Harlan Ellison

Both writers and marathon runners complain about the task. Even though most writers and runners agree that the pain is worth it, they still have to get through it. Like writer Dorothy Parker exclaimed, we don't like writing but we love having written.

Because writing takes up an enormous amount of physical, emotional, and mental energy, we need to find ways to conserve our energy. Meditation guru Belleruth Naparstek instructs listeners who take meditation walks to not look or smile at anyone because the actions deplete our energy reserves. It's not bad advice for writers, either.

In earlier chapters, you worked hard to let go of energy drains for the month. You let go of relationships that taxed your energy reserves. You set aside activities that bled your time. You also considered adding some helpful energy boosts: exercise, healthy food, naps, and energy renewing activities like doing art or washing dishes.

At this point in the marathon, you need to take a second look at your life. As humans, we tend to revert to our natural way of being. Even if we started the marathon determined to avoid eating junk food, staying up late watching television, and taking calls from our complaining friends, we easily revert to our old habits. We do what we know. Research shows that most people fail at their New Year's resolutions by the third Monday in January—about three weeks into the process. Choosing to write a book in twenty-six days is a resolution no matter when you do it. Before you hit the point where you give up on the project, take a look at your life:

1. CHECK FOR GOALS IN CONFLICT. One of the biggest challenges we have with accomplishing our goals is that they conflict with other goals. For example, let's say you plan to use this book to propel your career forward. You want to self-publish this book and use it as your business card, teaching other people how hiring you will help them solve their problems. At the same time, you have the goal of meeting and developing relationships with as many people as you can in the next month. Both are admirable goals. But they conflict with each other. You cannot dedicate time to both creating a product and meeting your potential customers at the same time. Think about your own life. Do you have goals that conflict with your writing marathon? If so, can you let go of the conflicting goal for the rest of the marathon so you can finish your book?

2. CHECK FOR ENERGY DRAINS. In order to do something big, something that requires a huge chunk of time, energy, and chutzpah, you need to let go of some of the things that drain your energy. Different activities drain each of us. Introverts find too much time with large groups of people to be tiring. Extroverts grow weary of being alone. Some people find outdoor sports to be invigorating while others tire after a walk around the block. Think about the activities and people that are draining your energy right now. Are any of these interfering with your writing marathon? If so, make a change. Rearrange your schedule so you get in your writing before you attack the activities that drain your energy. Set stronger boundaries, refusing to answer the phone or check e-mail before you get your work done. Finally, if you can, take a break from anyone or anything that consistently drains your energy. When we let go of practices that deplete our energy, we discover energy for the tasks that inspire us—like writing a book in twenty-six days!

3. ADD ENERGY BOOSTS. Energy boosts are practices that renew energy. In the midst of writing this book in a month, I got stuck at around 20,000 words. I was tired and didn't know if I could keep going. Instead of quitting, I wrote ahead so I could take two days off to replenish my energy. Besides sleeping as much as I could, I did an art project with my daughter, had coffee with a friend, and watched six episodes of *Buffy the Vampire Slayer*. When I got back to work on Monday morning, I was reenergized and ready to slay my own vampires. But I didn't stop there. I made sure I got my exercise every single day and took time to purchase some healthier snacks. As much as I love my brownies, I knew the sugar high was causing me to crash before I finished my daily writing.

In an earlier chapter, you created a list of ways you could boost your energy. Take a look at that list and make sure you get some of those in each day. Next, look at the Manage Your Energy chapter in the previous section. What other energy boosts can you add to increase your energy? Do it. You need it. Your book needs it!

WRITE ANYWAY

No matter what is going on in your life, know that ideal situations are not necessary for finishing a book. People who succeed in life do so because they have grit—the ability to work toward their goals whether they feel like it or not. Laura Hillenbrand, the best-selling author of *Seabiscuit: An American Legend*, has chronic fatigue syndrome. At times, she could only write a paragraph or two a day. She had to perch her laptop on books because looking down at the screen made the room spin. Yet she stuck with it. Her grit—anchored in her passion for the topic—kept her writing. A client of mine kept writing her book despite migraines, a bout of phlebitis, and multiple trips to the emergency room. An early book of ours was finished on time even though I took a break to have surgery—talk about an energy-depleting situation! I woke up in recovery to my husband asking me questions about one of the chapters.

You don't need to have the perfect amount of energy to write this book. But you do need to conserve the energy you have. Do what you can to use your energy to do this work—the writing that matters to you. You will be glad you did!

BE OPEN TO CHANGE

Writer's block is often a sign of a plot-gone-wrong.
—Antoinette Kuritz

When writing doesn't work, writers often blame themselves or the demon writer's block. Sometimes writers get stuck when an aspect of the book isn't working.

Chapter one nearly wrote itself. But fifteen pages into chapter two, my husband and I had no idea how to proceed. The project felt unwieldy. We had too much to say in such a short space. In addition to working on the book, *The Spiritual Leader's Guide to Self-Care*, we were expecting a baby in a few months. We could not afford writer's block! We needed to finish the bulk of the project before the baby made her appearance.

After several unproductive writing sessions and a lot of grousing at each other, we came to the same conclusion. The book's structure wasn't working. As Antoinette Kuritz advised, writer's block can sometimes be a sign of trouble with your book's structure.

We wrote to our editor and, with her help, restructured the book. The new structure, a fifty-two-chapter exercise-based book, worked better for us. Once we figured out the new outline, the writer's block disappeared. We turned in the book on time. (The baby appeared a week late!)

For us, the problem was book structure. For you, the problem might be something different: voice, style, or a topic that isn't working. Take a step back from your project and look at your work. Ask yourself:

- Could I write this if it were structured differently?
- Could I write this if I used a different voice (for example, first person instead of third person)?
- Could I write this if I used a different point of view?
- Could I write this if I used a different style? (For example, you might need to start by writing a case study or a list. Just changing the style might help you get into the action or content of the chapter.)
- Could I write this in dialogue form?

- Could I write this as a narrative?
- Could I write this if I had more information? (Note: If the chapter requires too much more information, you may need to set it aside for a different project or highlight it to finish later.)
- Could I write this after I had a few days break? (You may need to work on something else until the ideas for this chapter come together.)
- Does this repeat other chapters or scenes I have already written? (If so, you may need to scrap it or move your ideas from here to another chapter.)
- Could I write this scene after I have written a later scene?
- Does this need to be a summary of what happened instead of a scene?

Once you have analyzed why you are stuck, you will be able to fix the problem and move on. Two warnings. First, the problem you fix may impact the rest of the book. This is not the time to go back and fix the first thirty chapters you wrote. Save that for when you revise the book. Second, the problem you encounter in this chapter may not be the same problem you have the next time you get stuck. Put a little sticky note on the side of this book right next to the above questions so you can revisit them whenever you need to.

Remember: If you get stuck with the project, you don't have writer's block. You may just be bumping up against a problem with the book. You may need to change a few things. That's okay. Change happens.

FINISH ANYTHING

Your behavior influences others through a ripple effect.
A ripple effect works because everyone influences everyone else.
–JOHN HEIDER

My clients talk a lot about the ripple affect. They know that when the people around them change—their family members, friends, and colleagues—they are more likely to make changes in their own lives. They've also seen that when they make changes in their lives, their family members follow. A parent begins to exercise and his children start moving more, too. But there is one more way the ripple effect happens: When they make one change in their lives, other changes follow.

One client upped her daily exercise routine. She believes that because of that, she was able to stick to a daily reading program. Another client gave up television for Lent. He also saw a reduction in his alcohol and junk food consumption the same month. I started exercising again after a three-month break. Wouldn't you know—the more I exercised, the more I wrote. Coincidence? No.

Researchers have discovered that taking control in one area of your life affects other areas of your life. Australian researchers Megan Oaten and Ken Cheng headed up a study where participants embarked on a two-month physical exercise program. The study participants did aerobic activity, lifted weights, and practiced resistance training. The results? They consumed less caffeine, alcohol, and junk food. They smoked fewer cigarettes. They had better control over their emotions, spent less, and watched fewer hours of television. Why? Working on any hard goal strengthens your ability to self-regulate—to control your behavior. And that ability spreads to your actions in all parts of your life. Clearly change is contagious.

When you encounter writer's block in the middle of your twenty-six-day writing marathon, you might begin to believe you will never finish this project. Take the research we just learned about and apply it to the writing life. If you have success in one area of your life, it's going to spread to other areas of your life. Right now you need that success to spread to your writing life.

When I get stuck in a process that isn't working—and yet I am committed to the project—I do something I know I can finish and that will not fail. I bake cookies, plant flowers, or bead a bracelet! The simple joy of finishing a creative project boosts my energy and gets me back in the rhythm of finishing the task I have started.

Finish something. Choose a small, doable task you know you will succeed at—bake a cake, rake the lawn, or wash the dishes. Repetitive tasks have the added benefit of engaging your subconscious mind and bringing you those aha moments. Finishing another task will help you gain confidence. Before long, you will be back at your computer or in front of your notebook writing fast and furiously, completing chunk after chunk.

SUCCESS CREATES SUCCESS

Every NaNoWriMo winner I talked to was proud of their 50,000-word accomplishment—and they should be. NaNoWriMo success boosted the winners' writing confidence and spilled over into other areas as well. Winner Kristine Augustyn said, "Because I actually completed the novel I feel that I can do many more things. It has given me greater confidence and inspiration and in turn I have inspired others to try things." Kristine gained the confidence to start a new business, Badge of Intent. Other writers started exercise programs, revamped their eating habits, and gained the courage to submit their writing to agents. How is your writing success spilling over into the rest of your life?

WRITE ANYTHING

*Quantity produces quality. If you only
write a few things, you're doomed.*
—Ray Bradbury

A bookseller once said to me, "I don't think you have an unpublished thought." He was wrong. I have tons of unpublished thoughts. I also have an attic stacked with boxes of unpublished manuscripts. Writers write a lot. Not everything gets published. Nor should it. But the practice will improve your writing.

Natalie Goldberg encourages students to do writing practice for two years before actually writing anything to sell. The idea isn't a bad one. Practicing writing strengthens your writing muscles the way lifting weights strengthens your arms for tennis or swimming.

When my children were babies, I noticed that the more they slept, the more they slept. I didn't have to worry about a baby napping too much. Chances were if the baby took a good nap, she also slept at night. It's the same with writing. The more you write, the more you write. If you are feeling blocked, write something to loosen your writing muscles. Here are some ideas:

- How are you doing with the daily dump? Try to write one to three pages a day about anything, no matter how random it is.
- Write a letter about how hard the project is.
- Write a list of things to do before you die.
- Make a list of your favorite expletives.
- Do a writing exercise.
- Use a newspaper title, sentence from a poem, or sentence from a favorite book to spur your writing.

Prolific novelist Jodi Picoult reminds us that you cannot edit a blank page. She says, "Writer's block is for people who have the luxury of time; I started writing when I had three kids under the age of four. I used to write every ten minutes I got to sit in front of a computer. Now, when I have more time, I function the same way: If it's writing time, I write. I may write garbage, but you can always edit garbage. You can't edit a blank page."

So if you are feeling stuck on this project—don't stop writing. Write ANYTHING. Write garbage. Just put some words on paper.

ADD NINJAS AND STIR!

Without conflict, writing gets boring—for both writers and readers. NaNoWriMo participant Nicole Gustasa of Monterey, California, solved her novel's need for conflict this way: "Whenever I was stumped for what was going to happen next, I'd throw ninjas at my characters. I was writing a wacky screwball-comedy spy-and-nerd-on-the-run farce, so it worked well. Your mileage may vary, although personally I think serious literary fiction could benefit from a few ninjas." I like the spirit of this idea. Create momentum for your work by adding conflict, surprise, or just doing something different. If you get stuck, ask yourself how you might move forward if you added a diagram, a poem, or the opposing point of view.

WARM UP WITH POETRY

I warm up and break through the ice called writer's block by writing poetry. If I can't come up with a topic for a poem, I'll look at the headlines in newspapers or magazines and find something to write a poem about. Once I write the poem, I'm ready to return to longer work like a short story or novel.

—Lloyd Lofthouse

Sometimes writer's block strikes because we are weary. When we force ourselves to churn out work each day, focusing more on creating a finished product than on appreciating the process, we get tired. The words all sound the same. Nothing seems interesting anymore. Our mind seems as blank as the page in front of us.

Writing poetry can pull us out of our ennui. I like the practice of writing haiku poems because the form demands that the writer be both attentive and precise. In her book *Haiku: Asian Arts and Crafts for Creative Kids*, Patricia Donegan offers several concrete tips for writing haiku. I've pulled out my favorites for you:

- **FORM.** Traditionally, teachers have taught the seventeen-syllable haiku poem (5-7-5). Donegan teaches that the haiku poem is one breath long. As you write, read your poem aloud. Pay attention to your breath as you read.

- **FOCUS ON THE HERE AND NOW.** Write about the present moment. Write about something concrete you can see and describe. What do you see right now that inspires or perplexes you?

- **USE IMAGES.** Think about your haiku poem as a word-picture. How can you use descriptive images to capture what you see and feel?

- **USE A SEASON WORD.** Haiku poems tend to connect the reader (and writer) to nature and the flow of the seasons. What words or images connect your poem to the weather or the season?

- **SURPRISE.** Donegan believes that the haiku poem "should have an 'ah!' moment that wakes us up." How can you introduce the element of surprise into your poem?

My son's piano teacher says to him, "I don't care if you can play the piece fast. I want you to be precise first." Not bad advice for writers as well. I love the length of the haiku poem because it forces the writer to be precise. We must slow down and ponder what is in front of us. We must weigh all of the possible elements and choose the ones that work best. In the process of attending, pondering, and choosing, we may find a bit of joy.

PLAY WITH WORDS

NaNoWriMo winner Gail Brandeis, author of the novel *Self Storage*, gives this advice: "One thing I like to do is crack open the dictionary, find a word I haven't heard of before, and write a poem around it. Sometimes the poems are silly, sometimes they're painful, but they always get me excited about writing again."

Get out your dictionary, thesaurus, or rhyming dictionary and play with words. You could:

- Use the word to write an acrostic poem.
- Look up the word in the thesaurus and try to use all the synonyms and antonyms in a poem.
- Find the word in a rhyming dictionary and try to use as many rhyming words as you can to create a poem.
- Write your own definition for the word. Include synonyms, antonyms, and some made-up rhyming words.

GET INSPIRED

*There's no strict route to a U2 song. The only thing
that's consistent is the search for inspiration. It can
start from a drumbeat, a guitar part, a title, a lyric. An entire
piece of music can suddenly arrive. We subscribe to the
idea that there's no such thing as failure. There's just giving
up. We do not give up. We're relentless.*
–THE EDGE, U2 GUITARIST

One of my coaching colleagues has a saying: "Your mind is like a bad neighborhood at night. Don't go there alone."

No kidding.

Now that you are writing this book, you're going into that neighborhood alone every day.

Frightened yet?

I've written quite a bit in this book about how your environment primes your behavior. *Changing* your environment can prime you to be inspired. Think about how invigorated you feel when you go on vacation and explore a new city or store. Your imagination comes alive. All of a sudden, you have new ideas about how you could decorate your house, dress, or earn a living.

But when we are in the midst of a big project, living from task to task, life ceases to be an inspirational journey and becomes a series of chores to be crossed off our to-do list. We lose perspective. Our imagination shuts down. The chunks that once looked easy—even exciting—become complicated puzzles. I tend to cope with this experience by working even harder. I put in longer hours, postpone pleasures—and get even less done.

Once when my children were little, I experienced a week with several big deadlines and a boo-hoo baby. I paged through my commonplace book—a book of quotes I have collected over the years—for inspiration. I found this quote by author Angeles Arrien:

> When we go to a medicine person or healer because we are feeling
> disheartened, dispirited, or depressed, he or she might ask questions
> like: When did you stop singing? When did you stop dancing? When

did you stop being enchanted by stories? When did you begin finding discomfort in the sweet territory of silence?

OF COURSE! The solution to being overwhelmed will not be found in that which overwhelms us! The solution comes in stopping, in stepping away from our messy desks, piles of manuscript pages, or stacks of research—and nurturing our spirits. Play golf. Shoot hoops. Read a poem. Play with a baby. Skip down the driveway. Go fishing. Admire the tulips. Take off your shoes and wiggle your toes in the sand or the dirt. Splash in a puddle. Take a nap. Sing. Enter that parallel world where your to-do list doesn't exist. Then, when you return to your work, it won't seem nearly so daunting.

As you write through the twenty-six-day writing marathon, you will need to find ways to build inspiration into every single day. The daily inspiration will feed your work by bringing fresh insights into your subject material. It can also provide illustrations and ways to explain the points you are making.

Your inspiration break may take anywhere from thirty seconds to three hours. Take one every day. When you can, devote a whole day to an inspiration break. When you get back to work you will be refreshed and ready to go. Oh, and one more thing: Bring your note cards. When inspiration hits, you want to be ready to write it down.

LIST IT!

I encourage all of my clients to make a list of their top ten inspiration breaks. Keep this list near your computer so you can quickly access it when you need inspiration. To begin creating your list, name experiences that inspire you. Try to include activities you can connect to easily either at home or in the community. Include plenty of activities that are free; you won't want to pay to get inspired every day. Try to get a variety of experiences, and pay attention to how the activities connect to each of your five senses. Think about some of the following categories.

LEARNING. Educational experiences can often be extremely helpful, especially if they come from an area outside your expertise. Perhaps attending a lecture about how rocks form will give you an idea about explaining what goes into the foundation of a house. You can also learn by watching an educational program, helping out at an elementary school, or reading a book or periodical in an area you know little about.

CREATING. Stretching your mind around how to put something together—from changing a tire on your car to putting up a new set of shelves—will make you smarter. Figure out what you want to make and then watch a YouTube video, attend a class, or just try creating something on your own. Over the years I've tried making lefse, planting a garden, and crocheting an afghan. Each creative endeavor has brought me a life lesson that has inspired my writing.

MOVING. There's nothing like exercise to stretch your muscles and tickle your imagination. I'm not talking about the usual "climb on a treadmill and walk while watching television" exercise routine. No, I'm talking about trying something new. Take a dance class, try Pilates, ice skate, or walk with a two-year-old. Move your body in a way you haven't tried before and see if it inspires you.

LISTENING. Another way to get inspired is to listen to new music or other sounds. I'm infamous at my house for eavesdropping. I love overhearing what other people are saying, especially people from a different generation. You could also try learning new music. Ask five people of different generations and cultures to list their favorite songs. Go look those up online and listen. Or commit to listening to a song from a different country each week. You don't have to listen to music to become inspired. You can get a similar effect listening to the ambient sounds station on either iTunes or Pandora. Tune into the ocean or birds or whatever rocks your world.

SEEING. From observing nature to art to hardware parts, seeing something new might just kick an idea loose in your head. Take a break to visit a museum, wander through a hardware store, or look at trinkets in a junk store. Walk through your yard on your hands and knees and see what you can see. Visit a library with the goal of looking at old art books or other picture-laden tomes. Do what you can to challenge your eyes!

INSPIRATION BOX. Find an old decorative box, bag, or accordion file. Collect photos from magazines, newspapers, and old books. Gather together art museum postcards or greeting cards that stimulate your creativity. You might even pick up postcards or old family photos at garage sales. One writer I know cuts out favorite sayings. Once you have a stack of inspiring photos or sayings, put them in your container. Next time writer's block strikes, you're sure to find a photo or a quote to inspire you.

COLLECTIONS THAT INSPIRE

Just about any collection of items can inspire you. When you get stuck, use one of the items as a writing prompt. Try collecting:

- songs
- small objects like plastic animals, figurines, or erasers
- inspiration cards
- jokes
- limericks
- poems
- small toys like tops, rubber balls, windup toys, or marbles

SCENT AND TASTE. I always say I write better in San Diego because the smell of the ocean and the flowers inspire me. Our senses of smell and taste have great power over us. They can help us remember a fond or challenging time, and stir our ideas about new possibilities. Seek out new or comforting senses by cooking, visiting an arboretum, taking a walk outside, trying out a new restaurant, or simply lighting a fragrant candle.

Once you have your list of inspiration breaks, select one and make your plan for it. You might decide to write ahead so you can set aside a whole day for a field trip or a retreat.

Now: Go forth, get inspired, and write on!

WRITE YOUR DREAMS

*A word is a bud attempting to become a twig.
How can one not dream while writing? It is the pen which
dreams. The blank page gives the right to dream.*
—GASTON BACHELARD

What do you with your dreams? Some of us mumble them to our families over breakfast or dinner. Others write them down in a dream journal. Jacquelyn Mitchard took one of her dreams and molded it into the best-selling novel *The Deep End of the Ocean*. Author Stephenie Meyer was a mom and a homemaker when she had a dream that became the basis of her best-selling Twilight series.

Our nighttime dreams can become a rich source for our daytime writing. In our dreams, our minds weave together unrelated people, events, and objects and offer up rich stories with striking images and metaphors. These images and metaphors—and sometimes the whole stories—can find homes in our novels and nonfiction books.

Start by keeping a dream journal next to your bed. If you wake up with a dream in your mind, grab that journal and write it down. Try to capture as many details as possible, even if they are out of order. (Do it before you get up to use the bathroom. I find that moving can cause an already fleeting dream to fly away.) Later when you're fully awake, take a moment to read over your dreams and add any details that come to you. If you wrote down the dream out of order, take a moment to record the proper order. Underline or star any passages or images that interest you.

The next time you encounter writer's block, read through your dream journal. Is there an image, story, or idea you can use as a starting point? If you don't find something that relates to your current project, look for an image or metaphor that stirs your imagination. Write about that for a few minutes. Before long, you will have found the solution to your writer's block. Who knows, maybe you'll find the key to unlocking your book in your dreams!

NO BLANK PAGES

When I am about to write a speech or a chapter
of a book and I feel blocked, I simply find someone else's words
in another book and type them onto my computer.
Then, I go back and line by line and think, "Hmm, I
wouldn't say that that way; this is what I would say."
I replace their words with mine. The finished product doesn't
resemble what I started with at all. It's now what
I THINK—in my words. Works every time.
—Dr. Toni LaMotta

A memoir writer started every writing session by copying down a favorite poem in her journal. When she finished copying, she was ready to write. Dr. LaMotta, quoted above, takes the words of another writer and changes them until she's off on her own writing path. I start every writing session with yesterday's words. I add sentences, rewrite others, and before long, I am onto writing the next chunk of text.

What do all of these techniques have in common? They allow writers to overcome the blank page. While some writers face the blank page with energy and hopes of what will be, most of us dread it. The blank page just sits there, mocking us, waiting to be filled with brilliant prose. When we can't measure up, our inner critics go at us. Even the prolific author Sidney Sheldon said, "A blank piece of paper is God's way of telling us how hard it is to be God." So what's a writer to do? Never start with the blank page.

STOP AT THE GOOD PART

NaNoWriMo participant Elizabeth McKinney, a PR professional from Winston-Salem, North Carolina, had this advice: "In the pre-NaNo kickoff with Winston-Salem Writers, we learned to stop at an exciting point in the plot, to leave yourself something to automatically begin writing when you sat down the next day." Novelist Janet Fitch puts it this way: "I usually start with something that has some energy, like a compressed character or a situation that's wound up like a spring. Then all I have to do is let it go, let its energy carry the story." Novelist Haruki Murakami wrote something similar in his book *What I Talk About When I Talk About Running*: "I stop every day right at the point where I feel I can write more. Do that, and the next day's work goes surprisingly smoothly."

Avoid the blank page by never ending a day's writing at the natural end of a segment—a scene, paragraph, or chapter. Always leave yourself a little mess to clean up in the morning. Once you're done sweeping up those extra words, you'll be ready to move forward again.

WRITE NOW

Here are a few more tools for tackling that blank page:

- Take Dr. LaMotta's advice and begin by writing down a sentence or paragraph from the newspaper or a favorite book. Change words, expound on concepts, and add new ideas.

- Make a list of your ideas for the specific chunk you are working on. When you feel the urge to start writing about one of the ideas, go for it!

- Take a line or paragraph from your journal and use it as a starting point.

- Make a list of headlines from magazines, newspapers, and online news sites. Use one of these as the title of your chapter, something a character says, or an anecdote.

- Turn on the radio or tune into the conversation at the coffee shop or gym. Write down everything you hear (just don't get caught). Use these phrases when you are stuck for a bit of dialogue or an illustration.

WRITE WHAT
YOU KNOW

*If you are going to write you must become aware of this
richness in you and come to believe in it and know it is there so
that you can write opulently and with self-trust.*
—Brenda Ueland

Many writers have abandoned a day of writing or even a project because they get stuck on a tricky part. You don't know how to explain rocket science to a layperson. You're not sure how to put together a diagram that would sufficiently explain the progression of … well … of whatever it is you are writing about. Maybe you cannot figure out how the protagonist discovers that his girlfriend is cheating. I stopped working on my memoir for two years because I could not figure out how to structure the book.

When sports psychologist Caroline Silby wrote her first book, *Games Girls Play: Understanding and Guiding Young Female Athletes*, she got through the difficult parts by setting those aside for a time and writing what she knew. It's not a bad idea. When I started to work on my memoir again, I decided to set aside the idea of a perfect structure and simply write the book scene by scene, starting with the scenes I knew how to write.

If you're stuck, start by creating a page in your manuscript for every chunk in your table of contents or every scene in your novel's outline. You might just have a title or a few notes about setting and action on each page, but that is okay.

Review your table of contents or your scene outline. Put a checkmark next to every piece you think you could write in your sleep. Meaning, check the topics you know a lot about or the novel's scenes that are well developed in your head. Go to the pages you created for each of these topics or scenes and write those.

When you're done with writing what you really know well, the stuff you could write about while walking backwards and chewing gum, it's time to write what you know about the chunks you don't know as well. Look at what's left on your topic list or scene outline. What do you kind of know something about? Mark those items.

Go to the pages with the topic or scene title on them and list what you do know about each chunk. You might only know where the scene takes place or who is in it—that's enough. Write it down. Add what you need to know to write the chapter—or perhaps what you need to think about. Consider how you could combine your experience and expertise to write these chunks. Maybe you've never experienced a death in the family but you have experienced both love and loss. Combine those experiences and imagine the rest. Jot down these ideas. After a day or so off, you will be able to go back to these jottings and put together the chunk.

Once you have written about everything you know really well and everything you know kind of well, you will be left with the topics or scenes you think you know nothing about. Yikes! Wait, don't worry. This really isn't a problem. Remember: This is your book. Your area of expertise. Your characters. Your story. You must know something about even the things you think you know nothing about or it would not be part of your book. So, my dear reader, go to those pages in your manuscript and write down everything you think you know about the topics or scenes you don't think you know anything about.

Did you do it?

Apply the same process you applied before to these chapters: Give it a few days and get back to it. Chances are, with time, you will be able to write those chapters as well.

When novelist Janet Fitch wrote *White Oleander*, she wrote it out of order. She'd write any scene that had energy for her, print it out, and throw it in a box. When she was done, she put them in order. When I get stuck, I pretend I am writing to a client with a specific problem. When I start solving her problem, I forget about my problem with writer's block, and soon I am typing away!

Next time you get blocked on a chapter or even a paragraph, ask yourself: "So, what DO I know?" Write what you know (even if it is simply a description of the character's socks) until you stop feeling blocked.

You will be surprised at how much wisdom you have buried beneath all that useless information you carry around with you. You are a virtual treasure trove of valuable information and ideas.

QUESTION THE BLOCK

All writing is difficult. The most you can hope for is a day when it goes reasonably easily. Plumbers don't get plumber's block, and doctors don't get doctor's block; why should writers be the only profession that gives a special name to the difficulty of working, and then expects sympathy for it?
—Philip Pullman

Most of my clients have experienced writer's block. When it happens, we think we are the only ones who suffer so fiercely. We imagine that our favorite novelists produce their books easily and fully formed. As we hit our head on our desks, struggling to find any old word (not to mention the best word), we think, "Real writers don't have this problem. Professionals never get blocked. If I were good at this, I'd be done by now." Yeah, right.

Writers get writer's block. After years of writing professionally and coaching writers through blocks, I've learned that writer's block is not some mysterious curse that needs to be cured. Instead, writer's block is simply information. Writer's block teaches us that something about our writing project or process is not working. In that sense, writer's block is a gift. Like the pain that comes with a broken ankle, writer's block tells us what's broken. Once we know what is NOT working, we can fix it. Use the following questions to discover what writer's block has to teach you:

- **IS THIS THE RIGHT PROJECT FOR ME?** Sometimes we get blocked because we are working on a project that is not right for us. Yeah, I know—you've done the prep work. You thought this was the right project. If you're a professional writer, you have the added burden of knowing that writers write, no matter what. Ideally, we should be able to put together an article on either tree frogs or toe fungus with our eyes closed. But we can get embroiled in projects that don't work for us. Writer's block or procrastination can be our soul saying, "No." Let go of what doesn't work for you and move on.

- **IS THIS THE RIGHT TIME FOR THIS PROJECT?** We can love a project and desire to do it, but bump against writer's block because the timing is wrong.

Maybe we are trying to write a book while also launching a business or a teenager. Perhaps we don't have the distance from a difficult experience to write a memoir about it. Or maybe we should just wait until tomorrow when the kids are back at school and the house is quiet! If now is not the right time for this project, work on something else. Or, schedule a different time to write.

- **DO I HAVE THE INFORMATION I NEED TO DO THIS PROJECT?** Writer's block can happen when we don't know enough to write a chapter or book. We might have thought we were ready to write, but writer's block shows up to teach us we need to research more. Get thee to a library (or search engine)!

- **DO I BELIEVE I CAN DO THIS PROJECT?** Research on the effectiveness of medication reveals that when a patient believes a placebo will cure depression or a headache, it usually does. The same goes for us—if we believe we can write it, we can. It doesn't matter what we are writing, how much training we have, or how well connected we are; our belief in our ability to write well busts through any block we might face. If you don't believe you can write this particular project, you have two choices: Write as if you believe in yourself or dump the project and find a new one.

Most writers treat writer's block like it's the flu. We worry we can catch it from other writers. We have habits we hope will keep us safe from an untimely bout of writer's block. When we have writer's block, we try all sorts of home remedies to get rid of it. But what if we treated writer's block as nothing more than information? Writer's block shows up to inform us that something doesn't work. Once we fix the problem, we can move on. If not, there's always plumbing school.

GET HELP

Never doubt that a small group of committed people can change the world. Indeed it is the only thing that ever has.
—Margaret Mead

Alone we can do so little; together we can do so much.
—Helen Keller

I can do it myself!" I must hear that phrase a hundred times a day from my young daughter. It doesn't matter what the chore—putting on shoes, brushing her hair, pouring a glass of water—she wants to remind me that she is more capable than I give her credit for. Still, she yells, "I need help!" from time to time, too. No matter how big we get, we all need help.

We live in a culture that prizes independent achievement. We were founded on the value that every human being—not every family or community—should have the right and opportunity to pursue life, liberty, and happiness. We see these values acted out in our society. We clamor for stories of the little guy or gal overcoming negative circumstances to achieve something on their own. We honor individual heroes with awards. We reward *individuals* for getting Ph.D.s. Who ever heard of a cooperative doctorate degree?

We also view book writing as a solitary task. And it is. Even people who write books together must spend hours alone in a silent room putting the words to the paper. But when we get stuck we can't always see why we are stuck, we just know we are stuck. Another person's point of view can move us toward solving the situation.

Asking for help can be hard. Because we live in an independent culture, we often believe that asking for help is a sign of weakness or even failure. We tell ourselves lies like:

- "Real writers do it alone."
- "If I were smarter, I could do this without anyone's help."
- "If I ask for help and get it, it won't be my book anymore. It would be like cheating."

Of course, none of this is true. Real writers need and get help all the time. That's part of what makes a real writer a professional—she knows when she needs the support of other people. Knowing we don't know everything is also, as the old adage goes, the beginning of real wisdom. It's not cheating to get help. It is research. When you are a professional writer—and for this month you are—you use any resource you have to get your job done.

Just in case you don't recognize when you need help, here are humorous and serious signs that you need help:

- You've stared at the same passage on the same page every writing session for several sessions in a row.
- The text you are staring at begins to take on the shape of a golem, a dead relative, or your ex.
- You start pacing and talking to yourself in public.
- You begin talking to the text: "Tell me what to do, damn it!" Or worse yet, the text begins to talk to you. And you listen.
- You are finding it hard to string words together to talk to your family, let alone write anything down. Oh yeah, and you can't find your keys.
- You cannot sleep, you have trouble eating, or you get sick.
- You think about giving up.

Stop. Get help. Get out of your house and connect with someone who can help you RIGHT NOW! At least get out of your house and away from the project for a few hours. When you have calmed down and feel better, here are some ideas for getting help:

- **LIST IT.** Make a list of all the problems you are encountering. You might start with a phrase like, "I don't know how to …" or "If I really want to finish this book, I need to know …"

- **QUESTION.** Make a list of questions you have about the project. "I wonder how or why or what …"

- **CONNECT.** Take a look at your list of support people: editors, writing and accountability coaches, writing buddies, experts, your research and development team, and others. Who can help you with the problems and questions you have?

- **FIND AN EXPERT.** Yeah, you have a team. We went over that in an earlier chapter. But sometimes you need new people. Find someone who seems to know the information you need to know and ask them for help. It might just be another writer or writing coach who can tell you how he has dealt with the kind of situation you are facing.

- **RESEARCH.** Take an hour or even a day to do a research and development field trip. Yes, often the solution to one's crisis can be found in a book, periodical, or online. (When in doubt, look it up!) But sometimes you need to get out of your house and into a new environment. Looking stuff up in person can help you get a fresh view on your problem.

- **PARTY!** Sometimes you need to bounce ideas off of real live people, not the imaginary ones who live in your head. Have a research and development party. Give them food and drink. Promise them an acknowledgment in your forthcoming book. People love to eat. They also like to look smart and give advice. Let them. Present some of your toughest questions and let the party begin!

On an episode of *The Biggest Loser*, a former contestant talked about his first Ironman triathlon in Hawaii. Every athlete competes in a triathlon as a solo competitor. But this man did not do it alone. At the end of the grueling race, as he was trying to complete the marathon, he hit the proverbial wall. In the last mile, his family and friends surrounded him and ran with him, cheering and speaking encouraging words. The athlete finished the race.

Your marathon is no different. Yes, you are doing it in private. But you are not alone. Gather your cheering section around you, ask for help and some encouragement, and keep writing. Connect with the people and resources that can help get you out of your rut and across that finish line. I know you can do it!

GET IN THE ZONE

When we commit ourselves to writing for some part of each day we are happier, more enlightened, alive, lighthearted and generous to everyone else. Even our health improves.
—Brenda Ueland

Running in The Zone has to be one of the most satisfying experiences. When it all fits together it can seem effortless and intensely rewarding. But why are some times better than others? Is there anything we can do to help ourselves get into The Zone?
—Roy Palmer

Runners talk about getting into the zone, the place where all the variables—breathing, stride, and weather—work together to create the perfect run. Runner Roy Palmer has studied the zone for more than ten years to discover how to reach that elusive place. Palmer has reviewed the studies on running in the zone and reports these seven common characteristics. Runners:

- were totally absorbed in the activity
- experienced an inner clarity
- had a sense of ecstasy and being outside everyday reality
- were *in the moment*, focused on the present
- felt a deep passion for the activity
- had a sense of serenity, no anxiety about their performance
- had no sense of effort—it just happened

Writers know the zone, too. Every one of the above characteristics can be applied to the writing zone. When you write in the zone, you feel like you could write forever. Ideas come easily. You feel passion for what you say and you put sentences together effortlessly. You don't worry about what you will say next, whether you have met the word count, or if your writing is good enough. The usual intrusive thoughts—what should I make for dinner? Do my toenails need clipping? I should check e-mail—disappear. You are in the zone—writing fast and furiously and loving every minute of it.

Most writers have experienced the zone at least once in their writing careers. Even if you're a first-time marathon writer, you have probably had at least one writing session in the zone. The zone experience presents a few challenges for all writers but especially for beginning writers. First, once we've had a zonelike writing experience, we think writing should always be like that. One of my clients woke up on a Saturday with a full-fledged scene in his mind. He wrote it that morning. The challenge came when he tried to write the next scene, and it didn't come so easily. He lamented, wondering why his muse had left him. Second, once we've had a zonelike experience, we believe that all *real* writers compose their masterpieces in the zone every single day. So instead of writing, we beat ourselves up for NOT being in the zone or we try desperately to get into the zone. We believe that once we are real writers—once we sell a book for a bazillion bucks—we will be in the zone. Finally, many writers mistakenly credit the zone experience to a flash of inspiration. We look back at the zone experience and, whether it is true or not, believe it happened because inspiration struck. So we put our writing on hold while we wait for the magic muse to return and inspire us. When it doesn't, we feel like failures.

After working as a professional writer for nearly twenty years, I've gotten pretty cynical about the zone. Professional writers cobble together words into prose on a multitude of topics every single day. Some of the topics we are passionate about and could write while doing the complicated Ganda Bherundasana position in yoga. Other topics remind me of how I used to feel about the Christmas fruitcake (do I have to eat it?). But the zone happens whether I am writing about what I love or what I loathe. Here are some truths about the zone:

1. YOUR WRITING SESSION DOESN'T HAVE TO BE AN AMAZING, PLEASURABLE EXPERIENCE IN ORDER FOR YOU TO PRODUCE GREAT WORK. Some writers believe the writing process is downright painful. George Orwell said, "Writing a book is a long, exhausting struggle, like a long bout of some painful illness. One would never undertake such a thing if one were not driven by some demon whom one can neither resist nor understand." I disagree with Orwell. Sure, there are painful moments. There will be times when, like a runner entering the middle of the marathon, you feel like you have hit a wall. But you will also have times that are merely okay. Not good, not bad, but like an ordinary day at work. And here's the real truth: You can write good stuff whether you are in the zone or not.

2. THE ZONE EXPERIENCE HAS NOTHING TO DO WITH WHETHER YOU ARE A REAL OR PROFESSIONAL WRITER. In fact, I am beginning to think that writers who claim they were in the zone the whole time they were writing their masterpieces are lying. Writers are people who write, just like runners are people who run. If you feel good while you write, good for you. If you feel sucky while you are working, I am so sorry to hear that. But how you feel while you write doesn't have a thing to do with your professional status as a writer.

3. WRITERS GET INTO THE ZONE WHILE THEY ARE WRITING, NOT BEFORE. Inspiration doesn't ring like a school bell, telling you when to get in your seat and work. Inspiration is more like the announcements that come over the loudspeaker after you get into your seat. The announcements are going to come no matter what, but you have to be quiet and sit in your seat in order to hear them. In other words, inspiration strikes while you are already writing!

I'll be the first to admit that inspiration does strike at random moments. That's why I carry a pen and a stack of note cards with me wherever I go. But real writers never wait to be inspired. They know—just as you are learning—that inspiration strikes most frequently during the writing process. Even if you start your writing session with a brain that feels dull and fuzzy, chances are if you write persistently for any amount of time, you will get inspired.

Zone writing happens more than you think. It is not some amazing mystery reserved only for professionals and a few gifted individuals. It happens to anyone who writes regularly.

So how do you get in the zone?

You write every day or, at the very least, five days a week. What would you say to a runner who took one run a year and complained about never reaching the zone? You'd laugh at her, right? I would. How can anyone think that one run a year is going to get him in a zone? Yet plenty of writers abandon their great book because they tried to write for a few days and never felt it. If you only write once a week, it's going to be harder to get into the zone. As I said earlier in the book, the more you write, the more you write. And, the more you write, the more likely you are to find and stay in the zone.

Next, you look back at your zone times—the moments when your writing felt like it was effortless and fun—and write down everything about those writing sessions you can remember. What made success possible for you? Look at every internal and external factor you can think of, including environment, attitude, topic, and so forth.

When I did this exercise, I realized that the zone happened most often when:

- I wrote first thing in the morning, before I had communicated with anyone either in person or virtually.
- I was writing daily or nearly daily.
- I gave myself time to prewrite the day before—to jot down notes about the project before I began the actual writing session.

The list you compile will be longer and probably different than mine. If you can, try to re-create the environment that has produced the zone for you in the past. It will increase your chances of reaching the zone in your writing sessions. But please don't think that if you write in less-than-ideal conditions, you have to give up the zone. You don't. I've hit the zone with my kids screaming in the other room, while suffering through a nasty cold, and at the end of a long day of work. The zone happens. It happens most to people who write daily. Trust that the zone will happen for you, too.

FORGET IDEAL
AND FIND PLAN B

---

*The most successful people are
those who are good at Plan B.*
—James Yorke

For new writers and sensitive souls, a small interruption can upset the delicate balance—and ruin the writing day. Often writers tell me they can only write in the morning or when the house is perfectly still or when the moon is full. Some tell me they need to set aside a whole day to get anything done. Others need just the right paper or light or chocolate.

When I first started writing, I needed perfect conditions: a quiet house, an empty morning, and no worries about interruptions. A telephone call or the doorbell ringing could upset the delicate balance—and ruin the writing day. That fragility led to many arguments with my writer husband. It seemed I always needed to talk when he needed to write and vice versa. Then the babies came. Neither of them seemed to have any respect for our writing hours. They needed attention, food, and diaper changes during our precious writing time.

When I interviewed novelist Liam Callanan, author of *The Cloud Atlas* and *All Saints*, for my podcast *Always Write*, his baby daughter started crying. Not ideal—but real. I asked Liam how he managed to write novels with little children in the house and a job directing the Creative Writing Program at the University of Wisconsin, Milwaukee. He said, "Realize that there will never be ideal conditions."

As a writer, I usually juggle family duties, work, and writing. Liam's words—*there will never be ideal conditions*—have become an encouraging mantra. One week, up against several deadlines, I tried to write despite the after-lunch energy dive. My kids screamed in the background. The band next door practiced (loudly). I repeated Liam's words—*there will never be ideal conditions*—and managed to write an article and a promotional letter. At some point, I had to accept that *ideal* is for the television and romance novels. Here are some thoughts on how to loosen your grip on *ideal* and get real (or get a plan B).

PLAN AHEAD. Interruptions happen. Part of getting real is getting ready. Look back on the kinds of interruptions and roadblocks you have experienced in your writing over the past year. What sort of plan B would have helped you solve them? Examples include: writing less, working on a shorter portion of the project, writing in a different location, researching instead of writing, or turning off the phone.

GET SPECIFIC. Most writers I work with have a global idea of what they want to do during the week. For example, the first time I did National Novel Writing Month (and failed), I went into the month with this on my to-do list: "write novel." That's too big, even without interruptions. Take your big goal and break it down into really small steps. This year, my plan B steps will be really tiny turtle steps: choose character's name, write description of character's house, start scene list, and so forth. Each of these steps I could do in fifteen-minute slots. Many of them I could work on while cuddling a sick child.

GET CREATIVE. Do you remember the old saying, "Necessity is the mother of invention?" Crazy, challenging situations stimulate our creativity. Use your interruptions as an opportunity to get creative and design a fun plan B. Barbara Kingsolver wrote her first novel in a closet, in the middle of the night, while pregnant with her first child. In 2007, five of the ten best-selling books in Japan were written on cell phones via text message. And some of those writers were teens, composing their novels between classes. Talk about a plan B! If these writers can write without all the time in the world, you can, too!

You will not have ideal conditions throughout this writing marathon. Someone you live with will get sick and cough all over you or your computer. The neighbors will put on a new roof. The basement will flood. Tough. Get a plan B (and C and D)! Write through, around, and within the distractions. Write every day. Write every time you have a free moment. Start right now.

READ AND REVISE

Don't reread.
–CHRIS BATY

So you're blocked. You don't have one more original word to say. Your deadline is fast approaching and all you can do to get closer to reaching your total word count is to separate all contractions. So *they're* becomes *they are* but *you are* no closer to finishing your book. What do you do?

You go back to what you wrote yesterday and you reread it. Maybe you change a few words. Maybe you add a sentence or two. Pretty soon you will have an idea for another sentence or maybe you get some thoughts about how you want to put together another whole chunk. And there you go. Without pomp and circumstance, without a bottle of Jack, you are writing again.

What just happened? In *No Plot? No Problem!*, Chris Baty strongly urges his readers not to reread during the marathon and certainly not to rewrite. It's good advice. You don't want to get caught in the trap of revising your book before you have finished writing it. If that happens, you will never finish writing your book.

Using this technique, you don't revise the book. You rewrite a few sentences. You can use this tool successfully—and not get caught revising—if you follow these three rules:

- Focus on revising a set amount of text—maybe the last five lines you wrote yesterday. Don't allow yourself to review the manuscript beyond those few sentences.

- Keep your eye on what is happening now and what will happen next in your book. It's tempting to look at the big picture. Don't. This isn't the time. Instead, focus on how these five sentences can best lead into what you are writing today.

- Set a time limit. Ideally, this process of reading and revising will take just five minutes and then you will move on to write today's set of new words. If you notice that you are continually revising for more like twenty minutes, set a timer. Give yourself five minutes to rework yesterday's writing and then move on.

Why does reading and revising work to break through writer's block? When you read and revise, you don't tackle the blank page, you tackle a page with some words on it. This has the same effect as creeping into a cold swimming pool a bit at a time. As you step down into the water, you get warmer and warmer, until finally you feel ready to jump in and swim. By revising a few words, you get more comfortable and your brain forgets it was supposed to be afraid to write. Instead of panicking and freezing up, like you usually do when you have writer's block, your brain starts working. Before long, you are back to writing new words for your book. And that's always a good thing!

RUMINATE WELL

Many people hear voices when no one is there.
Some of them are called mad and are shut up in rooms
where they stare at the walls all day. Others are called
writers, and they do pretty much the same thing.
—ANONYMOUS

Bennett Cerf, a publisher and the cofounder of Random House, challenged beginning writers with these depressing tidbits from the lives of some of the famous writers in history:

> Coleridge was a drug addict. Poe was an alcoholic. Marlowe was killed by a man whom he was treacherously trying to stab. Pope took money to keep a woman's name out of a satire then wrote a piece so that she could still be recognized anyhow. Chatterton killed himself. Byron was accused of incest. Do you still want to be a writer—and if so, why?

Popular fiction and movies portray writers as brooding and depressed. Consider how *The Hours* portrayed Virginia Woolf or how Sylvia Plath's life unfolded in the movie *Sylvia*. Psychologists such as Martin Seligman suggest that ruminating—the practice of obsessively analyzing events—can cause depression. When we ruminate, we literally behave like a cow: chewing again what has been chewed slightly and swallowed. Psychologists think that people who consistently ruminate over bad events—especially the people who create unhelpful stories about those events—are more likely to be depressed.

Psychologists think rumination hurts us more when our stories about the bad events in our lives are:

- personal (It's about me and my character flaws: "I'm a bad writer.")

- pervasive (It's universal and applies to all situations: "I am doomed to a lifetime of writer's block" or "All publishers are unfair.")

- permanent (It will never change: "I'll never get anything published" or "No one will ever want to read my book.")

Far better to story your life in ways that are:

- external (It's not about me. It's about the situation or something else: "Maybe the editor didn't need a story about the proper use of commas" or "Of course it was hard to write with a punk band playing next door.")

- specific (The problem is related to a specific event: "I had trouble writing this article" or "This publisher is unfair.")

- temporary (It is a passing thing: "Maybe the editor doesn't have room for the story right now" or "My agent wasn't listening because she was distracted when I called.")

But ruminating doesn't always have to be bad. Instead, productive ruminating—thinking about a challenging piece of your project—can actually move your work forward. Select a difficult chunk of your book, a part that you don't know how to tackle. This might be a concept you are not sure how to explain, a chapter you don't know how to write, or an exercise you need to create. Be specific. Don't choose six chunks to ruminate on. With all of those thoughts circling your brain, you may give yourself motion sickness. Instead, choose one chunk. Here are some actions ideas for ruminating productively:

- Write your challenging chunk on an index card and take it with you throughout the day. Use some of the tools we have talked about to spur your thinking brain—visit the park (nature increases your ability to think well), do a repetitive action (repetitive actions bring aha moments), or exercise (moving your body increases blood flow to your brain and improves cognitive functioning).

- Write your challenging question or problem on a large piece of butcher-block paper. Brainstorm or mind map ideas. Sometimes it helps to tack up the problem in a central place so you will think about it whenever you pass by throughout the day.

- Carry a token that reminds you of your problem. Each time you touch the token, think about the writing problem and how you might solve it. Talk it over with a colleague, family member, or a close friend.

The answer might come to you while you are chewing it over or while you are doing something completely different. But rest assured, the answer will come. Next time you sit down to write, you will have your answer. And, with luck and a little bit of discipline, you'll be able to ruminate without sending your life down the drain of depression or debauchery!

THE GREAT ESCAPE

*I'm constantly raising the high bar on myself and setting
new challenges. Sometimes I'll get very frustrated and
am certain that I can be more creative or that I need
to find something wholly original to tackle. At that point, it's
best for me to go for a hike, read a favorite author,
or simply put my project away for a few days. Doing something
physical like digging holes or pulling weeds helps, too.*
—KRISTINE O'CONNELL GEORGE

Anything can and does happen during the writing marathon. In my own writing marathons I've had skunks move in under the porch, kids puke all night long, and work emergencies appear. The solution? When daily writing gets interrupted repeatedly, get out. Plan one or more short writing retreats off-site.

With multiple demands for my time and energy, my writing thoughts often get swallowed up in a host of other demands for my time and energy. Not so in an empty hotel room! I booked a room at a four-star hotel in downtown Milwaukee through Priceline. (Cheap!) I checked in at 3:00 P.M. on Friday and wrote steadily until my daughter joined me at 6:00 P.M. the next evening. Without Internet access or other demands on my time, I was free to think solely about my writing project. It was exactly what I needed to jump-start my writing.

Brendan McLeod, the 2007 winner of the three-day novel contest, didn't spend every minute of the fast-paced contest working on his book. For the course of the long weekend writing marathon, McLeod and his girlfriend wrote at an apartment near the beach. McLeod said, "No one can sit at a computer for seventy-two hours straight. I don't think that's how a book gets written. I went to the gym. I took walks. I played the guitar. The important thing is I kept the story in my head."

McLeod is onto something. The brain is a lazy organ. True, it has an enormous job. The brain basically runs the body—directing our organs and muscles to do their work. But when it comes to thinking, the brain has learned to rely on past experiences and connections to produce answers. In order for the brain to generate new images and connections, it needs to be in a circumstance where it cannot predict what will happen next. According to Gregory Berns, a professor of neuroeconomics, we can help our brain see new ideas and think differently. He says, "You need a novel stimulus—either a new piece of information or an unfamiliar environment—to jolt additional systems awake. The more radical the change, the greater the likelihood of fresh insights."

If you're feeling stuck and unable to get writing done right now, take a writing retreat. Even a night away from home will free up those brain cells and stimulate new ideas. You can get a similar experience by escaping your regular writing environment and working at a coffee shop, the public library, or a friend's house (while she is away).

Don't say you can't afford to change your environment. Get creative. One of my writing-coaching clients regularly uses Priceline to get the ridiculously low rate of forty-eight dollars a night in the Washington D.C. metro area. Monasteries and convents often rent rooms or guesthouses for a nominal fee. A colleague has found house sitting for friends with pets to be a good way to find a quiet writing space away from home. With a little imagination and effort, you will find the perfect writer's retreat.

Need a novel stimulus? Try:

- Changing your routine. Eat something new. Drive to work a new way. Exercise at a different time of day.
- Get up earlier than usual.
- Take a day trip on your own or, better yet, with a group.
- Stay up late and write.
- Watch a new TV show or movie.
- Buy a stack of magazines in a new field and read them.
- Visit the library and check out books on topics you know nothing about and read them.

TIMED WRITE

Get it down. Take chances. It may be bad,
but it's the only way you can do anything really good.
—William Faulkner

At a recent conference, the guest speaker gave us timed writing exercises. For two- or three-minute periods, we would write like crazy in response to phrases like, "I am ..." or "What I really want to say ..." We had been complaining about feeling blocked in our writing. But once we were forced to write against the clock, our writer's block disappeared. We focused on our work, writing quickly and intensely for these short periods.

I use the same tactic when I exercise. When I stop seeing results from my daily exercise routine, I increase the intensity in short timed periods. Whether I'm walking or pedaling my bike, I do a thirty-second sprint every three minutes. I'm able to increase my effort without feeling overwhelmed.

If your writing isn't working, a timer can help you get back on track. Here are some ideas:

1. TIMED WRITING SESSIONS. Choose a specific task and a short period of time (three to twenty minutes). Make rules: You must sit in the chair. You cannot check e-mail or surf Facebook while you are working. Then set the timer and write like crazy until it goes off. It may sound silly but it works.

2. BREAK REMINDERS. In the midst of a big project or a looming deadline, you may not have the luxury of writing in twenty-minute spurts. You may have to write around the clock to finish on time. In these cases, use your timer to remind you to take a break every thirty to forty-five minutes. Get up and do something active and repetitive for fifteen minutes (lift weights, wash dishes, stretch). You will be more energized for your next writing period.

3. FOCUS REMINDERS. Over the years, I've worked with many graduate students who are writing dissertations. Often the students get so lost in their research that they forgo writing time. Other clients start projects with great intentions but then get lost in exploring great new ideas. In these cases, it can be helpful to set a timer to go off every twenty to thirty minutes to remind us to get back to the writing task.

Most computers and cell phones come with timers. If you don't have access to either, you can use a simple kitchen timer or a website like Online Stopwatch (www.online -stopwatch.com). Play with the suggestions to see which one works best for you. Or, create your own method for using a timer to write now.

DAYDREAMS THAT WORK

One man's daydreaming is another man's novel.
—GREY LIVINGSTON

In the course of doing the twenty-six-day writing marathon, I discovered I needed time for something I didn't budget for: daydreaming. Idle moments create great books. As a writer and coach, I know the necessity of idle hands. Without daydreams and meandering walks, how would we birth new stories? Without lazy mornings and afternoon naps, how could we imagine new ideas? Without the time to listen to music and shoot hoops, how could anyone vision a different way of expressing their ideas?

Daydreaming allows us to wander into the world of our ideas. Idle moments create the space for us to listen to the music of our souls, to hear the whispering of the universe. In a more practical vein, daydreaming gives us time to conjure up the content we will write about. In the moments between the tasks—when no one wants or needs us, when our output doesn't matter—we are free to dream.

And guess what? Scientists have proven that when we daydream, the problem-solving function of our brain is hard at work. Actually, our brains are more active when we daydream than when we perform routine tasks. That means we can daydream about anything and come back to a problematic writing project with a solution.

Next time you feel stuck or blocked with your writing project—no matter what it is—take time to daydream and listen for the whispers of your soul. You will come back to your work refreshed. And you may find that daydreaming supports you in finding solutions to your life problems as well as your writing projects.

THE CARE AND FEEDING
OF YOUR CREATIVE LIFE

*[Creativity is] always there, filling us or else colliding with
whatever obstacles are places in its path. If it finds no inlet to
us, it backs up, gathers energy, and rams forward again until
it breaks through. The only ways we can avoid its insistent
energy are to continuously mount barriers against it, or to
allow it to be poisoned by destructive negativity and negligence.*
—CLARISSA PINKOLA ESTÉS

At the beginning of my professional writing career, I became friends with a woman who had just finished writing her first novel. I was in awe. This woman had done something I was just learning to do: set aside time to write a book that no one had assigned her to write. She had no external deadline. She wrote the novel because she wanted to write it. She got up before work and gave up her weekends to write because she dreamed of becoming a novelist. She possessed the grit to keep writing despite plenty of distractions. She did what all writers need to do: Show up and do the work.

I don't know where you are on your write-a-thon course. No doubt some of you finished your book in twenty-six days. If that is you, pat yourself on the back. Savor this amazing accomplishment. You have jumped over writing hurdles, pushed through procrastination, and crossed the finish line. I admire you! Some of you may have stalled somewhere in the middle of the course. The reasons will be different for each of you: Life duties interrupted your work, you got stuck on how to write a section of the book, or you ran out of energy. Hang in there. You can restart the race and still finish your book. Some of you are still moving forward—not yet done with the write-a-thon, but not running in place. Keep at it. This chapter is for all of you: the winners, the writers on break, and the writers still accumulating words.

In the above quote, Estés reminds us that all artists possess a powerful creative force that insists we pay attention to it. But artists also face obstacles—the barriers we create and the difficulties we encounter in the world. As writers, we need to protect our creative force against obstacles and poisons, much like we might protect a real river from pollution. There are literally thousands of books, including this one, to help you protect your creative force and keep writing. But at this point in the write-a-thon, you know better than anyone what makes your creative force thrive. In fact, you could write a book about it. Maybe you will call it *The Care and Feeding of My Creative Life* or *A Field Guide to How I Conquered the Write-A-Thon (and Lived to Tell About It)*.

In fact, I would like you to write a field guide just like that. You probably think I'm joking. You are already immersed in writing a book (or recovering from just finishing one) and now I am suggesting you write another book? Am I crazy? No, I am not crazy and I am not kidding. Despite the fact that you are trying to complete another book or have just finished one, I want you to write a mini field guide to completing the write-a-thon. Not a book really, more of a booklet—like the kind you get with a new appliance. Why? Here's the thing: Even though you know how to bust through every writing block imaginable and write like Joyce Carol Oates on speed, sometimes you forget to use what you know. Instead of writing, you stare at the blank page or beat your head against the desk and wonder what to do next. You're a little like an absentminded professor searching desperately for the glasses perched on his head. This chapter's exercises are designed to help you recall and use what you already know.

If you have finished the write-a-thon, the booklet will be your guide for the next write-a-thon. (You know you're going to do this again. If you had one book inside of you, you probably have more books inside of you!) If you are stalled midcourse, this guide will help you figure out how to restart and finish the write-a-thon. And if you are still writing, this exercise will help you understand how you can keep writing fast!

What follows is a series of five writing exercises. Most of them invite you to simply make lists about stuff you already know. Each list will become a chapter in your write-a-thon field guide. You can do all of the exercises or choose the ones you think will help you the most. Do them in the order they appear or in an order that works for you. Each exercise should take you about the same amount of time as it takes to do the daily dump writing—maybe even less. In fact, this would be a good daily dump activity. As you write, remember how writing productivity works: The more you write, the more you write. Doing these exercises might just increase your productivity for the day.

But hear this: Don't do anything that will distract you from your central purpose, which is to finish the write-a-thon. If this is not the right time to do these exercises, if you still feel energized to write your write-a-thon project, come back and complete these exercises when you need them.

Naming Strengths

Marathon runners know which part of the marathon they excel at. Some are slow and steady runners, skilled at endurance. Others love the sprint at the beginning and end of the race. It is no different with writers. We each have parts of the writing process we rock and other parts we struggle with. Now that you have been writing steadily for some time, you know your strengths. These strengths describe who you are as a writer and reveal the parts of the writing process you do best. Naming and using your strengths can help you finish your writing project.

1. MAKE A LIST OF YOUR STRENGTHS. Strengths can be classified in two ways—either as traits you possess or skills you perform. If you choose to name traits, you might articulate your strengths by listing characteristics such as curiosity, gratitude, playfulness, or sense of purpose. For example, your curiosity about what happens next keeps you writing when you get stuck on the logistics of a scene. You could also define your strengths by identifying skills you excel at, such as writing dialogue, researching, or revising. As you create your list of strengths, feel free to use a mixture of the two approaches. Here are examples for each approach to articulating strengths:

Naming characteristics.

- Playfulness. I like writing the first draft because I can play with the characters on the page. I am especially good at putting the characters in wacky situations to surprise them (and me)!
- Purpose. When I remember why I am writing this book, I can picture the people I want to help and talk directly to them.

Identifying skills.

- I am good at writing dialogue. I hear my characters talking to me all day at work. Sometimes I jot down notes on break. When I get home at night, I am able to recall their voices and write the dialogue.
- I love to do writing exercises. Whenever I get stuck, I do writing exercises and before long, I am working on the book again.

2. ONCE YOU HAVE A LIST OF YOUR STRENGTHS, add a few examples from the write-a-thon that show how and when you used these strengths. For example, the writer above with the strength of playfulness might write:

- I made the best use of my playfulness when I worked with friends at a write-in. I asked them for suggestions I could play with in my book, and it worked! Their off-the-wall ideas infused my novel with the fresh energy it needed.

The writer with the strength of purpose might record:

- I used my strong sense of purpose during each writing session. Asking myself why I was writing each section helped me write clearly.

Hold onto your list of strengths. It's part of the guidebook, and it is necessary for the next exercise.

Overcoming Challenges

You've heard it before, maybe from a parent or even a writing teacher: We can't be good at everything. We have weaknesses, too. The writing tasks that challenge us might not challenge our best friend. But that doesn't matter. Our challenges are the writing tasks that trip us up and make it hard for us to figure out what to do next.

1. MAKE A LIST OF YOUR CHALLENGES. These might be skills you struggle with, like plotting or writing a draft. Challenges might also be external issues that make getting writing done difficult for you, like limited time or a stressful job. Your list might look like this:

- I have a deadline at work at the same time as the write-a-thon.
- I worry that my writing is not good enough.
- I am not good at writing description.

2. ADD A FEW BRIEF EXAMPLES FROM THE WRITE-A-THON THAT SHOW HOW THESE CHALLENGES GOT IN THE WAY OF YOUR PROGRESS. The person who wrote, "I worry that my writing is not good enough" might write:

- I spent a whole Saturday obsessively rereading my book and comparing it to one of my favorite books in the genre—and it didn't measure up. In the meantime, I didn't get any writing done!
- Worrying interrupts my writing. I sometimes worry while writing, I question every bit of description and dialogue, wondering if it is inaccurate or boring.

3. OUR STRENGTHS NOT ONLY SUPPORT US IN DOING WHAT WE ARE GOOD AT; THEY ALSO CAN HELP US OVERCOME CHALLENGES. Recruit your strengths to help you defeat each of the challenges you listed above. Let's go back to the example of the worrier above. Perhaps she has the strength of curiosity. She might discover that curiosity could help her overcome worry in a very simple way. Instead of asking, "Is this good enough?" she might train herself to ask questions of the characters like, "What do you want to do next?"

Review your list of strengths. For each weakness or challenge, list three ways your strengths could help you overcome the challenge and keep writing.

Learning From Mistakes

Everyone makes mistakes during the write-a-thon. We forget that we don't have super-powers and take on too many other tasks during the twenty-six days we are supposed to be writing. We choose a project that is too big to finish in twenty-six days. We share our writing with a friend before it is ready and let his unhelpful critique stall us. But, as wise men and women have said for centuries, mistakes hold lessons. We learn more from our messes than our successes.

1. MAKE A LIST OF THE MISTAKES YOU MADE DURING THE WRITE-A-THON.

2. FOR EACH MISTAKE YOU LISTED, WRITE ONE TO THREE WAYS TO OVERCOME IT. These might be actual ways you overcame the mistake during the write-a-thon or ideas you have for the next time you encounter something like this. If you have difficulty finding a solution, look back at your strengths. How might they help with overcoming mistakes?

If the mistake you are working with is that you took on too many other tasks during the write-a-thon, your list might look like this:

- Say no to as many things as possible before the write-a-thon.
- Better late than never: Say no to outside tasks in the middle of the write-a-thon and preserve the time that is left.
- My strength is creativity. Instead of writing every day, as I had hoped, I got creative and did minimarathons on free days.

WRITE NOW

Recording Lessons

When I finished writing this book, I made a list for myself of what I learned from writing a book fast. Though I've been writing books fast for years, each time I participate in a write-a-thon, I learn something new about writing, my writing habits, and writing tools. All of these lessons will help me with the next write-a-thon.

You are also an expert at what has made this write-a-thon work for you. You accessed your strengths, overcame challenges, and learned from your mistakes. You have a lot to teach you! Make your own list of lessons, habits, and tools so you can successfully finish this write-a-thon or complete your next one. Here are a few items from my list as inspiration. Don't worry if your list is different than mine. It should be!

- Daily word counts work.
- When necessary, I can write at different times of day.
- Taking time off to do other activities helped me to write more.
- I had to say no to things I enjoy—coffee with friends, editing work.
- Doing homework at night—reading books, taking notes, jotting down ideas—helped me write the next morning.
- I got inspired while writing, not before—so hang in there and write.

The Summary Guide

True field guides are designed to be helpful in the field, while traipsing through tall grass and fighting the weather. For that reason, the information is narrowed down to the most essential elements, classified by type, and presented in a way that is easy to digest. You have just completed a number of exercises that have helped you discern your strengths, challenges, and lessons learned. This exercise helps you summarize this information in a quick and easy guide. Fill in any of the categories that are helpful to you. When you are done, you might choose to tape this to your office door, post it on your blog, or e-mail it to friends who are wondering why you haven't returned their phone calls for the last three weeks.

> Species Name: The write-a-thon writer
> Description
> Appearance before write-a-thon
> Appearance during write-a-thon
> Appearance after write-a-thon
> Zones of hardiness
> Preferred habitat
> Distinguishing habits
> Often confused with
> Preferred food
> Thrives on
> Cautions for approaching and handling the working writer
> Practices that endanger working writer

PUTTING IT ALL TOGETHER

You've made your lists. You know your strengths, habits, and preferred habitat. Next time writing challenges you, don't bother calling a colleague or hiring a writing coach. You know better than anyone how you can overcome writer's block and write fast because you have done it successfully. Open your field guide and follow your own advice. Then do what you were meant to do: Put your butt in the chair and write. Remember the adage: Writers write. We write whether we are busy, tired, sick, or discouraged. If you have slowed down or been sidelined on the write-a-thon, don't fret about it. Start again today. Write now. Finish your write-a-thon project.

PART THREE
RECOVERY

The worst mistake you can make—both physically and mentally—is not giving yourself time to recover.
—JOHN BINGHAM AND JENNY HADFIELD

First, congratulations. You did it! You finished your book. Whether this is your first book or your forty-first book, you have accomplished something very few people do. Celebrate that.

When runners finish a marathon, some collapse into bed while others go out to party. When you finish your writing marathon, you will probably have both urges. You may want to get as far away from the project as possible. After racing to meet this deadline, you will certainly need a break. You need to rest. Both your brain and body need time to recover. You may also need to take care of some of the tasks you have let lapse over the past twenty-six days. You know, like taking showers, dusting the furniture, and sorting through that pile of mail in the front hallway! Do it. Celebrate, rest, and recover. You deserve it.

Every writing teacher I've had has suggested that the real work of writing starts when the first draft is finished and the editing begins. Some writers like to dig into the editing in the midst of the marathon. I am not crazy about this idea. It's a little bit like a runner analyzing how she ran the marathon while still running it. It would be difficult and fruitless, if not impossible, to do both tasks at the same time. Writers who get blocked during the marathon may find that starting the day by reading and reworking the previous day's writing can give them confidence to move forward. Writers who get ideas for large rewrites or structural overhauls during the marathon can make notes about it in a separate document. But the bulk of the editing must wait until the book is finished and when the writer has had a sufficient period of rest.

Many writers want to quickly edit their work so they can submit it or show it to friends and family. I also discourage you from doing this. Your work is not ready. Like a roast just out of the oven, the project needs time to rest. Give it that. Let it sit. Get some distance from the project. With that distance, you will be able to see the book more clearly. Then, when you are ready, turn to this section. It highlights the steps you need to take to review and edit your book.

WHY REVISE?

---

*The time to begin writing an article is when you have
finished it to your satisfaction. By that time you begin to
clearly and logically perceive what it is you really want to say.*
—MARK TWAIN

When I read a good book, I want to quit writing. Who can compete? I'll tell you who: the writer who is committed to rewriting until the writing is right. It's all in the editing, friends. If you read a good book, it's good because the writer worked at it.

Veteran writers rewrite. They study their precious words and favorite phrases, and slash the ones that don't work. If you're going to write well, know that the first draft is only the beginning.

Many of my editing and writing coaching clients have come to me with finished manuscripts, paying me to offer suggestions for making it better. When I do, they confess their anger. One client said, "I was really pissed at your comments. I didn't want to change a thing." She told me it took her some time and a few talks with her husband before she accepted that she would need to revise her manuscript if she wanted to publish it. Another client lamented to me about the amount of hard work it would take to edit her book. I understand. I've been there. I once sent what I thought to be a brilliant chapter to my editor only to have her tell me it didn't work. I wanted to scream, "Doesn't work? I'm a professional!" Of course, I didn't scream because she was absolutely right. I took her advice and rewrote the chapter.

No one wants to hear bad news about his work. But better to hear it from a critique partner or an editor than to read it in a review.

Do you remember Sisyphus? He pushed the boulder up the hill all day. When he got to the top, it would roll to the bottom and he would start all over again. Sometimes writing and editing feels just like that. Put a word in; take it out. Write a chapter; delete half of it. But slowly the writing gets done, gets better, and finally—gets finished.

Here are some basic, global suggestions to help you revise your work:

- Take time off before you edit your book. The time gives you distance and distance gives you the ability to see your work more like the reader than the author.

- Create distance while you edit. Novelist Colum McCann reduces the computer font so he has to squint to see it. The small print gives him a sense of distance from the work and enables him to revise.

- Give yourself more time than you think you will need to edit your work. Review your work slowly and repeatedly.

- Schedule a day to read the whole book in one sitting. That first full read will teach you much about your book.

- Read your work aloud.

- Read your work in a different setting. One writer takes his printed manuscript to a park and reads it like he would another person's book. He asks himself, "What would I think if I bought this book?"

- Read your work backwards to catch spelling errors. When we read normally, our brains fix typographical errors, and we don't catch them. When we read backwards, we are more likely to notice these mistakes.

- Have a friend or colleague read your draft. Because they are not as familiar with your subject, they will be able to tell you where you are not communicating clearly.

- Know your blind spots. Each of us has types of mistakes we make repeatedly. Know the mistakes you make and check for them.

- Take frequent breaks. After forty-five minutes or ten pages, your brain needs a break. Wash the dishes, get a drink, do a yoga pose—anything to get the blood flowing back to your brain. You'll catch more problems and, in the end, your writing will sing.

Okay—so are you ready to start? Take a deep breath. Ready, set, GO!

THE FIRST READ

---

*Thank your readers and the critics who praise you, and
then ignore them. Write for the most intelligent, wittiest, wisest
audience in the universe: Write to please yourself.*
—HARLAN ELLISON

You've taken some time off. You've left your writing desk, closed your laptop, and walked away from your manuscript. Good. You need that time away from the project to get the distance you need to look at your work with fresh eyes. Once you've had your time off, you will begin the editing process by reading your book in one sitting, beginning to end.

If you've written your work by hand, get it entered into a computer. Print out your work so you can take it with you. Find a new environment. In order for this first reading to be effective, you cannot read your book in the same physical space that you created it. Take it to a coffee shop, work at a friend's office, or rent a hotel room. If it's warm, find a park bench. A new environment adds to your ability to read the book as if you were someone other than the author.

Before you head to that new environment, make sure you have the right supplies. Take a notebook to write revision notes to yourself about your book. You will also need a pen in a color you like. You might also want to take pads of sticky notes in different colors. I use one color to designate missing items—where I need to add a scene, a description, or a reference. I use other colors to note sections that need to be moved and chapters I need to read again. Some writers use different colored highlighters to track their changes or the movement of each character throughout the book.

Okay, you are ready to read! When you read your book, pretend that you are your ideal reader. Think about what your reader wants from you. Get in the mind-set of your audience and ask:

- How do I feel reading this book?
- What am I looking for—answers, help, entertainment, inspiration, a good story, or something else?
- What do I want to get from reading this book? Am I getting it?
- What parts of this book thrill me?

- What parts of this book annoy me? (Annoying your reader is not necessarily bad—you just need to be aware of when and why you are doing it.)
- What parts of this book work?
- What parts don't work?
- Is the material presented in an order that makes sense?
- What is missing?
- Is there repetition that needs to be cut?
- Does the book structure or the plot structure work? If not, how would I change it?

During this first read, don't get caught up in the details. Grammatical errors and small mistakes are details that can be fixed later. Use this reading to focus on the big picture. You want to learn if the book works as a whole.

Once you are done with this reading, make a list of items you need to change. It helps if you can prioritize your revisions. Often writers take care of the big revisions first. This may include shifting the order of the chapters, consolidating chapters, cutting a character, or adding scenes. Then add the pieces you didn't have time to write during the marathon: setting descriptions, callouts, exercises, a quotation to begin each chapter, or anything else that will make the work better. After working on fixing the big chunks and adding the missing pieces, writers move onto making each scene or paragraph work. They might add the bits of beautiful dialogue or supporting quotes they have been jotting down in their project journal. In the end, revising the manuscript is as much a process as writing it was. Give it time.

WRITE IT RIGHT: FIRST LINES

When in doubt, or wherever possible,
tell the whole story in the first sentence.
—JOHN IRVING

Do you want people to read what you write? Do you hope an agent or publisher might buy your story? And what about your potential reader? Here's a tip: Get that first line right.

People buy books based on great covers, catchy titles, and powerful first lines. Whether you're writing a book about finding Jesus, making a million dollars, or climbing Mount Everest, your first line better capture the reader's attention. The best first lines:

1. HOOK THE READER. Great first lines pique the reader's interest. Create some shock or mystery with that first line and you'll have the reader begging for more. Dan Brown did it in his mystery thriller *Angels & Demons*: "Physicist Leonardo Vetra smelled burning flesh, and he knew it was his own."

2. ESTABLISH VOICE. The first line reveals the tone and quality of the writing. Readers can hear if they want to spend some time with your work. Listen to how M.T. Anderson does it in his young adult novel *Feed*: "We went to the moon to have fun, but the moon turned out to completely suck."

3. ARE STICKY. A great first line haunts the reader. If a reader likes the line, sooner or later he'll be back to read the whole article or book. Almost everyone who reads knows how Herman Melville began his epic novel *Moby-Dick*: "Call me Ishmael."

So how do you create a great first line? Don't agonize over it. Don't wait to start a piece until you have the perfect first line. Write your draft. The perfect first line usually comes in the process of writing and revising. You'll know when you find your equivalent of "Call me Ishmael."

Need more examples? The *American Book Review*, a nonprofit journal, made a list of the one hundred best first lines. You can search for "best first lines" online and find it. Here's my favorite from Anita Brookner's novel *The Debut*: "Dr. Weiss, at forty, knew that her life had been ruined by literature."

MAKE YOUR WORDS COUNT

*Always and never are two words you should
always remember never to use.*
—WENDELL JOHNSON

spent many years writing children's stories. The practice of writing for children taught me that every word counts. In a 120-word children's story, a writer doesn't have room for meaningless, dull, or extraneous words.

Neither do you. Many writers mistakenly assume that because they are writing a longer book, it is okay to have a few sentences that don't work. It's not. Any sentence that doesn't work only confuses your reader—something a writer in today's market cannot afford to do. In our culture, people are already on information overload. Write a sentence that confuses, confounds, or irritates a reader, and you might just lose her for good. Yes, we put up with bad writing all the time. That doesn't mean we want to. The better you write, the better chances you have of getting that book contract and the readership to go with it.

Use these tips to improve your work and make your words count:

- Use meaningful, descriptive words. Words like *nice* or *interesting* don't tell the reader much. What word or phrase would more accurately describe the situation or action?

- Use active verbs. Don't let your subjects sit there, having things done to them. Get them up and moving! Instead of, "Fifty books were read by the class." try, "The children devoured fifty books."

- Twain gave great advice when he said, "Substitute 'damn' every time you're inclined to write 'very'; your editor will delete it and the writing will be just as it should be." Eliminate the word *very*, other words that modify adverbs and adjectives (e.g., *really*), and any other extraneous words such as *always, never, perhaps, quite, definitely, somewhat, I think, I believe.*

- Avoid adverbs. Yeah, some writers use them well. Most overuse them. If you cut about half of them, you will be on the right track.

- Don't change your verbs into nouns. For example, *investigate* becomes *investigation* and *explore* becomes *exploration*. When your characters make an investigation into the truth or begin an exploration, your readers fall asleep. But when your characters investigate and explore, readers pay attention.

- Cut clichés. We put clichés in our books because they are easy as pie to find. But they are not going to knock anyone's socks off. We are so used to reading clichés that we pass right over them. According to novelist Janet Fitch, "We read so that we can be moved by a new way of looking at things. A cliché is like a coin that has been handled too much. Once language has been overly handled, it no longer leaves a clear imprint." You don't want to lose your reader's attention. You want to hold it. So lose the clichés instead.

- Cut dictionary definitions and rhetorical questions. There are a few ways to mark your work as amateur writing. One is to begin your essay or chapter with a definition from the dictionary. Another is to use rhetorical questions. We use both as ways to begin chapters or chunks that challenge us. While the techniques work to get the draft written, once you are finished, go back and eliminate them.

- Don't use "quotation" marks, a bold font, or ALL CAPS to emphasize words. Write your sentences so your words and phrasing make your point.

- Check your writing for professional jargon. Unless a doctor is saying someone has abnormal bibasilar breathing sounds, cut it. And even then, if the average reader won't understand it, you might have your doctor speak in a way we can all understand.

- Shorten your sentences. Don't shorten all of them—that would sound choppy. One of my editors advises writers to keep longer sentences to twenty-five words or less. If you're not sure if your sixty-word sentence is too long, read it aloud. If the sentence leaves you gasping for air, shorten it. Your readers will thank you!

- Cut anything else that seems superfluous. Big words. Phrases that don't make sense. Quotations that don't add to your work.

Before you leave a sentence or a section behind, ask yourself this: Do I really need this to make my point? As the cliché goes, when in doubt, leave it out!

Brilliant writing emerges out of rewriting. So write. Then take the time to rewrite it right!

WHY HIRE AN EDITOR?

You'd be surprised how many famous novels have lived a good part of their histories being known as The *&$!* Book.
—Jan Burke

ere's the thing—sometimes you need to hire an editor. Let's say you finished the write-a-thon. You took a few weeks off and reread the book. You came up with a list of problems to fix. Your critique partner or writing group gave you another list of issues for you to address. You rewrote the book. But now that you're ready to submit it, you cannot actually tell if it really is good enough. Plus, you've read over the book so many times, the words are beginning to swim together and make no sense at all. You've begun to refer to the book with the four-letter words you will not let your children use. It might be time to hire an editor.

Ah, but what kind of an editor? When you look online you see development and copy and line editors. Some charge by the page and some by the word and others by the hour—but all look fairly pricey. What can you expect an editor to do? Should you worry about him stealing your work and selling it as his own? And the big question: How do you know if an editor is reputable or not? In this chapter, we will review the various types of editors and consider when to hire an editor.

TYPES OF EDITING

Editing roles, definitions, and tasks vary from editor to editor (and project to project) because of the individual styles of editors as well as the unique demands of clients. For example, an editor who is doing a development edit, which generally looks at content and organization, may point out or correct grammatical errors. Or an editor who is hired to simply copyedit a book may find that it needs a more extensive content edit. The following general definitions can be used as a basic guideline to types of editors and editing.

DEVELOPMENT EDITOR. A development editor works with a publishing house or in a freelance capacity to develop a manuscript from the concept stage through draft stage.

In some publishing houses, the development editor may actually do a good bit of the book-development work before hiring a writer to complete the project.

A freelance development editor usually works with a writer to develop a book from concept to outline to draft. If the editor is hired after the book is finished, the development editor may:

- Provide a manuscript evaluation, reading the manuscript for content and to address the specific concerns of the client.
- Show where the book needs more content or research.
- Point out content that is repetitive or doesn't work.
- Suggest changes in sentences, paragraphs, and organization so ideas or story work better.
- Catch inconsistencies.
- Do writing or rewriting.

COPY OR LINE EDITOR. A copy or line editor usually works with a manuscript after it has been through a development edit. The copy editor checks for clarity, organization, flow, and logic. The editor also reads for redundancies, sentence structure, spelling, punctuation, syntax, and word usage. The editor will query the writer to check permissions, errors, references, quotes, and so forth. If the copy editor works for a publishing house, she will edit so the manuscript fits the style of the particular house.

PROOFREADER. A proofreader reviews a manuscript for grammar, punctuation, and usage. He corrects typos and other errors, notes inconsistencies, and verifies links.

SUBSTANTIVE EDITING. Substantive editing requires that an editor identify and solve problems of clarity or accuracy. This often includes reorganizing paragraphs, sections, and chapters to improve the logical flow of the story or book. It may also include writing or rewriting segments to improve readability. In an ideal situation, the writer does substantive edits on her own work—often at the request of an agent or editor. If this is not possible, an editor can be hired for a substantive edit. This does cost quite a bit more than any other form of editing because of the time and effort required.

WHY HIRE AN EDITOR?

Though we'd love to think we can take a book from conception to publication all on our own, it actually takes a village to raise a book. An editor can be a helpful partner at many stages of the writing and publication process.

1. WHEN YOU GET STUCK. Maybe you didn't finish the twenty-six-day marathon—and not because you didn't try to write 50,000 words in a month. You bumped up against some structural or content issues with the book and couldn't figure out how to fix them. Early in the writing process or at any stage we get stuck, a development editor can help us understand and fix the structure of the book or address issues of plot, character, and setting.

2. WHEN YOU WONDER IF THE BOOK IS GOOD ENOUGH. You've finished and although you trust the opinions of your first readers, you want to hear what an expert thinks of your book. You are curious about what works, what doesn't work, and what you can do about it. You have two choices: You can hire someone to do a manuscript evaluation, a broad read of the book with an eye for content, flow, consistency, and marketability. Or you can hire a development editor who will look at all of the above and make suggestions for how you can fix those issues.

3. WHEN YOU WANT TO MAKE A GOOD FIRST IMPRESSION. Your book is done and has been read and critiqued for content and flow. You think you're ready to go. But wait. Some editors and agents, faced with a deluge of submissions, will look for reasons to dump your work. For that reason, it can be helpful to get someone to review your book for clarity and consistency. You will also need someone to address grammar issues and typographical errors. At the very least, you want a proofreader. You might want a copy editor to provide a more substantial look at the final copy of your book.

4. WHEN YOU ARE PUBLISHING THE BOOK ON YOUR OWN. You've decided to self-publish your book. Because you're doing it all on your own, you'll want to hire everyone you can to help: a development or content editor to make sure the book is organized well and makes sense; a copy editor to deal with issues of style and content; and a proofreader to check for minor errors. At the very end, you will probably want someone who can prepare your manuscript for publication, including typesetting, layout, and design.

5. WHEN YOU GET AN AGENT OR A PUBLISHER. When an agent or publisher accepts a book, it is by no means done. An agent will often give suggestions for revision before submitting it to editors. If several publishing houses reject your book, your agent might suggest you hire an outside editor to help you revise the book before the agent will submit it again. Once a publisher accepts your book, the publishing house will assign an editor to your project. The editor will help you further develop and edit the content of the book. No doubt you will be doing the bulk of the rewriting here. But the editor will be there to support you in creating the best book possible. Finally, copy editors and proofreaders will work to put your book in tip-top shape for publication.

Okay, so now you know you need an editor. You may even know what type of editor you need to hire. But how do you go about actually finding editors and then working with them? The next chapter gives you the information you need to do both.

WORKING WITH EDITORS

Never throw up on an editor.
—Ellen Datlow

Hiring an editor is a bit like hiring a babysitter for the first time. When I hired someone to watch my infant son, I contemplated staying home and watching the babysitter watch the baby so I could make sure she did it right. I didn't know about nanny-cam. Too bad there isn't an editor-cam, so we could watch an editor handle our precious manuscript. Hopefully, the following precautions will make the editor-cam moot.

1. KNOW WHAT YOU WANT. Make a list of the various tasks you want an editor to do. If you have specific concerns (Do I use too much jargon? Is chapter seven confusing?), note those, too. Choose the type of editor based on the kinds of concerns you have. If you have concerns that bridge a variety of editorial jobs, know that you might need to hire more than one editor.

2. ASK YOUR NETWORK FOR REFERRALS OF GOOD EDITORS. Talk to every writer you know. Post it on Facebook and Twitter. Invite the members of your critique group to share names. You will find the best editors through referrals from other writers.

3. DO YOUR RESEARCH. Review the websites and LinkedIn profiles of the editors you are considering. Research them online. Make sure there are no complaints about them.

4. ASK FOR A CONSULTATION. Almost all reputable editors will give you a complimentary consultation. Some will even do a free test edit, reviewing a few pages of your work so you can see how the editor works, and the editor can get a sense of how long it will take to edit your writing. Let the editor know about your list of concerns and issues for your book and what kind of an edit you want. Talk frankly about what you want from the editing process. Ask the editors what exactly they can provide and what their price points are. Also, have a conversation about the mechanics of the process—the format you would prefer the editing to take (written or in a word processing program). Also, find out how the editors tend to work—will they edit it all at once or pass it back to you for revisions? Ask for a written price quote.

5. SHOP AROUND. Talk to multiple editors. Check their credentials and referrals. Compare their credentials against what you are asking them to do. If you need to have a novel edited and they have only edited nonfiction, look somewhere else. But if you need someone to proofread your dissertation on the mating habits of bonobos and the editor happens to be a member of the Bonobo Fan Club, this might be a match made in heaven.

Check the editor's prices against the prices of the other editors in the area. Weigh price and qualifications together. You may pay less for a newbie but not receive the same level of editing you'd get with an experienced editor.

6. GET IT IN WRITING. Once you have hired an editor, ask them to put your agreement in writing. The agreement should contain a list of what the writer can expect the editor to do, how the process will work, how long it will take, and how much it will cost. The agreement will also include a payment schedule. Most editors ask for a portion of the payment up front and the rest upon satisfactory completion of the editing work. If the project is a long one, some will ask for a payment in the middle of the process.

HOW TO WORK WITH AN EDITOR

So you've taken the big leap of hiring an editor. Now how do you make the relationship work? Here are a few hints.

1. LET GO OF YOUR EGO. Your editor is not here to tell you you're a rock star who writes like the magic combination of Shakespeare and Charlotte Brontë! Your editor's job is to make the work better—to take it from passable to superb. Let your ego take a vacation with a good book and a bottle of wine while you work with the editor on improving your book.

2. REMEMBER YOU ARE ON THE SAME SIDE. When your manuscript looks like it had a bad run-in with a slasher, you may be tempted to lash out at your editor. No wonder—it will probably feel like she's just tried to lob off the arm of your new baby. Relax, take a deep breath, and remember—you are on the same side. You both want to end up with a great book. It just might take a little slashing to get there.

3. ASK QUESTIONS. It may take time to learn how best to communicate with your editor. As you work at understanding each other, ask questions. Invite the editor to clarify his statements, queries, and changes.

4. SAY THANK YOU! Editing can be a challenging task. The editor is working hard to improve your book. Yes, the editor will get paid—either by you or by the publishing house. But beyond that, the only credit the editor will receive is a note from you on the acknowledgment page. Let the editor know you are thankful for help birthing your book!

5. SEND CHOCOLATE. Refer your friends. What editor doesn't like a bar of good chocolate? Nothing says thank you like a small gift and a referral to all of your writerly friends!

HOW TO GET
YOUR QUERY REJECTED

---

*Only kings, editors, and people with tapeworm
have the right to use the editorial "we."*
—MARK TWAIN

You've finished writing your best book ever. You have had it critiqued and spent hours revising it. Now you are finally ready to send it out into the big exciting world of publishing. But first you must conquer one of the hardest writing assignments ever: the query letter. A query letter, well written and properly addressed, is designed to interest agents and editors in your project. Think of it as the key that opens the magical door to the publishing world. But here's the thing: Most writers fail at this crucial step because they have not figured out the basics of writing and submitting query letters.

I've worked as the editor of a devotional periodical for ten years. The job has given me the opportunity to understand the other side of the editor's desk. I am constantly amazed by how many writers ignore the basic rules of writing query letters. Whether you are submitting your query to an agent or editor, here are five ways to guarantee rejection.

1. GET THE NAME WRONG. Rachel, Michelle, and Michael are all beautiful names. But none of them are my name. I frequently get submissions addressed to these lovely people. If you want to guarantee a stack of rejection letters, address your letter to the agent or editor of another firm, misspell the name, or use a different name altogether.

2. GET THE GENDER WRONG. When I'm not being addressed as Michelle, writers are adding a male title to my name: *Dear Sir, Gentlemen, Mr.* If you're aiming to paper your bathroom with rejection letters, don't do your homework. Just address all of your queries to, "Gentlemen" or "Ma'am."

3. DON'T READ THE GUIDELINES. The denominational devotional periodical that I edit offers specific assignments to writers of religious devotions. Yet every week, I receive queries about potential articles on everything from the mating habits of newts to how to cure cancer. Sometimes I get queries for books. I cannot use any of these. I used to tell writers why I couldn't use their lovely query and encourage them to read the guidelines. Now I just send a rejection letter. Every agent, publisher, and publication has specific guidelines for what types of material they are looking for. If you want a rejection letter, don't read these guidelines.

4. DON'T PROOFREAD YOUR QUERY LETTER. I look for the writers who will turn in work on time with few mistakes. You can imagine what I think of query letters that have simple spelling, grammar, or punctuation mistakes. It's like showing up on a first date with ketchup stains on your shirt and food particles in your teeth. If you cannot bother to edit your query letter, how can I trust you'll edit your submission? Yeah, don't edit. I guarantee you will get rejected!

5. BUG THE EDITOR OR AGENT FOR AN ANSWER. I frequently receive e-mails from writers who say, "I sent you a submission last week, and I haven't heard from you yet. What did you think of my work?" Reading unsolicited submissions is only a small part of my part-time job as an editor. And, like most editors, I am inundated by submissions. Bugging an editor may get you an answer more quickly, but it's unlikely it will be the answer you want.

KEYS TO ACCEPTANCE

So there you have it, writers: several good ways to guarantee rejection. But what can you do to help guarantee acceptance? Here's what I look for in a query.

1. LOOK FOR A MATCH MADE IN HEAVEN. Okay, so finding the perfect agent or publisher for your book is not exactly like finding the right mate, but it's close. Do your homework. Agents and publishers all have specialties. Find out what kind of books and authors the agent represents before you submit. Some agents only do fiction while others specialize in a specific kind of nonfiction, like positive psychology or business management resources. If you are submitting directly to editors and publishers, know what kinds of books they publish. This information is readily available online through searchable databases. Writers can subscribe to Writer's Market (www.writersmarket.com) for a yearly fee. Agent Query (www.agentquery.com) offers a free database of agents.

I encourage clients to develop their list of publishers and agents by researching the top books in their field or genre. Writers can discover this information by reading the copyright page and the book's acknowledgments. After you have a list of people, research them. The best way to get a proposal accepted is to pitch it to the person who is already looking for it!

Before you send the query letter, triple-check the spelling of the name. Make sure the name on the letter matches the name on either the envelope or in the e-mail address. If you are unsure of the editor or agent's gender, don't use gender words.

2. HOOK THE READER. Agents and editors read constantly. We know pitches. We read query letters and proposals. At writing conferences, writers pitch their ideas to us over cold toast, while walking down the hallway, and even in the bathroom. That said, we are seeking the million-dollar idea, so we keep listening. But because we have heard so many pitches, we get bored easily. We need you to grab our attention with that first line. Write a first line (and paragraph) that hooks us.

3. INFORM THE READER. Tell us what you are proposing and why we need to pay attention to it. Don't assume we know that your book on the secret life of termites will be the first book to reveal these secrets clearly and has a quantifiable potential readership. Tell the reader what your book is and does, what genre it fits into, and who will buy it.

4. SELL YOURSELF. Forget that your mama chastised you for talking big about yourself. This is your chance to tell the agent or editor why you are the perfect person to write this book. Include education or experiences that help justify your status as an expert on this topic, your previous writing credits, and information about how many people are already paying attention to what you have to say. Try to leave out extraneous information and anything that makes you sound like an amateur—including references to a spouse, child, or parent having read the book and loved it.

5. BE POLITE. As you write the closing of your letter, remember all those things that your mama taught you to say—like *thank you* for reading my work, *please* let me know if you need any further information, and I've included a self-addressed stamped envelope for your response.

Finally, be patient. Agents and editors get hundreds of query letters a week from new writers. That's on top of the work they have to do to get paid—like submitting and editing the books already under contract. Once a week or once a month or, in some cases, once a quarter, when they have a spare moment, they sit down with a strong cup of coffee and read queries. Don't worry. They will get to your query sooner or later. Meanwhile, make a list of more agents and editors to submit to just in case you get rejected on the first round. Getting published takes time.

PERSISTENCE

A professional writer is an amateur who didn't quit.
—RICHARD BACH

Our family adopted an eleven-year-old Bichon named Muffin Man. This six-teen-pound dog has three great loves: treats, walks, and cuddles. When he wants any one of the three, he will employ one of his well-honed begging tricks. He follows me around the house, trying to guide me to the front door and his leash. Muffin dances backward and forward on two legs, tilting his little head to the side and making eyes at my daughter, begging for a treat. He sits attentively, tapping his feet rhythmically, silently pleading my husband to invite him to jump into his lap! No matter how many times we say "later" or "no" ("we'll walk you later," "no table treats," "no sitting on the sofa"), Muffin persists in asking for what he wants. Writers, we can learn from my dog!

Richard Bach said that a professional writer is an amateur who didn't quit. How true. In this complicated, competitive market, persistence might be your best asset. The writers who succeed continued writing and revising their books even after their family, friends, or a few dozen agents told them to give up and get a real job. They submitted their books to hundreds of agents and publishers until something clicked. Then the authors persistently marketed their books until readers started showing up.

Once, when I was frustrated by a series of rejections from agents, my writer husband sent me the following message of encouragement:

Rejection sucks but keep going. Randy Pausch in *The Last Lecture* said it best: *The brick walls are not there to keep us out. The brick walls are there to give us a chance to show how badly we want something. Because the brick walls are there to stop the people who don't want it badly enough. They're there to stop the other people.*

As writers, rejection is only one of the obstacles we face. If you've done the write-a-thon, you've faced obstacles. You've had to jump through hoops to find the time, energy, and space to write. You've been criticized for taking time away from work or family to write. Your writing has been critiqued and possibly rejected because the critic believes it's not good, not good enough, or not what he was looking for. Every day you get up and face the tyranny of the blank page. Whether you win or lose the battle against that page, almost no one really cares. Few people pat you on the back and cheer, "Wow, you did it!"

Well, writers—I'm here to say, "Congratulations! You did it!" Keep writing. When you encounter a brick wall, jump over it or knock it down. Don't let the critique or rejection of others stop you. Your writing matters. Writing has the power to transform your life—to make you healthier, happier, and more able to achieve your goals. Writing also has the power to transform the world. But none of this can happen unless you actually write. So keep at it!

P.S. Yes, it is hard to get published. There are fewer publishing houses looking for big-name authors who can promise thousands of readers. But there are also new, small publishing houses cropping up all over the place. Many authors choose to bypass traditional publishing and sell their books online. Authors with a large platform—a group of people who already follow and pay attention to them—can sell their books either as a self-published hard copy or e-book on their websites. Seth Godin made headlines in 2010 when he announced he would no longer use traditional publishing. In 2011, Godin launched The Domino Project as his online venue for releasing powerful idea books. Authors with a book and no platform at all can also use any number of self-publishing tools to produce either a hard copy or an e-book. Books can be sold from the back of the room when you speak, on your website, or from a site that sells e-book formats, like Amazon's Kindle or Barnes & Noble's PubIt! But before all of that, you must persist in writing and rewriting until you have a manuscript that shines. The key to all of the above tasks is persistence. Now, get back to that writing!

CONCLUSION: THE NEXT RACE

*But after I finish and some time has passed, I forget
all the pain and misery and am already planning how I can run
an even better time in the next race.*
—HARUKI MURAKAMI

Writers, you have done a remarkable thing. You have accomplished what 80 percent of Americans have dreamed of doing. You have written a book. The pain and suffering of the race was temporary. Your book is forever! Many of you have edited your books and sent out queries to editors and agents. A few of you are already working on publishing these books—either on your own or through a traditional publisher. Congratulations! Writing a book—like running a marathon—is an amazing, jaw-dropping accomplishment. You did it!

When I finish a book project, before I can celebrate, I clean. I put away all of the books I've yanked off the shelves during the write-a-thon. I pick the paper drafts off the floor and dump them in the recycling bin. I shelve the project binder and journal in my closet. A sort of emptiness settles in. I'm both giddy at the freedom from the constant deadline and at a loss for what to do with all the extra time. For the past twenty-six days or longer, my life has been shaped by one purpose: writing the book. I've built my days around this purpose. Everything I have done—from thinking to reading to exercise—has been in the service of the book. Now that the project is finished, I must order my days differently. I wonder if this is what empty nest syndrome feels like.

The empty feeling doesn't last long. In *The Courage to Start* John Bingham said, "We run simply because we are runners." It's the same with us: We write simply because we are writers. We cannot wait for the next NaNoWriMo to come along. As soon as we forget the pain and misery of this book, of this write-a-thon, we grab an empty journal and begin to plan the next race.

And so, dear writers, the journey is not over. You have finished one race. Be proud and happy for what you have accomplished. But know this: You have more races to run, more books to write. Take a break, celebrate, and begin again!

WATER STOPS, STRENGTH TRAINING, AND ESSENTIAL GEAR:
RESOURCES FOR THE WRITE-A-THON

Managing and Organizing Your Life

One Small Step Can Change Your Life: The Kaizen Way by Robert Maurer, Ph.D. Maurer uses practical examples to show how taking absurdly small steps toward goals can lead to lasting change.

Creating Your Best Life: The Ultimate Life List Guide by Caroline Adams Miller and Dr. Michael B. Frisch. Learn what types of goals work, how to set up a successful plan, and how to develop resilience.

The Power of Full Engagement: Managing Energy, Not Time, Is the Key to High Performance and Personal Renewal by Jim Loehr and Tony Schwartz. The authors present a program to support individuals in managing their physical, intellectual, emotional, and spiritual energy for both work and play.

Organizing From the Inside Out: The Foolproof System for Organizing Your Home, Your Office, and Your Life (second edition) by Julie Morgenstern. Organization expert Morgenstern teaches readers how to identify their organizational problems and create solutions based on their personal style and goals.

SHED Your Stuff, Change Your Life: A Four-Step Guide to Getting Unstuck by Julie Morgenstern. Morgenstern explains how letting go of old stuff and habits can transform one's life.

Take Time for Your Life: A Personal Coach's 7-Step Program for Creating the Life You Want by Cheryl Richardson. Richardson provides practical tools and exercises to help readers manage their own lives.

Writing Books Fast

No Plot? No Problem! A Low-Stress, High-Velocity Guide to Writing a Novel in 30 Days by Chris Baty. The founder of National Novel Writing Month (NaNoWriMo) offers up a fun, easy-to-read guide, divided into two sections and based on his experience and tips from fellow NaNoWriMo participants.

Book in a Month: The Fool-Proof System for Writing a Novel in 30 Days by Victoria Lynn Schmidt. This spiral-bound book provides a complete system for writing a novel in a month. It teaches time management and goal setting as well and offers worksheets for developing characters and tracking the plot.

First Draft in 30 Days: A Novel Writer's System for Building a Complete and Cohesive Manuscript by Karen S. Wiesner. Learn the building blocks of the novel and get a daily plan for outlining and drafting a novel.

Writing Advice

Escaping Into the Open: The Art of Writing True by Elizabeth Berg. Novelist Berg offers writing advice, exercises, and a glimpse of her journey from being a working mother to earning her living as a working writer.

The Giblin Guide to Writing Children's Books by James Cross Giblin. Former editor-in-chief of Clarion Books, Giblin provides advice on how to write nonfiction, fiction, and picture books for children.

On Writing: A Memoir of the Craft by Stephen King. Half memoir, half advice on the craft, King's book first shows readers what the writer's life is like and then tells them how to make it happen.

Bird by Bird: Some Instructions on Writing and Life by Anne Lamott. This now-classic text on writing and the writing process teaches memorable lessons on writing and life with both humor and tenderness.

Walking on Water: Reflections on Faith and Art by Madeleine L'Engle. The prolific author, best known for her beloved Newbery Award-winning book *A Wrinkle in Time*, describes how writing is a spiritual endeavor.

What I Talk About When I Talk About Running by Haruki Murakami. Novelist and marathon runner Murakami describes the running and writing life in a series of essays adapted from journal entries and articles.

Dear Genius: The Letters of Ursula Nordstrom collected and edited by Leonard S. Marcus. This volume of letters from one of the most-revered children's book editors gives the reader a rare and valuable glimpse into the life of writers such as Louise Fitzhugh, Shel Silverstein, and H.A. Rey.

If You Want to Write: A Book About Art, Independence, and Spirit by Brenda Ueland. This classic text on the writing process offers a pep talk for the tired, bedraggled writer.

Fiction Writing

How to Write a Damn Good Novel, How to Write a Damn Good Mystery, and *How to Write a Damn Good Thriller* by James N. Frey. Frey lays out a simple and clear plan for writing a novel, mystery, and thriller.

Write Away: One Novelist's Approach to Fiction and The Writing Life by Elizabeth George. The author of the popular series featuring Thomas Lynley and Barbara Havers shares her secrets for creating a novel.

Fiction Writer's Workshop by Josip Novakovich. Not only does Novakovich explain each step of creating good fiction, he offers multiple imaginative exercises to help writers master the craft.

Nonfiction Writing

Old Friend From Far Away: The Practice of Writing Memoir by Natalie Goldberg. Goldberg offers essays and exercises to support the reader in remembering their life stories and writing them down.

The Situation and the Story: The Art of Personal Narrative by Vivian Gornick. Essayist Gornick guides writers through personal narrative by recalling some of the best memoir and essay writing of the past century.

Will Write for Food: The Complete Guide to Writing Cookbooks, Blogs, Reviews, Memoir, and More by Dianne Jacob. Food writer Jacob teaches readers how to write about food for a variety of venues.

Publish Your Nonfiction Book: Strategies for Learning the Industry, Selling Your Book, and Building a Successful Career by Sharlene Martin and Anthony Flacco. This practical book written by an agent and a professional writer helps readers discover their market, build a platform, and create a sellable proposal and query.

Thinking Like Your Editor: How to Write Great Serious Nonfiction—and Get It Published by Susan Rabiner and Alfred Fortunato. An editor turned agent and a freelance editor and writer teach the basics of nonfiction writing: putting together a sellable proposal, creating a readable book, and marketing the finished book.

Fearless Confessions: A Writer's Guide to Memoir by Sue William Silverman. Memoirist Silverman offers tips, practical exercises, and examples on a wide variety of issues that face the memoir writer.

Writing About Your Life: A Journey Into the Past by William Zinsser. The author of the popular writing book *On Writing Well*, Zinsser takes the reader on a tour through his own writing history and, in doing so, teaches the reader how to write her own life story.

Writing Exercises

The Playful Way to Serious Writing: An Anything-Can-Happen Workbook to Inspire and Delight by Roberta Allen

Imaginative Writing: The Elements of Craft by Janet Burroway

Yoga for the Brain: Daily Writing Stretches That Keep Minds Flexible and Strong by Dawn DiPrince and Cheryl Miller Thurston

Wild Mind: Living the Writer's Life by Natalie Goldberg

The Write-Brain Workbook: 366 Exercises to Liberate Your Writing and *Take Ten for Writers: Generate Ideas and Stimulate Your Writing in Only 10 Minutes a Day* by Bonnie Neubauer

Poemcrazy: Freeing Your Life With Words by Susan Goldsmith Wooldridge

Revising, Submitting, and Publishing

The Indie Author Guide: Self-Publishing Strategies Anyone Can Use by April L. Hamilton. From publishing options to platform, Hamilton teaches readers how to navigate the world of self-publishing.

The ASJA Guide to Freelance Writing: A Professional Guide to the Business, for Nonfiction Writers of All Experience Levels edited by Timothy Harper. The best nonfiction writers in the field provide advice on topics like gathering ideas, setting up a business, and developing a specialty.

Six-Figure Freelancing: The Writer's Guide to Making More Money by Kelly James-Enger. Writing expert James-Enger teaches readers how she built a six-figure career and how they can do it, too.

How to Write a Book Proposal by Michael Larsen. Agent and author Larsen guides the reader through a step-by-step process in creating a sellable book proposal.

The Writing & Critique Group Survival Guide: How to Give and Receive Feedback, Self-Edit, and Make Revisions by Becky Levine. This guide provides tools for critiquing writing in multiple genres, suggestions for revising one's own writing, and worksheets for critique groups to use.

Self-Publishing for Dummies by Jason R. Rich. Rich offers a step-by-step guide for writers who want to publish their own books, providing information on everything from starting a own publishing company to marketing a book online.

WORKS CITED

For full works cited go to writersdigest.com/writing-articles/by-writing-goal/complete-first
-draft/write-a-thon-exclusive

MOVE FROM WANNABE TO WRITER

The Summer of The Great Grandmother
by Madeleine L'Engle
"Becoming a Writer"
by Gail Godwin in *A Writer on Her Work*
edited by Janet Sternburg

MAKE AFFIRMATIONS

*Marathoning for Mortals: A Regular Person's
Guide to the Joy of Running or Walking a Half-
Marathon or Marathon*
by John Bingham and Jenny Hadfield

TAKE YOURSELF SERIOUSLY

Dear Genius: The Letters of Ursula Nordstrom
collected and edited by Leonard S. Marcus

WHY WRITE? HOW WRITING HEALS

*Asthma Free in 21 Days: The Breakthrough
Mindbody Healing Program* by Kathryn
Shafer, Ph.D., and Fran Greenfield, M.A.
*Opening Up: The Healing Power of Expressing
Emotions* by James W. Pennebaker

PREWRITE

The Mind Map Book
by Tony Buzan with Barry Buzan

DISCOVER WRITING STRENGTHS

Now, Discover Your Strengths by Marcus
Buckingham and Donald O. Clifton

THE PROJECT JOURNAL

*Write Away: One Novelists Approach to Fiction
and The Writing Life* by Elizabeth George
"Ten Rules for Writing Fiction," in *The Guardian*

TAKE NOTE

How to Write a Great Novel by Alexandra Alter,
Wall Street Journal
'Writuals'—*Scribes Reveal Daily Routines*
by Kerry McKittrick, BBC News

THE STORY BIBLE

How to Write a Great Novel
by Alexandra Alter, *Wall Street Journal*

WHERE DO YOU GET YOUR IDEAS?

Gaiman's blog: http://www.neilgaiman.com/p/
Cool_Stuff/Essays/Essays_By_Neil/Where_
do_you_get_your_ideas%3F

THE WHO

"Rounding Up Your Characters" by Margaret
Maron in *Writing Mysteries* edited by Sue
Grafton with Jan Burke and Barry Zeman
"Characterization" by Michael Connelly in
Writing Mysteries edited by Sue Grafton with
Jan Burke and Barry Zeman
Screenplay: The Foundations of Screenwriting by
Syd Field
Cutting For Stone by Abraham Verghese
Two For the Dough by Janet Evanovich
Maisie Dobbs by Jacqueline Winspear
A Visit from the Goon Squad by Jennifer Egan
Catherine, Called Birdy by Karen Cushman
Holes by Louis Sachar
*Write Away: One Novelist's Approach to Fiction
and the Writing Life* by Elizabeth George
'Writuals'—*Scribes Reveal Daily Routines* by Kerry
McKittrick, BBC News
The Cruelest Month by Louise Penny

THE WHERE

"A Sense of Place" by Anne Wilson in *They Wrote
the Book: 13 Women Mystery Writers Tell All*
edited by Helen Windrath
The Girl With the Dragon Tattoo by Stieg Larsson
In Her Shoes by Jennifer Weiner

THE PLOT

*No Plot, No Problem: A Low-Stress, High Velocity
Guide to Writing a Novel in 30 Days*
by Chris Baty
Take Joy: A Writer's Guide to Loving the Craft by
Jane Yolen
"Outlining" by Robert Campbell in *Writing
Mysteries*, edited by Sue Grafton with Jan
Burke and Barry Zeman
How to Write a Great Novel by Alexandra Alter,
Wall Street Journal

POINT OF VIEW

*Write Away: One Novelist's Approach to Fiction
and the Writing Life* by Elizabeth George
The Spellman Files by Lisa Lutz
The Daughter of Time by Josephine Tey
Judy Moody by Megan McDonald
Seedfolks by Paul Fleischman
With No One as Witness by Elizabeth George
A Tale of Two Cities by Charles Dickens

"The Hills Like White Elephants," in
*The Complete Short Stories of Ernest
Hemingway* by Ernest Hemingway
How to Write a Great Novel by Alexandra Alter,
Wall Street Journal

RESEARCH THE NOVEL
On Writing: A Memoir of the Craft
by Stephen King
"Expertise and Research" by Faye Kellerman and
Jonathan Kellerman in *Writing Mysteries*,
edited by Sue Grafton with Jan Burke and
Barry Zeman

THE POWER OF PASSION
Stories from *Rotten Rejections: A Literary
Companion* edited by Andre Bernard

FIND YOUR PURPOSE
*The Power of Full Engagement: Managing Energy,
Not Time, Is the Key to High Performance
and Personal Renewal* by Jim Loehr and
Tony Schwartz

CREATE YOUR LIFE PRIORITY LIST
What I Talk About When I Talk About Running
by Haruki Murakami

MANAGE YOUR ENERGY
*Marathoning for Mortals: A Regular Person's
Guide to the Joy of Running or Walking a Half-
Marathon or Marathon* by John Bingham and
Jenny Hadfield
*The Power of Full Engagement: Managing Energy, Not
Time, Is the Key to High Performance and Personal
Renewal* by Jim Loehr and Tony Schwartz
*The Courage to Start: A Guide to Running for Your
Life* by John Bingham
What I Talk About When I Talk About Running
by Haruki Murakami
"Behaviorial Responses to Stress: Tend and Befriend,
Not Fight or Flight," Taylor, S. E., Klein, L.C.,
Lewis, B. P., Gruenewald, T. L., Gurung, R. A.
R., & Updegraff, J. A. *Psychology Review*

PRIME YOUR ENVIRONMENT
"Technology Tempts Us To Dawdle, Study Finds,"
by Seth Borenstein, AP
"Nancy Werlin: Get Thee to a Bread Store"
in *Novel Ideas* by Melody Joy Kramer and
Marc Silver

TAKE TINY STEPS
*One Small Step Can Change Your Life: The Kaizen
Way* by Robert Maurer, Ph.D.

Bird by Bird: Some Instructions on Writing and Life
by Anne Lamott

PUT YOUR BUTT IN THE CHAIR
"Laptime Reading" New Futures School http://www.
newfutureshigh.org/Reading/How%20toLearn.
html
From *How to Write a Great Novel*
by Alexandra Alter, *Wall Street Journal*
Snoopy's Guide to the Writing Life edited
by Barnaby Conrad and Monte Schulz

GET A LIFE!
"The Interview" with Alaa al Aswany, novelist and
dentist, by Rachel Cooke in *The Guardian*
"Jodi Picoult: You Can't Edit a Blank Page," in
Novel Ideas by Melody Joy Kramer and
Marc Silver, NPR

AVOID MONKEY MIND
Huston Smith, *The World's Religions*
From an interview with Hallowell on CNet:
http://news.cnet.com/Why-cant-you-pay-
attention-anymore/2008-1022_3-5637632.
html)

AVOID OVERWHELM
The Power of Little Steps; from the AP, 8/22/2006,
Ridgeville, SC

VISION DAILY
James Bauman, "The Gold Medal Mind,"
Psychology Today
The Secret by Rhonda Byrne

PAY YOURSELF FIRST
"A Way of Writing," by William Stafford in
Landmark Essays on Writing Process
edited by Sondra Perl

DROP EVERYTHING
*Coaching the Artist Within: Advice for Writers,
Actors, Visual Artists & Musicians from
America's Foremost Creativity Coach*
by Eric Maisel

MAKE MISTAKES
The High Flyer by Susan Howatch
Conquer Sabotage
Traveling Mercies: Some Thoughts on Faith
by Anne Lamott

OVERCOME PERFECTIONISM
From Interview with Mike Ness of *Social
Distortion* done by A.V. Club by Matt Schild

CONSERVE ENERGY
"You Think You're Tired?"
    by Mary A. Fischer in O *Magazine.*

FINISH ANYTHING
The Tao of Leadership Lao Tzu's Tao Te Ching
    Adapted for a New Age by John Heider

WRITE ANYTHING
"Jodi Picoult: You Can't Edit a Blank Page"
    in *Novel Ideas* by Melody Joy Kramer and
    Marc Silver, NPR

WARM UP WITH POETRY
Haiku: Asian Arts and Crafts for Creative Kids
    by Patricia Donegan
"Gayle Brandeis: A NaNoWriMo Success Story"
    in *Novel Ideas* by Melody Joy Kramer and
    Marc Silver, NPR

GET INSPIRED
"'Horizon'" Evolves with U2's Audacity,
    Creativity, and Innovation" by Edna
    Gunderson, *USA Today*
"Gateway to the Soul," in *Handbook for the Soul*
    edited by Richard Carlson

WRITE YOUR DREAMS
"Oprah Talks to Janet Fitch" in O *Magazine*
What I Talk About When I Talk About Running
    by Haruki Murakami

WRITE WHAT YOU KNOW
If You Want to Write by Brenda Ueland

GET IN THE ZONE
"Can We Train to Get in the Zone," Fitness
    Programs for Life. http://www.fitness-
    programs-for-life.com/in_the_zone.html

THE GREAT ESCAPE
Quoted in *Poetry Matters: Writing a Poem*
    from the Inside Out by Ralph Fletcher.
    The National Post

"Neuroscience Sheds New Light On Creativity"
    by Gregory Berns, adapted from the book
    Iconoclast, in *Fast Company*
For a list of monasteries, check out: *Monastery*
    Guest Houses of North America: A Visitor's
    Guide by Robert J. Regalbuto

THE CARE AND FEEDING OF
YOUR CREATIVE LIFE
Women Who Run With the Wolves: Myths and
    Stories of the Wild Woman Archetype by
    Clarissa Pinkola Estes, Ph.D.

PART THREE:
RECOVERY SECTION INTRODUCTION
Marathoning for Mortals: A Regular Person's
    Guide to the Joy of Running or Walking a Half-
    Marathon or Marathon by John Bingham and
    Jenny Hadfield

WRITE IT RIGHT: FIRST LINES
Getting Started by John Irving in *Writers on*
    Writing edited by Robert Pack and Jay Parini
Angels and Demons by Dan Brown
Feed by M.T. Anderson
The Debut by Anita Brookner

MAKE YOUR WORDS COUNT
"Oprah Talks to Janet Fitch" in O *Magazine*

WHY HIRE AN EDITOR?
"Revision" by Jan Burke in *Writing Mysteries*
    edited by Sue Grafton with Jan Burke and
    Barry Zeman

PERSISTENCE
The Last Lecture by Randy Pausch

CONCLUSION: THE NEXT RACE
What I Talk About When I Talk About Running
    by Haruki Murakami
The Courage to Start: A Guide to Running for Your
    Life by John Bingham

INDEX